# PROFILES IN BELIEF

THE RELIGIOUS BODIES OF THE UNITED STATES AND CANADA

## VOLUME III

HOLINESS AND PENTECOSTAL

## VOLUME IV

EVANGELICAL, FUNDAMENTALIST, AND OTHER CHRISTIAN BODIES

PROFILES IN BELIEF

# Profiles in Belief

## THE RELIGIOUS BODIES
## OF THE UNITED STATES AND CANADA

VOLUME III

HOLINESS AND PENTECOSTAL

By *ARTHUR CARL PIEPKORN*

Published in San Francisco by
HARPER & ROW, PUBLISHERS, INC.

1817

NEW YORK, HAGERSTOWN

SAN FRANCISCO, LONDON

PROFILES IN BELIEF: The Religious Bodies of the United States and Canada—Volume III —Holiness and Pentecostal. Copyright © 1979 by the Estate of Miriam S. Piepkorn. All rights reserved. Printed in the United States of America. No part of this book may be used or reproduced in any manner whatsoever without written permission except in the case of brief quotations embodied in critical articles and reviews. For information address Harper & Row, Publishers, Inc., 10 East 53rd Street, New York, N.Y. 10022. Published simultaneously in Canada by Fitzhenry & Whiteside Limited, Toronto.

FIRST EDITION

*Designed by Sidney Feinberg*

Library of Congress Cataloging in Publication Data

Piepkorn, Arthur Carl, 1907–1973.
  Profiles in belief.

  Includes bibliographies and indexes.
  CONTENTS: v. 1. Roman Catholic, Old Catholic,
Eastern Orthodox. v. 2. Protestant denominations. v. 4. Evangelical, fundamentalist,
and other Christian bodies. 1. Sects—North
America.     I. Title.
BR510.P53     1977     200′.973     76–9971
ISBN 0–06–066581–5

79 80 81 82 83 10 9 8 7 6 5 4 3 2 1

# Contents

v

**PART II**
**PENTECOSTAL CHURCHES**

viii     **Contents**

# Foreword

"One book is about one thing—at least the good ones are." Eugene Rosenstock-Huessey's famous dictum may seem inappropriate in the eyes of readers who might casually come across the present work. That it is a "good book" will be immediately apparent even to the casual user. But that it is "about one thing" may seem less obvious at first.

Arthur Carl Piepkorn's good and even great work seems to be about many things. It concerns itself with profiles of the many beliefs of millions of Americans who are separated into hundreds of religious bodies. Many of them, it may safely be presumed, will not even have been known by name to most readers before they acquaint themselves with the table of contents. Never before within the covers of several volumes in a single series will the student of American religion have been able to find convenient and reliable access to so many different religous groups. How can one in the midst of such variety think of Piepkorn's book as being "about one thing"?

The answer to that question, on second thought and longer acquaintance, could well be, "Easily!" For here is a single-minded attention to the one thing that is supposed to be at the heart of almost all of these religious groups, their beliefs. The telephone book includes many names, but it is "about one thing," and no one will mistake its purposes or its plot. So with Piepkorn's presentation of *The Religious Bodies of the United States and Canada.* It is precisely what its precise author's title claims it to be: *Profiles in Belief.*

Profile: it is a side view, an outline, a concise description. This book offers such an angle of vision. No individual can speak from within all these denominations and movements. To invite a separate speaker from each tradition would be to convoke a new Babel of tongues. Here we have something coherent and believable, the voice of a single informed observer. He establishes the "side view" and then invites criticism and approval by a member of each group to check on the accuracy of the portraits. This process assures evenness in tone and consistency in proportion without sacrificing either fairness or immediacy. While the description inevitably has had to grow long because of the number of groups presented, even its several volumes will be seen to be but an outline, something concise.

Beliefs: these by themselves do not constitute or exhaust all that a religion is or is experienced to be. For a full description the student will want to learn about social contexts and environments, about behavior patterns and practices of individuals and groups. But since these external marks purportedly grow out of the group's shared set of formal meanings and values and since these, in turn, derive from root beliefs, somewhere and somehow it is important to gain access to such beliefs. Had we all world enough and time it is possible that the knowledgeable could establish for themselves the profile of a large number of these religious bodies. But with the industry and intelligence for which he was noted, Dr. Piepkorn devoted years to the task of assembling the data for others. His profiles can be ends in themselves or instruments for further research. Of one thing we can be sure: they will force all thoughtful readers to take the beliefs more seriously than before.

Arthur Carl Piepkorn was a confessional Lutheran, but he does not use the confessional stance as a means of ranking the value of beliefs. Instead, that stance turned out to be the means of assuring readers that the author knew the importance of beliefs, knew what it was to confess a faith, was aware of the intellectual power that can reside in a religious tradition. If, as a book title of some years ago asserts, "beliefs have consequences," the opposite was also true for Piepkorn. He could look at behavior and practice and step back, in effect saying, "consequences also have beliefs."

This is not the place to read the narrative of American religion, be enthralled by anecdote, or ramble with a sage author dispensing practical advice. This is a very formal guide to belief systems. As an ecumenist of note, Dr. Piepkorn came to be emphatic about others' beliefs. As a military chaplain he had practical experience encountering people of faiths remote from his own in the American and Canadian contexts. As a teacher he knew how to get ideas across. As a confessor he valued faith. His book is certain to be a classic.

A classic is, among other things, a book behind which or around which one cannot easily go. Once it has appeared and come into common use it is a measure or benchmark for others. While the official title of this series is likely to endure, it is probably destined to be referred to in shorthand as "Piepkorn." If so, as the standard reference in the field, the designation will be a fitting tribute to the person who prepared himself well and spared himself not at all for the writing of this life work.

MARTIN E. MARTY
The University of Chicago

# Editor's Preface

Volume II in this series of *Profiles in Belief: The Religious Bodies of the United States and Canada* presented "Protestant Denominations," church bodies which in a direct way were shaped and influenced by the sixteenth-century Reformation in the Western church. Not described in that volume were two whole families of churches which in popular parlance are usually considered "Protestant" but were the result of significant movements within Protestantism in the United States and Canada in the latter part of the nineteenth and early part of the twentieth centuries. The church bodies which emerged from the Holiness and Pentecostal movements are the focus of Volume III.

If salvation and the work of Jesus Christ were the dominant themes of the Reformation movement that produced the Protestant denominations, then sanctification and the work of the Holy Spirit were the significant themes in the movements that resulted in the formation of Holiness and Pentecostal churches. The connection between the Holiness and Pentecostal movements is historical as well as thematic, as the material in this volume demonstrates. For some in both movements Holiness is a "second blessing" of God's grace. For those in the Pentecostal movement the baptism of the Holy Spirit as evidenced in the gift of tongues is either a "third blessing" or the second step in the Christian experience after conversion.

Arthur Carl Piepkorn had fairly well completed the material included in this volume by the time of his death five years ago. I have made some revisions to bring the material up to date. In my research I came upon several church bodies that had escaped even the meticulous scrutiny of Arthur Carl Piepkorn and have included them in his material. In addition I wrote the introductory chapters which survey the Holiness and Pentecostal movements (chapters 1 and 4).

I express gratitude to the many church-body officers who provided me with up-to-date information about their organizations; to the library staff of

Christ Seminary—Seminex, especially Mary Bischoff and Eleanor Sauer, for their help in locating reference works and bibliographical material; to my colleague, Thomas Rick, for providing the index; and to my secretary, Rosemary Lipka, for assistance in contacting church bodies and for her painstaking work of preparing the manuscript for publication.

Since the publication of Volume II the author's wife, Miriam Södegren Piepkorn, has gone on to join her husband among the saints in light. Volume III is dedicated to her memory.

JOHN H. TIETJEN
Christ Seminary—Seminex
St. Louis, Missouri

# Introduction

The apearance of Arthur Carl Piepkorn's multi-volume series on *The Religious Bodies of the United States and Canada* is of prime importance to all those Americans and Canadians who take a serious view of religion and contemporary national life. One of the most striking developments in twentieth century Christianity is the rapid growth of the Holiness and Pentecostal churches in America and around the world. With the growth of the Charismatic movement in the traditional denominations, a book such as this is all the more relevant to a basic understanding of the times.

It is only natural that the Holiness and Pentecostal churches should be considered in the same volume since they share so much historically and theologically. The Pentecostal movement emerged from the Holiness movement which in turn emerged from Methodism. Methodism, of course, had its roots in the Anglican and Catholic mystical traditions.

As the reader examines each church one will see that both the Holiness and Pentecostal groups teach in some way the idea of a "second blessing" beyond conversion, usually spoken of as "entire sanctification" or the "Baptism in the Holy Ghost." One can classify the various Holiness and Pentecostal groups by how they define and experience this subsequent blessing. Piepkorn has in each case done an excellent job of classifying these bodies. By summarizing the articles of faith, the general rules and the latest available statistics of each group, the author has produced an invaluable guide to what is a bewildering array of denominations, both great and small, in the Holiness and Pentecostal traditions.

Most of the bodies in this volume share in the Methodist tradition to some extent. Almost unanimously these groups are Arminian* in theology and centralized in government. For many, the articles of faith are largely verbatim copies of Wesley's twenty-five articles of religion, which in turn

* Arminianism, rooted in the teachings of James Arminius (1560–1609), stressed the universality of God's grace and human freedom to choose for and against salvation; it strongly influenced Methodism, especially in the United States. Cf. Vol. II, this series, pp. 277-279, 535, 556, 578-579.

were adapted from the thirty-nine articles of the Church of England. These Methodist theological roots bring to mind a comment from Dr. Charles Wynes of the University of Georgia when I explained to him the Methodist ties of most holiness churches; he said: "What would we do for denominations in America were it not for the Methodists?"

The relationship of the Pentecostal movement to the earlier Holiness movement is one that is subject to some debate. Most historians of religion in America recognize the fact that Pentecostalism arose from the milieu of the Holiness movement. In fact, the early ground-breaking dissertation of Merle E. Gaddis at the University of Chicago, entitled "Christian Perfection in America" (1929), classed the Pentecostal bodies along with the other Holiness bodies with little distinction. They were simply Holiness churches that had added the charism of glossolalia as evidence of their Pentecostal experience.

The classical Holiness churches that rejected the claims of the Pentecostal movement after 1906 made a clear line of demarcation between themselves and the new Pentecostals. To many of them Pentecostalism was "the Holiness movement gone to seed." Yet there is much truth in the Latin American Catholic scholar Ignacio Vergara's statement that "Pentecostalism is Methodism carried to its ultimate consequences." (*El Protestanismo En Chile*, 1962, pp. 126-127).

It is a matter of historical record that the first Pentecostal denominations in the world were established Holiness groups that added the Pentecostal experience to their Wesleyan system. Although the later "finished work" Pentecostals modified the initial teaching on sanctification, calling for a more progressive approach, they continued to consider themselves part of the movement to uphold holiness standards in the church and the world. Thus practically every Pentecostal group has a statement in its articles of faith on entire sanctification. Holiness standards for church membership are practically the same for both movements. For example, both Holiness and Pentecostal denominations unanimously forbid their members to use tobacco or alcoholic beverages. Both tend to stress the fact that outward appearance and behaviour give evidence of an inward work of grace in the heart.

Yet with the passage of time, it became evident that the Holiness and Pentecostal groups were in reality two major different movements. In the words of Prudencio Damboriena, the Holiness movement appeared "as a revivalist movement devoted to restoring the doctrine and practice of holiness among the people of God . . . ," while the Pentecostal movement arose as a dissident Holiness group which, "unsatisfied with internal sanctification, wanted to manifest it with charismatic signs. One cannot be disengaged from the other." (*Tongues As Of Fire*, 1969, p. 20)

Much bitterness was engendered during the early years of the twentieth century as the two movements struggled for a place in the sun. Yet, as Melvin

Dieter has suggested, these differences and conflicts "could be the strongest proof of the commonality of their origins. It is in one's family that one often has the most difficulty in establishing his identity and his role; it is especially dfficult when one is born a twin—even if only fraternal and not identical." (In Vinson Synan, *Aspects of Pentecostal-Charismatic Origins,* 1975, p. 76.)

Although Piepkorn was a Lutheran, he demonstrated an accurate understanding of the doctrinal and social concerns of the movements he examined. For those who have studied the Holiness and Pentecostal denominations, it is noteworthy that so many new ones appear here for the first time; and there are probably many more that remain to be discovered. One must also sympathize with the fact that after scores of groups were placed in the best categories available, the author finally ended the volume with a list of denominations that defied classification altogether.

Such is the kaleidoscopic nature of the Holiness and Pentecostal movements in North America. Yet, one is amazed at the similarities of doctrine of all the groups taken together. What emerges is a portrait of a large number of American Christians who are concerned about the deeper dimensions of spirituality and who are also greatly concerned about maintaining a separation from the world.

This then is a profile of the several million North American Christians whose belief in holiness or "Christian perfection" has led them to explore the heights and depths of what it means to be Baptized in the Holy Spirit. So those Christians from the world-wide membership of the Church of the Nazarene (441,093 members) to the faithful of the "Pentecostal Fire-Baptized Holiness Church of God of the Americas" (6,000 members) salute the labors of Arthur Carl Piepkorn in Volume III of this monumental work.

VINSON SYNAN
Oklahoma City

# PART I

## HOLINESS CHURCHES

# 1. The Holiness Movement

As the nineteenth century drew to a close, significant new church bodies emerged from a movement which for more than a generation had sought to recapture Wesleyan perfectionism in order to make American Methodists into a holy people. The participants in the Holiness movement[1] repeatedly disavowed any intention of separating from Methodism and forming a new church body. Yet, like Wesley himself, they found it necessary to establish extra-ecclesiastical organizations, which sometimes were interdenominational in membership, to promote their concerns. These organizations in turn sponsored missionary activity, which in time produced new denominations when opposition from the entrenched church establishment caused some in the Holiness movement to leave as "come-outers" and put out others. The church bodies spawned by the Holiness movement grew rapidly during the first three decades of the twentieth century as the new organizations appealed successfully to the many thousands of rural Americans who were moving into the cities at that time.

The Holiness movement had its origin among American Methodists and their commitment to John Wesley's teaching on holiness and Christian perfection.[2] Freely adapting Wesley's teachings to the situation of the American frontier, Methodism expanded rapidly in the New World. The Methodist Episcopal Church grew from 14,000 members at the end of the Revolutionary War to over 1 million members by 1845.[3]

As Methodists increased in numbers, criticism arose about widespread neglect of Christian perfection among American Methodists. In 1825 Timothy Merritt (1775–1845) published *The Christian's Manual, a Treatise on Christian Perfection* and in 1839 began printing the *Guide to Holiness,* a journal which became a major vehicle for the Holiness movement within American Methodism. The periodical was later purchased by Walter C. Palmer (1804–1883), a physician and prominent Methodist layman, whose wife, Phoebe (1807–1874), became editor and influenced Holiness believers inside and outside Methodism.

Phoebe Palmer began promoting her views on sanctification through "Tuesday Meetings for the Promotion of Holiness" in her home. She was convinced that the experience of entire sanctification was the cure for the ills of Methodism. In contrast to John Wesley's emphasis on the perfection of love as a process, Phoebe Palmer stressed entire sanctification as a present possibility. While Wesley urged his followers to develop a discipline for seeking perfect love, Mrs. Palmer urged her followers to follow a discipline for the sanctified life. She compared sanctification to baptism, an inward cleansing followed by a circumspect life. Entire sanctification was described as a second blessing, an experience of grace accompanied by emotional exuberance which enabled the one so sanctified to forsake inward sins such as pride and covetousness and to renounce unholy practices such as the use of tobacco and alcohol and membership in secret societies. By placing "all on the altar," it was possible to be instantly sanctified through the baptism of the Holy Ghost.[4]

Timothy Merritt, the Palmers, and others put down the roots of a movement that was to flower throughout the nineteenth century and produce the fruit of new church bodies at the turn of the twentieth century. The movement also played a part in the formation of several independent churches at the midpoint of the nineteenth century. One of these, the Free Methodist Church, was formed in 1860 after Benjamin Titus Roberts (1823–1893) was expelled from the Methodist Episcopal Church; yet he and his followers differed from the Holiness advocates within the latter church body not in basic teaching but in the intensity and fanaticism of their espousal of the Holiness movement; for some, that included vigorous antislavery activity. Most of the Holiness advocates stayed in the two major Methodist churches and rose to prominent positions within them.

Those eager for the revival of evangelical perfectionism turned to the camp meeting as the instrument by which to recover Methodism's theological heritage. During the first half of the nineteenth century the camp meeting had become a Methodist institution for revival. In 1867 several Holiness proponents on the eastern seaboard chose Vineland, New Jersey, as the site for a National Camp Meeting to foster Holiness. The event was a success, leading to the formation of the National Camp Meeting Association for the Promotion of Holiness.

The association sponsored more than fifty camp meetings over the next twenty-five years, changing its name in 1893 to the National Association for the Promotion of Holiness. Its leaders scrupulously avoided competition with the Methodist ecclesiastical organization and sought instead to save Methodism for Holiness. The need for administration and published materials led some of the leaders, like J. S. Inskip (1816–1884), to leave the pastoral ministry for the work of fulltime evangelists. Traveling thousands of miles annually, they made the movement nationwide in scope. The camp-meeting sites drew people back year after year, turning them into settled summer resorts.

Association leaders soon recognized the need for ongoing contact with their converts if they were not to be lost to the perfectionist cause. Since the churches themselves could not be trusted with the task, the National Association endorsed regional, state, and local associations modeled after the national organization. These associations provided worship services, conventions, revivals, and camp meetings to care for Holiness adherents. In local communities Holiness bands were organized to nurture seekers after perfection in their quest and to engage them in prayer. The official Methodist Church looked askance at the growing "associationism," especially when local and regional groups were vocal in their expression of dissatisfaction with the official church. From within these regional associations some insisted on separation from the Methodist Church and were labeled "come-outers."

Along with regionalization went evangelization in the Holiness movement. Methodist Bishop William Taylor (1821–1902) introduced "self-supporting" missions, and a number of Holiness advocates associated themselves with him as workers who provided their own support for their mission activity. "Faith missions" multiplied, and Holiness promoters used the method of self-supporting mission work to evangelize the rural population, which was moving into the cities as the nineteenth century drew to a close. City mission associations were established in major urban centers for the purpose of evangelization. Rescue homes, orphanages, and Bible schools developed out of the missions. One influential enterprise was the Peniel Mission founded by T. P. Ferguson (1853–1920) in Los Angeles in 1886. During the 1890s Ferguson's mission enterprise spread across the country and overseas. The missions were located in the poorer residential sections downtown in the cities, where people off the farm moved into homes and apartments vacated by the more prosperous who had moved uptown or to mushrooming suburbs. The camp-meeting approach of the missions reestablished the old-time religion for the migrants in their new communities.

The Holiness movement was not confined to the United States. Holiness advocates like Inskip and the Palmers took their cause across the border into Canada and overseas to England and around the world. Among those affected by the Holiness effort in England were William Booth (1829–1912), founder of the Salvation Army, and Thomas Dundas Harford Battersby (1823?–1883), vicar of Keswick. A series of summer conventions at Keswick became the English version of the American National Holiness Association.

Promoted primarily by Methodists, the Holiness movement did not stay within Methodist boundaries. Many in the Society of Friends identified with the Holiness cause. The Evangelical United Brethren Church and the Cumberland Presbyterian Church inserted sections on Holiness in their official documents. Under the leadership of Daniel S. Warner (1842–1895), a group seceded from the Winebrenner Church of God in 1880 to establish a new church under the Holiness banner, the Church of God, with headquarters in Anderson, Indiana. In addition to Methodists, the Holiness cause was supported by Presbyterians, Baptists, and Congregationalists.

The Holiness movement received strong support in the Methodist Church for several reasons. Some saw it as a bulwark against urban and progressive ministers who were gaining in numbers and influence and against the fashionable modes of dress that these ministers allowed their members to wear. Some supported the movement as a defense against the theological views of those who had been influenced by German higher critics and new theories of evolution. Many saw the movement as a means to unite Methodists of North and South after the Civil War came to an end. Others saw it as a means of saving the camp meeting and the "old-time" religious fervor.[5]

In the last decade of the nineteenth century a move toward the establishment of independent congregations developed within the Holiness movement. The argument for separation from the official Methodist Church was based on the claim that converts soon gave up their commitment to Holiness under the influence of pastors opposed to the Holiness teaching. Those who favored separation were convinced that the way to preserve the doctrine of Christian perfection was by establishing the primitive Wesleyan church outside the structures of Methodism. The expulsion of some proponents of Holiness hastened the move toward separation, which during the first decades of the twentieth century moved thousands of Methodists into Holiness sects.

Several independent New England congregations united in 1890 to form the Central Evangelical Holiness Association, which in turn joined with several Brooklyn, New York, independent congregations in the Association of Pentecostal Churches of America in 1896. A number of Pennsylvania congregations associated together as the Heavenly Recruits reorganized in 1894 as the Holiness Christian Association, renamed in 1897 the Holiness Christian Church.

The main battleground in the controversy over Holiness became the South and the Middle West, where the Holiness movement was having great effect. In the South the turning point in the struggle came at the General Conference of the Methodist Episcopal Church, South in 1894. There a statement was adopted disavowing the Holiness movement:

> But there has sprung up among us a party with holiness as a watchword; they have holiness associations, holiness meetings, holiness preachers, holiness evangelists, and holiness property. Religious experience is represented as if it consists of only two steps, the first step out of condemnation into peace and the next step into Christian perfection. The effect is to disparage the new birth, and all stages of spiritual growth from the blade to the full corn in the ear . . . . We do not question the sincerity and zeal of these brethren; we desire the church to profit by their earnest preaching and godly example; but we deplore their teaching and methods in so far as they claim a monopoly of the experience, practice, and advocacy of holiness, and separate themselves from the body of ministers and disciples.[6]

As opposition to Holiness advocacy increased, independent Holiness churches were formed through splits in Methodist congregations in widespread locations across the United States, and these united with like-minded congregations in support of mission activities, publishing enterprises, and educational or benevolent institutions. Though Holiness leaders spoke out against schism, they fellowshiped with separatist ministers and spoke at independent tabernacles. The action of the Methodist officials against Henry Clay Morrison (1857–1942) for his participation in a Dublin, Texas, camp meeting in 1896 convinced many Holiness supporters that the official church was against them. Two figures significant for the formation of new Holiness denominations who found it necessary to withdraw from the Methodist Church because of official opposition were Phineas F. Bresee (1838–1915) and Martin Wells Knapp (1853–1901).

Bresee was for a time associated with T. P. Ferguson at the Peniel Mission in Los Angeles. In 1895, three weeks after conducting services on his own in Los Angeles, Bresee organized the Church of the Nazarene there. He prospered through a program that succeeded in meeting the needs of homesick midwesterners newly arrived in Southern California by the thousands. Advertising itself as a simple, primitive church for the common people, the Church of the Nazarene grew rapidly, and additional churches were established in the first years of the twentieth century in other cities of California and throughout the Northwest and the Midwest.

Martin Knapp, an editor who settled in Cincinnati in 1892, launched an all-out evangelistic effort in 1895, which because of official disapproval caused him to become more independent. In 1897 Knapp formed the International Holiness Union and Prayer League committed to independent missionary activity and conducted on the faith principle. Though disavowing any intention to be an ecclesiastical body, the International Holiness Union assumed churchly functions, ordaining workers, acquiring property, and sponsoring missions. After Knapp's death in 1901, Seth Cook Rees (1854–1933) served as leader of the International Holiness Union, which in 1905 changed its name to the International Apostolic Holiness Union and Churches, and in 1913 to International Apostolic Holiness Church.

A series of mergers in 1907 and 1908 brought the Church of the Nazarene and several other groups together in the Pentecostal Church of the Nazarene, which over the next decade absorbed a number of additional Holiness groups and in 1919 dropped "Pentecostal" from its name to dissociate the group from the rapidly developing "tongues" movement.[7] It became one of the largest of the Holiness denominations to emerge from the movement.

The International Apostolic Holiness Church joined with several other Holiness groups to form the Pilgrim Holiness Church in 1922 and absorbed a number of other church bodies over the next few years. It, too, became a large Holiness denominatoin with major impact and helped form the Wesleyan Church in 1968.

A number of other independent Holiness churches were formed in the last decades of the nineteenth and first decades of the twentieth century,[8] and their ranks were swelled with Methodists committed to Christian perfection. From 1910 to 1920 five Holiness groups increased by almost 240 percent, while in comparison five mainline Protestant denominations grow by a little more than 20 percent. By 1930 the percentage rate of growth for the Holiness groups was at 300 percent over the membership in 1910, while the growth rate of the mainline denominations was down to 10 percent.[9]

But the growth rate dropped significantly in subsequent decades. The new churches were institutionalized. And in time the Holiness churches helped their members develop middle-class ways and moved with them to the suburbs. Institutionalization led to charges of forsaking the old ways of perfectionism. In efforts to recall the members to the principles of their founding, new church bodies were established in the mid-twentieth century.

## NOTES

1. The information in this chapter is based primarily on the excellent histories of the Holiness movement by Charles Edwin Jones, *Perfectionist Persuasion: The Holiness Movement and American Methodism, 1867–1936* (Metuchen, N.J.: The Scarecrow Press, Inc., 1974), and Vinson Synan,*The Holiness–Pentecostal Movement in the United States* (Grand Rapids, Mich.: Wm. B. Eerdmans Publishing Co., 1971).
2. For the Wesleyan legacy on holiness and Christian perfection, cf. chap. 15 in *Profiles in Belief: The Religious Bodies of the United States and Canada*, vol. II (San Francisco & New York: Harper

& Row, 1978).
3. For a description of Methodist development in America, cf. *Profiles in Belief*, vol. II, chap. 16.
4. Phoebe Palmer's teachings are described in Jones, pp. 4-5, and in Synan, p. 29.
5. Synan, pp. 40-42.
6. Ibid., pp. 50-51.
7. The relation of Pentecostalism to the Holiness movement is described in part II, below.
8. These are described in detail in chap. 2.
9. Edwin Scott Gaustad, *Historical Atlas of Religion in America* (New York: Harper & Row, 1962), pp. 121-122.

## BIBLIOGRAPHY

Clark, Elmer T. *The Small Sects in America*, rev. edn. Nashville: Abingdon-Cokesbury Press, 1949. This standard reference includes a short description of the Holiness movement in chap. 3, "Perfectionist or Subjectivist Sects," pp. 51-84.

Gaustad, Edwin Scott. *Historical Atlas of Religion in America*. New York: Harper & Row, 1962. Holiness bodies are described, pp. 121-126.

Greer, George Dixon. "A Psychological Study of Sanctification as a Second Work of Divine Grace." Unpublished Ph.D. dissertation, Drew University, 1936.

Jones, Charles Edwin. *A Guide to the Study of the Holiness Movement*. Metuchen, N.J.: The Scarecrow Press, Inc., and the American Theological Library Association, 1974. This is an invaluable bibliographical reference work for the Holiness movement, totaling 918 pp. and including, in addition to 536 pp. of bibliography, sections listing the schools and the major figures of the movement.

———. *Perfectionist Persuasion: The Holiness Movement and American Methodism, 1867–1936*. Metuchen, N.J.: The Scarecrow Press, Inc., 1974. A sociological study of the Holiness movement both inside and outside official Methodism.

Synan, Vinson. *The Holiness–Pentecostal Movement in the United States*. Grand Rapids, Mich.: Wm. B. Eerdmans Publishing Co., 1971. This major historical work examines the interrelation of the Holiness and Pentecostal movements.

Warburton, T. R. "Holiness Religion: An Anomaly of Sectarian Typologies," *Journal for the Scientific Study of Religion* 8 (1969).

# 2. Holiness Associations and Church Bodies

### Christian Holiness Association

The Christian Holiness Association began as the National Camp Meeting Association for the Promotion of Holiness in 1867 at the first national Holiness camp meeting in Vineland, New Jersey. Incorporated in 1889 in Iowa, it was known from 1893 to 1971 as the National Association for the Promotion of Holiness. It was reincorporated in 1952 in California and adopted the present form of its constitution in 1959.

In its early years the association saw itself as an instrument for reviving the Wesleyan doctrine of perfect love within American Methodism. At the turn of the twentieth century many of its members left their Methodist churches to establish new denominations committed to the cause of Holiness as a "second blessing" after conversion. In mid-twentieth century the association modified its emphasis on evangelistic revival and its publication program and espoused interdenominational fellowship as its major function. In recent years the association has devoted itself to theological discussions and plans for cooperation among Holiness churches.

Its constitution describes it as "an interchurch and interdenominational association" that seeks to "effect the closest possible fellowship and cooperation" among the proponents of the Wesleyan doctrine and experience of entire sanctification, "to secure the conversion of sinners, the entire sanctification of believers as a second definite work of grace, to promote a spiritual awakening, and to seek generally to edify the body of Christ." (It explicitly disavows as a purpose the organization of a church.) The means that it proposes to use to achieve its purpose include camp meetings, revivals, conventions, educational institutions, missionary societies, publications, and state and national organizations.

There are three types of membership: (1) individual; (2) auxiliary, open to interdenominational organizations and associations, camp meetings, churches, and educational institutions;[1] and (3) affiliate, open to denominations, conferences, districts, individual churches belonging to a larger fellowship not affiliated with the association, and denominationally related educational institutions and other religious groups.[2]

Article 9 of the constitution is an eight-article Statement of Faith that affirms the divine inspiration of both Testaments ("inerrant in the originals") and their final authority for life and truth; the Trinity; the death of Christ ("manifested in the flesh through the virgin birth") for the redemption of the human family, "all of whom may be saved from sin through faith in Him"; the fall, with death as its consequence; "the salvation of the human soul, including the new birth, and, as a subsequent work of God in the soul, a crisis, wrought by faith, whereby the heart is cleansed from all sin and filled with the Holy Spirit"; the retention of this gracious experience "by faith as expressed in a constant obedience to God's revealed will, thus giving us perfect cleansing moment by moment"; the church as the body of Christ, the members of which are "all those who are united by faith to Christ" and who acknowledge the duty of peaceful mutual fellowship and of pure and fervent mutual love; Christ's literal resurrection as the "living guarantee of the resurrection of all human beings, the believing saved to conscious eternal joy, and the unbelieving lost to conscious eternal punishment," and the personal return of Christ in power and great glory.

The central office is at 25 Beachway Drive, Indianapolis, Indiana 46224.

### Inter-Church Holiness Convention

The Inter-Church Holiness Convention came into existence over the year-end 1951–1952 and incorporated itself in 1956. It represents a response to the conviction of many adherents of Holiness denominations that by the mid-twentieth century the Holiness movement in the United States and elsewhere in the world had entered a critical stage where it needed a spiritual revival more than merely better organization and more precise doctrinal interpretation. They saw as the symptoms of this situation the appearance of worldly practices in the churches, schools, colleges, and general program of the Holiness denominations and the failure of the churches' leadership to speak out more aggressively against materialism, secularism, and doctrinal erosion.[3]

The convention's constitution lists among the purposes of the organization "to afford an opportunity for fellowship and cooperation among churches, groups, and individuals who are committed to the doctrine and life of Scriptural holiness as interpreted by John Wesley"; to witness to "the necessity of separation from all worldly influences, customs, and practices, and to encourage the maintenance of true Scriptural standards of holy living"; and to campaign against popular theories that "teach a 'holiness' which demands no death to the self-life, no separation from the world and worldly practices, no positive filling with the Holy Ghost, and which lightly passes over as 'non-essentials' those matters of outward living, dress, speech, and conduct which are taught by the word of God" or that demand "no holy conformity of life to the word of God, [but insist] on the necessity of certain 'signs,' such as the gift of tongues, as proof of the baptism with the Holy Ghost."[4] The organization seeks to accomplish its purposes chiefly by creating fellowships in different parts of the country, which sponsor periodic area conventions marked by prayer, Bible study, and evangelistic meetings, preceeded by fasting. These area conventions climax annually in a convention at Dayton, Ohio. There are thirty area fellowships. In addition the convention publishes a monthly periodical, the *Convention Herald*, with 12,000 subscribers, and republishes Holiness classics that are out of print, such as the *Standard Sermons* and other works of John Wesley and the writings of Asa Mahan, Samuel Chadwick, and others.

Membership in the convention is not exclusive; its members are in general also members of the Wesleyan Church, the Church of the Nazarene, the Free Methodist Church or of some other church body that stands in the Arminian-Wesleyan tradition.[5] The mailing address of the convention's headquarters is Box 3583, SR9, Salem, Ohio 44460.

## The Wesleyan Church

The Wesleyan Church came into existence in 1968 through a union of the Wesleyan Methodist Church of America with the Pilgrim Holiness Church.

The organizing convention of the Wesleyan Methodist Connection of America was held at Utica, New York, in 1843. Its founders were former members of the Methodist Episcopal Church. Their chief leader was the Reverend Orange Scott (1800–1847). They left the Methodist Episcopal Church partly out of opposition to episcopacy, but primarily in protest against slavery. In 1844 the General Conference added another dimension to the connection's concern by including among its articles of religion a statement on sanctification, the first denomination to do so. After the War between the States and the abolition of slavery, the connection felt justified in continuing its separate existence because in its view the specifically Wesleyan doctrine of entire sanctification and the connection's stand against intoxicating liquors and against lodges and secret societies could be maintained only in this way.

In 1891 it took the name Wesleyan Methodist Connection (or Church) of America, which it changed in 1947 to the Wesleyan Methodist Church of America. A number of independent religious bodies and agencies united with it in the course of time. Thus a large segment of the now dissolved Hephzibah Faith Missionary Society (organized 1892) of Tabor, Iowa, joined the Wesleyan Methodist Church in 1948. The Missionary Bands of the World joined it in 1958. (The Reverend Vivian A. Drake had organized this agency in 1885 among young people of the Free Methodist Church. It took the name Pentecost Bands of the World in 1898 and the name Missionary Bands of the World in 1925). (A third group was the Alliance of the Reformed Baptist Churches of Canada (organized in 1888); in 1966 its 63 churches and 2,600 members united with the Wesleyan Methodist Church as the latter's Atlantic Conference.

Meanwhile, in 1955, a proposed merger with the Free Methodist Church was rejected, in part because the general superintendents of the latter body are called bishops.

The Pilgrim Holiness Church was organized in 1897 by the Reverend Martin Wells Knapp, a Methodist minister, and Seth C. Rees, a former evangelist in the Society of Friends, as the International Holiness Union and Prayer League. Knapp in particular felt that the neglect of the regeneration of sinners, the entire sanctification of believers, divine healing, premillennialism, and the evangelization of the world demanded creation of an interdenominational union that would provide the older churches with stimuli to reformation. But the new organization rapidly developed into a denomination in its own right.

In 1900 it became the International Apostolic Holiness Union, in 1905 the International Apostolic Holiness Union and Churches, and in 1913 the International Apostolic Holiness Church.

The absorption in 1919 of the Indiana Conference of the Holiness Christian Church (organized in 1889 at Linwood, Pennsylvania, as the Holiness Christian Association, and subsequently renamed) resulted in a further change of name to International Holiness Church. The Pentecostal Rescue Mission of Binghamton, New York (begun in 1897) joined the International Holiness Church in 1922 as the latter's New York District. In the same year the Pilgrim Church of California (initially a Nazarene congregation that the district superintendent had "disorganized" in 1917, whereupon it had reorganized under a new charter as the Pilgrim-Pentecostal Church) joined the International Holiness Church, which thereupon called itself the Pilgrim Holiness Church.

Other mergers followed. The Pentecostal Brethren in Christ became part of the Ohio District in 1924. The People's Mission Church (founded in 1899), with headquarters at Colorado Springs, Colorado, joined in 1925. The Holiness Church of Del Monte, California (a predominantly rural body begun in 1880 as the Holiness Bands and later renamed) was received into the Pilgrim Holiness Church in 1946.

In 1959 a proposed union of the Wesleyan Methodist Church of America with the Pilgrim Holiness Church failed to pass the General Conference of the former by a single vote. In 1962 union negotiations were reopened. Both churches authorized the union in 1966 and in 1968 the union took place. Both churches suffered minor defections from their ranks in the process.

The articles of religion—article 2 of the Wesleyan Church's constitution —depend extensively on the Twenty-Five Articles of Religion of John Wesley, fortified with biblical demonstrations. There are articles on faith in the Holy Trinity; the Son of God; the Holy Ghost; the resurrection of Christ; the sufficiency and full authority of the Holy Scriptures for salvation (expanded beyond the Wesley original by an affirmation that the canonical books of the Old and New Testaments are "the inspired and infallibly written word of God, fully inerrant in their original manuscripts and superior to all human authority"); the Old Testament; relative duties ("the two great command-

ments are the measure and perfect rule of human duty, as well for the ordering and directing of families and nations, and all other social bodies, as for
individual acts"); original or birth sin; the atonement ("the offering of
Christ, once made through his sufferings and meritorious death on the cross,
is that perfect redemption and propitiation for the sins of the whole world,
both original and actual . . . sufficient for every individual of Adam's race");
free will (expanded beyond the Wesley original by explicitly affirming human
moral responsibility and the possibility of a fall from grace); the justification
of human beings; good works; sin after justification; regeneration ("that
work of the Holy Spirit by which the pardoned sinner becomes a child of
God"); entire sanctification ("effected by the baptism of the Holy Spirit . . .
subsequent to regeneration . . . wrought instantaneously . . . [with the crisis
of cleansing] preceded and followed by growth in grace and the knowledge
of our Lord and Saviour Jesus Christ . . . maintained by a continuing faith
in the sanctifying blood of Christ, and . . . evidenced by an obedient life");
the gifts of the Spirit ("the gifts of the Spirit, although different from natural
endowments, function through them for the edification of the whole
church");[6] the sacraments (abbreviated from the Wesley original); baptism[7]
("adult persons and the parents of each child . . . shall have the choice of
baptism by immersion, sprinkling, or pouring");[8] the Lord's Supper (abbreviated from the Wesley original);[9] the church ("the entire body of believers in
Jesus Christ . . . some of whom have gone to be with the Lord and others
of whom remain on the earth"); the second coming of Christ ("personal and
imminent"); the resurrection of the dead ("the resurrection of the righteous
dead at Christ's second coming and the resurrection of the wicked at a later
time"); the judgment of mankind; and destiny ("the eternal destiny of man
is determined by God's grace and man's response, evidenced inevitably by
his moral character which results from his personal and volitional choices
and not from any arbitrary decree of God; heaven . . . is the final abode of
those who choose the salvation which God provides, [while] hell is the final
abode of those who neglect this great salvation").[10]

   The "general rules"—article 3 of the constitution—inculcate the Christian
virtues and forbid the manufacture, sale, and use of alcoholic beverages,
harmful drugs, and tobacco. They also prohibit membership in secret societies
and oathbound lodges (but not in labor, civic, or other organizations that do
not contradict loyalty to Christ and the church).[11]

   The Wesleyan Church "recognizes the responsibility of the individual to
answer the call of his government and to enter into military service," but
"will lend moral support to any member who asks and claims exemption by
legal processes from military service as a sincere conscientious objector and
who asks to serve his country as a noncombatant."[12]

   It affirms Christ's willingness and power to heal the bodies as well as the
souls of human beings and encourages prayer for healing according to the
pattern set forth in the Bible.[13]

   The district conferences meet annually. The General Conference meets every four years. The general superintendents oversee geographic administrative areas and together form a board of general superintendents.

The headquarters of the Wesleyan Church are at Box 2000, Marion, Indiana 46952. There are 2,600 churches with an inclusive membership of more than 80,000. The Wesleyan Church carries on foreign missions in Latin America, the West Indies, Asia, Africa, Australia, New Guinea, and the Republic of the Philippines.

### Allegheny Wesleyan Methodist Connection

Most of the Wesleyan Methodist churches in Pennsylvania and Eastern Ohio left their church body in 1966 because of their opposition to the proposed merger of the Wesleyan Methodist Church of America and the Pilgrim Holiness Church. Claiming to be the Original Allegheny Conference of the Wesleyan Methodist Church, the group adopted its present name in 1968 when it reached a settlement with its former national body.

Convinced that the merger which produced the Wesleyan Church would only increase worldliness, the Allegheny Wesleyan Methodist Connection set out to recover original Wesleyan Methodist commitment to sanctification.[14]

The Allegheny Wesleyan Methodist Connection is congregational in polity in that local church property ownership and the call of the pastor are vested in the local congregation, and in that members of local church boards and committees are elected by the congregation in annual meetings. The church body is connectional in that each local congregation agrees to be governed by the Discipline of the Connection and to participate in the annual conference. All churches are represented in the conference by ministers and lay delegates.[15]

The connection does mission work in Haiti among Native Americans in the United States. It has approximately 100 congregations and 3,000 members. Headquarters are at 413 East Main Street, Titusville, Pennsylvania 16354.

### Congregational Methodist Church

The founders of the Congregational Methodist Church withdrew from the Methodist Episcopal Church, South, in 1852. Their reasons were dissatisfaction with the itinerant system, the absence of "republican elements" in the government of the parent church, the principle of "taxation without representation," which they saw embodied in the episcopal form of government, and what they regarded as inequalities within the ranks of the ministry. In 1887–1888 the Congregational Methodist Church suffered a severe reduction in size when two thirds of the members withdrew to join the Congregational Church. In 1941 a further rift resulted in the establishment of two rival general conferences, one of which called itself the Congregational Methodist

Church, while the other ultimately took the name First Congregational Methodist Church of the United States of America.

The Twenty-Five Articles of Religion have been part of the Discipline of the Congregational Methodist Church from the beginning. In view of the trend toward liberalism among American churches, the General Conference of 1957 felt impelled to add five articles designed to clarify and fix the conservative beliefs of the denomination. These new articles define regeneration as "the instantaneous impartation of spiritual life to the human soul by the Holy Ghost"; describe entire sanctification as "the second definite work of grace, subsequent to regeneration, by which a justified person is cleansed from the original or Adamic nature and is filled with the Holy Ghost"; identify "storehouse tithing and free will offerings" as the divinely given financial plan for the church; assert eternal retribution for the wicked; and affirm two resurrections of the dead, one of the saved at the premillennial coming of Christ and a second postmillennial resurrection of the unsaved.[16]

The baptism of infants is thought of chiefly as an act of dedication by the parents and minister.[17]

Local congregations elect their own pastors and care for their own affairs within the framework of the *Constitution and Government*. There are the usual local, district, and annual conferences, and a General Conference that meets every four years and that is the sovereign organ of the whole church.

There are 236 churches in eleven southern states, with a total membership of 20,022. The church body carries on foreign missions in Africa and Latin America, as well as among Mexican immigrants and North American Indians in the United States. Headquarters are at Highway 469, South Florence, Mississippi 39073, the home also of Wesley College.

**The Free Methodist Church of North America**

During the 1840s and the 1850s a minority of the Genesee (New York) Conference of the Methodist Episcopal Church had become increasingly concerned that the success of Methodism in the United States had been achieved at the cost of repudiation of the Wesleyan doctrine of entire sanctification. Holiness, they contended, had become a counsel of perfection for the few and an object of ridicule to many. The result was an invasion of the church by worldliness and laxity of discipline. Simplicity in worship was being lost as congregational singing declined in favor of choirs. Revivals and camp meetings were in diminishing use. Membership in secret oath-bound societies, toleration of slavery, pew sales, pew renting, and commercial methods in church finance were, in their opinion, additional evidence of the sad state into which American Methodism had fallen.

The contest between the two parties climaxed in the expulsion of one of the leaders of the minority group, Benjamin Titus Roberts (1823–1893) from the conference in 1858 by a vote of 54 to 34 with 28 abstentions. Other ministers shared his fate and the laypeople who supported them were "read out" of their congregations. Roberts's appeal to the General Conference of 1860, which reaffirmed the action of the Genesee Conference, made the issue a national one. A convention of lay supporters of the expellees' position, held in July 1860 at St. Charles, Illinois, in effect created a new denomination, the organization of which was perfected by a delegated convention of fifteen ministers and forty-five laymen at Pekin, New York, the following month. It adopted the name Free Methodist Church; for the founders the added adjective meant "*free* seats, *free*dom from ecclesiastical domination, *free*dom from sin, and *free*dom in worship."[18]

Half a century later, the 1910 meeting of the Genesee Conference confessed that the action of its meeting of 1858 had been both unjust and unwise and solemnly returned the credentials that the conference had canceled more than five decades before.

The Free Methodist Church is conservative in doctrine and evangelical in spirit, and holds to the tradition of free worship. It has maintained the position of its founding fathers except on one point. In 1943 it granted local option in the matter of choirs and instrumental music in the church and in 1955 it deleted the antichoir restriction altogether. In 1959–1960 the Holiness Movement Church of Canada became a part of the Free Methodist Church of North America.

At the time of its organization the Free Methodist Church modified the Twenty-five Articles of Religion. It deleted the articles on purgatory, on both kinds in the sacrament, and on the marriage of ministers as issues that were no longer relevant. It also omitted the article on the rulers of the United States of America and everything but the first sentence of the article on the sacraments. It added two articles that its leaders constructed from the writings of John Wesley.

One of these added articles, on entire sanctification, read: "Justified persons, while they do not outwardly commit sin, are nevertheless conscious of sin still remaining in the heart. They feel a natural tendency to evil, a proneness to depart from God and cleave to things of earth. Those who are sanctified wholly are saved from all inward sin—from evil thoughts and evil tempers. No wrong temper, none contrary to love, remains in the soul. Entire sanctification takes place subsequently, and is the work of God wrought instantaneously upon the concerned, believing soul. After a soul is cleansed from all sin, it is then fully prepared to grow in grace."[19]

This statement was found unsatisfactory as an article of religion and the Centenary General Conference substituted the following for it in 1960: "Entire sanctification is that work of the Holy Spirit, subsequent to regeneration, by which the fully consecrated believer, upon exercise of faith in the atoning blood of Christ, is cleansed in that moment from all inward sin and empowered for service. The resulting relationship is attested by the witness of the Holy Spirit and maintained by obedience and faith. Entire sanctification enables the believer to love God with all his heart, soul, strength, and mind, and his neighbor as himself, and prepares him for greater growth in grace."[20]

Against a growing Universalist insistence in the mid-nineteenth century that all human beings will finally be saved, the second new article on future reward and punishment was added.[21]

The founders of the Free Methodist Church also took over with little change the Wesleys' General Rules for the United Societies. The church's four Special Rules demand conformity to "the scriptural standards of attire," which forbid adorning oneself with "gold, pearls, or costly array"; forbid using and handling tobacco, opiates, and intoxicating beverages; prohibit membership in secret associations; and recognize no other ground for divorce than the Bible permits.

The Free Methodist Church has been exceptionally successful in developing its members' sense of stewardship, and it has consistently led the denominations of the United States in its per-capita contributions. In its missionary enterprise it has featured the indigenous principle of church development; almost 40 percent of its world membership is in its overseas churches. The Free Methodist Church carries on missions in India, Africa, the Dominican Republic, the Republic of China (Taiwan), Hong Kong, the Republic of the Philippines, Brazil, Paraguay, and Mexico.

The government of the Free Methodist Church is similar to that of major Methodism in North America, but with more limited powers given to the active bishops.[22] These are elected to four-year terms and are eligible for reelection only to retirement age. One or more elders superintend each of the thirty-six annual conferences in North America. The General Conference meets every four years. Laypeople have always had equal representation with ministers in the annual and general conferences.

The international headquarters of the Free Methodist Church of North America are at 901 College Avenue, Winona Lake, Indiana 46590. The headquarters for Canada are at 3 Harrowby Court, Islington, Ontario M9B 3H3. There are 1,058 churches in 40 states of the United States with an inclusive membership of 67,043 and 126 churches in 6 Canadian provines with a total membership of 5,043.

### Standard Church of America

The Holiness Movement Church, founded at Ottawa, Ontario, Canada by Ralph Cecil Horner (1854–1921) in 1895, merged with the Free Methodist Church in 1959. When Bishop Horner was asked to retire in 1919, he left the Holiness Movement Church and with his followers formed the Standard Church of America, incorporated at Watertown, New York, in 1919 and in Canada in 1920.

The Standard Church of America has the same doctrinal position as its parent body. Pastors are appointed by the Annual Conference for four-year terms. Statistics are not available, but the total membership is not above a few thousand. Headquarters are at Brockville, Ontario.[23]

## Holiness Baptist Association

The Holiness Baptist Association of Georgia and Florida was the result of a separation from the Little River Baptist Association over the teaching of Holiness. In 1893 two churches and several ministers were expelled from the Little River Baptist Association because of their teaching of sinless perfection and the baptism of the Holy Ghost. With two additional newly organized churches, they organized the Holiness Baptist Association at Pine City Church in Wilcox County, Georgia in 1894.

The church body operates a campground seven miles east of Douglas, Georgia on the Alma Highway. At an annual camp meeting in August the business of the association is conducted. The church body has 46 churches in Georgia and Florida with a baptized membership of about 2,000.[24]

## The Church of Christ (Holiness) U.S.A.

The beginnings of the Church of Christ (Holiness) U.S.A. are linked with the beginnings of the Church of God in Christ. In 1897 Charles Price Jones, Sr. (1865–1949), a black Baptist preacher, called an interdenominational Holiness convention into being at Jackson, Mississippi, after three years of searching for a faith that would make him "one of Wisdom's true sons and, like Abraham, 'a friend of God.' " Among his associates in this project was another Baptist, Elder Charles H. Mason. When persecution forced the movement to organize as a separate church body, it called itself the Church of God in Christ, the name that Mason asserted God had revealed to him. In 1906 Mason and a number of others went to Los Angeles and received the baptism of the Holy Spirit in the Azusa Street revival (described in chapter 4, below). Upon their return in 1907, the Holiness party of the movement under Jones withdrew the hand of fellowship from the Pentecostal party under Mason. Both groups continued to use the name Church of God in Christ. The Mason party began to reorganize immediately, while the Jones group waited until 1909, after the legal issues arising from the schism had been settled. The Jones group adopted the name Church of Christ (Holiness) U.S.A. not earlier than 1911.

Following the convention of 1920 King Hezekiah Burruss withdrew to found the Churches of God, Holiness, with headquarters in Atlanta.

Another schism in 1946–1947 involved a number of churches that followed the lead of Bishop William A. Washington, who took out of the larger fellowship the Bethel Church of Christ (Holiness) that he had incorporated in Los Angeles in 1915. Some of these joined together in the Assembly of the Associated Churches of Christ (Holiness); others became completely independent congregations. The year 1947 also saw the withdrawal of Bishop William E. Holman and a number of other clergymen, together with their congregations, to become the Evangelical Church of Christ (Holiness).

The church body's Articles of Faith affirm belief in the Trinity; Christ's deity and humanity; the Holy Spirit; the sixty-six books of the Bible as the revealed word of God; original sin; Christ's atonement for the whole human race; repentance as a sincere change of mind; justification, which removes the guilt of sin for all believers; regeneration, which removes the love of sin; sanctification, which removes the inclination to sin, as a necessary condition of fitness to see God; Christ's resurrection and second coming; believer's baptism by immersion;[25] the Lord's Supper; the gift of the Holy Ghost to every true believer; foot washing;[26] the spiritual gifts of 1 Corinthians 12–14, with the proviso that "no one gift is the specific sign or evidence of the Holy Spirit's presence" and that, while "the Bible endorses speaking in tongues or a gift of tongues," no one "really speaks in tongues unless he speaks a language understood by man"; and divine healing, although the church body does not "condemn physicians and medicines because the Bible does not."[27]

Since 1927 the government of the church has been episcopal, with one of the bishops (now eight in number) designated senior bishop. District conventions meet every six months, the General Convention every two years.

The headquarters are at 329 East Monument Street, Jackson, Mississippi 39202. At last report the church body had 159 churches from Michigan to California with a total membership of 9,289. Recent efforts to contact the church-body headquarters have been unsuccessful.

### [National Convention of] the Churches of God, Holiness

King Hezekiah Burruss began what became the mother-church of this black denomination with a congregation of eight in Atlanta, Georgia, in 1914. Growth over the next years was rapid. In 1920 the founder withdrew from the Church of Christ (Holiness), U.S.A. In 1922 he incorporated the National Convention of the Churches of God, Holiness. The convention holds that the New Testament "gives safe and clearly applied instructions on all methods of labor, sacred and secular," and it serves as the standard by which all doctrine is tested. The denomination believes in the inspiration of the Scriptures, the Trinity, justification, entire sanctification or perfection as something that is both present and ultimate, regeneration, the gift of the Holy Spirit as an act after conversion, and divine healing (although the denomination does not forbid medicine and the services of physicians and surgeons on principle). Baptism and the Lord's Supper are observed as ordinances. Foot washing is not regularly practiced. Direction of the church is largely concentrated in the hands of the national president or bishop, elected by the National Convention. From the beginning to his death in 1963 King Hezekiah Burruss held this office; it has now passed to his son, Titus Paul Burruss. The headquarters are at 170 Ashby Street, Northwest, Atlanta, Georgia 30314. Bishop Burruss claims for the Churches of God, Holiness, 42 churches with an inclusive membership of 25,600.[28]

### [Assembly of] the Associated Churches of Christ (Holiness)

Bishop William A. Washington (d. 1949) organized Bethel Church in Los Angeles, the first Church of Christ (Holiness) congregation on the West Coast of the United States. After a number of years of association with the Church of Christ (Holiness) U.S.A., Bethel Church and a number of other churches withdrew from the latter body in 1946–1947 "in order to work with freedom under their own charters."[29] Some of the withdrawing churches organized the Assembly of the Associated Churches of Christ (Holiness). The articles of faith of the Associated Churches of Christ (Holiness) are identical with those of the Church of Christ (Holiness) U.S.A.[30]

The headquarters of the association are at 1302 East Adams Boulevard, Los Angeles, California 90011. It comprises 6 churches and 1 mission in the Los Angeles area, with a total active membership of 2,008. The association's meetings are held twice each year.[31]

### Evangelical Church of Christ (Holiness)

Bishop William E. Holman organized a branch of the Church of Christ (Holiness) U.S.A. in Los Angeles. During the dissension that led in 1947 to the withdrawal of Bishop Washington and the churches that followed him, Bishop Holman, together with a number of other ministers and churches, also dissolved his connection with the Church of Christ (Holiness) U.S.A. To avoid confusion with the larger group, the Holman movement took the name Evangelical Church of Christ (Holiness).

The doctrines and practices of the Evangelical Church of Christ (Holiness) are identical with those of the Church of Christ (Holiness) U.S.A.

The church body counts 4 churches, in Washington, Omaha, Denver, and Los Angeles, and 2 missions in the last-named city. The total active membership is estimated at about 500. The headquarters are at 1938 Savannah Place, Southeast, Washington, D.C. 20020.[32]

### The Church of God (Anderson, Indiana)

The Church of God (Anderson, Indiana) finds its immediate antecedents generally in American frontier revivalism and more specifically in the Holiness movement of the last half of the nineteenth century. It finds remoter antecedents in the Wesleyan and Puritan movements in England, in Pietism in Germany, and in the radical wing of the sixteenth-century reformatory movements.

Among the pioneers of the Church of God (Anderson, Indiana), the most prominent was Daniel S. Warner (1842–1895), who had begun his ministerial career in the Ohio Eldership of the Churches of God in North America. Later he accepted the Wesleyan doctrine of perfection and joined the Holiness Association. The periodical that he edited, *The Gospel Trumpet*, drew together a company of likeminded individuals. In 1881 Warner and others declared themselves free from all human creeds and party names and committed themselves exclusively to the apostolic church of the living God. This year is considered as marking the beginning of the Church of God (Anderson, Indiana).

The Church of God (Anderson, Indiana) has never adopted a formal creed, and its open-ended commitment to "truth" has resulted in a considerable measure of doctrinal flexibility. Its theological position is basically trinitarian biblicism. Its major emphases fall under five heads.

First, a life-changing relationship to God is the essential precondition of authentic Christianity. Repentance and trust in Christ's forgiveness bring about a personal conversion that is the renewal of life at its deepest level.

Second, the believer must "go on to perfection," that is, he or she must experience an "infilling of the Holy Spirit" that infuses grace and power for service and makes the person perfect in love, in intention, and in attitude.

Third, the church is a divine institution composed exclusively of true believers and ruled by the Holy Spirit. Conversion by itself places the believer in the church and he or she needs to go through no church-joining formalities to belong either to the local congregation or to the universal church.

Fourth, God has only one church. The common experience of Christians in Christ produces a solidarity with all true believers of which Christian unity is an outgrowth. Basically unity is something that God gives, but Christians are under the obligation to attain "to the unity of the faith." The Church of God (Anderson, Indiana) does not belong to organized interdenominational councils and associations but sees itself as providing a strong witness to the validity of an undenominational Christianity and has many interdenominational working relationships.

Fifth, Christ will come again to dictate rewards and punishments at the time that God has appointed and without any millennial reign before or after his coming.

Believers who have reached an age of accountability receive baptism by immersion in water as a public testimony of their new relationship with Christ. In the Lord's Supper the bread symbolizes Christ's broken body, and unfermented grape juice symbolizes his blood; the Communion table is open "to all persons who would honestly draw near to Christ." On the Thursday evening before Easter men and women separately observe the custom of foot washing, to symbolize obedience and humble service to one's brother or sister in Christ and the servant role of the church. The gift of a minimum of one tenth of one's personal income is strongly recommended. Most members of the Church of God are not opposed to military service, but the church supports the position of those of its members who are conscientious objectors to war and to participation in the armed forces. Matters of dress and related matters are left to the educated Christian conscience.

Theologically the polity of the Church of God is charismatic. Functionally it is basically congregational, although it also incorporates elements deriving from presbyterial and episcopal sources. The fear of ecclesiasticism, the conviction that the Holy Ghost must determine policy and action in the church, and the absence of any formal structures within the movement during the first generation of its existence still exert an influence. The state assemblies coordinate the intercongregational work of the local churches and approve the ministers who are to receive *Yearbook* recognition. The General Assembly, which meets annually in connection with the international convention held each June at Anderson, Indiana, is the central policy-making agency of the church body.

The mailing address of the headquarters is Box 2420, Anderson, Indiana 46011. The Church of God has 2,251 congregations in the United States and Canada with a total membership of 166,259. Its main concentrations are in Ohio, Indiana, and Michigan, with lesser concentrations in Kentucky, West Virginia, Illinois, Missouri, Oklahoma, California, and western Canada. It conducts foreign missions in Africa, India, Australia, Japan, the islands of the Pacific Ocean, Europe, the Antilles, and Latin America.[33]

### The Church of God (Guthrie, Oklahoma)

The Church of God (Guthrie, Oklahoma) holds that God began to restore his church around 1880, in the "evening time" (Zechariah 14:7) of the world, through the labors of Daniel S. Warner and his associates. Around 1910, it declares, the majority of adherents of the movement began to compromise and abandon its original teachings,[34] which the Church of God (Guthrie, Oklahoma) continues to maintain in their original rigor. The majority group became known as the Church of God (Anderson, Indiana).

The unofficial organ of the Church of God (Guthrie, Oklahoma), *Faith and Victory,* has been published at Guthrie since 1923. Since 1938 the fellowship has held a national camp meeting at Neosho, Missouri.

The Church of God (Guthrie, Oklahoma) emphasizes holiness. In addition to justification for sinners, it teaches sanctification for believers—including the infilling of the Holy Spirit—as a second definite work of grace, although it does not hold that speaking in tongues is a necessary and unfailing evidence of the baptism with the Holy Spirit.[35]

Separation from the world precludes all participation in war, including noncombatant service in the armed forces and military training;[36] remarriage after divorce;[37] the use of alcoholic beverages and tobacco;[38] wearing any kind of adornment (including neckties); and television viewing.[39]

It acknowledges no discipline but the New Testament and affirms that it does not attempt to legislate on the teachings of the New Testament.

It teaches that the church that Jesus built includes all those who have been saved through the new birth. It reaches out the hand of fellowship to every true Christian and opposes all forms of "sectism," that is, denominationalism, including the exchange of pulpits with sectarian ministers by its clergy and their joining ministerial associations.[40] God gave the name "Church of God" to the church; all churches that accept any other name added by humans are laying a snare to divide God's people.

The Church of God (Guthrie, Oklahoma) follows Warner in opposing theological seminaries, honorific titles and academic degrees for ministers, a salaried clergy, instrumental music in worship, expensive churches, and the use of medicines and drugs for healing.[41]

The ordinances of the church include baptism by immersion, not to save the soul but to serve as a testimony of what has taken place in the soul;[42] the Lord's Supper; foot washing;[43] lifting up holy hands in worship; the holy kiss, brothers greeting brothers and sisters greeting sisters; divine healing;[44] and prayer and fasting, to which God responds by giving miracle-working powers, as he did to the primitive church.[45] It rejects both commercialized methods of obtaining financial support for the church and tithing "as a doctrine of the church" and as "a test of fellowship."[46] In its doctrine of the last things, it is nonmillennial and antirapture.[47]

The fellowship includes 36 local churches, mainly in Oklahoma, California, Louisiana, Missouri, and Kansas, with many adherents scattered over the United States and Canada who do not belong to any local church. It maintains no membership rolls. The subscription list to *Faith and Victory*, is currently about 7,000.[48]

Faith Publishing House, 920 West Mansur Avenue, Guthrie, Oklahoma 73044, which carries on an energetic tract, book, and magazine ministry, is a facility for the church, which the church uses to coordinate its efforts.

## The New Testament Church of God, Incorporated

In 1942 a group of ministers and laity who belonged to the Church of God (Anderson, Indiana) withdrew from that body because they felt that it had compromised the Fundamentalist position to which they stood committed. They incorporated their movement as the New Testament Church of God under the laws of Oklahoma in 1945.

The New Testament Church of God, Incorporated, consciously takes its stand in the tradition that Daniel S. Warner established in the latter part of the nineteenth century. It defines the church as the body of Christ and as the whole number of reborn believers. It emphasizes Christian unity on the basis of New Testament standards of faith and experience under the rule of the Holy Spirit and the headship of Christ, but it rejects denominational, organizational, and ecclesiastical criteria of fellowship. It accepts the New Testament in the King James Version as its only book of discipline, and believes in the divine inspiration of the Bible, the experience of holiness, and the establishment of the Kingdom of God here and now. It affirms the return of Christ, but disavows the idea of a millennial reign of Christ on earth. It awaits the fulfillment of the prophecies of the Revelation of St. John, the final judgment, the resurrection of the dead, the rewarding of the righteous, and the punishment of the wicked. Water baptism is by immersion; its members practice foot washing and observe the Lord's Supper as ordinances, but do not make them conditions of fellowship. It strongly opposes any cooperation with the National Council of the Churches of Christ in the United States of America.

There are currently about 800 churches in the United States and Canada that have associated themselves with the New Testament Church of God, Incorporated. These churches do not keep formal membership rolls, but leaders of the movement estimate the total overall membership of these churches at about 7,000. Each church retains its independence, but maintains contact and fellowship with the other churches through camp meetings, state assemblies, and regional conventions, as well as through radio broadcasting activities, a tract ministry, and a monthly journal, *The Seventh Trumpet*, whose editor is the "managing chairman" of the New Testament Church of God, Incorporated. The movement promotes foreign missions in 8 countries of Latin America, Asia, and Africa.[49]

### The Church of God (Holiness)

The immediate antecedents of the Church of God (Holiness) are to be found in the Southwestern Holiness Association, which S. P. Jacobs, a Methodist Episcopal preacher in North Topeka, Kansas, organized at Bismark Grove, Kansas in 1879, at a Holiness camp meeting. Leadership rapidly passed to the followers of J. H. Allen, a Methodist Episcopal local preacher, who had begun to preach Holiness doctrine energetically in Monroe City, Missouri and neighboring areas in the same year. Differences of opinion soon arose in the association. One group saw the association's function as that of propagating Holiness teaching within the existing denominations. The other group felt that the anti-Holiness views of the existing denominations demanded the withdrawal of the proponents of the Holiness view from these congregations and the organization of Holiness congregations on a new Testament pattern, with their own ministry and their own meeting places. The latter triumphed and in 1882, when the association applied for incorporation, it dropped the requirement that members of the association be members in good standing of some Christian church.

The first congregation in what was to become the Church of God (Holiness) was organized on this principle at Centralia, Missouri in 1883. Others came into being elsewhere with considerable rapidity. The association did not survive the controversy, and it held its last meeting in 1885. In 1888 the first convention of "true Holiness people," that is of the Independent Holiness congregations organized during the preceeding five years, was held at Fort Scott, Kansas. In 1895 the third convention adopted the name Church of God (Known as Independent Holiness People). Two years later another controversy came to a head—between the [Local Church] Sovereignty faction, and the [Elder] Supremacy faction. The proponents of Local Church Sovereignty held that the local church was the highest tribunal, from which there was no appeal, and that in life and doctrine the elders were responsible to local churches. Since the third and fourth conventions of 1895 had been held without authorization from the local churches, they argued, these conventions were an attempt to take authority away from the local churches and made those who accepted the authority of the conventions a sect. The proponents of Elder Supremacy accepted the elders as the interpreters of the church's doctrine, held that the elders were subject to a presbytery composed of elders, and urged that the pastor be regarded as the spiritual ruler and guide of the local church by the members and by the elders and evangelists who worked in the local church. The schism that resulted persisted from 1897 to 1922, when the Supremacy faction and all but twenty churches of the Sovereignty faction were reunited. In 1932 the Missionary Bands of the World united with the Church of God (Holiness), only to withdraw again in 1940; they subsequently (1958) joined the Wesleyan Methodist Church (now part of the Wesleyan Church).

The Church of God (Holiness) is basically Wesleyan in faith and practice. It accepts the King James Version of the Bible as its church manual and discipline. It has consistently stressed four main doctrines in its teaching: the new birth, entire sanctification, the "one New Testament church," and the premilliennial coming of Christ. It sees its ministry as not primarily social but spiritual and evangelistic. The cardinal doctrines of the Church of God (Holiness) include the Trinity ("only in official position or in the manner of manifestation and operation is there a classification of first, second, and third persons in the Trinity"); the incarnation ("there is no true analogy, but we may find in illustration some likeness: In our own existence there is a mortal body and an immaterial spirit; we are a curious combination of dust and deity"); the person of the Holy Spirit; the creation of humankind in perfection; the death of all human beings in Adam; Christ's atonement for all human beings through his perfect obedience; repentance, coupled with the forsaking of every known sin; saving faith; justification ("a judicial act of God by which he pardons full and freely of all guilt"), coupled with moral transformation; regeneration ("a radical moral change in man's character"); adoption ("justification, regeneration, and adoption are parts of one experience and occur at one time"); conversion ("that change in the total disposition and life of the sinner which is wrought when he is renewed by the spirit of God"); witness of the Spirit ("an indelible inner impression upon our spirit by which the Holy Spirit of God bears to us a conscious sense of peace with God"); sanctification ("an instantaneous work of the grace of God, though there may be a gradual process of learning and obedience on the part of the candidate as he approaches the experience, and . . . a grateful but more rapid growth in grace after the conscious reception of the Holy Spirit"); the church (consisting of every person who is saved by Christ's blood and properly designated simply as "the Church of God"); practical Christian living (including abstention from intoxicating beverages, tobacco, and habit-forming drugs; modesty in apparel; and marriage for life); Christ's second coming to catch away his saints; a general resurrection, with the millennium intervening between the resurrection of the just and that of the unjust; judgment for all persons; and everlasting heaven and hell.[50] The ministry consists of elder(s) and deacons, the former having authority in doctrinal and moral matters, the latter having, with the lay members of the church, authority in temporal and physical aspects of the church's business.[51]

The ordinances are baptism, with freedom as to mode, since baptism is a symbol, although there is an inclination to a single immersion with the candidate's face upward; and the Lord's Supper, where the "bread represents the broken body of Christ and the wine symbolizes his blood."[52]

The headquarters are at 7415 Metcalf Street, Overland Park, Kansas 66204. The General Convention meets annually. There are 135 churches in 20 states from Pennsylvania to the West Coast, with the strongest concentrations in Kansas and Missouri, and in the United States Virgin Islands. The total membership is estimated at 10,000. Foreign missions are conducted in Bolivia, Mexico, Haiti, Jamaica, the Cayman Islands, and the British Virgin Islands.[53]

### Churches of God (Independent Holiness People)

When the schism in the Independent Holiness movement that began in 1897 finally came to an end in 1922, twenty churches that had adhered to the Elder Supremacy principle refused to reunite with the former proponents of Local Church Sovereignty to form the Church of God (Holiness). Calling themselves the Churches of God (Independent Holiness People) they continued to affirm the declaration of principles that the convention held at Fort Scott, Kansas had adopted in 1897.

This declaration—which the movement disavows using as a creed or test of fellowship—asserts the sufficiency of the Holy Scriptures for belief, experience, and church polity; the determination to propagate and maintain the Independent Holiness Movement; the identity of the general or universal church with the whole body of God's spiritual children in the world; the character of the local church as an organic body; the inherent and independent autonomy of the local church; the amenability of the officers and members of the local church to the latter's authority and rightful jurisdiction in all matters of government and discipline; the voluntary character of the cooperation of local churches; the impropriety of officially investing the ministry with special and distinctive rights or prerogatives of government superior to the body of the local church; the necessity of including representatives of the local churches as well as ministers at general meetings or conventions; and the impropriety of introducing propositions of doctrine or discipline at such assemblies. It asserts the naturally sinful condition of all human beings; Christ's atonement as a full and complete satisfaction for all persons; the necessity of repentance; justification through faith in Christ; regeneration as a work of the Holy Spirit that accompanies justification; entire sanctification of the believer's nature from inherited sin as a subsequent work of the Holy Spirit; the sanctity of the Lord's Day; only two church ordinances, water baptism and the Lord's Supper; Christ's literal and personal second advent; the resurrection of the body; the judgment; the final glorification of the saints; and the rejection and eternal punishment of all impenitent and unsaved persons.[54]

The 1967 convention reasserted the movement's 1948 stand rejecting "the use of carnal weapons in putting down violence" and voicing conscientious objection "to using any means whatsoever in killing any human being in war."[55]

The Churches of God (Independent Holiness People) meet annually. The publication office of the movement's journal, *The Church Advocate and Good Way*, 1225 East First Street, Fort Scott, Kansas 66701, functions in lieu of a headquarters. There are 19 churches and mission stations in Oklahoma, Illinois, Iowa, Missouri, Kansas, Alabama, Colorado, Mississippi, California, Ohio, South Dakota, and Wyoming, with a total membership estimated at 1,100. The Churches of God (Independent Holiness People) support a foreign mission effort in Japan.[56]

### Peniel Missions, Incorporated

Peniel Missions, Incorporated is an outgrowth of a series of rescue missions, the first of which was organized in Los Angeles, California in 1886 by T. P. Ferguson and his wife, Mannie. Peniel Missions were opened in other cities, and through the impetus of the Peniel Missionary Society a chain of missions were developed in the United States and overseas. The name Peniel was chosen from Genesis 32:24-30 and is meant to connote spiritual triumph as a result of prevailing prayer.

In 1949 the Peniel work in Egypt and on the West Coast affiliated with the National Holiness Missionary Society. Under this arrangement rescue mission work in the United States continues under the old name.[57]

Peniel Missions, Incorporated, sees itself as an interdenominational faith work. "In doctrine it is Wesleyan. In spirit it seeks to be truly apostolic. Its watchword is 'Holiness unto the Lord.' "[58] Headquarters are at 4500 63rd Street, Sacramento, California 95820.

### Church of the Nazarene

"The Church of the Nazarene is composed of those persons who have voluntarily associated themselves together according to the doctrine and polity of said church, and who seek holy Christian fellowship, the conversion of sinners, the entire sanctification of believers, their upbuilding in holiness, and the simplicity and spiritual power manifest in the primitive New Testament Church, together with the preaching of the gospel to every creature."[59]

The name of the denomination goes back to 1895, when the First Church of the Nazarene was founded in Los Angeles. The organization as it stands today is the result of a long series of unions that span six decades. The first organized beginnings of any body now a part of the denomination are traceable to Providence, Rhode Island in 1886. A decade later the Central Holiness Association that had grown out of these beginnings and that had been formally organized in 1890 at Rock, Massachusetts joined the Association of Pentecostal Churches of America (1895) of Brooklyn. The First Church of the Nazarene began to organize likeminded congregations until the denomination extended as far East as Chicago. In 1907 the Association of Pentecostal Churches and the Nazarene group united at Chicago as the Pentecostal Church of the Nazarene.

In the meantime the New Testament Church of Christ (1894), with headquarters at Milan, Tennessee, and the Independent Holiness Church (1901), with headquarters at Van Alstyne, Texas, merged in 1904 as the Holiness Church of Christ. This body in turn joined the Pentecostal Church of the Nazarene in 1908.

In 1898 the Pentecostal Alliance had come into being at Nashville, Tennessee; under its altered name of Pentecostal Mission it joined the Pentecostal Church of the Nazarene in 1915, followed by the Laymen's Holiness Association (1917) of Minnesota, the Dakotas, and Montana in 1922, the Hephzibah Faith Missionary Association (1892) of Iowa in 1950, and the Gospel Workers Church of Canada (about 1900) in 1958. The denomination had become a transatlantic body as far back as 1915 when the Pentecostal Church of Scotland (1906) had united with it. In 1952 the International Holiness Mission of England (1907), and in 1955 the Calvary Holiness Church of Britain (1930) followed suit. To differentiate itself from the burgeoning Pentecostal movement with its stress on speaking in tongues, the denomination dropped "Pentecostal" from its name in 1919.

The Church of the Nazarene deems belief in the following brief statements as sufficient, since the denomination holds that the right and privilege of church membership rests upon the fact of the individual's being regenerated. The church can accordingly require only such avowals as are "essential to

Christian experience." The "agreed statement of beliefs"—which clearly exhibits the denomination's Wesleyan-Arminian doctrinal heritage—reads:

We believe—

1. In one God—the Father, Son, and Holy Spirit.

2. That the Old and New Testament Scriptures, given by plenary inspiration, contain all truth necessary to faith and Christian living.

3. That man is born with a fallen nature, and is, therefore, inclined to evil, and that continually.

4. That the finally impenitent are hopelessly and eternally lost.

5. That the atonement through Jesus Christ is for the whole human race; and that whoever repents and believes on the Lord Jesus Christ is justified and regenerated and saved from the dominion of sin.

6. That sinners are to be sanctified wholly, subsequent to regeneration through faith in the Lord Jesus Christ.

7. That the Holy Spirit bears witness to the new birth, and also to the entire sanctification of believers.

8. That our Lord will return, the dead will be raised, and the final judgment will take place.[60]

The fifteen Articles of Faith with which the constitution begins are somewhat more extensive and explicit. Thus they assert that "original sin continues to exist with the new life of the regenerate, until eradicated by the Baptism with the Holy Spirit." They define the atonement in terms of the meritorious death of Christ on the cross and assert that it is "graciously efficacious for the salvation of the irresponsible and for the children in innocency, but is efficacious for the salvation of those who reach the age of responsibility only when they repent and believe." A human being "cannot now turn and prepare himself by his own natural strength and works to faith and calling on God," but the grace of God enables "all who will to turn from sin to righteousness," believe on Jesus Christ, and follow good works acceptable in his sight. At the same time, even those "who have experienced regeneration and entire sanctification can apostasize and be lost."[61]

By God's "gracious and judicial act" of justification, "He grants full pardon of all guilt and complete release from the penalty of sins committed and acceptance as righteous" to those who believe on Jesus Christ as Lord and Savior. Regeneration, or the new birth, quickens spiritually the moral nature of the repentant believer and gives the person "a distinctively spiritual life, capable of faith, love, and obedience." Adoption constitutes the believer a child of God. "Justification, regeneration, and adoption are simultaneous in the experience of seekers after God, and are obtained upon the condition of faith, preceded by repentance."[62]

In his atonement Christ has made provision not only to save people from their sins but also to perfect them in love. The baptism with the Holy Spirit as an act of God subsequent to regeneration works entire sanctification—also known as "Christian perfection," "perfect love," "heart purity," "the fullness of the blessing," and "Christian holiness"—and "comprehends in one experience the cleansing of the heart from sin and the abiding indwelling of the Holy Spirit, empowering the believer for life and service."[63]

Baptism is a sacrament that signifies the believer's acceptance of the benefits of Christ's atonement. Young children may be baptized upon their parents' or guardians' assurance that they will receive the necessary Christian training. The mode of baptism may be sprinkling, pouring, or immersion. The Lord's Supper is a New Testament sacrament that declares the sacrificial death of Christ, through the merits of which believers have life and salvation. Communicants are to prepare themselves for reverent appreciation of its significance and only those who have faith in Christ and love for the saints should be called to take part in it. Divine healing is a biblical doctrine; Nazarenes are urged to offer the prayer of faith for the healing of the sick, but they should not refuse necessary providential means and agencies.[64]

The General Rules require members of the Church of the Nazarene to give evidence of salvation from their sins through a godly walk and vital piety. This forbids profaning the Lord's Day by unnecessary labor or business "or by the patronizing or reading of secular papers, or by holiday diversions"; using or trafficking in intoxicating beverages, promoting the licensing of places for their sale, or using tobacco in any of its forms; going to theaters, ballrooms, and circuses, taking part in lotteries and games of chance, and membership in or fellowship with oath-bound secret orders and societies.[65]

The Special Rules set forth total abstinence from all intoxicants [as] the Christian rule for the individual and total prohibition of the traffic in intoxicants [as] the duty of civil government." Those who obtain divorces on a ground other than adultery and remarry are ineligible for membership in the Church of the Nazarene, and the denomination positively forbids its ministers to solemnize the marriage of persons who do not have the "scriptural right to marry." Each member is to place his or her tithe faithfully and regularly in that local church to which the person belongs, as being "the only storehouse properly recognizable in a scriptural sense."[66]

The polity of the Church of the Nazarene is representative. The broad outlines of its organization are evidence of its Methodist heritage, but general superintendents take the place of bishops. The supreme doctrine-formulating, lawmaking, and elective body is the General Assembly, which meets once every four years. The General Board acts for the assembly between meetings. The headquarters are at 6401 The Paseo, Kansas City, Missouri 64131. With 4,733 churches and an inclusive membership of 441,093, it is the largest Holiness body. Its strength lies largely in the smaller communities of the Middle West. The Church of the Nazarene carries on foreign missions in 44 countries from India to Peru. It cooperates with, but is not an affiliate of, the National Holiness Association.

### The Fire Baptized Holiness Church (Wesleyan)

In the 1890s a Holiness revival penetrated the Methodist and Friends churches in the southern part of Labette and Montgomery counties in Kansas and led to the organization of the Neosho Valley Holiness Association. In 1904 the association incorporated itself under the name of the Fire Baptized Holiness Association of Southeastern Kansas. The church body adopted the present name in 1945.

The Articles of Faith have sections on the unity and Trinity of the God-head; the incarnation and sacrificial death of Christ for the original guilt and the actual transgressions of all humankind; the reproving role of the Holy Ghost; the inerrancy and infallibility of the Authorized (that is, King James) Version of the Bible "when freed from all errors and mistakes of translators, copyists, and printers"; original sin, the corruption of the nature of all the off-spring of Adam, which continues to exist after regeneration until the baptism of Holy Ghost and of fire eradicates it; Christ's full atonement for all sin; faith; justification and regeneration as simultaneous but separate acts; consecration as the total submission of the redeemed soul to the whole will of God; entire sanctification or the baptism with the Holy Ghost and fire; the witness of the Spirit as essential evidence of salvation and sanctification; growth in grace; willful sin after justification, which requires repentance before the soul may again be justified; the church ("composed of all persons who are born of the spirit"); divine healing through prayer ("we are not to sever fellowship from or pass judgment on those who use other providential means for the restoration of health"); the Christian Lord's Day; the typical and shadowy nature of the ordinances ("as an organization we are non-ordinance,[67] [although] we do not wish to criticize those of other denominations who observe them"); tongues as a spiritual gift enabling the recipient to speak an intelligible language ("the gift of tongues as an evidence of the Holy Ghost we hold to be unscriptural"); the imminence of Christ's personal and premillennial return for the rapture of his saints and his reign on the throne of David; the separation of the resurrection of the just from that of the unjust by the millennium; the immortality of the soul; the intermediate state of the souls of the departed in Sheol-Hades; the eternal destiny of every human being in either heaven or hell; the church body's motto, "love for all, malice toward none, living peaceably with all men"; the church body's goal, "love out of a pure heart"; and the church body's creed, the whole word of God, "inerrant, infallible, and sufficient," with preeminence accorded to the doctrines of "repentance, justification by faith, the cleansing of the heart from all sin by the baptism of the Holy Ghost and fire, divine healing, and the premillennial coming of the Lord."[68]

The general standards prohibit attendance at "the circus, the theater, the moving picture show, the dance, or places of gambling or reveling." The church body opposes television and forbids all elective or appointed officers of the organization or of the local churches to own or endorse television. Women must wear full-length sleeves, close-fitting necks, and skirts coming to half-way between ankle and knee; they may not bob or curl their hair or wear sheer or flesh-colored stockings. Neither sex may wear gaudy or transparent apparel or jewelry (including wedding rings). The church is "strictly opposed to war," and is unwilling that any of its "children should be compelled to engage in combat services." Ministers may not solemnize the marriage of a divorced person whose previous partner is still alive or perform a wedding ceremony in which rings are involved. Members may not use or sell intoxicating liquors, tobacco, or harmful drugs, or belong to oath-bound secret societies and lodges.[69] Tithing is the standard of giving.

The headquarters are at 600 College Avenue, Independence, Kansas 67301. The polity of the church body is broadly Methodist. The chief officer is the general superintendent. The General Assembly meets annually. There are 50 churches with an estimated inclusive membership of 1,200. The church body carries on foreign missions on Grenada in the Windward Islands.

### Christ's Sanctified Holy Church (West Columbia, South Carolina)

In 1887 Joseph Lynch, a class leader in the Methodist Episcopal Church on Chincoteague Island, Virginia, became persuaded that he could not be saved without Holiness. After he had received the blessing of sanctification as a separate and distinct blessing after justification, he began to attract others to his conviction, among them Sarah E. Collins, who joined him in proclaiming the Holiness message in 1889. When he and fifty followers petitioned the bishop of the conference for a "holy man of God to preach the gospel to them," they were forbidden to hold services in the local Methodist Episcopal church. In 1892 they organized the first congregation of Christ's Sanctified Holy Church. From Chincoteague Island members of the church moved down into North Carolina and Florida in their float houses, fishing and eeling for a livelihood and preaching the Holiness doctrine. Ultimately their travels took them over the whole southern part of the United States from the Carolinas to California and from Missouri to Louisiana and Texas, although they did not begin establishing churches until around 1940.

The Articles of Faith affirm the unity of God; the Trinity; the sufficiency and divine inspiration of the Bible; humanity's fall from native holiness; the formation of the divine purpose to redeem the human race by Jesus Christ; the work of the Holy Spirit striving with human beings prior to the coming of Christ; the deity and humanity of the incarnate Christ; his death for all people, his resurrection, ascension, and mediation; salvation for all human beings through his passion and death; the gift of pardon and holiness to human beings for the sake of Christ alone by faith; the grace of faith as the gift of God; instantaneous justification or absolute pardon of all actual sin;

the need for the purification and cleansing from all inbred sin; instantaneous sanctification of believers by the Holy Ghost; the possibility of a believer backsliding at any time during a life that is continually a time of probation; the conditional nature of the threats and promises in the Bible; the free will and agency of a human being as a necessary constituent of the person's rational soul; the existence in every human being of sufficient light and power, bestowed by Christ, to direct the operation of the will; and the universality of the atonement and of the Holy Spirit's enlightenment to put all people into a savable state, so that those who are lost are lost by their own fault.[70]

Christ's Sanctified Holy Church teaches that the one baptism is "to be baptized into Jesus Christ, being sanctified and made holy"; for that reason it does not practice water baptism. Ministers who join unequal persons— holy and unholy, white and black—together in marriage are to be expelled. Ministers receive no salary. Married persons who have left their spouses, except for fornication, must remain on probation. The discipline forbids festivals; denies full membership to persons who vote to license the sale of intoxicants or who use or sell tobacco; declares that "members should take no part in war";[71] withholds full membership from those who wear jewelry; and gives equal rights to women in all church work.[72] The Holy Communion is not observed.[73]

The conference meets as necessary on the call of "Board No. 1." The actual headquarters are at the Christ's Sanctified Holy Church Camp Ground, Perry, Georgia; the denomination's mailing address is 1024 Seminole Drive, West Columbia, South Carolina 29169. There are 18 churches in Alabama, Arizona, California, Delaware, Florida, Georgia, Louisiana, Mississippi, the Carolinas, Tennessee, and Virginia, with a total membership estimated at 1,175.[74]

### Christ's Sanctified Holy Church (Jennings, Louisiana)

Three followers of Joseph Lynch—Asher Fisher, Charlotte Gray, and Mary Hanson—came to West Lake, Louisiana, in 1903. They began a revival in the Colored Methodist Episcopal Church there and won a group of black converts who organized the Colored Church South on April 16, 1904. In 1908 a group of proponents of entire sanctification from North Carolina organized at Wichita, Kansas the first church of what has become the Northern District of Christ's Sanctified Holy Church. The latter name began to be widely used after 1910. It was officially adopted in 1922, when the church moved its headquarters from West Lake to Jennings, Louisiana.

It emphasizes the idea of "one Lord, one faith, one [spiritual] baptism," and stresses sanctification through faith as a gradual experience distinct from instantaneous justification through faith in Christ. The baptism of the Holy Spirit has speaking in tongues as its evidence. This experience may happen at any time and in any place, but it most frequently takes place during a "tarry meeting," where the worshipers have been taught to expect the phenomenon. Christ's Sanctified Holy Church regards water baptism as superfluous. In view of Christ's words in Mark 14:25, "I shall not drink again of the fruit of the vine until that day when I drink it new in the kingdom of God," Christ's Sanctified Holy Church does not serve the Lord's Supper, and contents itself with constant spiritual feasting with Christ. Men and women have equal status in the church and both are ordained to the diaconate and the ministry. If a member of the church body marries outside it, he or she is placed on probation for a six-month period during which he or she cannot take part in the services of the church. If by the end of that time the unholy partner has not been baptized with the Spirit, both are ejected from the church. Christ's Sanctified Holy Church forbids the sale and use of tobacco and alcoholic beverages, requires strict observance of its rules, and pledges its members to "expose all evil" to the church officials.

The conference meets annually. Between conferences, the five-person "Board No. 1" directs the church body's affairs. Its headquarters are at South Cutting Avenue and East Spencer Street, Jennings, Louisiana 70546. It claims 60 churches, mainly in Texas, Louisiana, Arkansas, and California, with an estimated total membership of 1,000.[75]

## Church of Daniel's Band

In 1893 a group of members of the Methodist Episcopal Church, concerned about a declining emphasis on holiness and evangelism in that denomination, withdrew and organized the Church of Daniel's Band at Marine City, Michigan, on February 3 of that year. The church body was incorporated the same month.

The first thirty of its thirty-seven Articles of Faith and Practice have to do with doctrine and draw extensively from the Methodist Articles of Religion. In addition to original depravity it knows an "acquired depravity" that consists of "all the thoughts of our defiled minds resulting from the original depravity of our moral nature." There are added articles on repentance ("godly sorrow for sin and forsaking it by turning to God"), conversion ("the forgiveness of actual transgressions of the law and the regeneration— the 'new birth'—of the soul by the Holy Ghost"), and entire sanctification ("by which the hereditary body of sin, or inherited depravity, is removed from the flesh"), the resurrection of the dead, and future reward and punishment. The church "consists of all people that are born again." The mode of baptism is optional. The Lord's Supper is "an emblem of the broken body of Christ." Following the article on Christian men's goods are added articles on divine healing ("all God's children should be exhorted to lay hold on this promise"), ordination, the support of the gospel ("offering ourselves a living sacrifice to God, with all that God has entrusted us with as stewards, to be used with an eye single to his glory"), marriage ("no believer should enter into this sacred agreement without positive leadings from God [who] commands his children to marry 'only in the Lord' "), divorce, intemperance, conformity to the world, the call to the ministry ("the sisters called should have all the privileges given the brethren"), and laying on of hands ("for the gift of the Holy Ghost, for the healing of the sick, and for the work of the ministry").[76]

There are two congregations in the vicinity of Midland, Michigan, with a total membership of about 100.[77]

## Holiness Christian Church of the United States of America, Incorporated

In 1882 three men and two women began to conduct open-air meetings in Philadelphia with a view to bringing nonchurchgoers to Christ. To provide for the spiritual care of their converts they began to organize churches as extensions of their evangelistic revival efforts. In 1889 they took the name the Heavenly Recruit Association, but five years later the Philadelphia church withdrew and as the custodian of the charter it claimed both the charter and the name. The remaining membership adopted the name Holiness Christian Church—and continued the work. Foreign missions were an integral part of the program almost from the beginning.

Domestic growth was westward; by 1908 a part of the Pennsylvania Conference felt sufficiently isolated that it joined the Pentecostal Church of the Nazarene, later a part of the Church of the Nazarene. In 1919 the Holiness Christian Church voted to merge with the International Apostolic Holiness Church to form the International Holiness Church, which became part of the Pilgrim Holiness Church (now part of the Wesleyan Church) in 1922.

The continuing Pennsylvania Conference opposed the 1919 merger and determined to carry on by itself as the Holiness Christian Church. It gradually expanded throughout eastern Pennsylvania, Maryland, Virginia, and West Virginia, and in 1945 it incorporated itself as the Holiness Christian Church of the United States of America. Despite the divisions of the past it maintains cordial fellowship with the Church of the Nazarene and with the Wesleyan Church.[78]

The Articles of Faith and General Rules reflect the wide range of denominational influences that touched the Holiness Christian Church in its history, particularly Methodism, the Evangelical Association, the United Brethren Church, the Mennonites, and the Brethren in Christ. There are articles on the Holy Trinity; Christ's resurrection; the sufficiency of the Bible for salvation; the inherent depravity of human nature; free will ("God graciously employs the means of enlightening and awakening the mind of the sinner to a sense of his poverty and wretchedness and then extends the invitation that 'Whosoever will may come' "); repentance; conversion ("this consists in justification . . . and the regeneration . . . while continuing in this regenerated state we do not commit sin"); sanctification ("embodies both the entire consecration or setting apart of the believer, as well as the cleansing of the heart from carnality, accompanied by the baptism of the Holy Spirit . . . obtained instantaneously and subsequent to the new birth"); sin after justification and sanctification; the ordinances, believer's baptism exclusively by single immersion ("not essential to salvation from sin nor a test of membership"), the Lord's Supper, and foot washing ("practice of our humility"); consecration of children under the age of accountability ("they need neither water baptism nor the sacraments"); divine healing for all of God's children ("but the piety of those who do not see or are unable to claim their privilege in this respect should not be questioned"); singing and music; the support of the gospel; marriage; divorce ("no divorce except for adultery"); intemperance ("no one shall be . . . retained as a member who is guilty of using alcoholic or intoxicating liquors as a beverage. . . . the raising of tobacco for human use is injurious to the soul as its personal use is injurious to the body, mind, and moral nature"); conformity to the world ("members should keep free from oath-bound secret societies and worldly amusements, such as dancing, moving picture shows, automobile and horse racing, and gambling . . . . church suppers and festivals are prohibited. We also insist on plainness and modesty in dress"); national reform ("[we] will use all our influence to have the Bible read in our public schools and have all laws recognizing and protecting the Lord's Day faithfully enforced. . . . all [inter]national differences should be settled by arbitration"); the call to the ministry; heaven; hell; Christ's second coming, the rapture, the tribulation, the millennium, and the resurrection of the unjust "to receive a just retribution"; warning against false doctrines (such as that "we are eternally saved once we have believed"; that "the gift of tongues must be obtained as an evidence [of the gift of the Holy Ghost]"; that "sickness is sin and error"; that "our salvation is dependent upon keeping the seventh day as the Sabbath"; and "the theory of evolution [and] the teaching of modernism").[79]

The headquarters are at Gibraltar, Pennsylvania 19524. The general superintendent is the chief administrative officer. The conference meets annually. There are approximately 30 churches with a total of 1,000 reported members. In 1945 the denomination took over a foreign mission in Jamaica.

### Church of God (Apostolic)

Elder Thomas J. Cox (d. 1943) organized the Christian Faith Band at Danville, Kentucky in 1897 and incorporated it under that designation in 1901. A predominantly black Holiness group, it adopted its present name in 1915 as "more scriptural," but because of some internal resistance to the change, incorporation under the new designation was postponed until 1919.

Local congregations admit members either by a letter of recommendation from another Christian congregation or by repentance for sin, a confession of faith made in the presence of the congregation and the pastor, and baptism by immersion in the name of Jesus Christ.

The Church of God (Apostolic) practices foot washing and celebrates the Lord's Supper with unleavened bread and wine (which the *Discipline* defines as unfermented grape juice in contrast to water) once a month. The Articles of Faith affirm one living and true God, the one substance of the Father and the Son, the unity of the Godhead, the need for repentance toward God, water baptism in the name of the Lord Jesus, and the initiatory right of those thus baptized to the baptism of the Holy Ghost and fire. The *Discipline* of the church body also teaches tithing; the premillennial second coming of Christ; the postmillennial resurrection, white throne judgment, and destruction of the dead who did not know God; obedience to the laws of the land, but not "in war, nor going to war"; the doctrine that "the Father, the Word, [and] the Holy Ghost . . . are manifested in the person of Jesus Christ"; speaking with other tongues as the accompaniment of the baptism of the Holy Ghost; instant sanctification that is carried on into holiness and godly living; divine healing (although the Church of God [Apostolic] does "not condemn those who are weak in faith for using medicine"); and justification by faith. The "Guide for Woman's Home Missionary Societies" appended to the *Discipline* concludes with the Apostles' Creed; in it "he descended into hell" is omitted and "the holy church of God" replaces "the holy catholic church."[80] Although the Church of God (Apostolic) does not regard itself as a Pentecostal body, it shares the general theological position of Pentecostal "Oneness" organizations.

The General Assembly is the highest authority in the church body. The general overseer or apostle, who is also the senior bishop, holds office for an indefinite term. Both men and women are admitted to the ministry. Annual conferences meet in each of the five districts. The general headquarters are at 11th Street and Highland Avenue, Winston-Salem, North Carolina 27101. There are 25 churches in Virginia, West Virginia, Georgia, the Carolinas, Florida, Pennsylvania, New York, and Michigan, with a membership estimated at 1,000.[81]

### The Metropolitan Church Association

A revival movement in the Metropolitan Methodist Church, Chicago, in 1894 led to the organization of the Metropolitan Church Association (chartered in 1899, incorporated in Wisconsin in 1918) to carry on evangelistic work in the city's slums. Sometimes called the [Church of the] Burning Bush, its work has expanded with the years to a point where it has centers in various parts of the United States (including the United States Virgin Islands) and foreign missions in India (7,000 members under native pastors), and the Republic of South Africa. Its Wesleyan theology strongly emphasizes holiness. It rejects all creeds "except such as may be found in the Scriptures themselves."

Its government, overseen by an annual General Assembly, also gives evidence of the Methodist origins of the association. Fifteen churches in the United States report 400 members.[82] International headquarters are at 323 Broad Street, Lake Geneva, Wisconsin 53147.

### Lumber River Annual Conference of the Holiness Methodist Church

The Lumber River Annual Conference of the Holiness Methodist Church is the present name of a Holiness body organized in North Carolina in 1900 as the Lumber River Mission Conference of the Holiness Methodist Church. It emphasizes Christ's atonement, "holiness in heart and life," the witness of the Spirit, and home missions. It does not have an itinerant ministry. Seven churches report 522 members.[83] The Annual Conference meets with the bishop as presiding officer. There are no central headquarters.

### The Church of God (Sanctified Church)

Convinced that the complete plan of salvation as set forth in the Bible required teaching two separate works of grace—justification and sanctification—some of the members of the black Mount Lebanon Baptist Church, Columbia, Tennessee, withdrew from that congregation in 1901. Under the leadership of Elders John C. Brown and Charlie W. Gray (1861–1945), they organized a church of their own, which they called the Church of God,[84] and erected a building on East Eighth Street in Columbia. To obviate legal difficulties that might arise from a confusion of their church with other churches that called themselves Churches of God, they added "(Sanctified Church)" to the original designation.

The new movement grew rapidly in central Tennessee and the first convention of the Church of God (Sanctified Church) was held in 1903 at Nashville. The assembly elected Elder John R. Inman (1848–1917) of Lebanon as chairman. His administration and that of his successor, Elder John Ledsay Rucker (1872–1946) of Knoxville, saw the continuation of an intensive program of revivals, evangelism, and church establishment that ultimately carried the movement into nine states, the Panama Canal Zone, and Jamaica.

Tentative efforts looking to union with the Church of Christ (Holiness) U.S.A. in 1924 were unsuccessful.[85]

In 1927 a schism divided the church body. Under the leadership of Elder Gray about one third of the churches withdrew and organized the Original Church of God (or Sanctified Church), while the remaining two thirds continued under Elder Rucker's leadership. Elder Theopolis Dickenson McGhee (1882–1965) of Detroit succeeded Elder Rucker as general overseer and was in turn succeeded by Elder Jesse E. Evans (b. 1903).[86]

The statement of faith, as set forth in the manual of the Church of God (Sanctified Church), consists of twenty-five articles. The first seven are identical with the statement of faith of the National Association of Evangelicals. The remaining articles affirm that the Bible is God's revelation; that original sin exists in all human beings until "eradicated or destroyed by the Holy Ghost through the blood of Christ"; that Christ atoned for the sins of the whole human race through the shedding of his blood; that the Spirit of God graciously helps the penitent heart to a sincere change of mind and a turning away from sin; that justification is a work of God that grants full pardon to all who believe and takes away the guilt of their sin; that regeneration is the work of God that gives believers spiritual life and takes from them their love of sin; and that sanctification is the act of divine grace that makes reborn believers holy and takes away their inclination to sin. They also affirm Christ's resurrection, ascension, and intercession; his second coming; believer's baptism by immersion; Christ's institution of the Lord's Supper; foot washing as an act of obedience to Christ's example; the gift of the Holy Ghost subsequent to conversion; the spiritual gifts of 1 Corinthians 12-14 (but in such a way that none of these gifts, including the gift of speaking in foreign tongues understood by human beings, is to be trusted or required as evidence of the Holy Spirit's presence); divine healing (without condemnation of physicians and medicines); the identity of the Church of God (Sanctified Church) with the body of Christ, in which he continues to do the will of God; the obligation of the Church of God (Sanctified Church) to seek the fellowship of all Christians who are sound in faith and doctrine; the conversion of sinners, the sanctification of believers, and the preaching of the gospel to every creature; and the necessity of persons seeking fellowship with the Church of God (Sanctified Church) to believe the statement of faith, particularly those articles that refer to the Trinity, the inspiration of the Bible, the sufficiency of the Bible as containing all truth necessary for Christian living, and the necessity of the sanctification of believers through faith in Jesus.[87]

The prohibitions of the general rules include the use of strong drinks and tobacco; going to extremes in dress or conduct; sodomy and adultery; going to any place of entertainment; reading unwholesome literature; and belonging to oath-bound secret orders and fraternities.[88]

The headquarters of the Church of God (Sanctified Church) are at 1037 Jefferson Street, Nashville, Tennessee 37208. There are 60 churches in eight states with an estimated 5,000 members and 12 churches in Jamaica.[89]

### Original Church of God or Sanctified Church

This is the branch of the Church of God (Sanctified Church) that followed Elder Charlie W. Gray (1861–1945) in the schism of 1927.[90]

Its *Hand Book* identifies the church as it is revealed in the New Testament with the body of Christ, with Christ as its head. It lists hearing and attention, repentance, faith, confession, and baptism as the steps in regeneration. It describes the baptism of the Holy Spirit as the "second blessing," a definite experience after regeneration that means holiness of heart and life. It names the Lord's Supper and foot washing as the ordinances of the church. It sees the ministry as composed of bishops, deacons, and elders. It regards Christ and the apostles as setting the example of ordination of the ministry. It holds that, while Elder Gray discouraged the ordination of women, the Bible does not determine the issue and the decision rests with the local church; but if a woman baptizes she does so "without Christ's or the apostles' authority." Marriage is a lifelong union that can be broken only on account of fornication. Tithing has biblical warrant but no special New Testament command.[91]

Negotiations are going on looking to a reunion with the Church of God (Sanctified Church).

The leadership of the Original Church of God or Sanctified Church claims about 85 churches and missions, with a total active membership estimated at 4,700.[92]

### Faith Mission Church

In the mid-1880s teams usually of four men—known as "Pentecost bands"—were sent out by Bishop Benjamin Titus Roberts of the Free Methodist Church to conduct revivals in various parts of the central United States. One of the major early leaders of the movement was Vivian A. Dake. In a number of places churches grew out of these revivals; some of these withdrew from the Free Methodist Church and in 1898 associated themselves as the Pentecost Bands of the World, with headquarters in Indianapolis. In 1925 they took the name of Missionary Bands of the World, Incorporated, and in 1958 they became a part of the Wesleyan Methodist Church (now part of the Wesleyan Church). Around the turn of the century a group from the Indianapolis headquarters established a church in Bedford, Indiana, and called it the Pentecost Faith Mission of Bedford. In 1963 it took the name Faith Mission Church.

Its articles of faith have sections on the Trinity; Christ; the Holy Spirit; the plenary inspiration of the Bible; original sin or depravity ("it continues to exist with the new life of the regenerate until eradicated by the baptism with the Holy Spirit"); the atonement ("[it] is the only ground of salvation and . . . it is sufficient for every individual"); free agency ("[a human being,] though in possession of the experience of regeneration, and entire sanctification, may fall from grace and apostatize . . . the doctrine of eternal security, or once in grace always in grace, or absolute final perseverance of the saints, is not in harmony with the teaching of the Scriptures"); repentance; justification, regeneration, and adoption ("simultaneous in the experience of seekers after God"); entire sanctification ("synonymous to and simultaneous with the baptism with the Holy Ghost and fire . . . the gift of tongues, so called, as proof of this baptism is opposed to the explicit word of God"); Christ's second coming; resurrection, judgment, destiny; water baptism ("a sacrament signifying acceptance of the benefits of the atonement. . . . young children

may be baptized"); the Lord's Supper; and divine healing ("[but] providential means and agencies when deemed necessary should not be refused").[93]
The Faith Mission Church has a membership of about 100.[94]

### Pillar of Fire

Alma White (1862–1946) was the wife of a Methodist Episcopal minister-evangelist in Colorado. From 1896 on she too conducted revivals in Denver and in many other western communities as far as Butte, Montana. In many of them she established what she called "Pentecostal Missions." She helped to organize the Colorado Holiness Association, and opened a training home for the education of converts who expressed a desire to devote their lives to missionary service. In 1902 the need for some kind of organization became evident, and she incorporated her work as "The Pentecostal Union." In 1905 she began publishing a bulletin for her movement and called it *Pillar of Fire*. Gradually the name of the widely circulated magazine displaced the corporate name of its sponsor in the minds of its readers, and in 1917 it became the official name of the body. From the start educational concerns bulked large in the organization's planning and operations; today the Pillar of Fire operates an educational system that begins with elementary schools and continues through college and Bible seminary. It was one of the first religious denominations to acquire its own radio stations.

Theologically the Pillar of Fire is a Fundamentalist Holiness body in the Primitive Methodist tradition. Its eleven-article Statement of Faith affirms the inspiration of the Scriptures; "repentance toward God and faith toward our Lord Jesus Christ"; justification by faith and entire sanctification as a second definite work of grace; the immortality of the soul and the resurrection of the body; the judgments that the Bible teaches; water baptism in whatever mode the candidate elects; the Lord's Supper; marriage as a divine institution; divine healing; Christ's premillennial coming and the restoration of the Jews; and eternal punishment for the wicked and life everlasting for the righteous.[95]

Since 1908 the Pillar of Fire's headquarters have been at Zarephath, New Jersey 08890. It ordains both men and women to the ministry. The form of government shows Methodist influence. There are district superintendents called presiding elders and a bishop. The foundress was the first to hold the latter office; her son, Arthur K. White, has succeeded her. There are 50 churches and centers in 17 states and the District of Columbia, with a total membership of about 4,500. There are also two centers in England and a foreign mission in Liberia.[96]

### Christian Nation Church of the United States of America

In 1892 Edward Day and seven others organized the Equality Evangelists at Mount Victory, Ohio. They met with little permanent success. Undaunted,

Day remarshaled the little company in 1894. In 1895 they reorganized at Marion, Ohio, as the Christian Nation Evangelists, and the next year they incorporated themselves as the Christian Nation Church. In this way they sought to create a community within which they could take care of their converts, since the opposition of the existing denominations in the area of the movement's operations made it impossible for the evangelists' converts to belong to these churches. It took its present name when it was reincorporated in 1961.

The Christian Nation Church of the United States of America is trinitarian. It teaches salvation by grace and not by the keeping of rules. It asserts that it opposes no organization that can bring a human being to the Lamb of God that takes away the sins of the world, but that it rejects the sympathy and cooperation of those who have a form of godliness but not its power. Of its own members it demands that they lead exemplary Christian lives.

Its statement of faith has to do chiefly with practice. It rejects as unbiblical the wearing of needless ornaments, gold, or expensive clothing; calls upon its members to dress neatly but in perfectly plain attire; forbids membership in societies and clubs, secret or not secret, composed even in part of unsaved and ungodly persons; denies membership to a divorced person whose former spouse is still alive; prohibits the sale and manufacture of liquor; limits activity on Sabbath, that is, Sunday, to necessary work only and discourages the use of public conveyances on that day as much as possible; calls for its members to marry only saved persons; discountenances dishonesty; encourages each husband and wife to raise as large a family as God gives them; forbids festivals, entertainments, and Christmas trees; rejects obtaining money from congregations except by free-will offerings; calls for the practice of tithing; discountenances jesting, worldly songs, vulgarity, and slang; requires the enforcement of "social purity"; recommends to its members that they do not resist any injury done to them; holds that every hour should be spent at some important line of work or study; recommends fasting and prayer for others and charity for the worthy sick and needy; condemns the use and sale of tobacco; believes in the fourfold gospel of justification, entire sanctification as a separate act of faith in believers subsequent to justification ("to be 'sanctified' is identical with [the] experience of 'being filled' or 'baptized with the Holy Ghost' "), divine healing ("promised to all who keep God's and nature's laws carefully and prayerfully"), and Christ's return ("perhaps soon, to take his bride the church with him to reign one thousand years before the final judgment"); affirms the unity in heart and love of all Christians, regardless of denomination or difference of doctrines not necessary to salvation; and accepts baptism (normally by immersion, although the mode is not insisted upon) and the Lord's Supper as biblical ordinances.[97]

The church's congress meets annually. The senior officer is the general overseer. It has no formal headquarters. There are 16 churches with an inclusive membership estimated at 3,000.[98]

## The Churches of Christ in Christian Union

In order to have greater freedom to preach and teach the Wesleyan-Arminian message of full salvation, five ministers and some sixty laypersons left the Christian Union in 1909 and organized the Churches of Christ in Christian Union. The 1940s ushered in a period of rapid expansion, especially after the Annual Council of 1945 authorized the organization of state and district councils. In 1952 the surviving remnants of the Reformed Methodist Church joined the Churches of Christ in Christian Union.[99]

The strongly evangelistic thrust of the denomination finds expression in revival campaigns, missionary conventions, and camp meetings. Its worship is simple, with little emphasis on form.

The Churches of Christ in Christian Union teach the Trinity; Christ's deity, incarnation, virgin birth, sinlessness, ascension, intercession, and pre-millennial return; the role of the Holy Spirit in convicting sinners of sin, regenerating the believers, and sanctifying consecrated Christians; the infallibility and sufficiency of the Bible; sin both as willful disobedience to God's known law and as the evil twist and corruption in human nature; the possibility of redemption through Christ's atoning death and resurrection, which has won for Christians regeneration and baptism by the Spirit into the body of Christ, entire sanctification and cleansing from the carnal mind, growth in grace after sanctification, and immortality of body and soul; water baptism and the Lord's Supper (with no prescribed mode of administration for either) as outward symbols of the inner life, faith, and hope of the participants, but not as saving ordinances; the dedication of children ("this *may* be by baptism"); the church as the totality of all believers, commissioned to take the gospel to every creature; Sunday as a day of rest and worship; and an eternal hereafter in heaven for believers and in perdition for the wicked.[100]

The denomination reports 260 churches in 15 states with 10,100 members. Its headquarters are at Circleville, Ohio 43113. The General Council meets every two years, the district councils annually. A general superintendent heads the organization. The denomination conducts foreign missions in cooperation with the World Gospel Mission in the West Indies, Mexico, and New Guinea.

## Church of the Gospel

Around the end of the nineteenth century the Reverend C. T. Pike became pastor of the Advent Christian Church in Pittsfield, Massachusetts. Later he and his wife developed an interest in the Holiness movement and they and many of the members of the congregation received the experience of entire sanctification. The Pikes withdrew from the Advent Christian Church, established a Holiness church in Pittsfield in 1911, and began to conduct revivals in various communities. In 1911 they incorporated the church body as the Church of God; to obviate confusion with other organizations that they had founded bearing the same name, the church body took the name Church of the Gospel in 1930.

The Church of the Gospel believes in baptism by immersion, sanctification as a second work of grace, anointing with oil and prayer for the healing of the sick, and Christ's imminent second coming. The Church of the Gospel stresses holiness of heart and its standards of discipleship are exacting. Membership in unions or lodges and the wearing of short skirts, short sleeves, silk stockings, and jewelry is prohibited. The Church of the Gospel holds that organized Christianity today has only the form of religion but denies its power.

The churches in Hudson Falls, New York, and Aroda, Virginia, own their own building. Elsewhere meetings are held in homes. Though the headquarters are at 20½ Walnut Street, Hudson Falls, New York 12839, the majority of the members live in Virginia. There are 3 congregations with a total membership of 50.

### The Missionary Methodist Church of America

About 1910–1912 controversies about the use of tobacco, the wearing of jewelry, membership in secret societies, tithing, and women preachers agitated the Wesleyan Methodist Church in North Carolina. In July 1913 about nine tenths of the members of the Wesleyan Methodist Church in Forest City withdrew, and some twenty-five or so of the seceders, led by the Reverend Henry Clay Sisk, organized the Holiness Methodist Church. A successful tent meeting at nearby Caroleen led to the organization of a second church the same year. When the annual conference became aware of the existence of the older Lumber River Conference of the Holiness Methodist Church in the same state it changed its name to the Missionary Methodist Church. An effort to unite the Missionary Methodist Church with the Congregational Methodist Church in 1942 failed because of the geographical distance between the bodies, differences in organization and doctrine, and attachment to the denominational name. In 1947 an effort at uniting the Missionary Methodist Church and the People's Christian Movement (founded 1937) also failed.[101] The latter body, also known as the People's Methodist Church, merged with the Evangelical Methodist Church (Wichita, Kansas) in 1962.

Missionary Methodists believe in the divine origin and inspiration of the Holy Scriptures; in Christ as the head of the church, and the Holy Scriptures as the only guide to faith; in the divine origin of the ministry of deacons, elders, and stewards in the church; in the equality in rank of all elders; and in the duty of Christians to take or send the gospel to every nation as part of their obligation to their brothers.

The *Doctrine, Creed and Rules* contains a twenty-one-part statement of belief modeled broadly on the conventional twenty-five Articles of Religion of Methodism. It omits the articles on works of supererogation, the church, purgatory, worship in a tongue not understood by the people, both kinds in the Lord's Supper, the marriage of ministers, the rulers of the United States of America, Christian men's goods, and a Christian's oath. It adds articles on "relative duties," that is, obligations to others, and on regeneration or the new birth, holiness and entire sanctification, the general resurrection of the dead, and the general or final judgment. The *Doctrine* retitles some of the remaining articles, extensively recasts some of them, and provides many of them with biblical documentation. Among the sacraments the *Doctrine* includes the washing of the brethren's feet.[102]

The church still prohibits the use of tobacco by its ministers; it now admits women to the ministry and urges tithing on its members. A divorced person whose spouse is still living may neither preach nor become a pastor.

Thirteen churches in North Carolina have a total membership of 1,708; there are 3 affiliated churches in Virginia. The Annual Conference is the highest lawmaking body. For over twenty-five years the denomination has been affiliated with the Oriental Missionary Society (with headquarters at Greenwood, Indiana) and has supported its foreign missionary endeavors in Haiti, Latin America, the Republic of China (Taiwan), India, Hong Kong, Japan, and Korea.[103]

### Kentucky Mountain Holiness Association

The work of the Kentucky Mountain Holiness Association, which now has congregations in eight eastern Kentucky counties, began in 1924, when Lela G. McConnell, who had just been ordained deacon in the Methodist Episcopal Church, came to Breathitt County, Kentucky, to begin a militant ministry of preaching and teaching that extended over four decades. The association, organized in 1925 and incorporated in 1931, maintains two elementary schools, a high school, a three-year college-level Bible institute for the training of fulltime Christian workers, a radio station, and a camp-meeting ground. Although interdenominational, this evangelistic body has a strong Methodist orientation. It explicitly affirms the Wesleyan-Arminian interpretation of Christian doctrine, including the plenary inspiration of the Bible; Christ's deity, virgin birth, vicarious atonement, bodily resurrection, and personal premillennial return; the deity of the Holy Spirit; the inheritance of the carnal nature by all people as a consequence of the fall; justification through faith; the resurrection and glorification of the saints; and the eternal punishment of the wicked. "True Christian holiness" or sanctification as a definite, instantaneous, second work of grace through faith that the Holy Spirit accomplishes and witnesses to in believers receives special emphasis.[104]

The association has 25 churches and missions; an estimate of the overall membership is not available. In addition to domestic missions among Mexicans, North American Indians, and Chinese, it maintains foreign missionaries in Africa, Asia, Latin America, Japan, the Republic of the Philippines, the Republic of China (Taiwan), Central and South America, and the islands of the Caribbean Sea.[105] Its headquarters are at Jackson, Kentucky 41339.

### Kodesh Church of Immanuel

The Reverend Frank Russell Killingsworth of Washington, D.C., founded the Kodesh Church of Immanuel at Philadelphia in October 1929 and incorporated it in 1930. He reports that when he prayed to God to reveal to him a name for the movement, God turned his mind to Isaiah 7:14. In a subsequent vision he saw very distinctly the Hebrew word *qôdesh*, "pure, sanctified, holy." He combined these insights into the name the church body now bears.

The theological position of this interracial but predominantly black church body stresses rebirth from above and entire sanctification. The latter is a second supernatural work of grace that is subsequent to rebirth and that is obtainable in this present life on the condition of absolute consecration and receptive faith. The denomination forbids the use of alcoholic beverages and tobacco, pride of dress and behavior, Sabbath desecration, dissolute dancing, membership in secret societies, and attendance at immoral theatrical presentations. It recognizes adultery as the only ground for divorce. It baptizes by pouring, sprinkling, or immersing. It practices divine healing, but not to the exclusion of scientific remedies or means. It regards love as the highest gift of God to human beings and sees the witness and fruit of the Holy Spirit as the only infallible evidence of a holy heart. It rejects tongue-speaking that is unintelligible and incomprehensible to the hearers. It teaches Christ's imminent and premillennial return. It draws its support from the tithes and free-will offerings of its members.

Annual assemblies endorse candidates for the ministry; the General Assembly, which meets once every four years, enacts church laws and consecrates the supervising elders. Six churches in Pennsylvania, Ohio, and Virginia have about 4,000 members. The denomination maintains a mission in Liberia.[106]

### The Apostolic Methodist Church

During the negotiations that finally led in (1939) to the formation of The Methodist Church, an itinerant Methodist minister in Florida, the Reverend E. H. Crowson (b. 1898) and his father, the Reverend F. L. Crowson (1876–1963), began to protest vehemently against what they called the modernistic tendencies in the then Methodist Episcopal Church, South. They charged it with declension from the historic Wesleyan position on holiness and on other fundamental issues. The Florida Conference, to which both Crowsons belonged, "located"—that is, deposed from the itinerant ministry—the younger Crowson for "unsuitability" in 1931. The next year he and a few others organized the Apostolic Methodist Church at Loughman, Florida.[107]

In general, the teaching of the Apostolic Methodist Church is that of the "second blessing" Holiness type of body. It stresses the Bible as the free and independent word of God. Its doctrine of the last things is premillennial. The *Discipline* of the body rejects "the papalistic type of episcopacy" and recognizes only two orders of the ministry—deacons and elders.[108]

The secretary of the General Assembly of the Apostolic Methodist Church, Pastor-Elder E. H. Crowson, receives mail at Box 1106, Kissimmee, Florida 32741. No information is available on the number of churches or the active membership of the Apostolic Methodist Church.[109]

## Oriental Missionary Society Holiness Conference of North America

The Oriental Missionary Society came into being in 1901. The scope of its work included Japanese immigrants to the West Coast of the United States. In 1920 six seminarians of Japanese ancestry—Henry T. Sakuma, George Yahiro, Paul Okamoto, Aya Okuda, Toshio Hirano, Hatsu Yano, and Hanako Yoneyama—all of whom were deeply concerned about the evangelization of their own people in California, united in a prayer fellowship. The next step was the organization of the Los Angeles Holiness Church in 1921. This independent, indigenous work branched out to other parts of California in 1924, then to other states,[110] and eventually, in 1932, to Hawaii. The Oriental Missionary Society Holiness Conference of North America came into being in 1934 as a means of coordinating the work of the participating churches. The relocation of Japanese immigrants in the continental United States during World War II brought the work of the conference to an almost complete stop, except in the case of the Honolulu Holiness Church (formerly the Japanese Holiness Church), which was able to function throughout the war. The churches in the continental United States reestablished themselves in 1945/1946. Because of the language problem, the conference has two divisions and each church has two separate congregations, one Japanese-speaking and the other English-speaking, and two pastors.

The statement of faith in its constitution commits the conference to the Bible in its entirety as the word of God revealed by his spirit and to the Apostles' Creed as its creedal basis. It places major emphasis on the "fourfold gospel." First, penitent believers in Christ are saved instantly, their sins are forgiven, and they are justified, regenerated, and made children of God. Second, Christ's blood and the baptism of the Holy Spirit is able to sanctify the regenerated heart, even though it still has original sin in it. Third, the power of God through faith can heal physical illness. Fourth, Christ's second coming will be premillennial.[111]

The conference believes that there are two ordinances, or sacraments, baptism and Holy Communion. It regards immersion as the formal mode of baptism, other modes as informal. Holy Communion is open to members of any church. Only ordained ministers may officiate in these ordinances.[112]

The conference's Southern California Ministers' Fellowship adopted a revised supplementary statement of faith in 1970. It affirms the Trinity; the divine inspiration of the Bible; the creation of human beings in the image of God and their separation from him through disobedience; salvation only by the grace of God through faith in Christ and in his redemptive act and by the work of the Holy Spirit; the initiation of spiritual growth and maturity in the believer by God's Spirit and by a conscious act of self-dedication on the part of the believer, and the effectuation of spiritual growth and maturity by the Holy Spirit's indwelling; the church as consisting of all who have been regenerated through faith and have been united into one body; and the church's vocation to worship God, preach the gospel, administer the ordinances, and care for and nurture the believers.[113]

The General Conference meets annually. A nine-member Executive Council implements the decisions of the conference.

The headquarters are at 3660 South Gramercy Place, Los Angeles, California 90018. There are seven churches in California, one in Honolulu. The total membership is estimated at just under 1,500.[114]

### God's Missionary Church

God's Missionary Church was formed in 1935 by members of the Pennsylvania–New Jersey District of the Pilgrim Holiness Church (now part of the Wesleyan Church) who were unhappy over trends in the parent body, which relaxed traditional Holiness structures. Those responsible for its founding are the Reverend William Straub and the Reverend Daniel W. Dubendorf. Avowedly missionary in approach, the church body takes over abandoned church buildings to serve as the sites for missionary outreach. It carries on foreign mission work in Haiti. Its 37 churches and 1,200 members are located primarily in Pennsylvania, though the church body is represented also in Florida, Maryland, Ohio, Indiana, and Arkansas. The headquarters are located at Penns Creek, Pennsylvania 17862.[115]

### Sanctified Church of Christ

In order to preserve the heritage of "true scriptural holiness," a small group of concerned people organized the Sanctified Church of Christ at Columbus, Georgia, in July 1937. The church lays particular stress on the experience of sanctification as a second definite, instantaneous work of grace. It regards its doctrine as in harmony with that of the Church of the Nazarene, the Wesleyan Church, and the Evangelical Methodist Church.

Seventeen articles of faith in twelve chapters affirm the Trinity; Christ's deity, incarnation, vicarious sacrifice, and exaltation; the activity of the Holy Ghost in and with the church; the sufficiency of the Bible, the inerrant and inspired word of God; humanity's creation and fall; the possibility that even human beings in the possession of forgiveness and sanctification may fall from grace and be eternally lost; original or inherent sin ("God does not forgive original sin in us and it continues to exist, though suppressed . . . until eradicated or destroyed by the baptism with the Holy Ghost"); the sufficiency of the atonement as the ground of salvation for every human being and its efficacy for "the irresponsible from birth, or for the righteous who have become irresponsible, and to children in innocency"; salvation only through faith, the gift of God, "exercised by humans with the aid of the Spirit, which aid is assured when the heart has met the divine condition" of Hebrews 5:9; the necessity of repentance; justification of the penitent soul that trusts in the merits of Christ's shed blood, as an act in which God pardons all past sins of commission; instantaneous sanctification, provided through the shed blood of Jesus and preceded by complete consecration, as an act of God subsequent to forgiveness "by which believers are made free from original sin or depravity," not in the sense of a "suppression or counteraction" but of "destruction and eradication" ("this experience is wrought by the baptism with the Holy Ghost and is that essential 'holiness without which no man shall see the Lord' "); the witness of the Spirit to the justification of the sinner and the sanctification of the believer; the personal return of Christ; the resurrection of the dead and a future judgment followed by everlasting life for "all who savingly believe in and obediently follow" Christ, and eternal suffering for the finally impenitent.[116]

The General Rules forbid slang; profaning the Lord's Day by unnecessary labor or business or holiday diversions; membership in oath-bound secret orders or fraternities (other than labor unions); wearing of shorts by either sex; men going shirtless; wearing of jewelry (including wedding rings); women plucking eyebrows, using cosmetics, or dying their hair; public or mixed bathing; transparent apparel or immodest attire; attending the theater, motion pictures, dances, circuses, carnivals; card playing; all competitive games or sports, including bowling and skating. They counsel women against wearing slacks, jeans, pedal pushers, and any clothing pertaining to men, as well as cutting their hair. They describe television as dangerous and detrimental to spirituality and urge that it be not watched.[117]

The Special Rules prohibit marriage between a holy and an unholy person, divorce (except for fornication), and remarriage after a divorce granted for reasons other than fornication or adultery. Members "called into war service . . . are to offer themselves" for noncombatant service.[118]

A council of twelve members is the chief legislative and ruling body. The Annual Conference consists of the council and delegates from the churches. The general superintendent presides over both. There is also a bishop; the only episcopal function that the constitution specifies is to ordain.

There are 7 churches in Georgia, Florida, Louisiana, Mississippi, Arkansas, and Tennessee. The total membership is nearly 1,000.[119] A recent letter to the bishop was returned marked "MOVED."

## Wesleyan Tabernacle Association

The Wesleyan Tabernacle Association came into being in 1937 "to promote Christian love and understanding among godly leaders of various undenominational holiness bodies," to "create a greater field of fellowship and service for holiness evangelistic preachers and singers," and to "offer credentials to worthy persons desiring them." It disclaims the intention of exercising "any jurisdiction over local congregations." The association meets annually.

Six Articles of Faith affirm God as Creator; Christ the Savior and head of the church; the Holy Spirit ("now the representative of the Godhead on earth"); the Trinity; the Bible ("infallibly true as originally given"); the plan of salvation as consisting of true repentance and faith to bring the forgiveness of sins and the experience of the new birth, followed by unconditional abandonment to God forever of all that we are and have and unwavering faith in the promise of the Father to bring the baptism of the Holy Spirit, an instantaneous experience received by faith, cleansing the heart of the recipient from all sin and endowing him with power for service; the resurrection of the body and the judgment of all human beings, followed by everlasting punishment for the wicked and eternal happiness for the righteous.[120]

The association recommends divine healing as a Bible doctrine and the offering of the prayer of faith for the healing of the sick. It further recommends water baptism "as an outward sign of an inward work wrought in the heart by the Holy Spirit" and the reverent observance of the Lord's Supper as "representing our redemption through Christ." It also recommends that its preacher proclaim from time to time the personal and premillennial return of the Lord.[121]

The moderator resides at 9841 South 82nd Avenue, Palos Hills, Illinois 60465. The association has 26 affiliated congregations in the United States and 104 in Haiti. No information is available about the total membership. It also enrolls 173 ordained ministers of both sexes, 53 licensed ministers, 10 song evangelists, and 19 commissioned Christian workers.[122]

## Emmanuel Association

The late Reverend Ralph J. Finch organized the Emmanuel Association in Carthage, Kentucky, in 1942, in order "to promote scriptural, practical, and personal holiness and holy living" and to "be uncompromising in its teaching and world wide in its field."

The association's Principles of Faith show the influence of the Twenty-five Articles of Religion of Methodism. There are paragraphs on each of the persons of the Holy Trinity; on the Holy Scriptures; on original sin ("it continues to exist after regeneration, though subdued, until eradicated and destroyed by the mighty baptism of the Holy Ghost and of Fire"); on living faith ("to be distinguished from intellectual confidence which may be in the possession of any unawakened soul"); on justification and regeneration ("though these two phases of the new birth occur simultaneously, they are, in fact, two separate and distinct acts"); on consecration; on entire sanctification or the baptism with the Holy Ghost ("whereby the heart of the believer is cleansed from all original sin and purified by the filling of the Holy Ghost"); on the witness of the Spirit ("none should think that they are either saved or sanctified until the Spirit of God has added His testimony"); on the possibility of sin after justification; on the possibility of sin after entire sanctification; on water baptism ("it is not to be held as being essential in bringing either justifying or sanctifying grace to one's heart. . . . the individual conscience should be satisfied as to the mode")[123]; on the Lord's Supper ("the elements used are representative[124] and the means whereby the body of Christ is received and eaten in the supper is faith"); on healing ("it is the privilege of every child of God to be healed in answer to the prayer of faith . . . yet we are not to sever fellowship from, or pass judgment on, those who use other providential means for the restoration of health"); on the Christian Sabbath ("of divine origin . . . we recognize the first day of the week as being the Christian Sabbath under the present dispensation"); and on the second coming of Christ ("personal and premillennial, also . . . imminent; . . . the rapture . . . may occur at any moment, [but] the revelation . . . will not occur until after the gathering of Israel, the manifestation of Antichrist and other prophesied events").[125]

Worldly amusements ("dances, shows, theaters, fairs, horse and auto races, places where gambling is indulged in, competitive games, festivals, church plays, and church picnics and socials . . . radio and television") are death to spiritual life. Modesty requires women to wear "dresses with full length sleeves, without low necks, and in length not more than nine inches from the floor" and not to patronize beauty parlors or to duplicate their work. Men and women are to avoid gaudy or transparent apparel and not wear jewelry (including wedding rings). In dressing their children they are to avoid short stockings, short sleeves, loud colors, and transparent apparel. Members of the association are to abstain from handling or using intoxicating liquors, tobacco, and habit-forming drugs, from worldly associations (including secret societies, oath-bound lodges, labor unions, and other organizations of both capital and labor), and from worldly business, pleasure seeking, and any occupation or travel that does not glorify God on Sunday. The local church must maintain a Christian day school or an association of Christian parents must employ Christian teachers to educate their children. Members of the association "cannot participate in war, war activities, or compulsory military training." While the association holds that "war, duelling, suicide, prenatal destruction of human life, and all other forms of wilful human life-taking are murder," it allows its members to seek protection under a civil law that is in harmony with the gospel. Ministers should "publicly enforce" the apostolic caution not to be unequally yoked together with unbelievers. No divorced and remarried person may belong to the association.[126]

The ministry of the association consists of local workers, licensed ministers, and ordained ministers; all three levels are open to both sexes.

The headquarters of the association are at West Cucharras and 27th Street, Colorado Springs, Colorado 80904. It reports 17 churches in 9 states and Canada, with a total estimated membership of 400. It supports a mission in Guatemala.[127]

## The Methodist Protestant Church

From the very organization of the Methodist Episcopal Church in 1784, some lay members were unhappy with the form of government that the body had adopted. In the second and third decades of the nineteenth century they began in considerable numbers to voice their dissatisfaction at the "exclusion of laymen from the councils of the church and the withholding from them of the right of suffrage." William S. Stockton, a Philadelphia layman, began publishing his *Wesleyan Repository* in 1821 in the interest of a reform on this point; in 1824 *The Mutual Rights of Ministers and Members of the Methodist Episcopal Church*, published at Baltimore, superseded the earlier journal. The 1824 General Conference rejected a large number of petitions placed before it for the admission of laymen "in the lawmaking department." To "ascertain the number of persons in the Methodist Episcopal Church friendly to a change in her government" and to present a united front at the next General Conference, the proponents of reform organized Union Societies. After the 1828 General Conference reiterated the position of the 1824 assembly, a number of annual conferences began to expel the readers and promoters of *The Mutual Rights*. The expellees and their supporters thereupon launched The Associated Methodist Churches in 1828. In 1830 they adopted the present title. As Americans, the framers of the constitution of the new church took as their model "the church without a bishop and the state without a king." As a necessary part of its organic law it affirmed the equality of all elders and secured to every adult layman the right to vote and to be represented in every church meeting.[128]

The bulk of the Methodist Protestant Church entered the union of 1939 which created The Methodist Church, but part of the membership felt that the union did not adequately stress the John Wesley type of holiness or sufficiently oppose modernism, socialism, and liberalism. This group convoked the 29th Quadrennial Session of the General Conference of the Methodist Protestant Church in 1944 to continue "its doctrine, its government, its faith, and its name."

The Methodist Protestant Church accepts the conventional Twenty-five Articles of Religion of Methodism with some changes. While most of these are minor, some are significant. Thus, for instance, the term "ordinance" consistently replaces the term "sacrament." The Methodist Protestant Church also adds articles on sanctification, on the resurrection of the dead, and on the general judgment. The General Conference of 1884 stipulated that those who enter the ministry of the Methodist Protestant Church avow acceptance of these doctrinal teachings and that "good faith toward the church forbids any teaching on their part which is at variance with them."[129]

The ritual's order for the administration of the Lord's Supper directs that it is to be administered at least once a month in churches with their own ministers.[130] The order for the baptism of infants conceives of this rite primarily as the parents' act of dedicating their children to God.[131]

The Methodist Protestant Church's stress on sanctification as a second work of grace distinguishes this body from the Southern Methodist Church, which has no such emphasis. The Methodist Protestant Church's belief in racial segregation as serving the best interest of both blacks and caucasians differentiates it from the Evangelical Methodist Church for whom this principle is not of major concern. The Methodist Protestant Church accepts literally the biblical account of creation. Its doctrine of the last things is premillennial.[132]

Sixty churches in Mississippi, Louisiana, and Alabama report 3,717 members. The denomination supports foreign missions in Belize, Jamaica, and Korea. The headquarters of the body are at 325 East McDowell Road. P.O. Box 1468, Jackson, Mississippi 39205.

## Holiness Gospel Mission

In 1945 a number of families wihdrew from the Evangelical United Brethren and Church of God denominations and formed the Holiness Gospel Mission. Its theology is generally that of the Wesleyan Methodist type with a strong Holiness emphasis. The mission functions through radio broadcasts, publications, and camp meetings and through three congregations in Pensylvania with a reported total of about 120 members. It conducts a foreign mission in the Bahamas. Its headquarters are at Route 2, Box 13, Etters, Pennsylvania 17319.[133]

## The Fundamental Methodist Church, Incorporated

Following the union of the three Methodist bodies that brought The Methodist Church into being in 1939, the congregation of the John Chapel Methodist Church, Ash Grove, Missouri, under the leadership of the Reverend Roy Keith, withdrew in 1942 in protest against what it called the modernism of the merged body. Two more congregations soon joined forces with the Ash Grove congregation and in 1944 the first Annual Conference of the Fundamental Methodist Church was organized. It was chartered in 1948.

The church body subscribes to twenty-eight articles of religion. In addition to the traditional Methodist twenty-five articles, which—like the General Rules—are for the most part taken over verbatim or with minor changes (such as the elimination of the word "sacrament" and the elision of the last paragraph in the article "Of the Rites and Ceremonies of Churches"), an article "Of Sanctification" is added after the article "Of Justification," and articles "Of the Resurrection of the Dead" and "Of the Judgments" are added after the article "Of the One Obligation [that is, Oblation] of Christ Finished on the Cross." Sanctification is described in the first of the added articles as a setting apart of the regenerated believer by the Holy Spirit which not only delivers him or her from the guilt of sin but washes the person from its pollution and saves the person from its power; it is also described as the continuing of God's grace by which the Christian grows in grace and in the knowledge of Christ. The added articles on the last things assert that the millennium will separate the resurrection and judgment of the just from the resurrection and Great White Throne judgment of the unjust. The article on baptism has been rewritten to require baptism "by emersion [that is, immersion]" as a sign of regeneration or the new birth, but not as the "door into the Fundamental Methodist Church"; it further provides that young children may be dedicated but they are not to be baptized.[134]

The statement of belief published in the annual minutes summarizes the articles of religion, describes "the representative type of church government [as] superior to the episcopal type," calls for support of the church through "storehouse tithing and freewill offerings," rejects the World Council of Churches and the National Council of the Churches of Christ in the United States of America along with local ministerial alliances that have constituencies which belong to the National Council, and affirms the obligation of the Fundamental Methodist Church to affiliate "with the Bible believing American Council of Christian Churches."

There is only one Annual Conference, that of Missouri. The headquarters are at 1028 North Broadway, Springfield, Missouri 65802. There are 15 churches and missions with an inclusive membership of 745.

## The Bible Holiness Movement

The Bible Holiness Movement was organized as the Bible Holiness Mission in Vancouver, British Columbia, Canada in 1949. In that year Wesley H. Wakefield took over the work of his father among the poor and underprivileged of Vancouver and organized the Bible Holiness Mission. The mission was incorporated in 1957 and adopted its present name in 1971. The organization does not require its members to sever relations with other groups but to live by the *Discipline* of the movement as the way to Christian service. The movement has been active in foreign mission work, especially in the Philippines.

Basically Wesleyan in theology, the Bible Holiness Movement has also been influenced by the principles of the Salvation Army.[135] The group affirms the total, but not absolute, depravity of humanity; that prevenient grace as an operation of the Holy Spirit is necessary to draw human beings and enable them to seek God; that the moral commands of the Old Testament, being an expression of God's eternal nature, were not abrogated at the cross but that added grace is conferred through redemption to fulfill them.

Like other Holiness groups, the Bible Holiness Movement teaches entire sanctification as a work of grace for the regenerate but differs from some groups on the means of attainment. "We affirm that there is indeed growth in Christian grace and holiness both before and subsequent to this experience, and that inasmuch as it deals with sin in an inward cleansing of the moral nature, definite repentance (rather than consecration) is the essential to a sanctifying faith. We also do not believe that this experience is the baptism with the Holy Ghost. We also believe in the necessity of a constant as well as an instant cleansing; the constant being a careful walking in the light of God." [136]

The Bible Holiness Movement teaches that atonement is a satisfaction of divine justice and law; that the sacraments are not just symbolic but a means of grace, though "not saving in their requirement or their administration"; and that eschatology is amillennial. On social issues, the group is opposed to war, allowing its members only noncombatant military service; to racism and all forms of racial discrimination and segregation; to abortion, viewing it as a form of murder; to alcoholic beverages, encouraging total abstinence; and to divorce, refusing to recognize remarriage while the divorced partner is alive. Birth control is left to the individual conscience. Members of the movement participate in labor unions and are active in credit unions and cooperatives. In polity the group is congregational.[137]

The Bible Holiness Movement has 5 churches in Canada and 2 in the United States with a total membership of 81, although adherents to the groups are about three times the membership total. The address of the headquarters is P.O. Box 223, Postal Station A, Vancouver, British Columbia, Canada.

## Bible Missionary Church

The Bible Missionary Union came into being in November 1955 as a result of a Holiness evangelistic campaign that the Reverend Glenn Griffith conducted in the fall of that year in the Nampa-Caldwell area of Idaho. Within a year other ministers and congregations in twenty states and three foreign missionary fields had associated themselves with the new movement. Most of the ministers were former elders in the Church of the Nazarene, from which they had withdrawn because of what they described as the parent body's "turn toward liberalism." In September 1956 the Reverend Elbert Dodd (b. 1902) joined the movement at its first General Conference at Denver, Colorado. This General Conference adopted the name Bible Missionary Church.

(Griffith himself subsequently withdrew from the organization and in 1959 helped organize the Wesleyan Holiness Association of Churches.)

The Bible Missionary Church explicitly declares itself in favor of Arminianism and against Calvinism, modernism, and formality, and claims "a God-given right to preach in every place" without apologizing for entering any field. Its Articles of Religion are an adaptation and expansion of the Articles of Faith of the Church of the Nazarene, with added articles on faith, the witness of the Spirit, growth in grace, the first day of the week as the Christian Sabbath under the present dispensation, and the invisible church.[138]

The general office of the Bible Missionary Church is at 1824 Jones Street, Duncan, Oklahoma 73533. The church body is presided over by a two-member board of general moderators. The General Conference meets every four years. District conferences meet annually. There are approximately 220 churches in 38 states; no estimate of the total active membership is available In addition to a mission among the Navajos in New Mexico, the Bible Missionary Church carries on foreign missions in Japan, Okinawa, New Guinea, Nigeria, Guyana, Mexico, and the West Indies.[139]

### Independent Holiness Churches

When the Holiness Movement Church of Canada prepared to unite with the Free Methodist Church, a merger which took place in 1959, a number of its congregations refused to participate in the union and were chartered in 1958 as the Independent Holiness Churches. The polity of the group is congregational. Ministers and wives and three lay delegates from each circuit comprise the Annual Conference. A General Conference meets biennially.

The doctrinal position of the Independent Holiness Churches is summarized in seven statements: (1) one God—the Father, the Son, and the Holy Spirit; (2) the plenary inspiration of the Scriptures; (3) the total moral depravity of the human race; (4) the universality and sufficiency of the atonement of Christ; (5) the obligation of all to repent and believe in Christ who by the Holy Spirit regenerates the penitent and saves them from the dominion of sin; (6) the privilege and duty of every believer to be entirely sanctified by faith after being justified; (7) the baptism of the Holy Spirit as the crowning credential of faith for the purpose of soul winning.[140]

Among rules which members are to observe are total abstinence from alcohol, drugs, and tobacco; repudiation of secret societies, games of chance, and worldly entertainment; fasting once a week; following Bible standards in modest dress; tithing; and daily Scripture reading. Adultery is considered the only justifiable cause for divorce; remarriage results in forfeiture of membership in the group.[141]

The Independent Holiness Churches comprise 12 churches in Canada and 1 in the United States with a total membership of 250. Headquarters are at 815 Princess Street, Kingston, Ontario, Canada.[142]

## The Wesleyan Holiness Association of Churches

Until the mid-1950s both the Reverend Glenn G. Griffith and the Reverend L. Wayne States were ministers in the Church of the Nazarene. In 1955 they left the Church of the Nazarene to organize the Bible Missionary Union, which subsequently took the name the Bible Missionary Church. Differences within the leadership of the latter body finally led to a break. Reportedly the issues involved such matters as the admission of divorced persons into membership. Charging that the reforms instituted by the Bible Missionary Church did not go far enough, the Reverend Messrs. Griffith and States withdrew in 1959 from the Bible Missionary Church to organize the Wesleyan Holiness Association of Churches. In December 1967 they incorporated it under the laws of Arizona.

In doctrine and practice the Wesleyan Holiness Association of Churches takes a strongly conservative position. The group is governed by a General Board and a General Conference of district leaders which include laity. The association includes about 75 congregations, which operate through Faith Missions to support fifteen missionaries on foreign fields.[143] The headquarters of the association are at 3213 West Camelback Road, Phoenix, Arizona 85017.

## Gospel Mission Corps

Early in the 1960s, Hightstown, New Jersey, was the focus of a number of evangelistic missionary efforts by ministers from nearby Pillar of Fire, Pilgrim Holiness (now Wesleyan), and Mennonite Brethren in Christ churches. Robert S. Turton III, a graduate of the Pillar of Fire Bible Seminary at Zarephath, established the Hightstown Gospel Mission Society as a nonsectarian, united, evangelistic Holiness church. As his work branched out to neighboring communities, the organization dropped Hightstown from its name and on the analogy of the Peace Corps incorporated itself as the Gospel Mission Corps.

In the article on "doctrine" in its constitution it affirms its belief in the fundamental doctrines of evangelical Christianity, specifically in the Bible; the Trinity; Christ's incarnation, sinlessness, and virgin birth; repentance and justification, the latter understood as the new birth; personal faith in Christ's shed blood; the "deeper life" as a "victorious Christian experience through sanctification or the baptism of the Holy Spirit for all who are fully consecrated to the Lord"; the immortality of the soul and the resurrection of the body; Christ's intercession and imminent premillennial return as a climax to this dispensation of grace; the future judgment and the eternal conscious destiny of each individual; "the spiritual unity of all born-again, Bible-believing Christians . . . regardless of race, nationality, or denominational affiliation"; believer's baptism in the name of the Father and of the Son and of the

Holy Ghost by pouring, immersion, or sprinkling, as the candidate may elect; the Lord's Supper "as the holy communion of the body and blood of Christ" in unleavened bread and unfermented wine; marriage ("the wedded life of believers is to be within the fellowship of Christ"); the dedication and Christian training of infants and children; anointing of the sick with oil and prayer ("some cases are cured instantaneously, some gradually, and other are like Paul's 'thorn in the flesh' "); obedience to appropriate authority ("[but] to swear by oath to a statement of truth and also the taking up of arms or weapons for the intent [and] purpose of destroying human life are both contrary to what Christ allows"); and worship, witnessing, and loving service.[144]

Serving or drinking beverage alcohol, the use of tobacco and narcotics, and "the vain use of unnecessary ornamentation (especially any of those articles which are strictly prohibited in Scripture)" are discountenanced. Conversely, fasting, abstinence, tithing, and the wearing of a head-covering by women engaged in public prayer, preaching, and Christian education are encouraged.[145] The ministers and workers of the corps receive no salary. The headquarters are at Box 175, Hightstown, New Jersey 08520. There are 8 churches with an estimated 160 members.[146]

### Evangelical Wesleyan Church

In 1963, at Grand Island, Nebraska, the Evangelical Wesleyan Church was formed by two church bodies which had been established by disaffected members of the Free Methodist Church. The Evangelical Wesleyan Church of North America was formed at Centerville, Pennsylvania, in 1958 by a Pennsylvania-based group within the Free Methodist Church. A Nebraska-based group of Free Methodists organized the Midwest Holiness Association at Ansley, Nebraska, in 1962. The two groups were formed because of the conviction of their members that liberal influences had succeeded in betraying the Free Methodist Church's fundamental convictions. They joined together to form the Evangelical Wesleyan Church to continue their commitment to historic Methodism.

In the Evangelical Wesleyan Church the articles of religion, the rules of discipline, and the patterns of worship and polity are Wesleyan. The group has approximately 25 churches in the United States with a total membership of 350. Headquarters are at 2400 Avenue East, Kearney, Nebraska 68847.[147]

### The Pilgrim Holiness Church of New York, Incorporated

The Pentecostal Rescue Mission of Binghamton, New York, was organized in 1897. In the next quarter of a century it grew to a conference of about sixteen churches and sponsored both charitable institutions and missions in Africa and South America as well as in Alaska. In 1922 the conference affiliated with the Pilgrim Holiness Church (now part of the Wesleyan

Church) as an autonomous district under the name of the New York Conference. With an increasing thrust toward centralization in the Pilgrim Holiness Church, the conference saw its prized autonomy jeopardized and it once more became an entirely independent body, in 1963, under the name of the Pilgrim Holiness Church of New York, Incorporated.

Since 1963 more than twenty churches either affiliated with the Pilgrim Holiness Church of New York, Incorporated, or were formed through the church body's missionary efforts. Ten of these churches were located in Indiana and Illinois. In 1967 the parent body authorized these churches to form a completely autonomous Midwest Conference of the Pilgrim Holiness Church of New York. In 1970 the Midwest Conference was chartered as the Pilgrim Holiness Church of the Midwest, Incorporated. In the same year, the midwestern body sponsored the formation of a third autonomous body, the Jamaica Conference, in the West Indies.

Each of the three conferences is completely independent and self-governing, but they share a strong bond of fellowship and a deep sense of common purpose. This feeling of community has found expression in the cooperation of the policy committees of the three bodies in creating disciplines that are to a large extent identical.

Theologically the Pilgrim Holiness Church of New York, Incorporated, sees itself as a conservatively evangelical Arminian-Wesleyan-Holiness body.

The headquarters are at 32 Cadillac Avenue, Albany, New York 12205. There are 50 churches in the United States and 2 in Canada, with a total active membership estimated at 1,250. The church body carries on foreign missions in South America and Mexico. In Canada the work is among Indians in Winnipeg in association with the Society of Indian Missions of Winner, South Dakota.[148]

## United Holiness Church

A number of conservative members of the Free Methodist Church, unhappy with trends in that church body, organized the United Holiness Church in Carson City, Michigan, in 1966. Wesleyan in theology, the group seeks to perpetuate the fervor and emphasis on sanctification which it believes characterized its parent body in the past.

The United Holiness Church affirms the Scriptures as the divinely inspired Word of God, inerrant, infallible, and the all-sufficient rule of faith and practice. It teaches one God, eternally existing in three persons; the virgin birth, sinless perfection, bodily resurrection and ascension of Jesus Christ; the creation of humanity in the image of God, its disobedience to God and consequent separation from God with physical death as a consequence and all the Adamic race born in sin and aberation from God; the vicarious substitutionary sacrifice of Jesus Christ, through whose shed blood all who believe in him are justified, born of the Spirit and adopted into the family of God; the personal, premillennial return of Jesus Christ; the bodily resurrection of the just and the unjust, with the everlasting blessedness of the saved and the everlasting punishment of the lost. The church body teaches that the baptism with the Holy Spirit is subsequent to regeneration, by which the heart is circumcised and the body of sin put off.[149]

The United Holiness Church has 30 congregations in the United States and 3 in Canada with a total membership of 500.[150] Wesleyan Bible Institute at Cedar Springs, Michigan 49319, a school with a two-year arts program and a four-year theology program, serves as headquarters.

## Church of the Bible Covenant

The concern of a considerable number of members of Holiness denominations in Indiana and in some other states about the direction that the church bodies to which they belonged seemed to be taking mounted during the mid-1960s. This led to the formation in January 1967 of a steering committee charged with investigating the possibility of the organization of a new denomination that would be aggressively evangelistic, consciously committed to conserve the original Holiness heritage, considerate of the individual conscience, and opposed to undemocratic ecclesiastical organization. As a result the Church of the Bible Covenant came into being on August 10, 1967, in a meeting held at the John T. Hatfield Campground in Cleveland, Indiana. Most of the fifty-two ministers who initially affiliated themselves with the new body had previously been members of the Church of the Nazarene, the Wesleyan Church, the Pilgrim Holiness Church, and the Bible Missionary Church.

The theology of the Church of the Bible Covenant is Wesleyan and Arminian. Its creedal statements—modeled extensively on the Methodist Twenty-five Articles—affirm the Trinity; Christ's incarnation, reconciling sacrifice, resurrection, and ascension; the Holy Spirit's activity in the church; the plenary inspiration of the Bible; original sin; Christ's meritorious and atoning death for all human sin as the only ground of salvation; the free bestowal of grace on all human beings, enabling them to turn from sin and to believe on Christ, and the possibility of apostasy even for those who have been regenerated and entirely sanctified; the need of repentance; the simultaneity of justification, regeneration, and adoption; entire sanctification as the instantaneous result of the baptism of the Holy Spirit when the believer presents himself to God as a living sacrifice; Christ's imminent second coming, preceded by the rapture of the living and resurrected saints; the resurrection of the dead, just and unjust; the final judgment; eternal life for believers and eternal punishment in hell for the finally impenitent; the sacraments of baptism and the Lord's Supper as the certain signs of God's grace; the prayer of faith for the healing of the sick (although providential means and agencies are not to be refused when they are deemed necessary); and the obligation of all human beings to order their individual social and political acts in such a way as to obey God and secure for all human beings the enjoyment of every natural right and of happiness in the exercise and possession of these rights.[151]

The General and Special Rules direct the members of the church to manifest the spirit of Christ in all of life; to practice courtesy, charity, truthfulness, kindness, mercy, and other virtues; to engage in private devotions and attendance on the "means of grace," to tithe as a minimum requirement of stewardship; to keep the Christian Sabbath, "a fundamental institution of God," as a day of rest and worship and on it to refrain from joyriding, secular reading, and secular radio listening; to shun tobacco, nonmedicinal narcotics, and liquor; to be separate from the world, refraining from dishonesty, from membership in secret orders, from games of chance, theatergoing, and card playing, from attendance at skating rinks, carnivals, bowling alleys, mixed swimming places, and professional, amateur, and intercollegiate sports, and from ownership of television sets; if they are women, to dress modestly and to avoid undue exposure of their bodies, face painting, and the wearing of rings, of ornamental jewelry, of shorn hair, and of masculine attire. They deplore the evils of divorce and remarriage; innocent parties who marry after they have been divorced because of the adultery of their first spouses are admitted to limited membership but may not serve as officers, teachers, or ministers. In the program of the local church the rules forbid fellowship halls, dramatics, award-giving contests, motion pictures, projected slides, athletic programs, and fund raising by means of bazaars and similar functions.[152]

The Church of the Bible Covenant opposes what it calls formalism in worship and considers "Spirit-led emotionalism" essential to the church's success. The church, which is headed by two general presiding officers, has as its supreme administrative organ the General Convention, held as often as advisable. A general board carries on the business of the church between conventions. The church body does not have a headquarters building;[153] it uses an agent in legal matters. There are reportedly 50 churches, chiefly in Indiana, Texas, Oklahoma, and Louisiana, as well as in other states, with an estimated membership of 1,000.

### The Evangelical Church of North America

Following a preliminary meeting of clergy and laity at Oregon City, Oregon, in 1967, the Evangelical Church of North America held its organizing conference in Portland, Oregon, on June 4 and 5, 1968. The constituency of the new body consisted of congregations of the Evangelical United Brethren Church that felt themselves unable to enter the union of their parent church body with The Methodist Church to form the United Methodist Church. A resolution of the organizing conference describes the Evangelical Church of North America as "orthodox in its beliefs, evangelical in its emphasis, and Wesleyan-Arminian in its interpretation of the scriptural meaning of salvation." It proposes to be in substance, as nearly as possible and practical, identical with the former Evangelical United Brethren Church in doctrine, polity, and program.

The twenty-three articles of faith are obviously indebted to John Wesley's Twenty-five Articles of Religion adopted in 1784, although there has been some adaptation of both language and content. The first nine articles are substantially the same as those drawn up by Wesley. They discuss the Trinity; the Son of God; the resurrection of Christ; the Holy Spirit; the Holy Scriptures; the Old Testament; depravity; prevenient grace and free will; and justification by faith.

An intercalated article treating regeneration and adoption defines regeneration as "the renewal of the heart of man after the image of God, through the word, by the act of the Holy Spirit, by which the believer receives the spirit of adoption and is enabled to serve God with the will and affections. The witness of the Spirit is an inward impression on the soul, by which the Spirit of God, the heavenly comforter, immediately convinces the regenerate believer that he has passed from death unto life, that his sins are all forgiven, and that he is a child of God."

The articles on good works and sin after justification substantially reproduce the Wesleyan articles.

Another intercalated article treats entire sanctification, which is described as an instantaneous cleansing from all inbred sin through faith in Jesus Christ, as subsequent to regeneration, and as taking place when the believer consecrates himself/herself as a living sacrifice to God. Consecration is a gradual process of devoting oneself to God and comes to completion at a point in time; it precedes and prepares the way for the act of faith that brings God's instantaneous sanctifying work to the soul. Entire sanctification does not deliver the believer from the infirmities, ignorance, and mistakes common to human beings, nor from the possibility of further sin.

The articles on the church, on the language to be used in public worship, on the sacraments, on the one sacrifice of Christ, and on the rites and ceremonies of the church again reflect the Wesleyan original. The article of civil government has been generalized; it further asserts that war and bloodshed are generally not in keeping with the gospel and spirit of Christ, but concedes that war is at times an unpleasant necessity in order to preserve orderly governments in the world. The article on a Christian's property reformulates Wesley's thought. The last two articles are new, treating the imminent second coming of Christ and the last judgment, the latter affirming eternal life without end for the believers and everlasting damnation for the impenitent and ungodly.[154]

In 1969 the local churches of the Holiness Methodist Church voted to join the Evangelical Church of North America and the council of administration of the former church body concurred. The council of superintendents of the Evangelical Church of North America acted favorably on the application. The Holiness Methodist churches in the western states joined the two existing conferences of the Evangelical Church of North America. The rest formed the nucleus of a new North Central Conference, with headquarters in Minneapolis.

The Northwestern Holiness Association had been founded at Grand Forks, North Dakota, in 1909[155] under the leadership of the Reverend William C. Ehlers (1868–1916), a Methodist minister. In 1920 it had changed its name to the Holiness Methodist Church. It took its articles of religion from Adam Clarke's *Commentary*, with some revision by Ehlers.[156]

Local churches of the Evangelical Church of North America hold title to their own property. The pastoral-appointment process follows a modified itinerant system.

The Evangelical Church of North America holds membership in the National Association of Evangelicals and in the Christian Holiness Association.

The whole church meets in conference annually. The office of the general superintendent is at 8719 John Drive, Indianapolis, Indiana 46234. There are 122 churches in the merged body with a total membership of 11,171.

Over fifty missionaries who are members of the local churches of the Evangelical Church of North America are serving under independent missionary boards. The church body cooperates with the World Gospel Mission and the Oriental Missionary Society and recommends them to the consideration and support of the local churches.

### Bible Methodist Connection of Churches

The participation of the Wesleyan Methodist Church in the merger that produced the Wesleyan Church in 1968 caused secession movements in that church body's conferences in Ohio, Tennessee, and Alabama. The Tennessee dissidents remained independent and have not responded to inquiries. In 1968 those in Alabama had organized the Bible Methodist Church and those in Ohio had formed the Wesleyan Connection of Churches. In 1970 the two groups united as the Bible Methodist Connection of Churches.

The church body is committed to Wesleyan Methodist theology as espoused by the Holiness movement. It is strongly congregational in polity and advocates conservative standards of dress and behavior. There are more than 60 congregations in the Alabama Conference with a membership of 1,200 and about 20 congregations in the Ohio Conference with approximately 300 members.[157] There are no central headquarters.

### NOTES

1. The auxiliary members include about 150 local associations and camp meetings, about 50 schools and colleges, including those sponsored by affiliated denominations; the foreign mission boards of the affiliated denominations; the World Gospel Mission, Marion, Indiana, with nearly 225 missionaries; the Oriental Missionary Society, Indianapolis, Indiana, with over 200 missionaries; and the Voice of China and Asia, Incorporated, with over 20 missionaries.

2. The affiliate members are the Brethren

in Christ Church, the Churches of Christ in Christian Union, the Evangelical Church of North America, the Evangelical Friends Alliance, the Evangelical Methodist Church, the Free Methodist Church of North America, the Holiness Christian Church of the United States of America, the Canadian Holiness Federation, The Church of the Nazarene, the Salvation Army, the Salvation Army in Canada, and the Wesleyan Church. Cooperating organizations are the Methodist Protestant Church, the Primitive Methodist Church, the Congregational Methodist Church, the Church of God (Anderson, Indiana), the Missionary Church and the Sanctified Church of Christ.

3. H. E. Schmul, editor of *Convention Herald*, official publication of the Inter-Denominational Holiness Convention, asserts in vol. 21, no. 9 (September 1967), p. 2: "The climactic struggle in the nominal holiness denominations over Bible holiness with standards is finished. For over fifteen years the name-brand holiness churches have been experiencing a continuing warfare between conservative and liberal elements. This warfare has culminated in mergers, separations and court action and a bad name for holiness in general. . . . By and large the forces for revision, change and compromise have won the field. . . . The basic issues were not doctrine or merger. . . . The basic issues were these: (a) simplicity and modesty of attire; (b) the wedding ring as a test of membership; (c) television as an entertainment evil; (d) centralized government (although some who have separated are as centralized as what they left); and (e) an educational system stressing the secular and athletics. In approximately ten years over 10,000 conservative holiness people and their ministers have left the old churches. In some cases entire conferences or districts have withdrawn. The issues were always pretty much the same."

4. Article II, *Constitution and Bylaws of the Inter-Church Holiness Convention* (Salem, Ohio: Inter-Church Holiness Convention, 1972) (12-page pamphlet), pp. 8-9.

5. Letter from the Reverend H. E. Schmul, executive secretary, Inter-Church Holiness Convention.

6. The Wesleyan Church also holds that "the relative value of the gifts of the Spirit is to be tested by their usefulness in the church and not by the ecstasy produced in the ones receiving them" (*The Discipline of the Wesleyan Church* [2nd printing; Marion, Ind.: The Wesleyan Publishing House, 1970], p. 31). It further declares that "to teach that speaking in an unknown tongue or that the gift of tongues is the necessary proof of the baptism with the Holy Spirit or of that entire sanctification which the baptism accomplishes" contradicts the Wesleyan Church's understanding of the Word of God (ibid., p. 53).

7. The formula is "I baptize you in the name of the Father and of the Son and of the Holy Spirit" (ibid., pp. 521, 522, 524).

8. Another option is the dedication of the child without the sacrament of baptism or dedication of the child through the sacrament of baptism (ibid., pp. 519-521). Baptism is seen as "the sign and seal of God's covenant of grace," as "not itself the door of salvation, but rather [as] an outward sign of the new birth which God has wrought" in the candidate's heart (ibid., pp. 519-521). At the baptism of adults the candidate affirms steadfast faith in the teachings of the Apostles' Creed, without the clause affirming Christ's descent into the nether-world, and with the church described as "universal" rather than "catholic" (ibid., p. 524).

9. Unfermented grape juice is prescribed, unleavened bread recommended (ibid., p. 533). The Lord's Supper, which is to be celebrated at least once a quarter in each local church, becomes "a medium through which God communicates grace to the heart[s]" of those who "rightly, worthily, and with faith receive" it (ibid., p. 32).

10. Ibid., pp. 25-34.
11. Ibid., pp. 34-37.
12. Ibid., p. 51.
13. Ibid., p. 53.
14. The church body's doctrine and discipline are described in *What We Believe: Doctrine and General Rules* (Titusville, Pa.: The Allegheny Wesleyan Methodist Connection, n.d.).

15. Four-page pamphlet entitled "Presenting the Allegheny Wesleyan Methodist Connection."

16. *Constitution and Government of the Congregational Methodist Church* (11th edn.; Dallas, Texas: The Messenger Press, 1960) (92-page brochure), pp. 61-62.

17. Ibid., pp. 67-69.

18. Ralph Stoody, "Other Branches of Methodism, 1960," in Emory Stevens Bucke, ed., *The History of American Methodism* (Nashville: Abingdon Press, 1964), vol. 3, pp. 589-592 (the quotation is on p. 590). See also Walter W. Benjamin, "The Free Methodists," ibid., vol. 2, pp. 339-360. The derisive name "Nazarites," which the majority group gave to the minority, was roundly repudiated by the founders of the Free Methodist Church and was welcomed only by the outer fringe of independents who refused to submit to any kind of denominational control.

19. Text in Benjamin, p. 356.

20. Walter S. Kendall and others, eds., *Doctrines and Discipline of the Free Methodist Church of North America 1964* (Winona Lake, Ind.: The Free Methodist Publishing House, 1965), p. 13.

21. Ibid.

22. The general superintendents have borne the title of bishop since 1907.

23. This description is based on Charles Edwin Jones, *A Guide to the Study of the Holiness Movement* (Metuchen, N.J.: The Scarecrow Press, Inc., and The American Theological Library Association, 1974), pp. 447-448.

24. The information on the Holiness Baptist Association was provided by Bishop R. W. Sapp of the Church of Jesus Christ, Rt. 6, Box 68, Dublin, Georgia 31021.

25. "The Holy Ghost baptized the whole church on the day of Pentecost because of the Jewish nation and the whole church in Cornelius' house because of the Gentile nation" and thereafter "he is never referred to as a baptism for there is but one baptism."

26. Not practiced by many local churches.

27. Otho Beale Cobbins, ed., *History of the Church of Christ (Holiness) U. S. A.* (New York: Vantage Press, 1966), pp. 83-86.

28. This writer gratefully acknowledges the assistance of Dr. Josephus R. Coan of the Interdenominational Theological Center, Atlanta, who interviewed Bishop Titus Paul Burruss on this writer's behalf.

29. *Manual of the History, Doctrine, Government, and Ritual of the Associated Churches of Christ (Holiness)* (San Pedro, Calif.: Assembly of the Associated Churches of Christ [Holiness], 1953) (47-page pamphlet), p. 5.

30. Ibid., pp. 7-9.

31. Letter from Bishop Whitfield Massengale.

32. This statement is based on a telephone conversation between the present writer and Bishop E. K. McFadden, senior bishop, Evangelical Church of Christ (Holiness), Washington, D.C.

33. The present writer gratefully acknowledges the assistance and counsel of the Reverend John W. V. Smith, chairman, department of church history, School of Theology, Anderson College, Anderson, Indiana, in the preparation of this section.

34. As an example of this kind of compromise, the Church of God (Guthrie, Oklahoma) sees a "drifting into worldliness of dress" (E. E. Byrum, "Marching along the By-Path" [pamphlet, reprinted from the *Gospel Trumpet* for September 15, 1910], p. 5). Byrum foresaw this as the first step toward a complete abandonment of the distinctive features of the movement. One of the events that precipitated the ultimate break was a resolution which the Church of God adopted at the camp meeting of 1911; it discouraged the wearing of neckties "as being unnecessary and as tending to the spirit of the world," but authorized their "being worn by those whose consciences do not forbid their doing so on occasions when their business or other extreme circumstances require it" (Lawrence D. Pruitt, *Eighty Years in the "Evening Light"* [pamphlet], p. 5). All the pamphlets cited in this section are published by Faith Publishing House, Guthrie, Oklahoma, and are undated.

35. Lawrence D. Pruitt, *Modern Pentecostalism* (pamphlet).

36. Lawrence D. Pruitt, *The Christian versus War* (pamphlet). The Church

of God (Guthrie, Oklahoma) defined its position on this point at the beginning of the American involvement in World War II.

37. Lula Bose, *Marriage and Divorce* (pamphlet).

38. Roy L. Guest, *Harmful and Sinful Tobacco Using* (pamphlet).

39. *The New Modern Cross* (pamphlet).

40. Daniel S. Warner, *The Church of God: What the Church of God Is and What It Is Not* (pamphlet); Otto Bolds, *Denominationalism—My Last Message to the Church* (pamphlet).

41. C. E. Orr, *Not a New Movement* (pamphlet).

42. Fred Pruitt, *Water Baptism* (pamphlet), p. 3.

43. T. H. Coffey, *The Forgotten Ordinance: Feet-Washing* (pamphlet).

44. The November 1966 issue of *Faith and Victory* contains over a column of prayer requests and four columns of testimonies.

45. *Church Membership* (pamphlet), pp. 12-13.

46. W. M. Pettigrew, Sr., *The Origin of Tithing* (pamphlet); Doris Guinup, *Modern Day Tithing Deprives God of All* (pamphlet).

47. George W. Stephenson, *Will There Be a Millennial Reign?* (pamphlet).

48. Letter from Lawrence D. Pruitt, editor, Faith Publishing House. From the beginning the Church of God (Guthrie, Oklahoma) took the position that all races are equal in spiritual matters and it has always received all nationalities and races into fellowship, although for reasons of expediency the church has never practiced or sanctioned black-white intermarriage. In Guthrie the presence of both races in the local church— one of the charter members was a black minister, G. W. Winn—inspired the derogatory nickname "Holstein Church of God" with reference to the black-and-white color of the Holstein breed of dairy cow. (Letter from Mr. Pruitt.)

49. Letters from the Reverend G. W. Pendleton, managing chairman, the New Testament Church of God, Incorporated, 307 Cockrell Hill Road, Dallas, Texas 75211.

50. I. C. Holland, "Cardinal Doctrines of the Church," Dale M. Yocum, ed., *The New Testament Church* (Over-

land Park, Kan.: Witt Printing Company, 1962) (64-page brochure), pp. 10-25; *Church of God (Holiness) Welcomes You* (4-page undated pamphlet).

51. E. W. Roy, "The Ministerial Orders of the Church," and Dale M. Yocum, "Organization and Administration of the Church," *New Testament Church*, pp. 26-46.

52. C. F. Croy, "Ordinances of the Church," *New Testament Church*, pp. 47-54; Clarence Eugene Cowen, *A History of the Church of God (Holiness)* (Overland Park, Kan.: Herald and Banner Press, 1949), p. 112.

53. Communication from church-body headquarters.

54. *A Declaration of Principles of the Churches of God (Independent Holiness People)*, (rev. edn.; Fort Scott, Kan.: Church Advocate and Good Way, n.d. [1963 or later]), (12-page pamphlet).

55. "The Convention of 1967," *The Church Advocate and Good Way*, vol. 51, no. 42 (October 26, 1967), 2.

56. Communication from Donald Rohrer, editor and business manager.

57. Charles Edwin Jones, *A Guide to the Study of the Holiness Movement* (Metuchen, N.J.: The Scarecrow Press, and the American Theological Library Association, 1974), p. 243.

58. Eight-page pamphlet entitled, "Peniel Missions: A Historical Statement."

59. "Church Constitution," para. 23, in John Riley and others, eds., *Manual of the Church of the Nazarene: History, Constitution, Government, Ritual—1964* (Kansas City, Mo.: Nazarene Publishing House, 1964), p. 33.

60. "Church Constitution," para. 24, pp. 33-34. It should be noted that the Church of the Nazarene commits itself officially only to Christ's personal second coming, not to a premillennial view.

61. Paras. 5-7, pp. 27-28.

62. Paras. 9-12, p. 29.

63. Para. 14, p. 30. Speaking in tongues is against the official practice, although not the explicit doctrinal stand, of the denomination.

64. Paras. 18-20, pp. 31-32. The ritual provides forms for the dedication or consecration of children in lieu of baptism, for the baptism of infants,

and for the baptism of believers (para. 582, pp. 263-266). The temperance stance of the denomination prescribes the use of unfermented wine—along with unleavened bread—in the Lord's Supper (para. 36, p. 46).

65. Para. 25, pp. 34-37.
66. Paras. 32-41, pp. 45-48.
67. This position reflects the Friends' influence on the Fire Baptized Holiness Church.
68. *Articles of Faith and By-Laws, The Fire Baptized Holiness Church* (n.p.: n.p., 1963) (63-page pamphlet), pp. 1-15.
69. Ibid., pp. 39-43.
70. "Articles of Faith," in Joseph B. Lynch and Sarah E. Collins, *The Doctrines and Discipline of Christ's Sanctified Holy Church* (rev. edn.; Columbia, S.C.: The R. L. Bryan Company, 1949), pp. 21-25. The original edition came out in 1893.
71. "Under no circumstances should one of our members take up arms or train with same" ("Statement of Christ's Sanctified Holy Church Concerning War" [1-page undated multilithed document]).
72. Lynch and Collins, *Doctrines and Discipline*, pp. 7-9, 17, 19-20.
73. E. Joseph Clelland, "The Doctrine of Christ's Sanctified Holy Church" (4-page undated typewritten document), p. 3.
74. Letter from the Reverend E. Joseph Clelland.
75. The present writer gratefully acknowledges the assistance of the Reverend James Brammeier, Ponca, Nebraska, then seminarian-assistant at Immanuel Church, Houston, Texas, who interviewed the Reverend James Boseley, the minister of the Christ's Sanctified Holy Church congregation at 4905 Nicholas Street, Houston, on behalf of this writer. Repeated efforts to obtain information from the leadership of the church were unsuccessful.
76. *The Doctrines and Discipline of the Church of Daniel's Band* (rev. edn., 30-page undated pamphlet), pp. 3-8. The bread in the Lord's Supper is to be "broken rather than cut," the wine in all cases to be "unfermented, containing nothing that could intoxicate" (ibid., p. 21).
77. The present writer gratefully acknowledges the assistance of the Rev-

erend Lawrence E. Witto, then associate pastor of St. John's Church, Midland, Michigan, who interviewed the Reverend Wesley Hoggard, Route 2, Midland, president of the Church of Daniel's Band, on behalf of this writer.
78. Ira W. Bechtel, "The Holiness Christian Heritage," a series of 35 articles published in *The Christian Messenger* between February 1958 and July 1962.
79. "Articles of Faith and General Rules," *The Doctrines and Discipline of the Holiness Christian Church of the United States of America, Incorporated* (n.p.: n.p., 1948), (74-page brochure), pp. 9-19; see also pp. 57-58.
80. *Discipline of the Church of God (Apostolic Inc.) (sic)* (Beckley, W. Va.: Church of God [Apostolic], n.d. [after 1943]) (40-page booklet), especially pp. 1-6, 8, 12, 18-21, 39-40. There is verbatim or near verbatim agreement in many crucial passages of the *Discipline* with the *Manual* of the Apostolic Overcoming Holy Church of God, Incorporated. A noteworthy instance is the section headed "Ethiopian: Who Is He? And Where Is He Spoken Of in The Bible?" (ibid., p. 21; compare with *Manual of the Apostolic Overcoming Holy Church of God, Incorporated* [Mobile, Ala.: Apostolic Overcoming Holy Church Publishing House, 1967], p. 11). While both bodies "embrace the same principles of Apostolicism," there has never been any organic connection between the two. Bishop David E. Smith, general overseer, Church of God (Apostolic), 125 Meadows Street, Beckley, West Virginia 25801, states in a letter to the present writer that the verbal agreements between the two manuals is "coincidental."
81. Letters from Bishop Smith.
82. Letter from the Reverend W. T. Pettengell, former president, the Metropolitan Church Association.
83. Communication from the Reverend C. N. Lowry, Rowland, North Carolina, secretary of the Lumber River Annual Conference of the Holiness Methodist Church.
84. On the basis of Acts 20:28.
85. Charles Price Jones, Sr., "The Tennessee Brethren *et al.*," in Otho Beale Cobbins, *History of Church of Christ*

*(Holiness) U.S.A. 1895–1965* (New York: Vantage Press, 1966), p. 435.

86. Letters from the Reverend H. C. Nesbitt, 1501 Twenty-First Avenue North, Nashville, Tennessee 37208.

87. *Manual of the Church of God* (rev. edn., Nashville, Tenn.: Curley Printing Company, 1952), pp. 13-18.

88. Ibid., p. 19.

89. Cited letters from the Reverend Mr. Nesbitt. The present writer gratefully acknowledges the assistance of the Reverend Harry D. Smith, then pastor, First Lutheran Church, Knoxville, Tennessee, who kindly interviewed Elder Evans on this writer's behalf.

90. Cf. previous section dealing with the Church of God (Sanctified Church).

91. *The Hand Book of the Original Church of God or Sanctified Church* (Nashville, Tenn.: The Original Church of God or Sanctified Church, 1945) (25-page booklet), pp. 5-20.

92. Telephone conversation with Bishop Thomas R. Jeffries, general chairman, Original Church of God or Sanctified Church, 653 Roscoe Street, Akron, Ohio 44306.

93. *The Doctrines and Discipline of the Faith Mission Church* (n.p.: n.p., n.d. [after 1963]) (20-page pamphlet), pp. 5-11.

94. Letter from the Reverend Ray Snow, pastor, Faith Mission Church, 1813 26th Street, Bedford, Indiana. In another letter the Reverend Mr. Snow states that his church is in no way connected with the Evangelistic Faith Missions, Incorporated, 921 Eighth Street, Bedford, Indiana, directed by the Reverend Victor Glenn. The Evangelistic Faith Missions have no local congregations in North America; the organization operates missions in a number of foreign countries. The present writer gratefully acknowledges the efforts of the Reverend Karl J. Dunker, pastor of Calvary Church, Bedford, Indiana, to secure information about the Faith Mission Church and the Evangelistic Faith Missions, Incorporated, on this writer's behalf.

95. "What We Believe," *Religious, Educational and Benevolent Activities of the Pillar of Fire Movement* (Zarephath, N.J.: Pillar of Fire, 1966) (32-page brochure), p. [14].

96. Letter, Bishop Arthur K. White, A.M., D.D., president, Pillar of Fire, Incorporated.

97. "What We Believe," in *Short History and Polity of the Christian Nation Church* (n.p.: Christian National Church, 1954) (21-page booklet), pp. 11-19. The gift of tongues is understood as involving the speaking of an actual language. The Christian Nation Church professes belief in the Father, Son, and Holy Ghost and "in being baptized in water as John the Baptist baptized Jesus" (letter from the Reverend Walter F. Clark, secretary, the Christian Nation Church of the United States of America, 345 Cedar Drive, Loveland, Ohio 45140.

98. Cited letter from the Reverend Mr. Clark.

99. Pliny Brett founded the Reformed Methodist Church in New England in 1814. In the course of the nineteenth century most of its local societies joined the Methodist Protestant Church. (Frederick E. Maser and George A. Singleton, "Further Branches of Methodism Are Founded," in Emory Stevens Bucke, ed., *The History of American Methodism* [Nashville: Abingdon Press, 1964], vol. 1, pp. 622-624).

100. Thomas Hermiz, *What We Teach: A Summary of the Doctrines of the Churches of Christ in Christian Union* (rev. edn.; Circleville, Ohio: The Advocate Publishing House, 1965) (16-page tract). The *Constitution and Bylaws of the Churches of Christ in Christian Union* (rev. edn.; Circleville, Ohio: The Advocate Publishing House, 1965), p. 8, lists the following "cardinal principles": "(1) The oneness of the church of Christ; (2) Christ the only Head; (3) the Bible the only rule of faith and practice; (4) good fruits the only condition of fellowship; (5) Christian union without controversy; (6) each local church governs itself [within the limitations of the denomination's constitution and bylaws]; (7) partisan political preaching discountenanced."

101. Dan S. Hardin, *History of Missionary Methodism 1913–1948* (Forest City, N.C.: Forest City Courier, 1948), pp. 7-8, 28, 32, 38-39.

102. *Doctrine, Creed and Rules for the Government of the Missionary Methodist Church of America* (Forest City, N.C.: The Courier Print, 1946), pp. 3-9.

103. Communications from the Reverend

Dan S. Hardin, Pastor, Forest City (N.C. 28043) Missionary Methodist Church.

104. "Doctrine," *Kentucky Mountain Bible Institute Catalog for 1967–1969* (Vancleve, Ky.: Kentucky Mountain Bible Institute, 1967), p. 13; *Pastors Manual* (Jackson, Ky.: Kentucky Mountain Holiness Association, 1960), p. 19.

105. Communication from Lela G. McConnell, L.H.D., president Kentucky Mountain Holiness Association.

106. Letters from the Reverend Frank Russell Killingsworth, D.D., 1509 S Street Northwest, Washington, D.C. 20009.

107. In 1933 the Florida Conference tried the elder Crowson and suspended him for one year; when the suspension came to an end he withdrew from the conference. The trial was precipitated in part by his publication of a 46-page pamphlet, *Anarchy Unmasked* (Kissimmee, Fla.: Acorn Print Shop, 1933).

108. *The Book of Discipline of the Apostolic Methodist Church* (Kissimmee, Fla.: Acorn Print Shop, 1932), pp. 6, 15, 40.

109. Repeated requests to the secretary of the General Assembly of the Apostolic Methodist Church, Pastor-Elder E. H. Crowson, for information about the present size of the church body were unsuccessful in eliciting a reply. (Pastor-Elder Crowson is also trustee of the Beacon News Service, the India Mission Fund, Incorporated.) According to Elmer T. Clark, *The Small Sects in America* (rev. edn.; Nashville: Abingdon-Cokesbury Press, 1949), p. 65 and n. 32, the Apostolic Methodist Church at that time had "one or two congregations and only a handful of members." There is no evidence of subsequent growth.

110. There were at one time churches as far away as Seattle, Washington, and Chicago, Illinois, but the churches outside California have either died out or united with other fellowships.

111. Article III, *The Revised Constitution* (Los Angeles, Calif.: Oriental Missionary Society Holiness Conference of North America, 1965) (7-page mimeographed document), p. 3. The Articles of Faith of the Oriental Missionary Society commit it to the inspiration and freedom from error of the original documents of the Bible; the Trinity; the deity, incarnation, universal substitutionary atonement, exaltation, and millennial return of Christ; the deity of the Holy Spirit and his operation in the church; the original innocence and purity of human beings, their free will, their sinful nature at birth, and their need of God's freely bestowed grace; the possibility of a Christian falling away and being lost; repentance, justification, the new birth or regeneration, adoption, and the witness of the Holy Spirit; the fullness of the Spirit (entire sanctification) as an act of the Holy Spirit subsequent to the new birth; the privilege of believers to ask God to heal the sick; the resurrection of all human beings, eternal life for the saved, and eternal punishment for the unsaved; and the spiritual unity of all true Christians in the church and the obligation of this church and its members to reach the whole world with the gospel.

112. Article VIII, ibid., p. 7.

113. "Statement of Faith," revised by the Southern California Holiness Ministers' Fellowship, April 14, 1970 (1-page mimeographed document).

114. Letters from the Reverend Bill Hara, minister, Honolulu (Hawaii) Holiness Church, and the Reverend Akira J. Kuroda, minister, Los Angeles Holiness Church.

115. This information was supplied by the Reverend Paul Miller, general superintendent.

116. *Discipline of Sanctified Church of Christ* (2nd printing; Columbus, Ga.: Sanctified Church of Christ, 1957), pp. 2-7. A footnote states that dissent on the second coming of Christ does not break or hinder church fellowship or membership.

117. Ibid., pp. 7-10.

118. Ibid., pp. 10-11.

119. Letter from Bishop M. L. Leary, Columbus, Georgia.

120. "Articles of Faith," *Wesleyan Tabernacle Association: Yearbook 1965* (New Castle, Ind.: Dale Printing Co., 1965), pp. 3-4.

121. Ibid., pp. 4-5.

122. Letter from the Reverend Thomas Reed, moderator.

123. *The Guidebook of the Emmanuel Association* (rev. edn.; Colorado Springs, Colo.: Emmanuel Associa-

tion, 1966) (48-page pamphlet), pp. 41-42, provides a form to be used "when parents desire to dedicate their children."

124. The form for the Lord's Supper, *Guidebook*, p. 40, speaks of the bread and wine as "emblems of His broken body and shed blood." The formula of distribution in each case begins "This represents."

125. "Principles of Faith," *Guidebook*, pp. 4-10.

126. "Principles of Holy Living," *Guidebook*, pp. 11-16.

127. Communication from O. F. Gault, treasurer.

128. T. H. Lewis, "Historical Sketch of the Origin of the Methodist Protestant Church," in F. L. Sharp, ed., *Constitution and Discipline of the Methodist Protestant Church, Revised by The General Conference of 1952* (Brookhaven, Miss.: The Methodist Protestant Church, 1952), pp. 8-14.

129. "Articles of Religion of the Methodist Protestant Church," ibid., pp. 33-42.

130. Ibid., pp. 138-144.

131. Ibid., pp. 145-148.

132. *The Methodist Protestant Church* (undated 4-page pamphlet), p. 4; communication from the Reverend B. F. Gerald, ed., *The Methodist Protestant Faith*.

133. Letter from Brother Eugene Winter, Holiness Gospel Mission.

134. Roy Keith and Carol Willoughby, eds., *History and Discipline of the Faith and Practice [of] The Fundamental Methodist Church, Incorporated* (rev. edn.; Springfield, Mo.: The Fundamental Methodist Church, 1964) (62-page pamphlet), pp. 37-45.

135. William J. Wakefield, the father of Wesley H. Wakefield, was a Salvation Army staff officer and one of their pioneers in the Canadian field.

136. Letter from Wesley H. Wakefield, president.

137. Ibid.

138. *Manual of the Bible Missionary Church, Incorporated* (Duncan, Okla.: Board of General Moderators of the Bible Missionary Church, 1967), pp. 3, 9-15.

139. Letter from the Reverend Carl A. Dillard, general secretary.

140. The doctrinal position is published in a mimeographed booklet, "Declaration of Rules and Doctrines," pp. 2-3.

141. Ibid., pp. 3-7.

142. Letter from the Reverend W. J. Woodland, president.

143. Letter from the Reverend Glenn Griffith, general superintendent, and the Reverend L. Wayne States, assistant general superintendent.

144. Article VIII ("Doctrine"), Constitution, *Manual of the Gospel Mission Corps, Incorporated* (Cranbury, N.J.: Gospel Mission Corps, n.d.), pp. 9-13.

145. Article IX ("Discipline"), ibid., pp. 14-17.

146. Communication from the Reverend Robert S. Turton III.

147. The information in this section is based on a letter from the Reverend Larry D. Smith, secretary of the General Conference and editor of the church body's publication, *The Earnest Christian*.

148. Letter from the Reverend Andrew J. Whitney, president, Pilgrim Holiness Church of New York, Incorporated.

149. The doctrinal views are presented in the Catalog of the School of Theology, Wesleyan Bible Institute, 1970–72, p. 9.

150. Letter from the Reverend E. D. Coxon, general superintendent.

151. "Creedal Statements," *Church of the Bible Covenant: Articles* (Indianapolis, Ind.: Church of the Bible Covenant, 1967) (23-page document), pp. 3-5.

152. "General and Special Rules," ibid., pp. 7-8.

153. The name and address of its presiding officer is Dr. Remiss Rehfeldt, Route 2, Box 66, Greenfield, Indiana 46140.

154. *The Discipline of the Evangelical Church of North America* (Milwaukie, Ore.: The Evangelical Church of North America, 1969), pp. 1-23.

155. On the developments that led to the founding of the association, see chap. 25, "The Northwestern Holiness Association," in William C. Ehlers, *Holiness and the Opposition* (Minneapolis, Minn.: Northwestern Holiness Publishing Company, 1915), pp. 229-242.

156. See "Articles of Religion," *Discipline of the Holiness Methodist Church* (rev. edn.; Minneapolis, Minn.: Holiness Methodist Publishing Board, 1964), pp. 34-44, and *What We Believe* (Minneapolis, Minn.: Holiness

Methodist Publishing Company, n.d.) (8-page pamphlet).

157. This information was supplied by the Reverend Jarrette D. Young, president of the Ohio Conference, 1705 Colum-bia Avenue, Middletown, Ohio 45042, and the Reverend V. O. Agar, president, Alabama Conference, Pell City, Alabama 35125.

## BIBLIOGRAPHY

Chapman, J. B. *The Nazarene Primer.* 11th printing. Kansas City, Mo.: Nazarene Publishing House, 1964.

Cobbins, Otho Beale, ed. *History of Church of Christ (Holiness) U.S.A.* New York: Vantage Press, 1966.

Cowen, Clarence Eugene. *A History of the Church of God (Holiness).* Overland Park, Kan.: Herald and Banner Press, 1949. This history, definitive to 1948, reproduces the author's doctoral dissertation in the department of history of the University of Missouri at Columbia. It exhibits great sensitivity to the doctrinal position of the Church of God (Holiness) in comparison with other Holiness churches.

*The Discipline of the Evangelical Church of North America 1969.* Milwaukie, Ore.: The Evangelical Church of North America, 1969.

*The Discipline of the Wesleyan Church.* 2nd printing. Marion, Ind.: The Wesleyan Publishing House, 1970.

Fowler, Wilton R., Jr., ed. *Minutes of the General Conference of the Congregational Methodist Church: The First through the Twentieth Sessions 1869–1945.* Tehuacana, Texas: Westminster College Print Shop, 1960.

Kendall, Walter S., and others, eds. *Doctrines and Discipline of the Free Methodist Church of North America 1964.* Winona Lake, Ind.: The Free Methodist Publishing House, 1965.

Marston, Leslie R. *From Age to Age a Living Witness.* Winona Lake, Ind.: Light and Life Press, 1960. Witness from a member of the Free Methodist Church of North America.

McConnell, Lela G. *The Pauline Ministry in the Kentucky Mountains, or, A Brief Account of the Kentucky Mountain Holiness Association.* 10th edition. Berne, Ind.: Economy Printing Concern, n.d. This volume chronicles the Association's history to 1942.

———. *Rewarding Faith Plus Works.* Jackson, Ky.: Kentucky Mountain Holiness Association, 1962. A description of the teaching of the Kentucky Mountain Holiness Association.

McDaniel, S. C. *The Origin and Early History of the Congregational Methodist Church.* Atlanta, Ga.: Jas. P. Harrison and Co., 1881. This useful source is available in an unaltered and undated reissue in litho-printed typescript published by the Westminster College Print Shop, Tehuacana, Texas.

McLeister, Ira Ford. *History of the Wesleyan Methodist Church.* Marion, Ind.: The Wesleyan Press, 1959.

Purkiser, W. T. *Adventures in Truth: A Biblical Catechism for Christian Youth.* 7th printing. Kansas City, Mo.: Nazarene Publishing House, 1964. A catechism of the teaching of the Church of the Nazarene.

———, ed. *Exploring Our Christian Faith.* 5th printing. Kansas City, Mo.: Beacon Hill Press, 1966. Eight Nazarene theologians here provide a contemporary "introduction to evangelical Wesleyan Christianity as understood in churches conventionally described as part of the holiness movement."

Riley, John, and others, eds. *Manual of the Church of the Nazarene: History, Constitution, Government, Ritual—1964.* Kansas City, Mo.: Nazarene Publishing House, 1964.

Schmul, H. E., and Fruin, E., eds. *Profile of the I. H. Convention: A 25 Year Historical Scan of the Inter Church Holiness Convention.* Salem, Ohio: I. H. Convention, n.d. [1978?].

Smith, John W. V. *Heralds of a Brighter Day.* Anderson, Indiana: Gospel Trumpet Company, 1955. Testimony from the Church of God (Anderson, Indiana).

———. *Truth Marches On.* Anderson, Indiana: Gospel Trumpet Company, 1956. Useful information about the position of the Church of God (Anderson, Indiana).

Smith, Timothy L. *Called unto Holiness: The Story of the Nazarenes: The Formative Years.* Kansas City, Mo.: Nazarene Publishing House, 1962. An excellent account of the history of the Church of the Nazarene down to 1933.

*So This Is the Church of God.* Anderson, Ind.: Executive Council of the Church of God, 1966. A 31-page illustrated brochure.

Taylor, Richard S. *Life in the Spirit.* Kansas City, Mo.: Beacon Hill Press, 1966. Teachings from within the Church of the Nazarene.

Yocum, Dale M., ed. *The New Testament Church.* Overland Park, Kan.: Witt Printing Company, 1962. This 64-page brochure was written by the members of the Commission on Unification of Orthodox Holiness Bodies at the request of the General Convention of the Church of God (Holiness), in part to provide "a small handbook of doctrinal truth about the New Testament church" (p. vi).

# 3. Social Action Bodies

## The Salvation Army

William Booth (1829–1912), the founder of the Salvation Army, preached his first sermon in Nottingham, England, at the age of seventeen. In 1855, while preparing for ordination (1858) in the Methodist New Connexion, he married Catherine Mumford, a remarkable woman destined to become "the Mother of the Army." In 1861 he regretfully resigned his ministry to be free to become an evangelistic preacher. By 1865 he had dedicated his life to the poverty-stricken, unchurched masses and had begun what he called the East London Christian Mission (later simply the Christian Mission) in Mile End Waste, the worst slums in London's East End. Initially he conceived of his work as supplementary to that of the churches, but this proved impractical. Many converts did not want to go where he sent them, and, when they did go, the congregation to which he sent them often would not accept them. Besides, Booth found that he needed his converts to help handle the mission to the Salvation Army.

At first Booth had organized his movement along the lines of Methodist polity, with annual conferences at which reports were made and programs planned. But the new name resulted in a revision both of the movement's organization and of its nomenclature. Booth published his Army's declaration of faith as Articles of War. Mission stations became "corps," members became "soldiers," evangelists became "officers." Converts were listed as "prisoners." Booth himself became "general." The military pattern provided a direct line of authority and a practical system of training personnel for effective action.

In spite of strong opposition both from the churches and from officialdom to the kind of evangelism that the Salvation Army employed, the work spread quickly over England, Scotland, and Wales. Booth then committed the Army to a policy of overseas expansion. He sent out pioneering parties to different countries. In adapting the work to overseas situations, Booth found it necessary to make some modifications in the Army's system of government, but it remained essentially an autocratic one. This evoked criticism, but during Booth's generalship no organized opposition emerged.

Upon Booth's death in 1912, his son William Bramwell Booth succeeded him. He gave the Army a great missionary impulse and laid the foundation for its youth program. The High Council's relief of the younger Booth as general in 1929 because it considered him physically unable to continue led to litigation; ultimately the council's action stood. Out of this crisis came certain constitutional reforms which made the international organization more vigorous and democratic.

The Salvation Army has a dual function. Its first purpose is religious, the salvation of human beings "by the power of the Holy Spirit combined with the influence of human ingenuity and love." The second purpose is that of a social agency. The international headquarters in London administers the Army's work in over seventy countries.

For the Salvation Army in the United States, the years from 1880 to 1904 were a formative era of struggle, hardship, and rapid growth. This period also saw two serious schisms. In October 1884, Major Thomas E. Moore, in violation of orders, sought to establish the Salvation Army in the United States as a corporation independent of General Booth's control. Booth removed Moore from office and the latter established an American Salvation Army. Without Booth's leadership and the international support of Booth's Army, Moore's organization gradually declined and in 1889 it disbanded. In January 1896, Ballington Booth, a son of General Booth and the national commander of the Army in the United States, received a new appointment. When public protest and Army-wide appeals failed to move the father to rescind the order, Ballington Booth and his wife withdrew from the Salvation Army and set up the Volunteers of America.

The period from 1904 to 1934, during which Evangeline Booth commanded the United States operation, was a period of further expansion, marked at first by gradual, and after World War I by mass, acceptance.

Since 1934 the Army has been in a phase of broader integration with other fund-raising agencies. This period has seen increasingly wider recognition and acceptance of Army personnel and programs both by religious denominations and by social welfare organizations.

In carrying out its religious and social welfare activities in all fifty of the United States, the national headquarters at 120 West 14th Street, New York, New York 10011, directs a force of over 5,100 officers and cadets, assisted by some 15,000 employees without rank and backed by a membership of 384,817. The Salvation Army functions through more than 8,500 centers and extension units of its own and in 300 welfare institutions. Its program in the United States includes the operation of treatment centers, hospitals, maternity homes (for about 10,000 unmarried mothers a year); children's camps, boys' and girls' clubs; community centers; mobile canteens; hotels and lodges for men and women; nurseries and settlement houses; missing persons bureaus;

Salvation Army–United Services Organization centers and Red Shield Clubs for servicemen; centers for the care of alcoholics; and a correctional services bureau that works with prisoners and their families. Clients receive services without respect to their race, color, or creed. Funds for the activities come from voluntary subscriptions, annual maintenance appeals, and participation in united community fund solicitations.

Converts from England started Salvation Army work in Canada in 1882 at London, Ontario. Officers from the United States established operations in the Dominion the same year. In spite of stormy beginnings, the Army's witness was effective and Canada became a separate command in 1884. The Army's League of Mercy—Salvationists of both sexes who visit hospitals, prisons, and needy homes—originated in Canada in 1892, the very years of "the split," the one serious interruption in the Army's progress in Canada, when differences of opinion about administration led to the withdrawal of a number of leading officers and many "soldiers." From 1900 to 1914 the Army's colonization scheme brought 200,000 English immigrants to Canada. In 1933 the international headquarters placed the work in Bermuda under the Canadian command. The Canadian command has 1,800 officers and cadets, assisted by over 4,800 employees without rank and backed (according to the government census of 1961) by a membership of 100,000, functioning through 600 corps and outposts and in nearly 200 institutions and schools. The program of the Salvation Army in Canada largely parallels that carried on in the United States. The headquarters for Canada and Bermuda are at 20 Albert Street, Toronto, Ontario M5G 1A6.

The basic unit of the Salvation Army is the corps, of which there may be several in a community. It corresponds to the congregation or parish of other denominations. Each corps has a commanding officer, ranging in rank from lieutenant to brigadier, who is responsible to one of forty-five divisions in the United States; a divisional commander supervises each division's activities. In the United States four territorial commanders direct the work in their respective territories. The national commander is the chief administrative officer and official spokesman at the national level.

Converts who desire to become soldiers sign the Articles of War and are enrolled during a corps meeting (worship service). This is the equivalent of acceptance into church membership. After this, as members they give volunteer service to the Army. Part of their commitment is to abstain from alcohol and tobacco. "Local officers"—layperson's with specific responsibilities—also refrain from tobacco. The officers, commissioned to full-time service, correspond in function to the clergy of other denominations.

Salvation Army worship services are simple. They reflect the determination of the early leaders to conduct services that would attract and hold converts from the poor, ignorant, and unchurched classes, whose greatest need was to understand clearly the power of God in their lives. Booth put his early converts at ease by creating an informal atmosphere in his services through joyous singing, instrumental music, clapping of hands, personal testimony, free prayer, and an open invitation to repentance. Currently Salvation Army services are likely to be more moderate in outward form, but they follow the same pattern and demonstrate the same lively spirit.

Not content with reaching only those who attend indoor services, the Salvation Army regularly proclaims the gospel on city streets.

Salvation Army music is distinctive. The Army has evolved a network of music camps, institutes, and bandmasters' training courses, and its many well-trained bands not only contribute to the Army's worship services, but also seek to provide a spiritual ministry of music to churches, hospitals, schools, and civic gatherings where they are invited to perform.

At dedication services Salvationist parents present their children to the Lord and pledge themselves to train their children for him. At most Army meetings seekers are exhorted to come to the Penitent Form, or Mercy-Seat, confessing their sin or failure to God and claiming salvation or sanctification in faith. Salvation Army solemnizes its members' marriages "under the flag." It discourages officers from marrying non-Salvationists unless the new partner intends to become a Salvation Army officer.

On principle, women have an absolute parity of privilege, position, and dignity with men.[1]

Ever since the Chancery Division of the High Court of Justice in England enrolled the "Foundation Deed" of the Salvation Army in 1878, the following eleven cardinal affirmations have constituted the "principle Doctrines" which the Army holds and teaches throughout the world:

1. We believe that the Scriptures of the Old and New Testaments were given by inspiration of God and that they only constitute the Divine rule of Christian faith and practice.

2. We believe there is only one God who is infinitely perfect, the Creator, Preserver, and Governor of all things, and who is the only proper object of religious worship.

3. We believe that there are three persons in the Godhead, the Father, the Son, and the Holy Ghost, undivided in essence and co-equal in power and glory.

4. We believe that in the person of Jesus Christ the Divine and human natures are united so that He is truly and properly God and truly and properly man.

5. We believe that our first parents were created in a state of innocency but that by their disobedience they lost their purity and happiness and that in consequence of their fall all men have become sinners totally depraved and as such are justly exposed to the wrath of God.

6. We believe that the Lord Jesus Christ has by his suffering and death made an atonement for the whole world so that whosoever will may be saved.

7. We believe that repentance toward God, faith in our Lord Jesus Christ, and regeneration by the Holy Spirit are necessary to salvation.

8. We believe that we are justified by grace through faith in our Lord Jesus Christ and that he that believeth hath the witness in himself.

9. We believe that continuance in a state of salvation depends upon continued obedient faith in Christ.[2]

10. We believe that it is the privilege of all believers to be "wholly sanctified" and that their "whole spirit and soul and body" may "be preserved blameless unto the coming of Our Lord Jesus Christ" (1 Thess. v. 23).[3]

11. We believe in the immortality of the soul, in the resurrection of the body, in the general judgment at the end of the world, in the eternal happiness of the righteous, and in the endless punishment of the wicked.[4]

Both the generally Arminian strain and the specifically Methodist stresses in Salvation Army doctrine appear clearly in these articles. Arminian is the insistence on a universal atonement, the conviction "that whosoever *will* may be saved," and the teaching that is is possible for even the "truly converted to fall away and be eternally lost." Unmistakably Methodist is the accent on perfection and entire sanctification.

The "principal Doctrines" receive an official commentary in *The Salvation Army Handbook of Doctrine.* "Issued by authority of The General," this volume has a General Order prefacing it: "It is required of Officers of all ranks that their teaching, in public and private, shall conform to our Doctrines as herein set forth."[5]

*The Handbook of Doctrine* reflects the milieu and the period that originally produced it. The treatment of the individual articles is evangelistic, thorough, strongly apologetic, and somewhat scholastic. The biblical documentation utilizes the proof-text method. The basic orientation is that of nineteenth-century English evangelicalism.

The fall of humankind's first parents was inexcusable and dreadful. Its consequences for the offenders was disastrous. Since Adam was the head and representative of the human race, his sin affected the whole of humankind, which now has a sinful nature; "this depravity or disposition of sin affects every part of man's being and renders him unable by his own efforts to deliver himself."[6] He also commits sinful acts that are the outcome of his sinful nature, but he does so by his own choice. "Man's greatest need is a way of deliverance from sin and its consequences, and this Jesus Christ, by his atoning work on man's behalf, has fully and freely provided."[7]

By his life, death, resurrection, and ascension, Jesus Christ revealed the nature of God, made known the Father's will, set humanity a perfect example, made an atonement for sin ("this is the most important of all"), and procured for humankind the presence and operation of the Holy Spirit in virtue of his accepted atonement on humanity's behalf.[8]

Christ's atoning sacrifice was sufficient for its purpose because he was truly human, he was truly God, he was perfectly holy ("deserving no punishment Himself, He could suffer for the sins of others"), he suffered voluntarily ("this made Him sacrifice supremely meritorious"), and his offering involved tremendous sacrifice on the part of his Father, the Lawgiver. The Bible speaks of the atonement in various ways. It describes Christ as a ransom and his work as redempton; it shows that Christ suffered in the sinner's stead, that is, on behalf of the whole of humankind; it calls him a propitiation for sin; and it affirms in him God, out of his immeasurable and unchangeable love, reconciled humankind with himself. The Bible never represents Christ as having paid the sinner's debt, but it shows that by his atonement he opened a way by which God could forgive the sinner's debt in a way that meets the requirements of both love and justice.[9]

The individual can experience the benefits of redemption only by the exercise of individual free will. God's predestination does not have to do with the destiny of particular individuals; "God foresaw who would receive Jesus, and predestinated (decided, settled from the very beginning) that those who did so should be made like Him and also that those who persevered in His choice or call should be finally justified and glorified." At the same time, "the only ground or merit of our salvation from first to last is to be ascribed to the love of God, as revealed in the work and sacrifice of Jesus Christ." But "man is free to accept or reject the Salvation which he in no way merits or deserves."[10]

"We know little as to how those who have never heard of Christ will finally be benefited by His sacrifice, but we can safely leave them to the mercy of God"; however, it is the solemn duty of Christians to take salvation to the heathen as quickly as possible.[11]

"Salvation takes place when the individual is regenerated and consists in deliverance from outward sin and the love of it. Sanctification takes place usually some time after regeneration, and is deliverance from both inward and outward sin—from sin in disposition as well as in deed." In other words, the unconverted person is under sin, the regenerated person is over sin, and a sanctified person is without sin. Sanctification is not divine or absolute perfection; nor is it sinless or "Adamic" perfection, "since the Fall has rendered us imperfect both in mind and body" and God expects us only "to love and serve Him to the best of our knowledge and ability"; nor is it infallibility, freedom from bodily or mental infirmities, freedom from temptation, a state of grace from which it is impossible to fall, or a state where further advance is impossible. In Army synonyms for entire sanctification are "holiness, a clean heart, perfect love, Christian perfection, full salvation, The Blessing."[12]

The Salvation Army breaks most radically with its theological antecedents in its doctrine of the sacraments, the discussion of which is relegated to an appendix in *The Salvation Army Handbook of Doctrine*, since the "principal Doctrines" do not advert to them. This appendix puts it plainly: "As it is

The Salvation Army's firm conviction that these ceremonies [baptism and the Lord's Supper] are not necessary to salvation nor essential to spiritual progress, we do not observe them." The supporting argument declares that Christ's religion is spiritual; that observance of certain ceremonies by the early Christians does not prove that we are bound to observe them; that Paul pointed out the uselessness and even danger of the observance of certain customs and ceremonies that the early Christian communities had carred over from the Jewish dispensation; that some who observe sacraments exhibit no spiritual change; and that many people rely on sacraments rather than on Christ, and sacraments thus are sometimes a hindrance to spiritual life. With specific reference to baptism the *Handbook* argues that the New Testament often uses baptism figuratively of suffering; that water baptism in Christ's time was even then an ancient form of initiation; that the one all-important baptism is the baptism of the Holy Spirit; that water baptism was evidently not intended to be perpetually observed; and that Matthew 28:19 and John 3:5 are to be figuratively interpreted. With reference to the Lord's Supper the *Handbook* argues that this is one of the most controversial subjects connected with the Christian religion; that Christ did not institute at his last Passover a religious ordinance to be permanently and universally observed; that consistency requires that those who interpret spiritually Christ's command to wash one another's feet should similarly interpret what he said about his body and blood; that 1 Corinthians 11:20–26 is to be interpreted spiritually; that the true communion of the body and blood of Christ is spiritual; and that the Salvation Army's stress is on obedience to the command that the Savior gave at his last supper, namely, to remember his death and to feed on him spiritually.[13]

## American Rescue Workers

Major Thomas E. Moore began to head the activities of the Salvation Army in the United States in 1882. He soon became aware of the resentment that some Americans at that time felt toward an organization under the autocratic control of a subject of the king of England. His first solution to the problem was to try in 1884 by an act of incorporation to establish the Army's United States operation as a domestic organization legally independent of London's control. This effort failed, so he withdrew from the Salvation Army and in 1885 he established the Salvation Army of America as a domestic rival to the English organization. He subsequently gave up his generalship and became a Baptist minister. His successor, along with all but about twenty-five posts, returned to the original Salvation Army, then headed in the United States by Commander Ballington Booth. In 1891 the continuing body incorporated itself as the American Salvation Army. In 1913 the organization renamed itself the American Rescue Workers. The constitution of this philanthropic, evangelistic, home-missionary body defines it in Article I as "a movement, military in its methods, organized for the reaching and uplifting of all sections of the people, and bringing them to the immediate knowledge and active service of God." Article II describes it as "composed of men and women who have given every evidence of a change of heart by the abandonment of all evil, unclean and worldly habits, by honesty of character, purity of life, and earnestness of purpose, and who live for the bettering and saving of humanity."[14] Article III affirms that it must ever be "an American institution, recognizing the spirit and justice of the Constitution, and it is not, and never shall be, controlled or governed by any foreign power whatsoever."[15]

The American Rescue Workers insist that they are a Christian church and not simply an organization. They define a church as "a congregation of faithful persons to whom the Word of God is preached and taught, and to whom the duly appointed Sacraments of Baptism and the Lord's Supper are administered." Since they administer both of these sacraments and receive the Word of God as their rule of faith and guide of action, they see their status as a church incontestably demonstrated.

Article XI of their constitution specifies their "cardinal doctrines," which their *Ritual and Manual* calls their Articles of Religion. These are an obvious adaptation of the "principal Doctrines" of the Salvation Army. They affirm one supreme Creator-God; the Trinity; the inspiration of the Bible; the manhood and Godhead of Jesus Christ "when upon earth"; the sinful propensity of human beings as a consequence of the fall; the universality of Christ's atonement and "that whosoever will call upon Him and accept His overtures of grace may be saved"; the necessity of salvation of repentence, faith in Jesus Christ, and regeneration through the operation of the Holy Spirit; the Holy Spirit's inward witness of acceptance by God to each person thus saved; cleansing in heart from inbred sin; the immortality of the soul, the general resurrection of all persons, and a divine judgment with everlasting consequences.[16] Article XIII of the constitution obligates the American Rescue Workers to "maintain and retain the most friendly relationship with the evangelical churches of God." Membership in the American Rescue Workers is not exclusive; a soldier may continue as a member of any church.

Only the general in command or a staff officer may administer the sacraments and the rite of marriage. Infants may be bapized by putting water on the candidate's head or by immersion.[17] Adults may be baptized by sprinkling, pouring, or immersion, as the candidate may elect; if he has received baptism in infancy, "a second baptism is unnecessary."[18] Whenever practicable, "the pure, unfermented juice of the grape" is to be used at the Lord's Supper; the text of the order for the celebration of the Lord's Supper derives from the Anglican Book of Common Prayer with some change in the sequence of parts.[19] Both women and men are admitted to ordination as officers, that is, ministers.

A fifteen-member national board elects the commander in chief for a ten-year term. National headquarters at 2827 Frankford Avenue, Philadelphia, Pennsylvania 19134, oversee 25 churches with 2,700 members. Support for the American Rescue Workers' evangelistic and philanthropic activities comes from voluntary contributions.

## The National Society of the Volunteers of America

On March 8, 1896, Commander Ballington Booth and his wife, Maud, withdrew from the Salvation Army and "after serious thought and careful deliberation" founded the Volunteers of America at a public rally held at the Cooper Union in New York. For the preceding seven years, Booth, the first general and commander in chief of the new organization, had headed the work of the Salvation Army in the United States. In undertaking the formation of the new organization the Booths acted upon the advice and encouragement of a large number of nationally prominent religious, political, and industrial leaders. Thus the Volunteers of America came into being in response to a desire for a distinctively American philanthropic and evangelistic society that recognized "the spirit and justice of the Constitution of the United States and [that] is not and never shall be controlled or governed by any foreign power whatsoever," in the words of the constitution of the National Society of the Volunteers of America, Article III.

The new organization reflected the intensely nationalistic and anti-English mood of America in the period in which it came into being. While it espoused democratic principles of self-government, it patterned its methods, doctrines, and aims after the organization with which the Booths had been associated. Article I of the constitution describes the organization as "a movement military in its methods, organized for the reaching and uplifting of all sections of people and bringing them to the immediate knowledge and service of God." The United States Army provides in a broad way the model for the operation of the Volunteers of America. All officers wear military uniforms and bear military titles. The commander in chief is elected for a five-year term. The motto of the Volunteers of America is "The Lord My Banner."

The organization considers its spiritual work its real work. It regards its extensive benevolent, philanthropic, and humanitarian endeavors as having only secondary importance. These are only means to the end of bringing the gospel to the neglected and unchurched. The organization undertakes no charitable work in any place until after it has begun spiritual work. The Volunteers of America must therefore be considered in a sense a church body, although the organization on principle neither proselytizes nor seeks to build up a denominational church membership. Its 572 posts propose to function as undenominational religious centers; they try to achieve their purpose by means of mission churches that they establish (usually in economically depressed areas), Sunday and vacation Bible schools, evangelistic and consecration meetings, and religious services held in prisons. The Volunteers encourage the individual who comes to an awareness of the need of God in his life through their missionary efforts to return to the denomination of his family or to feel "at liberty to go into any church that [he] may desire," according to Article XIV of the constitution. At the same time, 31,218 persons avail themselves of the option not to join other churches and regard the Volunteers of America as their only church home. The headquarters are at 340 West 85th Street, New York, New York 10024.

Article XI of the constitution sets forth these "cardinal doctrines" as the organization's theological base:

> We believe in one supreme God, who is "from everlasting to everlasting," who is infinitely perfect, benevolent, and wise, who is omnipotent and omnipresent, and who is creator and ruler of heaven and earth.
>
> We believe in a Triune God—the Father, Son, and the Holy Ghost. We believe these three Persons are one, and while separate in office, are undivided in essence, co-equal in power and glory, and that all men everywhere ought to worship and serve this Triune God.
>
> We believe the contents of the Bible to have been given by inspiration of God, and the Scriptures form the Divine rule of all true, Godly faith and Christian practice.
>
> We believe that Jesus Christ, when upon earth, was truly man and yet was as truly God—the Divine and human being blended in the one Being, hence His ability to feel and suffer as a man and yet supremely love and triumph as the Godhead.
>
> We believe that our first parents were created without sin, but by listening to the tempter and obeying his voice fell from grace and lost their purity and peace; and that in consequence of their disobedience and fall all men have become sinful by propensity and are consequently exposed to the wrath of God.
>
> We believe that Jesus Christ, the only begotten Son of God, by the sacrifice of His life, made an atonement for all men, and that whosoever will call upon Him and accept His overtures of grace shall be saved.
>
> We believe that in order to be saved it is necessary (a) to repent toward God; (b) to believe with the heart in Jesus Christ; and (c) to become regenerated through the operation of the Holy Spirit.
>
> We believe that the Spirit beareth witness with our spirit that we are the children of God, thus giving the inward witness of acceptance by God.
>
> We believe that the Scriptures teach and urge all Christians to be cleansed in heart from inbred sin, so that they may walk uprightly and serve Him without fear in holiness and righteousness all the days of their lives.
>
> We believe the soul shall never die; that we shall be raised again; that the world shall be judged by God; and that the punishment of the wicked shall be eternal, and the joy and reward of the righteous will be everlasting before the throne of God.

Article XV directs that the Volunteers of America shall observe the Lord's Supper (with unfermented wine) and that the ordained officers of the society shall administer the sacrament in accordance with the society's ritual. It also directs the observance of baptism by all members who desire it and authorizes the society's ordained officers to baptize the children of members, but provides that "the observance of this sacrament is not to be considered as an essential condition of membership."

In keeping with Ballington Booth's thesis that "you cannot preach to a man when he is hungry," the Volunteers of America operates nearly 600 centers throughout the United States in which it carries on a wide variety of social welfare and institutional work. These include family centers to provide counseling services, recreational activities, and educational programs; emergency homes for homeless men, women, and children; summer camps; housing and clubs for older people; school clothing programs for children from underprivileged families; residences for young women away from home; disaster services; maternity homes; salvage and rehabilitation programs for handicapped persons; day-care centers and family day-care programs; and youth programs designed to prevent juvenile delinquency. Particularly siginificant is the correctional-services program. To this program Maud Booth devoted much of her time and for it she was called the "Little Mother of the Prisons." It is designed to help prisoners and their families and to assist former prison inmates to become self-supporting and law-abiding citizens.

## Grace and Hope Mission

With thirteen dollars in cash and a great deal of faith in God, Mamie E. Caskie (1880–1959) and Jennie E. Goranflo, (1880–1941) opened a gospel mission in Baltimore, Maryland, in 1914. In 1919 they incorporated it as the Grace and Hope Mission. In the 1920s they began to extend their work to blighted areas of other cities. While the approach of the mission is to all, its special concern is for families and children in crowded urban slums, and for homeless and transient men. Evangelistic services are held several evenings each week at all the chapels of the mission.

The mission's ten-article Doctrinal Statement affirms the inspiration of the Bible; the unity of the true God; the Trinity; the sentence of death on all human beings as a result of the fall of our first parents; salvation wholly through God's grace and mercy, Christ's full atonement for all sin through his death on the cross, and full justification through faith in him; conversion or regeneration as a gracious miracle of new birth; the need of sanctification in the sense of separation from ungodliness for a life of holiness; the peril of backsliding, although the backslider can have forgiveness and cleansing; Christ's return as the comforting hope of the church; and the resurrection of the just to life and of the unjust to damnation.[20]

The officers and missionaries of the Grace and Hope Mission are all single women. The mission sisters wear an identifying uniform of black, trimmed with red, with the badge of the mission on it. The headquarters are at 4 South Gay Street, Baltimore, Maryland 21202. There are 14 centers in cities within a triangle formed by Buffalo, Boston, and Norfolk. Appointments for the following year are made at an annual conference. The nature of the mission's ministry makes the keeping of membership statistics impossible, but it is estimated that at any given time the average number of persons associated with the mission's centers is about 800.

## NOTES

1. Evangeline Cory Booth (1865–1890) became the fourth general of the Salvation Army in 1934. See P. W. Wilson, *General Evangeline Booth of The Salvation Army* (New York: Charles Scribner's Sons, 1948).

2. *The Salvation Army Handbook of Doctrine* (London: International Headquarters of the Salvation Army, 1965), p. 2, prints this official comment on the ninth article: "*That is to say*, We believe that the Scriptures teach that not only does continuance in the favour of God depend upon continued faith in, and obedience to, Christ, but that it is possible for those who have been truly converted to fall away and be eternally lost."

3. *The Salvation Army Handbook of Doctrine* (op. cit.) prints this official comment on the tenth article: "*That is to say*, We believe that after conversion there remain in the heart of the believer inclinations to evil, or roots of bitterness, which, unless overpowered by Divine grace, produce actual sin; but that these evil tendencies can be entirely taken away by the Spirit of God, and the whole heart, thus cleansed from everything contrary to the will of God, or entirely sanctified, will then produce the fruit of the Spirit only. And we believe that persons thus entirely sanctified may, by the power of God, be kept unblameable and unreprovable before him."

4. This statement is widely reprinted in Salvation Army literature. It is here quoted from *The Salvation Army Handbook of Doctrine*, pp. 1-2.

5. Ibid., p. ii.

6. Chapter V, section IV, 2(a) (ibid., p. 49).

7. Chapter V, section IV, 6, final note, (b) (ibid., p. 55).

8. Chapter VI, section I, 5 (ibid., pp. 58-59).

9. Chapter VI, section I, 7-13 (ibid., pp. 60-67).

10. Chapter VI, section III (ibid., pp. 70-75).

11. Chapter VIII, section V (ibid., pp. 103-104).

12. Chapter X, section I, 3-6 (ibid., pp. 118-124).

13. Appendix (ibid., pp. 160-167).

14. When a "soldier" is admitted "under the flags" he takes this obligation: "Having received with all my heart the salvation offered to me by the tender mercy of Jehovah, I do here and now publicly acknowledge God to be my Father and King, Jesus Christ to be my Saviour, and the Holy Ghost to be my Guide, Comforter and Strength; and that I will love, serve, worship, and obey this glorious God for ever, God helping me" (*The American Rescue Workers Ritual and Manual* [Philadelphia: American Rescue Workers, n. d.], pp. 22-23).

15. The standard of the American Rescue Workers is the Stars and Stripes. The banner of the organization has a blue ground for purity, a five-pointed red star for the blood of Christ, a border of deep blue for heavenliness, a fringe of yellow for the fire of the Holy Ghost, and a small American flag in the upper left corner.

16. *Ritual and Manual*, p. [1].

17. Ibid., p. 5.

18. Ibid., p. 10.
19. Ibid., pp. 30-39. All of the orders in the *Ritual and Manual* show a strong dependence on the Book of Common Prayer.
20. "Doctrinal Statement," *Grace and Hope Evangel*, vol. 37, no. 3 (October 1964), 2.

## BIBLIOGRAPHY

Begbie, Harold. *Life of General Booth.* 2 vols. London: The Macmillan Co., 1920.

Bishop, Edward. *Blood and Fire—The Story of General William Booth and the Salvation Army.* Chicago: Moody Press, 1965. A popularly written sympathetic biography by a non-Salvationist.

Booth, William. *In Darkest England and the Way Out.* London: International Headquarters of the Salvation Army, 1890.

Brown, Arnold. *"What Hath God Wrought?" The History of the Salvation Army in Canada 1882–1914.* 2nd edn. Toronto: The Salvation Army Printing and Publishing House, 1957. A history of the Salvation Army in Canada down to the beginning of World War I, designed more for readability than for documentary purposes.

Collier, Richard. *The General Next to God: The Story of William Booth and the Salvation Army.* New York: E. P. Dutton and Co., 1965.

Ervine, St. John Greer. *God's Soldier: William Booth.* 2 vols. New York: The Macmillan Co., 1934.

*General Orders for Conducting Salvation Army Ceremonies.* London: Salvationist Publishing and Supplies, 1966.

Hall, Clarence Wilbur, and Brengle, Samuel Logan. *Portrait of a Prophet.* New York: National Headquarters of the Salvation Army, 1933.

*Orders and Regulations for Officers of the Salvation Army.* Rev. edn. London: International Headquarters of the Salvation Army, 1950.

Orsborn, Albert. *The House of My Pilgrimage.* London: Salvationist Publishing and Supplies, 1958. Orsborn was the sixth General of the Salvation Army.

Pean, Charles. *The Conquest of Devil's Island.* London: Max Parrish, 1953.

*The Salvation Army Directory.* 3rd edn. (1954), 2nd printing. London: Salvationist Publishing and Supplies, 1962. A catechism for new Salvationists and a manual for cadets designed to prepare them for *The Salvation Army Handbook of Doctrine.*

*The Salvation Army Handbook of Doctrine.* 4th edn. (1935), 6th printing. London: International Headquarters of the Salvation Army, 1965.

*The Salvation Army Yearbook.* London: Salvationist Publishing and Supplies. Published annually.

Sandall, Robert, and Wiggins, Arch R. *The History of the Salvation Army.* 4 vols. New York: Thomas Nelson and Sons, 1947–1964.

Welty, Susan Fulton. *Look Up and Hope! The Motto of the Volunteer Prison League: The Life of Maud Ballington Booth.* New York: Thomas Nelson Sons, 1961.

Wisbey, Herbert Andrew, Jr. *History of the Volunteers of America.* New York: The Volunteers of America, 1954. An account of the Volunteers of America from the beginnings to 1952, by the organization's official historian.

————. "Religion in Action: A History of the Salvation Army in the United States." New York: Unpublished doctoral dissertation of Columbia University, 1951.

————. *Soldiers without Swords: A History of the Salvation Army in the United States.* New York: Macmillan Co., 1955. A revision of *Religion in Action.*

# PART II

---

# PENTECOSTAL CHURCHES

---

# 4. The Pentecostal Movement

Between 1901 and 1906 the Pentecostal movement emerged from the Holiness movement that had been flourishing among Wesleyan Methodists for a half century[1] and represented a major theological division within the ranks of Holiness advocates. Calling for baptism with the Holy Spirit as a "third blessing" to follow the "second blessing" of sanctification, the Pentecostals claimed that speaking in tongues was the evidence which proved that one had been baptized with the Holy Spirit. The movement spread rapidly through the United States and Canada, embracing people beyond the Holiness movement, and was carried overseas where it became a major religious force especially in South America and Africa. After the movement was institutionalized in new church denominations in the first half of the twentieth century, it emerged again from 1960 on as the Charismatic movement within mainline Christian denominations, Protestant and Roman Catholic.

The roots of the Pentecostal movement lie deep within the Holiness movement.[2] The advocates of entire sanctification repeatedly prayed for a new Pentecost and described the "second blessing" of Christian perfection as the baptism with the Holy Spirit. The gift of holiness was often accompanied by ecstatic emotional experiences, which included jerks and twitchings of the body, trances, and on occasion even speaking in tongues.

A forerunner of the Pentecostal movement was Benjamin Hardin Irwin, a member of the Iowa Holiness Association who became convinced that there was a third experience beyond sanctification called "the baptism with the Holy Ghost and fire" or simply "the fire." Hardin began to preach his doctrine throughout the Middle West, and many who came to his meetings professed to receive the "baptism of fire." When the leadership of the Iowa Holiness Association repudiated Irwin for his "third blessing heresy," he established the Iowa Fire Baptized Holiness Association in 1895 and similar associations in other states, which he united as the Fire Baptized Holiness Church in 1898. In time speaking with tongues became a common experience among those who received "the fire."[3]

One of those who attended Irwin's meetings was Charles Fox Parham (1873–1929) who, while rejecting the emotional extremes of the meetings, was impressed with the idea of a "third experience" of a "baptism with the Holy Ghost and fire." Dissociating himself from the Methodist Episcopal Church as a "come-outer,"[4] Parham started Bethel Bible School near Topeka, Kansas, in 1900. He and his students came to the conclusion from their study of the book of Acts that speaking with other tongues was the one scriptural evidence for the baptism with the Holy Spirit. After midnight in a watchnight service as 1901 began, one of Parham's students, Agnes N. Ozman, asked him to lay hands on her head and to pray for her to be baptized with the Holy Spirit as evidenced by speaking in tongues. As Parham reported the event, a halo seemed to surround her head and face and she began to speak in the Chinese language.[5] Before many days most of the other students and then Parham himself testified that they had experienced Spirit baptism and had spoken in "other tongues."

Parham closed his school and engaged in evangelistic activities to spread his "Pentecostal" ministry. Over four years of activity he and his followers spread the "Full Gospel," including an emphasis on healing, through Kansas and Missouri and into Texas, Alabama, and Florida, raising up thousands of Pentecostal believers. In 1905 at a Bible school which he had established in Houston, Parham had among his students a black Holiness preacher, William J. Seymour, a short, stocky man, with only one eye and little religious training, whom Parham convinced that the only biblical evidence for the baptism with the Spirit was the act of speaking with other tongues, though Seymour himself did not at the time share the experience.

In Parham's services in Houston, Neely Terry, a black woman from Los Angeles, befriended Seymour. When she returned to Los Angeles she prevailed on her small black Holiness mission to invite Seymour to be their pastor. Seymour accepted, and on his arrival in Los Angeles affirmed in his first sermon that everyone truly baptized with the Spirit would speak in tongues. The leader of the congregation was appalled at the teaching and locked Seymour out. Invited to stay in the home of Richard Asbury, Seymour conducted services there and on April 9, 1906, together with several others began to speak with other tongues. The house was soon too small for the huge crowds that gathered to hear Seymour speak. After a search for other quarters, Seymour used an old abandoned Methodist church building at 312 Azusa Street to continue the meetings.

So began the famous Azusa Street revival in Los Angeles in April 1906. At first hundreds, then thousands, flocked to the Apostolic Faith Gospel Mission on Azusa Street to witness the new Pentecost in "the American Jerusalem."[6] The revival was reported regularly in the secular and religious press as it continued for three years. Holiness leaders from all over the country made pilgrimages to the Azusa Street mission to see for themselves and in many cases to receive their own Pentecostal experience. Some of the visitors were later to become leaders of denominations of Pentecostal believers, and the list of those Pentecostal leaders baptized with the Spirit at the mission was long indeed.

Among those who became prominent in the Pentecostal movement was Florence Crawford, who brought the Apostolic Faith movement to the Pacific Northwest. Another was William H. Durham, who became an outstanding Pentecostal leader in Chicago. "Elder" Sturdevant, a black preacher, brought the Los Angeles experience to New York City. A. H. Argue carried the Pentecostal message to Winnipeg in Canada.

The Azusa Street revival had a significant impact on the Holiness churches in the southern and southeastern United States. Speaking in tongues had occurred there as a phenomenon of Holiness revivals and had been a significant feature of the Camp Creek revival in North Carolina in 1896. News of the events at the Azusa Street mission were reported in church periodicals in the South and were received favorably. In 1906 G. B. Cashwell of Dunn, North Carolina, made a trip to Los Angeles and received the Pentecostal experience there. Returning to North Carolina, he became an Apostle of Pentecost to the South and succeeded in winning several Holiness denominations and adherents of other church bodies to the Pentecostal cause, including Joseph Hillery King (1869–1946) of the Fire Baptized Holiness Church, and Ambrose Jessup Tomlinson (1865–1943) of the Church of God (Cleveland, Tennessee).

Another visitor to the Azusa Street mission who assisted the Pentecostal cause in the South was Charles Harrison Mason (1866–1961) of the Church of God in Christ in Memphis, Tennessee. Mason won out in a contest with his church body's leadership for control of the organization. The Church of God in Christ in time became the largest black Pentecostal group in the world.

From its beginnings in the United States the Pentecostal movement spread rapidly throughout the world. A Norwegian Methodist pastor, Thomas Ball Barratt (1862–1940), who was on tour in the United States in 1906, had correspondence with Seymour and received the Pentecostal experience at a service in New York City. Returning to Oslo, he brought the Pentecostal revival to Norway and from there to all of Northern Europe.[7]

Speaking in tongues occurred in 1906 among the prayer bands and evangelistic missions conducted by the widows and orphans of a home sponsored by Pandita Ramabai in Mukti, India. Their witness, strengthened by Pentecostal missionaries newly arrived from the United States and Great Britain, spread the Pentecostal revival throughout India and to other parts of Asia by 1909. The Pentecostal movement was brought to China in 1908 and to Korea in 1909.

American evangelists John G. Lohe and Thomas Hezmalhalch first brought the Pentecostal message to the African continent sometime before 1910. They began their work in Johannesburg, Union of South Africa. Other

American and British evangelists spread Pentecostalism into central and western Africa in the next few years, leading to the establishment of large independent church bodies.

The gift of tongues spread in South America first within a Methodist church in Valparaiso, Chile, in 1907. When the pastor, Willis C. Hoover, was disciplined, his supporters left the Methodist Church to establish the Methodist Pentecostal Church, and the Pentecostal movement spread rapidly throughout Chile. The movement was brought to São Paulo, Brazil, by Louis Francescan in 1910, who founded *Congregacioni Christiani*, a major Pentecostal church body in Brazil. Another major Pentecostal organization—the *Assembléias de Deus do Brasil*— was begun in 1910 by two Swedish-Americon missionaries. The spread of the movement throughout South America has made the Pentecostal denomination the largest Protestant group there.[8]

As it grew and spread, the Pentecostal movement met with vigorous opposition. Many of the leaders and organizations of the Holiness movement rejected and opposed the Pentecostal teaching that had emerged from their midst. They criticized the Azusa Street revival both for emotional excesses and for heretical distortion in insisting on speaking in tongues as the evidence of the baptism with the Holy Spirit. Alma White (1862–1946), leader of the Pillar of Fire organization, denounced Seymour and Parham as "rulers of spiritual Sodom," speaking in tongues as "this satanic gibberish," and Pentecostal services as "the climax of demon worship."[9] The largest of the Holiness denominations, the Pentecostal Church of the Nazarene, became a center of anti-Pentecostal sentiment and in 1919 at its General Assembly deleted "Pentecostal" from its name so that the Church of the Nazarene might not be confused with those who insist on speaking in tongues as "evidence of holiness."[10] Other Holiness denominations followed the lead of the Nazarenes in dissociating themselves from Pentecostalism. As the Pentecostal movement touched adherents of other denominations, those church bodies repudiated the movement. In the South some Pentecostal promoters were subjected to physical abuse and persecution.

During the first years of the Pentecostal movement there was little interest in forming a new denomination. Most of its leaders thought of themselves as Spirit-filled members of the denominations of which they were members and sought to share with others in their denominations the gift they had received. The opposition of the already established denominations led naturally enough to the formation of new Pentecostal organizations. Proliferation of new organizations took place for several reasons. Major doctrinal controversies split the Pentecostals. There was no united leadership. And those baptized with the Spirit were as diverse in doctrine and practice as the many different denominations from which they came.

As Pentecostal centers or assemblies developed outside the established churches, there was a gradual recognition of the need to associate them in organizational networks. Parham led the way with his Apostolic Faith movement. In the South there were existing Holiness church organizations which had adopted the Pentecostal message, and it was possible to relate organizationally to these denominations. Among the largest of these were the Church of God in Cleveland, Tennessee, the Pentecostal Holiness Church formed in 1911 by independent holiness groups that had embraced Pentecostalism, and the Church of God in Christ, a black church body which for a number of years provided ordination credentials for many Pentecostal preachers not otherwise affiliated with a church body.

In the early years of the Pentecostal movement a major doctrinal controversy over sanctification as a second work of grace split the Pentecostals and separated the Pentecostals of the Holiness movement from those who came from churches not affected by the Wesleyan tradition. The Pentecostal movement began with the view that baptism with the Holy Spirit as evidenced by speaking in tongues was a "third blessing," which came after the "second blessing" of sanctification. Early Pentecostal leaders like Parham, Seymour, Tomlinson, and Mason continued to maintain the place of sanctification as the "second blessing," which cleanses from sin and prepares for the reception of the Holy Spirit. A problem arose within the Pentecostal movement when those of non-Wesleyan, especially Baptist, backgrounds described the Christian experience as involving only two steps, conversion and baptism with the Holy Spirit.

Protagonist in the attack on sanctification as a second work of grace was W. H. Durham of Chicago, Illinois, who had received the baptism with the Spirit at the Azusa Street revival and had brought Pentecostalism to his North Avenue Mission. In 1910 Durham advanced his notion of "the finished work," rejecting sanctification as a second work of grace and assigning it to the act of conversion based on "the finished work of Christ on Calvary."[11] When Durham advanced his views at the Azusa Street mission, Seymour, who had been away on a trip, returned to lock him out of the mission. In acrimonious debate Parham criticized the teaching and so did the southern Pentecostal groups. But most of the Pentecostal denominations established after 1911 espoused it as part of their statements of faith.

As "the finished work" theory spread, calls were heard for a united denominational home for all who espoused the view. A number of groups met in Hot Springs, Arkansas, 1914 and created a new denomination, the General Council of the Assemblies of God. The new church body espoused "the finished work" teaching and became the first major Pentecostal body outside the Wesleyan tradition. From the beginning the Assemblies of God was one of the largest Pentecostal organizations and wielded considerable influence on the rest of the movement.

A new controversy almost destroyed the young Assemblies of God church body. The issue became known as the "Jesus only" or the "Pentecostal unitarian" question. It arose at a camp meeting in Los Angeles in 1913 when an evangelist, R. E. McAlister, claimed that the apostoles baptized only in the name of Jesus. Deeply impressed was one of the leading figures of the Pentecostal movement on the West Coast, Frank J. Ewart. After spending a year in thinking the doctrine through, in 1914 Ewart began teaching that there was only one personality in the Godhead, Jesus Christ, and that the terms "Father" and "Holy Spirit" were titles used to designate different aspects of Christ's person.[12] The notion of a "Trinity" was an error foisted on the church by the bishop of Rome and anyone baptized with the trinitarian formula was not baptized at all. Ewart and Glenn A. Cook, one of Ewart's converts, rebaptized themselves and launched a campaign to convert the Pentecostal movement to their "oneness" or "Jesus only" belief.

The controversy over "oneness" came to a head in the Assemblies of God General Council in St. Louis in 1916. The trinitarian faction prevailed, committing the church body to a document which affirmed the rightness of calling the Godhead a "trinity or as of one Being of three persons."[13] The "oneness" advocates joined together in forming the Pentecostal Assemblies of the World and a number of other independent organizations.

By 1920 the general lines of Pentecostal organization had been established. The movement was divided into equal factions over the question of sanctification as a second blessing or as a finished work. About one fourth of all Pentecostals eventually sided with the "oneness" view. The movement grew phenomenally in the first decades of the twentieth century[14] and was ultimately described by some not as another denomination but as a "third force" in Christendom.[15]

Begun in hostility, the Pentecostal movement was ultimately tolerated as a phenomenon here to stay and finally won acceptance in the larger community. The appeal of Pentecostalism was at first to the lower classes of society; as their members rose on the economic scale, the Pentecostal churches rose with them and became middle-class institutions. In time, store-front churches and frame tabernacles gave way to more permanent structures. From 1940 on Pentecostals demonstrated keen interest in education for their members and their clergy and developed Bible institutes and colleges. In recent years Pentecostals have shown increasing concern to deal with social problems like drug addiction. Inevitably, some Pentecostals accused the majority of abandoning Pentecostal practices prominent at the beginning of the movement, and new Pentecostal groups were organized, including the New Order of the Latter Rain; the World Church; Wings of Healing, Full Gospel Fellowship of Ministers and Churches, International; and the Gospel Assemblies.

Fundamentalist and evangelical in the theological temperament, the Pentecostals were nevertheless rejected by the Fundamentalists. In 1928 at a Chicago convention American Fundamentalists rejected the Pentecostal movement as "a real menace in many churches and a real injury to the same testimony of Fundamental Christians" and went on record "as unreservedly opposed to Modern Pentecostalism, including the speaking with unknown tongues, and the fanatical healing known as general healing in the atonement."[16] Gradually the hostility between the groups was tempered. In 1943 Pentecostals were represented in strength at a meeting in Chicago which organized the National Association of Evangelicals, and the major Pentecostal groups subsequently decided to join the NAE.

As early as 1911 Thomas Ball Barratt of Norway had appealed for some simple structure to express the spiritual union among the world's Pentecostals. Unity conferences sponsored from time to time over the next decades were unsuccessful. The first World Pentecostal Fellowship met in Zurich, Switzerland, in 1947. Over the ensuing years world conferences helped allay fears about the possible consequences of such meetings. The World Pentecostal Conference provides a rallying center for the Pentecostals throughout the world, whose total numbers are estimated to be anywhere from 12 million to 35 million.

Out of the 1947 World Pentecostal Fellowship came the stimulus for an organization to unite the Pentecostals of North America. At Des Moines, Iowa, in 1948 the Pentecostal Fellowship of North America was organized as the voice for almost 1 million Pentecostals. Founding members included the Assemblies of God, the Church of God, the Pentecostal Holiness Church, the International Church of the Foursquare Gospel, and the Open Bible Standard Church. By the second meeting in 1949 the membership comprised fourteen groups, including the Pentecostal Assemblies of Canada. Not included were the black Pentecostal bodies, the oneness Pentecostals, and the Tomlinson branches of the Church of God.

The Pentecostal movement emerged in a new form known as the Charismatic movement[17] within mainline Christian churches from 1960 on. In 1960 Dennis J. Bennett, rector of St. Mark's Episcopal Church in Van Nuys, California, informed his congregation that he had received the baptism with the Spirit, precipitating a controversy within the congregation and the Episcopal denomination. Pentecostal practices emerged in other denominations as well, including the American Baptist Convention, the American Lutheran Church, the Evangelical United Brethren, The Methodist Church, the Reformed Church in America, and the United Presbyterian Church. By the 1970s the Charismatic movement was a phenomenon in most denominations, and informal structures were established to unite charismatics within denominational families. Major regional and national conferences of charismatics were held cutting across denominational lines.

The Charismatic movement spread to the Roman Catholic Church with an outbreak at Duquesne University in 1966 and at Notre Dame University in 1967. Kevin Ranaghan, theology professor at Notre Dame University, became a chief apologist for the movement.[18] The hierarchy of the Roman Catholic Church took note of the movement in 1969 and encouraged its development as a legitimate movement within the denomination.[19]

Though there has been considerable controversy over the charismatic phenomenon within Protestant and Roman Catholic churches, the Charismatic movement has until this point remained within the denominations and has not resulted in the formation of independent, charismatic church bodies.

Though some believe the Charismatic movement to be a spontaneous development of the working of the Holy Spirit, others argue that there is a link between the Charismatic movement and the earlier Pentecostal movement through personalities and organization of the latter.[20] Especially influential were the television broadcasts of Oral Roberts and the work of the Full Gospel Business Men's Fellowship International. David J. du Plessis (d. 1905), for a long time general secretary of the World Pentecostal Conference, has worked indefatigably to forge links with non-Pentecostals and charismatics.

## NOTES

1. For a description of the Holiness movement cf. chap. 1 above.
2. For a carefully documented historical account of the Holiness movement as the source of Pentecostalism, cf. Vinson Synan, *The Holiness-Pentecostal Movement in the United States* (Grand Rapids, Mich.: Wm. B. Eerdmans Publishing Company, 1971).
3. The views and influence of Irwin are described in Synan, pp. 61-68.
4. "Come-outism" as an aspect of the Holiness movement is described in chap. 1, above.
5. Parham's words are quoted in John T. Nichol, *Pentecostalism* (New York: Harper & Row, 1966), p. 28.
6. The phrase was used by Frank Bartleman, a Holiness advocate who often was on the same platform with Seymour, in an article in *The Way of Faith*, a publication in South Carolina which reported the Los Angeles revival in detail, quoted in Synan, p. 109.
7. Nils Bloch-Hoell, *The Pentecostal Movement: Its Origin, Development, and Distinctive Character* (New York: Humanities Press, 1964), pp. 65-86, 178-179.
8. The spread of the Pentecostal movement in other parts of the world is described in detail in W. J. Hollenweger, *The Pentecostals: The Charismatic Movement in the Churches* (Minneapolis, Minn.: Augsburg Publishing House, 1972), pp. 63-287.
9. Quoted in Synan, p. 143.
10. Nichol, p. 72.
11. Durham's views and the controversy over them are described in Synan, pp. 147-153.
12. Ewart's teaching is presented in Synan, p. 155.
13. Quoted in Synan, p. 157.
14. Edwin Gaustad, *Historical Atlas of Religion in America* (New York: Harper & Row, 1962), pp. 121-126.
15. So Henry Pitney Van Dusen in *Life* XLIV (June 9, 1958): 113-124.
16. The resolution is quoted in Nichol, p. 208.
17. The literature on the Charismatic movement is voluminous and growing. Cf. David J. du Plessis, *The Spirit Bade Me Go: The Astounding Move of God in the Denominational Churches* (Plainfield, N.J.: Logos International, 1970); Michael P. Hamilton, ed., *The Charismatic Movement* (Grand Rapids, Mich.: Wm. B. Eerdmans Publishing Company, 1975); Vinson Synan, ed., *Aspects of Pentecostal-Charismatic Origins* (Plainfield, N.J.: Logos International, 1975); Richard Quebedeaux, *The New Charismatics: The Origins, Development, and Significance of Neo-Pentecostalism* (Garden City, N.Y.: Doubleday, 1976).
18. Cf. Kevin and Dorothy Ranaghan, *Catholic Pentecostals* (Paramus, N.J.: Paulist Press, 1969).
19. For a description of the Charismatic movement within Roman Catholicism, cf. also Prudencio Damboriena, S.J., *Tongues as of Fire: Pentecostalism in Contemporary Christianity* (Washington, D.C.: Corpus Books, 1969); J. Massingberd Ford, *The Pentecostal Experience: A New Direction for American Catholics* (Paramus, N.J.: Paulist Press, 1970); Edward D. O'Connor, C.S.C., *The Pentecostal*

*Movement in the Catholic Church* (Notre Dame, Ind.: Ave Maria Press, 1971).

20. Nichol, p. 241, follows Russell T. Hitt

in arguing a connection between the two movements; Hollenweger, pp. 6-7, takes a similar position.

# BIBLIOGRAPHY

Bloch-Hoell, Nils. *The Pentecostal Movement: Its Origin, Development, and Distinctive Character*. New York: Humanities Press, 1964.

Damboriena, Prudencio, S.J. *Tongues as of Fire: Pentecostalism in Contemporary Christianity*. Washington, D.C.: Corpus Books, 1969.

Du Plessis, David J. *The Spirit Bade Me Go: The Astounding Move of God in the Denominational Churches*. Plainfield, N.J.: Logo International, 1970.

Faupel, David W. *The American Pentecostal Movement: A Bibliographical Essay*. First Monograph of the Society for Pentecostal Studies, 1972.

Ford, J. Massingberd. *The Pentecostal Experience: A New Direction for American Catholics*. Paramus, N.J.: Paulist Press, 1970.

Foster, Fred J. *Think It Not Strange: A History of the Oneness Movement*. St. Louis, Mo.: Pentecostal Publishing House, 1965.

Hamilton, Michael P., ed. *The Charismatic Movement*. Grand Rapids, Mich.: Wm. B. Eerdmans Publishing Company, 1975.

Kendrick, Klaude. *The Promise Fulfilled: A History of the Modern Pentecostal Movement*. Springfield, Mo.: Gospel Publishing House, 1961.

O'Connor, Edward D., C.S.C. *The Pentecostal Movement in the Catholic Church*. Notre Dame, Ind.: Ave Maria Press, 1971.

———, ed. *Perspectives on Charismatic Renewal*. Notre Dame, Ind.: University of Notre Dame Press, 1975.

Paulk, Earl P., Jr. *Your Pentecostal Neighbor*. Cleveland, Tenn.: Pathway Press, 1958.

Quebedeaux, Richard. *The New Charismatics: The Origin, Development, and Significance of Neo-Pentecostalism*. Garden City, N.Y.: Doubleday, 1976.

Ranaghan, Kevin and Dorothy. *Catholic Pentecostals*. Paramus, N.J.: Paulist Press, Deus Books, 1969.

Sherrill, John L. *They Speak with Other Tongues*. New York: McGraw-Hill, 1964.

Wagner, C. Peter. *Look Out! The Pentecostals Are Coming*. Carol Stream, Ill.: Creation House, 1973.

# 5. Trinitarian Pentecostal Bodies

## The Pentecostal Fellowship of North America

The first formal effort looking toward cooperative fellowship among all Pentecostal bodies took place in 1946. In that year the call went out for the first world conference of Pentecostal believers, held at Zurich, Switzerland, in 1947.[1]

The success of this first international effort encouraged the trinitarian Pentecostal bodies of North America to attempt the organization of a continent-wide fellowship of their own. As a result the Pentecostal Fellowship of North America held its constituting convention at Des Moines, Iowa, in October 1948.

Its objectives include provision of a vehicle of expression and coordination for common efforts, including missionary and evangelistic efforts throughout the world; demonstration to the world of the essential unity of Spirit-baptized Pentecostal Christians; promotion of the efficiency of the member bodies by making necessary services available to them; and encouragement of the principles of comity for the nurture of the body of Christ.[2]

The statement of doctrinal truth to which all member bodies subscribe is identical with that of the National Association of Evangelicals, except for the insertion of the following affirmation as the fifth in the series: "We believe that the full gospel includes holiness of heart and life, healing for the body, and baptism in the Holy Spirit, with the initial evidence of speaking in other tongues as the Spirit gives utterance."[3]

Membership is open to Pentecostal institutions, churches, and groups of churches[4] who subscribe to the Statement of Faith and the constitution of the fellowship.

The Pentecostal Fellowship of North America has no headquarters of its own; its officers are officials of the member bodies. Its journal, *PFNA News*, is published at 1445 Boonville Avenue, Springfield, Missouri 65802.

## The United Holy Church of America, Incorporated

The United Holy Church of America, Incorporated, exists chiefly along the eastern seaboard. It is a black Pentecostal body that began in a revival held by the Reverend Isaac Cheshier at Method, a suburb of Raleigh, North Carolina, in 1886 under the name of United Holiness Convention. By 1894 it had established headquarters at Durham. As the revival spread elsewhere in the state, some of the converts left their churches and formed Holiness associations ("come-outers"). Other converts remained in their previous denominations ("in-church people") until criticism forced them into Holiness congregations. In 1900 a meeting of the various groups that the revival had brought into being, notably the United Holiness Convention and the Big Kahara Association, resulted in a denominational organization under the name Holy Church of North Carolina. A schism over the necessity of the Lord's Supper for salvation was healed in 1907. Expansion of the movement ultimately led to the adoption of the name United Holy Church of America in 1916; incorporation took place in 1918. The church teaches justification through faith; water baptism by immersion; entire sanctification as an instantaneous second work of grace; baptism of the Spirit accompanied by various gifts, including the gift of tongues; divine healing (but not to the exclusion of medicine); observance of the Lord's Supper; foot washing; the imminent premillennial return of Christ; and a literal hell of fire for the lost. Members are forbidden to belong to secret societies, to wear ornaments, and to dress extravagantly. The church reports just under 29,000 members in 470 churches. The church is governed by bishops (who use the style "Right Reverend"), one of whom is the general president. Its headquarters are at 159 West Coulter Street, Philadelphia, Pennsylvania 19144.[5]

## The Mount Sinai Holy Church of America, Incorporated

During the early 1920s, Elder Ida Robinson (d. 1946) was the youthful pastor of Mount Olive Holy Church in Philadelphia. At that time it was a small mission affiliated with the United Holy Church of America. Elder Robinson dreamed dreams and saw visions of a great church being born under her ministry in Philadelphia and of people coming into it from the North, the South, the East, and the West. In 1924, after she and her flock had prayed and fasted for ten days, she believed that the Holy Spirit commanded her, "Come out on Mount Sinai." She understood these words as an order to establish her own work for God. Within a few months she and her supporters had chartered the Mount Sinai Holy Church of America, Incorporated, of which she became the first bishop. Under her leadership and that of her successor, Bishop Elmira Jeffries (d. 1964), the church body expanded along the entire Atlantic seaboard from Florida to Massachusetts and into California. While the church body has had male leaders in many official posts, it has been noteworthy for the extent and degree that women have taken a responsible part in its growth and direction.

The doctrinal sections of its manual commit the Mount Sinai Holy Church of America to preach Christ, his birth, baptism, works, teachings, crucifixion, resurrection, ascension, and literal second coming under two appearances, one to catch away his waiting bride, the other to execute judgment on the world at the Great White Throne judgment; repentance toward God; the need for restitution, since "the blood of Jesus will never blot out any sin that we can make right"; sanctification as a definite second work of grace; the baptism of the Holy Ghost as the gift of power on the sanctified life of a believer, accompanied by speaking with tongues; healing of the body as included in Christ's atonement, as well as the casting out of devils; the great tribulation before Christ's second coming; the new heaven and the new earth; and an eternal heaven and an eternal hell.[6]

The church insists on the indissolubility of marriage; allows separations only on account of unchastity and without the privilege of remarriage to another spouse; observes the ordinances of water baptism by immersion in the name of the Father and of the Son and of the Holy Ghost, the Lord's Supper with unleavened bread and the unfermented juice of the vine (not water) as its elements, the washing of the saints' feet, and the blessing (or dedication) of children with prayer; calls for the exclusion of evil and immoral persons, those who live in idleness, busybodies, and members of secret societies from the congregation; regards as public offenses such behavior as the teaching of false doctrines, disregard of authority, contention and strife, immoral conduct, covetousness, and going to law; prohibits the sale and use of intoxicants, narcotics, and tobacco in all its forms; requires candidates for membership to forgo superfluous ornaments in their dress; takes a firm stand against war; bans fairs, festivals, feasts, and every other kind of abomination from its houses of worship; and insists upon the payment of tithes by all.[7]

The "questions and answers for ministers" include affirmations that the Bible is the Word of God; that it does not contradict itself; that there are three persons in the Trinity; and that water baptism is essential to salvation when seen as an act of obedience to Christ's command.[8]

The headquarters are at 1601 North Broad Street, Philadelphia, 19122. Here the annual convocations are held. There are four geographical districts in the United States with 91 churches and an estimated total active membership of 7,000.[9] Foreign missions are carried on in Cuba and Guyana.

### The Pentecostal Holiness Church, Incorporated

In the 1890s Benjamin Hardin Irwin, a lawyer turned Holiness preacher, popularized what became known as the "third blessing heresy," the teaching that there was a religious experience, the "baptism of fire," beyond salvation and sanctification. By 1895 his movement had established itself in ten states from Iowa to Texas and from Kansas to South Carolina. Incorporated at Anderson, South Carolina, in 1898 as the Fire-Baptized Holiness Association, it took the name Fire-Baptized Holiness Church in 1902. By 1907 it had completely accepted the Pentecostal revival that radiated from the Azusa Street Mission[10] in Los Angeles.

Also during the 1890s A. B. Crumpler's energetic promotion of the doctrine of sanctification forced his withdrawal from the Methodist ministry. Under his influences the Pentecostal Holiness Church came into being in 1901—probably at Fayetteville, North Carolina. The adjective "Pentecostal" was dropped the next year, but from 1907 on many of the group's preachers and ministers received the baptism of the Holy Spirit in Pentecostal revivals. Although Crumpler rejected the charismatic experience and in 1908 withdrew from the body he had founded, the Holiness Church committed itself to the Pentecostal principle and in 1909 restored the adjective "Pentecostal" to its name.

The two bodies merged in 1911 at Falcon, North Carolina, as the Pentecostal Holiness Church.

In the meantime Nickels John Holmes, a Southern Presbyterian minister, found his Synod of South Carolina questioning the stress that he was placing on sanctification and divine healing. He withdrew and with a number of like-minded colleagues from Georgia and the Carolinas founded the Tabernacle Presbyterian Church as a Presbyterian Holiness denomination. In the course of time, Holmes, together with many of his followers, had a Pentecostal experience, and in 1915 his organization joined the Pentecostal Holiness Church. In 1920 a small group of ministers in the Georgia Conference withdrew and organized the Congregational Holiness Church the next year.

The twelve Articles of Faith in the denomination's *Discipline* constitute in general a synthesis of the Wesleyan doctrine of instantaneous sanctification as a second definite work of grace with the Pentecostal baptism with the Holy Spirit. The denomination disavows the doctrine of "absolute perfection" and teaches that sanctification is progressive as well as instantaneous. It regards divine healing for the body as the privilege of Christians in every age and as "the more excellent way," but it also acknowledges and appreciates the work of medical science in relieving human suffering. It offers parents the option of requesting either dedication or baptism for their children. Candidates for baptism need not be immersed, but may choose another of the modes of baptism that evangelical denominations use. It does not practice foot washing.[11]

The organization of the Pentecostal Holiness Church reveals strong Methodist influence. The chief officer of the denomination is a general superintendent, who holds the honorary title of bishop. The representative general conference, composed of both ministers and laity, meets every four years. The representative annual conferences assign pastorates and examine and approve candidates for the ministry. District conferences meet every three months.

The address of the headquarters of the Pentecostal Holiness Church is Box 12609, Oklahoma City, Oklahoma 73112. The inclusive membership of 135,410 is distributed over 2,340 churches; there are about 25 churches in Canada and 8 in Great Britain. It maintains missions in Africa, India, Hong Kong, the Republic of the Philippines, and Central and South America.

### Congregational Holiness Church

The action of the General Board of the Pentecostal Holiness Church in 1920—described by a later General Board as "irregular and illegal"—in dropping the Reverend Watson Sorrow and the Reverend Hugh Bowling from the ministerial roll before affording them a trial before their state board resulted in the withdrawal of a number of ministers and churches of the Georgia Conference from the Pentecostal Holiness Church. The issue was divine healing. Sorrow held that "since God had placed remedies here He intended that these remedies should be used if a person expected to be healed."[12] The two expellees, together with their supporters, organized the Congregational Holiness Church in January 1921. They inserted "Congregational" in the title to affirm their intention to ensure a democratic government for the new body. The separation took place quite peacefully and the relations between the two bodies have been good. In 1944 representatives of both church bodies agreed that there was no essential difference in doctrine and government between them and proposed reunion of the two churches. The proposal foundered on opposition among some of the members of the Congregational Holiness Church. In 1946 Sorrow and his church withdrew from the body that he had helped to found.

The Articles of Faith affirm the Trinity; the Bible as the inspired Word of God; justification when the individual repents of his or her sins and believes in Christ; baptism with the Holy Ghost and speaking with tongues as the initiatory evidence; divine healing, but without condemning medical science; the merits of atonement as the source of every blessing, including divine healing; Christ's imminent personal and premillennial second coming; the redemption of all saints who are faithful to the end, while rejecting the "once in grace always in grace" theory; eternal punishment for those who die out of Christ and glory forever for those who die in him; and the entire spiritual church as the bride of Christ. The church requires all its ministers to speak the same thing and to avoid division in doctrine concerning its Articles of Faith.[13]

It forbids its members to use tobacco, slang, alcoholic beverages, and other things that are contrary to holy living; to belong to oath-bound secret societies (although they may belong to labor unions that are not oath-bound); to wear shorts or bathing suits; to go to places of worldly entertainment such as theaters, ballrooms, circuses, swimming pools, and public ballgames; and to gamble. It enjoins simple and modest dress and the keeping of the first day of the week as the Holy Sabbath.[14]

It believes "war to be at variance with the principles of the Gospel and that God's children should not take up arms against their fellow-men."[15]

It accepts water baptism by immersion in the name of the Father and of the Son and of the Holy Ghost and invites all Christians to partake of the Lord's Supper and foot washing.[16]

The Congregational Holiness Church encourages women to exercise all their spiritual gifts but does not ordain them.

The church body comprises eight conferences in nine states: Alabama, Florida, Georgia, Illinois, Kentucky, North Carolina, South Carolina, Texas, and Virginia. It carries on foreign missions in Brazil, Costa Rica, Honduras, Guatemala, Mexico, and Spain. It has about 150 churches with a membership of more than 5,000. Headquarters are at Route 1, Box 325, Griffin, Georgia 30223.

### First Interdenominational Christian Association

In 1946 the Reverend Watson Sorrow withdrew from the Congregational Holiness Church that he had helped to found and launched the First Inter-denominational Christian Association. In 1947 it received a charter from the state of Georgia.

The bases of association are belief in the Trinity; the Bible as the inspired Word of God; eternal salvation for those who die in Christ and eternal loss for those who die out of him; spiritual rebirth, sanctification, and the baptism with the Holy Ghost, with speaking in other tongues as evidence; Christ's second coming; liberty of conscience in the mode of water baptism and in the matter of foot washing; divine healing; the full gospel and holy living; open Communion; the consolidation of all Christian bodies on firm Bible grounds; the support of God's work through tithes and offerings; "clean, honest Christian institutions, such as orphan homes, Bible schools, and so on"; evangelism; and the effort to achieve "the highest goal possible in Christ."[17]

The General Association has no authority over local associations, and the latter assume no obligations other than "Christian fellowship." While several other churches have set themselves up on the basis of the association's rule of faith, the association is practically limited to Calvary Temple Holiness Church, 1061 Memorial Drive, Southeast, Atlanta, Georgia 30316. This church has 100 members, but a larger number of worshipers.[18]

### Door of Faith Churches of Hawaii

The Reverend Mildred Johnson[19] (b. 1911) came to Hawaii in 1936 as a missionary of the Pentecostal Holiness Church. She had previously spent ten years as a Pentecostal minister and missionary in the southeastern United States. Her initial stay in Honolulu was brief. On her way to the island of Molokai she lost her purse, which contained all the money that she had. A native Hawaiian woman took her in. A service that she conducted in her benefactress's home initiated a revival that in three weeks spread across the island. With a $100 love-offering that her native Hawaiian listeners gave her she opened a store-front church in Honolulu. Her marriage made it necessary to establish her expanding work on an independent basis. In 1940 the Door of Faith Churches received a charter from the territorial government. It has since become an international denomination.

Although it is administratively altogether independent, the Hawaii-based body holds the same position in doctrine and practice as the Pentecostal Holiness Church. It stresses salvation, water baptism by immersion, sanctification, baptism in the Spirit, and in general a "signs following" ministry (Mark 16:20; Acts 2:4). It does not forbid military service to its members.

The headquarters are at 1161 Young Street, Honolulu 96814. There are 40 churches and missions in Hawaii with a total active membership estimated at between 3,000 and 4,000. In addition there are 10 churches in Indonesia, 40 in the Republic of the Philippines, and 2 on Okinawa. The Honolulu Bible School of the church body graduated 100 students in 1979.[20]

### The Church of God of the Mountain Assembly, Incorporated

In 1895 a number of preachers in the United Baptist Church of the South Union Association in Kentucky, among them the Reverend John H. Parks (1861–1943) and the Reverend Steve N. Bryant (1867–1939), began to preach that sanctified Christians could live without sin and that regenerated Christians could be lost. These views stirred up a lively controversy and in 1903 the association resolved to expel any minister who preached that regenerated Christians could be lost.

In 1907 the churches of these expellees and their followers organized the Church of God at Jellico Creek Church near the mouth of Ryans Creek in Whitley County, Kentucky. Moderate but consistent growth, as well as external opposition and persecution and internal controversy, especially about the use of tobacco, marked the early years of the new body. In 1911, to avoid confusion with other organizations calling themselves Church of God, the church body added "of the Mountain Assembly" to its name. It incorporated itself in 1917.

There were close relations with the Church of God (Cleveland, Tennessee), then headed by Ambrose Jessup Tomlinson, early in the history of the Church of God of the Mountain Assembly. Transient consideration was even given to the possibility of a merger of the two bodies, but the single meeting that was held led nowhere. But in 1923–1924 a considerable number of ministers of the Church of God of the Mountain Assembly withdrew and joined the Church of God (Cleveland, Tennessee). Another schism in 1946 saw the loss of about a quarter of the membership to the Churches of God of the Original Mountain Assembly. Negotiation looking toward possible union with the Pentecostal Church of Christ in 1950 failed.[21]

The Church of God of the Mountain Assembly accepts the New Testament as its creed and teachings; advises the use of the King James Version of the Bible by its members; and teaches regeneration, immersion of believers in the name of the Father and of the Son and of the Holy Ghost, sanctification following regeneration, the baptism of the Holy Ghost after sanctification with speaking in tongues as evidence, holiness, the fruit of the Spirit of Galatians 5:22-23, the spiritual gifts of the church of I Corinthians 12:8-10, the signs of Mark 16:17-18, divine healing, the Lord's Supper, washing the saints' feet, tithing and giving, restitution when possible, the millennium, the resurrection of the dead, and eternal life for the righteous. It commands total abstinence from strong drink; keeping the Sabbath day (that is, Sunday) holy; and modesty on the part of its women members. It prohibits wearing expressions of pride, such as gold ornaments (including rings, bracelets, and lockets); uncleanness, including the use of tobacco in any form; women members from cutting their hair; swearing; "going to war and killing"; and "infants being taken into the church" ("all children under twelve years of age are under question by the church").[22]

Ministers are either bishops (ordained ministers) or evangelists, the latter licensed annually; both have the authority to preach the gospel, baptize, administer the Lord's Supper and the washing of the saints' feet, and be pastor of a congregation. Women evangelists are licensed only to preach. Congregations elect their pastors every two years. The penalty for fornication by a minister of either sex is revocation of license or ordination and suspension from preaching and conducting revivals for ten years.[23]

The headquarters are at Florence Avenue, Jellico, Tennessee 37762, where the General Assembly meets every year. The highest officer is the general overseer. With the gradual emigration of elements of the mountain population into other communities, the Church of God of the Mountain Assembly has spread into 13 states across the country. There are 105 churches with a reported total membership of 4,000. The Church of God of the Mountain Assembly conducts foreign missions in Jamaica and Haiti and is building camp grounds in Hillsboro, Ohio, and a Bible school at Jellico, Tennessee.[24]

### Churches of God of the Original Mountain Assembly, Incorporated

In the 1939 meeting of the Church of God of the Mountain Assembly, the Reverend A. J. Long was elected to succeed the recently deceased founder, Steve N. Bryant, as moderator. In 1944 the church body made a number of changes in its government in the interest of better coordination and greater centralization, and the senior officer of the church body received the title of general overseer. Long, who had helped to draft the reorganization plan, was elected to the new office, and in 1945 he was reelected. When he failed of reelection in 1946, he led a group of opponents of the 1944 reorganization— fourteen other preachers, eight deacons, and approximately two hundred laypeople—out of the Church of God of the Mountain Assembly. He and his followers gathered at Williamsburg, Kentucky, reaffirmed their faith "in the principles embodied in the old platform of the Church of God set in order at Ryan's Creek, Kentucky, by Brothers S[teve] N. Bryant, J[ohn] E. Parks, and others in the year of 1907 A.D." The churches represented in the meeting called themselves the Churches of God of the Original Mountain Assembly, reasserted the form and principles of government in force in the parent body until 1944, reaffirmed the covenant originally adopted in 1917, and accepted the 1917 Articles of Faith as "some of our Articles of Faith."[25]

The body is trinitarian and baptizes by immersion in the name of the Father, the Son, and the Holy Ghost. The statement of the "teachings of the Church of God at the Original Mountain Assembly," as published in the annual minute book, are identical or substantially so with those of the parent group on regeneration; water baptism; sanctification; baptism of the Holy Ghost; holiness; fruit of the Spirit; spiritual gifts of the church; the Lord's Supper; washing the saints' feet; tithing and giving; total abstinence from strong drink; against women members cutting their hair; against uncleanliness (*sic*); against the use of tobacco; against infants being baptized into the church; signs following the believer(s); against ear-bobs, bracelets, and lockets; the resurrection of the dead; and eternal happiness for the righteous and eternal punishment for the wicked. The statements on divine healing, the wrongfulness of "Christians to take up war arms and go to war," the millennium, and the modesty required of sisters of the church appear in somewhat expanded form in the teachings of the Churches of God of the Original Mountain Assembly. New in the latter are the requirement that pastors and deacons shall work together in harmony, the quotation from I Timothy 2:12 ("I suffer not a woman to teach, nor to usurp authority over the man, but be in silence"), and the teaching "against the doctrine of snake-handling."[26]

The General Assembly meets annually at the headquarters tabernacle in Williamsburg, Kentucky. The office of general overseer later replaced that of moderator. A council of 12 elders is chosen from among the ordained ministers. Deacons are either ordained or appointed. There are 11 churches in Kentucky, Tennessee, and Ohio; no information is available on the total membership.

## Apostolic Faith Movement

One of the major early centers of the Pentecostal movement was at Topeka, Kansas. Its leader was Charles Fox Parham (1875–1929). After his teen-age conversion he became successively a Congregationalist, a Methodist, and a Holiness preacher. About the turn of the century, following a tour of the major evangelistic and healing centers in the eastern United States, he established a Bible school at Topeka for ministers and lay Christians "who were willing to forsake all, sell what they had, give it away, and enter the school for study and prayer, where all . . . together might trust God for food, fuel, rent, and clothing."[27] At the watch-night service on December 31, 1900, the students at the school began to receive the baptism of the Holy Spirit evidenced by speaking in foreign languages. Efforts to spread the revival during the next two years had little success, but beginning with a preaching campaign in Galena, Kansas, in 1903 Parham succeeded in establishing Apostolic Faith[28] assemblies in Kansas, in southwestern Missouri, and, in 1905, in Galveston and Houston, Texas. Out of the Houston campaign came William J. Seymour, the black evangelist who began the West Coast Pentecostal revival with his preaching at the Azusa Street Mission in Los Angeles.

In 1906 Parham began to issue ministerial credentials.[29] But he was also persuaded that "the spirit of organization" was fatal to the work of the Holy Spirit. For that reason Parham strenuously disavowed efforts to organize the Pentecostal movement above the local level. His ideal was a community chapel in each locality where church members could "express a larger faith in God than they could in their own creed-bound institutions" and where the unchurched" might find a place to work for God" and both groups could together "maintain a great revival spirit the year round." He stressed local sovereignty and wanted the control of each chapel's affairs vested in a board of elders who together with the regular attendants would invite the pastors and evangelists; the pastors and evangelists in turn would constitute an itinerant ministry.[30]

Parham's ideals found institutional expression in the loosely organized Apostolic Faith Movement, the leadership of which has concentrated its energies on the publication of a periodical, *The Apostolic Faith*, and the operation of the Apostolic Faith Bible School at 1009 Lincoln Avenue, Baxter Springs, Kansas 67713, which also serves as the movement's headquarters.

Its doctrinal teachings affirm the Trinity; repentance and subsequent consecration as acts of human beings and conversion or justification and subsequent sanctification as separate and definite acts of God; baptism of the Holy Ghost with the speaking of other tongues as initial evidence, but without fanaticism; divine healing; the ordinances of water baptism by immersion, the Lord's Supper, and foot washing; Christ's second coming and millennial reign; conditional immortality; the final destruction of the wicked; and the giving of tithes and offerings. The movement forbids divorce and subsequent remarriage.[31]

The lack of organization precludes an accurate estimate of the number of adherents. In 1951 a survey showed that there were 136 ministers and 83 churches throughout a 13-state region affiliated with the movement.[32] The fact that the circulation of *The Apostolic Faith* increased by slightly over 7 percent (from 2,800 to 3,000 families) between 1951 and 1967 may provide an index to the status of the movement as of the latter date.[33] Recent efforts to communicate with the organization have been unsuccessful.

## Full Gospel Evangelistic Association

In the late 1940s the Apostolic Faith Movement (see preceding section) of Baxter Springs, Kansas, began to condemn the taking of offerings in church, using the professional services of medical doctors, visiting churches not in fellowship with the movement, and going into foreign missionary work. Uncomfortable in this climate of opinion, several ministers formed the Ministerial and Missionary Alliance of the Original Trinity Apostolic Faith, Incorporated, only to be disfellowshiped, along with the congregations, by the Apostolic Faith Bible School.[34] The result was the formation in 1952 of the Full Gospel Evangelistic Association with about forty ministers of both sexes as charter members. The new organization established its headquarters first at Katy, Texas, and then, in 1967, at 106 North Pennsylvania Street, Webb City, Missouri 64870.

The declaration of faith commits the association to the verbal inspiration of the Bible; the Trinity; Christ's virgin birth, crucifixion, resurrection, ascension, and intercession; the sinfulness of all human beings and their need of repentance and forgiveness; justification, regeneration, and the new birth worked by faith in Christ's blood; holiness as the standard of living for God's people; the baptism of the Holy Ghost; speaking with other tongues as evidence of the baptism of the Holy Ghost; water baptism of repentant believers by immersion in the name of the Father and the Son and the Holy Ghost; divine healing provided for all in the atonement; the Lord's Supper and washing of the saints' feet; Christ's premillennial second coming to resurrect the righteous dead, to catch away the living saints, and to reign on the earth a thousand years; and the bodily resurrection of the righteous to eternal life and of the wicked to eternal separation from God.[35]

There are 30 churches and missions in 7 states, with a total estimated membership of more than 4,000. The association carries on foreign missions in Mexico, Nicaragua, and in the Republic of China (Taiwan). With other independent churches it operates the Kingsway Language School in Pharr, Texas.[36]

## The Apostolic Faith [Mission]

In 1906 Mrs. Florence Louise Reed Crawford (1872–1936) received the baptism of the Holy Spirit at the Azusa Street Mission in Los Angeles and recovered from a series of long-term illnesses and injuries. She immediately began to conduct a series of revival campaigns in Salem, Oregon, Seattle, the Twin Cities, and Winnipeg. While she was in Minneapolis she felt that God was moving her to establish her headquarters in Portland, Oregon. Here she organized The Apostolic Faith in 1907.

A noteworthy feature of her movement's evangelistic work has been its willingness to experiment with a variety of means for proclaiming its message, including cross-country buses, motorboats to establish contact with seamen in local ports, its own seagoing vesel, and airplanes. It has always emphasized the printed word and its presses currently produce materials in over seventy languages and dialects.

It is explicitly trinitarian and fundamentalist, affirms the inspiration of the Bible, insists on repentance toward God and restitution, and teaches the importance of living a daily life of Christian holiness based on three definite and separate spiritual experiences—justification and regeneration following faith in God, entire sanctification which eradicates the sin principle of the inbred sinful nature and makes a person holy, and the baptism of the Holy Ghost with speaking with tongues as the accompanying evidence. It sees the atonement as providing the healing of sickness and disease for God's people. Its doctrine of the last things emphasizes Christ's literal, visible, and imminent second coming, with two appearances; the first appearance is for the rapture, followed by the tribulation, and the second appearance is to exercise judgment on the ungodly, followed by the millennium, the Great White Throne judgment, the new heaven and the new earth, and eternal heaven and eternal hell. The Apostolic Faith regards marriage as binding for life and allows no remarriage after divorce. As ordinances it observes water baptism by a single immersion in the name of the Father and of the Son and of the Holy Ghost, the Lord's Supper, and washing of the disciples' feet.[37]

Its members are to avoid all worldly amusements and sinful pleasures, such as dancing, card playing, theatergoing, smoking, and drinking, and are not to marry unbelievers. The women are to dress modestly and avoid extreme fads, facial makeup, and bobbed hair. Men are to dress conservatively and neatly.

The churches do not solicit funds and do not take offerings in their services; the faithful are expected to place tithes and free-will offerings in an offering box near the entrance.

In addition to Sunday services, the churches hold regular week-night evangelistic meetings and send out groups of workers to the streets, to retirement homes, to hospitals, and to penal institutions.

The worship of The Apostolic Faith avoids ceremonialism and formalism, including vestments for the ministers and prayerbooks. Its services are mainly evangelistic. The sermon is "preached directly from the Bible under the anointing of the Holy Spirit." After the regular services, the ministers anoint the sick and the afflicted and pray for them.

The governing body of the organization is a board of five trustees, with the general overseer as chairman. The Portland headquarters direct the activities of the local congregations.

In 1909 Jackson White became leader of the Minneapolis branch of The Apostolic Faith. About 1915 he withdrew from the parent body to organize a rival Apostolic Faith Mission, taking with him a considerable number of followers. After his death, his widow, Mrs. Martha White, and Miss Minnie Hanson continued to lead the movement. It did not long survive them.

In 1919 some of the leaders of the Eugene (Oregon) branch withdrew from The Apostolic Faith, because of Mrs. Crawford's requirement that remarried divorcees separate, and organized the Bible Standard, Incorporated, now merged into the Open Bible Standard Churches.

In parts of the Midwest and the South, many "oneness" assemblies have adopted the designation "Apostolic Faith." To prevent confusion with these assemblies, local churches of The Apostolic Faith have frequently put the adjective "Trinitarian" in parentheses after their name.

There are 45 churches in the United States, including Puerto Rico and the United States Virgin Islands, with an inclusive membership of 4,100, and 2 churches in Canada, with a total membership of 120. The Apostolic Faith also maintains foreign missions in 39 countries of Latin America, the Antilles, Europe, Africa, Lebanon, Jordan, Korea, and Japan.

## The Church of God in Christ

Charles Harrison Mason began his career as a minister of the Missionary Baptist Church in Tennessee. In the last decade of the nineteenth century he and some of his fellow ministers came so profoundly under the influence of the Holiness movement that their fellow Baptists expelled them. In 1895 Mason and Elder C. P. Jones founded a church in Memphis. While he was walking along a street in Little Rock, Arkansas, in 1897, Mason reported, the Lord revealed to him the name that his church should take in order to differentiate between true and false followers of Christ—the Church of God in Christ. As the biblical basis for the name, God pointed him to I Thessalonians 2:14; II Thessalonians 1:1; and Galatians 1:22.

In 1906 Mason and two supporters spent five weeks in Los Angeles at the Azusa Street Mission and received the baptism of the Spirit with the gift of speaking in tongues. In the meantime, Glen A. Cook, himself recently returned from Los Angeles, was preaching Pentecostal doctrine to the Memphis congregation. Upon Mason's return to Memphis, his insistence on the need for the baptism of the Holy Spirit and speaking in tongues led at the General Assembly of 1907 to the withdrawal of the non-Pentecostal faction headed by Jones. Mason called another meeting of like-minded clergy for later in the same year. It organized under the old name and elected Mason as general overseer of the fourteen or so churches that had grown up in Tennessee, Arkansas, Mississippi, and Oklahoma, with the title of chief apostle (bishop). In the course of time it has become the largest black Pentecostal denomination in the world.

In 1915 sixteen Baptists in Enid, Oklahoma, most of them in the family of the Reverend J. H. Morris, received the baptism of the Holy Spirit; under the leadership of E. J. Morris they formed an organization which they called the Church of God in Christ. In 1921 they joined Mason's church, but in 1925 the Enid group again withdrew as a result of dissensions arising over a state charter and called itself the Free Church of God in Christ. It differed from Mason's church only in its greater stress on divine healing. In the late 1940s it had about 40 churches and 900 members; subsequently it seems to have died out completely.[38]

In 1933 the increasing complexity of administering the growing church body required the delegation of authority to five regional bishops as assistants to the chief bishop. Out of this grew an episcopal system, with a bishop over each state and with superintendents presiding over the districts within a state.

The denomination's doctrinal position is almost identical with that of the Church of God (Cleveland, Tennessee) or the Pentecostal Holiness Church.

The Church of God in Christ is explicitly trinitarian. It holds that man is by nature sinful and must be born again; that the Holy Scriptures contain all that is necessary to salvation and are a complete and infallible standard in matters of religion and morals; that the universe has a personal Creator; that science must accommodate itself to revelation; and that the church is both visible and invisible and is composed of baptized members who are saved by grace through faith, sanctified through the truth, and redeemed through Christ's blood.

Essential to the church's organization are the three ordinances: (1) water baptism administered in the name of the Father and of the Son and of the Holy Ghost as a symbol of regeneration and a public profession of faith and discipleship; (2) the Lord's Supper as a sacramental rite commemorating Christ's death and suffering; and (3) foot washing as an indication of humility.

Repentance makes sinners see and be sensible of their sins; regeneration is the work of the Spirit that changes and renovates the soul by the spirit and graces of God. Justification is the state in which sinners are made judicially acceptable to God when they accept in faith the substitution of the just for the unjust. Sanctification is separation from worldliness and dedication to divinely sacred purposes. While it is possible to have the Spirit and not speak in tongues, speaking with other tongues is an accompaniment of a full and Pentecostal baptism of the Holy Ghost. Divine healing—the process of being cured of sickness and disease by faith in God's power—is part of the church's faith and practice. Perfection is a quality in believers that will find the highest degree of accomplishment in the world to come.

The denomination also believes in the second coming of Christ, the rapture of his bride, the church, to meet him in the air, and his reign on earth in millennial power and glory.

The government of the church must be in harmony with II Timothy 3:16; Ephesians 4:11-12; and I Corinthians 12:28. The legal and governmental authorities must support a marriage if it is to be lawful; divine law requires marriage in the Lord and forbids being equally yoked together with unbelievers. Fornication is the only ground for divorce. Common-law marriage and remarriage without a divorce are unlawful marriages and the church does not support or endorse them.[39]

The Christian Sabbath is the first day of the week.

State and district conferences and the national convocation meet annually. In addition to 83 bishoprics in the United States, there are 3 in Canada, 1 in

England, and 1 in British Honduras. The Church of God in Christ claims 4,100 churches with 420,500 members. Headquarters are at 938 Mason Street, Memphis, Tennessee 38126. The denomination carries on foreign missions in Africa, Thailand, Jamaica, and Haiti. Church officials have not responded to recent efforts to communicate with them.

### The Church of God in Christ, International

Fourteen bishops of the Church of God in Christ withdrew from that church body in 1969 to establish The Church of God in Christ, International. Disagreement over polity and governmental authority led to the separation. Like its predecessor organization, the church body is Wesleyan in theology, emphasizing sanctification as a second work of grace, and Pentecostal in teaching, stressing baptism with the Holy Spirit evidenced by speaking with tongues. The General Assembly is the governing authority and meets annually. Headquarters are at 1905 Columbia Avenue, Philadelphia, Pennsylvania 19121.[40]

### The Fire Baptized Holiness Church of God in the Americas

The Fire Baptized Holiness Church of God in the Americas traces its history back to the organization of the Fire Baptized Holiness Association of America at Anderson, South Carolina, in 1898. With the increase of antiblack prejudice during the next decade, the black membership and the white membership of the association agreed to an amicable separation at another general council held in Anderson in 1908. The white group ultimately became part of the Pentecostal Holiness Church, while the black membership, 925 strong, led by W. E. Fuller, Sr. (1875–1958), organized the Colored Fire-Baptized Holiness Church. In 1922 it designated its general overseer a bishop and adopted the name Fire Baptized Holiness Church of God. It adopted its present name in 1926.[41]

The basis of union affirms the organization's belief that Christ shed his blood for the remission of past sins, for the regeneration of penitent sinners, and for their salvation from sin and from sinning; that justification is by faith alone through Christ's blood; that Christ's blood cleanses the justified believer from all indwelling sin and from its pollution; that sanctification is an instantaneous second work of grace which the justified believer can obtain by faith; that the sanctified believer can obtain the baptism of the Holy Ghost and fire, of which speaking with other tongues is the initial evidence, by an act of appropriating faith; that the atonement includes divine healing; and that Christ's second coming is imminent, personal, and premilliennial.[42]

The General Council is the governing authority and meets every four years. The clergy is composed of bishops and elders. There are no headquarters, but the church body's Fuller Press is at 130 Jackson Street, Northeast, Atlanta, Georgia 30312. There are about 500 churches with an inclusive membership over 6,000.

## Assemblies of God

The General Council of the Assemblies of God came into being in response to an increasingly felt need for something more than regional associations of Pentecostal Christians. The initial leadership came for the most part out of two groups of Pentecostals, one in southwestern United States, the other in the Southeast. The southwestern group, which included Eudorus N. Bell, a former Southern Baptist minister and an alumnus of the University of Chicago, Howard A. Goss, W. F. Carothers, Arch P. Collins, and Daniel C. O. Opperman, dated back to 1906. Organized under Charles Fox Parham's leadership with the name Apostolic Faith, they had withdrawn from Parkham in 1909. The southeastern group had organized itself in 1911 as the Church of God in a meeting at Dothan, Alabama, which H. G. Rodgers had called. The same year this group secured the permission of Elder Charles H. Mason to use the name "Church of God in Christ."

During 1912 and 1913 the two groups, with a combined membership of over three hundred ministers, united. The fact that some of the members had come from Baptist backgrounds, while others had a Holiness tradition behind them, made for a measure of doctrinal confusion, notably on such issues as sanctification. Sensing the inadequacy of their very loose organization, the leader of the united association issued an invitation before the year was out in which they called upon all "Pentecostal Saints and Churches of God in Christ" to meet at Hot Springs, Arkansas, the next year in a "general council." This conference was to try to achieve better understanding and a direly needed unity of teaching, to consider how to conserve the movement's work at home and abroad, to consult on the protection of funds for missionary endeavors, to look into the chartering of churches under a legal name, and to explore the establishment of a Bible training school.

The invitation stirred up militant opposition by other Pentecostals, who attacked the proposed organization as un-Pentecostal and unbiblical. In spite of it the "general council" met in 1914, with 120 delegates from twenty states and several foreign countries. The participants recognized themselves as members of the "General Assembly of God (which is God's organism)." For individual congregations they recommended the name Assembly of God; for the individual assemblies taken together they urged the designation Assemblies of God. They solved the problem of organization by affirming the sovereignty of each local affiliated church and by defining the relationship of the local assembly with the council as one of equality, unity, and cooperation. The problem of doctrinal definition defied immediate solution. The convention contented itself with declaring that since God had given "the holy inspired

Scriptures . . . as the sufficient rule for faith and practice, we therefore shall not add or take from it."[43]

The "oneness" controversy was already in the making. When the new body adopted its Statement of Fundamental Truths in 1916, their explicit trinitarian character triggered the defection of 156 ministers, including some of the leaders, and the creation of a rival "oneness" body, the Pentecostal Assemblies of the World.

Under the leadership of J. Roswell Flower, John W. Welch, and others, the Assemblies of God survived the schism. When the denomination moved its headquarters to Springfield, Missouri, in 1918, it listed over five hundred ministers and ninety-one missionaries in affiliation with it.[44]

In 1919 the Western Canada District Council of the Assemblies of God came into being, and in 1921 the Pentecostal Assemblies of Canada became the Eastern District Council of the Assemblies of God. But the arrangement proved undesirable from the start, and shortly thereafter both district councils withdrew and united as the Pentecostal Assemblies of Canada.

The Spanish Eastern District of the Assemblies of God covers Puerto Rico and the Spanish-speaking churches of most of the United States east of the Mississippi.[45]

The sixteen-article Statement of Fundamental Truths affirms the Bible as the inspired Word of God and "the infallible rule of faith and conduct"; the revelation of the one true God "as embodying the principles of relationship and association, i.e., as Father, Son, and Holy Ghost," explained in such a way as to preclude the "oneness" position; Christ's deity; humanity's fall and redemption in Christ; the appearance of the salvation-bringing grace of God to all persons and their salvation by the washing of rebirth and justification by grace through faith; the direct witness of the Spirit to the believer as inward evidence of salvation and a holy life as its outward evidence; believer's baptism by immersion as an outward symbol of cleansing; the Lord's Supper as the symbol of human beings' sharing in Christ's divine nature, as a memorial of his suffering and death, and as a prophecy of his second coming; the baptism in the Holy Ghost and fire as an experience distinct from and subsequent to the new birth, with speaking in other tongues as the initial physical sign; entire sanctification; the church as the body of Christ, of which each Spirit-born believer is an integral part; a divinely called and biblically ordained ministry for the evangelization of the world and the edifying of Christ's body; divine healing provided for in the atonement; the resurrection of the departed believers and their translation along with those who are alive at Christ's coming; Christ's millennial reign; everlasting punishment for the devils and those not found in the Book of Life; and the new heavens and the new earth.[46]

With its impressive growth over the years, the organization of the Assemblies of God has become more complex. The General Council, which meets every two years, is the highest legislative and policy-making body. It elects sixteen executive presbyters, one of whom is the general superintendent, to execute the council's mandates between sessions. Each district has its own annual district convention and its own district council or presbytery.

The largest Pentecostal body in the United States, the General Council of the Assemblies of God has 9,140 local congregations with 1,299,468 members. In addition to its ambitious publishing program and its domestic missionary efforts among foreign language groups, North American Indians, the Jews of New York and Chicago, prisoners, the deaf, and the blind, the denomination has more than 800 missionaries serving in 71 foreign countries. The headquarters are at 1445 Boonville Avenue, Springfield, Missouri 65802.

### The Pentecostal Church of God of Puerto Rico
### (Iglesia de Dios Pentecostal de Puerto Rico)

Pentecostal missionaries on their way from California to the Orient in 1912 stopped long enough on the island of Oahu in Hawaii to convert a number of Puerto Rican immigrants at the Government Experimental Station near Honolulu to form a congregation with Francisco D. Ortiz, Sr., as pastor. A member of this congregation, Juan L. Lugo, returned to California in search of new employment. Here he felt himself called to return to Puerto Rico as a missionary in 1916. On the way from California he passed through St. Louis and met the secretary of the newly organized General Council of the Assemblies of God. Lugo and two fellow members of the Oahu congregation, Salomón Feliciano Quiñones and his wife, Dionisia, arrived in Ponce, Puerto Rico, within a day of each other. Out of their first street-corner service came the beginning of a church in Ponce. Lugo and Feliciano extended their work to a number of communities in the south and southwestern parts of Puerto Rico. By 1920, when Feliciano left for the continental United States, they had started eight congregations, and a number of additional returnees from Hawaii and California, notably Francisco D. Ortiz, Sr. and Jr., had swelled the ranks of the missionaries. In 1921 the congregations, grown to thirteen in number, held a convention in Arecibo and organized the Pentecostal Church of God (Iglesia de Dios Pentecostal); they incorporated themselves under that name in February 1922.

For the next twenty-five years the Puerto Rican movement considered itself an organic part of the Assemblies of God. Finally, in 1947 the Assemblies of God refused to make the Puerto Rican church a domestic district and ruled that because of the distance involved and the difference in language, the Puerto Rican organization was national and sovereign and its tie with the Springfield headquarters merely spiritual. As more members of the Puerto Rican church emigrated to the continental United States, difficulties arose; some joined the Assemblies of God, but others remained tenaciously loyal to the Puerto Rican church. In 1954 the two bodies resolved the problem on a stop-gap basis; the Puerto Rican church agreed not to open missions in the continental United States and to transfer those ministers that had already emigrated or that would emigrate to the Spanish Eastern District of the Assemblies of God (with the exception of the pastor of one church in New York City); the Spanish Eastern District in turn agreed that ministers migrating between Puerto Rico and the continental United States could retain their credentials with the body that had originally recognized their ordination, and that Puerto Ricans in the continental United States would be allowed to retain their insular membership for six months. These arrangements did not prove successful, and in 1955 the Assemblies of God proposed the close union that it had refused eight years earlier. This time the Puerto Rican church rejected the proposal and in September 1956 it formally declared itself sovereign although reaffirming its desire for "friendship and fellowship with the General Council of the Assemblies of God."

In 1957 it formed an autonomous district of some thirty churches in New York and adjoining states, the Latin American Council of the Pentecostal Church of God of Puerto Rico; actually the council is independent in every way with the exception of its mission work, which the Puerto Rican church continues to coordinate. Shortly after the establishment of the New York District, the Puerto Rican church organized five churches in the Chicago area into a presbytery under the direct supervision of the Puerto Rican headquarters, but in cooperation with the New York District. By 1964 this presbytery had expanded into other midwestern states and into the Mexican state of Tamaulipas; in that year the Puerto Rican headquarters reorganized it as the Midwest America District, with congregations in Ohio, Illinois, Michigan, Florida, Texas, Indiana, and Wisconsin. The work of the Puerto Rican church in the United States Virgin Islands began in the 1940s. Missionary work began in Haiti in 1948 and in that same year the Puerto Rican church absorbed the Assemblies of God missionaries in Cuba. Since achieving full sovereignty in 1956, the Puerto Rican church has begun missions in seven other Latin American countries, as well as in Spain and Portugal.[47]

A seventeen-section Statement of Fundamental Doctrines reflects the history of the Pentecostal Church of God of Puerto Rico. It is a faithful translation of the Statement of Fundamental Truths of the Assemblies of God into Spanish, with two exceptions. The Puerto Rican church has expanded Article II on "the one true God" in such a way as explicitly to reject the "oneness" view. It has also intercalated after the eleventh article an additional article on the support of the ministry by means of tithes and offerings. It declares that tithing is the plan that God designed from the beginning for the support of the ministry and directs that tithes are to be used exclusively for that purpose and for the propagation of the gospel.[48]

The headquarters of the Pentecostal Church of God of Puerto Rico are at Barrio Caimito, Río Piedras. The church has 220 congregations and nearly 600 preaching stations on Puerto Rico, with over 20,000 adult members. In the United States Virgin Islands it has 3 churches and 245 adult members.

Apart from the autonomous Latin-American Council of the Pentecostal Church of God of Puerto Rico in New York and adjacent states, it has 94 churches with 5,000 adult members in the continental United States.[49] Church officials have not responded to recent efforts to communicate with the organization.

### The Pentecostal Assemblies of Canada

The year 1919 was important for the Pentecostal Assemblies of Canada for two reasons. In Montreal the Pentecostal Assemblies of Canada received their Dominion charter. In Moose Jaw, Saskatchewan, Pentecostal Christians from the four western provinces decided to unite as the Western Canada District Council of the United-States-based Assemblies of God. Two years later the eastern group followed the example of their coreligionists in Canada West and became the Eastern Canadian District Council of the Assemblies of God. But it was not long before everyone realized that the Canadian Pentecostals could not function effectively as part of a denomination with headquarters in the United States. Differences in national temperament and differences in situation of which the American leadership could not always take account in the formulation of policy played in the decision to effect an amicable separation.

Thus the Pentecostal Assemblies of Canada have continued to function as the Canadian counterpart of the Assemblies of God, but with significant differences. One factor was the influence that James Eustace Purdle, a former Anglican clergyman, who headed the Canadian denomination's first theological college during the entire second quarter of the twentieth century, exerted upon the students.[50] Another factor was a reluctance on the part of the Canadians to overstress differences of teaching and practice and their willingness to allow a considerable degree of doctrinal latitude. A third was the relatively larger number of foreign-language Pentecostal congregations in Canada, chiefly in French, Slavic, German, and Finnish communities; about one out of ten local assemblies is non-English-speaking.

The Statement of Fundamental and Essential Truths approved by the Pentecostal Assemblies of Canada appeals to the Bible as the all-sufficient rule of faith and practice. It discusses the inspiration, infallibility, and adequacy of the Bible; the Holy Trinity carefully described so as to preclude the "oneness" view; the resurrection; humanity's fall and redemption; sin; Christ's substitutionary atonement; the new birth; repentance ("a change of mind toward God") and faith ("simple reliance or dependence on Christ"); justification ("a judicial act of God whereby the sinner is declared righteous"); the believer's obedience to God as the antithesis of "the dangerous doctrine called Antinomianism"; entire sanctification experienced as both instantaneous and progressive; the baptism of the Holy Spirit with speaking in other tongues as the initial physical sign ("our Distinctive Testimony"); the Lord's Supper as symbol, memorial, and prophecy; water baptism by single immersion "signifying the believer's identification with Christ"; the church as a living organism; a divinely called and biblically ordained ministry for the evangelization of the world and the edification of the church; divine healing provided for in the atonement; the imminent and premillennial coming of Christ; everlasting punishment for the wicked in the lake of fire; and the new heavens and the new earth. The Pentecostal Assemblies of Canada disapprove of divorce among Christians except for fornication; recommend that divorced persons do not remarry; prohibit ordination of divorced persons with living former spouses; and counsel ministers not to officiate at marriages of divorced persons with surviving former spouses. The Pentecostal Assemblies also hold that "all Christians should conscientiously and systematically tithe their income to God."[51]

The Pentecostal Assemblies of Canada report 850 churches with an inclusive membership of 170,000. The headquarters are at 10 Overlea Boulevard, Toronto, Ontario M4H 1A5. More than 220 missionaries are engaged in work in 15 foreign fields. The church body is associated with the Pentecostal Assemblies of Newfoundland, though the latter is a separate and autonomous organization.[52]

## The Pentecostal Assemblies of Newfoundland

The first Pentecostal Assembly in Newfoundland opened on Easter Sunday, 1911. The number of assemblies had grown sufficiently by 1925 to secure governmental recognition as a registered movement. In 1932 the association expanded its field of labors to Labrador by means of a coastal vessel, *The Gospel Messenger*. There are currently 147 assemblies with 30,000 members.[53] Although organizationally separate from the Pentecostal Assemblies of Canada, the Pentecostal Assemblies of Newfoundland stand committed to the same Statement of Fundamental and Essential Truths. Headquarters are at 57 Thorburn, St. John's, Newfoundland A1B 3M2.

## The Italian Pentecostal Church of Canada

In 1913 a few members of an Italian Presbyterian church in Hamilton, Ontario, banded together for prayer and received a Pentecostal experience of baptism in the Holy Spirit. Out of this event grew the Italian Pentecostal Church of Canada. From Hamilton the work spread to Toronto and ultimately to Montreal. Early leaders were Luigi Ippolito and Ferdinand Zaffuto. The Montreal church received a government charter in 1926; it was extended to the denomination in 1958. Although autonomous, the Italian Pentecostal Church of Canada maintains close ties with and shares the doctrinal position of the Pentecostal Assemblies of Canada. There are 16 churches in Ontario and Quebec with 2,640 members. The headquarters of the denomination are

at 6724 Fabre Street, Montreal, Quebec H2G 2Z6. It carries on its North
American work in both Italian and English; it also carries on an active missionary program in Italy.[54]

## Calvary Pentecostal Church, Incorporated

The founders of what became the Calvary Pentecostal Church, Incorporated, were originally ministers of the Assemblies of God. They left the parent
organization in the 1920s because of what they regarded as unwarranted in-
terference by the denominational authorities in the affairs of local congregations and organized a ministerial fellowship of their own. In 1932 they and
their congregations incorporated the Calvary Pentecostal Church at Olympia,
Washington. In the course of time the church established flourishing missions
in India, Brazil, and the Republic of the Philippines. A contest of wills between the Executive Board of the church body and some of the ministers of
the church, beginning in the mid-1950s, led to the withdrawal of twenty-one
of the twenty-five local churches and to the loss of all of the foreign missions
except those in the Philippines.

The church body's statement of fundamentals makes the principle that
"the Bible contains all that is ever necessary as a rule for our faith and
practice" the basis of fellowship. It affirms the inspiration of the Bible;
the one God; the eternal preexistence and deity of Christ; the personality of the
Holy Spirit; the Trinity; the fall of humanity and the atonement through the
blood of God's Son as the only hope for the redemption of human beings;
repentance, confession, faith, cleansing by Christ's blood, regeneration, and
renewing of the Holy Spirit as conditions of salvation; the church as the
body of Christ; believer's baptism; the Lord's Supper;[55] the baptism of the
Spirit as distinct from and subsequent to the new birth; speaking with other
tongues as evidence of the baptism with the Holy Ghost; the necessity of a life
of holiness; divine healing provided for in the atonement; Christ's second
coming; the millennium; the everlasting lake of fire; and the new heavens
and the new earth.[56]

Calvary Pentecostal Church disapproves of divorce except for unchastity
and of the marriage of Christians with unsaved persons.[57] It affirms that its
members "cannot conscientiously participate in war and armed resistance
which involves the actual taking of human life."[58]

Theologically Calvary Pentecostal Church takes a strongly conservative
and antiecumenical position. It is concerned about retaining the traditional
Pentecostal emotionalism, but it seeks to train it so that it does not run
rampant.

The headquarters of Calvary Pentecostal Church, Incorporated, were at
1856 Bigelow Avenue, Olympia, Washington 98506. The chief officer is the
general superintendent. There are 4 churches in the United States, with a total
membership estimated at just under 1,500. The church body continues to

carry on its foreign missionary work in the Philippines. Recent efforts to contact the organization have been unsuccessful.

## Iglesia Pentecostal de Jesucristo, Incorporada, en Puerto Rico
## (Pentecostal Church of Jesus Christ, Incorporated, in Puerto Rico)

Under the leadership of its pastor, Felix Rivera Cardona, a congregation of the Pentecostal Church of God in Barrio Balboa, Mayaguez, Puerto Rico, withdrew in 1938 from the parent body over a disciplinary issue and took the name Iglesia Pentecostal Jesucristo, Incorporada, en Puerto Rico (Pentecostal Church of Jesus Christ, Incorporated, in Puerto Rico). A second congregation came into being at Sabana Grande the following year. The work gradually expanded into the southern and eastern sections of the commonwealth.

The organization's doctrinal stress is on repentance toward God, baptism with the Holy Spirit, divine healing, and the second coming of Christ. It practices water baptism by immersion and the Lord's Supper in unleavened bread and the fruit of the vine. Above the level of missionary it has a ministry of three classes: exhorter, preacher, and ordained minister.

In the course of time it followed some of its people to the continental United States. In addition to 35 congregations and 50 preaching-places in Puerto Rico, with an active membership of over 3,000, it has congregations in New York, Chicago, Milwaukee, Gary, and elsewhere. In New York it maintains the International Bible Institute. It also has congregations in Haiti. The headquarters of the organization are at Yauco, Puerto Rico.[59]

## Latin-American Council of the Pentecostal Church of God
## of New York, Incorporated (Concilio Latino-Americano de la Iglesia
## de Dios Pentecostal de New York, Incorporado)

The Latin-American Council of the Pentecostal Church of God of New York, Incorporated, began its work in 1951 as an offshoot of the Concilio de la Iglesia de Dios Pentecostal of Puerto Rico. In 1956 it became an autonomous agency, although it maintains "affiliation" with the Concilio of Puerto Rico and contributes to the support of the parent body. A three-year school of theology (unaccredited), with an enrollment of about five hundred, trains the council's missionaries, preachers, and ministers.

The council affirms its purpose to represent as far as it is possible to do so the body of Christ as the New Testament describes it, with particular stress on the principles of unity, cooperation, and equality. It commits itself to the Bible as the all-sufficient rule of faith and practice. The seventeen-article statement of the fundamental doctrines that the council regards as essential to a complete ministry is identical with that of the Puerto Rican mother church.[60]

The council is neutral in the matter of participation in war and in the armed forces and leaves the matter to the conscience of its members according to the light and the inferences of the New Testament.[61] It takes a strong position against divorce, counsels its members not to engage in political activity beyond exercising the right to vote, and requires them to abstain from membership in secret societies.[62]

The council has about 75 churches in Greater New York with a membership estimated at 8,000. Its headquarters are at 115 East 125th Street, New York, New York 10035. It carries on foreign missionary work in Central America, the Netherlands Antilles, and elsewhere.[63] Recent efforts to contact the group have been unsuccessful.

## The Church of God of the Apostolic Faith, Incorporated

James Obediah McKinzie (1872–1919), Edwin Alvie Buckles (1877–1938), Oscar Harrison Myers (1889–1956), and Joseph Plummer Rhoades (1884–1959) were all Pentecostal ministers who received the baptism of the Holy Spirit as a result of the revival that had begun in Topeka, Kansas, in 1901. With the passage of time it became clear to them that some kind of church government was necessary for their movement to survive. For that reason they met in 1914 at the Cross Roads Mission, near Ozark, Arkansas, under McKinzie's chairmanship, and organized the general conference of the Church of God of the Apostolic Faith.

While the church is in this way linked historically with the Apostolic Faith Movement of Topeka, it stands very close theologically to the Apostolic Faith Mission of Portland, Oregon. The doctrinal section of the Articles of Faith that serve as the basis of fellowship in the Church of God of the Apostolic Faith reveals many borrowings from the "Bible doctrines" of the Portland body, even though the sequence of some paragraphs is slightly different.

The Church of God of the Apostolic Faith teaches "the personality of the three-fold Godhead." It affirms the identity of its gospel with that proclaimed to the early church by Paul and the other apostles. It declares that the content of its preaching is Christ's birth, baptism, works, teachings, crucifixion, death, burial, resurrection, ascension, and "soon coming."

Specifically, the Church of God of the Apostolic Faith teaches repentance toward God; justification through repentance and faith in Christ and his atonement; sanctification as a second, definite work that the Holy Spirit brings about in the heart with the blood of Jesus; the baptism of the Holy Ghost as a gift of power on a sanctified life, with speaking in other tongues as evidence of the experience; healing for the body purchased in the atonement; the revealing of the Antichrist and the great tribulation as preludes to the second coming of Jesus; water baptism of believers by a single immersion in the name of the Father, Son, and Holy Ghost; the necessity of restitution; tithing as an ordinance of God; the sacrament of the Lord's Supper, followed by the washing of one another's feet; marriage for life with no divorce and remarriage while the first spouse is alive; an eternal heaven and an eternal hell; the church as the body of the Christ and each believer's need for some visible church affiliation; conscientious objection to taking up arms against fellow human beings (although noncombatant service in the armed forces is permitted); the millennium; and thereafter the "great white throne judgment."[64]

The rules of Christian conduct call for conformity to the precepts of the Bible. They prohibit traffic in and the use of intoxicants and habit-forming drugs (including tobacco). They require modesty in apparel and neatness in appearance.[65]

The General Conference meets annually. The governing body of the church is a seven-minister General Presbytery, of which the general superintendent and his two assistants are members. The pastor is the highest authority in the local church. Property is deeded to the church body for the benefit of the respective local churches.[66]

The headquarters of the Church of God of the Apostolic Faith are at 2530 West Cameron, Tulsa, Oklahoma 74127. There are 27 churches in Oklahoma, Arkansas, Missouri, Kansas, New Mexico, and California, with a total active membership in excess of 1,400. Its mission in Mexico is called Iglesia Cristiana Evangelica Mexicana.[67]

## The International Pentecostal Church of Christ

On August 10, 1976, two Pentecostal groups, the International Pentecostal Assemblies and the Pentecostal Church of Christ, completed ten years of association in a consolidation of the two groups under the name the International Pentecostal Church of Christ.

The International Pentecostal Assemblies had been formed in 1936 through the union of the National and International Pentecostal Missionary Union (organized in 1914 by Philip Wittich) and of the Association of Pentecostal Assemblies (organized in 1921 by Mrs. Elizabeth A. Sexton, her daughter Dr. Hattie M. Barth [1876–1956], and Paul T. Barth [1872–1942]). The new group was to be "a cooperative fellowship, dedicated to the task of carrying the full gospel to the ends of the earth."[68]

The Basis of Fellowship of the International Pentecostal Assemblies affirmed belief in the verbal inspiration of the Bible, "inerrable in the original writings"; the Trinity; justification by faith through the atonement; sanctification as a work of grace subsequent to justification; baptism in the Holy Spirit, accompanied with speaking in other tongues; the spiritual gifts of I Corinthians 12; healing in the atonement; Christ's premillennial return; the resurrection of the just before the millennium and of the unjust after it; heaven and hell; a personal devil; Sunday as the Lord's rest day under the new covenant; the Lord's Supper and water baptism by immersion "in the name of the

Father and of the Son and of the Holy Ghost"; the optional observance of foot washing; and "war to be at variance with the principles of the Gospel."[69]

The Pentecostal Church of Christ was formed on May 10, 1917, by ministers who had been part of a movement led by John Stroup, an evangelist in South Solon, Ohio, who had experienced the Holy Spirit baptism and had begun to preach his faith and experience in the area where Ohio, Kentucky, and West Virginia meet. Initially only an organization of ministers, it responded to the need for an organization of the churches which they served. Stroup was chosen as the first bishop.

The faith of the Pentecostal Church of Christ was that of a Holiness Pentecostal group, with stress on the divine inspiration of the Bible; the Trinity; Christ's virgin birth, vicarious atonement, resurrection, and imminent return; justification through faith; salvation as a prerequisite for water baptism and church membership; sanctification as a second, definite work of grace; divine healing; and the baptism of sanctified believers with the Holy Ghost to give them greater power for spiritual service, with speaking in other tongues as the initial evidence.[70]

After the consolidation the headquarters of the International Pentecostal Church of Christ was established at P.O. Box 263, London, Ohio 43140. The church body has 90 churches with approximately 3,000 members.[71]

### The Apostolic Church (in Canada and in the United States of America)

The Welsh revival of 1904–1905 prepared the way for British Pentecostalism. One group of British Pentecostals, led by W. O. Hutchinson, organized the Apostolic Faith Church with headquarters at Winton, Bournemouth, in 1908. This body attempted to give precedence to the Holy Spirit in everything and taught that one of the primary purposes of the "gifts of the Spirit" is to bring a revelation of divine truth by means either of prophecy or of tongues and their interpretation. In this way, the Apostolic Faith Church held, it is possible to discover God's will in the appointment of church officers and similar matters having to do with the government of the church. The extravagances that marked the application of this principle in the Apostolic Faith Church repelled some of its members and ministers, among them the Reverend Daniel Powell Williams, who led a nucleus of like-minded persons out of the organization and founded another church body that in 1916 took the name of the Apostolic Church. Its headquarters in Penygroes, South Wales, direct churches in the British Isles, Canada, Australia, New Zealand, the United States, and a half dozen European countries, as well as foreign missions in the West Indies, Africa, India, Ceylon, New Guinea, and the New Hebrides.

Its Eleven Tenets affirm the Trinity; the utter depravity of human nature, the need for repentance and regeneration, and the eternal doom of the finally impenitent; Christ's virgin birth, sinless life, atoning death, resurrection, ascension, intercession, second coming and millennial reign; the justification and sanctification of believers through Christ's finished work; the baptism of the Holy Ghost evidenced by speaking in tongues; the nine gifts of the Holy Ghost for the upbuilding, exhortation, and comfort of Christ's body, the church; water baptism administered to believers fifteen years of age or older by complete immersion as a symbol of burial and resurrection with Christ and the Lord's Supper observed on the first day of every week with the bread portraying Christ's body and the wine portraying his blood; the divine inspiration and authority of the Bible; church government by apostles, prophets, evangelists, pastors and teachers, elders and deacons ("they are revealed and are to be called to their office by the Holy Spirit; the Spirit may reveal His call to and through the Apostleship; the Spirit may also reveal His call by prophetical ministry"); the possibility of falling from grace; and the obligatory nature of tithes and offerings.[72]

The doctrine that most clearly sets the Apostolic Church off from other Pentecostals is that if the church in the twentieth century has recovered the experiences of the first-century Christian community—speaking in tongues and the gifts of the Holy Spirit—there must also be the restoration of the first-century apostolic and prophetic offices, with the incumbents of these offices possessed of the same rights and privileges as their primitive counterparts.[73]

The Apostolic Church came to Canada in 1924. It currently has 13 churches, of which 8 are in Ontario and the remainder in Quebec, Nova Scotia, and Alberta. The total membership is about 700. The Canadian headquarters are at 27 Castlefield Avenue, Toronto. The Canadian churches carry on missions in Jamaica, Brazil, and Barbados.[74] There are two autonomous groups of churches in the United States. The 4 churches in Pennsylvania, with a total membership of about 150 people, are supervised from Williamsburg, Pennsylvania 16693.[75] The 3 churches in California with 100 members, in addition to a mission at Lodi, are supervised from 10841 Chapman Avenue, Garden Grove, California 92640.[76]

### Free Gospel Church, Incorporated

Two brothers, the Reverend Frank Casley and the Reverend William Casley, secured a charter for the Free Gospel Church from the commonwealth of Pennsylvania in 1916.

The Free Gospel Church believes in the plenary inspiration of the Bible; the Trinity; Christ's preexistence, virgin birth, and deity; the deity and personality of the Holy Spirit; the vicarious atonement through Christ's death and resurrection; complete salvation by grace through faith in Christ's blood; the life of holiness; water baptism by immersion; the Lord's Supper; tithing; the church as the sum total of reborn believers; a divinely called and biblically ordained ministry for the evangelization of the world and the edification of the body of Christ; divine healing; baptism with the Holy Spirit accompanied by speaking in tongues; the gifts of the Holy Spirit; Christ's personal and imminent return; eternal life for believers; everlasting punishment for the impenitent; Christ's millennial reign; and the new heavens and the new earth.[77]

The address of headquarters is Box 311, Turtle Creek, Pennsylvania 15145. There are 25 churches in Pennsylvania, Ohio, West Virginia, Maryland, and New Jersey that are affiliated or in fellowship with the Free Gospel Church, Incorporated. The total membership of these churches is estimated at 2,000. The Free Gospel Church carries on foreign missions in Sierra Leone, India, and the Republic of the Philippines.[78] Recent efforts to communicate with the church body have been unsuccessful.

### The Pentecostal Church of God

Not all the Pentecostal ministers who attended the meeting at Hot Springs, Arkansas, in April 1914 out of which the General Council of the Assemblies of God came into being affiliated with the new organization. Fearful that they and their congregations would lose their cherished freedom and apprehensive of the ecclesiasticism that they sensed in the Statement of Fundamental Truths that the "oneness" controversy called forth, they waited cautiously for five years. Then in 1919 they organized the Pentecostal Assemblies of the United States of America at Chicago. In 1922 they changed the name to Pentecostal Church of God and adopted a constitutional declaration: "We deem it advisable, in order to avoid creating unscriptural lines of fellowship and disfellowship, to affiliate on the basic principles of love, righteousness, and truth, with due recognition of each other, allowing liberty of conscience in matters of personal conviction." After disavowing a fellowship based on a doctrinal statement, they affirmed their acceptance of "the Word of God in its entirety, conducting ourselves in harmony with its divine principles."[79] The 1933 convention moved the headquarters from Ottumwa, Iowa, to Kansas City, Missouri. Since 1950 the headquarters have been in Joplin, Missouri 64801 (presently at Messenger Plaza, 221 Main Street).

Its Statement of Faith, adopted in 1933, affirms the verbal inspiration of the Bible; the Trinity in unity; Christ's deity, virgin birth, sinless life, miracles, vicarious and atoning death on the cross, resurrection, ascension, and personal return; the essentiality for salvation of regeneration by the Holy Ghost through faith in Christ's shed blood; a life of holiness through sanctification as a definite but progressive work of grace; the baptism of the Holy Ghost subsequent to the new birth, with speaking in tongues as the initial physical evidence; water baptism by immersion for believers only in the name of the Father and of the Son and of the Holy Ghost; the provision for divine healing in the atonement and its availability to all true believers; Christ's premillennial second coming to resurrect the righteous dead and catch away the living saints to meet him in the air; and the bodily resurrection of both the saved and the lost, the former to life, the latter to damnation.[80]

The General Convention, which meets every two years, is the highest governing body of the denomination. The general superintendent is assisted by three regional assistant superintendents.

In addition to an aggressive program of evangelism among North American Indians, the Pentecostal Church of God carries on foreign missions in Taiwan, the Republic of the Philippines, Brazil, Trinidad, Jamaica, Haiti, Guatemala, Mexico, Belize, Portugal, Spain, England, Indonesia, Japan, Lebanon, and Israel. It reports 2,000 churches at home and abroad with a total membership of 150,000.[81]

### Pentecostal Fire-Baptized Holiness Church

In August 1918 a group of members of the Pentecostal Holiness Church— itself at the time a seven-year-old union of the Pentecostal Holiness Church and of an earlier Pentecostal Fire-Baptized Holiness Church—withdrew because of disagreements about the wearing of adornments and elaborate dress and organized a new Pentecostal Fire-Baptized Holiness Church at Nicholson, Georgia. In November 1919 the Pentecostal Fire-Baptized Holiness Church banded together with the Pentecostal Free-Will Baptist Church (organized in 1919); the united body took the name Pentecostal Fire-Baptized Holiness Church.

The basis of union for the new body affirms justification by faith; the shedding of Christ's blood for the remission of past sins, for the regeneration of penitent sinners, for salvation from sin and sinning, and for the complete cleansing of the justified believer from all indwelling sin and from its pollution after rebirth; entire sanctification as an instantaneous second work of grace obtainable by faith; the Pentecostal baptism with the Holy Ghost and fire by the fully cleansed believer's act of appropriating faith, with speaking in other tongues as its initial evidence; divine healing as part of the atonement; Christ's imminent, personal, premillennial return; antagonism to war and prohibition of participation in it by members of the denomination; and opposition to Christian Science, Spiritualism, Unitarianism, Universalism, the Church of Jesus Christ of Latter-Day Saints, Seventh-day Adventism, and a number of other teachings.[82]

Chapters IX through XLVII of the *Discipline* develop this position at length with sections on the Bible; the Deity and the three Persons of the Trinity; creation; humankind's primitive state and fall; divine and human government; Christ's mediation and atonement; the universal gospel call to all persons; repentance; faith; the experiences of justification, regeneration, sanctification, and baptism with the Holy Ghost; the Christian possibilities of perseverance, apostasy or backsliding, restoration, and achievements (including obedience to the command to "heal the sick, cleanse the lepers, raise the dead, and cast out devils"); the church; the gospel ministry (including women as well as men); the ordinances of believer's baptism by immersion, the Lord's Supper (with the emblems representing Christ's body and blood), foot washing ("not a compulsory but a voluntary obligation which brings to the participant greater reward than an obligatory duty"), anointing of the sick with oil, and the laying on of hands for ordination, healing, imparting the Holy Ghost, and casting out devils; death and the intermediate state; Christ's return after the first resurrection of the deceased saints and the translation of the living saints, to be followed by the millennium; the final resurrection; the general judgment and final retribution; sin; grace; perfection; hope; love; humility; surrender and consecration; sacrifice; gifts of the Spirit; prayer; fasting; conviction; confession; forgiveness; restitution; temperance; usury; conscience; giving; filthiness; and the tongue.[83]

Under penalty of having their names erased from the church's rolls, members must renounce oath-bound secret societies, labor unions, social clubs, corrupt partisan politics; the use or handling of tobacco, morphine, intoxicants, and cola beverages; attending fairs, swimming pools or shows of any kind; wearing of jewelry, gold, feathers, flowers, costly apparel, neckties, hobble or split skirts, low necks, short sleeves, indecent dress, or ornamentation; bobbing or waving of hair; participating in manual labor or business on the Lord's Day for which pecuniary remuneration is received for service rendered; and riding in any kind of public or private transportation, buying or selling anything at all, cooking food, or preparing fuel (except in emergencies) on the Lord's Day. Churches must not engage in festivals, ice cream suppers, oyster stews, fairs, bazaars, or other amusements or traffic for their support, and members must pay tithes of their net incomes and give free-will offerings for the spread of the gospel.[84]

The worship of the Pentecostal Fire-Baptized Holiness Church stresses spontaneity; "joyous demonstrations," such as shouting, crying, and hand-clapping, often mark the services.

The organization of the church is congregational. The delegated General Convention meets every two years. The headquarters of the church are at Toccoa, Georgia 30577. It has 41 churches in Georgia, Alabama, and the Carolinas with an estimated 500 members. It supports foreign missions in Mexico. Church officials have not responded to recent requests for information.

### Emmanuel Holiness Church

To emphasize their dissent from some of the decisions of the 1953 General Conference of the Pentecostal Fire-Baptized Holiness Church, a number of delegates withdrew and organized the Emmanuel Holiness Church at Whiteville, North Carolina. The creed of the latter body is an expanded adaptation of the Apostles' Creed: "The cruel hands of the Roman soldiers" replaces "Pontius Pilate"; "he descended into hell" is replaced by "but quickened by the Spirit, by which also he went and preached unto the spirits in prison"; after "I believe" and before "in the Holy Ghost" the words "in sanctification as a second definite work of grace and" are inserted; and "the holy catholic church" is replaced by "the Christian church."[85] The basis of Union is substantially identical with that of the Pentecostal Fire-Baptized Holiness Church, except that Article 8 reads: "We forbid that our members participate in actual combat service, in taking of arms in war, if their conviction is objective."[86] The Emmanuel Holiness Church took over most of the general rules of the older church body; one significant difference is the fact that in the Emmanuel Holiness Church being "in double marriage" debars a person not from membership in the church but merely from preaching; another is the resolution of the Emmanuel Holiness Church, while welcoming "all nationalities of people" into the church body, "that we are opposed to the act of integration of the races."[87] The Articles of Faith affirm belief in the Trinity; Christ's incarnation and atonement for both original sin and actual guilt; his resurrection, ascension, session, and "return to judge all men at the last day"; the double procession and deity of the Holy Spirit; and eternal life for the righteous and unending torture in hell for the wicked.[88]

State assemblies meet annually and the General Assembly meets every two years. The general superintendent resides at Social Circle, Georgia 30279. There are 73 churches in 7 states with a reported membership of 1,462. Recent efforts to communicate with the church body have been unsuccessful.

### Bethel Temple

The Reverend William Henry Offiler (1875–1957) founded a Pentecostal congregation in Seattle, Washington, in 1914, and called it Bethel Temple.[89] In the course of time other congregations came into being under its inspiration and on the same model, each independent and autonomous but in fellowship with the others, and all cooperating together, particularly in foreign mission endeavors.

The eleven-article Doctrinal Statement affirms the inspiration of the Bible; the Trinity; Christ's preexistence, virgin birth, miracles, sacrificial death, literal resurrection, and translation to glory; the blood of Christ as the complete atonement for sin; the new birth; divine healing in the atonement; water baptism by immersion "in the name of the Father and of the Son and of the Holy Ghost—the LORD JESUS CHRIST, A triune God with a triune name";[90] baptism with the Holy Spirit according to Acts 2:4; heaven and hell, and two resurrections; holy living as the standard of Christian experience; and the perfection of the church, the marriage of the Lamb, the binding of Satan, Christ's premillennial second coming, the purging of the earth for the establishment of his Kingdom, and the millennial reign of Christ and his church, followed by the final judgment.[91]

The headquarters of the fellowship are at 2033 Second Avenue, Seattle, Washington 98121. There are 12 churches in Washington, 2 in Minnesota, and 1 in Wisconsin. The mother church in Seattle has 300 members; information about the membership of the other churches is not available. The fellowship sponsors foreign missions in Europe, New Guinea, Japan, and Indonesia.[92]

### Open Bible Standard Churches, Incorporated

The strongly evangelistic and missionary-minded Open Bible Standard Churches, Incorporated, came into being in 1935 when the Bible Standard Church, Incorporated, of Eugene, Oregon, merged with the Open Bible Evangelistic Association of Des Moines. The present name goes back to 1935.

The Bible Standard Church, Incorporated, dated back to 1919. In that year its founders under the leadership of Fred Hornschuh had withdrawn from Florence Louise Crawford's Apostolic Faith Mission in Portland, Oregon, when she refused to abandon her position that her mission was the only true church (and that its members for that reason could not fellowship with other Pentecostal Christians) and her insistence that remarried divorcees separate before being admitted to church membership.

The Open Bible Evangelistic Association resulted from the 1932 withdrawal of the Iowa and Minnesota divisions from Aimee Semple McPherson's Church of the Foursquare Gospel under the leadership of John R. Richey, less over doctrinal than administrative issues.

Theologically the Open Bible Standard Churches, Incorporated, are typically Pentecostal—fundamental, evangelical, missionary, premillennial, with strong stress on the atoning blood of Christ, the baptism of the Holy Spirit attested by speaking in tongues, water baptism by immersion, sanctification, and divine healing.[93] They operate on a modified congregational basis. An annual general conference of ministers and lay delegates from the local congregations determines programs and policies of intercongregational concern. The denomination numbers 275 churches in the continental United States and Puerto Rico with an inclusive membership of 25,000. It maintains missions in Jamaica, Cuba, Trinidad, Argentina, Liberia, Guinea, and Japan, and carries on evangelistic work in Okinawa. The headquarters are at 2020 Bell Avenue, Des Moines, Iowa 50315.

### The Holiness Church of God, Incorporated

The Holiness Church of God, Incorporated, has roots in the Kimberley Park Holiness Church at Winston-Salem, North Carolina, that go back a century. As the Pentecostal movement spread into that part of North Carolina it brought into being the "Big May Meeting" at Madison, North Carolina, in 1917, which Elder James A. Foust led until 1920. In that year the congregations that supported the meeting took the name Holiness Church of God. In 1928 the leaders incorporated it at Winston-Salem.

Its teachings are typical of Pentecostalism erected on a Holiness foundation. Trinitarian in theology, it lays key stress on entire sanctification; on the baptism of the Holy Spirit with speaking in tongues as the initial evidence; on water baptism in the name of the Father and of the Son and of the Holy Ghost; on divine healing; and on Christ's premillennial return.[94]

The general chief administrative officer is the presiding bishop. The assembly meets annually. Elders serve as overseers of the 5 districts along the eastern seaboard among which the 28 churches, which have a total membership of 927, are divided. The headquarters are at Winston-Salem.

### The General Assembly and Church of the First Born

The General Assembly and Church of the First Born is a loosely organized fellowship that takes its name from Hebrews 12:23. One of the largest and most influential congregations, the General Assembly and Church of the First Born, 2719 Tindall Avenue, Indianapolis, Indiana, was founded in 1896.[95]

The Articles of Faith affirm belief "in God, the Eternal Father, and His Son, Jesus Christ, and in the Holy Ghost"; salvation for all persons through Christ's atonement by obedience to the laws and ordinances of the gospel, that is, faith in Christ, repentance, believer's baptism by immersion for the forgiveness of sins, and laying on of hands for the gift of the Holy Ghost; in the same organization as that of the primitive church, with apostles, prophets, pastors, teachers, evangelists, and so on; in spiritual gifts such as those of tongues, prophecy, revelation, visions, healing, and interpretation of tongues; in the Bible as the Word of God and in the necessity of living by every word of the New Testament; in the privilege of worshiping God according to the dictates of each person's conscience; and in doing good to all persons. In 1965 the fellowship added an additional article, which commands obedience to civil government as far as this is possible in harmony with the divine law, but which teaches the young men of the fellowship "to serve their country in any capacity except to bear arms."[96]

Members of the General Assembly and Church of the First Born reject totally the use of medicines and all recourse to physicians, surgeons, and other members of the medical profession in cases of illness. They trust completely in God for divine healing, mediated through prayers and through anointing with oil by the elders of the church. The congregations protest court rulings which require the inoculation of children of members against childhood diseases. On the other hand, the group regards dentists and optometrists not as medical personnel but as technicians who provide mechanical devices and services.

The General Assembly and Church of the First Born also teaches against the use of tobacco and intoxicating beverages.

The Lord's Supper is served at frequent intervals and regularly after each baptism. Immediately following the Lord's Supper, the rite of foot washing takes place, the men washing the men's feet, the women washing the women's feet. The "greeting of the church" or the "kiss of charity" follows the foot washing.

The five signs of Mark 16:17-18—casting out demons, speaking in new tongues, picking up serpents safely, not being hurt by drinking any deadly thing, and laying hands on the sick for their recovery—are reportedly an integral part of the life of the churches in the fellowship.

A sympathetic observer commends the emphasis of the General Assembly and Church of the First Born on the study of the Bible and describes the fellowship in these terms: "Generally they are a happy group, strict in their rearing of children, frowning on many of the pleasures of the world, but finding much joy and strength in their associations with one another."[97]

The elders (or bishops) are the administrative heads of the church. After they have shown themselves "approved of God," they are ordained for life by the laying on of hands of the presbytery with fasting and prayer. They receive no special schooling or training, and since they are filled with the Holy Spirit they do not prepare their sermons beforehand. They receive no pay and support themselves with other employment. The voluntary contributions of the members maintain the church.

The General Assembly and Church of the First Born has no central headquarters and maintains no statistics. The Indianapolis congregation, which provides a considerable measure of leadership, reports records of associated churches in Arkansas, California, Colorado, Illinois, Indiana, Kansas, Kentucky, Maryland, Missouri, Nevada, Oregon, Ohio, Texas, Washington, and West Virginia.[98] A concentration of about thirty churches reportedly exists in the vicinity of Oklahoma City.[99]

The churches in the fellowship conduct no foreign missions and generally make little effort to convert outsiders, although occasionally they sponsor revivals with visiting elders at the homes of the community to encourage participation in the service. The congregations depend for their growth chiefly on the relatively large families of members.

### Church of God of the Union Assembly, Incorporated

The Church of God of the Union Assembly, Incorporated, traces its history back to a single little congregation in Center, Jackson County, Georgia. By 1920 the movement that began in Center had spread sufficiently to warrant the superior court of Bartow County to charter the Union Assembly of the Church of God, Incorporated. The next year it was incorporated under the laws of the state of Georgia.[100] In 1950 it adopted its present name.[101]

The Church of God of the Union Assembly is a trinitarian body[102] which administers believer's baptism by immersion[103] in the name of the Father and of the Son and of the Holy Ghost.[104]

It teaches the necessity of repentance; justification through faith in Jesus Christ; power, forgiveness, remission, sanctification, the Holy Ghost, the redemption of the church, the redemption of the body, and the resurrection through his blood; the baptism of the Holy Ghost, with stammering lips and speaking in other tongues as evidence of the baptism of the Holy Ghost and as the fruit of the Spirit; Christ as the spiritual head of the church; the Lord's Supper and foot washing;[105] the healing of the body by faith;[106] and the church's God-given power to overcome the world.[107]

Tithing, it holds, has no biblical basis. Neither Jesus nor any of his apostles paid tithes, received tithes, or commanded anyone else to pay or receive them.[108]

There are significant differences between the Church of God of the Union Assembly and most other Pentecostal churches in the doctrine of the last things. It teaches, for instance, that the Kingdom of Jesus is not to be looked for in some future millennium, but is already here. It is a spiritual Kingdom. It was at hand when John the Baptist came preaching. Christ's first coming, his death, burial, resurrection, and ascension brought the Kingdom about. It came with power at Pentecost. Its fruits are those set forth in Galatians 5:22. They are in error who say that at Christ's premillennial coming he will take the righteous away and leave the wicked on earth. On the contrary, the teaching that "Christ is coming here to reign on this earth a thousand years" is a deception. His second coming will be simultaneous with the end, and he will take the bad and leave the good.[109]

In the same vein, the Church of God of the Union Assembly teaches that the "first resurrection" involved our Lord and the crowd of 144,000 male Jews who rose with him when he rose from the dead. The second ("last" or "judgment") resurrection will take place on the last day and will comprise the "blood-washed crowd" of the just and all the unjust.[110]

The Church of God of the Union Assembly also holds that the dragon, the serpent, and the devil of Revelation 20:1–2 is a human being who was ruling when Jesus was born.[111] It believes that the two olive trees of Zechariah 3 and the two witnesses of Revelation 11 are idential; both cases have to do with Elijah (that is, John the Baptist) and Jesus.[112] It stresses the priority of preachers over prophets in the New Testament church.[113] It teaches that there are three heavens. The first is an exalted heaven, from which the devil was driven out and which is to be destroyed; it is identical with the first earth, the earth of people that passes away. The second heaven is the second man Adam. The third heaven is the paradise of God. Similarly, there are three births. The first is the natural or earthly birth from a human mother, which puts a person in the first or earthly heaven. The second birth is of the water and of the spirit, which puts a person in the second man Adam, or second heaven. The third birth, being born from the dead, puts a person in the paradise of God. Again, when the Bible talks about an earth that is to be burned up or pass away, it means the earth or world of people. The earth that the meek will inherit for ever after the "judgment resurrection" is the earth that we live on, renewed and with the curse removed.[114]

The prohibitions and directives of the church body's general rules regulate minutely many aspects of the lives of members of the Church of God of the Union Assembly.

Among the activities prohibited to all members of the church body are attendance at public motion-picture shows, public ballgames, and public swimming pools that do not segregate the sexes; the use of tobacco,[115] intoxicating drinks, or narcotics ("dope"); "taking up arms and going to war";[116] attendance at meetings held by a dismissed preacher; putting permanent waves in one's hair; chewing gum in church; the use of artificial hair coloring; keeping company with sinners as sweethearts; marrying a person who is not a member of the Church of God of the Union Assembly; and vilification of anyone for belonging or not belonging to a labor union or "any worthy and respectable lodge."

The prohibitions laid upon women members of the church body forbid them to bob, trim, curl,[117] or tease their hair; to wear sleeveless or knee-length dresses;[118] to wear slacks[119] or shorts in public; to paint their faces, lips, fingernails, or toenails; to use fingernail polish or fingernail hardener; to pluck their eyebrows; to apply eyebrow sticks; to color their eyelashes; and to go without hose when at church or in town.[120]

All ministers must once each month notify the state or general overseer of their whereabouts and activities, either by a personal letter or through a church paper or other means. Ministers may not discuss new questions of doctrine outside a ministers' meeting or the annual assembly of the church body. Only ministers whom the annual assembly has approved may conduct debates or discussions with preachers of other church bodies. There is a strong stress on revivals in the Church of God of the Union Assembly, but ministers are "asked to use good judgment concerning holding revivals and not to wear out one church with meetings when there is plenty of preaching to be done elsewhere." A minister is not allowed to marry "a sinner girl" or to remarry if his wife has left him without a Bible excuse, nor may ministers "ride around in automobiles or be in company with women when their wives or someone else is not with them." After preaching a sermon they are not "to talk around for 30 or 40 minutes" and thus undo all the good that they may have done. A minister who "goes out and partakes of the world and commits adultery and fornication" must prove himself for twelve months before he will be reinstated as a minister. Candidates for ordination must undergo a twelve-month probationary period and must demonstrate a satisfactory mastery of the teachings of the church body.[121]

The assembly meets annually at the national headquarters in Dalton, Georgia, early in July. The biblically indicated purpose of the assembly is to agree on doctrine, to settle issues and to send forth decrees and laws for the churches, and to oversee the churches.[122] The "official and only ruling and governing body" of the Church of God of the Union Assembly, Incorporated, is the fifteen-member Supreme Council. At the head of the church body is the

general overseer.[123] Individual states and groups of states have state overseers and state assemblies called "ministers' meetings."

The headquarters of the Church of God of the Union Assembly, Incorporated, are at Dalton, Georgia 30720, where the mailing address is Box
1323. According to its leadership, the church body operates in seventeen
states.[124] No information is available on the number of churches or the total
active membership.[125]

### Latin American Council of Christian Churches
### (Concilio Latino-Americano de Iglesias Cristianas)

Francisco Olazabal was a moderately prominent Methodist minister in
Mexico and California who associated himself with the Assemblies of God
from 1918 to 1923.[126] His subsequent evangelistic activities covered all the
states that border on Mexico as well as Puerto Rico. In 1923 he incorporated
the Concilio Latino-Americano de Iglesias Cristianas. After Olazabal's death,
the task of organizing and leading the council fell on Dr. Miguel Guillen,
Brownsville, Texas, who became president for life in 1956. In 1954 the
council established the Cladic Seminary at 2804 Whittier Boulevard, Los
Angeles, with one-year, two-year, and three-year curricula to train men and
women in various capacities in the different fields of the council's work.[127]

The council, a "full Gospel" organization, sets forth its doctrinal position
in twenty-three articles of faith. They cover the Sacred Scriptures; the Trinity,
described in such a way as to exclude the "oneness" position; the fall of
humankind; the plan of redemption; salvation by grace; repentance and
acceptance of Jesus Christ; the new birth; the daily Christian life; baptism as
a sublime and solemn symbol reminding us that we must regard ourselves as
dead to sin, and the Lord's Supper as a commemoration and observance in
which the breaking of the bread is a type of the Bread of Life; the baptism
of the Holy Spirit; life in the fullness of the Spirit; the gifts and fruits of the
Holy Spirit, including tongues and the interpretation of tongues; moderation;
divine healing; Christ's personal and imminent second coming; the obligation
of those who have been reborn into the invisible church, the family and body
of Christ, to affiliate with the visible church of Christ on earth; civil government; the last judgment; heaven; hell, and evangelism as the great mission of
the church on earth.[128]

The council, which meets every two years, is headed by a president and
a general superintendent whom the president appoints. Its headquarters are
at 328 East Jefferson Street, Brownsville, Texas 78520. There are ten districts, covering California, Arizona, New Mexico, Texas, Colorado, Illinois,
Indiana, Michigan, Ohio, and five states of the Republic of Mexico.[129] The
"Assembly of Mexico" is headed by a superintendent whom the president of
the council nominates. Work is also carried on in Mexico City and in New
York. No information is available on the total number of churches and
missions that the council operates or their inclusive membership.[130]

### International Church of the Foursquare Gospel

Ontario-born Aimee Kennedy Semple McPherson (1890–1944) was converted at the age of seventeen under the preaching of a Pentecostal evangelist, whom she married shortly afterward and with whom she went to China as a missionary couple. When her husband died of malaria in 1910, she returned to North America and remarried, only to feel the tug of the pulpit draw her back into an evangelistic ministry that covered a large part of the United States. In 1921 she had a vision of the Foursquare Gospel on the basis of Ezekiel 1:4-28 while conducting a revival in Oakland, California. Less than two years later she dedicated Angelus Temple, Los Angeles, a structure with a seating capacity of 5,300. In 1924 she established her own radio station. In 1925 she founded L.I.F.E. Bible College. In 1927 she incorporated the International Church of the Foursquare Gospel based on a belief in Jesus as the Savior, the Baptizer, the Healer, and the Coming King. She was immensely energetic, unconventional, fluent, physically attractive, controversial, thoroughly human, and gifted with a magnetic personality and a flair for publicity and the dramatic. Her concern for the "have-nots" in society won their loyalty and kept them "faithful to her even during the times when she was allegedly involved in family quarrels, lawsuits, and [a] kidnaping incident."[131] After 1944 the leadership of Angelus Temple and the Church of the Foursquare Gospel passed to Rolf McPherson, son of the foundress.

For Angelus Temple and the International Church of the Foursquare Gospel; Mrs. McPherson compiled a twenty-two-article Declaration of Faith,[132] which the Church of the Foursquare Gospel has summarized in these terms:

We believe that (1) The Bible is the inspired Word of God. (2) God is Triune: Father, Son, and Holy Spirit. (3) Man was created in God's image, but by disobedience fell from perfection. (4) Christ died for us, signing the pardon of all who believe on His name. (5) By grace we are saved through faith. (6) Upon repentance and acceptance of Christ, through the merits of His shed blood, we are justified before God. (7) A change takes place in the heart and life as a result of the new birth. (8) We are daily to grow in the the faith. (9) [Water] baptism by immersion is an outward sign of an inward work; the Lord's Supper is to be commemorated by the symbolical use of the bread and the juice of the vine.[133] (10) The incoming of the Holy Spirit is after the same manner as in Bible days.[134] (11) It is the will of God that we walk in the Spirit daily. (12) The Holy Spirit has gifts to bestow upon the Christian, and we should show spiritual fruit as evidence of a Spirit-filled life. (13) The experience and daily walk of the believer should never lead him into extremes. (14) Christ still heals the sick as He did in Bible days. (15) The second coming of Christ is imminent. (16) We are to identify ourselves with the visible church of Christ. (17) Rulers should be upheld at all times except in things opposed to the will of God. (18) Sinners shall stand before the judgment bar of God and Christians before the judgment seat of Christ. (19) Heaven is the eternal home of believers, and (20) hell is the place of eternal torment for unbelievers. (21) Soul-winning is the one big business of the church. (22) Tithes and offerings is the method ordained of God for the support and spread of His cause.[135]

The minimum membership age is eight. At eighteen members are qualified to take part in all the spiritual and temporal affairs of the church. The chain of responsibility runs from the individual member through the pastor of the chartered local church to the latter's next superior, to one of the ten district supervisors, to the board of directors, to the missionary cabinet, to the executive council, and finally to the annual international convention, where each chartered local church is represented by its pastor and one delegate for each fifty members or fraction of that number.

Angelus Temple, 1100 Glendale Boulevard, Los Angeles, California 90026, is the international headquarters. There are 760 churches in the United States with a total membership of 119,436 and 30 churches in Canada, especially in British Columbia, with a total membership of 1,896. The denomination supports approximately 3,800 missionaries and indigenous workers in 29 countries in Latin America, Europe, Africa, the Far East, and the Pacific Islands, and the number of churches overseas has grown by 1,388 to a total of 4,025 in the past five years.[136]

## General Council, Christian Church of North America

Chicago is in a sense the cradle of the Pentecostal movement among Italian Americans. Luigi Francescon was one of the Waldensian founders of the Italian Presbyterian Church in Chicago in 1892. In 1903 he and a group of eighteen others in the congregation, persuaded of the necessity of baptism by immersion, received baptism in this manner from a fellow member who in turn had been thus baptized a few days before by an adherent of the Church of the Brethren. Before the end of the year the Francescon group withdrew from the Italian Presbyterian Church in Chicago over the immersion issue. In 1907 Francescon received the baptism of the Holy Spirit in the North Avenue Church of Chicago, of which the Reverend W. H. Durham was the pastor. Francescon and others who had had a similar experience carried the Pentecostal message to fellow Italians across the United States, in the European homeland, and in the Italian communities of Brazil and Argentina. Ror the first two decades the work remained largely unorganized. In 1927 a meeting of Italian Pentecostal ministers convened in Niagara Falls, New York, "in order to unite against those who believed in eating blood."[137] The outcome was the Unorganized Italian Christian Church in the United States. "Unorganized" was dropped from the name in 1939 and "Italian" in 1942. The movement was incorporated at Pittsburgh, Pennsylvania, in 1948, as the General Council, Christian Church of North America. The church body is gradually losing its distinctively Italian identity, although on an overall basis at least half its membership is still of Italian extraction.

The Christian Church of North America sees itself as identical with the Assemblies of God in faith and practice. Theologically it stands in the Holiness wing of the Pentecostal movement. It believes in the Bible as the infallible Word of God; the Trinity; Christ's deity, incarnation, virgin birth, and redemptive death ("not only for the primitive transgressions, but also for the actual sins of man"); the existence of a personal devil; regeneration only through faith in Christ; water baptism of adult believers by single immersion in the name of the Father and of the Son and of the Holy Ghost (and the dedication of children to God); the baptism in the Holy Ghost, with the sign of speaking in tongues; the Lord's Supper; abstention from things offered to idols, blood, things strangled, and fornication; divine healing as part of the atonement and the anointing of the sick with oil accompanied by prayer; Christ's premillennial return and the rapture of the living believers; and the bodily resurrection of the unjust to everlasting punishment and of the righteous to life eternal.[138]

It rejects "the excesses tolerated or practiced among some" Pentecostal churches.[139] Its code of ethics defers to the individual's conviction and the public conscience in matters where the Bible gives no positive direction. Women are to dress modestly and their wearing of a head-covering at worship is favored. The church body forbids gambling, drunkenness, the use of tobacco, social vices, public theaters, dancing, and the intermarriage of Christians with unbelievers. It takes a conservative position on divorce and remarriage and encourages total abstinence from alcoholic beverages. Some ministers support themselves by secular occupations. At the Lord's Supper it permits chalices or individual glasses and allows the use of wine or grape juice.[140]

The headquarters are at 1818 State Street, Sharon, Pennsylvania 16146. The local churches are autonomous. The General Council meets annually. The general overseer is assisted by three assistant general overseers. The church body reports 111 churches in the United States, with a total membership of about 8,500. The General Council carries on foreign missions in Belgium, Italy, the Republic of the Philippines, and Mexico; in addition "approved workers" and national missionaries supported by individual congregations function in Tunisia, Uruguay, Australia, Argentina, Kenya, and India.[141] Missionaries are also at work in Canada and in Puerto Rico.

### Carolina Evangelistic Association (Garr Memorial Church)

Shortly after evangelist Alfred Goodrich Garr (1874–1944) was converted to Pentecostalism in Los Angeles, he set out in 1908 to preach the Pentecostal message among the Chinese of Hong Kong. Subsequently he conducted extensive evangelistic and healing campaigns in Japan, China, India, and the United States. In 1930 he and his wife, together with Alfred Goodrich Garr, Jr., began a revival campaign in Charlotte, North Carolina. The campaign led to the founding of the Carolina Evangelistic Association and the erection of the Garr Memorial Church (formerly the Garr Auditorium) in Charlotte. The association is the corporate body through which the Garr Memorial Church operates a summer camp, conducts a radio ministry, ordains qualified ministers, and receives offerings for distribution to missionary agencies. Upon Garr's death, his widow, Hannah Erickson Garr, assisted by his son, assumed the administration of the association and the congregation.[142]

The Garr Memorial Church describes itself as a "Full Gospel" church. In line with Garr's wishes, the association and the congregation have remained independent, although they fellowship with the Assemblies of God, the International Church of the Foursquare Gospel, and similar church bodies in the mainline Pentecostal tradition. The association is a member of the Pentecostal Fellowship of North America.

From Garr Memorial Church 103 persons entered fulltime religious service during the first thirty-six years of its existence. In addition to a variety of ministries in Charlotte and elsewhere in the Carolinas, the association provides varying amounts of support to foreign missions in fourteen countries; the most extensive support goes to operations in Brazil. The total membership of the Garr Memorial Church is about 1,000.[143] The church is located at 200 Tuckaseegee Road, Charlotte, North Carolina 28208.

### Defenders of the Christian Faith Movement, Incorporated (Movimiento Defensores de la fe de Puerto Rico, Incorporado)

Juan Francisco Rodríguez-Rivera was born (1897) in the southern mountains of Puerto Rico, near Maunabo. While a member of the Methodist Church he underwent a conversion experience and in 1917 and 1918 he was a preacher on Vieques Island. After two years in Santo Domingo as a government schoolteacher and part-time colporteur-minister, he returned to Puerto Rico and from 1921 to 1931 he was a Christian and Missionary Alliance minister. During 1931 Rodríguez was a member of the committee that invited Gerald B. Winrod (1900–1957) of Wichita, Kansas, founder of the Defenders of the Christian Faith and editor of The Defender Magazine, to hold a series of missionary conferences in Christian and Misisonary Alliance churches in Puerto Rico. Winrod decided to initiate a missionary effort of his own on the island and engaged Rodríguez to oversee the production of a Spanish edition of The Defender Magazine, to be known as El Defensor Hispano, and to open a Defenders of the Faith center in Arecibo. The congregation that Rodríguez had founded in Guayma left the Christian and Missionary Alliance and became the first Puerto Rican congregation of the new movement, which regards 1931 as the year of its founding. Initially the Defenders of the Faith was to be an interdenominational evangelistic movement; it was not to have members or to oversee churches. Its sole purpose was to hold evangelistic campaigns; the converts that these would make were to unite with existing congregations. For three years Rodríguez sponsored revivals in cooperation with Baptists, Methodists, the Christian and Missionary Alliance, the United Evangelical Church of Puerto Rico, and the Disciples of Christ. In 1932 he accompanied Francisco Olazábal on the latter's evangelical campaign in New York's Harlem. In 1933 Rodríguez moved his office to Río Piedras, where in 1934 he conducted a protracted evangelistic campaign which Olazábal joined for two months. The success of this effort stimulated the organization of Defenders of the Faith congregations in Río Piedras and in other cities. Sensing the need for more than correspondence-school training for the ministers of the new organization, Rodríguez, with Winrod's assistance, opened the Defenders Theological Seminary in Río Piedras in 1945. In the same year the Defenders had begun work in the continental United States, and in 1947 they initiated efforts in Santo Domingo.

The creed of the movement affirms belief in the Bible as the inspired source of faith; God the Father; Christ the Redeemer; the Holy Spirit of God and of Christ; the church as Christ's body, composed of all those who through faith are children of God; the obligation to proclaim the gospel and to manifest the fruit of the Spirit in character and conduct; the freedom of the church to create the institutions and to name the officers who will carry out the church's purposes; the sacraments of baptism by immersion and the Lord's Supper; and, in compliance with the law of Christ, baptism by immersion and the duty not only to proclaim the gospel, but also to carry on works of charity and operate institutions of mercy, sustain human liberty, free the oppressed, achieve civic justice, and repulse all iniquity.

The autonomy of the local congregations extends to details of belief and practice, as long as the basic trinitarian confession is not jeopardized. Some of the local congregations are Pentecostal in faith, worship, and government; others are Baptist; others do not fit neatly into any conventional denominational pattern.

Annual assemblies are held separately in Puerto Rico and in the continental United States. Each of the two areas has a central committee that directs its affairs. The Puerto Rico headquarters' address is P.O. Box 7598, Barrio Obrero Station, Santurce; it supervises 68 churches, chapels, and missions with a total membership of about 6,000. Originally somewhat antiecumenical, the movement has in recent years developed very cordial relations with the Evangelical Council in Puerto Rico. In the continental United States there are 14 churches and missions in 7 states from coast to coast, with an inclusive membership of about 2,000.[144]

### The Church by the Side of the Road (Seattle, Washington)

In 1924 some of the supporters of a community Sunday school that met at the Thorndyke School in Seattle, Washington, received the Pentecostal baptism of the Holy Spirit. A few years later, with the outlook for the continued use of the public school building becoming more and more doubtful and with dissension developing within the community Sunday school itself over the experience of the Pentecostal group, the latter first joined Bethel Temple as a branch mission and then developed into an independent congregation in 1933. In 1936 it founded a branch of its own, the Little Chapel of the Church by the Side of the Road, now a completely separate congregation. The mother church, which cooperates with the Northwest District Council of the Assemblies of God, is located at South 148th Street and Highway 99, Seattle, Washington 98166.

Its tenets of faith affirm the inspiration of the Bible; the one, true, self-existent God; Jesus as the eternal Son of God; the Holy Spirit; the Trinity; the fall of humankind and its redemption through the atoning blood of Christ; salvation by God's grace through the washing of regeneration and renewing of the Holy Spirit, evidenced by the witness of the Spirit and a holy life; the possibility of falling from grace, although this must not be allowed to rob believers of their assurance of salvation; the church as the body of Christ; believer's baptism by immersion; the Lord's Supper as a symbol of participation in his divine nature; filling with the Holy Ghost as the promise of the Father to all believers, initially evidenced by speaking with other tongues; entire sanctification; divine healing for the body provided for through the atonement; Christ's imminent return the blessed hope of the church; Christ's millennial reign; the lake of fire for the devil and his followers; new heavens and a new earth; the indissolubility of marriage except for unchastity, with remarriage possible only after the death of the first partner; and marriage only with the saved.[145]

The total constituency of the Church by the Side of the Road is estimated at 500, with an enrolled membership of 175.[146] The Church by the Side of the Road supports foreign missionaries in Indonesia.

### The Filipino Assemblies of the First-Born, Incorporated

In 1933 an immigrant clergyman from the Philippines, the Reverend Julian Bernabe (b. 1898), founded the Filipino Assemblies of the First-Born[147] at Stockton, California. Before the end of the year he moved the headquarters of the new movement to Fresno, in 1942 to San Francisco, and in 1943 to Delano, California.

The Statement of Fundamental Truths of the Filipino Assemblies of the First-Born is identical with the parallel statement of the Assemblies of God.[148]

The leadership of the Filipino Assemblies of the First-Born feels that the organization can minister more effectively to Filipino immigrants if it maintains its administrative independence.

The Assemblies declare themselves "as against going to war," and as unable "conscientiously [to] participate in the actual destruction of human lives," although they declare their willingness to "serve in any capacity outside of taking up arms if required to do so."[149]

The organization meets in convention annually. The senior executive officer is the general superintendent. The headquarters for the United States are at 1229 Glenwood, Delano, California 93215. There are 15 churches on the North American mainland, all in California, and 17 in Hawaii. The total active membership is estimated at 325.[150] A Philippines branch was organized in 1947; its headquarters are at Caba, La Unión.

### Iglesia de Cristo en las Antillas (Church of Christ in the Antilles)

Francisco Olazábal's evangelistic and divine healing services in Puerto Rico in 1934 stimulated the emergence of other Pentecostal movements. A congregation came into being in that same year in the barrio La Dolores of Río Grande. The movement expanded under native leadership in the northeastern part of Puerto Rico; by 1935 twelve other congregations had been founded and participated in the first general council of the Iglesia de Cristo en las Antillas. At the 1938 assembly the majority adopted the name Iglesia de Cristo Misionera (Missionary Church of Christ), but the mother church in La Dolores of Río Grande refused to accept the new name. It withdrew from the fellowship and began organizing new churches on its own initiative.

Its basic doctrines include the infallibility of the Bible; God as the almighty Creator; good and evil angels; the bliss of human beings as dependent on their acceptance of God's revelation through Christ; sin as separating God and humanity and cleansed only through faith in Christ's blood; Christ as Savior of the world through his expiatory death on the cross; the Holy Spirit as the third Person of the Trinity; baptism in the Holy Trinity; the church; Christ's second coming, when the righteous will receive everlasting life and the evil everlasting condemnation. Baptism in water is only by immersion in the name of the Father and of the Son and of the Holy Spirit; the baptism in the Holy Spirit manifests itself through its fruits and gifts, notably through the gift of tongues.[151]

The headquarters' address is Box 273, Río Grande, Puerto Rico 00745. There are 17 churches with an inclusive membership of 1,700.

### Iglesia de Cristo Misionera (Missionary Church of Christ)

From 1934 to 1938 the Iglesia de Cristo Misionera and the Iglesia de Cristo en las Antillas share a common history. At the 1938 assembly of the

Iglesia de Cristo en las Antillas a majority of the churches represented adopted the name Iglesia de Cristo Misionera to make the scope of the body more inclusive. Although this decision led to the withdrawal of the mother church of the organization, the majority group under the new name expanded into other Puerto Rican communities.

Its Declaration of Principles affirms faith in the Bible; water baptism for the forgiveness of sins; the baptism of the Holy Spirit and his gifts; the Lord's Supper ("that it is the sacrifice of Christ on the cross, wounded for our sins"); matrimony as a divine institution; the dedication of children; the Trinity; the general resurrection; the obligation of tithing and bringing offerings; the sanctification of the believer throughout earthly life; divine healing ("by means of the prayer of faith the Lord will heal the sick person"); reverent worship; the prayerful relation between God and the Christian on the basis of Christ's intercession; fasts and vigils as a means of increasing consecration; faith, hope, and love as the great benefit of Christ's work; Sunday as a day of worship; the commemoration of Pentecost; the power of the Spirit in vanquishing the world, the flesh, and the devil; prophecy without fanaticism and anything else inconsistent with sound doctrine; the millennium; the resurrection of the departed faithful who are in Paradise before the millennium and of the wicked for the Great White Throne judgment at the end of the millennium; the saints, angels, and cherubim as God's messengers but not as recipients of adoration; the cross as a type of the persecution a Christian must bear but not as an object of worship; obedience to earthly government; an apostolic ministry of spiritual, holy, and instructed men who do not belong to secret societies; the free use of foods and the complete abstention from the use and sale of intoxicating beverages; and the government of the church through ministers, deacons, and presbyters.[152]

The headquarters are at Apartado 26, Saint Just, Puerto Rico 00750. There are about 60 churches with 4,500 members.[153]

### Grace Gospel Evangelistic Association International, Incorporated

In the mid-1930s a number of West Coast Pentecostals with a Calvinistic theological orientation became increasingly uncomfortable in the presence of what they regarded as Arminian and Pentecostal extremes that they were encountering. They reportedly came together more or less spontaneously and out of this meeting the Grace Gospel Evangelistic Association International, Incorporated, emerged. It is trinitarian, administers water baptism by immersion in the name of the Father and of the Son and of the Holy Ghost, and stresses the charismatic gifts of the Holy Spirit. Its overall theological accent is conservatively Pentecostal. Its organization is congregational.

The corporate headquarters are at Longview, Washington. Most of its congregations in the United States are on the Pacific Coast, but they also include groups in Pennsylvania and Oklahoma. No information is available on the total number of congregations or the total membership. Churches of the association sponsor missions in Jamaica, Colombia, Japan, the Republic of China (Taiwan), and India.[154]

## Concilio Olazábal de Iglesias Latino-Americano, Incorporado
### (Olazabal Latin-American Council of Churches, Incorporated)

In 1936 a number of Spanish-speaking Pentecostal ministers and churches organized the Concilio Olazábal de Iglesias Latino-Americano, Incorporado, named after the Latin-American Pentecostal missionary and evangelist, Francisco Olazábal.

Its doctrinal position is typically "full gospel" Trinitarian Pentecostal. Its statement of fundamental teaching affirms the truthfulness and normative character of the Bible. Salvation is the rebirth of the sorrowing penitent so that he or she loves God and hates sin. Water baptism by immersion in the name of the Father and of the Son and of the Holy Spirit for salvation and the Holy Supper as a memorial of Christ's past sacrifice are sacraments that He himself established. He will return to raise his own into eternity. Prayer confirms believers in the faith and fasting weakens the desires of the body; both are necessary. The perfection of Christ's church requires the baptism of the Holy Spirit. God established matrimony as the lifelong union of the two partners. Tithing is a blessing, but merciful concern for others is unlimited. The council practices communion with all Christians and commends the Golden Rule.[155]

The council's constitution and bylaws declare that its members "do not favor the taking up of arms to participate in war" and that "conscientiously [they] are unable to participate in the actual destruction of human lives."[156]

The council has 7 churches and missions in California and Arizona with a membership of 275 and 4 in Mexico with nearly 100 members. [157] Its headquarters are at Tabernaculo Bethesda, 1925 East First Street, Los Angeles, California 90033. It conducts its work primarily in Spanish but also in English.

## Pentecostal Evangelical Church

The Pentecostal Evangelical Church, founded n 1936, is a ministerial fellowship, a sponsor of foreign missions and orphanages, and an association of churches.

The Statement of Doctrine in its bylaws lists succinctly the following emphases: "Inspiration of the Scripture; Trinity of the Godhead; repentance and regeneration; water baptism [by immersion]; baptism of the Holy Spirit [available to all who ask for it] with initial evidence [that is, speaking with tongues]; the [communion of the] Lord's supper; divine healing [provided for in the atonement as the privilege of all believers]; and holy living." The Statement of Fundamental Truths expands these points, and adds several sections on the last things which teach the resurrection of the faithful departed at Christ's coming, the rapture of the saints, the visible millennial reign of Christ and his saints, the resurrection of the wicked to eternal punishment, and a new heaven and a new earth.[158]

Local churches are autonomous and may establish their own standard for membership, but the district conferences, which meet annually if possible, and the general conference, which meets every two years, retain the right "to approve scriptural doctrine and conduct and to disapprove unscriptural doctrine and conduct."[159]

About 200 ministers belong to the church, of whom about 10 percent are foreign missionaries that the church supports in the Republic of the Philippines, India, Bolivia, and Guyana. The 23 local churches have an estimated inclusive membership of 1,150. The church is also at work in Alaska and in the Yukon Territory. The headquarters are in Spokane, Washington.[160]

### The Overcomers Church (Evangelical)

James D. Varey organized The Overcomers Church (Evangelical) in 1939. It was incorporated in 1945.

It holds that Christ came to this world to establish the Kingdom of God, over which he will rule visibly when he returns. Citizens of this Kingdom have a more abundant life, full joy, peace that passes understanding, power over all wrong emotions, power against the devil, power with God, and union with Christ. The "divine government" of this Kingdom operates through apostles, prophets, teachers, pastors, with elders, deacons, and deaconesses in the individual assemblies. The Overcomers Church holds that since Christ is the same, the church of today can have any of the gifts and miracles that the early church had if the church of today is willing to pay the spiritual price.

The fundamental doctrinal beliefs of The Overcomers Church include the divine inspiration and authority of the Bible; the Trinity; salvation and rebirth into the Kingdom of God through personal repentance and faith in the atoning blood of Christ; his deity, second coming, and millennial reign; water baptism of believers by a single complete face-upward immersion in the name of the Father and of the Son and of the Holy Ghost, administered where possible out-of-doors in running water; the Lord's Supper; the maintenance of the church exclusively through tithes and offerings; the baptism of the Holy Spirit with speaking in other tongues as the initial evidence; the nine gifts of the Holy Spirit (I Corinthians 12 and 14) (including the gift of healing); the "divine government" of the church; divine revelation through direct outward communication and direct inward revelation; the gift of prophecy; open and mental visions; the gift of tongues and of the interpretation of tongues; and dreams and signs. The voice gifts of the Holy Spirit are exercised in public rarely and only by the leaders of the meeting; at home others may exercise these gifts only in the presence of a "called-out" apostle or pastor. All emotionalism is strictly banned from the services of the church.

Young children are dedicated at a special service. Reception of the emblems of Christ's death at the Communion service is open to all "born again" believers over thirteen, but the emblems are not knowingly given to persons who have been excommunicated from The Overcomers Church. Ministers and assistant ministers are set apart by anointing and the laying on of hands. The clergy wear clerical collars, preaching gowns, and stoles, and a special vestment at the Communion service.[161] Applicants for membership must have been "born again" and must establish their competence by a rigorous pre-membership examination.

The headquarters of The Overcomers Church (Evangelical) are at 312 Palmerston Boulevard, Toronto, Canada. The single congregation at 506 College Street, Toronto, has an estimated strength of 125. In addition there are approximately 100 churches, mission prayer halls, and other centers in foreign countries, chiefly in India and Malaysia.

**Christ Faith Mission**

Established in 1939 in the "Old Pisgah" Tabernacle, 6026 Echo, Los Angeles, California 90042, Christ Faith Mission emphasizes salvation, healing, and the baptism in the Holy Spirit in its teaching. Its theology is trinitarian. Water baptism is administered in the name of "God the Father, Jesus Christ the Son, and the Blessed Holy Spirit." Participation in military service is left to the individual conscience. Christ Faith Mission publishes the *Herald of Hope* in five languages. The single congregation maintains no membership rolls.[162]

**The Assembly of Christian Churches, Incorporated**
**(La Asamblea de Iglesias Cristianas)**

After the death of the distinguished Mexican-born Latin-American Pentecostal evangelist, Francisco Olazábal (1886–1937), one of the churches that he founded, Bethel Christian Temple, 7 West 110th Street, New York, invited a number of Spanish-speaking Pentecostal churches and their pastors to plan a missionary crusade among the Spanish-speaking residents of New York and Puerto Rico. This was in 1939. Out of this effort grew the Assembly of Christian Churches, Incorporated (known in Puerto Rico, where work was begun in 1940, as La Asamblea de Iglesias Cristianas), which Bishop Carlos Sepúlveda, formerly a Presbyterian minister, headed until 1967.[163]

The teachings of the Assembly of Christian Churches are similar to those of the Assemblies of God. The office of bishop is elective. In addition to the continental United States (where it is incorporated in Washington, D.C., New York, Illinois, and California), Puerto Rico, and the United States Virgin Islands, the Assembly of Christian Churches has expanded into the Dominican Republic, Central and South America, and India. Except for an English-speaking congregation in St. Croix, United States Virgin Islands, with a membership of about 100, and another in Bombay, India, the Assembly of

Christian Churches carries on its work in Spanish. There are 60 churches in the continental United States, with an estimated total membership of 800. There are 54 churches in Puerto Rico, with an estimated membership of 1,200.[164] The Puerto Rican headquarters are at Calle 37, S.O. 860, Las Lomas, Río Piedras 00926.

### La Iglesia de Dios (The Church of God), Incorporada

Nine adherents of the Pentecostal faith founded La Iglesia de Dios (The Church of God) at Fajardo in eastern Puerto Rico in 1939. Growth was rapid as the church expanded westward and southwestward until it occupied the eastern, northeastern, and southeastern sectors of the island. More recently it has expanded into the United States and into the Virgin Islands.

La Iglesia de Dios, Incorporada, is Pentecostal in faith and practice. Its strongly biblical and largely outline-statement of "fundamental doctrines" has forty-nine chapters. It covers the Sacred Scriptures as the invariable rule of faith and behavior; the attributes and names of God; the angels; humankind; sin; Our Lord Jesus Christ; the atonement achieved on the cross and commemorated in the Lord's Supper; salvation; the Trinity; baptism ("John's baptism was not Christian baptism"; "one ought to administer [baptism] in the name of the Triune God"; Matthew 28:19 contains the formula for baptizing Gentiles, while Acts 2:38 illustrates how Peter as apostle to the circumcision administered it among the Jews; the baptism of the Holy Spirit has spiritual signs); abstinence from eating blood or animals smothered or strangled ("not to obey this command is to depreciate the Holy Spirit who gave it to the Gentiles"); the Christian woman's dress and behavior; the Lord's Supper and the washing of feet; tithes, offerings, and gifts; the veil with which the woman ought to cover herself in the assembly ("not a doctrine arising out of the Roman Catholic church, but one of biblical origin, and many orthodox churches have applied it through the centuries"); repentance; the new birth through the baptism of water and of the Holy Spirit; the gifts and manifestations of the Holy Spirit; the necessity of the fruits of the Spirit; divine healing as one of the signs of the Church of God; the gift of prophecy; Saturday as the only biblical day of rest; vices; the church as the body of Christ ("it ought to maintain itself separate from the state"); prayer; fasting; vigils; children and their dedication to the Lord; how a Christian ought to live in the company of others; the government of the church directed by the Holy Spirit; the second coming of Christ (two phases: the rapture of the church and the day of Christ's revelation); the resurrection of the dead; everlasting life for the just; everlasting punishment for the godless and impenitent; the need of being united for prayer; forbidden oaths; Christian marriage; Christian holiness; woman and her collaboration in the work of God ("they ought not be ordained to the ministry, but they can serve as deaconesses or missionaries under supervision"); restitution where it is possible; the changes that God made of old names; witchcraft prohibited and condemned by the Scriptures; the moral law as an unchangeable code; the ceremonial law abolished; the state of the departed ("as a divine essence, the spirit cannot die, much less be annihilated"); greed condemned; the final judgment; civil government.[165]

There are 70 churches in Puerto Rico, 18 in the continental United States (New York, Connecticut, Pennsylvania, New Jersey, Ohio, California, Illinois, Florida), and 2 in the Virgin Islands. The total membership averages 5,500, not counting children under twelve. The president receives mail at Box 7389, Barrio Obrero Station, San Juan, Puerto Rico 00916.[166]

La Iglesia de Dios, Incorporada, has no connection with other denominations of the same name.

### The Anchor Bay Evangelistic Association

In 1916 Roy John Turner, a doctor of medicine at New Baltimore, Michigan, a little northeast of Detroit on Lake St. Clair, and his wife, Blanche, accepted the Pentecostal full gospel. For five years after 1918 they conducted services in their home; in 1923 they built Bethel Temple. From 1938 to 1940 Turner served in an executive capacity at Angelus Temple of the International Church of the Foursquare Gospel in Los Angeles. Upon his return to New Baltimore in 1940 the Turners organized the Anchor Bay Evangelistic Association. Since Turner's death his wife and daughter have carried on the work at Bethel Temple, Anchor Bay Evangelistic Association, and its training school, the Anchor Bay Bible Institute.

The association's eighteen Articles of Faith declare its belief in the Bible as the inspired Word of God; the Trinity; the fall of humankind; the plan of redemption, centering around Christ's death by divine appointment as an atonement for sin, so that upon simple faith and acceptance of Christ all who call on him may be justified through his blood; the new birth as a definite experience of salvation and conversion from a life of sin to a life of righteousness; daily Christian living; water baptism by immersion in the name of the Father, the Son, and the Holy Ghost as an outward sign of an inward work; the Lord's Supper as a memorial of Christ's suffering and death, with the broken bread a type of the broken body of the Bread which came down from heaven and the wine a reminder of his shed blood; the baptism of the Holy Spirit as a definite experience subsequent to the new birth; the gifts and fruits of the Spirit; entire sanctification as the will of God for every believer; divine healing provided in the atonement as the privilege of all believers; the rapture of the church and the millennial reign of Christ and his saints on earth; everlasting life for believers; everlasting grief, regret, and torment for those who rejected Christ; a new heaven and a new earth; a ministry divinely called for soul-saving and for the spread of the gospel to the whole world; the church as the body of Christ comprising every believer born of the Spirit; and the obligation of each believer to identify self with the visible church on earth and to live in unity and fellowship.[167]

No information is available about the number of churches and missions in the United States and Canada that belong to the Anchor Bay Evangelistic Association or their total inclusive membership. The headquarters of the association are at Base and Main Streets, New Baltimore, Michigan 48047. The association supports missionaries in Africa, India, the Republic of the Philippines, and Indonesia.

### The Lamb of God Church

The Reverend Mother Rose H. Soares, a Pentecostalist minister with an Assemblies of God background, founded the Lamb of God Church in 1942 shortly before her death. It has no published statement of faith, but subscribes generally to trinitarian Pentecostal principles. It administers water baptism by immersion in the name of the Father, the Son, and the Holy Spirit.

The Lamb of God Church has grown to three local congregations, all on the island of Oahu, with a total active membership of about 300. It also maintains a Bible school for the training of missionaries. The headquarters are at 612 Isenberg Street, Honolulu, Hawaii 96817.[168]

### International Christian Churches

The Reverend Franco Manuel, a Disciples of Christ minister from the Philippines who had emigrated to Hawaii, founded the International Christian Churches in Honolulu in 1943. The organization has no statement of faith and its beliefs are an amalgam of Restoration and Pentecostal elements, so that it describes itself as "Christian [that is, Restoration movement] by confession, Pentecostal by persuasion." It administers water baptism by immersion in the name of the Father, the Son, and the Holy Spirit. It stresses the activity of the Holy Spirit in the life of the individual believer. It affirms the baptism of the Holy Spirit and regards speaking in tongues as the Holy Spirit gives utterance as evidence that the individual has received the baptism of the Holy Spirit.

The headquarters of the movement are at 2322 Kanealei Avenue, Honolulu, Hawaii 96813, where the only church on United States soil is located. The Honolulu congregation has an active membership estimated at "several hundred."

In 1961 the Hawaii congregation began work in the Republic of the Philippines.[169] During the following decade the number of churches in that country grew to seven. These branch churches are organizationally independent of the mother church and of each other.[170]

### Shiloh Chapel

Shiloh Chapel, Colorado Springs, Colorado, is a single independent, nondenominational congregation with a trinitarian Pentecostal orientation. Launched in the early 1940s, it has a membership of about 200.[171]

**The Alpha and Omega Pentecostal Church of America, Incorporated**

On March 12, 1945, Mrs. Magdelene Mabe Phillips (b. 1905) withdrew from the Holiness church body of which she had been a member and with eight other persons organized the Alpha and Omega Church of God Tabernacle. The next month it took the name Alpha and Omega Pentecostal Church; subsequently it adopted its present designation, the Alpha and Omega Pentecostal Church of America, Incorporated. In 1964, following the secession of the then presiding officer, Charles E. Waters, Sr., to form the True Fellowship Pentecostal Church of America, the brother of the foundress and a co-founder, the Reverend John Mabe, became the overseer.

Its articles of faith affirm the unity and Trinity of the Godhead; Christ's resurrection, ascension, session, and return; the deity of the Holy Ghost; eternal life with God in heaven for the finally righteous and unending torture in hell for the persistently wicked; the shedding of Christ's blood for the remission of sins, for the regeneration of persistent sinners, and for salvation from sin and sinning; justification by faith alone; the complete cleansing of the justified sinner from all indwelling sin and its pollution; entire sanctification as a definite second work of grace; the availability of the Pentecostal baptism of the Holy Ghost and fire through an act of appropriating faith by the fully cleansed believer, with speaking with other tongues as initial evidence; divine healing in the atonement; and Christ's imminent premillennial second coming. Its general rules include prohibitions of the use of tobacco, intoxicating or detrimental drinks or drugs; of immodest and extravagant styles of dress, short dresses, short sleeves, low necks, cosmetics, earrings, painted fingernails; and of divorce. The general rules also require members to observe the first day of the week as the Sabbath "according to the teachings of the Old and New Testaments." Water baptism is administered by immersion in the name of the Father, Son, and Holy Spirit.

The headquarters are at 3023 Clifton Avenue, Baltimore, Maryland 21216. The church body consists of 2 organized churches and 1 mission in that city, with an estimated total membership of 400.[172]

**The True Fellowship Pentecostal Church of America, Incorporated**

In 1964 the Reverend Charles E. Waters, Sr. (b. 1917), the third presiding officer of the Alpha and Omega Pentecostal Church of America, withdrew from that body to found the True Fellowship Pentecostal Church of America, Incorporated. Its theology is trinitarian and it administers baptism in the name of the Father, Son, and Holy Spirit.

The headquarters are at 4238 Pimlico Road, Baltimore, Maryland 21215. The 2 congregations that comprise the church body are both in Baltimore. The total active membership is estimated as in excess of 25.[173]

### Elim Missionary Assemblies

The Elim Faith Home and Bible Training School in Rochester, New York, exerted a profound influence on the Pentecostal movement in its early days. When it closed its doors in the early 1920s, an alumnus of the training school, Ivan Q. Spencer, established the Elim Bible Institute at Hornell, New York, as an independent Pentecostal school in 1924. In 1933 some of its graduates formed the Elim Ministerial Fellowship; with the inclusion of congregations as well as ministers in 1946 the Elim Missionary Assemblies came into being. A primary purpose of the Elim Missionary Assemblies—which describe themselves as "a Christ-centered worldwide revival fellowship"—is to assist the graduates of the Elim Bible Institute, located since 1951, along with the Elim Missionary Assemblies' headquarters, in Lima, New York.

In their doctrine the assemblies are Pentecostal in the trinitarian tradition; in their organization they are congregational.

They include about 75 churches, the majority in New York and Pennsylvania. The total membership numbers about 4,500. Seventy-five missionaries in 15 foreign countries, chiefly in East Africa and South America, give the assemblies an enviable missionary-member ratio.[174] The headquarters are in Lima, New York 14485.

### Samaria Iglesia Evangélica (Samaria Evangelical Church)

Born at Quebrada Vuelta, Fajardo, Puerto Rico, of Roman Catholic parents in 1903, Julio Guzmán Silva had by his late twenties combined a belief in spiritualism and in dreams with his native religion. In 1934, after a series of disconcerting dreams, he attended the Baptist church in Palmer, joined it, and soon became one of its responsible leaders. He continued to study the Bible, to pray, and to fast, and reports that he "received great baths of the Holy Spirit" along with the gift of healing and the ability to drive out demons. When the Baptist church expelled him in 1941, he initiated services in his home. In 1945 he began to engage in the ministry on a fulltime basis. Two years later the congregation in Palmer began to branch out and the Samaria Iglesia Evangélica came into being as a full-fledged denomination. It opens a new field by preaching in the plaza and then establishing preaching points in friendly homes in the town. It has reportedly expanded into the Puerto Rican population of New York, but no information is available on this aspect of its activities.

There 25 congregations in Puerto Rico, with an estimated membership of 750. The headquarters' address is P.O. Box 269, Fajardo, Puerto Rico.[175]

### United Apostolic Faith Church

One segment of the early British Pentecostal movement formed the Apostolic Faith Church under the leadership of W. O. Hutchinson, with headquarters at Bournemouth. In 1916 the Welsh assemblies withdrew to form the Apostolic Church of Wales. The assemblies in England and Scotland then organized the United Apostolic Faith Church, with headquarters in London, under the leadership first of the Reverend James Brooke (1883–1960) and later of his son, the Reverend Percy J. Brooke. An assembly of the original Apostolic Faith Church existed from around 1912 on in Toronto, Canada, but during World War II it became all but extinct through lack of proper oversight. The work was revived in 1947, and became associated with the United Apostolic Faith Church.

The United Apostolic Faith Church believes in the Bible; the divine unity and Trinity; the universal depravity of human beings; full and free salvation for all human beings purchased by Christ when he died on the cross; restitution; water baptism of believers by total immersion ("an act of obedience and of our complete union with Christ") in the name of the Father and of the Son and of the Holy Spirit; the dedication of infants; baptism in the Holy Spirit evidenced by the gift of tongues; the blood of the everlasting convenant for redemption, cleansing, sanctification, peace, justification, access to God, and overcoming power; divine healing for the whole human being in the atonement; the restoration of the church with nine manifestations of the Spirit, nine fruits of the Spirit, and the five ministry gifts of I Corinthians 12:28 and Ephesians 4:11; the return of Christ to rule in Jerusalem for a thousand years; the resurrection of both the just and the unjust; tithes and offerings; the Lord's Supper; deliverance for the whole person through the ministry of exorcism, or casting out of demons; holy matrimony as a type of the union between Christ and his church; and local church government through a presbytery of pastor and elders under Christ.[176]

There are 7 churches in Ontario, with a total membership of 1,000. In conjunction with the British mother church, the Canadian branch carries on missionary work in South Africa, Nigeria, Rhodesia, and Taiwan.[177] The Canadian headquarters are 2 Delbert Drive, Scarborough, Ontario M1P 1X1.

## Iglesia Evangélica Congregacional, Incorporada, de Puerto Rico (Evangelical Congregational Church, Incorporated, of Puerto Rico)

In the late 1930s some of the members of the congregation of the Iglesia Evangélica Unida in the Barrio Aguacate de Yabucoa, Puerto Rico, received the baptism of the Holy Spirit and fire. This led to their separation from the congregation and the creation in 1937 of a council which they called Hermanos Unidos en Cristo (United Brothers in Christ). Eleven years later, with the establishment of a number of other organized congregations, they dissolved the council and reorganized in October 1948 as the Iglesia Evangélica Congregacional, Incorporada, de Puerto Rico.

The church's Declaration of Principles and Beliefs affirms the Holy Scriptures; the Trinity; Christ's expiatory sacrifice and resurrection; two resurrections of human beings, of the just and the unjust; believer's baptism by immersion[178] for the remission of sins; the baptism of the Holy Spirit and its gifts; the Lord's Supper as a symbol of Christ's sacrifice on the cross; the solemnity of marriage as a divine institution; the obligation to bring tithes and offerings into God's house; the sanctification of the believer during this life as a condition of entering the Kingdom of God; the practice of fasting and keeping vigils as a means of grace and consecration in order to work in the Lord's name; the day of the Lord as the day of hope and salvation of the Gentiles; the ministry of prophets as in the primitive church; Christ's visible second coming, the rapture of the church, and the millennial age; and the dedication of infants in place of infant baptism. The church rejects prayers and novenas for the departed and does not believe that speaking in tongues is the only sign of the Holy Spirit's sealing.

Members must secure the permission of their pastor to visit other groups and churches and must keep the Lord's Day according to His word. Women may serve as missionaries and deaconesses. Male members may not wear their shirts loose, nor may they wear neck-chains or shirts with short sleeves or with exaggerated collars. Women must wear moderate hairdos and may not cut their hair. Their dresses may not have short sleeves or expose too much of their shoulders and necks. Their skirts and the general cut of their clothes must be appropriate to a woman who professes holiness. They must wear stockings in public and at church services and must avoid rings, necklaces, bracelets, wristwatches, expensive pins, all kinds of adornment, hoop skirts (*ropa de kan kan*), and excessively expensive fabrics, Neither sex may wear the clothing of the other. A female member who submits to sterilization to avoid bearing children is to be expelled from the church for life; so is her husband if he consents to the operation.[179]

There are 7 congregations in Puerto Rico, 2 in Chicago, and 1 in Gary, Indiana. The total membership is estimated at 575.[180] The headquarters' address is Box 396, Humacao, Puerto Rico 00661. Recent efforts to communicate with the church body have been unsuccessful.

## Independent Assemblies of God International

Many of the local Pentecostal "assemblies of God" that chose not to place themselves under the General Council of the Assemblies of God when that body came into being in 1914 were congregations of Scandinavian immigrants whom the Pentecostal movement in their homelands had converted. The Filadelfiaförsamling in Stockholm, of which Pethrus Lewi [Johansson] Pethrus was the pastor from 1911 on, and the Fildelfiamenighet in Oslo, of which Thomas Ball Barratt became pastor from 1916 until his death in 1940, had been particularly influential in this connection. These Scandinavian Pentecostals held that the organization of each local church should reflect the pattern of the Acts of the Apostles and the New Testament letters. Each church was to be sovereign and autonomous, with its only rules and bylaws the Bible and with responsibility for the discipline and conduct of all its members, including the ministers, vested in each local church.

It soon became apparent, however, that absolute independence had its disadvantages, and a number of loose federations of these independent local assemblies came into being. About 1918 a group of churches and ministers in the northwestern states organized the Scandinavian Assemblies of God in the United States, Canada, and Other Lands. Another fellowship of independent churches came into being at a regional gathering of Full Gospel ministers held at St. Paul, Minnesota, in 1922. A third group was an incorporated body that called itself the Scandinavian Independent Assemblies of God. This group was based in Chicago and included among its leaders Bengt Magnus Johnson, the founder of the Lakeview Gospel Church in that city; A. A. Holmgren, a former Baptist minister; Gunnar Wingren, a Pentecostal missionary who scored impressive successes in Brazil; Arthur Frederick Johnson; and Elmer Claude Erickson.

In 1935 the last-named group dissolved its corporation and united with the other groups as well as with other independent Pentecostal churches to form the Independent Assemblies of God. The united body gradually lost its Scandinavian character to a considerable extent.

The "Latter Rain" controversy among Pentecostals that began in western Canada in 1947[181] divided the Independent Assemblies of God. One group hailed this new outpouring of the Holy Spirit as "the present move of God" and "Bible deliverance" and formed the Independent Assemblies of God International; at the same time they rejected the extreme doctrines and practices that attended some phases of the outpouring. The more conservative group continued as the Independent Assemblies of God (Unincorporated), later changing its name to Fellowship of Christian Assemblies (Unincorporated).

The Independent Assemblies of God International believe in the Trinity, the virgin birth and deity of Christ, the necessity of repentance for salvation, water baptism for believers after salvation, the verbal inspiration of the Holy Scriptures, the baptism of the Holy Ghost evidenced by speaking in other tongues, the literal return of Christ, and eternal life for believers and eternal damnation for the wicked.

All meetings of the Independent Assemblies of God International are free conventions; they have no legislative authority. The local churches and their ministers may accept or reject any of the insights that the open Bible studies at these conventions may bring out.

A major function of the denominational organization is to confirm the status of member ministers and member churches with governmental agencies. Thus it claims approximately 1,800 ordained and licensed ministers, evangelists and missionaries, including a number of husband-and-wife teams, in 34 states, 6 provinces of Canada, Puerto Rico, and 32 foreign countries in Latin America, Europe, Africa, and Asia. The heaviest concentrations are in

Ontario, New York, Illinois, Texas, and California. The Independent Assemblies of God International claim 300 churches registered with the headquarters and an additional 200 more or less closely connected with it; the total membership of all these churches is estimated at 90,000.[182] The headquarters are at 3840 Fifth Avenue, San Diego, California 92103.

## Fellowship of Christian Assemblies (Unincorporated)

The Fellowship of Christian Assemblies (Unincorporated) share a common history with the Independent Assemblies of God International down to 1948. They stand committed to the Pentecostal distinctives as taught by the Assemblies of God, of whose literature this group makes extensive use. A typical congregational "platform of faith" is that of Westgate Chapel, Edmonds, Washington. It affirms belief in the Bible; the Trinity; salvation, manifested inwardly through the direct witness of the Spirit and outwardly through a life of righteousness and true holiness; water baptism by immersion in the name of the Father and of the Son and of the Holy Ghost; the Lord's Supper; the baptism of the Holy Spirit, with speaking in other tongues as evidence; the nine gifts of the Spirit; the nine fruits of the Spirit; divine healing accomplished through Christ's sacrifice; Christ's imminent second coming; and everlasting punishment for the wicked.[183]

The fellowship sees the New Testament as requiring the principle of local congregational autonomy, with the authority of the Bible replacing the authority that the apostles exercised in the primitive church. The New Testament is also seen as requiring spiritual fellowship, voluntary cooperation, and loving interaction among the local assemblies, resulting in an identifiable family of churches with identifiable forms of cooperative effort.[184]

The fellowship meets annually; it holds a national convention in odd-numbered years, a national ministers' institute in even-numbered years. The fellowship's monthly journal, *Conviction,* is published by the Fellowship Press, 657 West 18th Street, Los Angeles, California 90015. There are about 100 churches in 20 states from coast to coast and in four Canadian provinces; the total membership is estimated at about 17,000. Major foreign mission fields sponsored by the local assemblies are in Mexico, Africa, South America, Japan, and India.[185]

## Thea Jones Evangelistic Association, Incorporated

The Reverend Thea F. Jones incorporated the Thea Jones Evangelistic Association in Cleveland, Bradley County, Tennessee, in 1949. In 1954 he transferred the arena of his activities to Pennsylvania. Here the association acquired the old Philadelphia Metropolitan Opera House (the "Met") at 858 North Broad Street, Philadelphia, Pennsylvania 19146.

The association's statement of belief commits it to faith in God the Father as Creator; Christ's divine Sonship, virgin birth, death, and saving resurrection; the power of his blood; the gift of the Holy Ghost, the third person of the Trinity; unselfish living; holiness as a work in the heart; water baptism by immersion in the name of the Father, Son, and Holy Ghost; heaven as the home of the saved; hell as "eternal damnation and annihilation from God"; the nine gifts of the Holy Spirit; the five ministries of the Church; the prayer of faith that saves the sick; regeneration and sanctification of the heart; Christ's premillennial second coming; eternal judgment for the wicked; and the use of the Bible in winning souls.[186]

The single congregation claims a cumulative membership of over 22,-000.[187] The actual active membership has been estimated at 6,000.[188]

### Faith Chapel (Zephyrhills, Florida)

In 1926 Mrs. Anna Rosenberger began to found congregations of Pentecostal Sabbath-keepers in various German-speaking cities of her native Switzerland. Her husband, Elder George Rosenberger (d. 1965), joined her in this venture in 1940. In 1951 they came to the United States. They established themselves at Zephyrhills, Florida. With this as their headquarters, they began a ministry chiefly to German-speaking Americans, although they continued to divide their time between Switzerland and the United States conducting revivals. Mrs. Rosenberger has been carrying on the work alone since her husband's death.

Faith Chapel is trinitarian. It teaches the sinfulness and guilt of all human beings; the substitutionary suffering and death of Christ; the need for a confession of guilt and the acceptance of God's reconciliation; believer's baptism by immersion in water in the name of the Father, the Son, and the Holy Spirit; the signs of Mark 16:16-18 and the spiritual gifts of I Corinthians 12 and 14; speaking in tongues in the public services only in order and only if there is an interpreter present (if none is present, adherents may speak in tongues only at home); the necessity of keeping all of the Ten Commandments, including the observance of Saturday as the Sabbath; God's final judgment on the basis of the Ten Commandments; everlasting life only through faith in Christ's death and blood; the possibility through faith of not sinning any more; the new birth from the Father through Christ's resurrection; the necessity of putting off the "old man" and of putting on the "new man"; Christ's imminent return and the rapture of the believers to meet him in the air and afterward to reign as kings and priests on a new earth.

Faith Chapel is located at 607 23rd Street, Zephyrhills, Florida 33599. The number of worshipers varies with the season and has gone as high as 128.[189]

## The Full Gospel Church Association, Incorporated

The Reverend Dennis W. Thorn organized the Full Gospel Church Association, Incorporated, at Amarillo, Texas, in 1952 in order to bring together as many as possible of the small independent Pentecostal churches and missions, most of them with memberships between 10 and 100, in the southern and western parts of the United States. The association uses the King James Version of the Bible, and requires each church to have an "altar of God" in its building as a condition of recognition. Its articles of faith affirm belief in the Bible as the inspired Word of God; the Trinity; humankind's creation in holiness; humankind's fall; God's altar; sanctification; baptism with the Holy Ghost evidenced by speaking with other tongues; the Spirit-filled life and true holiness; water baptism by immersion in the name of the Father, and of the Son, and of the Holy Ghost; the Lord's Supper with the broken bread and the juice of the vine as types of Christ's broken body and shed blood; foot washing; the church as the body of Christ; the gifts and fruits of the Spirit; divine healing in the atonement; tithing; heaven; the final judgment and the eternal hell or lake of fire; and Christ's second coming for the rapture of his saints and the revelation of his millennial Kingdom. It regards worldwide evangelism as the supreme privilege and duty of the church; leaves participation in combat and the taking of life in time of war to the individual's conscience; and forbids disloyalty, insubordination, and criticism of the association by its ministerial members.[190]

The general board of directors meets four times a year; its executive directors are the supreme council of the association. The general convention meets at the call of the general board. The headquarters of the association are at Box 265, Amarillo, Texas 79105. Since 1955 it has belonged to the National Association of Evangelicals. There are 72 churches holding active charters with the association; these churches have an inclusive membership estimated at 2,010. The association carries on foreign missions in Mexico, the Republic of the Philippines, and Africa.[191]

## Bethany Chapel (Long Beach, California)

The Reverend and Mrs. David Schoch founded Bethany Chapel at Long Beach, California, in 1953, and incorporated the Bethany Chapel Missionary Society the following year. In its teachings Bethany Chapel apparently shares the trinitarian, Arminian, and premillennial position of the Apostolic Church that grew out of the Welsh Pentecostal revival of 1904–1905. Radio and prayer ministries occupy a significant role in the work of Bethany Chapel. In 1964 it established a Bible school for the training of ministers and missionaries. The society conducts missions in Brazil, Africa, Japan, and New Zealand. The membership of Bethany Chapel is estimated at 300.[192] Bethany Chapel is located at 2201 East Sixth Street, Long Beach, California 90814.

**Hall Deliverance Foundation, Incorporated (Clothing of Power Church)**

Reared a Methodist, the Reverend Franklin Hall began his ministry as a Pentecostal evangelist in 1932. He incorporated the Hall Deliverance Foundation at San Diego, California, in 1956. In 1960 he transferred his base of activity to Phoenix and Scottsdale, Arizona. In 1966 he began to publish the quarterly journal *Miracle Word*.

The doctrinal position of his movement is basically Pentecostal. The major differences between his teaching and that of most Pentecostal movements consist of his extraordinary stress on fasting and his insistence that full baptism with the Holy Spirit includes the unquenchable and undying "Holy Ghost fire" and "body-felt salvation." He holds that Christ redeemed the bodies and the souls of human beings from the "Adamic curse of sickness" as well as from "the Adamic curse of sin" by his vicarious sufferings at the "two trees," the "whipping post tree," where he was scourged and received the stripes by which human beings are healed, and the "tree of the cross" on Golgotha, where he shed his blood for human beings. The movement affirms the tangibility of both phases of salvation, the awareness that Jesus is in the believer's soul and the perceptible enveloping of the believer's body by the "glory substance" of "Holy Ghost fire" that flows from Christ's warm glorified body. This "Holy Ghost sun tan of healing" upon the believer's flesh burns away the chaff, that is, disease-producing toxemia, protects the recipient from sickness, enables him to bring forth the fruit of the Spirit described in Galatians 5:22-23, and guarantees survival in holocausts. He is no longer affected by weariness and can break the enslaving chains of food addiction, surfeiting, wrong environment, fear, worry, and timidity.[193]

The Hall Deliverance Foundation is trinitarian and administers baptism in the name of the Father, Son, and Holy Spirit. As its doctrinal basis it professes the Apostles' Creed (in the plural: "We believe"), with "the holy catholic church" replaced by "the one holy universal world church."[194]

The headquarters of the Hall Deliverance Foundation, Incorporated, are at 9840 North 15th Street, Phoenix, Arizona 85020. A "Clothing of Power" convention is held annually in Phoenix.[195] There are 32 affiliated churches from Arizona to New York that have been opened largely as a result of Hall's cross-country evangelistic ministry, with an estimated total active members of more than 2,000. Another 20 affiliated churches are overseas.[196]

**Chinese-American New Testament Missionary Fellowship**

In 1955 Missouri-born Hong C. Sit, pastor of the Chinese Southern Baptist Church in Houston, Texas, received the baptism of the Holy Spirit, evidenced by speaking in other tongues, and determined to dedicate his life to evangelizing the Chinese of the Far East. In the light of his experience he felt that it would be fruitless to apply to a missionary society for support in the implementation of his purpose. On October 1956 he resigned his pastorate and organized the Chinese-American New Testament Missionary Fellowship with a view to reaching "by direct evangelism and through New Testament churches" Chinese whom Christianity had not succeeded in touching. In the furtherance of his purpose he founded Grace Chapel, now located at 1055 Bingle Road, Houston, Texas 77055, and the bilingual Chinese-American New Testament Missionary Bible School for the training of missionaries. During the first decade the latter agency produced three graduates who are actively engaged in missionary work. In addition, Sit himself spent three years in missionary work in the Far East and in Australia.

The theology of the movement combines Reformed, Baptist, and Pentecostal emphases. It stresses the sovereignty and grace of God; the necessity of faith, understood as taking God at his word; believers' baptism by immersion; the dedication of children; and the charismatic gifts of the Spirit, especially speaking in tongues, prophecy, and healing.

Grace Chapel maintains no membership roster. The average Sunday morning attendance is about 125; the total number of adherents is estimated at 200. The fellowship, which operates on the faith-mission principle, supports missionaries in Hong Kong and in the Republic of China (Taiwan) and contributes to the support of missionaries in Japan, Mexico, Colombia, and Brazil.

### Miracle Revival Fellowship

Evangelist A. A. Allen (d. 1970) entered the ministry in 1936. Increasingly repelled by what he describes as "denominationalism" even in the Full Gospel movement, he organized the Miracle Revival Fellowship in 1956 for two purposes: (1) to provide independent Pentecostal ministers and congregations with an undenominational kind of "fellowship without bondage" that transcends doctrinal differences and (2) to secure for these churches the benefits of tax exemption as independent religious corporations, exemption from Selective Service for their ministers, the use of public property, radio, and television, and freedom of speech, freedom of assembly, and freedom to exercise an apostolic ministry of healing. Membership in the Miracle Revival Fellowship entitles the ordained minister-member to a minister's fellowship card. On the principle that every believer should be an exhorter who heals the sick and casts out devils, the fellowship offers exhorter's credentials that certify the holders as qualified gospel workers to unordained applicants who belong to the fellowship and who feel a call to some kind of Christian ministry.[197]

Beginning in 1958 Allen attempted to create a Christian municipality at Miracle Valley, Arizona 85645. Here the Miracle Valley Bible College prepares students for the fellowship's ministry through both resident and correspondence courses; here Miracle Films produces visual records of Allen's domestic and foreign evangelist campaigns for screen and television use; here Miracle Revival Fellowship radio programs are taped; here Miracle Records are recorded; and here *Miracle Magazine* (which claims over 1.5 million readers) is published.[198]

The fellowship's doctrinal statement does not compel members to agree on all points of doctrine, but it states that "contention and confusion due to any such difference of doctrine will not be tolerated." It affirms belief in the verbal inspiration of the Bible; the deity, incarnation and saviorhood of Christ; his death, resurrection, and ascension; the bodily resurrection of the just to everlasting rewards and the unjust to everlasting, conscious suffering; Christ's appearance for the rapture of the living believers who are prepared for it; the filling of all believers with the Holy Spirit, with the speaking of an unlearned tongue as the initial physical evidence of this experience; personal holiness; the Trinity; the expression of true faith in living service for God and fellow human beings; the unity of Christians on the basis of the "essential doctrine that Jesus Christ, the Son of God, came in the flesh, died for our sins, and rose again"; miracles accompanying the preaching of the gospel as a witness in every nation; living fellowship between believers; and the unity of blood of all nations of men.[199] Baptism is for believers only and is by immersion.

The Miracle Revival Fellowship has belonging to it an estimated 500 churches in the United States and Canada, with about 10,000 members. It carries on foreign missions in the Republic of the Philippines and a number of countries of Latin America.[200]

## Pentecostal Free Will Baptist Church, Incorporated

The Pentecostal Free Will Baptist Church, Incorporated, traces its Free Will Baptist ancestry back to the late eighteenth century, when Benjamin Randall began to preach his doctrines of "free will" and of sanctification as an instantaneous work of God's grace among the Baptists of northern New England. From here Randall's type of doctrine filtered down into North Carolina. In 1855 the Cape Fear Conference of Free Will Baptists furnished the first organization at the conference level. In 1908 the growing conference divided by establishing the Wilmington Conference; it repeated the process in 1911 by establishing the New River Conference. During this period most of the Free Will Baptists of North Carolina had accepted the Pentecostal doctrine of baptism with the Holy Spirit accompanied by speaking in tongues as initial evidence. In 1912 the Cape Fear Conference suffered a minor schism when a group of ministers and laity who rejected both the doctrine of sanctification and the doctrine of the Pentecostal baptism with the Holy Spirit withdrew. In 1943 the three North Carolina conferences joined with a like-minded conference in South Carolina, the Free Will Baptist Church of Pentecostal Faith, to form a general conference. By the 1950s the North Carolina conferences wanted organic union. At this point the South Carolina body with-drew. The North Carolina conferences consolidated as the Pentecostal Free Will Baptist Church, Incorporated, in 1959. Negotiations looking to eventual organic union are continuing with the Free Will Baptist Church of Pente-costal Faith.

Current emphases of the Pentecostal Free Will Baptist Church are on the establishment of churches in urban centers, development of an educated ministry, literature production and promotion, and efficient utilization of its central organization.[201]

Its basic statement of faith, "This We Believe," asserts the inspiration of the Bible; the Trinity; Christ's deity and saviorhood; the necessity of repen-tance for the forgiveness of sins; justification by faith alone and the absolute essentiality of the new birth through faith in Christ's blood; sanctification as a second definite, instantaneous work of grace subsequent to regeneration; the Pentecostal baptism of the Holy Ghost with speaking in other tongues as initial evidence; water baptism of believers in the name of the Father and of the Son and of the Holy Spirit; divine healing as a blessing provided in the atonement; the sacrament of the Lord's supper as commemorating his death and anticipating his second coming; foot washing; the personal, premillennial second coming of Christ; and the bodily resurrection of the saved to life eternal and of the lost to everlasting punishment.[202]

Nineteen of the articles under the head of "Faith" in the *Discipline* expand the shorter statement. They discuss the Bible; the true God; divine government and providences; creation, humanity's primitive state, and the fall; Christ; the Holy Spirit; Christ's atonement and mediation; the gospel call ("coextensive with the atonement of all men"); salvation (with sections on regeneration, repentance, faith, justification, sanctification from the human being's side and God's side, the baptism of the Holy Ghost, divine healing, and Christ's second coming); gifts of the Spirit; perseverance of the saints; death and the intermediate state; the resurrection, final judgment, and rewards; the Sabbath (including a protest against such activities as unnecessary buying and selling, "attending meetings of worldly amusements, visiting pleasure resorts, [and] promiscuous and questionable joy-riding" on Sunday; worldy and sinful amusements; temperance ("members who persist in the use or selling of intoxicating liquors, after they have been admonished, are to be excluded"); tithing of net total income from all sources to the local church, in addition to free-will offerings; divorce ("the Board of Deacons of the local church and the pastor in charge . . . shall have the power to make a final decision in the matter"); and the church.[203] Among the requirements for entering the ministry are that the candidate not be guilty of using tobacco and if divorced should not remarry as long as the former spouse is alive.[204]

The denomination's headquarters' address is Box 1081, Dunn, North Carolina 28334. It has 128 churches in North Carolia, Virginia, and Hawaii with a total membership of 10,000. It carries on foreign missions in India, Mexico, and the Republic of the Philippines.

## Free Will Baptist Church of the Pentecostal Faith

Some Free Will Baptists in South Carolina accepted the Pentecostal message before 1920, but the bulk of them who became Pentecostalists did so in the 1920s and the early 1930s. The individual congregations maintained their autonomy, but a South Carolina conference of Pentecostal Free Will Baptists came into being in 1923. In 1943 this conference joined three like-minded conferences in North Carolina in a general conference. Within this framework the four conferences engaged in limited cooperative efforts, notably the production of educational materials.

The South Carolina conference felt itself more conservative in doctrine and practice, and in 1958 it severed its fellowship with the North Carolina conferences. The following year, while the North Carolina conferences were uniting in the Pentecostal Free Will Baptist Church, the South Carolina conference incorporated itself under the intentionally different name of Free-Will Baptist Church of the Pentecostal Faith. It ratified its discipline in 1961 and adopted a new constitution in 1965. Union with the Pentecostal Free Will Baptist Church and with the Pentecostal Holiness Church has been under recent discussion; the obstacles are chiefly nontheological and have to do with such matters as the ministers' retirement program and the conduct of missions.

The faith of the Free-Will Baptist Church of Pentecostal Faith, as set forth in its discipline, has sections on the Bible; the true God; divine government and providences; creation, the primitive state of humankind, and the fall; Christ; the Holy Spirit; the atonement and mediation of Christ; the gospel call ("coextensive with the atonement of all men . . . so that salvation is rendered equally possible to all"); repentance; faith; regeneration; justification; sanctification ("[on] man's side a complete consecration of himself and all he is to God and His service [and on God's side] an instantaneous work of God's grace . . . subsequent to regeneration"); the baptism of the Holy Ghost with the speaking in other tongues as evidence; the gifts of the Spirit; the perseverance of the saints ("their future obedience and final salvation are neither determined nor certain"); the Lord's Day ("by authority of the apostles [the first day of the week] is observed as the Christian sabbath"); worldly and sinful amusements; temperance ("members . . . who persist in the use of intoxicating liquors, after they have been admonished, are to be excluded; we believe that the use of tobacco in any form is in direct opposition to the principles of gospel temperance"); tithing; divorce ("only one scriptural reason for divorce, and that is fornication . . . . [No Scripture] sets either the husband or wife free to marry again so long as both parties live"); the church; the gospel ministry; believer's baptism by immersion in the name of the Father and of the Son and of the Holy Ghost, the Lord's Supper ("Christ made the [bread] the emblem of His broken body and the cup the emblem of His shed blood"), foot washing, and the laying on of hands as ordinances of the gospel;

death and the intermediate state; Christ's second coming "to close the gospel dispensation, glorify His saints, and judge the world"; the resurrection; and the general judgment and future retribution.[205]

The headquarters' address is P.O. Box 278, Elgin, South Carolina 29045. The conference meets annually. Five districts are under district pastors. There are 38 churches and missions (including one in Georgia and two in North Carolina) with a total membership of 1,300. The church body carries on foreign missions in Mexico, Costa Rica, and the Argentine Republic.[206]

### Gospel Harvester Evangelistic Association (Atlanta, Georgia)

The Gospel Harvester Evangelistic Association of Atlanta, Georgia, takes its name from Matthew 9:36-38. Its founders, Earl P. Paulk, Jr., Donald L. Paulk, and Harry A. Mushegan, all ordained ministers, organized the association on Easter Day, 1961.

The association's Declaration of Faith affirms the inspiration of the whole Bible; the Trinity; Christ's incarnation, virgin birth, death, and rising again; salvation through repentance and faith in the shed blood of Christ; divine healing through the atonement; water baptism by immersion in the name of the Father and of the Son and of the Holy Ghost; the Lord's Supper; the baptism of the Holy Spirit as a definite experience for all believers subsequent to conversion to endue them with power and equip them for service; Christ's personal, imminent, and premillennial coming; daily sanctification and a holy, separated life; the resurrection of the dead, the final judgment, and a literal heaven and hell.[207]

The local conference controls the association. Each church has its own quarterly conference. Seven pastors, missionaries, and evangelists comprise the ministerial membership; there are 2 congregations in Atlanta, with about 800 members.[208] The headquarters are at 836 Euclid Avenue, Northeast, Atlanta, Georgia 30307.

### Gospel Harvesters Evangelistic Association, Incorporated (Buffalo, New York)

Evangelist Rose Pezzino incorporated the Gospel Harvesters Evangelistic Association in 1962.

The association's statement of faith and practice has paragraphs on the inspiration of the Scriptures; the Trinity; the fall, redemption, and salvation of human beings; the baptism of the Spirit; divine healing; the second coming and the millennial reign of Christ; the lake of fire; and the new heavens and the new earth. The text of most of these paragraphs appears to be a condensed and nearly verbatim abbreviation of the Statement of Fundamental Truths of the Assemblies of God. The association's statement stresses the "total[ly] depraved condition" of human beings, the "literal" nature of Christ's return and his millennial reign, and the final passing away of "this earth which has been polluted by sin."[209]

The headquarters of the association are at 1159 Seneca Street, Buffalo, New York 14210. The foundress claims "many groups" of supporters in the southern states, as well as a group in Toronto, Canada. Since 1963 the association has sponsored an affiliated association in Manila, Republic of the Philippines, and maintains an office at Jabalpur, Madhya Pradesh, India. The foundress estimates her worldwide following at 2,000.[210] The association has no connection with the similarly named association in Atlanta, Georgia.

### The Alpha and Omega Christian Church

In 1962 a dissatisfied group of Filipino immigrants to Hawaii who belonged to the Pearl City Full Gospel Mission withdrew under the leadership of Alejandro B. Fagaragan. They organized the Alpha and Omega Christian Church, with headquarters at 96-171 Kamehameha Highway, Pearl City, Honolulu, Hawaii 87682. Fagaragan became the new congregation's minister. In 1966 some of the members of the church returned to the Philippines and organized a congregation at Dingras in the province of Ilocos Norte on the northwest tip of Luzon.[211] After a disastrous flood in 1968, which all but destroyed the Pearl City church, the bulk of the membership in Hawaii reportedly fell away.

The Alpha and Omega Christian Church believes in the inspiration of the Bible; the Trinity; Christ's deity, virgin birth, atoning death, bodily resurrection, and ascension; evangelistic and missionary fervor and endeavor; salvation through Christ's redeeming blood; God's keeping power; sanctification, holiness of heart, and the overcoming life; the baptism of the Holy Spirit, the present ministry of the Spirit in and through the believer as manifested in the five ministries of Ephesians 4:11 as they are being restored in the end-time revival, the gifts of the Spirit of I Corinthians 12:8-11, and the fruit of the Spirit of Galatians 5:22-23; divine healing to be obtained on the basis of the atonement; Christ's imminent personal return in power and glory, his millennial reign, and his everlasting dominion; the resurrection of the saved to eternal life and the resurrection of the lost to eternal punishment.[212]

The two congregations described comprise the church body. No information is available on the size of the active membership.[213]

### United Evangelical Churches

In 1959 two Monrovia, California, Methodist ministers, the Reverend Charles J. Hardin and the Reverend Merrill H. Eve (d. 1962), sharers of a common vision of a fellowship that they could regard as genuinely evangelical and Spirit-led, formed a ministerial group. Out of it there grew in 1964, under the leadership of Hardin and of an Assemblies of God minister, the Reverend

Delbert Hosteller, also a Monrovia clergyman, the United Evangelical Churches. The fellowship describes itself as open to persons of all denominations who share its evangelical heritage and its belief in the Spirit's moving in this day.

The fellowship's "tenets of faith" affirm belief in the Bible as the inspired, infallible, and authoritative Word of God; in one God eternally existent in three personalities, Father, Son, and Holy Spirit; in Christ's virgin birth, miracles, sinlessness, atoning death, bodily resurrection, ascension, and personal return in power and glory; in the total inability of human beings to save themselves by their unaided effort; in salvation through a complete commitment to Christ and rebirth by the Holy Spirit; in the present ministry of the Holy Spirit, whose indwelling empowers Christians to live victorious lives and who imparts to the church miraculous gifts and ministries;[214] and in the appearance of every human being before Christ's judgment seat to give an account of his or her stewardship of the earthly life.[215]

The fellowship sees itself as organized like a denomination for the purpose of granting ministerial credentials and publishing religious materials; at the same time membership in the fellowship does not affect membership in any existing denomination. It regards itself as an association in which the members have a keen sense of obligation to the other members individually and collectively. It recognizes the oneness of all who are baptized in the Spirit into Christ's body, but it does not oppose denominational names and distinctions. The membership consists chiefly of ministers, missionaries, chaplains, and lay groups. Member churches and groups retain their autonomy.[216]

The headquarters' address of the United Evangelical Churches is Box 28, Monrovia, California 91016. Affiliated with the fellowship are 32 churches, groups, and agencies, plus 23 others whose directors belong to the United Evangelical Churches. The ministerial membership is estimated at 250. No information on the total membership is available. Missionary members of the fellowship are active in Central and South America, and in the Middle and Far East.[217]

# NOTES

1. Further world conferences have since been held every three years.
2. See Klaude Kenrick, *The Promise Fulfilled: A History of the Modern Pentecostal Movement* (Springfield, Mo.: Gospel Publishing House, 1961), pp. 210-214; John Thomas Nichol, *Pentecostalism* (New York: Harper & Row, 1966), pp. 215-218.
3. *Pentecostal Fellowship of North America: Origin, Progress, Program, Objectives, Doctrines, Membership* (rev. edn.; Los Angeles: Pentecostal

Fellowship of North America, 1966) (a 6-page pamphlet), p. [4].
4. The following Pentecostal denominations belong to the Pentecostal Fellowship of North America: Anchor Bay Evangelistic Association; Assemblies of God; Carolina Evangelistic Association; Christian Church of North America; Church of God of Apostolic Faith; Church of God (Cleveland, Tennessee); Church of God of the Mountain Assembly; Congregational Holiness Church; Elim

Fellowship; Emmanuel Holiness Church; Free Gospel Church, Incorporated; Free Will Baptist Church of Pentecostal Faith; International Church of the Foursquare Gospel; International Pentecostal Assemblies; Italian Pentecostal Church of Canada; Open Bible Standard Churches, Incorporated; Pentecostal Assemblies of Canada; Pentecostal Assemblies of Newfoundland and Labrador; Pentecostal Church of God of America; Pentecostal Church of Christ; Pentecostal Free-Will Baptist Church; Pentecostal Holiness Church; and Pentecostal Holiness Church of Canada.

5. This writer's repeated efforts to obtain authoritative information from the leadership of the United Holy Church of America, Incorporated were unsuccessful.

6. *Manual of Mount Sinai Holy Church of America* (rev. edn.; Philadelphia, Penn.: Mount Sinai Holy Church of America, 1947) (48-page pamphlet), pp. 11-13.

7. Ibid., pp. 14-26.

8. Ibid., pp. 39-46.

9. Letter from Bishop Mary E. Jackson, president and senior bishop, Mount Sinai Holy Church of America, Incorporated. There has been no response to recent efforts to communicate with church body officers.

10. The Azusa Street Mission is described in chap. 4, above.

11. Klaude Kendrick, *The Promise Fulfilled: A History of the Modern Pentecostal Movement* (Springfield, Mo.: Gospel Publishing House, 1961), pp. 184-185; John Thomas Nichol, *Pentecostalism* (New York: Harper & Row, 1966), pp. 106-107.

12. Joseph Campbell, *The Pentecostal Holiness Church 1898–1948* (Franklin Springs, Ga.: The Publishing House of the Pentecostal Holiness Church, 1951), p. 277.

13. *Discipline of the Congregational Holiness Church* (rev. edn.; Greenwood, S.C.: Congregational Holiness Publishing House, 1964) (16-page pamphlet), pp. 2-3. See also the extensive exposition of the doctrine of the church body in B. L. Cox, *History and Doctrine of the Congregational Holiness Church* (Greenwood, S.C.: Congregational Holiness Publishing House,

1958) (80-page brochure), pp. 14-80.

14. Ibid., pp. 3-4.

15. Ibid., pp. 4-5.

16. Ibid., p. 6.

17. *First Interdenominational Christian Association: Our Rules and Faith* (Atlanta, Ga.: Calvary Temple, n.d.) (4-page pamphlete), pp. 1-2.

18. Letter from the Reverend John W. Sorrow, Sr., 2885 Grand Avenue, Southwest, Atlanta, associate pastor, Calvary Temple Holiness Church.

19. She became Mrs. Mildred Johnson Brostek after her marriage in 1938 to a United States Army officer.

20. Letter from the Reverend Mildred Johnson Brostek, general superintendent and founder, Door of Faith Churches of Hawaii.

21. Luther Gibson, *History of the Church of God, Mountain Assembly* (Jellico, Tenn.: Church of God of the Mountain Assembly, 1954) (53-page pamphlet).

22. "Teachings of the Church of God," *Minutes, Church of God of the Mountain Assembly, Incorporated, 1966* (Jellico, Tenn.: Church of God of the Mountain Assembly, 1966), pp. 4-5.

23. Ibid., pp. 13, 16.

24. Communication from J. L. Cox, Jr., general secretary.

25. They number their annual assemblies from 1906—so that the one held in 1968, for instance, is counted as the 62nd—to stress their conviction that they are the true continuation of the original movement.

26. "Teachings of the Church of God at the Original Mountain Assembly," *Minutes of the Churches of God of the Original Mountain Assembly, Incorporated, 1967–1968* (Williamsburg, Ky.: Churches of God of the Original Mountain Assembly, 1967), pp. 26-27.

27. Charles Fox Parham, "The Latter Rain: The Story of the Origin of the Original Apostolic or Pentecostal Movements" (10-page hektographed reproduction of an article published in *The Apostolic Faith* in 1926), p. 1.

28. Parham seems to have coined the name; it is a synonym for "Full Gospel" or "Pentecostal."

29. Gordon F. Atter, *The Third Force* (rev. edn.; Peterborough, Ontario: The College Press, 1965), p. 92.

30. Parham, p. 8. See also Lula A. Parham, *Movement History* (Baxter Springs, Kan.: Apostolic Faith Bible School, 1966) (12-page mimeographed brochure), and Gail Schultz, *Life of Charles Fox Parham* (Baxter Springs, Kan.: Apostolic Faith Bible School, n.d.) (6-page hektographed pamphlet).

31. *Doctrinal Teachings of the Apostolic Faith Movement* (Baxter Springs, Kan.: Apostolic Faith Bible School, n.d.) (6-page tract). Holiness influence is apparent in the view of sanctification as a "second, definite work of grace." Foot washing and a policy of faith in financial matters also differentiate this movement from most other Pentecostals. (See John Thomas Nichol, *Pentecostalism* [New York: Harper & Row, 1966], p. 97, n. 12).

32. *The Apostolic Faith* 28 (April 1951): 10-11.

33. Communication from Elder Paul A. Clonton, superintendent, Apostolic Faith Bible School, Baxter Springs, Kansas.

34. Noel McNeill, "As of a Rushing Mighty Wind" (unpublished manuscript), p. 76.

35. *Full Gospel Evangelistic Association* (undated 4-page tract), p. [4].

36. Communication from the Reverend Elvis O. Bishop, P.O. Box 315, Perryton, Texas 79070.

37. *A Historical Account of the Apostolic Faith: A Trinitarian-Fundamental Evangelistic Organization* (Portland, Ore.: The Apostolic Faith, 1965), pp. 48-50.

38. Elmer T. Clark, *The Small Sects in America* (rev. edn.; Nashville: Abingdon-Cokesbury Press, 1949), p. 119. At the present writer's request the Reverend Earl F. Krupp, pastor of the Church of the Redeemer, Enid, Oklahoma, undertook a careful investigation of the Enid area in the spring of 1967 without being able to find any traces of the Free Church of God in Christ. The Church of God in Christ (Pentecostal), listed by Clark (p. 110) as having 9 churches and 200 members likewise could not be traced; a letter addressed to its bishop at Bluefield, West Virginia, in February 1967 came back endorsed: "Addressee unknown."

39. "Articles of Religion," in the official *Manual of the Church of God in Christ* (7th edn.; Memphis: The Church of God in Christ, 1957), pp. 42-66; Charles Harrison Mason, "Doctrine of the Church of God in Christ," in C. A. Ashworth and U. E. Miller, eds., *1960–1961 Yearbook of the Church of God in Christ* (Memphis: Church of God in Christ, 1960), pp. 152-153.

40. This material is based on the information about the church body in *Yearbook of American and Canadian Churches 1977*, edited by Constant H. Jacquet, Jr. (Nashville: Abingdon, 1977), pp. 44-45.

41. *Discipline of the F.B.H. Church of God in the Americas* (Atlanta: The Fuller Press, 1962), pp. 9-13.

42. Ibid., pp. 13-14.

43. For the full text of the "Preamble and Resolution on Constitution," see Klaude Kendrick, *The Promise Fulfilled: A History of the Modern Pentecostal Movement* (Springfield, Mo.: Gospel Publishing House, 1961), pp. 84-85. According to Harmon Alden Johnson of the School of World Mission and Institute of Church Work, Fuller Theological Seminary, Pasadena, California, the first registered use of the name "Assembly of God" occurred on June 18, 1911, when the newly established Pentecostal church in Belém, Pará, Brazil, registered with the government as Sociedad Evangélica "Assembleia de Deus" (letter from the Reverend Mr. Johnson to the present writer).

44. See S. C. Burnett, *Early History of the Assemblies of God* (Springfield, Mo.: Assemblies of God, 1958) (27-page mimeographed pamphlet). In the course of time the Assemblies of God absorbed a considerable number of previously independent churches. A case in point is the Full Gospel Tabernacle, Reedley, California, a member of the consultative council of the National Interreligious Service Board for Conscientious Objectors. An independent tabernacle, it joined the Assemblies of God in the 1930s.

45. Frederick L. Whitam and others, *A Report on the Protestant Spanish Community in New York City* (New

York: The Protestant Council of the City of New York, 1960), p. 36.

46. *General Council of the Assemblies of God Statement of Fundamental Truths (Article V—Constitution, Revised 1961)* (undated 4-page pamphlet).

47. *Puerto Rico para Cristo: A History of the Progress of the Evangelical Missions on the Island of Puerto Rico* (Cuernavaca, Mexico: Centro Intercultural de Documentacion, 1969), pp. 3/37-3/48.

48. Article V ("Doctrinas Fundamentales"), *Constitución y Reglamento de la Iglesia de Dios Pentecostal "The Pentecostal Church of God, Inc."* (rev. edn., Río Piedras, Puerto Rico: Iglésia de Dios Pentecostal, 1954) (56-page pamphlet), pp. 4-9.

49. Letters from the Reverend Andrés Ríos, general secretary, the Pentecostal Church of God, Incorporated, of Puerto Rico.

50. *Concerning the Faith,* a catechism by Dr. Purdie which the Pentecostal Assemblies of Canada put out in 1951, included the so-called Apostles', Nicene, and Athanasian creeds.

51. *Statement of Fundamental and Essential Truths* (Toronto: The Pentecostal Assemblies of Canada, 1957) (7-page pamphlet).

52. Letter of the Reverend Earl Kulbeck, director of Public Relations.

53. Letters from the Reverend A. Stanley Bursey, president, and Roy D. King, secretary-treasurer.

54. Letter from the Reverend Daniel Ippolito, general superintendent, the Italian Pentecostal Church of Canada.

55. *What We Believe and Why? An Examination of the Statement of Faith of the Calvary Pentecostal Church* (undated 18-page mimeographed study outline), p. 7, says of water baptism: "We are not baptized to get saved, but because we are." The same lesson describes the Lord's Supper as both a memorial and "a sacramental experience in which I look past the emblems and discern the body and blood of Jesus in a spiritual sense." It also states that some of the Calvary Pentecostal churches practice foot washing, although this is "not a set doctrine."

56. "Scriptural Statement of Fundamentals," *Constitution and By-Laws of the Calvary Pentecostal Church,* 16th edn.; Olympia, Wash.: Calvary Pentecostal Church, 1962) (21-page pamphlet), pp. 3-6.

57. Ibid., p. 15.

58. Ibid., p. 16.

59. Letter of the Reverend Felix Rivera Cardona, Mayaguez, Puerto Rico, founder and presbyter-general of the council of the Iglesia Pentecostal de Jesucristo, Incorporada, en Puerto Rico.

60. Articles IV ("Principios") and 5 ("Doctrinas Fundamentales"), "Declaracion Constitucional," *Constitución y Reglamento del Concilio Latino-Americano de la Iglesia de Dios Pentecostal de New York, Incorporado* (New York: Latin-American Council of the Pentecostal Church of God, 1958), pp. 3-12.

61. Communication from the Reverend Abelardo Berrios, president, Latin-American Council of the Pentecostal Church of God, Incorporated.

62. Article VI ("Acuerdos Esenciales"), "Reglamento," *Constitución y Reglamento,* p. 22.

63. Letter from the Reverend Abelardo Berrios; Frederick L. Whitam and others, *A Report on the Protestant Spanish Community in New York City* (New York: The Protestant Council of the City of New York, 1960), p. 37.

64. *The Articles of Faith of the General Conference of the Church of God of the Apostolic Faith, Incorporated* (rev. edn. Tulsa, Okla.: The Church of God of the Apostolic Faith, 1966) (27-page pamphlet), pp. 2-6.

65. Ibid., pp. 7-8.

66. Ibid., pp. 9-18.

67. This name rather than the name of the parent body was adopted for the work in Mexico because of the association of the designation "Apostolic Faith" with the "oneness" movement in Latin American Pentecostalism. The Articles of Faith of the Mexican daughter church show great indebtedness to the Declaration of Faith compiled by Aimee Semple McPherson, foundress of the Church of the Foursquare Gospel (see *Articulos de Fe* [Reynosa, Tamaulipas, Mexico: Iglesia Cristiana Evangelica Mexicana, n.d.] [8-page pamphlet]).

68. L. Sigsbee Miller, "The International

Pentecostal Assemblies," *Pentecostal Evangel* 45 (August 18, 1957): 20; quoted in John Thomas Nichol, *Pentecostalism* (New York: Harper & Row, 1966), p. 143.

69. *General Principles of the International Pentecostal Assemblies* (Atlanta, Ga.: International Pentecostal Assemblies, n.d.) (8-page pamphlet).

70. Horace Ward, Jr. *An Introduction to the Pentecostal Church of Christ* (London, Ohio: The Pentecostal Church of Christ) (6-page pamphlet), p. 4.

71. Communication from Chester I. Miller, general overseer.

72. On the early history of the Apostolic Church, see Gordon F. Atter, *The Third Force* (rev. edn.; Peterborough, Ontario: The College Press, 1965), pp. 105, 137; John Thomas Nichol, *Pentecostalism* (New York: Harper & Row, 1966), pp. 84, 161-162, 180-182.

73. *Fundamentals: A Brief Statement of Fundamental Truths Contained in the Scriptures and Believed and Taught by the Apostolic Church* (Bradford, Yorkshire: Apostolic Church Publishing Office, n.d.) (31-page pamphlet).

74. Letters from the Reverend David H. Sture and the Reverend Stanley M. Hammond.

75. Letter from the Reverend Richard A. Gardner, Williamsburg, Penn.

76. Communication from the Reverend Dwight L. Niswander, Garden Grove, Calif.

77. "Our Doctrinal Bases," *Free Gospel [Bible] Institute (Pentecostal), Export, Pennsylvania: Official Catalogue* (Export, Penn.: The Free Gospel [Bible] Institute, 1966) (26-page pamphlet), p. 2.

78. Letter from the Reverend Chester H. Heath, trustee, Free Gospel Church, Incorporated.

79. Quoted in Klaude Kendrick, *The Promise Fulfilled: A History of the Modern Pentecostal Movement* (Springfield: Gospel Publishing House, 1961), pp. 146-147.

80. "Statement of Faith," *The Pentecostal Messenger*, 1965 Enlargement issue, p. 17.

81. Communication from the Reverend Roy M. Chappell.

82. "Basis of Union," chap. I, *Discipline and General Rules of the Pentecostal*

*Fire-Baptized Holiness Church* (Toccoa, Ga.: Pentecostal Fire-Baptized Holiness Church, 1961), pp. 6-7.

83. Ibid., pp. 21-49.

84. Chap. II ("General Rules"), ibid., pp. 7-10.

85. "Creed and Covenant," *Discipline of the Emmanuel Holiness Church* (n.p.: n.p., 1963) (24-page pamphlet), p. 4.

86. Ibid., p. 5.

87. Ibid., pp. 6-9.

88. Ibid., pp. 5-6.

89. "Ministry of Pastor Offiler," *Pentecostal Power*, vol. 12, no. 17 (August–September 1965), pp. 1, 4.

90. "There is a God who is Triune in both Nature and Being. A Three-in-One. God revealed as the Father, Son, and Holy Ghost. It is also true that this Triune God has a Triune Name. A Three-in-One Name. That Name is the Lord-Jesus-Christ. Consequently, when the disciples were commanded to baptize the converts in the Name of the Father and of the Son and of the Holy Ghost and they, under the supreme control of the Spirit, baptized them in the Name of the Lord-Jesus-Christ, the revelation was complete" (W. H. Offiler, *God and His Name: A Message for Today* [2nd edn.; Seattle, Wash.: W. H. Offiler, 1932], p. 92). "The Name of the Father, the great 'I Am,' is revealed as the Lord! The Name of the Son is unquestionably Jesus, while the appellation of the Spirit is manifested in the Christ" (ibid., pp. 83-84). "The Name Christ means the Anointed, and it has pleased God that the Holy Spirit should be comprehended under this name" (ibid., p. 82).

91. "Doctrinal Statement," *Bethel Temple Bible School Catalog 1964–1965* (Seattle, Wash.: Bethel Temple Bible School, 1964), p. [15].

92. Communication from M. Greene, secretary.

93. See "Articles of Faith," *Minister's Manual* (Des Moines, Iowa: Open Bible Standard Churches, 1967), pp. 42-48.

94. Letter from the Reverend B. McKenney, presiding bishop, the Holiness Church of God, Incorporated, 602 East Elm Street, Graham, North Carolina 27253.

95. According to a one-page undated printed broadside, the General Assem-

bly and Church of the First Born holds that the earliest reference to it in North America is in a volume in the rare-book collection of the University of Texas library at Austin, *Post Boy*, written by a certain Guildon and published in 1702. Actually the volume in question is English, not American. The title of the first edition of the work reads C[harles] G[ildon] (1665–1724), *The Post Boy Rob'd, or the Pacquet Broke Open, Consisting of Five Hundred Letters to Persons of Several Qualities*, ed. John Dunton (London: John Dunton, 1692). A second and expanded edition came out on the press of B. Mills for John Sprint, London, in 1706; this seems to be the edition to which the University of Texas copy belongs (letters to Mrs. June Moll, librarian, Miriam Lutcher Stark Library, the University of Texas, Austin). A still more expanded third edition, with a slight change in the main title, was published in London in 1719 for A. Bettesworth. Gildon based his work on *Il Corriere svalligiato*, which an Italian satirist, the Piacenza-born Augustinian canon regular Ferrante Pallavicino (1618?–1644), published under the pseudonym Ginifaccio Spironcini, in the year in which he was executed at Avignon. There are also seventeenth-century translations into French and German. The passage quoted in the broadside is part of the Gildon volume's Letter LXVI, "giving an exact, tho' short, and impartial Account of the several Sects of Christianity in the World, especially those in England." The Church of the First-Born appears as the forty-second in a series of forty-six denominations, of which all those from number twenty-three to the end seem to be British. The other names that the volume gives to the Church of the First-Born are "Visionaries," "Revelation-Men," and "Behemists," that is, disciples of Jacob Boehme (1575-1624) (Gildon, pp. 330? [230]–331). From this it appears that the Church of the First-Born of the Gildon volume was an enthusiastic and mystical movement.

96. *The General Assembly and Church of the First Born: Who We Are and What We Believe*, undated 3-page pamphlet distributed in 1967 by the General Assembly and Church of the First Born, Pleasant View, Colorado; "Articles of Faith," 1-page typewritten enclosure to a letter of the Reverend J. Ray Hamner, elder, the General Assembly and Church of the First Born, 2719 Tindall Avenue, Indianapolis, Indiana. The two statements are not identical. Thus the printed version includes this tenet: "We believe that [people] will be punished for their own sins and not for Adam's transgression."

97. Letter of the Reverend Dale Schultz, pastor of Trinity Church, Cortez, Colorado, whose assistance in securing information about the General Assembly and Church of the First Born this writer gratefully acknowledges.

98. Cited letter of Elder Hamner.

99. Cited letter of the Reverend Mr. Schultz.

100. Letter from the Honorable Ben W. Fortson, secretary of state and ex-officio corporation commissioner, State of Georgia, Atlanta, Georgia.

101. Jesse F. Pratt, *Minutes of the Church of God of the Union Assembly, Incorporated* (rev. edn.; Dalton, Ga.: Church of God of the Union Assembly, 1965) (31-page pamphlet), p. 1.

102. According to the Church of God of the Union Assembly, Incorporated, the Father, Son, and Holy Ghost are the three stars in heaven. The dragon's tail that swept down a third of the stars of heaven and cast them to the earth (Revelation 12:3-4) is the prophet who teaches lies (Isaiah 9:15). When Jesus was on earth a third of the stars of heaven was on earth. When he returned to the Father he sent the Holy Ghost back to the earth, so that a third of the stars of heaven is still here. (Ibid., p. 19.)

103. The baptism of Jesus is an example for the church to follow. It must baptize by immersion because Jesus was immersed. "John put Jesus down in the water because the word said he went up straightway out of the water. He couldn't have went out if he hadn't been in" (ibid., p. 21).

104. The formula prescribed for the ministers of the Church of God of the Union Assembly is: "In obedience to the commandment of our great Lord and Master, I indeed baptize thee, my

brother [or sister], in the name of the Father and of the Son and of the Holy Ghost" (ibid., p. 10).

105. "All members of the Church of God of the Union Assembly must take part in the Communion service and foot washing. If they don't they will have to make it right with the church or be dismissed from the church" (ibid., pp. 5-6).

106. "All members of the church are forbidden to use medicine, vaccinations, or shots of any kind, but are taught by the church to live by faith." An exception is made in the case of new members "who have recently taken up fellowship with the church" and future members. On the basis of Romans 14:1 ("As for the man who is weak in faith, welcome him, but not for disputes over opinions") these are to receive "time to grow in the faith until they attain to the teaching of the Church of God of the Union Assembly as found in James [5:13-15]" (ibid., pp. 6-7, 28).

107. Ibid., pp. 11-12.

108. Jesse F. Pratt, *The Tithing System Fully Explained* (Dalton, Ga.: The Southerner, n.d.) (16-page pamphlet). "Paying tithes didn't help to justify the pharisee. Here is what is going to get you into heaven, dear friend. 'You saw me hungry and you gave me meat, you saw me thirsty and you gave me drink.' These went into eternal life. . . . Get out from under the law; Christ is the end of the law. 'A new commandment I give unto you that ye love one another' " (ibid., pp. 14, 16). The curator of the James V. Geisendorfer Collection of Original Source Materials on American Minority Religious Groups in the library of Bethany Lutheran Seminary, Mankato, Minnesota, kindly shared the collection's copy of *The Tithing System Fully Explained* with the present writer.

109. Pratt, *Minutes*, pp. 16-17; Jesse F. Pratt, *The Throne of David* (Dalton, Ga.: Jesse F. Pratt, n.d.) (5-page folder); Jesse F. Pratt, *When Shall We Look for the Kingdom? Fully Explained* (Dalton, Ga.: Jesse F. Pratt, n.d.) (11-page pamphlet).

110. Pratt, *Minutes*, pp. 15-16; Jesse F. Pratt, *The First Resurrection—The Key to the Bible* (Dalton, Ga.: The

Southerner, n.d.) (15-page pamphlet).

111. Pratt, *Minutes*, p. 18.

112. Ibid., p. 14.

113. Ibid., p. 15.

114. Ibid., pp. 20-25.

115. The Church of God of the Union Assembly does not forbid raising tobacco for a livelihood or handling tobacco in the course of one's employment as a freight handler or a store employee (ibid., p. 4).

116. Members who enter the armed services must abide by the general rule of the church on the use of medicines, vaccinations, and "shots." They may "go to the battle fronts and help the wounded and be of service in any other way" that does not violate their consciences and beliefs (ibid., pp. 26-28).

117. Rollers may be used to make the hair manageable, so that women members of the church can fix their hair "in a way that becometh saints" (ibid., p. 5).

118. "Collars and necklines of the dresses must be worn high enough to look like Holiness" (ibid.).

119. If they are employed in factories where they are required to wear slacks at work, women members of the Church of God of the Union Assembly may do so, but they are then to wear dresses to and from work. While "culottes of proper length are not forbidden," slacks "that are too tight" are prohibited under all circumstances. (ibid., p. 7).

120. But "women [may] wear anklets to work" (ibid., p. 6). The twenty-six general rules of the church body are spelled out, ibid., pp. 4-7.

121. The thirty [thirty-one] rules for ministers are spelled out, ibid., pp. 7-10. Deacons enjoy considerable prestige in the Church of God of the Union Assembly. "All ministers of the Church of the God of the Union Assembly are required to obey when a deacon calls them to order and asks them to sit down. Then the deacon is required to give a Bible reason for asking the preacher to sit down. If the deacon fails to give a Bible reason he will have to make a confession to the preacher or be dismissed" (ibid., p. 8).

122. Ibid., pp. 12-13.

123. The incumbent is Elder Jesse F. Pratt,

301 Robinwood Drive, Dalton, Georgia, consistently referred to as "our Great Leader." In 1961 the Supreme Council of the Church of God of the Union Assembly, Incorporated, ordered that the national moderator, Elder Jesse F. Pratt, was to "have the complete power and full authority to transact any and all business that he may deem necessary and proper for the benefit of the Church of God of the Union Assembly, Incorporated . . . without confirmation of [the supreme council] or of any other organ of the church [and to] have complete power and authority to operate all affairs and businesses of the church, both from a business standpoint and from an ecclesiastical view." Explicitly this power included buying and selling property of all kinds, employing and discharging employees of the church body and its enterprises, and borrowing money with the church's property as security. (Pratt, *Minutes*, pp. 29-30.)

124. Telephone conversation with Elder Jesse F. Pratt.

125. The repeated efforts of this writer to obtain information about the total number of churches and the total membership of the Church of God of the Union Assembly, Incorporated, directly from the church body's headquarters were unsuccessful. *Quarterly News* (an organ of the church body published four times a year out of Box 345, Salome, Arizona), vol. 2, no. 3 (March 1969), carries the official minutes of the Georgia state ministers' meeting, with 70 ministers and 50 deacons present; the Ohio-Indiana-Kentucky-Illinois state ministers' meeting with 61 ministers present; and the Florida state ministers' meeting with 9 ministers and 4 deacons present. Other states in which activities of the church body were reported on included Alabama, Arizona, Arkansas, Louisiana, North Carolina, Tennessee, and Texas.

126. Elmer T. Clark, *The Small Sects in America* (rev. edn.; Nashville: Abingdon-Cokesbury Press, 1949), p. 105; letter from the Reverend Bartlett Peterson, general secretary, General Council of the Assemblies of God, Springfield, Missouri.

127. *Cladic Seminary Catalog 1965–1966* (Los Angeles, Calif.: Cladic Seminary,

1965) (19-page pamphlet), p. 4.

128. Chap. III, *Concilio Latino-Americano de Iglesias Cristianas: Constitución y Reformas 1923 a 1962* (Brownsville, Texas: Concilio Latino-Americano de Iglesias Cristianas, 1962) (34-page brochure), pp. 2-9.

129. Chap. VI, *Constitución*, pp. 10-11.

130. Miss Adela Tanguma, secretary, Latin American Council of Christian Churches, Brownsville, Texas, stated in a letter to the present writer that she was not authorized to provide the requested information.

There are about twenty churches in the Los Angeles area alone (*Cladic Seminary Catalog*, p. 4). This writer gratefully acknowledges the efforts of the Reverend Harry H. Smith, retired pastor of the Iglesia Evangélica Luterana, Brownsville, Texas, to secure information for him about the Latin American Council of Christian Churches.

131. John Thomas Nichol, *Pentecostalism* (New York: Harper & Row, 1966), p. 120. See also Klaude Kendrick, *The Promise Fulfilled: A History of the Modern Pentecostal Movement* (Springfield, Mo.: Gospel Publishing House, 1961), pp. 152-163. For a biography of Mrs. McPherson, see Lately Thomas (pseudonym of Robert V. P. Steele), *The Vanishing Evangelist* (New York: Viking Press, 1959), and *Storming Heaven: The Lives and Turmoils of Minnie Kennedy and Aimee Semple McPherson* (New York: Morrow, 1971).

132. Full text in Aimee Semple McPherson, *Declaration of Faith* (Los Angeles, Calif.: Angelus Temple and the International Church of the Foursquare Gospel, n.d.) (30-page pamphlet.

133. The Declaration of Faith reads at this point: "We believe in the commemoration and observing of the Lord's supper by the sacred use of the broken bread, a precious type of the Bread of Life, even Jesus Christ, whose body was broken for us; and by the juice of the vine, a blessed type which should ever remind the participant of the shed blood of the Saviour, who is the true Vine of which His children are the branches" (ibid., pp. 15-16).

134. The reference is to the Pentecostal Baptism of the Holy Spirit by the lay-

ing on of hands with speaking in other tongues as evidence, on which Mrs. McPherson laid much stress (ibid., pp. 16-17).

135. *Presenting—International Church of the Foursquare Gospel* (Los Angeles, Calif.: International Church of the Foursquare Gospel, n.d.) (6-page pamphlet), p. [4].

136. Letter from the Reverend Rolf K. McPherson, D.D., president, International Church of the Foursquare Gospel.

137. Letter from the Reverend Joseph Fiorentino, assistant general overseer, General Council, Christian Church of North America. See also the article, "Unorganized Italian Churches of North America: History, Doctrine and Organization," in T. F. Murphy, ed., *Religious Bodies: 1936* II/1 (Washington, D.C.: United States Government Printing Office, 1941), 755.

138. "What We Believe," in Guy Bongiovanni, *The Christian Church of North America* (Pittsburgh, Penn.: Publication Department of the Christian Church of North America, n.d.) (16-page pamphlet), pp. 10-12.

139. "Who We Are," ibid., p. 3.

140. Ibid., pp. 12-16.

141. Joseph Fiorentino, *In the Power of His Spirit—A Summary of the Italian Pentecostal Movement in the U.S.A. and Abroad* (n.p.: Christian Church of North America, n.d.) (17-page pamphlet), p. 11. There are a great many independent Italian-American Pentecostal congregations; Fiorentino (op. cit.) estimates their number at close to 100.

142. See *Twentieth Anniversary of the Garr Auditorium 1930–1950* (Charlotte, N.C.: Garr Auditorium, 1950) (40-page brochure).

143. Letters from the Reverend Dan O. White, Garr Memorial Church.

144. Letters from the Reverend Thomas J. Liggett, then executive secretary for Latin America, the United Christian Missionary Society, 222 South Downey Avenue, Indianapolis, Indiana; from the Reverend Juan Francisco Rodríguez, general superintendent, Movimiento Defensores de la Fe de Puerto Rico, Incorporado, P.O. Box 20178, Río Piedras, Puerto Rico; and the Reverend Licinio Rolón,

president, Movimiento Defensores de la Fe de Puerto Rico, Incorporado; Donald Troy Moore, *Puerto Rico para Cristo: A History of the Progress of the Evangelical Missions on the Island of Puerto Rico* (Cuernavaca, Mexico: Centro Intercultural de Documentacion, 1969), pp. 4/27-4/33.

145. Article III ("Tenets of the Faith"), *Constitution of the Church by the Side of the Road* (undated mimeographed document), pp. 1-6; "We Believe," *Dedication Service Folder, the Church by the Side of the Road, Seattle, Washington, September 9-10, 1962,* p. [11].

146. Letter from the Reverend Howard S. May, pastor, Church by the Side of the Road.

147. The name is an allusion to Hebrews 12:23.

148. Article VI ("Statement of Fundamental Truths"), *Constitution and By-Laws* (rev. edn.; Delano, Calif.: The Filipino Assemblies of the First-Born, 1963) (23-page pamphlet), pp. 3-7.

149. Article XII ("Military Service"), ibid., p. 11.

150. The present writer gratefully acknowledges the assistance of the Reverend Theodore L. Brohm, pastor, the Church of Our Saviour, Delano, California, who personally interviewed the Reverend Felix Antolin Fabrigas, director, missionary department, the Filipino Assemblies of the First-Born, on this writer's behalf.

151. *Constitucion y Reglamento de la Mision de Iglesias de Cristo en las Antillas* (rev. edn.; Río Grande, Puerto Rico: Iglesia de Cristo en las Antillas, 1963) (9-page multilithed document), pp. 3-4.

152. "Declaración de Principios," in *Constitución y Reglamento de la Iglesia de Cristo Misionera* (rev. edn.; Río Piedras, Puerto Rico: Nacional Imprenta y Offset, 1962), pp. 10-15.

153. Donald Troy Moore, *Puerto Rico para Cristo: A History of the Progress of the Evangelical Missions on the Island of Puerto Rico* (Cuernavaca, Mexico: Centro Intercultural de Documentacion, 1969), pp. 4/33-4/35 and 5/13.

154. Letter from the Reverend John D. Kennington, chairman, Grace Gospel Evangelistic Association International, Incorporated, 909 Northeast Thirtieth

Street, Portland, Oregon 97232.

155. "Nuestra Doctrina Fundamental," *El Revelador Cristiano*, November 1964, p. [2].

156. *Statements of Religious Bodies on the Conscientious Objector*, 4th edn. by Michael C. Yoder (Washington, D.C.: National Service Board for Religious Objectors, 1963), pp. 48-49.

157. Ibid.

158. Article 1 ("Statement of Doctrine"), *General By-Laws of the Pentecostal Evangelical Church* (rev. edn.; Spokane, Wash.: Pentecostal Evangelical Church, 1966) (20-page pamphlet), p. 2; "The Fundamental Truths (Abridged)" (2-page mimeographed document, undated).

159. Article 11 ("Local Churches"), *General By-Laws*, pp. 15-16.

160. Letter from the Reverend Ernest Beroth, general bishop of the Pentecostal Evangelical Church.

161. *The Manual and Constitution of the Overcomers Church* (Toronto, Ontario: The International Council of the Overcomers Church, 1951), pp. 97-102; letters from the Reverend James D. Varey, B.A., B.D., D.D., life president of the International Council, the Overcomers Church (Evangelical).

162. Communication from Christ Faith Mission, Los Angeles; Noel McNeill, "As of a Rushing Mighty Wind" (unpublished manuscript), pp. 91-92. McNeill estimates the functioning membership at 500 (ibid., p. 135).

163. Letter from the Reverend Carlos Sepúlveda, Brooklyn, New York.

164. Communication from the Reverend Carlos Bermudez, executive secretary, the Assembly of Christian Churches, Incorporated, and editor of the church body's monthly *La Voz Evangélica*, 561 Cauldwell Avenue, Bronx, New York.

165. *Doctrinas Fundamentales de la Iglesia de Dios, Incorporada* (3rd edn.; Juncos: Imprenta Junquña, 1966) (28-page pamphlet). The printed form has only forty-eight chapters; it lacks the first chapter through an accidental oversight (letter of the Reverend Benita Cintrón Santana, president of the Iglesia de Dios, Incorporada).

166. Cited letter from the Reverend Benito Cintrón Santana; *La Voz Apostólica*, vol. 24, nos. 4-6 (April–June 1967), 2. La Iglesia de Dios, Incorporada,

began its work in the continental United States in 1954 under the name the Non-Sectarian Church of God; it took the legal name La Iglesia de Dios, Incorporada, for its work in the continental United States in 1961. It officially began its work in the Virgin Islands in 1957.

167. *Articles of Faith* (New Baltimore, Mich.: Anchor Bay Evangelistic Association, n.d.) (16-page pamphlet). The Anchor Bay Evangelistic Association, as a member both of the National Association of Evangelicals and of the Pentecostal Fellowship of North America, shares the doctrinal positions of these two organizations.

168. The present writer gratefully acknowledges the kindness of the Reverend Frederick L. von Husen, pastor, Trinity Church, Wahiawa, Hawaii, in securing information about the Lamb of God Church on this writer's behalf.

169. Douglas J. Elwood, *Churches and Sects in the Philippines: A Descriptive Study of Contemporary Religious Group Movements* (Dumaguete City, Republic of the Philippines: Silliman University, 1968), p. 104.

170. The present writer gratefully acknowledges the assistance of the Reverend Frederick L. von Husen, pastor, Trinity Church, Wahiawa, Hawaii, who interviewed the Hawaiian leadership of the International Christian Churches on behalf of this writer.

171. Information provided by the Reverend Mabel Griffith, pastor of Shiloh Chapel, 1724 East Pikes Peak Avenue, Colorado Springs, Colorado 80909.

172. This section is based on printed material provided by the Reverend John Mabe, overseer, Alpha and Omega Pentecostal Church of America. The Baltimore body has no connection with the Alpha and Omega Christian Church, another Pentecostal body whose headquarters are in Pearl City, Hawaii.

173. Letter from the Right Reverend Charles E. Waters, Baltimore, Maryland, senior and presiding bishop, the True Fellowship Pentecostal Church of America, Incorporated.

174. Letters from the Reverend Carlton Spencer, chairperson, Elim Missionary Assemblies; John Thomas Nichol, *Pentecostalism* (New York:

Harper & Row, 1966), pp. 128-129.

175. Donald Troy Moore, *Puerto Rico para Cristo: A History of the Progress of the Evangelical Missions on the Island of Puerto Rico* (Cuernavaca, Mexico: Centro Intercultural de Documentacion, 1969), pp. 4/40-4/41 and 5/13. Repeated efforts by this writer to obtain information about the Samaria Iglesia Evangélica directly from its leadership were unsuccessful.

176. H. A. Maxwell Whyte, *Our History and Tenets* (undated 4-page tract), pp. [3]-[4].

177. Letter from the Reverend H. A. Maxwell Whyte, pastor, United Apostolic Faith Church, Scarborough, Ontario.

178. The church admits baptism by sprinkling in the case of helpless invalids or of ill persons at the point of death.

179. "La Constitución de la Iglesia Evangélica Congregacional, Incorporada, de Puerto Rico" (8-page undated typewritten document provided by the Reverend Antonio Jaime López, president, Iglesia Evangélical Congregacional, Humacao, Puerto Rico.

180. Letter from President López.

181. On the "Latter Rain" controversy, see Gordon F. Atter, *The Third Force* (rev. edn.; Peterborough, Ontario: The College Press, 1965), pp. 141-145.

182. Communication from the Reverend T. A. Lanes, secretary.

183. Article II ("Platform of Faith"), By-Laws, *Articles of Incorporation and By-Laws of Westgate Chapel* (Edmonds, Wash.: Westgate Chapel, 1962) (18-page pamphlet), pp. 6-8.

184. E. C. Erickson and Henry Jauhiainen, *Independent Assemblies of God: An Experience in Inter-Church Fellowship* (n.p.: Independent Assemblies of God, 1959) (12-page pamphlet), pp. 5-12.

185. Communication from church body headquarters.

186. *Scripture References: Thus We Believe* (1-page mimeographed document).

187. Letter from the Reverend Dr. Thea F. Jones, pastor, Thea Jones Evangelistic Association, Incorporated (Philadelphia's Evangelistic Center).

188. Noel McNeill, "As of a Rushing Mighty Wind" (unpublished manuscript), p. 138.

189. Letter from Mrs. Anna Rosenberger. See also Anna Rosenberger, *The Accomplished Redemption: Experiences* (Zephyrhills, Fla.: Anna Rosenberger, 1962) (63-page brochure).

190. Dennis W. Thorn, *The Full Gospel Church Association, Incorporated: Constitution, Faith, and Teaching* (Amarillo, Texas: The Full Gospel Church Association, 1958) (33-page pamphlet), pp. 5-30.

191. Communication from the Reverend Dennis W. Thorn, president.

192. Noel McNeill, "As of a Rushing Mighty Wind" (unpublished manuscript), p. 96. Repeated efforts to obtain information directly from the leadership of Bethany Chapel were unsuccessful.

193. Hall has cautioned adherents not to claim in their public testimony to have "the Holy Ghost clothing of power" all over them and "the precious warm fire covering of the Lord Jesus body" on their own bodies when in fact they become ill, have headaches, wear glasses, and get tired (*Miracle Word*, consecutive no. 8 [Winter 1968], 5). If they really possess these blessings on the designated portions of their body, the movement holds, they will remain well.

194. Letter from Myrtle Page, 821 South 28th Avenue, Phoenix, Arizona, president, Hall Deliverance Foundation, Incorporated.

195. The 1968 convention, for instance, featured one speaker "unusually anointed to impart [Holy Ghost] clothing in the mouth and on the gums," as well as on other parts of the body. Another, from Detroit, Michigan, imparted "fire covering of protection [on the body against] riots and snipers." (*Miracle Word*, vol. 3, no. 4 [Fall 1968], 16; communication from the Reverend Franklin Hall, ed., *Miracle Word*, Box 11157, Phoenix, Arizona 85061.)

196. Letter from the Reverend Mr. Hall.

197. A. A. Allen, *Miracle Revival Fellowship* (Miracle Valley, Ariz.: Miracle Revival Fellowship, n.d.) (10-page folder). Allen's opposition to "denominationalism" may explain why Noel McNeill states that Allen's "ministry has been unacceptable to the majority of the Pentecostal organizations in North America" ("As of a Rushing Mighty Wind" [unpublished manuscript], p. 94).

198. McNeill, p. 95; *Miracle Valley Bible College: Eleventh Catalog [1967–1969]* (Miracle Valley, Ariz.: Miracle Valley Bible College, 1967). At the time of Allen's death, United Press International stated that he published 55 million pieces of literature annually and that *Miracle Magazine* had a circulation of 350,000 ("The Rev. A. A. Allen Dies; Evangelist," *St. Louis Post-Dispatch*, June 13, 1970, 7A). About the same time a critical examination of Allen's radio programs was included in an article by Rice University sociologist William C. Martin, "The God-Hucksters of Radio: 'Keep Those Cards and Letters Coming In,'" *The Atlantic Monthly*, vol. 225, no. 6 (June 1970), 51-56. Martin called Allen and Garner Ted Armstrong of the World-Wide Church of God "the two giants of radio religion."

199. "Doctrinal Statement" (undated 1-page document). See also William Hedgepeth, "Brother A. A. Allen on the Gospel Train: He Feels, He Heals, and He Turns You on with God," *Look*, vol. 33, no. 20 (October 7, 1969), 23-31.

200. McNeill, p. 137. Membership in the Miracle Revival Fellowship is not "considered a limitation of fellowship among believers. Any member, whether ministerial or lay member, shall be free at all times to enjoy fellowship with any believer or group of believers with whom he finds a unity of spirit." (Article IX, "Articles of Incorporation of Miracle Revival Fellowship," in A. A. Allen, *Prisons with Stained Glass Windows* [Miracle Valley, Arizona: A. A. Allen Revivals, 1963], p. 113.)

201. Herbert F. Carter and Ruth K. Moore, "History of the Pentecostal Free Will Baptist Church, Incorporated," in Herbert Carter and others, *Discipline of the Pentecostal Free Will Baptist Church, Incorporated* (Dunn, N.C.: Pentecostal Free Will Baptist Church, n.d.), pp. 5-16.

202. "This We Believe," ibid., pp. 3-4.

203. Articles 1 through 19, "Faith," ibid., pp. 17-31.

204. Article 20, ibid., pp. 31-32.

205. "Faith," in *Faith and Government of the Free Will Baptist Church of the Pentecostal Faith* (Elgin, S.C.: Free Will Baptist Church of the Pentecostal Faith, 1961) (48-page pamphlet), pp. 3-21. For an elaboration of the statement of faith, see Ray Rumsey, *Fundamentals of the Faith* (Florence, S.C.: Free Will Baptist Church Conference —Pentecostal Faith, n.d.) (two 40-page pamphlets).

206. The present writer gratefully acknowledges the assistance of the Reverend William J. Meyer, then pastor of the Church of the Holy Spirit, Columbia, South Carolina, who interviewed the Reverend W. Dalton McIntire, general superintendent, Free Will Baptist Church of the Pentecostal Faith, on this writer's behalf.

207. See *Gospel Harvester Tabernacle* (Atlanta, Ga.: Gospel Harvester Evangelistic Association, n.d.) (8-page pamphlet), p. [6]. On the experience of the baptism of the Holy Spirit, the association holds that "while the Holy Spirit of God dwells in all those regenerated by faith in the Son of God, there remains an experience for believers who desire to become effective witnesses, the results and effectiveness in witness being the primary evidence of the experience; further evidences may be similar to those experienced in the Apostolic church (Acts 2:1-4; 10:44-48; 19:1-7; 1 Corinthians 12-14)" (letter from the Reverend Earl P. Paulk, Jr., president, Gospel Harvester Evangelistic Association).

208. Letter from the Reverend Mr. Earl Paulk.

209. "Statement of Faith and Practice of [the] Gospel Harvesters Evangelistic Association, Incorporated, Buffalo, New York" (undated 2-page typescript).

210. Letter from the Reverend Rose Pezzino, president and founder, Gospel Harvesters Evangelistic Association, Incorporated.

211. Douglas J. Elwood, *Churches and Sects in the Philippines: A Descriptive Study of Contemporary Religious Group Movements* (Dumaguete City, Republic of the Philippines: Silliman University, 1968), pp. 78, 180. The congregation in the Philippines apparently has fewer than 100 members.

212. Letter from the Reverend Carmelo B. Cabacungan, president-founder, the Alpha and Omega Christian Church

and Bible School, Incorporated—Philippines.

213. For the information here given about the Hawaiian mother church of this body, the present writer is indebted to the Reverend John F. Mulholland of the religious education department of the Kamehameha Schools, Kapalama Heights, Honolulu, Hawaii. Repeated efforts by the present writer to obtain information directly from the Pearl City headquarters of the Alpha and Omega Christian Church were unsuccessful.

214. These miraculous gifts and ministries include divine healing as a part of the gospel, speaking with tongues as evidence of the baptism of the Holy Spirit, and reproducing Christ's "mighty signs and wonders through the eternal Spirit."

215. "Tenets of Faith," in Charles Farah, Jr., *United Evangelical Churches: Vision* (Monrovia, Calif.: United Evangelical Churches, n.d.) (14-page tract), pp. 11-12.

216. Ronald R. Pottinger, *Why U.E.C.?* (Monrovia, Calif.: United Evangelical Churches, 1968) (3-page folder).

217. Letter from the Reverend Charles J. Hardin, president, United Evangelical Churches.

# BIBLIOGRAPHY

Allen, A. A. *Prisons with Stained Glass Windows.* Miracle Valley, Ariz.: A. A. Allen Revivals, 1963. Publication of the Miracle Revival Fellowship.

Atter, Gordon F. *The Third Force*, rev. edn. Peterborough, Ontario: The College Press, 1965.

Baxter, Mrs. J. R. (Ma), and Videt Polk, compilers. *Select Church Songs: A Select Collection of Songs Suitable for Every Worshipful, Religious Service.* Dallas, Texas: Stamps-Baxter Music and Printing Company, 1965. This songbook is widely used in Free Will Baptist Churches of the Pentecostal Faith.

Brumback, Carl. *Suddenly from Heaven.* Springfield, Mo.: Gospel Publishing House, 1961. The authoritative history of the Assemblies of God.

Campbell, Joseph E. *The Pentecostal Holiness Church 1898–1948.* Franklin Springs, Ga.: Advocate Press, 1951.

Cox, B. L. *History and Doctrine of the Congregational Holiness Church.* Greenwood, S.C.: Congregational Holiness Publishing House, 1958.

Gibson, Luther. *History of the Church of God, Mountain Assembly.* Jellico, Tenn.: Church of God of the Mountain Assembly, 1954. A 53-page pamphlet.

*A Historical Account of the Apostolic Faith: A Trinitarian-Fundamental Evangelistic Organization.* Portland, Ore.: The Apostolic Faith, 1965. A history of the Apostolic Faith organization established by Florence Crawford in 1907.

Hoover, Mario G. *Origin and Structural Development of the Assemblies of God.* Springfield, Mo.: Mario G. Hoover, 1970. A reproduction of the author's 1968 master of arts thesis in history, presented to the Southwest Missouri State College, Springfield, Missouri.

Kendrick, Klaude. *The Promise Fulfilled: A History of the Modern Pentecostal Movement.* Springfield, Mo.: Gospel Publishing House, 1961.

Kulbeck, Gloria Grace. *What God Hath Wrought: A History of the Pentecostal Assemblies of Canada.* Ed. Walter E. McAlister and George R. Upton. Toronto: The Pentecostal Assemblies of Canada, 1958. This is the definitive work on the denomination. Earl O. Kulbeck, "A Brief History of the Pentecostal Assemblies of Canada," in T. Johnstone, *Canada's Centennial: Our Spiritual Heritage* (32-page pamphlet) (Toronto: Full Gospel Publishing House, 1967) pp. 20-32, brings the account up to date.

McPherson, Aimee Semple, and Stiffler, Georgia. *The Foursquare Gospel.* Los Angeles, Calif.: Echo Park Evangelistic Association, 1946. The last literary effort of the foundress, in which she set forth the doctrines and tenets of the International Church of the Foursquare Gospel.

———. *This Is That: Personal Experiences, Sermons, and Writings.* Los Angeles, Calif.: Echo Park Evangelistic Association, 1923. The autobiography of the foundress of the International Church of the Foursquare Gospel.

Mitchell, Clarence G. *Starving Sheep and Overfed Shepherds.* Miracle Valley, Ariz.: A. A. Allen Revivals, 1963. Publication of the Miracle Revival Fellowship.

Paulk, Earl P., Jr. *Your Pentecostal Neighbor.* Cleveland, Tenn.: Pathway Press, 1958. The author of this book, "written in the hope of bringing together the fundamental beliefs of the Pentecostal believer into one book," was at the time of its publication a minister in the Church of God (Cleveland, Tennessee), from which he later separated "for personal and governmental reasons."

Synan, Joseph Alexander, and others, eds. *The Pentecostal Holiness Manual 1965.* Franklin Springs, Ga.: Board of Publications, Pentecostal Holiness Church, 1965. The *Manual* furnishes helpful theological perspectives in the "Doctrinal Exegesis" (pp. 15-27), by Bishop Joseph Hillery King, and in the "Doctrinal Amplification" (pp. 27-36), by Bishop Synan.

# 6. The Church of God (Cleveland, Tennessee) and Related Organizations

## The Church of God (Cleveland, Tennessee)

Near Cokercreek, Monroe County, Tennessee, a seventy-two-year-old licensed Baptist minister and two companions began in 1884 to devote themselves to prayer and to study of the Bible and of church history to try to find a way out of "the morass of tradition, legalism, and ecclesiolatry" into which they felt that the Christianity of the Smoky Mountains had fallen in their time. The minister was Richard G. Spurling, Sr. (1812–1886); his companions were his son, Richard G. Spurling, Jr., also a licensed Baptist minister, and John Plemons. After two years of failure to revitalize the worship of the churches of their community, they concluded that the trouble was more basic, that the Reformers of the sixteenth century had "failed to reform from creeds; they adopted the law of faith when they should have adopted the law of love; . . . they failed to reserve a right of way for the leadership of the Holy Ghost and conscience." In addition, Spurling and his followers concluded "that God's church existed only where his law and government was observed by his children."[1] Accordingly, on August 19, 1886, nine persons, including the two Spurlings, meeting in the Barney Creek Meetinghouse near the confluence of Barney and Coker creeks in Monroe County, organized the Christian Union "to restore primitive Christianity and bring about the union of all denominations."[2]

For a decade the movement languished. Then three laymen in the area caught the holiness vision, William Martin, a Methodist, and Joe M. Tipton and Milton McNabb, Baptists. With considerable success they began to proclaim Holiness as not only possible but as natural for Christians. Almost simultaneously a group of Baptists fourteen miles away in Cherokee County, North Carolina, became aroused and began to hold prayer meetings in their homes. They invited the three Cokercreek lay evangelists to conduct a revival, which swept the area and culminated in ecstatic experiences in which more than a hundred participants began to "speak in tongues."

The Cokercreek and Cherokee County congregations united and provided a spiritual home for the converts to the Holiness idea when their own denominations expelled them. The next six years were a period of violent opposition and persecution. The movement survived this phase, only to be brought to the brink of disaster by a wave of fanatical excesses. Only twenty were left to reconstitute the decimated congregation as The Holiness Church at Camp Creek in 1902.

The following year a Quaker colporteur of the American Bible Society "found" the church at Camp Creek and joined it. He was Ambrose Jessup Tomlinson (1865–1963). Spurling, M. S. Lemons, and W. F. Bryant evangelized the mountains of North Carolina, Tennessee, and Georgia. In 1904 Tomlinson established himself at Cleveland, Bradford County, Tennessee. In 1905 three more churches were organized and in 1906 the first annual General Assembly was held at Camp Creek. At the second assembly, held in Cleveland, Tennessee, which had become the center of the movement, the name Church of God was adopted on the basis of I Corinthians 1:2 and Acts 20:28, and considerable emphasis was placed on spiritual gifts, divine healing, and the baptism of the Holy Ghost. At the third assembly, on January 12, 1908, Tomlinson finally "came through" and received the baptism of the Holy Ghost himself.[3]

In 1909 a minor schism occurred, when J. H. Simpson and J. B. Goins seceded because of the parent body's teaching concerning tongues. In that year Tomlinson became general moderator of the organization, a position that he held for fourteen years. In 1910 his title was changed to general overseer, and in 1914 the assembly made him general overseer for life. At his own suggestion the assembly authorized a Council of Twelve [Elders] and in 1917 he appointed the first two members of the council and with their help appointed the remaining ten. In 1919 J. L. Scott withdrew to continue as the leader of the (Original) Church of God. In 1922 the body's financial situation, which had deteriorated to a critical condition, constrained the assembly to appoint a committee on better government; the assembly adopted the committee's recommendations, including the annual election of all officers, and appointed a committee of three to investigate all departments of the church. On the basis of its findings, the Council of Twelve impeached Tomlinson and two of its own members.[4]

Tomlinson, supported by the two elders and a small group of ministers and laypeople, insisted that he and his supporters constituted the Church of God. The "(Ten) Elders Church," as the majority group was known, secured an injunction in 1924, ultimately sustained in 1927 by the Supreme Court of Tennessee, forbidding Tomlinson and his followers from "representing themselves to be connected in any way with the Church of God."

These traumatic events affected the public image of the Church of God more than it did its growth. The membership in the United States and Canada has shown increases every year except for the years 1928 and 1929. In 1961 a number of ministers in Atlanta, led by Earl F. Paulk, withdrew to found the

Gospel Harvesters Evangelistic Association. The 1967 assembly ended forty years of strict racial segregation by voting to merge the 10,000 black members of the Colored Churches District with the white districts.

In 1910 the Church of God journal *Evangel* devoted an issue to the prominent doctrines of the church, drafted by a committee composed of Lemons, Spurling, McLain, and Tomlinson. The statement declared that "the Church of God stands for the whole Bible rightly divided" and "the New Testament as the only rule for government and discipline." The teachings are specifically listed as repentance; justification; regeneration; new birth; sanctification subsequent to justification;[5] holiness; water baptism by immersion; baptism with the Holy Ghost subsequent to cleansing as the enduement of power for service; speaking in tongues as the evidence of the baptism with the Holy Ghost; the full restoration of the gifts of I Corinthians 12 and 14 to the church; the signs of Mark 16:17-20 following the believers; fruits of the Spirit; divine healing provided for all in the atonement; the Lord's Supper; washing the saints' feet; tithing and giving; restitution where possible; Christ's premillennial second coming, first for the resurrection of the dead saints and the rapture of the living and second to reign on earth for a thousand years; resurrection; eternal life for the righteous; eternal punishment without liberation or annihilation for the wicked; total abstinence from all liquor or strong drinks, from tobacco, and from narcotics; meats and drinks;[6] and the Sabbath.[7]

These teachings are "the chief expression of Church of God theology, ethical teaching, and sacraments."[8] With slight amendments—such as the prohibitions, added in 1915, of wearing gold for ornament or decoration, of membership in lodges and of swearing oaths, and the point on divorce and remarriage, added in 1954—they have been published annually in the assembly minutes. After discussion, the 1930 assembly declared them to be its "official findings and interpretations."[9]

The 1945 assembly ruled that while nations can and should settle their differences without going to war, members will not lose their status in the church by engaging in combatant service in war; on the other hand, the church will support the constitutional rights of a selectee "who has conscientious objections to combatant service."[10]

In 1948 the assembly adopted a declaration of faith in the verbal inspiration of the Bible; the Trinity; Christ's sonship, virgin birth, death, resurrection, ascension, and intercession; the universal sinfulness of human beings and the need of repentance for forgiveness of sins; justification, regeneration, and the new birth as wrought by faith in Christ's blood; sanctification subsequent to the new birth, through faith in Christ's blood, "through the word and by the Holy Ghost"; holiness as God's standard of living for his people; the baptism of the Holy Ghost subsequent to a clean heart; speaking with tongues as the initial evidence of the baptism of the Holy Ghost; baptism of all who repent by immersion in the name of the Father, and of the Son, and of the

Holy Ghost;[11] divine healing provided in the atonement; the Lord's Supper and washing of the saints' feet; Christ's premillennial second coming for the resurrection of the righteous dead, the rapture of the living saints, and his reign on earth for a thousand years; and in the bodily resurrection to eternal life or eternal punishment.[12]

The General Assembly meets every two years and is the highest governing body. A general council of all ordained ministers (called bishops until 1948) prepares recommendations on polity or doctrine for the assembly. An executive committee of six officers (elected for four years), headed by the general overseer and his three assistants, and twelve counselors (elected for two years) form the Executive Council, which functions as the highest administrative body between general assemblies.

The headquarters are at Keith and 25th, Northwest, Cleveland, Tennessee 37311. There are 4,467 churches in the United States, chiefly in the southeastern states, with an inclusive membership of 343,249.[13] The Church of God (Cleveland, Tennessee) carries on foreign missions in Africa,[14] Europe, the Middle East, Latin America, the Caribbean, the Gilbert Islands, Hong Kong, India, Indonesia, Japan, Korea, Okinawa, and the Republic of the Philippines.

### The (Original) Church of God, Incorporated

In 1886 Richard Spurling, Sr., and his companions founded the first congregation in the United States "to set together . . . and to transact business" as "The Church of God."[15] With its affiliated branches, the Christian Union, as it called itself, helped in the establishment of the Church of God (Cleveland, Tennessee), but in 1909 it withdrew over a wide variety of questions including divorce and tithing, and in 1922 it incorporated as the (Original) Church of God.

As the basis of fellowship the (Original) Church of God has a thirty-item chapter on "Doctrine" in its *Manual*. It stands for "the whole Bible, rightly divided"; repentance that includes godly sorrow arising from love to God, a hatred of sin, a love of holiness, a fixed resolution to forsake sin, and an expectation of favor and forgiveness; restitution through repayment and confession; generation; justification ("that act of God's free grace by which we receive remission of sins"); sanctification as "the second definite work of grace wrought with the blood of Christ through faith in Him"; entire sanctification ("otained by knowledge of the Scriptures and perfect obedience to them"); baptism or filling with the Spirit; speaking with other tongues ("every man, woman or child who is filled with the Holy Ghost WILL *Speak With Other Tongues*"); divine healing ("obtained by faith, laying on of hands, the anointing with oil, and by special gift"), not as "a test of fellowship but as an individual matter" between each believer and God; the full working of all the gifts in the church; signs following believers "exactly as the 16th chapter of Mark sets forth"; fruits of the Spirit with a corresponding stand against all the works of the flesh; Christ's premillennial second coming; eternal life for the righteous and eternal punishment for the wicked; total abstinence from all intoxicants and tobacco and from all uncleanness and filthiness of the flesh as a precondition of membership; nonresistance ("We believe it to be wrong for Christians to take up arms and go to war . . . therefore, we would rather our members not engage in war"); the Sunday Sabbath as a day of voluntary worship and service; opposition to members swearing; lifelong marriage, with fornication as the only ground for divorce and remarriage, but without going back beyond a person's conversion from a sinful past; the tribulation under the imminent "ten-toe government of Daniel"; the millennium; the doom of the unbelieving dead; a new heaven and a new earth; avoidance of wearing gold for decoration; modest apparel appropriate to the wearer's sex and without jewelry and bodily ornamentation ("it is unthinkable that a Christian woman would put on . . . pants, shorts, shirts, etc."); humility and contrition; and separation of church and state.[16]

The ordinances of the church are water baptism by complete burial in water and with the trinitarian formula as "the only legal authoritative ceremony"; the Lord's Supper "as many as three or four times a year," with only those who are of like faith and at peace with God and human beings participating; washing of the saints' feet invariably and immediately after the Lord's Supper; tithing into the church treasury as God's Storehouse for the support of the ministry by the laity and into the general office by the ministry; and free-will offerings as often as each local church deems necessary.[17]

About 75 churches belong to the (Original) Church of God. They have a total membership estimated at 18,000. The General Assembly meets annually. The headquarters' address is at Box 3086, Chattanooga, Tennessee 37404.

### The Church of God of Prophecy

The Church of God of Prophecy—the name it has borne since 1952—sees itself as the legitimate continuation of the church that Ambrose Jessup Tomlinson (1865–1943) "found" in 1903 and that adopted the name Church of God in 1907. After the "disruption in the organization" that took place in 1923, Tomlinson rallied the little company of ministers that remained loyal to him and in November of the same year he held what he called the eighteenth annual assembly of the Church of God. His continued use of the name "Church of God" for the group that he headed resulted in a suit by the Church of God (Cleveland, Tennessee) to enjoin him and his supporters from "representing themselves to be connected in any way with the Church of God."[18] The suit was decided in favor of the plaintiff in 1924; Tomlinson immediately filed a cross bill. The litigation went on for twenty-nine years; finally the Supreme Court of Tennessee sustained the original decision, and the organization that Tomlinson had headed after 1923 accepted its present designation as "its business name for use in secular affairs in order to distinguish itself from other groups using 'Church of God.' " It continues to use the simple designation "Church of God" for itself in all its worship services.[19]

After Tomlinson's death his son Milton succeeded as general overseer. When Milton Tomlinson's brother Homer refused to submit to the action of the General Assembly that confirmed Milton as general overseer, the presbytery—consisting of the general overseer and the state overseers—expelled Homer Tomlinson from the denomination. A large segment chiefly of the urban congregations, followed him out and became the nucleus of the Church of God (Huntsville, Alabama).

The Church of God of Prophecy sees its "Twenty-Nine Important Bible Truths" not as a creed but as a roster of Bible beliefs. These teachings include acceptance of the whole Bible rightly divided, with the New Testament as the only rule of faith and practice; the necessity of the new birth, which is the result of repentance, justification, and regeneration; restitution for past wrongs; sanctification as a second work of grace that the Holy Ghost works instantaneously in the believer's heart through the blood of Christ; a life of holiness, which refrains from liquor, strong drink, tobacco, narcotics, the wearing of gold for ornament or decoration, membership in lodges, and oath-taking; withholding of membership from those living with a second marital companion (except where the former companion has died or is a fornicator, defined as one who is married to another's companion); baptism with the Holy Ghost accompanied by speaking in other tongues; immersion of believers in the name of the Father, and of the Son, and of the Holy Ghost; divine healing provided for in the atonement and accomplished by the power of God; the full restoration of the spiritual gifts imparted to the church, of the fruit of the Spirit, and of the signs and wonders that followed the ministry of the apostles; the Lord's Supper and the washing of the saints' feet; tithing and free-will contributions; Christ's premilliennial second coming for the resurrection of the dead saints and the rapture of the living saints to take part in the Lamb's marriage supper; his millennial reign on earth, followed by the resurrection of the wicked; and the reward of eternal life for the faithful and eternal punishment without liberation or annihilation for the unconverted. The "Twenty-Nine Important Bible Truths" are seen as implying the inspiration of the Bible, the Trinity, the apostasy of the church that Christ established on earth and its reappearance in the world today "as a visible, organized body operating in the world to provide one fold for all of God's sheep," and the distinction between the Kingdom of God ("all born-again children of God everywhere") and the Church of God.[20]

The government of the Church of God of Prophecy is described as theocratic. The annual General Assembly is judicial, not executive or legislative; it merely interprets the Bible and sets forth recommendations concerning the work of the church. All questions are settled by unanimous agreement and are ratified by each local congregation. The general overseer, selected by the unanimous vote of the General Assembly, holds office indefinitely. He serves as chairman of all but two standing committees; he also appoints the majority of the chairmen and members of other committees, as well as a number of administrative officials and the state and territorial overseers. The state or territorial overseers moderate an annual state or territorial convention and appoint the pastors of the local churches. ("Female members may attend [the quarterly business meetings of the local churches] and pray silently, but they do not take any part in discussions or decisions.") The ministry consists of bishops and deacons, who are the ordained ministers, male and female evangelists, and lay ministers. Female ministers and lay ministers of both sexes may serve as pastors but in that case do not moderate the business sessions; they may not establish churches, baptize, or administer the Lord's Supper and the foot washing ordinance.[21]

The headquarters are at Bible Place, Cleveland, Tennessee 37311. There are 1,755 churches in the United States and Canada, with a total membership of 62,743. The Church of God of Prophecy carries on foreign missions on six continents; more than half its total membership is outside the United States.[22]

### The Church of God House of Prayer

As overseer in Maine, Harrison W. Poteat supervised the work of the Church of God founded by Ambrose Jessup Tominson until the schism of 1923 and thereafter of the Church of God (Cleveland, Tennessee) in six northeastern states for a total of over twenty years. In 1933 he established the work of the latter body on Prince Edward Island, Canada.[23]

In 1939, after breaking with the Cleveland headquarters, Poteat founded the Church of God House of Prayer, and took with him into it many of the churches and congregations that he had supervised.[24] During the thirteen years that he was general overseer of the new denomination it attracted supporters in other states.[25] The parent church body brought suit to recover occupany of a number of local properties. When the courts ruled in the plaintiff's favor, the new denomination lost both buildings and members. Other congregations, including the church in Cleveland, Tennessee, withdrew and became independent congregations.[26]

The doctrinal position of the Church of God House of Prayer is substantially identical with the Arminian-Pentecostal theology of the Church of God (Cleveland, Tennessee).

The Church of God House of Prayer describes itself as "undenominational in purpose, apostolic in doctrine, theocratic in government, universal in scope, fundamental in principle, Christian in conduct, biblical in faith and practice."[27]

Specific emphases of its Declaration of Bible Order include the following. The Bible is the inspired Word of God, but the Church of God House of Prayer relies on the New Testament for church government and rules of

Christian conduct. Godly sorrow impels repentance, and restitution and conversion follow repentance. The vicarious atonement makes possible the spiritual or new birth, without which there is no spiritual life. Those who are begotten of God do not commit sin; therefore they are justified and accounted just in the sight of God by faith in the blood of Jesus. Those who are reborn and justified "may also be sanctified with the blood." The atonement provides healing for the body and complete deliverance for those whom evil spirits possess. Christ transmits the gifts of healing and power over demons to the church by the power of the Holy Ghost. The laying on of hands imparts divine healing and baptism with the Holy Ghost and ordains to Christian service. Water baptism is by immersion in the name of the Father and of the Son and of the Holy Ghost; baptism of the Spirit, the gift of power for service upon a sanctified life, has speaking with tongues as its initial evidence. The sacrament, or Lord's Supper, to be celebrated at least quarterly and on the night before Good Friday for true believers only, has as its purpose to show Christ's death; the elements consist of bread and unfermented fruit of the vine. Foot washing is for believers only. The resurrection to life will take place when Christ descends into the air, where the saints will meet him and will be kept during the great tribulation. Thereafter Christ will reign on earth with his saints for a thousand years, after which the resurrection to damnation and the eternal judgment will take place.[28]

The local churches are regarded as integral parts of the General Assembly and as subject to the assembly and its duly appointed officials. The General Assembly meets annually. The local pastor appoints the deacons. Women may be licensed as evangelists or exhorters.

There are 24 churches in the eastern part of the United States and 2 in eastern Canada, with an estimated total membership of 1,200. The Reverend Charles MacNevin, the present general superintendent and the third to hold the office, resides in Markleysburg, Pennsylvania. Incorporation of the church body was completed in 1966.[29]

### The Church of God (Huntsville, Alabama)
### (The Church of God, World Headquarters)

From 1886, when Richard B. Spurling, Sr., and his companions organized the Christian Union, to 1943, when Ambrose Jessup Tomlinson died, the organizations now known as the Church of God (Huntsville, Alabama), the Church of God of Prophecy, and the Church of God (Cleveland, Tennessee) shared in varying degrees not only a common name but a common history.[30]

After the division in the "Tomlinson Church of God" that followed the elder Tomlinson's death, his older son, Homer A. Tomlinson (1892–1968), observed thirty days of mourning for his father. Then, persuaded that he was still the general overseer of the authentic Church of God by his father's choice, he convoked an assembly of the whole church in New York in December

1943. At this assembly, in his own words, "in mighty anointings [he] was confirmed in his position."[31] Beginning with a single church, his own, in New York, he reorganized as the Church of God, World Headquarters, those of his father's followers who were loyal to him and resumed his evangelistic activities.

The first twenty-nine published teachings of the Church of God (Huntsville, Alabama) are identical, almost word for word, with the twenty-nine teachings of the Church of God (Cleveland, Tennessee). The major stress falls on the positions enunciated by Ambrose Jessup Tomlinson on divine healing, sanctification, the baptism of the Holy Spirit with speaking in tongues as evidence, Christ's premilliennial second coming, and the signs of Mark 16: 17-18, that are to follow believers.[32] The Church of God *Book of Doctrines 1903 to 1970* has sections on the Bible as truth, the universal sinfulness of human beings, repentance, justification, sanctification, and the baptism with the Holy Ghost. Under "Ordinances of the Lord" it treats of baptism of believers by immersion in water in the name of the Father and of the Son and of the Holy Ghost, the Lord's Supper in unleavened bread and unfermented grape juice, tithing and giving, and the healing of the body provided in the atonement. A third section discusses the name, the organization, and the officers of the Church of God. The last section takes up church practices: women are not to speak, that is, take up the reins of government, in the church; speaking in tongues is not to be forbidden; a woman's covering is her hair, not supplementary headgear; total abstinence from alcoholic beverages, tobacco, and drugs is to be observed; no meats (specifically pork) or drinks are to be forbidden; inward adornment of the heart is more important than outward adornment, and ultimately Christians will learn how to exemplify the Spirit of Christ while putting off worldly pride; swearing of oaths and membership in lodges is inconsistent with membership in the Church of God: God bestows nine gifts of the Spirit on the church. The thirtieth teaching of the Church of God, the kingdom of God on earth, implies that the Church of God holds the keys to the Kingdom of God, that the saints will be set up in the government of the nations, that preaching will bring forth the Kingdom of God, and that war budgets ought to be used on behalf of the needy. The final chapter discusses Christ's early return, the rapture, the millennium, and the "four judgments."[33]

Homer A. Tomlinson taught in the official newspaper of the Church of God (Huntsville, Alabama) that Jesus is not God, but only the Son of God.[34] In 1953 he urged upon his church three objectives: (1) peace on earth and an end to war among nations by a wholesale intercontinental population transfer of 280 million people; (2) the abolition of poverty; and (3) development of a glorious church, "holy and without blemish."[35] In announcing a new autobiographical history of the Church of God movement in December 1967, Tomlinson promised that the years 1968 through 1974 would take their place as "the seven best years of history" since the seven good years of Joseph in Egypt; he called on his church and the whole world to be ready by October 7, 1975, for Christ's second coming.[36]

Tomlinson was an indefatigable traveler with a flair for the dramatic. In 1943 he visited forty-three countries "to proclaim revival of religion." In 1952 he went to sixty-nine lands, "going boldly for peace on earth" and holding aloft "the All-Nations banner of love given him by his father."[37] Beginning in 1954 he visited the capitals of 101 nations over the next twelve years. Persuaded that he had been chosen in a revelation to be "the king of all nations of men in righteousness," he enthroned himself in some public place in each capital, promising the nation in question that its days of wars were over. For this ceremony he habitually wore a scarlet academic gown, a crown "with 14 tines" on his head and the red, white, and purple banner of the Church of God (Huntsville, Alabama) suspended from his neck. The 101st "coronation" took place on Friday, October 7, 1966, in Zion Square in Jerusalem coincident with the opening of the church's world headquarters near Jaffa Gate, Jerusalem.[38] By standing and kneeling in prayer at the Brandenburg Gate that divides East and West Berlin in 1952, Tomlinson asserts that he kept the "cold war" from erupting into a "hot war" for the next sixteen years.[39]

For the period August 1 to September 9, 1967, he announced a forty-day fast for "peace on earth" after what he described as the biblical pattern, taking only an occasional cup of black coffee and drinking sparingly of water and fruit juices, principally of the white grapes of Eshcol "flown in especially for him from the Holy Land."[40]

In 1952, in 1960, in 1964, and again in 1968 Tomlinson ran for the presidency of the United States of America as the Theocratic Party's candidate with the slogan "government under God through men of God."[41] The perennial platform of the Theocratic Party, drafted by Tomlinson, its chairman, has four sets of twelve laws each. The first set, for individuals, consists of the Ten Commandments, plus the injunctions, "This is my beloved son, hear ye him," and "Love one another." The second set, for world government, calls for one gathering of nations under one world ruler, with each nation choosing a national ruler subject to the world ruler's approval. Nations which do not unite with the others or which resort to war will suffer drought and plague. An annual October gathering (in which only men would be heard, while women would keep silent) would not pass laws, but only make recommendations. Adherence to the laws of the platform would be as the result of teaching, not force. All nations would bring a tenth of their national income to Jerusalem. The third set of laws, for individual nations, calls for the union of church and state in Jesus, but with freedom of worship and liberty. Tithes instead of taxes would support the church-state, which would follow the new revelations that it would receive for government and peace. the 1965 scale of wages, profits, and progress would be maintained by unlimited production and free enterprise. All nations and races would be equal.

Wars, crime, delinquency, divorces, and the use of tobacco, intoxicants, and narcotics would be abolished. There would be Bible reading and prayer in all schools. Roman and English law would be abandoned for new civil and criminal codes. These new codes would constitute the fourth set of principles. Repentant criminals would be forgiven 490 times, but unrepentant criminals would be punished under the present codes. The jury system would give way to trial before godly judges, who would execute punishment by their word and not by force. The punishment would affect the body; it might take the form of sickness or it might even be death. Prisons would become refuges and cities of safety, to give criminals time to repent. Thieves would show their repentance by restoring fourfold what they had taken. Civil litigants would award adversaries double, and covetous persons would be sentenced to lose everything. During the changeover to these new principles, all repentant prisoners would be set free and civil litigants would withdraw all pending actions and would reconsider.[42]

Officials in the Church of God (Huntsville, Alabama) are appointed, not elected. The authority of the bishop of the Church of God (formerly general overseer)[43] is greater than that of the head of the Church of God (Cleveland, Tennessee) or the Church of God of Prophecy.

The Church of God (Huntsville, Alabama) holds two assemblies annually, a national assembly in the United States, usually in the Middle West, and an October "world assembly" in Jerusalem. The latter is linked with a tour of the Holy Land.

Since Homer Tomlinson's death, the general overseership of the church body has devolved on his chosen successor, Bishop Voy M. Bullen, and the headquarters for the United States of America has been moved from Queens Village, New York, to 2504 Arrow Wood Drive, Southeast, Huntsville, Alabama 35803. The Church of God (Huntsville, Alabama) claims 1,933 churches with a total membership of 75,290 in the United States and in foreign missions in Panama, Haiti, Israel, Nigeria, and Ghana.

## The Church of God (1957 Reformation)

By accepting the jurisdiction of the assembly of the Church of God of Prophecy, General Overseer M. A. Tomlinson in 1956 vacated the seat of authority as the anointed leader of the Church of God, according to Grady R. Kent (1909–1964). For claiming to be a prophet in the spirit and power of John the Revelator and for declaring that not the assembly but the anointed leader was the highest authority, Kent himself was excommunicated by the assembly of 1957. Thereupon, he asserted, "the almighty works of God and the circumstances and need brought about [his] appointment as chief bishop" of the Church of God of All Nations that he and his three hundred supporters proceeded to organize.[44] The phrase "Of All Nations" was dropped from the name in 1962. Tomlinson's followers regard his action in 1957 as "the great reformation of the church which brought about the restoration of all things" spoken of in Acts 3:20–21.[45]

The twenty-four basic Bible teachings of the Church of God (1957 Reformation) declare that human beings must be born again in three steps: repentance, justification, and regeneration; that sanctification (identified with the remission of sins) is the second definite work of grace, which purges believers from their Adamic nature; that after cleansing or sanctification the baptism of the Holy Ghost, with speaking in tongues as the initial evidence, must take place; and that water baptism is to be performed by immersion. They call for holiness, the fruit of the Spirit, abstinence from narcotics (especially smoking), and tithing and giving; affirm the necessity of the five gifts of the ministry and the nine gifts of the Spirit; require twelve gentile apostles in the Church of God; direct the annual participation in the Passover (Lord's) Supper and in the washing of the saints' feet in connection with it; prescribe breadbreaking (observed about three times a year) on the basis of I Corinthians 10:17 and Acts 2:42, 46; assert that signs will follow the believers, that divine healing is provided for in the atonement, and that intoxicating beverages are in the same category as narcotics; demand restitution wherever possible; prohibit the taking of oaths and the wearing of gold or jewelry for ornament; reaffirm the early church's teaching on forbidden meats; identify Saturday as the Sabbath in the restoration of all things; affirm that the millennium will separate the resurrection to eternal life from the resurrection to eternal punishment; assert the premillennial return of Christ for the rapture of the saints during the three and a half years of the indignation, to be followed by his return for his millennial reign; oppose divorce and remarriage; and prohibit making a person with two living companions a bishop, deacon, or licensed prophetess.[46] These teachings are not regarded as the whole of the teachings of the Bible.[47] Again, the Church of God (1957 Reformation) does not regard its members as the only born-again believers, nor does it hold that membership in the Church of God (1957 Reformation) is a prerequisite for eternal life.

The Church of God (1957 Reformation) denounces the observance of Easter, Halloween, and Christmas. It rejects the Roman calendar in favor of the Jewish calendar. It observes February 13 (the anniversary of the day "when the church fell into the hands of Chief Bishop Kent") as "Reformation Day"; the 14th of Abib (Passover); Pentecost; the 2nd of Zif (the marking of Mount Hattin in 1962 as he place where Jesus esablished his church); June 13 ("the Arise, Shine," the anniversary of the day when Ambrose Jessup Tomlinson "found" the Church of God); the 15th to the 23rd of Tishri (Tabernacles); and the feast of Hannakuk (*sic*) or Lights on December 25 (not for the lighting of candles but to send an offering to the church headquarters for Jewish work).[48]

The government of the Church of God (1957 Reformation) is theocratic. The chief bishop, as the thirteenth apostle, rules in Christ's stead. He is assisted by the four corners, the twelve apostles, the seventy, and the seven. The ministry consists of bishops and deacons. A state bishop presides over a state or territory, a pastor over a local church. Women may be licensed as prophetesses and female servants. The sacraments are marriage; the Lord's Supper (observed at least three times a year and received by each member at least once, preferably on the 14th of Abib); and water baptism with the formula "In obedience to the command of our Lord and Savior Jesus Christ we baptize our brother (or sister) in the name of Jehovah God, the Father, Jesus Christ the Son, and the Holy Spirit, the Spirit of God," whereupon the candidate is immersed.[49]

The Church of God (1957 Reformation) recognizes the right of the nation to resort to arms to protect its rights and liberty when peaceful methods fail. It permits its young men to serve in the armed forces in unarmed, noncombatant, conscientious-objector status.[50]

The General Assembly meets twice a year. The headquarters are at Jerusalem Acres (Box 1207), Cleveland, Tennessee 37311. There are 30 churches in the United States and Canada, with an estimated total membership of 30,000. The Church of God (1957 Reformation) carries on foreign operations in Mexico, the Caribbean, India, Nigeria, England, Finland, and Israel. In 1976 it opened a school to train ministers and laypeople for work in the church body.[51]

## NOTES

1. Charles W. Conn, *Like a Mighty Army Moves the Church of God 1886–1955* (Cleveland, Tenn.: Church of God Publishing House, 1955), pp. 6-7, quoting L. Howard Juillerat, ed., *Brief History of the Church of God* (Cleveland, Tenn.: Church of God Publishing House, 1922), pp. 7-8. The authorship of the *Brief History* is uncertain.

2. Elmer T. Clark, *The Small Sects in America* (rev. edn.; Nashville, Tenn.: Abingdon-Cokesbury Press, 1949), p. 100. Conn, p. 7, cites this statement approvingly.

3. For Tomlinson's own vivid description of this experience, see chap. 4, "Endued with Power from on High; A. J. Tomlinson Receives the Holy Ghost," *Diary of A. J. Tomlinson*, ed. Homer A. Tomlinson (Queen's Village, N.Y.: The Church of God, World Headquarters, 1949), vol. 1, pp. 27-30. See also Lillie Duggar, *A. J. Tomlinson, Former General Overseer of the Church of God* (Cleveland, Tenn.: White Wing Publishing House, 1964), pp. 52-53 ("He has given his version of what took place on the twelfth day

of January, 1908, when he *finally* received the Holy Ghost" [emphasis added]). In recent years, Homer A. Tomlinson, appealing to the testimony of unnamed witnesses, has asserted that his father "received the Holy Ghost speaking in other tongues in 1896, but it was his first experience and he hardly knew at the moment that he had received the actual experience." Homer Tomlinson sees his father's description of the 1908 experience as "a vision of the great missionary tasks before the Church of God" (*The Church of God*, August 15, 1966, p. 4).

4. Conn, p. 178, n. 12, lists the fifteen charges against Tomlinson. For Tomlinson's own account of the "split," see *Diary of A. J. Tomlinson*, ed. Homer A. Tomlinson (Queens Village, N.Y.: The Church of God, 1953), vol. 2, pp. 13-15. See also Duggar, pp. 194-217. The "Tomlinson Church of God," since the division of 1943, is represented by the Church of God of Prophecy and the Church of God (Huntsville, Alabama).

5. A controversy about the question if

sanctification is an instanteous or "definite" work of grace or if it is progressive came to a head in 1944, but was left unresolved (Conn, p. 271). John Bernard Oliver, "Some Newer Religious Groups" (New Haven, Conn.: unpublished Ph.D. Dissertation, Yale University, 1946) described the Church of God as "extremely puritanical in matters relative to recreation, luxury, and sex." In adition to the actions noted in the "teachings," bobbed hair on a woman, attending motion pictures, and speculating in the stock market were also seen as impermissible evidences of "worldliness" (cited in John Thomas Nichol, *Pentecostalism* [New York: Harper & Row, 1966], pp. 101-102).

6. The biblical documentation is Romans 14:2-17; I Corinthians 8:8; I Timothy 4:1-5.

7. The biblical documentation is Hosea 2:11; Romans 13:1-2; 14:5-6; Colossians 2:16-17.

8. Conn, p. 119, n. 11.

9. Ibid., p. 120.

10. Ibid., p. 312.

11. Baptism may be repeated. Thus it is recommended that all ministers who shall apply for membership in the Church of God be baptized in water. Baptism in water is required of a minister whose license has been revoked and who goes into open sin before he is reinstated. Reinstatement is possible, for instance, after five years if a minister is found guilty of adultery or fornication, and after one year if he or she is found guilty of unseemly or unbecoming conduct with the opposite sex. ("Supplement to the Minutes," *Minutes of the 51st General Assembly of the Church of God* [Cleveland, Tenn.: Church of God Publishing House, 1966], p. 77).

12. Conn, pp. 280-282. For expositions of this declaration of faith see Ralph E. Day, *Manual of Instruction in the Faith of the Church for Young People (Ages 12 through 24 Years)* (cover title: *Our Church of God Faith*) (Cleveland, Tenn.: Pathway Press, 1959) (95-page brochure), and James L. Slay, *This We Believe* (Cleveland, Tenn.: Pathway Press, 1963), a lay theology in the form of a workers' training correspondence course.

13. Included are the Iglesia de Dios (Mission Board) of Puerto Rico, which joined the Church of God (Cleveland, Tennessee), in 1944, and its continental North American extension, the Eastern Spanish District of the Church of God. See Donald Troy Moore, *Puerto Rico para Cristo: A History of the Progress of the Evangelical Missions on the Island of Puerto Rico* (Cuernavaca, Mexico: Centro Intercultural de Documentacion [CIDOC], 1969), pp. 4/42-4/43. The Western Spanish District includes the Spanish-speaking churches of the territory from Texas to California.

14. The Full Gospel Church of God in South Africa merged organizationally with the Church of God (Cleveland, Tennessee) in 1951 (Conn, pp. 283-288). The 90,000 white and black members of this segment of the Church of God are separated according to the apartheid policy of the Republic of South Africa.

15. "A Brief History of 'The (Original) Church of God,' " in *Manual or Discipline of the (Original) Church of God, Incorporated* (Chattanooga, Tenn.: The [Original] Church of God, 1966), p. 61.

16. Ibid., pp. 16-29.

17. Ibid., pp. 34-39. Grape juice, not wine, is used in the Lord's Supper. The vessels, wash pans, glasses, and pitchers, used for the Lord's Supper and foot washing are dedicated to the Lord and are not to be used for any other purpose (ibid., p. 40).

18. Quoted in John Thomas Nichol, *Pentecostalism* (New York: Harper & Row, 1966), p. 138.

19. *These Truths about the Church of God of Prophecy* (Cleveland, Tenn.: The Church of God of Prophecy, n.d.) (18-page pamphlet), p. 4.

20. Ibid., pp. 5-9; *Twenty-Nine Important Bible Truths* (12-page undated pamphlet); letter from the Reverend A. T. Wagar, manager, Church Benefit Association.

21. *These Truths about the Church of God of Prophecy*, p. 13.

22. Cited letter from the Reverend Mr. Wagar. The Church of God of Prophecy has its own flag of red (for Christ's blood), white (for purity), blue (for truth), and purple (for kingship), with a scepter, a star, and a crown on it. It "never takes precedence over the national flag of any country" (ibid., p. 17). The Church of Prophecy Marker

Association has erected markers at the Fields of the Wood near Murphy, North Carolina, where the Church of God movement originated in 1903; at the site of the First Assembly of the Church of God in Cherokee County, North Carolina; on Mount Hattin, Israel, where the Church of God of Prophecy believes that Christ organized his church; and on the island of Nassau, The Bahamas, to commemorate Columbus' discovery of America (ibid., p. 15).

23. Charles W. Conn, *Where the Saints Have Trod: A History of Church of God Missions* (Cleveland, Tenn.: Pathway Press, 1959), p. 27.

24. It was popularly known as "Bishop Poteat's Church of God" (Elmer T. Clark, *The Small Sects in America* [rev. edn.; Nashville: Abingdon-Cokesbury Press, 1949], p. 104).

25. Letter from the Reverend Homer A. Tomlinson, bishop, the Church of God (Huntsville, Alabama).

26. Letter from the Reverend M. E. Littlefield, 910 17th Street, Northwest, Cleveland, Tennessee.

27. Howard Carr, ed., *Declaration of Bible Order of the Church of God House of Prayer* (rev. edn.; Markleysburg, Pennsylvania: Church of God House of Prayer, 1964) (16-page pamphlet), p. [2].

28. Ibid., pp. 12-15.

29. Communications from the Reverend Charles MacNevin, general superintendent, the Church of God House of Prayer. Other designations that the church body considered prior to incorporation were the Church of God, United Churches of God, and Evangelical Church of Christ (Carr, p. [16]).

30. Homer A. Tomlinson referred to the three groups respectively as the Third Part, the Second Part, and the First Part of the Church of God movement by way of allusion to Zechariah 13:8-9.

31. *Diary of A. J. Tomlinson*, ed. Homer A. Tomlinson (Queens Village, N.Y.: The Church of God, World Headquarters, 1953), vol. 2, p. 110.

32. For the text of the twenty-nine teachings of the Church of God (Huntsville, Alabama), see *The Church of God*, vol. 27, no. 5 (May 1970), 3. The thirtieth teaching has since been added. The signs of Mark 16:17-18 include protection against venomous snakes, immunity to the drinking of lethal poison, and the ability to raise the dead (ibid., vol. 23, no. 16 [August 15, 1966], 4).

33. *The Book of Doctrines 1903–1970 Issued in the Interest of the Church of God* (Huntsville, Alabama: Church of God Publishing House, 1970). The baptismal formula appears on p. 65.

34. "Jesus is not God. . . . Jesus himself nearly always referred to himself as 'the Son of Man,' though he did not hesitate to identify himself as the Son of God. . . . [St. Paul] said that Jesus would himself turn the kingdom, his Father's kingdom, over to the God of Abraham, and he would be all in all, while Jesus himself would be just one of the brethren. . . . Our brethren of Israel, of Islam, can now realize that we as Christians hold to the same God the Father, the God of Abraham, even as they do. We count Jesus the Son of God even as we count them, all of them, the sons of God, the children of God, if they walk in the ways of righteousness. . . . The great God of heaven and earth through Jesus would show that men and women of this flesh could live without sin, could be a blessing to others. . . . Jesus set the example for goodness and righteousness. We come in his name to the Father . . . for then, by referring to him, the Father knows that we will be among those who want goodness and righteousness, as Jesus proclaimed. Jesus is not here now, nor his apostles, but we are here, and are now doing far more than Jesus did. . . . [Jesus] sent forth only eighty-two missionaries. . . . From 1926 to 1936, in just ten years, the one church I served as pastor, located at 9010 168th St., Jamaica, New York, sent forth more than ten thousand missionaries, the best trained in all history of Christian missions for the work, to every nation in the world" (ibid., vol. 24, no. 11 [June 1, 1967], 1-2).

35. *Diary*, 2: 114, 122.

36. News release, " 'Seven Years of Good' to Start Jan. 1st," the Church of God, Queens Village, New York, dated December 15, 1967; *The Church of God*, vol. 25, no. 1 (January 1, 1968), 1; no. 2 (February 1, 1968), 1.

37. *Diary*, 2: 113.

38. *The Church of God*, vol. 24, no. 11 (June 1, 1967), 1; no. 13 (July 1,

1967), 1; William Whitworth, "Profiles on the Tide of the Times: Bishop Homer A. Tomlinson," *The New Yorker*, vol. 42, no. 31 (September 24, 1966), 67-108. Tomlinson noted that the only capitals that refused to allow him to proceed with his coronation rite were Saigon, South Vietnam; Hanoi, North Vietnam; and Washington, D.C. In the tradition of his predecessor, Bishop Voy M. Bullen and his wife on October 24, 1969, raised the banner of the Church of God, World Headquarters, over Mount Zion, Jerusalem, in token that on that day "by pure faith the Church of God in the 3d World Assembly restored the Kingdom of God to all Israel" (*The Church of God*, vol. 27, no. 4 [April 4, 1970], 1).

39. *The Church of God*, vol. 24, no. 11 (June 1, 1967), 2.

40. Ibid., vol. 24, no. 14 (August 1, 1967), 1. After losing twenty-five pounds in twenty-five days, Tomlinson discontinued his fast, but ate sparingly of solid food for the remainder of the forty days (ibid., no. 16 [October 1, 1967], 3).

41. Ibid., vol. 25, no. 2 (February 1, 1968), 1,3; no. 3 (March 1, 1968), 1; no. 7 (July 1, 1968), 2. In 1967 Tomlinson was the keynote speaker at the convention which kicked off the Theocratic Party's 1968 campaign. Church of God Bishop William ("Bill") R. Rogers of Fulton, Missouri, was apparently to have been the standard bearer. His announced strategy plans called for him to perform "Joshua-Jericho 'exploits' " around every county courthouse and state capitol in all fifty states. He would walk six times around the building "with steady military cadence of 160 ft. per minute, silent, speaking to none, save to kneel in prayer to Almighty God for the blessings of God upon the whole state" or county. On the seventh round the athletic forty-four-year old bishop would "start with a leap and a shout, blow his 37-inch hunting horn (from a Texas Longhorn) to all the voters of the state [or county, and] race around the . . . edifice at breakneck speed in his fervor" (ibid., vol. 24, no. 10 [May 15, 1967], 1; 2-page flyer headed "Bill Rogers for U. S. President, 1968"). But on February 13, 1968, Tomlinson suddenly announced that he would propose Lyndon

B. Johnson as the Theocratic Party's candidate at its nominating convention, because he "has led America half-way into the Kingdom of God by his help for the poor, the sick and the afflicted, the children and the aged, in the greatest manifestation of Christian love this age has ever known." Ultimately, however, the party nominated Tomlinson for the presidency for the fourth time.

42. *The Church of God*, vol. 25, no. 6 (June 1, 1968), 2. Tomlinson's activity in the Theocratic Party was in a sense a reversal of the position which the Church of God movement took in 1908, when it affirmed its opposition "to the union of church and State under any circumstances." At the same time, Tomlinson's political activities revealed a social concern that Pentecostalism's critics claim not to find generally in the movement.

43. The title was changed in 1966, although Tomlinson continued to use it. The 1966 assembly also abolished the office of state overseer, partly because of "the number of overseers who have left the church and formed other church bodies" (*St. Louis Post-Dispatch*, August 20, 1966).

44. Grady R. Kent, *Treatise of the 1957 Reformation Stand* (Cleveland, Tenn.: Church Publishing Company, n.d.) (20-page tract), pp. [11]-[15]. As a reminder of his protest on February 13, 1957, Kent grew a beard, which he wore until his death in 1964; while wearing a beard is not obligatory in the Church of God (1957 Reformation), many of the male members do so (ibid., pp. [17]-[20]).

45. *Basic Bible Teachings* (Church Publishing Company: Cleveland, Tenn.: n.d.) (32-page pamphlet), p. 4.

46. Ibid., pp. 5-27. Its ensign consists of a white field with two horizontal strips of blue, the scepter of David, the emblem of the Church of God (1957 Reformation) (a star of David and a seven-branched candlestick upon a cross), and a crown (ibid., pp. 29-31).

47. The Declaration of Faith of the Church of God (1957 Reformation) affirms belief in the Trinity; Christ as God's atonement; his virgin birth; his humanity and divinity; his death, burial, and resurrection after three days and three nights in the earth; his ascension; his gift of the baptism of the Holy

Spirit on Pentecost; his establishment of the Church of God; the continuation of the apostolic order; the falling away of the early church and its resurrection at the end of the Dark Ages; the cessation of the existence of the Church of God in 325; the apostles' doctrine; human fallibility; the Anointed of God as the head of the Church of God and the mutual spokesman between the church and God; the Old and New Testaments rightly divided; water baptism by immersion; the Lord's Supper and foot washing; the indissolubility of marriage except for fornication; the full restoration of all things; the restoration and everlasting salvation of the twelve tribes of Israel; Christ's bodily second coming for the rapture; his return to earth three and a half years later to set up his millennial reign in Jerusalem; eternal life for the righteous and eternal punishment (without liberation or annihilation) for the wicked; and the new heaven and the new earth (Grady R. Kent and Marion W. Hall, *The Church of God Business Guide and Spiritual Manual* [Cleveland, Tenn.: The Church of God, 1966] [42-page mimeographed document], pp. 37-40).

48. Ibid., pp. 9-13.
49. Ibid., pp. 14-31. The revelation of the marriage covenant to be used for church members is awaited. Wine (not grape juice) is used in the Lord's Supper.
50. Ibid., p. 37.
51. Letter from Bishop Robert S. Somerville, chief bishop, the Church of God.

## BIBLIOGRAPHY

*The Body of Christ: A Searching Analysis in Lesson Form of the Divine Church as It Is Outlined in Holy Scripture.* Cleveland, Tenn.: Bible Training Camp of the Church of God of Prophecy, n.d. This 99-page brochure contains a 15-lesson course on the doctrine of the church as taught in the Church of God of Prophecy.

Conn, Charles W. *Like a Mighty Army Moves the Church of God 1886-1955.* Cleveland, Tenn.: Church of God Publishing House, 1955.

————. *Where the Saints Have Trod: A History of Church of God Missions.* Cleveland, Tenn.: Pathway Press, 1959.

*Diary of A[mbrose] J[essup] Tomlinson.* Ed. Homer A. Tomlinson. 3 vols. Queens Village, N.Y.: The Church of God, World Headquarters, 1949–1955.

Duggar, Lillie. *A. J. Tomlinson: Former General Overseer of the Church of God.* Cleveland, Tenn.: White Wing Publishing House, 1964. The author was Tomlinson's private secretary.

Tomlinson, Homer A. *The Shout of a King.* Queens Village, N.Y.: The Church of God, World Headquarters, 1968.

# 7. "Oneness" Pentecostal Bodies

## United Pentecostal Church International

The Assemblies of God were organized in 1914. To avoid destructive doctrinal controversy the organization adopted the principle that "Holy inspired Scripture" is "the all-sufficient rule for faith and practice." But the "oneness" (i.e., nontrinitarian) movement that was to bring about a major split was already under way. At the Los Angeles camp meeting of 1913, R. E. McAlister spoke forcefully on baptizing "as the first-century church had, that is, in the name of Jesus Christ." At the same meeting John G. Scheppe, after a night of prayer, "was given a glimpse of the power of the blessed name of Jesus."[1] Although baptism in the name of Jesus in Pentecostal circles can be traced back at least to 1902,[2] the idea now began to catch on rapidly. Even outstanding leaders of the movement accepted rebaptism in the name of Jesus. The New Issue, as it was called, was soon linked with an affirmation of the complete identity of the Father, the Son, and the Holy Spirit, and a corresponding denial of the doctrine of the Trinity. In 1916 the Assemblies of God rejected the "oneness message" by adopting a strongly trinitarian Statement of Fundamental Truths. Through this action the organization lost over a quarter of its ministers, including two members of the Executive Presbytery, and its missionary giving shrank to under $5,000.

The proponents of "oneness" thus expelled from the Assemblies of God organized the General Assembly of the Apostolic Assemblies early in 1917. In order to secure exemption of their ministers from selective service they found it expedient to unite with the much smaller, racially integrated Pentecostal Assemblies of the World, a West Coast "oneness" body organized in 1914, and to retain the latter name for the merged organization.

In 1924 a considerable proportion of the white membership, especially in the South, withdrew because of the problems with which the biracial character of the organization confronted them. The following year the withdrawing constituency formally organized three new bodies: (1) the Pentecostal Ministerial Alliance at Jackson, Tennessee; (2) the Emanuel's Church in Jesus Christ, composed of persons who regarded the Ministerial Alliance as too loosely organized and not sufficiently emphatic on "oneness" and baptism in the name of Jesus, at Houston, Texas; and (3) the Apostolic Churches of Jesus Christ at St. Louis. The latter two merged in 1928 under the name of the St. Louis group.

In 1931 the still interracial Pentecostal Assemblies of the World (except for a black fraction led by Bishop Samuel Grimes) merged with the Apostolic Churches of Jesus Christ to form the Pentecostal Assemblies of Jesus Christ. The Pentecostal Ministerial Alliance reorganized itself in 1932 to "include the local churches as an integral part of the organization" and took the name Pentecostal Church, Incorporated. In 1937 most of the black members of the Pentecostal Assemblies of Jesus Christ returned en masse to the Pentecostal Assemblies of the World. This left the Pentecostal Church, Incorporated, and the Pentecostal Assemblies of Jesus Christ as the two major white proponents of the "oneness" doctrine.

A number of concerns tended to separate the two bodies. One group of issues centered about the standards concerning modest attire and worldly pleasures that some of the Pentecostals had brought with them out of their former Holiness affiliations. More serious was the issue of the essentiality of water baptism in the name of Jesus for the new birth and therewith for eligibility to participate in the rapture of the bride of Christ at Christ's return. On this point a majority of members of the Pentecostal Assemblies of Jesus Christ took a strongly affirmative position, while a majority in the Pentecostal Church, Incorporated, inclined to view the baptism of the Holy Spirit as the essential requirement. But the desire for unification in the two bodies proved to be stronger than these divisive issues. In 1945 the groups united as the United Pentecostal Church International on the basis of a Fundamental Doctrine Statement, which declared:

> The basic and fundamental doctrine of this organization shall be the Bible standard of full salvation, which is repentance, baptism in water by immersion in the name of the Lord Jesus Christ, and the baptism of the Holy Ghost with the initial sign of speaking with other tongues as the Spirit gives utterance.
>
> We shall endeavor to keep the unity of the Spirit until we all come into the unity of the faith, at the same time admonishing all brethren that they shall not contend for their different views to the disunity of the body.[3]

The teaching of the United Pentecostal Church International about God is characteristic: "[The] one true God manifested Himself in the Old Testament in divers ways; in the Son while He walked among men; as the Holy Spirit after the ascension. The one true God, the Jehovah of the Old Testament, took upon Himself the form of man, and as the Son of man, was born of the virgin Mary."[4] It insists that "the scriptural mode of baptism is immersion, and is only for those who have fully repented, having turned from their sins and a love of the world. It should be administered by a duly authorized minister of the Gospel, in obedience to the Word of God, and in the name of our Lord Jesus Christ, according to the Acts of the Apostles 2:38; 8:16; 10:48; 19:5; thus obeying and fulfilling Matthew 28:19."[5] Christ instituted "the use of literal bread and the fruit of the vine, which are partaken of, literally, as emblems of His broken body and shed blood. There is also a spiritual significance and blessing in partaking of the sacrament." Foot washing "is a divine insitution. It is well to follow [Our Lord's] example and wash one another's feet, thus manifesting the spirit of humility."[6]

The church disapproves of its members "indulging in any activities which are not conducive to good Christianity and Godly living, such as theaters, dances, mixed bathing, women cutting their hair, make-up, any apparel that immodestly exposes the body, all worldly sports and amusements, and unwholesome radio programs and music. Furthermore, because of the display of all these evils on television, we disapprove of any of our people having television sets in their homes."[7] It teaches "the restitution of all things" (Acts 3:21), but it "cannot find where the devil, his angels, and all sinners are included."[8] The church affirms "unswerving loyalty to our government." It disavows "contempt for law or magistrates, to be disloyal to our Government and in sympathy with our enemies, or to be unwilling to sacrifice for the preservation of our commonwealth." Since 1940 it holds that its members "can be consistent in serving our Government in certain noncombatant capacities," but it declares "against participating in combatant service in war, armed insurrection, property destruction, aiding or abetting in or the actual destruction of human life." Since 1930 it asserts that its membership "cannot conscientiously affiliate with any union, boycott, or organization which will force or bind any of its members to belong to any organization; perform any duties contrary to our conscience, or receive any mark, without our right to affirm or reject same."

It explicitly holds "that the people of God should have no connection whatever with secret societies, or any other organization or body wherein there is a fellowship with unbelievers, bound by an oath."[9] When a married person commits fornication, "the innocent party may be free to remarry only in the Lord." To raise a higher standard for the ministry, it recommends that divorced "ministers do not marry again."[10] Its doctrine of the last things includes the "translation of saints" and a premillennial "second coming of Jesus."[11]

The United Pentecostal Church International has about 2,800 churches in the United States and about 125 in Canada, with an inclusive membership of 440,000. Its headquarters are at 8855 Dunn Road, Hazelwood, Missouri 63042. It sponsors the widely heard radio program "Harvestime," and supports 196 foreign missionaries in 46 foreign countries.[12] The church is divided into sovereign statewide or multistate districts headed by superintendents elected for two-year terms. Current emphases are on (1) revival (based on prayer, on the "desperate action" of fasting, on faithfulness in church attendance, on tithing, on offerings and other duties, and on the recapture of the wisdom of personal work); (2) Sunday schools, as important agencies for evangelization, indoctrination, and service; (3) Bible colleges as a source of ministers and missionaries; and (4) home and foreign missions.

## Pentecostal Assemblies of the World, Incorporated

One of the first corporate expressions of the "oneness" movement in Pentecostal circles was a small West Coast body called the Pentecostal Assemblies of the World, organized in 1914. General Assembly of the Apostolic Assemblies, formed in 1917 by "oneness" adherents who had withdrawn from the General Council of the Assemblies of God, merged with the Pentecostal Assemblies of the World shortly afterward. The united body retained the name of the smaller group. It incorporated itself in 1919 and established its headquarters in Indianapolis, where a leading black evangelist, Elder (later Bishop) Garfield T. Haywood, headed a large "oneness" congregation. The national scope of the integrated body created problems, particularly when it came to meetings in the segregated South, and in 1924 the bulk of the white members withdrew to form the Apostolic Church of Jesus Christ in St. Louis, the Emanuel's Church in Jesus Christ in Houston, and the Pentecostal Ministerial Alliance in Jackson, Tennessee. The first two united in 1928, and in 1931 the merged body undertook to unite again with the Pentecostal Assemblies of the World as the Pentecostal Assemblies of Jesus Christ. But Bishop Samuel Grimes, a prominent black leader of the Pentecostal Assemblies of the World, together with some supporters, refused to enter the merger and renewed the charter of the Pentecostal Assemblies of the World in order to keep the name and the organization alive. Problems created by segregation once more arose within the Pentecostal Assemblies of Jesus Christ, and in 1937 most of the black members withdrew to rejoin Bishop Grimes's Pentecostal Assemblies of the World.

Today the Pentecostal Assemblies of the World remains an interracial body. It affirms that its "creed, discipline, rules of order and doctrine is the Word of God as taught and revealed by the Holy Ghost." The denomination's *Minute Book* spells out eighteen specific points. Membership in the body of Christ is obtained through a baptism of water and Spirit, and God alone blots out the names of sinners. But as a matter of legal record, a local congregation should keep a list of the persons subject to its rule. God's standard of salvation demands a Holy-Spirit-filled life. Repentance from the heart is the only ground on which God accepts sinners. On divine healing the denomination holds that the Lord is our Healer and that with his stripes we are healed. Melchizedek gave the first Communion to Abraham in bread and wine; water and grape juice are unauthorized substitutes for wine that the formal church has invented in modern times. Foot washing has as much a divine command as any other ordinance. Jesus is coming to earth again personally. Tithing and free-will offering are God's plan for carrying on the church's work, not begging, rallying, giving socials, shows and concerts, or collecting on the streets. We should rather suffer wrong than do wrong; we are not "to take up any weapon of destruction to slay another, whether in our own defense or the defense of others." It is our duty to obey all requirements of the law that do not contradict God's Word or require bearing arms. "The people of God should have no connection with secret societies"; they may hold membership and offices in unions that are not oath-bound and that do not require them to picket or bar others from their work. The translation of the saints and the millennium are near; at the end of the millennium the Great White Throne judgment will take place. To escape the judgment of God and to enjoy the glory of life eternal, the individual "must be thoroughly saved from his sins, wholly sanctified, and filled with the Holy Ghost."[13]

When both husband and wife have received the baptism of the Spirit, and are thus "believers," divorce is permitted only on the ground of fornication, broadly understood to include other sexual offenses. When one party is a "believer" and the other an "unbeliever," the believer may remarry if the unbeliever secures a divorce. Where both parties are "believers" divorce and remarriage are simply forbidden.[14]

Communion with foot washing is to be observed at least twice a year.[15] "Foot washing ties us in fellowship with our brothers and Communion ties us in fellowship with Christ's suffering." Sins or faults or failings "for best results . . . should be confessed to the pastor," who "is specifically called of God for this purpose and is given a grace to bear things that others are not prepared to bear."[16]

The denomination encourages its members to abstain from food and water until the evening meal once a week.[17]

The denomination's organization resembles that of Methodism. A board of bishops, headed by a presiding bishop, presides over the annual General Convention, the highest deliberative body.[18]

Several years ago the denomination had 527 churches in the United States, with an inclusive membership estimated at 45,000. The denomination conducted foreign missions in the Bahamas, Jamaica, Haiti, England, Liberia, and Nigeria. Recent efforts to contact the organization have been unsuccessful. The headquarters are at 3040 North Illinois Street, Indianapolis, Indiana 46208.

### The Church of the Little Children

Early in this century John Quincy Adams (1891–1951) withdrew from the Baptist ministry because of differences of opinion with his colleagues on the baptism of the Holy Spirit. In 1916 he founded the charismatic Church of the Little Children at Abbott, Texas; in the 1930s he transferred his base of operations to Gunn, Alberta, Canada, where he died. His widow returned to the United States and succeeded him as superintendent of the denomination.

The theology of the movement is eclectic, although basically dispensational and "oneness" Pentecostal (that is, nontrinitarian). The Church of the Little Children identifies Jesus precisely with the Jehovah of the Old Testament. The dogma of the "infernal" Trinity (described originally as the apotheosis of Nimrod, Cush, and Semiramis), observance of Sunday as the Sabbath, the celebration of Christmas and Easter,[19] shaving the male beard, wearing neckties, and using names of days and weeks that incorporate the names of pagan deities (such as "Wednesdays" and "March") are vestiges of Babylonian phallic worship.[20]

Water baptism must be the immersion of believers in the name of Jesus. There is no service of dedication or blessing of infants. Local churches observe the Lord's Supper—the only legitimate act of eating and drinking in honor and memory of Christ—with unleavened bread and wine as often as they wish and practice foot washing on the monthly Sabbath. The outpouring of the Holy Spirit and the gift of tongues (understood as foreign languages that the speakers do not natively speak or understand) have taken place and the world is now in the period of God's last judgments on it prior to the "translation."

The Church of the Little Children accepts the Bible literally as interpreted in the writings of Adams. It teaches divine healing and rejects modern medicine and the services of physicians. Conscientious objection is a tenet of its faith; noncombatant service is not acceptable, but the local churches apparently do not enforce the latter requirement rigidly. Members of the church are committed to acts of love toward little children and seek to ensure that no child is in want or hungry. In its literature the Church of the Little Children opposes Masonry, Christian Science, Jehovah's Witnesses, New Thought, Unity, and trinitarian Christian denominations (especially the Roman Catholic Church). It has no manual other than the works of Adams.

The organization of the denomination is loose. It owns no church edifices and operates from the homes of members in each community. The head of each local community is divinely chosen, but bears no special identifying title. Assemblies "in congregation" were held periodically from 1936 on at Gunn and later at Black Rock, Arkansas, the present headquarters, but the superintendent discontinued them because of the hardship that attendance worked on the members.

Several years ago there were eight "home-churches" in Arkansas, Missouri, Montana, Nebraska, Wyoming, and Saskatchewan. The superintendent maintains a tract ministry by mail.[21]

### Apostolic Overcoming Holy Church of God, Incorporated

According to his autobiography, William Thomas Phillips (b. 1893) was a member of the Methodist Church when he learned the Holiness message, in a tent-meeting evangelistic service in Birmingham, Alabama, from the

Reverend Frank W. Williams. In 1913 Williams ordained Phillips and in 1916 the latter began his career as an evangelist.[22] In March 1917, according to the official historical statement of the Apostolic Overcoming Holy Church of God, Incorporated, "the Holy Ghost in a body of elders" at Mobile, Alabama, selected him as bishop and father of the Ethiopian[23] Overcoming Holy Church of God. He incorporated the new denomination in 1920; in 1927 Apostolic replaced Ethiopian in the corporate name.[24]

The denomination's doctrine of God is that of the "oneness" movement: God is one Personality and one Person; Jesus Christ is the only, invisible God and there is no other beside him; the Father, the Word, and the Holy Ghost are manifested in the person of Jesus Christ, the image of the invisible God,[25] who died on the cross and rose again from the dead by his own merits. Justification is by faith, but "no man is justified with God as long as he is doing what God says not to do."[26] Jesus shed his blood to sanctify the people. Sanctification—described both as a process and as instantaneous—is a second work of grace that begins in regeneration; it affects the whole person. The Christian is "justified by one means of grace and sanctified by another means of grace." Holiness requires members of the church to refrain from intoxicating beverages, snuff, tobacco, morphine and other habit-forming drugs.[27] Speaking in tongues is the true evidence of the baptism of the Holy Spirit. Members of the Church are to expect divine healing ("[but] we do not condemn those who are weak in faith, but exhort and nourish and cherish them until they become strong").[28] At the end of time Christ will come again in a glorified body and the saints will be resurrected and changed from mortality into immortality. The millennium will follow. At its conclusion the Great White Throne judgment will take place and fire will rain out of heaven and destroy the wicked,[29] and the saints will inherit the earth for ever.

Baptism is by immersion in the name of Jesus for the remission of sins.[30] The baptism of the Holy Ghost is to be sought after water baptism. Communion in the natural emblems of bread and wine ("we are under the Melchizedek priesthood, who gave Abraham bread and wine") is carried out whenever the Lord leads the pastor, bishop, or overseer to do so.[31] Foot washing, brothers washing brothers' feet and sisters the feet of sisters, is a divine ordinance.[32] Tithing is the divinely appointed financial system of the church. Members, ministers, and officers tithe into the churches in which they hold membership; pastors (who are unsalaried), bishops, elders, and traveling evangelists must pay tithes to the senior bishop, who pays tithes to the Poor Treasury.[33] Members may not marry unsaved persons,[34] nor may they attend churches of other denominations on the meeting days and nights of the Apostolic Overcoming Church of God, "because it is against the church and the word of God."[35]

The officers of the church are apostles, who bear the title of senior or junior bishop, overseers, evangelists, pastors, and helps.[36] Women may teach and preach on a parity with men.[37] Power is concentrated in the cabinet board of executive officers (bishops and overseers), with the senior bishop—who uses the style "the Right Reverend"—as executive head. The members of the board hold office for an unlimited period of time, although the board is reappointed every four years.

The order of service consists of "voluntary singing, prayer in one accord (kneeling around the altar); Scripture lesson expounded; testimonies given with praise; consecration; a free-will offering, with praise and thanksgiving blessings; announcements; presentation of speakers; sermon; altar calls, with praise and prayer; tarrying, praises and prayer; the apostolic benediction."[38]

The denomination claims an estimated 300 churches in 21 states from coast to coast with a total membership of 75,000, the same figure that the denomination reported in 1956. It carries on foreign missions in Africa, India, and the West Indies. The headquarters are at 514 10th Avenue, West, Birmingham, Alabama 35204.

### Church of the Lord Jesus Christ of the Apostolic Faith

Apostle-Bishop Sherrod C. Johnson (1897–1961), a native of Pine Tree Quarter, Edgecomb County, North Carolina, began his ministry in a church at 1524 South 17th Street, Philadelphia in 1919. Out of this grew the Church of the Lord Jesus Christ of the Apostolic Faith. The multiracial but predominantly black church body is part of the "oneness" movement in Pentecostalism.

It believes that the Roman Catholic Church and the "false churches" that have developed out of it are the "backslidden church spoken of by John [the Divine]." It feels that the church of the Lord Jesus Christ of the Apostolic Faith has restored the apostolic faith in its simplicity and that Jesus Christ is its only real founder.[39]

It holds that Jesus Christ is the Father, Son, and Holy Ghost and that he was the Son of God only from the beginning of his virgin conception in Mary's body until his death on the cross. It rejects as unbiblical the position that there are three distinct persons in the Godhead. Father, Son, and Holy Ghost in its view are only titles or manifestations of the one God.

It rejects baptism in the name of the Father and of the Son and of the Holy Ghost and requires believer's baptism "in the name of the Lord Jesus Christ" as the only valid kind. It rejects sprinkling as a form of baptism and insists on immersion, accompanied by the new birth of the Holy Ghost and speaking in another language as the Spirit gives utterance. In lieu of the baptism of infants it "offers [babies] to the Lord."

It calls for a holy life in this world; teaches the divine healing of believers through anointing with oil and prayer; insists that Communion be given in bread and wine ("not bread and water, or bread and soda water, or bread and grape juice") and that it be observed more than once a year; requires foot washing after Communion and tithing; denies that women are called and sent to preach the gospel; rejects keeping the Saturday Sabbath and other Old Testament festivals and refraining from certain foods in this dispensation; condemns worldliness (such as wearing nylon stockings, shoes with exposed toes and heels, painted lips and enameled nails, straightening one's hair, going to beauty parlors, looking at television,[40] and women wearing any article of male apparel); denounces the prohibition of marriage for clergymen; condemns remarriage after a divorce secured for any reason during the lifetime of the other partner; affirms that the Bible is dependable regardless of the language into which it has been translated; prohibits membership in oath-bound secret societies; approves the use of mechanical musical instruments in the New Testament church; demands that women wear a head-covering when praying and prophesying; declares that Cain's wife was his sister ("we should marry our spiritual sisters as they married their natural sisters"); holds that the penitent thief on the cross was "saved without water" because baptism in water and the Spirit had not yet been preached; and sees the Church[es] of Christ[41] and others as making a mistake in "taking communion every Sunday."

It insists on the multiracial character of the church and on abstaining from blood and things strangled ("a saint cannot eat blood pudding or anything that is polluted"); condemns both the religious observance of Christmas, Lent, Palm Sunday, Good Friday, and Easter and the popular observance of traditional customs associated with these "heathen" days and seasons; prefers simple ordinal numbers to designate the months to the traditional month names; denies that a person "goes to heaven as soon as he dies"; rejects the idea of the crucifixion of Jesus on Friday; and conscientiously opposes "participation in combat and noncombat [military] service in any form," wearing military and naval uniforms, taking "up any weapon of destruction to slay another, whether in our defense or in the defense of others," taking oaths, and pledging allegiance to any national state or flag. It explicitly provides that a member need not give up his life insurance policies, welfare check, mother's assistance, or "blind pension," turn his property over to the church, or abstain from medical treatment, medicine, or medical care.[42]

The headquarters of the Church of the Lord Jesus Christ of the Apostolic Faith are at 22nd and Bainbridge streets, Philadelphia, Pennsylvania 19146. The church at large, the General Assembly, and the board of officials are presided over by the general overseer, who also bears the titles of apostle, bishop, and pastor and is referred to as "His Excellency" and "His Eminence." There are five districts in the United States, each presided over by a district overseer. There are 92 churches in thirty states, most of them in the Southeast; no information is available on the total active membership. All churches begin their Sunday morning services at eleven and their Sunday evening services at seven-thirty. The church body also has churches in the West Indies, British Honduras, the west coast of Africa, and England.

## Church of Our Lord Jesus Christ of the Apostolic Faith, Incorporated

Bishop Robert Clarence Lawson (d. 1961) reportedly organized the Church of Christ of the Apostolic Faith at Columbus, Ohio, as a "oneness" black Pentecostal body in 1919 and established its headquarters at New York. In 1931 it became the Church of Our Lord Jesus Christ of the Apostolic Faith, Incorporated.

It professes to draw its creed, disciplines, and rules of order exclusively from the Bible. It holds that the Father, Son, and Holy Spirit are three different manifestations of the one God, and administers water baptism in the name of the Lord Jesus Christ. Its theological emphases otherwise are those of Pentecostal churches generally: salvation through the blood of Christ; water baptism by immersion; spiritual baptism with the Holy Ghost, with speaking in other tongues as the witness of the gift of the Spirit; and Christ's premillennial return. In addition to water baptism, it observes the Lord's Supper and foot washing as ordinances.

A serious schism divided the body in 1957, when a considerable segment of the churches seceded to form the Bible Way Churches of Our Lord Jesus Christ World Wide.

The chief administrative officer is the senior apostle, one of the seven bishops of the denomination. Headquarters are at 2081 7th Avenue, New York, New York 10027. A national convocation meets annually.

No statistics since the 1957 schism are available. The denomination reportedly carries on foreign operations in the British West Indies, Africa, and the Republic of the Philippines.[43]

## The Bible Way Churches of Our Lord Jesus Christ World Wide, Incorporated

In 1957 Elders Smallwood E. Williams, John S. Beane, McKinley Williams, Winfield Showell, and Joseph Moore led approximately 70 congregations out of the Church of Our Lord Jesus Christ of the Apostolic Faith, Incorporated, and organized the Bible Way Churches of Our Lord Jesus Christ of the Apostolic Faith, Incorporated, at a national Pentecostal ministerial conference held in Washington, D.C. The reasons they assigned for their withdrawal from the parent body were what they called its intolerable authoritarianism and certain of its administrative practices that they felt they could not harmonize with the collective leadership of the apostles in the New Testament. The assembly chose as bishops all five of the above-named elders.

The new denomination perpetuated the "oneness" Pentecostal theology of the group from which they had come. Their official doctrinal statement affirms the Bible as the inspired Word of God; the unity of God ("[The Father, the Son, and the Holy Ghost] are three manifestations of the one God"); the identity of the Father and the Son ("God as Father, being a Spirit, had no blood to shed, so he prepared a body of flesh and blood [for Himself]"); the Holy Ghost as the manifestation of the Spirit of the Creator and of the resurrected Christ ("not the third person in the Godhead"); the continuing guilt of Adam's sin; salvation through the blood of Christ, repentance, water baptism, the baptism of the Holy Ghost, and a godly life; the unqualified essentiality of immersion in the name of the Lord Jesus Christ; the baptism of the Spirit evidenced by speaking in other tongues; the difference between speaking in other tongues and gift of tongues; the need of holiness and of separation from all worldiness; divine healing purchased by the blood of Christ; the imminent second coming of Christ for the rapture of his bride; the resurrection of all the dead; the universal judgment; everlasting punishment for the unjust and life eternal for the righteous.[44]

Members must attend all church business meetings and Holy Communion services; may not use tobacco or intoxicating drinks; are requested to give 10 percent of their income as an offering to God; and may not, if divorced, remarry while the original partner is still alive. On the other hand, the denomination brands as fanaticism the prohibition of straightening or shampooing one's hair and the forbidding of toeless or heelless shoes and neckties.[45] At an annual service of humiliation the members of the church ceremonially wash one another's feet in imitation of Christ's example.

The ministry consists of a presiding bishop, five other bishops, an honorary bishop, five junior bishops, five associate bishops, district elders, pastors, and ministers without churches. Women may serve as missionaries, social missionaries, and junior missionaries. The general convocation meets annually.

The headquarters of the church body are at 1130 New Jersey Avenue, Northwest, Washington, D.C. 20011. It claims approximately 300 churches and missions in the United States with a membership of about 25,000. It carries on foreign operations in the British West Indies, in Liberia, and in England.[46]

### Apostolic Church of Jesus

Mottie Crawford came to Pueblo, Colorado, in 1923 empowered with the gift of healing. Her converts included Antonio Sanches and, later, his brother George. By 1927 their preaching of their newfound conviction had won enough converts among fellow members of the Spanish-speaking community in Pueblo to organize the Apostolic Church of Jesus. With further growth and expansion, they incorporated the new denomination in 1936.

The Apostolic Church of Jesus stresses that the name of the Father, the Son, and the Holy Ghost is Jesus; that Jesus is the Almighty God; and that beside him there is no God. It teaches that "the three-god people" have received their trinitarian doctrine from the Roman Catholic Church, and that churches which preach three distinct persons in the Godhead are accursed and in dividing the Godhead are following the spirit of Antichrist. Its other doctrines and practices are those common to "oneness" Pentecostal denominations.

In addition to the mother church in Pueblo, the denomination has churches and missions in Denver, Westminster, Colorado Springs, Delta, Walsenburg, Fort Garland, San Luis, and Trinidad, Colorado; in Velarde, New Mexico; and in San Francisco and Palo Alto, Califorinia. The 12 centers, which carry on their work in both Spanish and English, have a total membership estimated at 300.[47]

## The Apostolic Faith Church

In 1923, several years after Charles Lochbaum (1876–1962) and his wife, Ada Beatrice Lochbaum (1877–1949), had received the baptism of the Holy Ghost at a prayer meeting of "oneness" Pentecostal believers in California, they came to Hawaii and founded the Apostolic Faith Church in Honolulu.

Its teachings conform almost throughout to the classic "oneness" Pentecostal pattern. There is only one person in God. The name of the Father is Jesus, the name of the Son is Jesus, and the name of the Holy Ghost is Jesus. Salvation requires repentance toward God and restitution. Justification and sanctification are separate and distinct acts of God's grace through faith. The baptism of the Holy Ghost is the gift of power on the sanctified life and is accompanied by speaking with tongues. The atonement destroys sickness and disease. Christ's premillennial second coming has two appearances, the rapture of the waiting bride and judgment on the ungodly. The tribulation will be followed by a literal millennial reign, and this by the Great White Throne judgment. Water baptism is to be by a single immersion in the name of Jesus. The Lord's Supper, to be celebrated at night, "brings healing to our bodies if we discern the Lord's body."[48] In lieu of baptism, infants are blessed.

The headquarters are at 1043 Middle Street, Kalihi, Honolulu, Hawaii 96819. There are five churches, all in Hawaii. They keep no membership rosters on the ground that when believers receive baptism in the name of Jesus Christ their names are written in heaven.

## The Church of Jesus Christ

Under the leadership of Bishop M. K. Lawson, a number of "oneness" Pentecostals organized the Church of Jesus Christ in 1927. Chief doctrines of the church body are repentance and baptism in the name of Jesus Christ and the infilling of the Holy Ghost.

The Lord's Supper is considered to be an expression of union and fellowship; foot washing is viewed as a sign of humility. Marriage must take place only between fellow church members. The civil government should be respected and obeyed except in its use of armed force. Members are expected to live a life of holiness; those who sin willfully are excluded from the membership. The future holds rewards for the faithful and punishment for the wicked. Members refuse to take oaths before magistrates and oppose secret societies.

A general assembly meets each year in August. The congregations are relatively autonomous. Officers of the church include bishops, elders, evangelists, deacons, and deaconesses. Most ministers are self-supporting, earning a living through secular employment, and ordinarily serve more than one but not more than two congregations. *The Messenger* is the church body's official periodical. Bishop R. W. Sapp broadcasts "The Voice of Truth" as the church body's radio ministry .

Headquarters of the Church of Jesus Christ were moved in 1975 from Cleveland, Tennessee, to 5336 Orbank Road, Kingsport, Tennessee 37660. Membership is approximately 37,500 served by 500 ministers. Foreign missions are conducted in Mexico, Jamaica, England, Africa, and India.[49]

### Church of Jesus Christ, Inc.

A number of members of the Church of Jesus Christ in Indiana and Illinois withdrew from the parent body to incorporate a new church body in the late 1940s. Reasons for the withdrawal are not clear. There are 12 ministers and a membership of about 500. Headquarters are located in the congregation in Bloomington, Indiana, where Bishop Ralph Johnson presides.

### The United Church of Jesus Christ

In 1948 a number of members of the Church of Jesus Christ left the parent body and formed the United Church of Jesus Christ. Adherents maintain that the name of Jesus Christ should be called over the person being baptized while he or she is under the water. They use wine mixed with water for the Lord's Supper and apply the term "Reverend" to their ministers. Headquarters are at the congregation at Highway 68, Sweetwater, Tennessee 37874. Chairperson of the church body is W. C. Gibson. Membership is approximately 1,250 with 25 churches and 100 ministers.

### Assemblies of the Lord Jesus Christ

In 1934 a number of members of the Church of Jesus Christ left the parent body over their dissatisfaction with the leadership of Bishop M. K. Lawson and their desire to use grape juice instead of wine for Communion. In 1952 they merged with three other groups to form the Assemblies of the Lord Jesus Christ. Their teachings are similar to those of the parent body with several exceptions. They use grape juice instead of wine for Communion. They allow several formulas for the name in baptism, either the Lord Jesus Christ, the Lord Jesus, or Jesus Christ. They do not object to the term "Reverend" applied to their ministers. They call their leader "Chairman" instead of "Bishop" and do not use the term "Elder" in reference to their ministers. The church body operates a publishing house and a bookstore in Memphis, Tennessee, where their periodical, *The Apostolic Witness*, is published. In 1964 they had about 120 churches in 22 states and 4 foreign countries with a membership of 6,300.

### The Universal Church of Jesus Christ

Because of a disagreement over the Lord's Supper, a number of members of the Church of Jesus Christ withdrew in the 1950s and formed the Universal Church of Jesus Christ. Regarded as apostate by all the church bodies in the orbit of the Church of Jesus Christ, this group has no fellowship with the parent body. It teaches that Communion is spiritual, denies the second coming of Christ, rejects the rapture of the saints, does not wash feet, or maintain a specific Holiness standard. Headquarters are in the congregation at Fort White, Florida, where its chairperson, Elder Earl Fairess, is pastor. Its membership has been in decline.

### The Holiness Church of Jesus Christ

The Holiness Church of Jesus Christ was formed in the late 1950s and early 1960s by those who came under the influential ministry of Bishop L. H. Webb. Headquarters are in Kingsport, Tennessee. Bishop Mack G. Arnold presides. No record of membership is available. Between ten and fifteen churches are located in four states.

### The Church of Jesus Christ of Georgia

Formed by several Georgia members of the Church of Jesus Christ in the 1960s, this church body has only 2 churches and 4 ministers with a membership of less than 100. Chairperson is Elder Wilbur Childers of Ranger, Georgia. The teaching is identical with that of the parent body except that a minister divorced and remarried must after conversion live alone or return to his first wife.

### The Church of Jesus Christ Ministerial Alliance

This group withdrew from the Church of Jesus Christ in 1962 over a disagreement on ministerial courtesy in connection with the death of Bishop M. K. Lawson. There are no doctrinal differences between it and the parent body. It has 300 ministers, 85 churches, and approximately 6,000 members. It carries on mission work in Jamaica, Trinidad, the Bahamas, England, and Australia. Headquarters are at the congregation at 2797 Bryant Street, Portage,

Indiana 46368. Bishop J. Richard Lee presides. Efforts at reunion with the parent body were begun in 1975.

### First Church of Jesus Christ

Formed by members of the Church of Jesus Christ who withdrew in the late 1960s, this group has 40 churches with 43 ministers and 2,200 members. Headquarters are at the congregation at 1100 East Lincoln Street, Tullahoma, Tennessee 37388. Bishop H. E. Honea presides.

### The Primitive Church of Jesus Christ

Formed in 1971, this offshoot of the Church of Jesus Christ has headquarters at Highway 19 North, Inglis, Florida. No information is available on the number of churches, ministers, or members.

### The Associated Brotherhood of Christians

In 1933, near Thomastown, Mississippi, a group of "oneness" or "Jesus Name" Pentecostal ministers organized the Associated Ministers of Jesus Christ. The founders were ministers whom other Pentecostal organizations had refused credentials because of doctrinal differences. In the early 1940s the association incorporated as the Associated Brotherhood of Christians. The organization's intention is to effect a oneness of heart and soul among all Christians and to induce them to be tolerant where doctrinal agreement is not possible.

The brotherhood sees "the basis for Christian fellowship among all blood-washed Spirit-filled people" in what it calls the "Bread of life message" or "spiritual communion." It holds that salvation is "not contingent upon the observance of the 'literal sacrament of the Lord's supper' " with material elements, and that the important thing is "the proper discernment of 'the Lord's body.' " All believers are participants in Christ's body and are eligible to receive the benefits of his broken body as revealed through the Spirit.[50]

The Articles of Faith, which all members are obligated not to oppose even though they may not be in agreement with every doctrinal point, teach the infallibility of the Bible; the unity of the Godhead ("God has revealed himself as Father in creation, as Son in redemption, and as the Holy Ghost in this church age"; "Jesus is the name of God for this dispensation"); the fallibility of human beings; Christ's vicarious suffering; his crucifixion and resurrection; salvation in the present dispensation by grace through faith; God's establishment of a new covenant for this dispensation in which the Mosaic statutes are not binding; the church as a spiritual house; church membership based on repentance, water baptism by immersion in the name of [the Lord] Jesus [Christ], and the baptism of the Holy Ghost of which speaking in other tongues is the sign and witness; holiness; divine healing provided for in the atonement; the nine gifts of the Spirit of I Corinthians 12 and 14; Communion by "partaking of the flesh and blood of the Lord through the Spirit" without "partaking of the natural or literal elements" ("but with due Christian courtesy we respect those who may hold an opposite view"); the second coming of Christ; the resurrection of the dead; the judgment of all human beings; total abstinence from all alcoholic drinks; the reception by believers of their redeemed bodies at Christ's second appearing; and the "seven principles of the doctrine of Christ" set forth in Hebrews 6:1-2.

The articles reject "washing feet in public as a church ordinance"; divorce and remarriage except in proved cases of fornication as defined by the Scriptures; "free love, spiritual companionship, social purity, or any other kindred teachings that might lead to immoral conduct"; the absolute security of believers; the obligation to refrain from tea, coffee, and meats forbidden by the Mosaic law; and participation in war. Members of the Brotherhood are obliged "to register as conscientious objectors to war in any form" or "to register as an objector to combat duty where the bearing of arms is required."[51]

Each church is regarded as an independent unit of which the "militant supervisory head is the pastor," who has full responsibility for selecting subordinate officials of the church. Tithes and offerings are deemed "the financial plan for the support of the gospel work," but each pastor has power to organize the plan most suitable for his church's situation. Churches are not established in the vicinity of existing churches of "like faith," except by mutual agreement. The chairman of the Official Board presides at the annual General Conference. State presbyters, appointed by the Official Board, oversee the work in their respective states.[52]

The headquarters are at 221 East Lowery Street, Hot Springs, Arkansas 71901. The brotherhood comprises about 40 churches, with an estimated total membership of 2,000, and about 100 ministers in 6 states.[53]

### Assemblies of the Lord Jesus Christ

In March 1952 three "oneness" Pentecostal bodies, the Assemblies of the Church of Jesus Christ, the Jesus Only Apostolic Church of God, and the Church of the Lord Jesus Christ merged at Memphis, Tennessee, into a single racially integrated organization under the name Assemblies of the Lord Jesus Christ.

The Articles of Faith of the united body affirm one eternal God who "has revealed Himself as the Father of creation, through His Son in redemption, and as the Holy Spirit by animation" and who "manifested Himself in the Old Testament in divers ways, in the Son while He walked among men, as the Holy Spirit after the ascension." They further affirm that "the Jehovah of the Old Testament took upon Himself the form of man and as the son of man was born of the virgin Mary"; that there is no salvation except in the name of Jesus; that man by his transgression lost his standing but that we have redemption in Christ's redemption through His blood; that "a Christian, to keep saved, must walk with God and keep himself in the love of God and the grace of God"; that Melchizedek gave the first Communion to Abraham in bread and wine and that Christ evidently administered it the same way; that the washing of feet is "as much a divine command as any other"; that divine "healing for the body is in the atonement"; and that repentance is the ground on which God will accept a sinner.

They teach believer's baptism by immersion in the name of Jesus Christ, administered by a duly authorized minister of the gospel; Holy Spirit baptism, with the evidence of speaking with other tongues; holiness and abstention from all appearance of evil; tithing; and the indissolubility of marriage, except for fornication ("no minister shall be accepted . . . who has married for the second time, after his conversion, unless the first marriage was terminated by death"). They prohibit members of the Assemblies of the Lord Jesus Christ from any connection with secret societies or organizations "wherein is a fellowship of unbelievers bound by an oath." They teach Christ's imminent personal return and the translation of the saints followed by the tribulation on earth, a literal millennium, and the final Great White Throne judgment.

They affirm civil government as a divine ordinance, but "declare against combatant service in war, armed insurrection, property destruction, aiding or abetting in or the actual destruction of human life." They approve service, "no matter how hard or dangerous," to the government "in certain noncombatant capacities, but not in the bearing of arms." They prohibit affiliation with any union, boycott, or organization which will force its members to perform any duties contrary to conscience, "or receive any mark without our right to affirm or reject the same." They also disapprove of public school students attending shows, dances, dancing classes, and theaters, "engaging in school activities against their religious scruples, and wearing gymnasium clothes which immodestly expose the body."[54]

The headquarters of the Assemblies of the Lord Jesus Christ are at 3403 Summer Avenue, Memphis, Tennessee 38122. About 400 ministers in the United States and Canada make up the organization.[55] The churches of which they are pastors are affiliated with the organization only in states or areas where this is necessary for tax and other exemptions. In any case the churches which members of the Assemblies serve as pastors are sovereign within themselves. No information is available about the total membership of these churches. The General Conference meets annually.

### Pentecostal Church of Zion, Incorporated

Luther S. Howard (b. 1903) was a boy of twelve living near Spring Lick, Kentucky, when he received the baptism of the Holy Spirit after hearing Pentecostal evangelist George Taylor preach in 1915. True to a vocation that he began to sense in connection with this experience, he received ordination in the Holy Bible Mission Workers at Louisville, Kentucky, in 1920. The organization, founded in 1919 by C. T. Adams (1875–1939) and presided over, after him, from 1929 to 1942 by C. L. Pennington (1880?–1942) and from 1942 to 1953 by the latter's widow, did not long survive Mrs. Pennington's death in the last-cited year. The Indiana ministers who had belonged to it organized the Pentecostal Church of Zion, Incorporated, in 1954 and elected Elder Howard as president. In 1964 he was chosen bishop of the church body.

The Pentecostal Church of Zion takes a "oneness" position on the doctrine of God. It does "not have a closed creed, but believes that [it is] to grow in grace and knowledge of the word of God." If anyone believing to have new light on the Word of God can prove the point to the satisfaction of the board of directors, the doctrine will be adopted.

The first fifteen of its Articles of Religion commit ministers and members of the Pentecostal Church of Zion, Incorporated, to the Bible as the uniquely inspired and infallible Word of God; to God as Creator and to a rejection of the doctrine of evolution; to Jesus as the virgin-born Son of God, outside of whom God has no body; to the Holy Ghost as Comforter; to the redemptive blood of Christ; to the necessity of accepting Christ as personal Savior, of baptism "in the name of the Lord Jesus Christ" by immersion, and of receiving the Holy Ghost with the evidence of speaking in tongues; to belief in the possibility of backsliding and of subsequent forgiveness; to the keeping of the Ten Commandments, including the observance of the Sabbath from Friday sunset to Saturday sunset; to the biblical organization of the church; to tithes and offerings for the support of the church; to the observance of the Levitical law of clean and unclean foods; to abstinence from alcohol, tobacco, and the habitual use of narcotic drugs; to prayer for and anointing of the sick; to belief in the punishment of the wicked after their resurrection and judgment at the end of the millennium; and to the avoidance of worldliness (including attendance at motion pictures, pool halls, dances, and public recreation centers; excessive wearing of jewelry and cosmetics, card-playing; and mixed swimming).

On the last seven of its Articles of Religion the Pentecostal Church of Zion, Incorporated, permits differences of opinion among its members. These authorize a child to come to the altar and repent at any age that he or she feels the need to do so; hold that "the passover [or so-called Lord's Supper] is now celebrated through communion of the Holy Ghost daily and is not to be kept through the symbols [of bread and unfermented grape juice] literally";[56] declare that Christ's crucifixion and death took place on Wednesday and his resurrection on Saturday; see the regathering of literal Israel to the land of Palestine from 1948 on as sign that Christ's second coming is very near; divide the Kingdom of Heaven into three phases, that is (1) the church on earth, (2) the millennial reign of Christ and his saints, and (3) Christ's everlasting reign on a earth under a new heaven; describe the state of the dead as unconsciousness; and call for all members to wear modest street apparel.[57]

The ministry consists of four orders: deacon-deaconess; preacher-evangelist; elder; and bishop. The last named, who holds office for life, is the highest authority, subject to the Board of Directors. The Annual Meeting of the church body is normally held at the headquarters in July.

The headquarters are at Zion College of Theology, French Lick, Indiana 47432. There are 15 churches, nine in Indiana, the remainder in Oklahoma, Alabama, Tennessee, Oregon, Illinois, and Mississippi. The estimated active membership is 500.[58]

### International Ministerial Association, Incorporated
### (Houston, Texas)

The International Ministerial Association, Incorporated, came into being in 1954 to promote cooperation and closer fellowship among "oneness" Pentecostal ministers and churches.

Its doctrinal position commits the members to belief in the Bible as the inspired and, in its original writings, infallible Word of God; in one God who "has revealed himself as Father in creation, through his Son in redemption, and as the Holy Spirit by emanation"; in the incarnation, deity, and mediatorship of Christ; in the fall of the first human beings, by which sin entered the world; the necessity of repentance; in redemption solely by the shed blood of the dying and risen Christ and justification through faith in his finished work; in believer's baptism by immersion "in the name of Jesus Christ"; in the baptism of the Holy Spirit, evidenced by speaking in other tongues, as "the standard of the normal Christian experience"; in divine healing in the atonement; in Communion, foot washing, and tithing; in the manifestation of the nine gifts of the Spirit (I Corinthians 12 and 14) in today's church; in the fruit of the Spirit in the form of the believer's godliness and holy living; in the personal pretribulational second coming of Christ, followed by the millennium; in a distinct judgment for believers only, at which their work will be judged and rewarded; and in a final judgment of the wicked after which they will be cast into the lake of fire burning with brimstone.[59]

At the same time, "differences of opinion on doctrine are not a bar to membership as long as there [is] no contention and the pulpits and churches of others are respected and not molested." Membership in the association is not exclusive and members may belong to other "religious organizations."[60]

The headquarters of the International Ministerial Association, Incorporated, are at 1312 North 67th Street, Houston, Texas 77011. A general international conference of the association meets annually. Individual membership is open to ministers, exhorters, and missionaries. Churches whose pastors belong to the association may become associate members. In the United States there are 440 individual members and 117 churches. In Canada there are 4 individual members. No estimate is available on the total active membership of the churches in the United States and Canada that hold associate membership in the association. In 16 countries outside of the United States and Canada, there are 412 missionaries and indigenous personnel who are members.[61]

## International Evangelism Crusades, Incorporated

In 1959 the Reverend Frank E. Stranges and two associates founded International Evangelism Crusades, Incorporated, at Palo Alto, California, as a voluntary interracial fellowship of licensed and ordained ministers. Its doctrinal statement puts it in the "oneness" tradition of Pentecostalism. It accepts the entire Bible as truth; holds that there is only one God, the Maker and Creator of all things, and that Jesus Christ is "the Son of God who was one with the Father before the foundations of the world"; proclaims personal salvation through faith in Christ, divine healing through faith in the Bible and Christ, the baptism and indwelling of the Holy Ghost with speaking in tongues as the external evidence, the nine gifts of the Spirit, and the personal premillennial return of Christ as the hope of all Christians. It observes the ordinances of water baptism by immersion and the Lord's Supper.[62] Both men and women are eligible for the ministry. Members may belong to other fellowships if they choose.

The headquarters are at 7970 Woodman Avenue, Van Nuys, California 91402. The fellowship claims an estimated membership of 6,000 in the Netherlands, England, Finland, Lebanon, Hong Kong, the Marshall Islands, the British West Indies, and other countries. In the United States and Canada minister-members serve about 30 churches with an estimated membership of 2,000.[63]

## Apostolic Gospel Church of Jesus Christ (Bible Apostolic Churches)

The Reverend Donald Abernathy, a Pentecostal preacher, founded the First Apostolic Gospel Church, an integrated but predominantly Caucasian congregation, in Bell Gardens, a suburb of Los Angeles, California, in 1963. During the next years four other Pentecostal churches in the area were attracted to the position of the Bell Gardens congregation and associated themselves loosely with it.

In July 1968 Abernathy reported that in a series of visions God had revealed to him that the entire West Coast of North America would fall into the sea as a result of an earthquake. The Los Angeles area would be the hardest hit. Abernathy communicated his vision to some of the other churches with which his congregation was in fellowship. Among them was the Bible Apostolic Church at Port Hueneme. Its pastor, the Reverend Robert Theobold, declared that he had received a divine confirmation of his colleague's visions.

As a result, the members of the five congregations decided to quit their jobs, sell their homes, and move to safety. The church in Avenal went to Kennett, Missouri, the church in Porterville to Independence, Missouri, the church in Port Hueneme to Murfreesboro, Tennessee, and the churches in Lompoc and Bell Gardens to Georgia, the latter congregation to Atlanta.

These churches belong to the "oneness" wing of Pentecostalism. The Atlanta congregation, for instance, professes to accept the Bible as its creed, discipline, rules of order, and doctrine. It affirms that baptism by water and Spirit is the only way to enter the true church, the body of Christ, the members of which have their names kept on record in heaven. It immerses candidates for water baptism in the name of the Lord Jesus Christ; the baptism of the Spirit has as initial evidence speaking in tongues. It describes the divine standard of salvation as a holy, Spirit-filled life, with Pentecostal signs follow-ing. It believes in repentance and in the remission of sins; in divine healing to the exclusion of medicines and the services of doctors or hospitals, either for preventative or curative purposes; in the Lord's Supper administered in bread and grape juice as Melchizedek gave the first Communion to Abraham; in foot washing as a divine ordinance; in Christ's personal coming again; in tithes and free-will offerings as the divine plan for the support of the church and the ministry; in the duty of obedience to the civil government in all law-ful requirements ("[but] we cannot take up arms against any man or support those who do so; therefore our members do not serve in the armed forces"); in the translation of the righteous dead and of those who are living holy lives at the imminent end of the present order of things; in the millennium; in the final Great White Throne judgment at the end of the millennium; and in the casting of Satan and of those whose names are not written in the Book of Life into the lake of fire.

It demands a wholly sanctified life that discountenances exposing the body by wearing bathing suits; that disallows slacks, shorts, tight-fitting or straight-cut skirts, dresses with hemlines shorter than halfway between the knee and ankle, and short hair for women, and long hair, short sleeves, and tight-fitting pants for men; and that refrains from the wearing of jewelry. It holds that the church for which Christ will return is a perfect church, marked by the fruits of the Spirit listed in Galatians 5:22-23; that for the church's perfecting, the offices of apostle, prophet, evangelist, pastor, and teacher are indispensable; and that the members of the church must possess and use for the profit of all the spiritual gifts listed in I Corinthians 12:1-11. The trustees of the church must meet the requirements that the Pastoral Letters set forth for bishops and elders.[64]

The five churches maintain contact by letter, telephone, and periodic fel-lowship meetings. The total membership of the five Bible Apostolic churches, as they call themselves, is 540.

### The Jesus Church

While Samuel E. Officer was preaching one night in 1941, a vision came to him that made him realize that there is no Trinity and that the Godhead is only one person, God manifest in the flesh. Three years later he organized the Church of Jesus. It soon became apparent to him, he says, that *Church of Jesus* was not an appropriate name, since it declares that the church is "of Jesus," whereas the church is also called by his name. In 1955 he persuaded the church to adopt its present name.

The Jesus Church holds that the God the Father became man, that the Holy Spirit is not a person but God's power, and that the Father, Son, and Holy Ghost have only one proper name and that name is Jesus. Father, Holy Ghost, Christ, and Lord are titles, not names.[65]

Baptism in the Jesus Church is administered "in the name of Jesus," although the formula "I baptize you in the name of the Father and of the Son and of the Holy Ghost" is acceptable, provided it is spoken in the realization that Father and Holy Ghost are designations for Jesus. "Water baptism in Jesus is for the washing away of sins. There is no other plan for the blood of Jesus to atone for our sins."[66] The mode of baptism is immersion; both adults and infants may receive baptism. The Jesus Church observes the Lord's Supper and practices foot washing.

Speaking with tongues is the mark of the baptism of the Holy Ghost. Christ did not rise from the dead on the first day of the week but at the end of the Sabbath, Officer holds, and for that reason and because it regards the Saturday Sabbath as a permanent part of the Decalogue, the Jesus Church keeps Saturday as its Sabbath for weekly rest and worship. In its stress on holiness it prohibits the use of alcoholic beverages and tobacco, condemns divorce (except in cases of fornication), and forbids women to wear tight and short clothing, cut their hair, and use cosmetics. Its doctrine of the last things is premillennial, although it does not regard Christ's return as imminent. The Jesus Church teaches that Judah, together with the ten lost tribes, will be restored and rule the nations and that the church will reign over Israel.[67]

The Jesus Church is interracial. Local churches are organized in bands, each headed by an elder whom the pastor or bishop supervises. The pastor-bishop and deacon constitute the local "seat of authority" or presbytery. Parallel organizations exist at the state level. When the Jesus Church expands beyond the United States, Officer envisions a similar organization at the national and international levels.[68]

The Jesus Church claims about 500 ministers in 25 states. Information on the number of churches and the overall membership of the denomination is not available. The mailing address of the headquarters is Box 652, Cleveland, Tennessee 37311.

## The Seventh Day Pentecostal Church of the Living God

The late Charles Gamble founded the Seventh Day Pentecostal Church of the Living God in Washington, D.C., in the 1940s, and became its first bishop. In the course of time a number of daughter congregations came into being in the area around the capital and in nearby states.

The church holds the conventional "oneness" Pentecostal positions on the "oneness" of the Godhead, on water baptism by immersion "in the name of Jesus Christ," on the baptism of the Holy Spirit with speaking in other tongues as evidence, on divine healing as included in the atonement, and on the personal premillennial coming of Christ. Since it feels itself bound to a literal understanding of the Bible and sees the Scriptures as demanding the continued observance of the Saturday Sabbath, it has added this tenet to its belief and practice.

The Seventh Day Pentecostal Church of the Living God engages in limited fellowship with other Pentecostal groups and with other Sabbatarian groups but does not regard itself as in affiliation with any of them.

The mother church is located at 1443 South Euclid Avenue, Washington, D.C. 20009. There are altogether 4 churches in the District of Columbia and nearby states, with a total active membership of less than 1,000.[69]

## NOTES

1. Fred J. Foster, *Think It Not Strange: A History of the Oneness Movement* (St. Louis: Pentecostal Publishing House, 1965), pp. 51-52.
2. Ibid., pp. 56, 71.
3. *Manual, United Pentecostal Church* (St. Louis: Pentecostal Publishing House, 1964), p. 19. It is also included among the "Articles of Faith."
4. *What We Believe and Teach: Articles of Faith of the United Pentecostal Church* (St. Louis: Pentecostal Publishing House, [1946]), p. 3.
5. Ibid., p. 6.
6. Ibid., p. 9.
7. Ibid., p. 10. Disapproved "Public School Activities" include "attending shows, dances, dancing classes, theaters, engaging in school activities against their religious scruples, and wearing gymnasium clothes which immodestly expose the body" (p. 15).
8. Ibid., p. 11.
9. Ibid., pp. 11-13.
10. Ibid., p. 13.
11. Ibid., pp. 13-14.
12. Letter from Robert L. McFarland, general secretary.
13. *1966 Minute Book of the Pentecostal Assemblies of the World, Inc.* (Indianapolis, Ind.: Pentecostal Assemblies of the World, 1966), pp. 9-12.
14. Ibid., pp. 47-48.
15. Ibid., p. 46.
16. F. L. Smith, *What Every Saint Should Know* (East Orange, N.J.: The Lutho Press, n.d.), pp. 7-8.
17. Ibid., pp. 2-3.
18. *1966 Minute Book*, pp. 112-140.
19. Jeremiah 10:2-4 is seen as forbidding Christmas trees and Isaiah 65:11-12 as prohibiting Christmas feasting. The symbols of fecundity that attach to Easter, such as eggs, rabbits, fish, hot cross buns, and crosses, identify it as "Ishtar" (or "Prostitute") Sunday. John Quincy Adams, *Christmas Means Slaughter* (Black Rock, Ark.: The Gathering Call, 1953) (pamphlet), pp. 15-18; *Babylon: Just What Is It?* (Gunn, Alberta: John Quincy Adams, 1938) (pamphlet), p. 7; *Wake Up to Phallus Worship* (Gunn, Alberta: The Gathering Call, 1941) (pamphlet), p. 13; "Mourn the Easter Apostasy," in *The Gathering Call* 2 (no year), 99-128.
20. Adams, *Wake Up to Phallus Worship*, pp. 25, 36; *Babylon: Just What Is It?* pp. 9-11, 18-19.
21. Communication from Edgar C. Wenzlaff, superintendent.
22. Letter from the Right Reverend W. T. Phillips, Th.B., D.D., LL.D., senior bishop, the Apostolic Overcoming Holy Church of God, Incorporated; William Thomas Phillips, *Excerpts from the Life of Rt. Rev. W. T. Phillips and Fundamentals of the Apostolic Overcoming Holy Church of God, Inc.* (Mobile, Ala.: A.O.H. Church Pub-

lishing House, 1967) (14-page pamphlet), pp. 1-4; "Autobiography of Bishop William Thomas Phillips" (1-page mimeographed document).

23. The denomination's *Manual* (rev. edn.; Mobile, Ala.: A.O.H. Publishing House, 1962) (56-page brochure), p. 11, notes that "Christianity has existed in Ethiopia since the days of the Eunuch" (Acts 8:26-39), and that "Ethiopian" is the name that God gave to black people, while "Negro" or "nigger" is a white curse name. There is verbatim or near verbatim agreement in many crucial passages of the *Manual* with the *Discipline* of the Church of God (Apostolic), Incorporated. The two bodies have not had any connection with each other.

24. Ibid., p. 2; John Thomas Nichol, *Pentecostalism* (New York: Harper & Row, 1966), pp. 130-131; Elmer T. Clark, *The Small Sects in America* (rev. edn.; Nashville: Abingdon-Cokesbury Press, 1949), p. 122.

25. *Excerpts*, pp. 6-7; *Manual*, p. 8.

26. *Manual*, p. 10.

27. *Excerpts*, p. 11; *Manual*, pp. 6, 8, 10.

28. *Manual*, p. 6.

29. *Excerpts*, pp. 12-14; *Manual*, pp. 6-8.

30. *Excerpts*, pp. 8-10; *Manual*, p. 9.

31. *Manual*, p. 6.

32. Ibid., p. 7.

33. Ibid., pp. 5, 18, 26. The Poor Treasury is in the hands of a Banking Committee.

34. *Manual*, p. 5.

35. Ibid., p. 19.

36. Ibid., p. 5.

37. Ibid., p. 7.

38. Ibid., p. 4; Nichol, p. 131.

39. Letter from Bishop S. McDowell Shelton, general overseer, Church of the Lord Jesus Christ of the Apostolic Faith.

40. The Church of the Lord Jesus Christ of the Apostolic Faith nevertheless makes extensive use of radio broadcasting both in North America and overseas.

41. The churches of the Restoration movement practice Communion every Sunday; cf. chap. 18 in vol. II, this series.

42. Sherrod C. Johnson, *Is Jesus Christ the Son of God Now?* (Philadelphia: Church of the Lord Jesus Christ of the Apostolic Faith, n.d.) (8-page tract); Johnson, *21 Burning Subjects: Who Is This That Defies and Challenges the Whole Religious World on These Subjects* (Philadelphia: The Church of the Lord Jesus Christ of the Apostolic Faith, n.d.) (24-page tract); S. McDowell Shelton, *B[ible] S[tudy]*, vol. I, nos. 1-5 (Philadelphia: Church of the Lord Jesus Christ of the Apostolic Faith, n.d.); Johnson, *The Christmas Spirit is a False Spirit* (Philadelphia: The Church of the Lord Jesus Christ of the Apostolic Faith, n.d.) (6-page folder); Johnson, *Are You False?* (Philadelphia: Bishop S. McDowell Shelton, n.d.); Johnson, *False Lent and Pagan Festivals* (Philadelphia: The Church of the Lord Jesus Christ of the Apostolic Faith, n.d.); letter from Bishop Shelton to Local Selective Service Board No. 104, St. Louis, Missouri, file "per His Excellency/o," dated December 19, 1968, subject not stated, with enclosure; *The Whole Truth*, vol. 21, nos. 11-12 (November–December, 1968), inside back cover.

43. The present writer's repeated efforts to obtain information from the leadership of the Church of Our Lord Jesus Christ of the Apostolic Faith, Incorporated, were unsuccessful.

44. Smallwood E. Williams, ed., *Brief History and Doctrine of the Bible Way Churches of Our Lord Jesus Christ World Wide* (Washington, D.C.: Bible Way Churches of Our Lord Jesus Christ World Wide, n.d.), pp. 5-13.

45. Ibid., pp. 16-20.

46. Communication from Bishop Smallwood E. Williams.

47. Information provided by the Reverend Raymond P. Vigil, secretary of the board, Apostolic Church of Jesus, 1818 East First Street, Pueblo, Colorado 81001.

48. "What Is the Kingdom of God Message," *Kingdom of God Crusader*, vol. 5, no. 18 (August 1963), 6; "The Apostolic Faith Church Doctrines," ibid., p. 3.

49. The information for this section and the following material on the derivatives of the parent church body was supplied by Bishop R. W. Sapp, Rt. 6, Box 68, Dublin, Georgia 31021.

50. *Articles of Faith of the Associated Brotherhood of Christians* (n.p.: n.p., 1958) (17-page printed pamphlet), p. 5.

51. Ibid, pp. 7-11.

52. Ibid., pp. 11-14.

53. See Noel McNeill, "As of a Rushing Mighty Wind" (unpublished manuscript), pp. 103, 135. The Apostolic Fellowship of Southern California, to which McNeill refers, seems never to have actually been organized. This writer gratefully acknowledges the assistance of the Reverend Arnold G. Kuntz, then pastor of Bethany Church, Long Beach, California, who interviewed the Reverend Joseph Thornton, pastor of the Pentecostal Faith Tabernacle, 133 East Chandler Street, Wilmington, California, a member of the Associated Brotherhood of Christians, on this writer's behalf.

54. "Articles of Faith of the Assemblies of the Lord Jesus Christ," *Constitution—Rules—Articles of Faith* (rev. edn.; Memphis, Tenn.: Apostolic Publishing House, 1965), pp. 9-15.

55. Letter from the Reverend Frank Schocke, secretary, Assemblies of the Lord Jesus Christ.

56. With the discontinuance of a literal observance of the Lord's Supper in 1968 the associated ordinance of foot washing has also fallen into disuse.

57. "Articles of Religion," in *What We Believe and Why* (French Lick, Ind.: Pentecostal Church of Zion, 1966) (39-page brochure), with typed-in correction of Article 17, "Concerning the keeping of the Passover (or so called Lord's Supper)," replacing the old like-numbered article, "The Lord's Supper and Feet Washing."

58. Letter from Evangelist Erma L. Jones, secretary, Pentecostal Church of Zion.

59. "Doctrinal Position," *Constitution, International Ministerial Association, Incorporated* (12-page undated pamphlet), pp. 3-5.

60. Article 1 ("membership"), "By-Laws," ibid., p. 6.

61. Letters from the Reverend W. E. Kidson, International Ministerial Association, Incorporated.

62. "Doctrinal Statement," *International Evangelism Crusades, Incorporated* (8-page undated mimeographed folder), p. [3]; letter from the Reverend Frank E. Stranges, Ph.D., B.Th., D.D., president, International Evangelism Crusades, Incorporated. Dr. Stranges is also director of instructors, Faith Bible College and Faith Theological Seminary, the fellowship's correspondence training agency.

63. Noel McNeill, "As of a Rushing Mighty Wind" (unpublished manuscript), p. 137; cited folder and letter from Dr. Stranges.

64. "By-Laws of the Apostolic Gospel Church of Jesus Christ" (undated typescript document), pp. 4-10; letter from the Reverend Donald Abernathy. For a description of the church at Kennett, Missouri, see Dickson Terry, "They Fled California in Fear," *St. Louis* (Missouri) *Post-Dispatch*, March 2, 1969, p. 3G.

65. Samuel E. Officer, *Fulness of the Godhead* (undated pamphlet).

66. Samuel E. Officer, *Have You Been Baptized in the Name?* (undated pamphlet).

67. Sam E. Officer, "You Are Walking Like Men," in *Light of the World*, vol. 12, no. 6 (April–June 1966), 1-3; "We Believe," ibid., vol. 13, no. 1 (January–March 1968), 2.

68. Sam E. Officer, *Wise Master Builders and the Wheel of Fortune* (undated pamphlet), pp. 11-14; Officer, *The Jesus Church in Divine Order* (undated pamphlet).

69. Letter from Bishop Theron B. Johnson, Sr., general overseer, The Seventh Day Pentecostal Church of the Living God, 317 West Park Avenue, Pleasantville, New Jersey.

# BIBLIOGRAPHY

Foster, Fred J. *Think It Not Strange: A History of the Oneness Movement.* St. Louis: Pentecostal Publishing House, 1965.

*Manual, United Pentecostal Church.* St. Louis: United Pentecostal Church, 1964.

Nichol, John Thomas. *Pentecostalism.* New York: Harper & Row, 1966. Especially pp. 118-119.

Smith, F. L. *What Every Saint Should Know.* East Orange, N.J.: The Lutho Press, n.d. A description of the teachings of the Pentecostal Assemblies of the World, Incorporated.

Williams, Smallwood E., ed. *Brief History and Doctrine of the Bible Way Churches of Our Lord Jesus Christ World Wide.* Washington, D.C.: Bible Way Churches of Our Lord Jesus Christ World Wide, n.d.

# 8. Other Pentecostal Bodies

It is not possible to classify all Pentecostal church bodies as either trinitarian or "oneness." Some refuse to regard the question as divisive of fellowship, although a majority of their ministers and members may incline in one direction or the other. In other cases it is not possible to determine with certainty what the position of a given Pentecostal church body really is.

## Church of God by Faith

Elder John Bright founded the Church of God by Faith at Jacksonville Heights, Florida, in 1919. It stresses the idea of "one Lord, one faith, one baptism"; teaches regeneration, sanctification, and the baptism with the Holy Ghost and with fire, accompanied by speaking in tongues; describes the Word of God as the communion of Christ's body and blood; and calls for the isolation of willful sinners from God and from the church.

The senior officer is the bishop. The General Assembly meets three times a year. The headquarters are at 3220 Haines Street, Jacksonville, Florida 32206. There are 105 churches in the eastern states from Florida to New York, with an estimated total membership of 4,500.[1]

## Apostolic Church of Pentecost of Canada, Incorporated

At the end of the second decade of this century, the Pentecostal Assemblies of Canada were in the process of uniting with the Assemblies of God. Within the former body a number of ministers, including one of the founders, Franklin Small (d. 1961) of Winnipeg, held the "oneness" position on the Godhead. Small and some others who shared his views withdrew and formed a new body, chartered in 1921 as the Apostolic Church of Pentecost.

In 1927 a group of Pentecostal believers in southern Saskatchewan, who also stressed water baptism in the name of Jesus and held a Calvinistic view of the grace of God, secured a provincial charter in 1927 as the Full Gospel Missions. In 1948 the Dominion chartered the body under the new name of

Evangelical Churches of Pentecost. The Apostolic Churches of Pentecost and most of the Evangelical Churches of Pentecost merged in 1953.

The fourteen-item Statement of Faith of the Apostolic Church of Pentecost of Canada, Incorporated, affirms belief (1) in the verbal inspiration of the Bible; (2) "in the existence of one True God who has revealed himself to this world as the Father, as the Son, and as the Holy Spirit"; (3) "in the Savior of men, the Lord Jesus Christ, conceived of the Holy Spirit, born of the Virgin Mary, very God and very man"; (4) in the creation, test, and fall of humankind, as recorded in Genesis, and humanity's total spiritual depravity and inability to attain to divine righteousness; (5) in the gospel of the grace of God in Christ's death, burial, and resurrection; (6) in salvation by grace alone through faith in Christ's perfect and sufficient work on our behalf; (7) in believer's baptism by immersion "in the name of our Lord Jesus Christ"; (8) in the baptism with the Holy Spirit as an experience subsequent to salvation, with speaking in tongues as evidence; (9) in the gifts of the spirit exercised and practiced as in the early church; (10) in the Lord's memorial for believers; (11) in divine healing of the body; (12) in eternal life for believers and eternal punishment for unbelievers; (13) in the Spirit-filled life of separation from the world and the perfecting of holiness; and (14) in Christ's personal return for his church.[2]

This Statement of Faith receives considerable amplification in the twenty-seven-section Articles of Faith of the General Bylaws. Section 5 of these, for instance, affirms that "the Holy Spirit, proceeding from the Father through the Son, is one substance, very and eternal God." With reference to the Son, Section 6 includes these statements: "In Him (Christ) dwelleth all the fulness of the Godhead (Trinity) bodily (or corporeally). . . . the title 'Son of God' is that which belongs to Christ's miraculous conception. . . . Christ is all of God, and God is all of Christ. . . . Deity has no Father, but God clothed in flesh has (referring to His Sonship), hence God and man are joined together in one person, which is Christ the Lord. . . . The idea of an eternal Sonship plus His incarnation is unwarranted and unsupported by Scripture. . . . Christ could not be God in any proper sense of the word and have a Father as touching Deity."[3] Section 17 affirms that "the body of Christ is given, taken, and eaten in [the Lord's] supper only in a spiritual manner by faith." Section 18 cites Matthew 19:14 in support of the dedication of children. Sections 19-24 teach a premillennial doctrine of the last things, with the rapture of the church and of the faithful departed, the judgment of the saints, a literal millennium, and the White Throne judgment of the unbelieving.[4]

In some areas fellowship exists between the Apostolic Church of Pentecost and other Pentecostal bodies. The general offices of the denomination are at 4—3026 Taylor Street East, Saskatoon, Saskatechewan S7H 4J2. There are 165 churches in the Dominion, mostly west of the Great Lakes, with an estimated membership of about 15,000. The denomination conducts foreign missions in 11 fields in Japan, Africa, India, Jordan, and Latin America.[5]

### The Evangelical Churches of Pentecost, Incorporated

A Pentecostal revival in Saskatchewan, Canada, in 1913 led to the opening of a Full Gospel camp at Trossachs. The witnessing of a nucleus of young men who were converted in this camp resulted in the opening of a number of local Full Gospel churches in the province. In 1927 the Reverend Allan Hoffman Gillett (1895–1967) of Radville, Saskatchewan, secured a provincial charter for the Full Gospel Mission. Some ministers who accepted credentials under this charter began to work in Alberta, Manitoba, and British Columbia. In June 1946 the ministers in the movement incorporated themselves as the Evangelical Churches of Pentecost. When this body united with the Apostolic Church of Pentecost in 1953, a number of ministers of the Evangelical Churches of Pentecost refused to enter the union and continued to operate as the Full Gospel Ministers Fellowship, Incorporated. Their major reasons for not entering the union appear to have been their "amillennial" position in the doctrine of the last things and their concern that the local churches would lose some of their cherished sovereignty. In the fifteen years that followed, some of these inhibitions began to be overcome. The Full Gospel Ministers Fellowship, Incorporated, has resumed the name of the Evangelical Churches of Pentecost, Incorporated.

The Statement of Faith affirms the verbal inspiration of the accepted canon of the Bible; the "tri-unity" of the Godhead; the Genesis account of the creation, test, and fall of human beings and their total spiritual depravity; the saviorhood and virgin birth of Jesus Christ, "very God and very man"; the gospel of God's grace in Christ's death for our sins, his burial, and his resurrection; salvation by grace alone through faith in the sufficient work of the cross; Christ's bodily ascension, enthronement, and return, "at which time there will be the general resurrection and final judgment"; believer's water baptism by immersion "on the name of our Lord Jesus Christ"; the baptism of the Holy Spirit as an experience subsequent to salvation, evidenced by speaking with other tongues; the gifts of the Spirit enumerated in I Corinthians 12 and 14; a Spirit-filled life of holiness and of separation from the world; divine healing; "the Lord's memorial" or Supper; eternal life for believers and eternal punishment for unbelievers; the reality and personality of Satan; and the sovereign autonomy of the local church.

Despite its name, the organization is now actually a fellowship of 48 ministers, evangelists, and missionaries; the churches of which members of the fellowship are pastors do not as such belong to the organization. All but three of the members are Canadians; the rest are citizens of the United States of America. The international headquarters are at 85 East 10th Avenue, Vancouver, British Columbia, Canada. The 19 churches in three provinces of Canada and the 3 churches in as many states of the United States whose pastors belong to the fellowship have a total membership estimated at over

3,000 persons. Individual churches whose pastors belong to the Evangelical Churches of Pentecost support foreign missions in Upper Volta and Japan. The organization also supplies credentials to missionaries in South India and Mexico, as well as in Upper Volta.[6]

## The United House of Prayer for All People, Church on the Rock of the Apostolic Faith, Incorporated

According to the official account, Charles Manuel (Emanuel) Grace (1884–1960) was born in Portugal and emigrated to New Bedford, Massachusetts, in 1903. Around 1919 he built the first House of Prayer with his own hands in West Wareham, Massachusetts.[7] In 1926 he extended his activity to the urban areas of the southern United States, where he conducted racially integrated services. The following year he incorporated the United House of Prayer for All People, Church on the Rock of the Apostolic Faith, in the national capital. "Sweet Daddy" Grace, as his followers called him, concentrated on the areas touched by urban blight and took "the rocks that no one would use and built his church."[8]

Upon his death he was succeeded by Elder Walter McCollough, senior minister of the mother church ("mother house") in Washington, D.C. Members of the United House of Prayer believe that "just as Elijah's mighty Spirit of Christ was left for Elisha, so was the Spirit of Christ reincarnated into Bishop W. McCollough, known to his followers as Sweet Daddy Grace McCollough."[9]

The United House of Prayer for All People describes the Bible as its guidebook; the Apostles' Creed as the basis of its faith; and the establishment, maintenance, and perpetuation of the doctrines of Christianity and the apostolic faith as its purpose.[10] The idea of "one Lord, one faith, and one baptism" is expanded to include "one leader," that is, the Sweet Daddy Grace for the time being, "to teach the same."[11]

Baptism is by immersion and is seen as "unto repentance of sins."[12] In the Lord's Supper the bread is seen as a memorial of Christ's broken body and the wine of his blood.[13]

The United House of Prayer for All People stresses the biblical basis for praising God with the dance and with instruments in its services.[14] Pneumatic phenomena such as speaking in tongues, collapsing in a trance, uncontrollable jerking of the limbs, and dancing are characteristic of the movement's services.[15]

In addition to Christmas, New Year's Eve, and Easter, the calendar of the United House of Prayer contains a series of anniversaries directly related to the movement: the founder's death, January 12; the founder's birth, January 25; Bishop McCollough's first (1960) election, February 6; Daddy McCollough's resurrection (second [1962] election), April 8; the founder's coming to America, May 3; Sweet Daddy McCollough's birth, May 22; Daddy

McCollough's crucifixion (the restraining order imposed on him by the court in 1960), August 25; and "Hurricane Week," the Thursday, Friday, and Saturday nights after October 22 to commemorate the Hurricane Services of prayer in October 1962, when the prayers and supplications of the members of the United House of Prayer for All Nations are believed to have turned back the missiles set in Cuba for American shores and the Soviet ships headed for American soil, "thus saving the nation."[16] Other celebrations take place on the second Sunday in April (Grace labor day), on May 30 (the annual Memorial Day parade in Washington, followed by a memorial service for the founder), and on "Grace Emmanuel Day," kept in each state to commemorate the establishment of the House of Prayer within its boundaries.[17]

The United House of Prayer for All People maintains low-rent apartment buildings in a number of communities for its members. It provides opportunities to its people for employment as members of the construction teams that build new temples and renovate and repair the organization's properties, as rent collection agents, as clerical office workers, and in a variety of professional positions (including attorneys, accountants, bookkeepers, architects, and engineers). The United House of Prayer for All People also markets to its membership a full line of "Grace McCollough" or "House of Prayer" products, including hair preparations, toothpaste, creams, lotions, perfumes, toilet waters, coffee, tea, olive oil, and soap; "in purchasing the House of Prayer products," the members are told, "[they] not only receive the benefit of first-class products, but also healing, and the proceeds are returned to the House of Prayer treasurer."[18]

The membership of the United House of Prayer meets "in convocation," actually a series of regional convocations, from July through September each year; convocations are held for periods up to two weeks in Buffalo, New Haven, New York, Philadelphia, Baltimore, Washington, Newport News, Columbia, Savannah, Augusta, and Charlotte successively.[19] In addition the General Assembly (elders, ministers, and congregational representatives) meets annually. The General Council (chairmen of each state and district, plus appointees) is described as "the governing body that helps enforce the by-laws and rules the United House of Prayer for All People."[20]

The headquarters ("God's White House") are at 601 M Street, Northwest, Washington, D.C. 20001. There are 137 churches and missions from coast to coast, with the largest number in the southeastern states; the total active membership is estimated at 27,500.

## True Grace Memorial House of Prayer for All People

Even after the 1962 court-authorized election of Bishop Walter McCollough confirmed him as leader of the United House of Prayer for All People, some members of the church body continued to be dissatisfied with various aspects of the new bishop's teaching and administration and withdrew.

Twelve of these dissidents in the city of Washington sought the aid of Elder Thomas O. Johnson (d. 1970), a pastor in the Grace organization for twenty-three years, in establishing a congregation of their own. In August 1962 they dedicated a church at 205 V Street, Northwest, under the name of True Grace Memorial House of Prayer. Repeated suits by the McCollough group to compel the new organization to delete "House of Prayer" from its name failed. Three other congregations were founded in Philadelphia, in Savannah, Georgia, and in Hollywood, Florida, shortly afterward.

All regard the late Bishop Grace as their founder and claim to stand in the authentic Grace tradition.

The original four congregations have grown to six. Although they have a common heritage, differences in the worship traditions that they have developed have frustrated the effort to organize them into a single body. The Washington congregation claims a membership of about 200; no information is available on the size of the others.[21]

### Gospel Assembly Churches (Anonymous Pentecostal Christians)

Louisville-born William Sowders (1878–1952) had a Methodist background, but he was nearly thirty when he was "directed" to religion. A voice reportedly came to him while he was rowing on a river in southern Illinois and said: "Son, I want you to go and preach." He preached for five years around Olmsted, Illinois. Then he went to Evansville, Indiana, where he founded a Bible school in which he taught young men the fundamentals of what he called the Gospel of the Kingdom. In 1927 he returned to Louisville and founded the Gospel Tabernacle. One of his innovations in Louisville was the "School of the Prophets," a Sunday afternoon service of up to four hours in length, during which questions of doctrine and practice were thoroughly discussed. In 1935 he purchased a 350-acre tract of land near Shepherdsville, Kentucky, and converted it into the Gospel of the Kingdom campground. Other early leaders included Robert Shelton, George Aubrey, and Frank Knight. At the height of the movement there were reportedly some 300 churches in 31 states, with an estimated 75,000 adherents.[22]

Serious internal struggles racked the movement after the death of Sowders. The majority of the churches followed the Reverend Tom M. Jolly of St. Louis, Missouri. Another group followed the Reverend Reynolds Edward Dawkins (d. 1965). In 1965 about thirteen assemblies under Jolly's leadership separated from the main body.[23]

The movement has no published statement of doctrine and professes to stand solely upon the Bible, which it interprets dispensationally.[24] The distinctive tenets of the movement are broadly those associated with Pentecostalism, although at least some of the ministers in the movement are reluctant to concede that they belong in this classification.

The commonly held doctrine of God avoids commitment either to the classic trinitarian view or to the "oneness" Pentecostal view of the Godhead. It sees the Father as God. The Son, preexistent and incarnate in Jesus Christ, is a god in the sense that he is the son of the Almighty. The Holy Spirit is the life of the Father and the Son, but in no sense "a god."[25]

The movement holds that there are three baptisms. The first is water baptism, the "baptism of John." This takes place by immersion "in the Lord's name." But this does not imply any fixed form of words to be spoken as baptism is administered. If those involved in the rite are not "in the Lord's name," no form of words will validate the action. If they are "in the Lord's name," no form of words is essential. Thus whether or not a form of words is to be used and what form of words is actually used are matters left to the baptizing minister's discretion.[26] The second baptism is the baptism of the Holy Spirit. Speaking with tongues (in the sense of Acts 2:4-11, not of I Corinthians 12:10 and 14:6-19) as the Holy Spirit gives utterance is seen as the initial evidence of the baptism with the Holy Spirit.[27] The third baptism is the baptism of fire, administered by the unbelieving world to members of the body of Christ in the form of persecution.

On the Lord's Supper there are diverging opinions. At the beginning of the movement it was felt that an observance of the Lord's Supper with material elements was unnecessary and that the Lord's Supper was in fact being observed spiritually whenever the members of the body of Christ gathered together for services. But over the years some ministers in the movement have come to feel that observance of the Lord's Supper with material elements is becoming increasingly desirable.[28]

The healing of physical illnesses is regarded as having been included in Christ's atonement, and he is believed to be able to heal even after a doctor has given a patient up.

The dispensationalist orientation of the movement disposes its adherents to profound interest in the Jewish nation. The first dispensation is seen as spanning the time from creation to the flood, the second the period from the flood to the giving of the Mosaic law, the third from Moses to the death of Jesus in A.D. 33. The fourth period extends to the end of this dispensation, which will take place before the year 2000. In each dispensation God has preserved a small remnant to carry his Word forward into the next dispensation. At this point in history the people that belong to the body of Christ are this remnant (Revelation 12:17). Its responsibility is to bring God's Word to the Jewish nation. Once converted itself, the Jewish nation will then convert the rest of the nations of the earth by such apostolic activities as preaching and healing. The events of the first Pentecost foreshow the special fitness of the Jewish nation for this ministry of proclamation. The rule of the Jewish nation over the world will continue for a thousand years; this will happen concurrently with Christ's millennial reign upon the earth.

Typical in its attitude toward missionary activity is the Gospel Assembly, Des Moines, Iowa. It describes itself as evangelistically minded and affirms its desire to carry the message of salvation through Christ to all persons. It sees conversion as conferring the hope of a future life and seeks to help its converts live inspired and happy lives in this present world.[29]

On the basis of their understanding of prophecy the churches in this movement hold that they alone make up the true body of Christ. The Roman Catholic Church in their view is the harlot of the Revelation of St. John the Divine and all the other denominations are daughters of the harlot.[30] None of the denominations of Christendom have the seven pillars that support the true church—God, Christ, apostles, prophets, pastors, evangelists, and teachers. Some (but not all) of the churches of the movement believe that any religious body that has been incorporated under the laws of a civil power has turned its back on Christ, and is refusing to let him be its head.

The local churches are highly organized and emphasize strongly the need for identical belief on every major point of doctrine.

Student ministers receive their training by observing the ministers to whom they are assigned and by attending the conferences of the fellowship, where doctrinal matters are discussed and decided.

The movement regards total conscientious objection to war and military service as the only position that a person genuinely dedicated to the Lord can possibly take, and the local church will support such a member in his stand if he is drafted.

The Gospel Assembly Churches have no formal headquarters, although the Gospel Assembly Ministers Fund, 100 North Military Highway, Norfolk, Virginia 23502, performs some headquarters functions. The *Ministers' Address Directory*, provided "as a guide for those seeking fellowship in the body of Christ," lists 92 local assemblies in 22 states from Florida and Georgia to Oregon and Washington.[31] There is also a mission in Haiti. The total active membership of these assemblies is estimated as in excess of 10,000. Nearly three quarters of the local congregations call themselves Gospel Assembly or Gospel Assembly Church.[32]

### The Body of Christ (B'nai Shalom)

"Are you dedicated in this hour to help set the church in order and restore Israel?" This question confronts the worshiper from the wall behind the platform of the Gospel of Peace Tabernacle in St. Louis and indicates the two emphases that differentiate the body[33] of Christ (B'nai Shalom)[34] from the other groups that have developed out of the work initiated by William Sowders early in the twentieth century. These emphases are the establishment of the "apostolic order" in the church and the restoration of Israel.

In the divisions that took place in the Gospel of the Kingdom movement after the death of Sowders in 1952, one of the major groups was led by Elder Reynolds Edward Dawkins (d. 1965). His followers regard him as "apostle and builder of the body of Christ,"[35] and in their teaching they avail themselves directly of the revelations that Dawkins believed that he had received.[36]

The year 1959, the body of Christ holds, initiated the final period of "Gentile times." Some time before this Dawkins had had a vision in which he was instructed to assist in the beginning of the work in Palestine. In 1963 he led the B'nai Shalom up Mount Zion in Jerusalem as a symbol of their looking forward to the early restoration of Israel.[37]

Following Dawkins's death, the body of Christ, according to Dawkins's successor, Elder Richard Tate, began a "series of experiments in leadership" that replaced Dawkins's "apostolic order" with "presbyterian or board rule." Some of the proponents of "presbyterian order" withdrew from the body of Christ during the next four years.[38] Tate confesses that he himself was "deceived by personalities and [had] almost been persuaded to abandon the revelations on [apostolic] order."[39]

In its dispensational understanding of the Bible, and in its teaching about the Godhead, baptism, the Lord's Supper,[40] healing as included in Christ's atonement, the apostasy of visible Christendom,[41] and conscientious objection to war and military service, the body of Christ stands very close to the other fellowships that developed out of Sowders' Gospel of the Kingdom movement.

The Body of Christ holds that Jesus introduced the "apostolic order."[42] Paul described it in Romans 13, where the "higher powers" of verse 1 refer not to civil but to ecclesiastical powers. To hold up the body of Christ, God uses the "five-gifted ministry"—the pastor, the teacher, the evangelist, the prophet, and, over all these, the apostle.[43] The prophet deserves tribute, the teacher custom, the pastor fear, and the evangelist honor. The apostle is the higher power to which all are subject and he deserves to receive all that his subordinates receive and more.[44] To "get in trouble with God" all that one needs to do is "to resist the ordinances of God which have been laid down by an apostolic ministry."[45]

Paul initiated an interim order that was not based on twelve apostles but on companies of seven. God is seen as leaving the Jewish nation in Acts 28:28 and as returning and blessing it in Hebrews 13:20-21. The gospel that Paul established between Acts and Hebrews is not the same gospel as that of the twelve apostles, because God designed it for the building of a work among the Gentiles. It was not his intention to bless all of Gentile humanity, but "to use it as an assembling ground for the formation of a special people made up of both Jew and Gentile, the body of Christ." God does not live among the Gentiles any more than among the Jews, "unless apostolic order is on the scene. And there is not eternal life outside that body."[46]

The world is now in the beginning of the seventh millennial day. It is evening time (as the Jewish calendar reckons days); "darkness has covered the earth, and gross darkness the professed religious leadership."[47]

Paul foresaw at the close of the age that he started the coming of another apostle. Only this other apostle would be able to discern and build on the foundation successfully. If others trying to help him would seek to build the body of Christ anywhere in the world, they would have to build according to this new apostle's pattern. This new apostle was Dawkins, "the builder, the ending of the Gentile age." His building of seven works throughout the world is the "last of God's visit among the Gentiles."[48]

The greatest vocation of the present time is the restoration of Israel.[49] It is the foundation of the message of the body of Christ. The "New Jerusalem" is "natural Israel restored to the favor of God and founded on the Twelve Apostles and from this the love of God flowing out to the rest of the world."[50]

Before this age closes, the body of Christ foresees the establishment of "strongholds" in America, Europe, Asia, and Africa—the four corners of the earth.[51] They will warn the nations that the set time when God will begin to favor the nation of Israel has arrived and they will provide places where the Jewish people can find comfort and rest on their homeward journey to the Holy Land. The body of Christ stresses the peril of its whole-souled commitment to Israel and anticipates a future Day of Atonement when people from the four corners of the earth will give their very lives like lambs for the restoration of Israel on the restored brazen altar in the outer court of the temple.[52]

Like its divinely commissioned character, the corporate aspect of the body of Christ receives great stress. The great threat to its integrity is the individuality of its members. Persons come forth as members of the body only when they have "died out" their old individualist spirit. Every member of the body of Christ must fulfill in himself or herself the teaching of the death, burial, and resurrection of Jesus. After going to the same church in Nazareth for thirty years, Jesus made the sacrifice of declaring himself, making enemies of his friends, and alienating his family. Then he buried himself in his work for three and a half years in Jerusalem, the heart of the earth, and on Pentecost came forth as a member—in this case, the head—of a body with many members.[53] It will be in the form of this anointed body, composed of Jews and Gentiles who have lost their identity, that Jesus will judge the nations.[54]

The body takes precedence over everything else as far as the love of its members is concerned.[55] "Overcomers" are members of the body who give their lives "for three years, living wholly for the body of Christ, not erring from the truth,"[56] or who give at least 51 percent of their time, money, effort, and life into the body of Christ.[57]

The role of women in the body of Christ is receiving increasing stress in the fellowship.[58]

General gatherings of various kinds are held in different parts of the country and in Israel as a means of providing mutual encouragement.[59]

The headquarters of the body of Christ (B'nai Shalom) are at the Gospel of Peace Camp Ground, 5607 South 7th Street, Phoenix, Arizona 85040. The

Peace Publishers and Company, 6401 South Eighth Place, Phoenix, functions "as the financial arm of the body of Christ." There are 8 churches in the United States, with an estimated total active membership of about 1,000.[60] There are also affiliates in Jamaica, Holland, Hong Kong, India, Nigeria (where there are 11 churches), and Israel.[61]

## Gospel Assembly

The origins of the Gospel Assembly are described as going back to the founding of the Gospel Assembly Church in Louisville, Kentucky, in the second decade of the twentieth century. In 1952 the Reverend Tom M. Jolly, who had been ordained in Louisville in 1934 and had founded the Eldorado (Illinois) Gospel Assembly the same year, assumed, as an additional duty, the pastorate of the ten-year-old Gospel Tabernacle in St. Louis after the death of the Reverend Dudley Fraze. Three years later he removed to St. Louis and subsequently changed the name of the Gospel Tabernacle to the Gospel Assembly.[62] The church was linked with the Gospel Assembly movement until 1965, when reportedly about thirteen churches in the movement joined Jolly in disassociating themselves from it.

Jolly describes his church as "an autonomous, independent, unorganized, unaffiliated church" that "fellowship[s] all Christians and works with them as far as possible."[63]

Between 1965 and 1970 the congregations linked with Jolly grew in number to about 30. They are located from Kansas City, Missouri, eastward to the Atlantic coast.[64] The total active membership is estimated at about 4,000.

## Association of Seventh Day Pentecostal Assemblies

After functioning as an informal fellowship from 1931 on, the Association of Seventh Day Pentecostal Assemblies was incorporated in 1967.

It upholds the principle of local autonomy and exercises no authority over either the pastors or the people of the local assemblies. It takes no position on the "oneness"/trinitarian issue, although there are no ministerial members that take an explicitly trinitarian stand. Baptism is administered either in the name of Jesus or (with slight differences in terminology from minister to minister) "in the name of the Father, God, and of the Son, Jesus Christ, and of the Holy Spirit."[65] The fellowship believes in the blood of Jesus for the remission of sins; in believer's baptism by immersion in water; in sanctification by Christ's blood, by the Spirit, and by the Word; in the Spirit as the guide to the truth and in truth's liberating power; in the baptism of the Holy Spirit as rest for the soul and endowment of power for service; in keeping the Saturday Sabbath as rest for the body; in the millennium as rest for both soul and body; in divine healing; in the equality of all Ten Commandments; in the church as Christ's body and in the endeavor to keep the unity of the Spirit in the bond of peace as a condition of fellowship in the church; in the achievement of unity by believers lifting up their voices together in song; in eye-to-eye vision when Christ brings Zion again;[66] in Christ's personal and imminent second coming as the blessed hope of the church; in Christ as the only helper of everyone; and in the preaching of the whole gospel for the whole person.[67]

The headquarters are at 4700 Northeast 119th Street, Vancouver, Washington 98665. There are 9 local assemblies on the West Coast, 2 in Canada, and 1 in Indiana whose ministers belong to the association. The total membership of these assemblies is estimated at 350.[68] The Association supports foreign missions in Costa Rica, Brazil, and South Africa, but the individual assemblies are free to support missionaries of their own choice.[69]

## California Evangelistic Association

Oscar C. Harms incorporated the movement known as the California Evangelistic Association at Long Beach, California, in 1934. He had gone to California for reasons of health. He stood at the side of an irrigation ditch one day and believed that he heard the voice of God calling him to preach the gospel. This he immediately began to do. An Advent Christian Church invited him to be its pastor and while he was so serving he received an "infilling of the Holy Spirit" that gave him a Pentecostal direction and moved him to establish an independent church, Colonial Tabernacle, the association's Long Beach mother church. The association adopted its present constitution in 1939.

Article IV of the association's constitution consists of a "statement of Fundamental Truths," adopted "for the purpose of maintaining general unity" and to cover the immediate needs of the association. This statement affirms the inspiration of the Scriptures as "the infallible rule of faith and conduct" and as "superior to conscience and reason." It acknowledges one true God, the creator of the universe and the Father of our Lord Jesus Christ.[70] It asserts the fall of human beings by voluntary transgression. The conditions of salvation are (1) the grace of God through the preaching of repentance toward God and of faith toward the Lord Jesus Christ and (2) the washing of regeneration and renewing of the Holy Spirit. The inward evidence of salvation is the direct witness of the Spirit, the outward evidence a life of true holiness. Baptism by immersion in water is the believer's declaration that he or she has been buried with Christ and raised with him to walk in newness of life. The Lord's Supper is a symbol that expresses a person's sharing of the divine nature, a memorial of Christ's suffering and death, and a prophecy of his second coming. All believers should expect and seek the baptism of the Holy Ghost as a wonderful experience distinct from and subsequent to the new birth; with the baptism of the Holy Ghost comes the enduement of power for life and service, and the bestowment of the gifts needed for the work of the ministry. Its initial evidence is speaking with other tongues and its subsequent proof the manifestation of spiritual power in public testimony and service.

The statement calls for entire sanctification; defines the church as the body of Christ; describes each believer as an integral part of the general assembly and church of the first born; calls for a divinely called and scripturally ordained ministry; makes divine healing the privilege of believers; asserts the resurrection and translation of the faithful departed as the blessed hope of the church; and teaches the everlasting reign of Jesus on earth,[71] the everlasting destruction of the devil, his angels and all those not named in the Book of Life, and new heavens and a new earth.[72]

The members of the association's churches may refuse combatant service in wartime, but are ready to serve the government "in any way consistent with noncombative service."[73] Membership implies a renunciation of smoking, of drinking alcoholic beverages, and of attendance at motion pictures. Wives of ministers receive credentials on a parity with their husbands.

Each local assembly is autonomous. There are 62 assemblies distributed over two districts, one comprising California, the other Oregon and Washington. The total membership is estimated at 4,700. Headquarters are at 1800 East Anaheim Boulevard, Long Beach, California 90813. The association maintains missionaries in Zambia, Mexico, Colombia, Brazil, and Italy.[74]

### Damascus Christian Church, Incorporated

In 1939 Francisco Rosado and his wife, Leoncia, both of them Pentecostal ministers, began an independent work among the Spanish-speaking population of New York City, which they incorporated as the Damascus Christian Church. It has since spread into New Jersey, the United States Virgin Islands, and Cuba.[75]

The church is headed by a bishop. A small council of officers and a mission committee carry on the church body's administration. The Damascus Christian Church, Incorporated, reportedly has ten churches and a total membership of about 1,000.[76]

### Wings of Healing, Incorporated

Dr. Thomas Wyatt[77] was a young farmer when he was converted in the Methodist Church at Ira, Iowa. After a dramatic recovery from an illness reportedly pronounced incurable and probably terminal, he became a Methodist minister. Some years later he received the baptism of the Holy Spirit. In 1937 he began a ministry of revival and healing in Portland, Oregon, where he initiated the Wings of Healing radio broadcast and established the Wings of Healing Temple in 1942. Although unquestionably Pentecostal and dispensationalist in its position and thrust, Wings of Healing has affirmed its desire to serve "all mankind, regardless of color, class, or creed" and to be "active on the frontiers of human want around the world" in an effort "to meet the needs of all men, spiritually, physically, economically, and socially."[78] In 1953 Wyatt undertook a healing crusade in Africa that attracted wide attention. In 1959 he moved the headquarters of his activities to Los Angeles. Since his death in 1964, his widow, née Evelyn Mae Smith, has continued his work.[79]

Among the "landmarks of our faith" Wings of Healing includes belief in the Bible as the Word of God; in Christ, the only begotten Son of God who "went about doing good, and healing all that were oppressed of the devil"; in repentance; in salvation by grace through faith; in the baptism of the Holy Spirit for every child of God; in deliverance from sin and worldliness; in personal responsibility to walk in the light and carry the gospel to every creature; in divine healing as "a gift of God provided in the atonement" that "can be brought into effect by faith";[80] in heaven, where goodness reigns, and in hell, where evil will be imprisoned; in the church of Jesus Christ "made up of those whose names are written in heaven"; in the imminence of the Kingdom of Heaven; in the need for spiritual landmarks to "serve as bearing points from which to survey the new territories we are called upon to possess"; in the ordinances of water baptism and the partaking of Communion, but not emphasized "to a point where people look upon the baptismal water and the communion bread and wine as Deity"; and in sanctification that can be found only in service.[81]

Strongly opposed to Communism, Wings of Healing lists as the "issues of this day" revolution against spiritual poverty, economic poverty, the carnality of divisive religion, illiteracy, racial discrimination, political tryranny, and sickness and disease.[82]

The bulk of the effort of Wings of Healing, Incorporated, goes into its international radio ministry,[83] its citywide rallies ("deliverance crusades") throughout the United States and Canada, its publications (notably *The March of Faith*), its foreign missions (especially in Africa, India, the Near East, and Latin America), its concentrated training programs for missionary workers, and its ministry of intercession for the sick in response to letters and telegrams sent to the Los Angeles headquarters. There are two congregations (in Los Angeles and Portland), with a predominantly floating and transitional total membership estimated at an average of 2,000 persons. The movement stresses its "interdenominational" ministry rather than the building of a denominational membership. The headquarters are at 847 South Grand Avenue, Los Angeles, California 90017.

## Evangelical Bible Church [Evangelical Church of God]

In 1947 the Reverend Frederick Bradshaw Marine (b. 1897) of Baltimore, Maryland, who had become a Pentecostalist over twenty years before, organized the Evangelical Bible Church. It sees as its mission to contend for the original Pentecostal faith without compromise. Its particular concern is the establishment of foreign missions that will give the fullest possible scope to the indigenous members and ministers.

The "doctrines and teachings" of the Evangelical Bible Church affirm that the Bible is the inspired and authoritative will, testament, and very Word of God. Christ abolished the Old Covenant and its law, including the Ten Commandments, on the cross. The New Covenant, with the laws and commandments given by Christ and the apostles, now takes the place of the Old Covenant. The Bible deals with three classes of people, the Jews, the Gentiles, and the Church of God. The three persons of the one Godhead are separate and distinct, each with his own body. The Father is a real person with a body and bodily parts like those of a man, that is, with a personal soul and soul passions, and with a personal spirit and spirit faculties. Ever since God the Son became man, he has replaced his spirit body with a human body. Devils, angels and other living spirit creatures are personal beings. Satan, angels, the pre-Adamite inhabitants of the earth, the demons, and human beings are free moral agents in revolt against their creator. Sin is both the outward transgression of the law and the inward spirit of the devil. The penalty for sin is eternal death. The Bible doctrine of salvation includes conviction, repentance, forgiveness, conversion, regeneration, adoption, new birth, sonship, atonement, righteousness, restitution, consecration, healing and health in the atonement, sanctification, justification, providence, and holiness. Of the seven baptisms in the Bible three are for all believers: the baptism into Christ when the candidate is born again through the agency of the Holy Spirit; baptism into the Holy Spirit through the agency of Christ; and baptism into water through the agency of the minister. Those who have the full baptism in the Spirit have unlimited grace and power, including the power to speak in tongues, to cast out demons, to be immune from poisons and to control wild beasts, to heal the sick through prayer, to raise the dead, to bind and loose anything, to destroy Satan's works, to get answers to every prayer, to have soul health, to control the elements, and to do miracles. The New Testament program for the church is to preach the gospel and to confirm the gospel. Christians are free in all things that the New Testament neither commands nor forbids. But they may not use intoxicating beverages, tobacco, and drugs, or indulge in evil and harmful habits and practices or in worldly pleasures. They may not belong to worldly organizations, and in case of war they may "serve in noncombatant forces according to their own conscience."

Each local church in affiliation with the Evangelical Bible Church has the right to order its own local affairs, but it may not take any action contrary to the Bible as the Evangelical Bible Church interprets it. The three ordinances are water baptism, the Lord's Supper, and the washing of the saints' feet. Christians are to support the church and the propagation of the gospel with tithes and voluntary offerings. The soul and spirit of every human being is immortal and is fully conscious after death. Since Christ's resurrection all the righteous go at death into heaven, while all the wicked go to hell. The first resurrection, before the millennium, involves the righteous. The second resurrection, after the millennium, involves the wicked. Christ's coming in the air will be followed successively by seven years of tribulation, the millennium, and the renovation by fire of the present heaven and earth. Thereafter the natural life of human beings and all living creatures on earth will be perpetual.[84]

The growth of the Evangelical Bible Church has been modest. The headquarters are at 2444 Washington Boulevard, Baltimore, Maryland 21230. There are 4 congregations in Maryland, and a mission in Pennsylvania. The total active membership of these five centers is estimated at 250. The Evangelical Bible Church sponsors a foreign mission in the Republic of the Philippines under the name of the Evangelical Church of God.

## Glad Tidings Missionary Society

The Glad Tidings Missionary Society came into being in the year 1950 as an extension of the work of the Glad Tidings Temple in Vancouver, British Columbia, Canada.

Its doctrinal position, developed through the "examination of all truth in the light of the word of God," teaches salvation through faith in Christ as Savior; believer's baptism through immersion in the name of the Lord Jesus Christ; sanctification as a work of the Spirit that separates believers from the world; divine healing provided for in the atonement; baptism in the Holy Ghost, evidenced by speaking in tongues; the nine gifts of the Spirit set forth in I Corinthians 12 imparted by prophecy with the laying on of hands; the five ministry gifts of Ephesians 4:11; the joy of the Lord; praise and worship; and Christ's second coming.[85]

The headquarters is the mother church at 3456 Fraser Street, Vancouver, British Columbia. In addition to the mother church and a rescue mission in Vancouver, there are 5 "fellowship" churches in British Columbia and 2 in the state of Washington, all of which are directly supervised by the mother church, and 6 "associated" churches—two in Alberta, one in British Columbia, and three in the state of Washington. The total membership is estimated at 1,200. The society supports missionaries in the Republic of China (Taiwan), Africa, and the Arctic, and provides partial support to missionaries in India, Hong Kong, Latin America, and the West Indies. The society cooperates with the Bethany Missionary Society of California.

## The World Church (The Universal World Church, Incorporated

In 1952 O. L. Jaggers, a minister of the Assemblies of God from 1943 to 1952, founded both the Universal World Church in Los Angeles and the World Fellowship of the World Church.[86]

An applicant is received into membership in the World Church by immersion after accepting Christ as personal Lord and Savior through repentance of sins and faith in his name. The Universal World Church calls this "the first process of the new birth and the new creation."

A member may thereafter receive the "genuine baptism with the Holy Spirit of resurrection power and fire," which the Universal World Church calls "the second process of the new birth and the new creation."

After this a member is eligible for what the Universal World Church calls "the third process of the new birth and the new creation," the "transubstantiation communion." Once every three months, at the "golden altar," twenty-four elders of the Universal World Church, wearing robes and crowns, perform "through faith in Christ" and "by the power of God" what the Universal World Church calls "the miracle of changing the bread and wine into the sacred body and blood of the Lord Jesus Christ" so that the communicants by partaking of Christ's body and blood may enjoy the benefits of his divine life.[87]

As the founder of the Universal World Church describes its organization, he himself is the president and the arch-elder; under him are the 24 elders, who constitute the executive committee; "'some 144 bishops" worldwide, one for each of the United States and "the remainder in some 70 countries of the world"; and 3,170 licensed and ordained ministers,[88] who function in "some 800 congregations" in the United States and other countries. All bishops and ordained ministers must be graduates of the University of the World Church.[89] A convention of the clergy and of laity whom they appoint meets annually.

The World Fellowship of the World Church is the "holding corporation for other World Churches throughout the world" and the ministerial organization in which ministers are licensed and ordained.

The Los Angeles mother church of the Universal World Church is located at 123 North Lake Street, Los Angeles, California 90026. The founder claims for it an active membership of 11,000.[90]

## American Evangelistic Association

In 1954 the Reverend John E. Douglas and seventeen other independent Pentecostal ministers founded the American Evangelistic Association in Baltimore. Their purpose was to create a cooperative agency that would establish doctrinal, ethical, and moral standards for independent Pentecostal ministers; provide them with credentials attesting their licensed or ordained status; and coordinate their churches' missionary, education, and charitable efforts in foreign countries.

Membership is open to ministers, not to their churches. The headquarters are at 2200 Mount Royal Terrace, Baltimore, Maryland 21217. Douglas claims a total active membership in excess of 100,000 for the churches served by the licensed and ordained ministers that belong to the association. The highest membership concentration is in the vicinity of Baltimore.

The missionary department of the association operates out of Dallas, Texas. It coordinates missionary activities in India, Hong Kong, and Korea; operates forty-two orphanages in various parts of the world; and publishes the magazine *World Evangelism.*

Since 1955 the association has cooperated with other Pentecostal minister-ial fellowships in conducting a "Christian Fellowship Convention" in a differ-ent city each year.[91]

### First Deliverance Church (Atlanta, Georgia)

After seventeen years as traveling evangelists in North America and Brazil, Lillian and William Fitch organized the First Deliverance Church in Atlanta, Georgia, in 1956.

It has no formulated creed or doctrine; the sources of its faith and prac-tices are the Bible, divine revelations, and other impartations of the Spirit. It regards the Bible as the inspired Word of God and as the infallible rule of faith and conduct, and it holds that the Bible is not contrary to reason and science, but that in many cases scientific discoveries substantiate and fulfill the Bible. It affirms the spirituality and the oneness of God; as the Father, he is the eternally self-existent creator of all things; as the Son, he is the Word made flesh; as the Holy Ghost, he dwells in human beings and gives them his attributes and power in the measure that a given human being repents of sin and yields self to God. God is good, love, intelligence, immutability, and eter-nity. The sinless Christ, the Word made flesh, is the perfect example for human beings, and his life, death, and resurrection made possible the deliver-ance of human beings from everything that has an ill effect upon their minds, bodies, spirits, or souls. Human beings, created good, fell from their holy state by voluntary transgression; their only hope of redemption lies in Christ. God has given human beings the power to create. They can exercise this power only when they are full of love; human beings who free themselves from prejudice, pride, bigotry, selfishness, hatred, and the works of the flesh become gods. Sickness is the result of sin; if human beings did not sin, there would be no sickness. God did not make human beings to die; they die because of sin and if they keep their minds clear of evil and free from fear, they can live. Salva-tion is deliverance from sin by God's grace; the mercy and unmerited favor of God, not obedience to the law, saves human beings. Sanctification, the act of cleansing oneself and setting oneself apart for God's use, follows conversion. The baptism of the Holy Ghost—the "one baptism" into the "one body"—follows sanctification; the sign of the baptism with the Holy Spirit is speaking in an unknown tongue. The new birth, the experience of being born again, follows conversion, sanctification, and filling with the Holy Spirit; a person who has experienced the new birth is in a state where the carnal nature of human beings has died and the spiritual person has come alive and where one can do the works that Jesus did. The visible church is the worldwide body of believers in Christ or a local assembly of believers. The invisible church is the body of Christ and inhabits the hearts, minds, and souls of believers; it possesses the virtues, power, and authority that Christ has. Individuals who continue in sin and unrighteousness will not obtain eternal life. Those who receive the Spirit of God, believe on his name, walk uprightly, and speak the truth in their hearts enter eternal life after passing through death. Those who have come to possess all of God's attributes, keep Christ's sayings, eat his flesh and drink his blood, and purify themselves as he is pure will not die, but will be changed in the twinkling of an eye.

In addition to daily prayer and Bible reading, a characteristic feature of the First Deliverance Church's practice is the monthly "shut-in fast." For a period of three consecutive days and nights each month the participants in the fast remain in the church building and refrain from food during this period. In addition, members of the church may engage in longer fasts, either by personal choice or in response to what they believe to be divine prompting.[92] A "denial" normally lasts for ninety days, but it may be shorter: during a "denial" the participants normally do not eat except between five in the evening and midnight. A "vigil" may be called for one or more days; during this time the participants assemble at the church for several hours of sustained prayer and praise daily.

The First Deliverance Church has its headquarters at 65 Hardwick Street, Southeast, Atlanta, Georgia 30315; its membership totals 840. It has 9 loosely affiliated churches and missions in Florida, Georgia, Oklahoma, Ohio, and California. No information is available on the membership of these affiliated congregations.[93]

### Rainbow Revival Church, Incorporated

Eldridge Plunkett and his wife, Ruth, Pentecostal evangelists since 1942, incorporated the Rainbow Revival Church in 1957. In addition to services at the Rainbow Revival Church every Sunday, the church carries on an extensive program by correspondence. It provides mimeographed "written church services" consisting of "paragraph sermons" about 250 words in length, extolling the death of Jesus on the cross to pay for the sin of human beings, recommending the use of its prayer handkerchiefs ("requesting a prayer handkerchief each week is better than once a month"), and encouraging liberal giving ("people don't have to give to have prayers answered, but it helps"). These are accompanied by testimonials from correspondents (usually identified only by initials and state of residence) describing recoveries from injuries (an abraded cornea, for example) and illnesses (tuberculosis, stomach ulcer, a running eye, a sore leg, a mole and a tumor, for example) through the application of prayer handkerchiefs and reporting the answering of other petitions. The mimeographed sheets also contain blanks on which correspondents can report the number of chapters of the Bible that they have read and the number of minutes that they have "prayed and praised" each day of the current week. There are other blanks on which they can indicate the amount that they are sending to the Rainbow Revival and on which they can check off the kind of intercession they want offered on their behalf (healing for self or a loved one; an unspoken personal request; improvement in financial circumstances; a better job; more Holy Ghost power and joy; intercession for a particular individual; finding Jesus Christ as personal Savior; the baptism of the Holy Ghost). Four-page mimeographed instructions on seeking the baptism with the Holy Ghost and speaking in tongues are sent on request.

The "co-pastors" of the Rainbow Revival Church, which is located at 890 South Crenshaw Boulevard, Los Angeles, California 90005, claim an average active mailing list of 6,000 to 7,000 persons.[94]

### God's House of Prayer for All Nations

Since the 1960s a number of Full Gospel congregations, some all-black, others interracial, have been organized under the name God's House of Prayer for All Nations. The largest concentration of these congregations is reportedly in the Chicago area. The individual congregations are autonomous and operate under their own charters; there is no formal intercongregational organization. They reportedly obtain most of their printed materials from the late A. A. Allen's Miracle Revival Fellowship in Miracle Valley, Arizona.

A more or less typical congregation is God's House of Prayer for All Nations, Incorporated, Peoria, Illinois, organized in 1964 by the Reverend Tommie Lawrence, a former minister of the Church of God in Christ, who calls himself pastor, chief apostle, founder, and senior bishop of God's House of Prayer of All Nations. Its charter affirms its acceptance of the Bible as its rule of faith and practice; its loyalty to the United States; its opposition "to war in all its forms or the preparation for war in any form" and the willingness of its members to serve in any capacity "that will not conflict with our conscientious scruples in this respect"; the desire of its members to let God have his way in their lives; the necessity of repentance and of faith in the atonement of the blood of Jesus; the "Deity of God the Father, the Deity of Jesus the Son of God, and the Deity of the Holy Ghost"; water baptism by immersion "in the name of Jesus Christ, which is the name of the Father, Son and Holy Ghost";[95] the signs of Mark 16:17-18 as following faith; the baptism of the Holy Ghost with the accompanying evidence of speaking with other tongues; worship in spirit and truth; divine healing in response to the prayer of a righteous believer and of the church; and the Lord's Supper, in which the bread and the fruit of the vine represent Christ's body and blood.[96]

Bishop Lawrence's church is located at 1801 Northeast Madison Street, Peoria, Illinois 61603. No membership figures are available.[97]

## Bold Living Society (Bold Bible Living)

In 1961 the Reverend Don Gossett, a former editor of *Faith Digest*, the monthly magazine of the Tulsa-based T. L. Osborn Evangelistic Association, organized the Bold Living Society of Canada near Cloverdale, British Columbia. The principal outreach of the society is by radio, chiefly in western Canada and in the West Indies. Gossett supplements this radio ministry with personally led evangelistic campaigns on the North American continent and in the West Indies (frequently in cooperation with local churches of the Assemblies of God and of the Apostolic Church of Pentecost of Canada, as well as in cooperation with other "fundamental" churches), the monthly magazine, *Bold Living*, and the publication of six books a year. Within a generally Pentecostal theology, the stress of the Bold Living Society is on victorious Christian living in the spirit of Romans 8:37 and Proverbs 28:1, on overcoming fear, on developing confidence and courage, and on daring to do God's will.

The headquarters of the Bold Living Society of Canada are at 5574 King George Highway, Cloverdale, British Columbia; the headquarters of Bold Bible Living, the United States counterpart, are at Box 2, Blaine, Washington 98230. The two Canadian congregations of the movement have an estimated membership of 100;[98] the Bold Living Fellowship has about 5,000 members.[99]

## Full Gospel Fellowship of Churches and Ministers International

In a reaction "against the bureaucratic machinery of the older, more highly organized Pentecostal denominations,"[100] a group of Pentecostal ministers met in Dallas, Texas, in September 1962 and organized the Full Gospel Fellowship of Churches and Ministers International—"the voice of Twentieth Century Pentecost," as it describes itself—to provide a medium through which churches might "work harmoniously in cooperation with each other." The constitution specifies that the fellowship "is not to any degree and shall never have any ecclesiastical authority" and that it "shall never attempt to exercise a single attribute of power or authority over any church or over the messengers of the churches in such wise as to limit the sovereignty of the churches."[101]

Originally it planned to offer ministerial recognition to ministers who had no credentials with other organizations, but in the light of its self-image as "a fellowship of the body of Christ rather than a closed communion," it has expanded this purpose to invite "all ministers and churches, regardless of denomination, which believe in the principles of the Full Gospel Fellowship" of the unity of the Body of Christ and the sovereignty of the local church, to join.[102] Other purposes are to provide tax-exempt status to its affiliated churches and to encourage the formation of regional groups that would carry on fellowship meetings and other cooperative activities for the good of all the member churches.

The fellowship's Tenets of Faith are "the doctrine of Christ" (II John 9-11) as found in Hebrews 6:1-2: Repentance from dead works, faith toward God, the doctrine of baptisms, the laying on of hands, the resurrection of the dead, eternal judgment, and the going on to perfection. It seeks to follow what it sees as the example of the apostolic church and does not require uniformity of belief in other matters; it "stands for apostolic liberty of conscience but disapproves of any who would use that liberty to divide brethren."[103]

On the issue of the Trinity, or the "oneness" of God, and on the baptismal formula to be employed, it allows its members complete individual freedom; the great majority of them would reportedly be on the trinitarian side, but without making it an issue. It excludes from its fellowship those who reject a part or all of the "doctrine of Christ" as stated, those who are immoral, those who are unruly or walk disorderly, those who cause divisions, leaders who are domineering, quarrelsome, and sectarian, and those who defile their separation from the world.[104]

It recognizes "the unity of the Body of Christ and the ministry—gifts God has set in the church, as described in I Cor. 12, [and] declares itself strongly for the supernatural ministry and the operation of the ministry-gifts in the assembly in accordance with the divine order of their manifestation, as set forth . . . in I Cor. 14." It disavows legalism in its spirit, but "stands for Bible righteousness in living and personal conduct in accordance with the Scriptures."[105]

The fellowship has grown rapidly. It has 1,649 ministerial members (about one third pastors, the rest evangelists, missionaries, teachers, and assistant ministers). There are 265 affiliated churches, including 2 churches in Canada, and 56 in Africa, Europe, the West Indies, and the Republic of the Philippines, with an estimated total membership of 21,000. In addition, the independent churches whose pastors are members of the fellowship have approximately the same total estimated membership. Another 300 pastors, heading independent churches with an estimated 30,000 adherents altogether, work with the fellowship without belonging to it.[106]

The direction of the fellowship's work is in the hands of an executive board which appoints an executive secretary. The headquarters' address of the fellowship was Box 8992, Dallas, Texas 75216. Recent efforts to contact the church body at that address have been unsuccessful.

## NOTES

1. Letter from Elder J. E. McKnight, Gainesville, Florida.
2. "Statement of Faith," *End Times Messenger*, vol. 31, no. 2 (February 1967), 2.
3. The Reverend F. Assman, clerk, Apostolic Church of Pentecost of Canada, Incorporated, notes in a

letter to the present writer: "At the time of incorporation in 1921 [the 'Oneness' teaching] seems to have been a much stronger issue as a doctrinal point than it is today. There are a number within our ranks that believe in the Triune aspect of the Godhead, but for the main part our Articles of

Faith are of the Oneness teaching."
Gordon Atter, *The Third Force* (2nd
edn.; Peterborough, Ontario: The
College Press, 1965), p. 103, speaks of
"many trinitarians in their ranks"
and "some amillennialists." He concludes that "their basis of fellowship
is rather broad."

4. *General Bylaws and Articles of Faith*
(rev. edn.; Saskatoon, Saskatchewan:
Apostolic Church of Pentecost of
Canada, Incorporated, 1965), pp. 3-
15.

5. Letter from the Reverend Mr. Assman.

6. Letters from the Reverend Lester
Arthur Pritchard, secretary-treasurer,
The Evangelical Churches of Pente-
cost, Incorporated, and from Thelma
(Mrs. Lester Arthur) Pritchard.

7. *The Truth and Facts of the United
House of Prayer for All People and
the Most Honorable Bishop W. Mc-
Collough, Leader* (Washington, D.C.:
The United House of Prayer for All
People, 1968), p. 1. A month after
Bishop Grace's death, after the federal
government had filed a $5,900,000 in-
come tax claim (subsequently settled
for $1,940,000) against his estate,
Don Oberdorfer, "Evangelist's Multi-
Million Dollar Kingdom on Earth:
'Sweet Daddy' Grace Refined the
Method of Receiving Donations into
Colorful and Profitable Art," *St. Louis
Post-Dispatch*, February 12, 1960, D2,
declared that Grace, "a newcomer
from Portugal's Cape Verde Islands,
. . . began as a ship's cook, small
groceryman, and patent medicine
salesman in New Bedford, Massachusetts." Albert Nathaniel Whiting,
"The United House of Prayer for All
People: A Case Study of a Charismatic Sect" (Washington, D.C.:
School of Social Sciences and Public
Affairs, The American University, unpublished doctoral dissertation, 1952),
p. 79, n. 1, describes Grace as a
former "cook for a southern railway
company."

8. *The Truth and Facts*, p. 2. Whiting's
careful sociological analysis (op. cit.,
pp. 95-96, for example) confirms
this. Sweet Daddy Grace is still regarded in the United House of Prayer
for All People as the prophet referred
to in John 1:21 and the comforter
promised in John 15:26 and 16:7.

Ephesians 2:8—"by Grace[!] are ye
saved through faith"—is also applied
to him. (*Grace Magazine*, May 1970,
p. 4.) For evaluations of Sweet Daddy
Grace by his followers during his lifetime, see Whiting, pp. 66-70.

9. *The Truth and Facts*, p. 3. In the first
(1960) election of a successor to the
founder, Elder McCollough received
118 (54.6%) of the 216 votes cast by
the elders present. The election was
challenged in the courts and in 1961
Bishop McCollough was restrained
from using the title of bishop and
from exercising the powers of the
late founder. At a second, court-
authorized election in 1962, Daddy
McCollough received 410 (88.7%)
of the votes cast; the electors in this
instance consisted of all ministers and
elders of the United House of Prayer
and two representatives from each
congregation (ibid., pp. 31, 47-61).
A group of dissident pastors and laypeople withdrew and organized the
True Grace Memorial House of
Prayer for All People with churches
in Philadelphia; Washington, D.C.;
Savannah, Georgia; and Hollywood,
Florida (ibid., p. 61).

10. Ibid., pp. viii and 2. Whiting, p. 81,
observed that the theology of the
United House of Prayer for All
People "has a traditional Judaic-
Christian foundation with a configura-
tion of distinguishing supplementary
beliefs," namely, the imminence of
the end of the world, preparation for
salvation through sanctification and
the reception of the Holy Spirit, and
"ultimate salvation through membership in the House of Prayer and
through the agency of God's man
'Grace' who was sent to establish the
church of Christ and gather unto him
those eligible for salvation."

11. *The Truth and Facts*, p. 2. Bishop Mc-
Collough is officially referred to as
"His Eminence, the Holy Anointed
Prophet of God, the Most Honorable
Bishop W. McCollough" (ibid., p. iii).
Other titles include "Precious Daddy"
(p. 33), "the Supreme Sweet Daddy
McCollough" (p. 79), and "God's
chief executive here on earth" (p. 91).
The May 1970 issue of *Grace Maga-
zine*, the monthly organ of the United
House of Prayer, describes him as
"Head and Leader of the United

House of Prayer for All People, conqueror of sin, healer of the sick, advocate of peace and goodwill, great counselor and humanitarian whose divine wisdom has caused this great organization to be tightly bound that the many congregations will stand together as one" (p. 2), "the key man" (p. 7), "the only one who is carrying the Christ today" (p. 10), "my Lord and your Lord ruling on this earth today" (p. 11), "my guide, my counselor, and my Saviour" (ibid.), "truly an angel and messenger of God, the one that God reveals his secrets to" (p. 12), "sweet Dad" (ibid.), the one "who was sent to save the world" (p. 14), and "the only one that has power over Satan to make him take his hands off your body" (ibid.). The same issue of the magazine reports a case where members of the United House of Prayer in Rocky Mount, North Carolina, "began calling on Sweet Daddy Grace McCollough" in their "holy mountain," or church building, on behalf of a dying young fellow member, "when the power of Sweet Daddy Grace McCollough began to move on him, he got up, and today he is well." The report concludes: "Saints, pray for us in Rocky Mount that we will ever praise Daddy's Holy Name" (ibid., p. 12). Another report describes a member of a Washington, D.C. congregation who was about to undergo an operation; in the hospital she recalled Daddy Grace McCollough, saying, "When you call him, he would check to see if you were a faithful member and had you paid your tithes, before he would pray. So I began to pray in the spirit and I told Sweet Daddy you know I am your child, I paid my tithes, and I do work in the House of Prayer. Please let me know that you will be with me by letting me see you tonight. That morning at about 5 o'clock Sweet Daddy came in the hospital in the spirit. I awakened rejoicing and saying, 'Thank You, Daddy' " (ibid., p. 11). The church body's manual of discipline, *The Supreme Laws for the Government of the United House of Prayer for All People, Church on the Rock of the Apostolic Faith*, revised edition (Washington, D.C.: The United House of Prayer for All

People, n.d.) (21-page pamphlet), provides that whenever the General Council sits as the highest court of appeal in the church body, the bishop is always to be addressed as "Your Honor Supreme" (p. 1). *The Supreme Laws* regularly refer to him as "the Supreme" and "our Supreme." Violations of the rules set forth in *The Supreme Laws* are punishable with warnings and fines of from $1.00 to $100.00 "and maybe other punishment." An elder may incur a fine of up to $100.00 by establishing a House of Prayer for All People without the bishop's consent; speaking cruelly to a member of the General Council, minister, another elder, or a member of the church, if it is his third offense; riding males or females in his car for immoral purposes or selfish intentions, if it is his second offense; staying, stopping in, or living in a single sister's home alone, or walking the streets with sisters; escaping trial before a local state council; acting disorderly with the opposite sex, if it is his second offense; failing to comply with an order to make a report on any church funds entrusted to him, failing to forward a weekly report of all church income and expenses and to transmit tithes weekly to the Washington headquarters; helping secretaries fix books or change records; teaching against the rules of the Supreme Laws; failing to have a sign reading "United House of Prayer for All People" on the body of his car; failing to display a picture of Bishop McCollough "in the proper place over the throne in which he reigns"; and failing to display on the front of the church building a sign reading "The United House of Prayer for All People" (ibid., pp. 2, 4-6, 11, 13, 16-19).

12. More than 1,000 candidates have been baptized at one time "during convocation" (*The Truth and Facts*, p. 82). Baptism is repeated in the United House of Prayer for All Nations. "As often as one sins, they are to be baptized unto repentance. As the waters of Jordan come [to the place of convocation] by faith and wash them clean and the sins are carried by Jordan's water down to the Dead Sea, never to rise up against them anymore. This is a very sacred ceremony

for in the water there is healing, there are blessings and salvation to them that believe" (*Grace Magazine*, May 1970, p. 9).

13. *The Truth and Facts*, p. 93.

14. Ibid., pp. viii, 95-96.

15. In a description of "a quite ordinary meeting of the group, held in midweek and in the absence of Bishop Grace," Elmer T. Clark, *The Small Sects in America* (rev. edn.; Nashville: Abingdon-Cokesbury Press, 1949), pp. 143-144, noted four stages in the "seizure": (1) Rhythmic swaying, with eyes closed or uplifted, accompanied by "inarticulate mutterings akin to an unknown tongue"; (2) falling prone on the ground in a state of trance or coma; (3) twitchings that increased in intensity "until the jerking body bounded about on the ground like a ball," accompanied by a return to consciousness or to a semiconscious state, with the individual struggling to his feet; (4) "a wild dance, which gradually emerged and eliminated the jerks," followed by the "lifting" of a song by "a circle of hand-clapping, laughing, ejaculating saints."

16. Currently the "Hurricane Services" are the occasion to pray for the power to "overcome any manner of danger, be healed of sickness, [and] increase our faith."

17. *Grace Magazine*, May 1970, pp. 8-9.

18. *The Truth and Facts*, pp. 77-79, 85, 91.

19. *Grace Magazine*, May 1970, p. 8.

20. *The Truth and Facts*, p. 84.

21. *The Truth and Facts*, p. 61; letter from the True Grace Memorial House of Prayer, Washington, D.C.

22. Thomas Tomizawa, "Split by Death of Leader Here: Gospel of Kingdom Members Summoned for Unity Talks," *The Louisville Times*, June 15, 1960, p. 16. Another estimate puts the maximum at 150 churches. Elmer T. Clark, *The Small Sects in America* (rev. edn.; Nashville: Abingdon-Cokesbury Press, 1949), p. 105, credits the movement with as many as 500 local assemblies. Sowders' own congregation had 750 members.

23. Letter from Mr. Clifton T. Chalk, executive administrator, Gospel Assembly Ministers' Fund. The present writer has found it difficult to obtain precise information about the causes of these divisions and the courses that they have taken. The Gospel of the Kingdom Campground at Shepherdsville, of which Mrs. Mary E. Mills, 1430 South 28th Street, Louisville, Kentucky, one of William Sowders's closest co-workers, is secretary, was reopened in 1958 and seeks to occupy a neutral position over against the various divisions within the movement.

24. Sowders insisted that his movement was "undenominational." He is quoted as telling his congregation at a School of the Prophets session: "If they ask you if you are a Protestant, tell them, no! If they ask you if you are a Catholic, no! Then, what are you? You are a Christian. They can't beat that!" (Tomizawa, loc. cit.) The movement still rejects the use of any "denominational" name for its assemblies and their members.

25. See Lloyd L. Goodwin, *The Mystery of the Godhead* (Des Moines, Iowa: Gospel Assembly Church, n.d. [after 1967]) (26-page brochure). Clark (loc. cit.) can be read to give the incorrect impression that the movement was a "Father Only" group. Clark describes a "Father Only" group as one which, on the analogy of the "Jesus Only" groups, "reject[s] the trinitarian formula and baptize[s] only in the name of the Father." The present writer has found no concrete evidence of the present (or past) existence of groups that correspond to this description.

26. See Lloyd L. Goodwin, *Water Baptism That Is Scriptural* (Des Moines, Iowa: Gospel Assembly Church, n.d.) (23-page brochure).

27. In the church services of the movement speaking in tongues is allowed and even encouraged, but the service does not revolve around speaking in tongues. The focal point of any service is given by the nature of the service itself; on one occasion, for example, the service may be for teaching, while on another it may be for evangelism. As Clark (op. cit.) describes the services of the assemblies, "a member propounds a doctrine and challenges any other member to 'cross' him, thus opening a free-for-all discussion which may continue for hours." Clark indicates as the purpose

of this kind of debate the development of "a unity of spirit among those who differ in points of doctrine, and thus lead to the ultimate goal of unity in both spirit and doctrine." While the movement has always provided opportunity for the discussion of doctrine, the statements of Clark at this point are regarded by ministers of the movement as grossly misleading.

28. Reportedly a few of them have actually observed the Lord's Supper with bread and fermented wine. Other considerations that have been urged for not observing the "meal" include the fact that the consequences of unworthy eating and drinking of the material elements are potentially so dire that its observance would imperil the health and even the lives of the participants. Some day, proponents of this view hold, the people will become perfect enough to take the meal, but now is not yet the time; when the time comes, the Spirit will indicate it.

29. *Do You Want Peace?* (Des Moines, Iowa: Gospel Assembly Church, n.d.) (4-page leaflet).

30. See Lloyd L. Goodwin, *Mystery Babylon the Great, The Mother of Harlots* (Des Moines, Iowa: Gospel Assembly Church, n.d.) (42-page brochure).

31. *Ministers' Address Directory 1970* (Norfolk, Va.: Gospel Assembly Ministers' Fund, 1970) (35-page pamphlet), pp. 32-35.

32. This article synthesizes information obtained from a series of telephone conversations with a minister of the movement who desires to remain unnamed and from correspondence with Mr. Clifford T. Chalk, Gospel Assembly Ministers' Fund, 100 North Military Highway, Norfolk, Virginia, and with the Reverend Lloyd L. Goodwin, minister of the Gospel Assembly Church, Sixth and Clinton, Des Moines, Iowa. The present writer also acknowledges gratefully the helpfulness of the Reverend Carl A. Eberhard, D.D., retired pastor, Concordia Church, Louisville, Kentucky.

33. The members of this fellowship are insistent that "body" must not be capitalized, since this would tend to make it a denominational name.

34. More correctly b*e*nei shalom, literally, "sons of wholeness" (or "peace"), a Hebrew name that the members of the body of Christ apply to themselves to underline their concern for the Jewish community.

35. J. L. Heard, in *B'nai Shalom*, vol. 5, no. 2 (May 1968), p. 8. *B'nai Shalom* is the quarterly publication of the body of Christ.

36. Richard Tate, *Alpha and Omega* (2nd edn.; Phoenix, Ariz.: Peace Publishers and Company, 1969) (14-page pamphlet), p. 1.

37. Richard Tate, editorial, *B'nai Shalom*, vol. 7, no. 1 (February 1970), inside front cover, and ibid., vol. 6, no. 4 (November 1969), p. 1.

38. Among them Orville J. Wallace and Bronson McArthy.

39. Tate, *Alpha and Omega*, pp. 1-2.

40. References to the Communion are not infrequent in the literature of the body of Christ. Dawkins, for instance, in *The Principles of the Doctrine of Christ* (Phoenix, Ariz.: Peace Publishers and Company, n.d. [1963 or later]) (14-page pamphlet), refers to "every member of the body of Christ, who has made the vow and sealed it in the communion" (p. 1). He further states: "Paul cautioned the people before they took the communion what would happen to them; that they would get sick, some of them would go to the grave, and so on, if they took the communion unworthily. To be worthy you must abide by the principle[*sic*] teachings" (p. 3). Again he asks: "How would it be possible for someone who has tasted of this wonderful spirit that we drink of, taken the communion with us, signed the vow with us, promised to work for each other . . . and then [whisper and talk and say] hurtful things to destroy the influence of a brother or sister?" (p. 12). In the *B'nai Shalom*, vol. 5, no. 2 (May 1968), there are three references to the Communion. James McKnight says of the bread that according to Paul is the body of Christ that when one takes hold of it and feasts on it, or perhaps chokes it down, it is supposed to furnish sustenance, to give the recipient life, and to blend him more completely into the one great bread of which Jesus is the original author (p. 6). Edith McArthy, "Woman's Voice," writes about making a covenant, and sealing it at the

Communion table, to remain with the body of Christ throughout life (p. 9). Irving Goldberg recalls that he was determined to become a member of the body of Christ by being baptized and by taking the cup of the Communion (p. 11). These references are to be given a spiritual interpretation. Elder Daniel J. Sturgeon, pastor of the Gospel of Peace Tabernacle, 5117 Virginia Avenue, Saint Louis, stated in a telephone conversation that the body of Christ does not practice the Lord's Supper with material elements.

41. Dawkins is said to have refused "to be identified in any way with the blasphemous ways of Christendom" (Richard Tate, *The body of Christ* [Phoenix, Ariz.: Peace Publishers and Company, n.d.] [10-page pamphlet], p. [ii]). Christendom is described as "a sort of spiritual insanity" (ibid., p. 1). Its whole legacy "is division and animal distrust, veneered with a guilt complex" (ibid., p. 2). "Blasphemous Christendom" and "religious hypocrisy" are used synonymously ("The Eastern Gate," *B'nai Shalom*, vol. 6, no. 4 [November 1969], p. 31).

42. Tate, *Alpha and Omega*, p. 5.

43. Reynolds Edward Dawkins, *Higher Powers* (Phoenix, Ariz.: Peace Publishers and Company, n.d.) (16-page leaflet), p. 2. "This ordained ministry has an order and each soul is to be subject to that order and to the one over [him]" (ibid., p. 2).

44. Ibid., p. 5.

45. Ibid., p. 3.

46. Tate, *Alpha and Omega*, p. 7.

47. Ibid., pp. 12-13. The Revelation to John was meant for the seventh millennium. Its meaning has been hidden so long, "because God intended the people to be in semi-darkness until he was ready for this apostolic church to come to the front" (Reynolds Edward Dawkins, *Rightly Dividing the Word of God* [Phoenix, Ariz.: Peace Publishers and Company, n.d.] [16-page leaflet], p. 2). The Revelation to John is also the most detailed prophecy of the close of the Gentile age, "with the greater portion actually to be fulfilled between 1964 and 1974" (Tate, *Alpha and Omega*, p. 9).

48. Tate, *Alpha and Omega*, pp. 7-8.

49. Tate, *The body of Christ*, p. 4.

50. Tate, *Alpha and Omega*, p. 9.

51. Richard Tate, *In My Father's House* (Phoenix, Ariz.: Peace Publishers and Company, n.d.) (11-page pamphlet), p. 8. "Most of the latter day church restoration effort has been among those familiar with or actually speaking English. The King James Bible, written in and for English speaking people, was one cornerstone of the great Reformation period, during which a door of liberty was opened from the stifling hell of the Dark Ages. This being true, a closer study should be made of the sequence of the letters in the English word, 'ASIA.' After finding, as Elder Dawkins did, that A-S-I-A are the initial letters of America, Scandinavia, India, and Africa, it becomes easier to see that the seven churches [of Asia] are symbolic descriptions of seven works which are to exist on these four corners of the earth . . . . The seven churches are the 'Menorah,' or seven branched candlestick, and the lights of them are the seven stars or ministers who are in attendance to these works" (Tate, *Alpha and Omega*, p. 10).

52. Richard Tate, "For Zion's Sake," *B'nai Shalom*, vol. 6, no. 4 (November 1969), p. 3.

53. Richard Tate, editorial, *B'nai Shalom*, vol. 5, no. 2 (May 1968), inside front cover.

54. "The Eastern Gate," *B'nai Shalom*, vol. 6, no. 4 (November 1969), p. 31.

55. "We don't have to love everyone. We should only love those in the body of Christ who are giving their lives for it, and we certainly don't have to love God's enemies. We are not required to love those who come in unawares, turning the grace of God into lasciviousness; they are rotten, and they seek to bring everyone down to their level. We must be delivered from these people. That doesn't mean that we must kill them; it just means that we should shun them" (Dawkins, *The Principles of the Doctrine of Christ*, p. 8).

56. Ibid., p. 10.

57. Dawkins, "The Church of Ephesus," *B'nai Shalom*, vol. 5, no. 2 (May 1968), p. 12.

58. At a service in the Gospel of Peace Tabernacle, St. Louis, in July 1970, which the present writer attended, of the 57 persons present, 11 were adult males. These included, in addition to

Elder Richard Tate, several other visiting leaders. There were about 20 grown women, the balance teen-agers and younger children.

59. Thus, for instance, 47 members of the movement from the United States and abroad met in Israel in the fall of 1969. This assembly climaxed with a symbolic march up Mount Zion on Erev Simchat Torah ("Eve of the Rejoicing in the Law") on October 3. See *B'nai Shalom*, vol. 6, no. 4 (November 1969).

60. Elder Dawkins looked forward to seeing seven strong centers established in America, with seven smaller gathering places around each center (J. L. Heard, in *B'nai Shalom*, vol. 5, no. 2 [May 1968], p. 8).

61. The present writer acknowledges the kindness of the Reverend Eugene A. Beyer, pastor, Mount Calvary Church, Phoenix, Arizona, in securing information on this writer's behalf from Elder Tate.

62. "3 St. Louis Area Residents Killed in Auto Mishaps," *St. Louis Post-Dispatch*, January 31, 1952, p. 16A; "Eldorado Church Plans Anniversary Open House," ibid., November 7, 1954; "Gospel Tabernacle Non-Denominational," ibid., December 4, 1957.

63. Letter from the Reverend Tom M. Jolly, minister, Gospel Assembly, St. Louis, Missouri.

64. Telephone conversation with the Reverend Mr. Jolly. The efforts of the present writer to obtain authoritative information about the details of the Gospel Assembly's current doctrinal position were unsuccessful.

65. This is the formula that the chairman of the association, Elder Garver C. Gray, Vancouver, Washington, uses. He explains in a letter to the present writer that he is neither an adherent of the "oneness" view nor a trinitarian; he does not regard the Holy Spirit as a person, but as the personality that caused the Son to be the image of the Father.

66. The reference is to Isaiah 52:8 (KJV).

67. "Association of Seventh Day Pentecostal Assemblies Clarify (*sic*) Position" (undated 1-page printed announcement).

68. Letters from Elder Gray.

69. The Los Angeles, California, assembly, for example, supports the Jerusalem Church of God (Seventh-Day) in Israel. In 1952 Elder Andrew N. Dugger, who had been a leader in the organization of the Church of God (Seventh-Day) (Salem, West Virginia), left that body and established the Jerusalem Church of God as a "Messianic order" of Judaism. Its members describe themselves, regardless of their individual racial and ethnic backgrounds, as "Jews believing in Jesus as the Messiah born in Bethlehem." It engages in an energetic magazine, tract, and book publication ministry in both English and Hebrew. Its doctrinal position is generally that of the Church of God (Seventh-Day) (Salem, West Virginia); it does not, however, grant ministerial recognition to persons who have remarried after being divorced or who have married divorced persons (letter from Elder Andrew N. Dugger). On Dugger's role in the founding of the Church of God (Seventh-Day) (Salem, West Virginia), see Andrew N. Dugger and Clarence O. Dodd, *A History of the True Religion Traced from 33 A. D. to Date* (2nd edn.; Jerusalem, Israel: The Mount Zion Reporter, 1968), pp. 298-306.

70. The statement refrains from touching on the issue raised by the "oneness" controversy in the Pentecostal movement and makes no statement about the Trinity or about the Godhood of the Holy Spirit. Paragraph 3 calls Christ the Son of God and paragraph 6 refers to his divine nature.

71. The association is "amillennial," that is, it denies a millennial reign of Christ. The association regards as a distinctive difference the fact that in its interpretation of the Revelation of St. John the Divine it takes a "historical" position in contrast to the "futurist" interpretation of most Pentecostals.

72. *Constitution and By-Laws of the California Evangelistic Association, a Corporation, Adopted February 20, 1939* (Long Beach, Calif.: California Evangelistic Association, 1939) (pamphlet), Articles IV and V (pp. 2-6).

73. Ibid., Article XVII (p. 16).

74. Communication from R. H. Harms, president.

75. Frederick L. Whitam and others, *A Report on the Protestant Spanish Community in New York City* (New

York: The Protestant Council of the City of New York, 1960), p. 40.

76. Noel McNeill, "As of a Rushing Mighty Wind" (unpublished manuscript), p. 136. Repeated efforts by this writer to obtain information about the Damascus Christian Church, Incorporated, from the Reverend Enrique Melendez, bishop of the church body, were unsuccessful.

77. He received his doctorate of divinity in 1962 from the International Free Protestant Episcopal University, London, of which the Most Reverend Charles Dennis Boltwood, D.D., L.L.D., bishop-primus of the Free Protestant Episcopal Church, is rector.

78. Thomas Wyatt, *Key to the Kingdom* (Hollywood: Oxford Press, 1961), p. 124.

79. *A Memorial Tribute to Thomas Wyatt —Man of Vision* (Los Angeles, Calif.: Wings of Healing, 1964) (48-page brochure). See also Basil Miller, *Grappling with Destiny: The Biography of a Dream* (Hollywood, Calif.: Cathedral/Vantage Press, 1962).

80. Wings of Healing holds that no affliction comes from God and "that He wants to deliver you from its cruel clutches" (Evelyn Wyatt, "Is It Saintly to Suffer?" *The March of Faith*, vol. 22, no. 2 [February 1967], pp. 4-5).

81. Thomas Wyatt, *The Birth and Growth of a World-Wide Ministry* (Los Angeles, Calif.: Wings of Healing, 1960) (16-page pamphlet), pp. 9-13. On the Trinity-"oneness" question, Wings of Healing believes in one God, who has chosen to manifest himself in three forms, Father, Son, and Holy Spirit. It favors the trinitarian formula of baptism as opposed to the "oneness" formula, but it contends for nonsectarian fellowship among all God's people, in the conviction that the experience of water baptism and the heart condition of the candidate are of more importance than the form of words spoken at the time of immersion, just as the heart condition of a deceased person is more important than the words which a minister speaks at the interment of the remains (letter of Mrs. Evelyn Wyatt, president, Wings of Healing).

82. Ibid., p. 14.

83. In a 1967 three-state poll, one third of the Wings of Healing listeners that responded stated that they did not attend church in their communities (*The March of Faith*, vol. 22, no. 4 [May–June 1967], p. 14).

84. [*Bible*] *Doctrines, Teachings, and By-Laws of the Evangelical Bible Church* (Baltimore, Md.: The Evangelical Bible Church, 1960) (28-page pamphlet), pp. 3-23.

85. *Introducing Glad Tidings Temple* (undated 8-page tract), pp. [3]-[5]. The Glad Tidings Missionary Society does not see the "oneness" and the trinitarian views of God as mutually exclusive. It holds that "Lord Jesus Christ" is the name that reveals God to the church and that for that reason the church should baptize in this name, but the church is to believe in the Father, Son, and Holy Ghost (letter, Glad Tidings Missionary Society, dated March 26, 1958).

86. John Thomas Nichol, *Pentecostalism* (New York: Harper & Row, 1966), p. 329, attributes the founding of the World Church to Jaggers's feeling "that the *charismata* no longer had precedence among the larger Pentecostal groups."

87. Descriptions of services in the Los Angeles mother church have been published by Pete Martin, "Faith and Fear for $1.07," *Christian Herald*, July 1967, pp. 13-14, 42-46, 48-49, and by Aubrey B. Haines, "Miss Velma Descends," *Christian Century* 83 (1966): 992, 994.

88. A leading minister in the Universal World Church is the founder's wife, Miss Velma Jaggers, reportedly a first cousin whom he married in 1957 (so Martin, pp. 48-49).

89. The University of the World Church in Los Angeles is not listed in *Education Directory* of the United States Office of Education. In a letter from Dr. O. L. Jaggers, founder-president, the World Church, to the present writer he states that he is a teacher and a professor of genetics in the university and that "some of the best known and renowned professors teach in the University, some of which are Nobel Prize winners."

90. Cited letter from Dr. Jaggers. Dan L. Thrapp, "The Background Story," *Christian Herald*, July 1967, pp. 15-16, 59, estimated that "Jaggers prob-

ably has, at the outside, one thousand two hundred adherents" and added: "The figure may be optimistic" (p. 59).

91. See Noel McNeill, "As of a Rushing Mighty Wind" (unpublished manuscript), pp. 94, 135; McNeill estimated the number of churches represented by their ministers at 100, and the total active membership of these churches at about 5,000. The present writer gratefully acknowledges the assistance of the Reverend George A. Loose, then pastor, Emmanuel Church, Baltimore, Maryland, who interviewed the Reverend John E. Douglas by telephone on this writer's behalf.

92. The Reverend Lillian G. Fitch states that she has completed three 30-day fasts, one 40-day fast, and many shorter fasts. From May 19, 1965, to May 19, 1966, she remained constantly in church, carried on a full program of ministrations and spiritual counseling, fasted three days a week, and spent two hours in Bible reading and four hours in prayer daily.

93. Letter from the Reverend Lillian G. Fitch, pastor, First Deliverance Church, Atlanta, Georgia.

94. Letter from the Reverend Eldridge M. Plunkett, evangelist-pastor, Rainbow Revival Church, Incorporated, Box 75855, Los Angeles, California. The curator of the James V. Geisendorfer Collection of Original Source Materials on American Minority Religious Groups, Bethany Lutheran Seminary Library, Mankato, Minnesota, has graciously made the collection's materials on the Rainbow Revival Church, Incorporated, available to the present writer.

95. The 1964 charter prescribed the form-

ula "in the name of the Father and of the Son and of the Holy Ghost." Baptism in the name of Jesus is necessary, according to Bishop Lawrence, "because the church is the bride of Christ and every bride takes her husband's name, which is also the name of her husband's father."

96. Typescript copy of the 1964 amended charter of incorporation of God's House of Prayer for All Nations, with Bishop Lawrence's handwritten revisions.

97. The present writer gratefully acknowledges the assistance of the Reverend John A. Strohschein, then seminarian-assistant at Christ Church, Peoria, Illinois, who personally interviewed Bishop Lawrence on this writer's behalf.

98. Noel McNeill, "As of a Rushing Mighty Wind" (unpublished manuscript), p. [135].

99. Letter from the Reverend Don Gossett.

100. John Thomas Nichol, *Pentecostalism* (New York: Harper & Row, 1966), p. 239.

101. Article 2 ("Nature of the Fellowship"), *Constitution* (rev. edn.; Dallas, Texas: Full Gospel Fellowship of Churches and Ministers International, 1967), p. 3.

102. Ibid., p. 4.

103. Article 14 ("Tenets of Faith"), ibid., pp. 13-14.

104. Article 15 ("Exclusions from the Fellowship of the Body of Christ"), ibid., p. 14.

105. Article 2, ibid., p. 7.

106. Letter of the Reverend Elwood H. Jensen, D.D., executive secretary, Full Gospel Fellowship of Churches and Ministers International.

## BIBLIOGRAPHY

*The Truth and Facts of the United House of Prayer for All People and the Most Honorable Bishop W. McCollough, Leader.* Washington, D.C.: The United House of Prayer for All People, 1968.

Whiting, Albert Nathaniel. "The United House of Prayer for All People: A Case Study of a Charismatic Sect." Washington, D.C.: School of Social Sciences and Public Affairs, The American University, unpublished doctoral dissertation, 1952.

Williams, Chancellor. "The Socio-economic Significance of the Store-Front Church Movement in the United States since 1920." Washington, D.C.: American University, unpublished doctoral dissertation, 1949.

# Index

251

PROFILES IN BELIEF

# Profiles in Belief

## THE RELIGIOUS BODIES
## OF THE UNITED STATES AND CANADA

VOLUME IV

### EVANGELICAL, FUNDAMENTALIST, AND OTHER CHRISTIAN BODIES

*By ARTHUR CARL PIEPKORN*

Published in San Francisco by
HARPER & ROW, PUBLISHERS, INC.

1817

NEW YORK, HAGERSTOWN

SAN FRANCISCO, LONDON

FIRST EDITION

*Designed by Sidney Feinberg*

Library of Congress Cataloging in Publication Data (Revised)
Piepkorn, Arthur Carl, 1907-1973.
  Profiles in belief.

  Includes bibliographies and indexes.
  CONTENTS: v. 1. Roman Catholic.     Old Catholic.
Eastern Orthodox.  v. 2. Protestant denominations.  v. 3. Holiness and
Pentecostal churches.
  1. Sects—North America.  I. Title.
BR510.P53   1977       200'.973       76-9971
ISBN 0-06-066581-5

79 80 81 82 83 10 9 8 7 6 5 4 3 2 1

# Contents

# Foreword

"One book is about one thing—at least the good ones are." Eugene Rosenstock-Huessey's famous dictum may seem inappropriate in the eyes of readers who might casually come across the present work. That it is a "good book" will be immediately apparent even to the casual user. But that it is "about one thing" may seem less obvious at first.

Arthur Carl Piepkorn's good and even great work seems to be about many things. It concerns itself with profiles of the many beliefs of millions of Americans who are separated into hundreds of religious bodies. Many of them, it may safely be presumed, will not even have been known by name to most readers before they acquaint themselves with the table of contents. Never before within the covers of several volumes in a single series will the student of American religion have been able to find convenient and reliable access to so many different religous groups. How can one in the midst of such variety think of Piepkorn's book as being "about one thing"?

The answer to that question, on second thought and longer acquaintance, could well be, "Easily!" For here is a single-minded attention to the one thing that is supposed to be at the heart of almost all of these religious groups, their beliefs. The telephone book includes many names, but it is "about one thing," and no one will mistake its purposes or its plot. So with Piepkorn's presentation of *The Religious Bodies of the United States and Canada*. It is precisely what its precise author's title claims it to be: *Profiles in Belief*.

Profile: it is a side view, an outline, a concise description. This book offers such an angle of vision. No individual can speak from within all these denominations and movements. To invite a separate speaker from each tradition would be to convoke a new Babel of tongues. Here we have something coherent and believable, the voice of a single informed observer. He establishes the "side view" and then invites criticism and approval by a member of each group to check on the accuracy of the portraits. This process assures evenness in tone and consistency in proportion without sacrificing either fairness or immediacy. While the description inevitably has had to grow long because of the number of groups presented, even its several volumes will be seen to be but an outline, something concise.

Beliefs: these by themselves do not constitute or exhaust all that a religion is or is experienced to be. For a full description the student will want to learn about social contexts and environments, about behavior patterns and practices of individuals and groups. But since these external marks purportedly grow out of the group's shared set of formal meanings and values and since these, in turn, derive from root beliefs, somewhere and somehow it is important to gain access to such beliefs. Had we all world enough and time it is possible that the knowledgeable could establish for themselves the profile of a large number of these religious bodies. But with the industry and intelligence for which he was noted, Dr. Piepkorn devoted years to the task of assembling the data for others. His profiles can be ends in themselves or instruments for further research. Of one thing we can be sure: they will force all thoughtful readers to take the beliefs more seriously than before.

Arthur Carl Piepkorn was a confessional Lutheran, but he does not use the confessional stance as a means of ranking the value of beliefs. Instead, that stance turned out to be the means of assuring readers that the author knew the importance of beliefs, knew what it was to confess a faith, was aware of the intellectual power that can reside in a religious tradition. If, as a book title of some years ago asserts, "beliefs have consequences," the opposite was also true for Piepkorn. He could look at behavior and practice and step back, in effect saying, "consequences also have beliefs."

This is not the place to read the narrative of American religion, be enthralled by anecdote, or ramble with a sage author dispensing practical advice. This is a very formal guide to belief systems. As an ecumenist of note, Dr. Piepkorn came to be emphatic about others' beliefs. As a military chaplain he had practical experience encountering people of faiths remote from his own in the American and Canadian contexts. As a teacher he knew how to get ideas across. As a confessor he valued faith. His book is certain to be a classic.

A classic is, among other things, a book behind which or around which one cannot easily go. Once it has appeared and come into common use it is a measure or benchmark for others. While the official title of this series is likely to endure, it is probably destined to be referred to in shorthand as "Piepkorn." If so, as the standard reference in the field, the designation will be a fitting tribute to the person who prepared himself well and spared himself not at all for the writing of this life work.

MARTIN E. MARTY
The University of Chicago

# Editor's Preface

Categorizing religious bodies and church denominations is an almost impossible task. Arthur Carl Piepkorn, prior to his death in 1973, arranged the voluminous material that he had assembled by grouping similar religious organizations in separate chapters. Subsequent to his death the decision was made to publish his massive manuscript in seven volumes, making it necessary to find more inclusive categories for his separate chapters. And for the sake of readability the individual volumes were divided into several parts where possible, bringing together additional groupings of religious bodies.

Volume I was simple enough; its title for the religious bodies described in its pages is "Roman Catholic, Old Catholic, and Eastern Orthodox." The title is descriptive enough but not completely accurate, since Part I deals with "Pre- and Non-Chalcedonian Churches," which are not, strictly speaking, embraced by any of the three denominations in the title.

Volume II was more difficult. It is entitled "Protestant Denominations," since the churches described in it are those which in a direct way have been shaped and influenced by the sixteenth-century Reformation and in popular parlance are referred to as Protestant. Yet the adherents of some of the churches described in its pages, Lutherans and Anglicans among them, object to the Protestant label. And a large number of churches usually described as Protestant were not included in the volume but were left for treatment in subsequent volumes with different titles.

Volume III deals with church bodies that were formed under the influence of the Holiness and Pentecostal movements of the nineteenth and early twentieth centuries. Those churches are described as "Protestant" and could have been treated in separate sections in the previous volume. On the other hand, some of those church bodies specifically categorize themselves as "Fundamentalist" or "Evangelical," and they therefore could have been reserved for treatment in the present volume.

The issue is even more complicated for the church bodies included in Volume IV, entitled "Evangelical, Fundamentalist, and Other Christian Bodies." They are all popularly labeled "Protestant" and, like the church bodies in Volume III, could have been dealt with in separate sections in Volume II. On the other hand, not all of the church bodies that consider themselves to be "Evangelical" or "Fundamental" are included in Volume IV; some of them, indeed some of the most important of them, have been described as part of other denominational categories in volumes II and III. And as a final complication, the category "Other Christian Bodies" surely does not do justice to the church bodies included under it, since they each have a distinctiveness of their own.

Confident that other categories could have been devised for presenting the material, I invite the reader to focus less upon the category and more upon the description of each individual denomination, where the effort has been made to let the people of the denomination speak for themselves. In any event, Volume IV completes the listing and description of religious bodies that are usually considered Christian denominations (though even that claim is open to challenge, as subsequent volumes will make clear).

Most of the material in Volume IV was written by Arthur Carl Piepkorn prior to his death five years ago. I brought the material up to date and wrote the introductory chapter on "The Evangelical and Fundamentalist Movements" (Chapter 1).

I am grateful to the library staff of Christ Seminary—Seminex for their assistance in providing bibliographical and reference material; to my colleague, Thomas Rick, for the index; and to my secretary, Rosemary Lipka, for her work in contacting church bodies for information and in typing the manuscript.

In the midst of his many scholarly and professional activities Arthur Carl Piepkorn was a family man. He and his wife Miriam, who has now joined him in the heavenly mansions, had four daughters. To the other women in Arthur Carl Piepkorn's life—his daughters Mary Eckart, Felicity Steere, Faith Hoffman, and Angela van Goidsenhoven—this volume is affectionately dedicated.

JOHN H. TIETJEN
Christ Seminary—Seminex
St. Louis, Missouri

# Introduction

During the late '70s, the evangelicals have been a talking point everywhere. Their growing churches, highly visible campus and youth ministries, phenomenally successful publishing and other media efforts, and unlikely "twice-born" national celebrities, such as Charles Colson, Jeb Magruder, Johnny Cash, Anita Bryant, Graham Kerr ("the Galloping Gourmet"), Eldridge Cleaver, and Jimmy Carter, have caught the eye of Protestant liberals, Roman Catholics, and secular journalists. Meanwhile, the new social and political activism of younger evangelicals has been a great encouragement to burned-out liberal and radical theologians and denominational-ecumenical leaders. Magazine writer Garry Wills insists that "evangelical chic" is impending.

In a widely publicized survey based upon in-person interviews with more than 1500 adults (18 and over) in more than 300 scientifically selected localities in the United States during August 27–30, 1976, The Gallup Poll discovered that one person in three (34 percent) has been *born again*—that is, has had a turning point in his or her life marked by a commitment to Jesus Christ. The figure works out to nearly 50 million American adults. Among Protestants alone, nearly half (48 percent) declare that they have had a born-again experience. And 18 percent of Catholics also admit that they are born-again Christians.

On the basis of his survey-research data, George Gallup, Jr., termed 1976 *The Year of the Evangelical*, and suggested that the United States may be in an early stage of a profound religious revival, with born-again Christians providing a powerful thrust.

The word evangelical comes from the Greek *euangelion*, the evangel, or good news. Broadly speaking, an evangelical is a person who is devoted to the good news that God has sent us a Savior and that we can be partakers of God's redemptive grace in Jesus Christ (I Corinthians 15:1–8). But historically, the term *evangelical* has taken on different meanings in divergent cultural contexts. It has applied since the Reformation to the Protestant churches by reason of their claim to base their teaching preeminently on the gospel, the good news. The word sometimes signifies all the Protestant churches in Germany. It is also used in Germany and Switzerland to distinguish the Lutheran group of Protestant churches (Evangelical) as contrasted with the Calvinist (Reformed) group. In the United States, evangelical most often refers to the school of theology that lays special stress on personal conversion and salvation by faith in the atoning death of Christ.

In *The Young Evangelicals* (1974), I defined an evangelical as a person who attests to the truth of, and acts upon, three major theological principles: (1) the full authority of Scripture in matters of faith and conduct; (2) the necessity of personal faith in Jesus Christ as Savior and Lord (conversion); and (3) the urgency of seeking the conversion of sinful men and women to Christ (evangelism). According to Gallup in 1976, about one in five Americans (18 percent)—the "hardcore evangelicals"—share these three affirmations together, though many others are committed to one or two of the principles.

Within this somewhat inclusive definition, we can discern at least three highly visible evangelical subgroups, the members of which work out their salvation in radically different ways—the fundamentalists, the charismatics, and the direct descendants of the neo-evangelicals.

The fundamentalists constitute the strict subgroups within evangelical Christianity. As a movement, fundamentalism emerged at the turn of the century and took on recognizable form after World War I. The name of the still-thriving movement is derived from a series of twelve short booklets entitled *The Fundamentals* (1910–15), written by a number of prominent theological conservatives and distributed widely throughout the English-speaking world. These doctrinal tracts were penned in defense of traditional orthodoxy, which was being challenged in the Protestant seminaries and denominational hierarchies by the gradual acceptance of biblical higher criticism, evolutionary theory, and the Social Gospel. By way of reaction, fundamentalism became an *opposition* movement against the modernists (or liberals) who had departed from orthodox belief; it was in that opposition that fundamentalists found their identity. They have insisted on the verbal inerrancy of Scripture and its literal interpretation. But the fundamentalists have also tended to live in a cultural time warp, rejecting almost all of the values not only of religious liberalism but also of the wider society as a whole. For them there is not much difference between religious liberalism and out-and-out secularism.

The charismatics represent a second major subgroup within evangelical Christianity. Participants in charismatic renewal (whose name is derived from the Greek *charismata*, gifts) are generally orthodox in belief, are born-again Christians, and witness to their faith. Their religious identity, however, is not centered so much on the defense of doctrinal formulations as it is on the experience and testimony that *precede* doctrine. The charismatic experience—most often seen as subsequent to conversion—is termed *baptism in the Holy*

*Spirit* (after the pattern in the Book of Acts), by which a believer, in the course of prayer, is "filled with the Spirit" and receives one or more of the spiritual gifts mentioned by Paul in I Corinthians 12–14 and elsewhere in the New Testament. Charismatics usually feel that the ability to "speak in tongues" as a prayer language (one of the gifts cited and practiced by Paul) is the best evidence of Spirit baptism. Other prominent gifts emphasized within charismatic renewal include divine healing and prophecy. The movement itself has been a more middle-class expression of the older denominational or "classical" pentecostalism, which is still thriving and from which charismatic renewal descends (see Volume III). Pentecostalism, very much akin to fundamentalism doctrinally and culturally, arose at the turn of the century and gets its name from the Day of Pentecost, when the church was founded and the Holy Spirit became manifest. The pentecostals, like the fundamentalists, formed their own very exclusive denominations. Charismatics, however, have tended to remain in or join churches that are part of an historic mainline denomination, hoping, by the practice of their spiritual gifts in the life of that church, to become a force for denominational renewal.

A third major subgroup within evangelical Christianity is represented by the direct descendants of fundamentalism, who first called themselves neo-evangelicals. These Christians broke with the stricter fundamentalists in the early '40s, reaffirming the basic tenets of orthodoxy, but rejecting what they saw in fundamentalism as theological and cultural excesses—anti-intellectualism, sectarianism, social unconcern, and an almost complete repudiaation of the values of the wider society. In the '60s and '70s, the term *neo-evangelical* has generally been replaced by the most historic and inclusive designation, evangelical. These evangelicals created their own distinctive denominations (like the fundamentalists), but many of them remain in the historic—albeit predominantly liberal—mainline Protestant denominations, with an increasing number in Roman Catholicism as well. To the American public at large, *they* are the evangelicals.

The churches and other religious groupings of many, if not most, non-charismatic evangelicals and fundamentalists have been included in Volume II, while most of the "holiness" and pentecostal evangelicals are discussed in Volume III. Volume IV, however, is comprised mainly of brief essays on a few important fundamentalist and evangelical interdenominational fellowships, and longer treatment of churches and denominations relatively unknown within mainline Protestantism and Catholicism, such as The Christian and Missionary Alliance, Plymouth Brethren, and numerous independent evangelical and fundamentalist congregations (from the Church of the Open Door in Los Angeles to the Church of the Saviour in Washington, D.C.). The sections on the Friends or Quakers (including their evangelical components), Adventists, small dispensational bodies, and other strict fundamentalist groupings are especially fascinating and helpful, as are the discussions of various (fringe groups" like the Berkeley Free Church (now dead), Christadelphians, Herbert W. Armstrong's Worldwide Church of God, and the proto-pentecostal Catholic Apostolic Church (though many evangelical scholars would question their inclusion here with other more "orthodox" churches).

Piepkorn has done an excellent job in attempting to describe the evangelicals and their subgroups fairly and objectively, both in this volume and in the others. *Profiles in Belief*, when completed, will surely be a standard reference work for scholars of American religion for decades to come.

RICHARD QUEBEDEAUX
Nevada City, California

# PART I

## EVANGELICAL AND FUNDAMENTALIST CHURCHES

# 1. The Evangelical and Fundamentalist Movements

In mid-twentieth century the adjective "evangelical" gained new meaning as a noun as large numbers of Christians from a wide variety of denominations identified themselves as Evangelicals to describe their basic theological orientation. The term "Evangelical" was used to describe a new movement, which crossed denominational lines and was expressed through the formation of a series of new organizations, including the National Association of Evangelicals, the Billy Graham Evangelistic Association, the journal *Christianity Today*, and Fuller Theological Seminary. The designation "Evangelical" was chosen to leave behind the negative associations with the description "Fundamentalist" and to identify with the heart and center of Protestant orthodoxy.

The new Evangelicalism and the Fundamentalism from which it emerged are closely related though there are significant differences. Both are descriptions of schools of theological thought whose proponents are members of a wide variety of denominations. Neither school of thought has resulted in a particular denominational expression, though some denominations gladly accept the Fundamentalist or Evangelical label to characterize their basic theological stance. The position that its proponents today affirm as Evangelical was in another age identified as Fundamental. Both groups share a common theological heritage and have much in common; yet neither wants to be confused with the other. Evangelicals have specifically rejected certain features historically associated with Fundamentalism and resent it when observers do not discriminate between their position and that of Fundamentalism. Though some Fundamentalists belong to the National Association of Evangelicals and support Evangelical causes like the Billy Graham crusades, most Fundamentalists reject the Evangelical position as a compromise in the direction of liberalism. Recently some leading Evangelicals have resorted to long-standing Fundamentalist views to warn against deviation from "orthodox" teaching in the Evangelical ranks.

As one historian has observed, Evangelicalism is "a battle-torn flag that has waved over many different Protestant encampments ever since the Reformation, sometimes over more than one at the same time."[1] The followers of Martin Luther in the sixteenth-century Reformation were called Evangelical because of their focus on the Gospel as justification by grace for Christ's sake through faith, and the followers of Luther to this day designate their churches as Evangelical Lutheran.

A widespread movement known as the Evangelical revival developed in eighteenth-century Europe and America. It was represented by Pietism in Germany, Methodism in England, and the Great Awakening in America. A number of churches, notably the Methodist Church, emerged from the movement, which also produced the evangelical party within the Anglican communion.[2]

With the Great Awakening as its source, Evangelicalism emerged as the dominant force of nineteenth-century Christianity. Revivalism was its central feature as Christians of most denominations adopted the revival system to carry out their mission and purpose. Major revivals erupted periodically during the nineteenth century as a result of evangelistic efforts; especially noteworthy were the contributions of Charles G. Finney (1792–1875) and Dwight L. Moody (1837–1899). Related to revivalism was the Voluntary Movement, which sought to rally and unite the converted across denominational lines in support of a variety of causes identified with the church's mission and the needs of society. A welter of Voluntary societies were created to channel the energies released by revivalism into various missionary, educational, and social causes. Among these were the American Home Missionary Society, the American Bible Society, the American Temperance Society, and the American Peace Society. Revivalism and Voluntaryism played significant roles in providing recruits for the abolitionist cause prior to the Civil War and in championing the rights of women in education and in society.[3]

In the years following the Civil War dramatic changes occurred in the intellectual climate of American society which challenged prevailing Protestant theology and seemed to many to threaten their understanding of the Christian faith. Psychological studies tended to reduce religion to phenomena of anthropology and sociology. New comparative studies of religion challenged the uniqueness of Christianity. Darvin's theory of evolution and new methods of biblical study, especially the higher criticism of the German universities, called the authority of the Bible into question.

In the church a major new theological emphasis on the Kingdom of God and the responsibility of the church for society developed in the latter part of the nineteenth century, later called the "Social Gospel." Drawing upon the new biblical criticism, it concentrated on the ethical teachings of the Scriptures rather than the traditional teachings of God's revelation. With the optimistic spirit of the times it was convinced that efforts of social reform could establish the Kingdom of God on earth.

Many in the church were challenged by the new movements in theology and American thought and adapted their theological understanding and ecclesiastical practice to them. In time they were described as Liberals or Modernists. They became a significant segment of most of the major denominations.

Others resisted and rejected the new influences in the name of Christian orthodoxy, and ultimately came to be known as Fundamentalists. Two major centers helped shape the emerging Fundamentalism. The first was Old School Presbyterianism headed by Princeton Theological Seminarary, where Archibald Alexander Hodge (1823–1886) and Benjamin Warfield (1851–1921) had developed a doctrine of inspiration which became a major apologetic for scriptural authority in the Fundamentalist-Modernist controversy. The second center was a school of theology known as Dispensationalism, a schematization of history according to a timetable of dispensations developed by J. N. Darby (1800–1882) in England and popularized by the Scofield Reference Bible (1909), which proposed eschatological views that had the effect of calling into question efforts to improve society.

Those in the churches who saw the new theology as a threat to the Christian faith rallied their forces to take a stand against further inroads. A number of heresy trials, especially among the Northern Presbyterians, cost liberal ministers and seminary professors their positions but served to elicit popular support for the cause of those who were ousted.

From 1910 to 1915 a series of ten small volumes were published entitled *The Fundamentals: A Testimony to the Truth*. They were edited by evangelist Reuben Archer Torrey (1856–1928) and Amzi C. Dixon (1854–1925), pastor of Moody Church in Chicago, and were financed by two Los Angeles businessmen, Milton and Lyman Stewart. The volumes were sent free to ministers, evangelists, missionaries, Sunday school superintendents, and any other likely prospect; ultimately three million copies were distributed. The short treatises in these volumes set forth the fundamentals of the faith, five of which came to be regarded as the absolute essentials of the Christian revelation: the verbal inspiration or inerrancy of the Bible, the virgin birth of Jesus, his substitutionary atonement, his bodily resurrection, and his imminent and visible return.[4]

Through the 1920s the acrimony of the controversy between Fundamentalists and Modernists became more intense. Within several major denominations Fundamentalists organized to reverse the Liberal tide. In the Northern Baptist Convention the National Federation of Fundamentalists and the Baptist Bible Union led the attack on Modernism but did not succeed in committing the denomination to their position. The Northern Presbyterians were seriously divided by the controversy. In 1929 J. Gresham Machen (1881–1937) resigned from the faculty of Princeton Theological Seminary to found a more orthodox school, Westminster Theological Seminary. When in 1933 Machen led the way in forming an independent mission board, he was expelled from his denomination in 1936. With about one hundred ministers and many congregations he helped establish the Orthodox Presbyterian Church that year.[5]

Fundamentalists organized across denominational lines to assist one another in their common cause. In 1919 William B. Riley launched the World's Christian Fundamentals Association in Philadelphia, meeting annually in convention and organizing Bible conferences across the nation.[6] Among other organizations were the Christian Fundamentals League formed in 1919, the Anti-Evolution League of America established in 1924, and the Defenders of the Christian Faith launched in 1925.

A climax of sorts was reached in 1925 with the trial of John Scopes in Dayton, Tennessee, for violating a Tennessee statute forbidding the teaching of evolution in tax-supported schools. National attention focused on the debates by the attorneys, William Jennings Bryan and Clarence Darrow, and served to discredit Fundamentalism as narrow and bigoted obscurantism.

Fundamentalism failed in its efforts to capture the major American denominations, resulting in the formation of a number of splinter groups by Fundamentalists who left those organizations. Others organized independently of the denominations and work through separate Fundamentalist colleges and seminaries, missionary and evangelistic associations, publishing houses and periodicals.

Considerable diversity exists among those who describe themselves as Fundamentalists today. They are united in their affirmation of the five fundamentals of the faith bequeathed by the Fundamentalist-Modernist controversy. In addition they are Dispensationalists and hold to premillennial eschatological views. In their affirmation of biblical inerrancy they insist on a strictly literal interpretation of biblical texts. They are united, too, in their insistence on separation from the historic denominations and their "unbelieving" theologians and ministers. Some Fundamentalists espouse political and social conservatism for theological reasons and take a vigorous anticommunist stand.[7] Others reject alliances with the political ultraconservatives on the grounds that the religious and political spheres should be kept apart and because theologically they see sanctification in personal rather than social terms.

The strident tradition of the Fundamentalist-Modernist controversy continues in a number of organizations and individuals. Carl McIntire (b. 1906) went with J. Gresham Machen in establishing Westminster Theological Seminary and, with him, was dismissed from the Presbyterian Church in 1936. However, McIntire broke with Machen's Orthodox Presbyterian Church after the latter's death in 1937 and established the Bible Presbyterian Church and Faith Theological Seminary. In 1941 he founded the American Council of Christian Churches and in 1948 the International Council of Christian Churches, both small and weak organizations of Fundamentalist denominations. Through his Twentieth Century Reformation movement in Collingswood, New Jersey, through the pages of a weekly journal, *Christian Beacon*, and through a Philadelphia radio station, McIntire has carried on crusades against the National and World Councils of Churches, the Revised Standard Version of the Bible, civil rights, foreign aid, and Communism.

Strident Fundamentalism is represented also by the Bob Jones University in Greenville, South Carolina; Major Edgar Bundy's Church League of America in Wheaton, Illinois; Dr. Fred Schwarz's Christian Anti-Communism Crusade, and Billy James Hargis's Christian Crusade in Tulsa, Oklahoma.

A more open Fundamentalism[8] is reflected in the work of Hal Lindsey, author of the best seller, *The Late Great Planet Earth*, a popular presentation of Dispensational eschatological views. Institutional centers for this type of Fundamentalism are the Moody Bible Institute in Chicago, Talbot Theological Seminary in La Mirada, California, and Dallas Theological Seminary, a respected school of theology which is noted for its theological scholarship. This Fundamentalism is represented by a number of smaller denominations, Pentecostal bodies, independent and nondenominational Bible churches, and by the more conservative elements of the Jesus People.[9]

In reaction to the negative connotations associated with Fundamentalism, a number of younger theologians sparked a new movement under the Evangelical banner in the 1940s. In 1942 some 150 delegates representing 40 denominations met in St. Louis for a National Conference for United Action among Evangelicals and at that meeting launched the National Association of Evangelicals (NAE). A year later at the constitutional convention in Chicago the NAE adopted a statement of faith which members were required to sign on joining and renewing membership annually. The statement affirms:[10]

1. We believe the Bible to be the inspired, the only infallible, authoritative word of God.

2. We believe that there is one God, eternally existent in three persons, Father, Son, and Holy Ghost.

3. We believe in the deity of our Lord Jesus Christ, in His virgin birth, in His sinless life, in His miracles, in His vicarious and atoning death through His shed blood, in His bodily resurrection, in His ascension to the right hand of the Father, and in His personal return in power and glory.

4. We believe that for the salvation of lost and sinful man regeneration by the Holy Spirit is absolutely essential.

5. We believe in the present ministry of the Holy Spirit by whose indwelling the Christian is enabled to live a godly life.

6. We believe in the resurrection of both the saved and the lost; they that are saved unto the resurrection of life and they that are lost unto the resurrection of damnation.

7. We believe in the spiritual unity of believers in our Lord Jesus Christ.

The National Association of Evangelicals was founded by denominations and individuals who were eager for an instrument of cooperation in between what they regarded as the liberal Federal Council of Churches (later the National Council of the Churches of Christ in the United States of America) and the ultra-Fundamentalist American Council of Christian Churches. The new organization was supposed to serve as an instrument for a united evangelical witness. Areas of cooperation that were specified were evangelism, government relations, radio broadcasting, public relations, promotion of the separation of church and state, Christian education, and securing freedom for mission work at home and abroad.

In 1947 a number of Evangelicals, including Charles Fuller, noted for his radio program, the "Old-Fashioned Revival Hour," and Harold John Ockenga, then pastor of the Park Street Church, Boston, decided to establish Fuller Theological Seminary on the basis of the estate and the name of Fuller's father, Henry. Ockenga was chosen president, and the first faculty included Carl F. Henry and Harold Lindsell, who were later to become editors of the journal *Christianity Today*. The seminary became a major resource in the Evangelical cause, providing pastoral leadership, theological guidance, and missionary impetus.

A rallying cause for the emerging Evangelicalism was a new revival movement launched by Billy (William Franklin) Graham (b. 1918) in 1949 and organized as the Billy Graham Evangelistic Association in 1950. Uniting the nineteenth-century revival tradition with the twentieth-century means of mass communication, advertising, and organization, Billy Graham became one of the most prominent personalities in the world. He shared the theological stance of those who were self-consciously seeking to be Evangelical in contrast to Fundamentalist and Liberal, and to many he was the embodiment of the Evangelical cause. Graham reflected some of the social concern which the Evangelicals were advocating. Though he is convinced that his mission is to change individuals whose calling is to change society, he took significant action during the struggle for civil rights in the 1960s by refusing to speak to segregated audiences here and abroad.

Just as significant for the Evangelical movement was the decision in 1956 to publish a biweekly journal to enable Evangelicals to speak to one another and to the world about their convictions and their concerns. Ever since, *Christianity Today* has been the major voice for Evangelicalism in the United States and Canada. Its first editor, Carl F. H. Henry, is an articulate academician with scholarly credentials,[11] whose editorial work earned the respect of many church people beyond the Evangelical ranks. The pages of *Christianity Today* urged its readers to be socially concerned as well as theologically orthodox.

The Evangelicals are by no means united in their understanding of what it means to be orthodox in doctrine. They do agree in affirming three major theological principles.[12] First, they affirm the complete reliability and final authority of the Bible in matters of faith and practice. Included in that affirmation is the conviction that the Bible is the inspired Word of God. Second, they affirm the necessity of a personal faith in Jesus Christ as Savior from sin and commitment to him as Lord. An experience of a personal relation with Jesus Christ is for the Evangelicals the heart of what it means to be Christian. Third, they affirm the urgency of reaching out to convert sinners to Christ. Evangelicals are united in a movement to evangelize the world for Christ.

Almost a generation after the emergence of Evangelicalism from Fundamentalism new stirrings occurred in the Evangelical ranks, producing what one observer has called New Evangelicalism.[13] Theologically, the New Evangelicals combine an acceptance of historical criticism with the traditional view of the reliability and authority of the inspired Scriptures. "The old concepts of infallibility and inerrancy are being reinterpreted to the point that a number of Evangelical scholars are saying that the *teaching* of Scripture (i.e., matters of faith and practice) rather than the text itself is without error."[14] In reaction to this emphasis Harold Lindsell, until recently editor of *Christianity Today*, has sounded an alarm against these developments in Evangelical ranks and warns that Christian teaching cannot survive without the bulwark of scriptural inerrancy.[15]

The New Evangelicals have also displayed a renewed interest in the social dimension of the Gospel. "For them, individual conversion is the precondition for revolutionary social transformation, yet conversion *by itself* is not enough to bring about such change. It must be supplemented by a practical social involvement together with all men and women of good will."[16] The new interest in the social dimension of the Gospel was reflected in a 1973 Evangelical workshop which produced "A Declaration of Evangelical Social Concern," which, among other things, called on Evangelicals "to demonstrate repentance in a Christian discipleship that confronts the social and political injustice of our nation."[17] The connection between evangelism and social responsibility was clearly articulated at the International Congress on World Evangelization at Lausanne, Switzerland, July 16–25, 1974, sponsored primarily by Evangelicals.[18]

Other characteristics of the New Evangelicalism include a rejection of Dispensationalism, a readiness for dialogue with mainstream denominations and representatives of other religions, and a wrestling with issues posed by geology and biology.

The new Evangelicals are represented theologically in the work of George Ladd and other professors at Fuller Theological Seminary. The interconnection between evangelism and social concern is embodied in the activity of black evangelist Tom Skinner. The concerns of the New Evangelicals are carried forward by many organizations, notably the Inter-Varsity Christian Fellowship and the Christian World Liberation Front. A significant journal is *Sojourners*, edited by Jim Wallis.

Since they represent schools of thought and not denominations, "Fundamentalist" and "Evangelical" are not yet apt labels for neatly categorizing churches in a published series dealing with religious bodies. As the membership lists of the American Council of Christian Churches and the National

Association of Evangelicals attest, the Evangelical ranks include many more church bodies than are described in the following chapters. Indeed, many of the more important Fundamentalist or Evangelical church bodies have already been described in previous volumes in chapters on Presbyterian or Baptist or Methodist or Holiness or Pentecostal or other denominations. The following chapters are devoted to Fundamentalist or Evangelical organizations not already described under some other denominational category.

## NOTES

1. Syndey E. Ahlstrom traces the use of the term in "From Puritanism to Evangelicalism," *The Evangelicals*, ed. David F. Wells and John D. Woodbridge (Nashville: Abingdon Press, 1975), pp. 269-289; the quotation is from p. 269.
2. The eighteenth-century Evangelical revival is described in Bruce L. Shelley, *Evangelicalism in America* (Grand Rapids, Mich.: W. B. Eerdmans Publishing Company, 1967), pp. 25-43.
3. Donald W. Dayton, *Discovering an Evangelical Heritage* (New York: Harper & Row, 1976) presents a number of case studies to show how deeply involved nineteenth-century Evangelicalism was in social reform in order to call present-day Evangelicals to recover their heritage in that area.
4. *The Fundamentals* themselves do not identify five essential doctrines; Ernest R. Sandeen, *The Origins of Fundamentalism: Toward a Historical Interpretation* (Philadelphia: Fortress Press, 1968), p. 22, challenges the accuracy of a historical assessment of Stewart G. Cole, *The History of Fundamentalism* (Hamden, Conn.: Archon Books, 1963 [reprint of the 1931 edition]), p. 34, repeated by many historians of Fundamentalism, that the 1895 Niagara Bible Conference had put forth a five points statement of doctrine; Sandeen, loc. cit., claims that Fundamentalists "did not define themselves in relation to any five particular points" and that "their innovations were more significant than their preservations."
5. For a description of the controversy within the denominations, cf. Norman F. Furniss, *The Fundamentalist Controversy 1918–1931* (New Haven:

Yale University Press, 1954).
6. The Association is described in Cole, pp. 298-317.
7. See Erling Jorstad, *The Politics of Doomsday: Fundamentalists of the Far Right* (Nashville: Abingdon Press, 1970); Gary K. Clabaugh, *Thunder on the Right: The Protestant Fundamentalists* (Chicago: Nelson-Hall Company, 1974).
8. Richard Quebedeaux, *The Young Evangelicals* (New York: Harper & Row, 1974), pp. 18-28, distinguishes between Separatist and Open Fundamentalism in setting both apart from Evangelicals.
9. For a description of the Jesus People, see Erling Jorstad, *That New-time Religion: The Jesus Revival in America* (Minneapolis, Minn.: Augsburg Publishing House, 1972).
10. Shelley, pp. 71-72.
11. See Carl F. Henry, *God, Revelation and Authority* (Waco, Texas: Word Books, 1976).
12. This description is based on the analysis by Quebedeaux, especially pp. 3-4.
13. Donald G. Bloesch, *The Evangelical Renaissance* (Grand Rapids, Mich.: W. B. Eerdmans Publishing Company, 1973), pp. 30-47, describes the "New Evangelicalism."
14. Quebedeaux, pp. 37-38.
15. See Harold Lindsell, *The Battle for the Bible* (Grand Rapids, Mich.: Zondervan, 1976).
16. Quebedeaux, p. 38.
17. Ronald J. Sider, ed., *The Chicago Declaration* (Carol Stream, Ill.: Creation House, 1974); the quotation is from p. 1.
18. C. René Padilla, ed., *The New Face of Evangelicalism* (Downer's Grove, Ill.: Inter-Varsity Press, 1976).

# BIBLIOGRAPHY

## FUNDAMENTALISM

Clabaugh, Gary K. *Thunder on the Right: The Protestant Fundamentalists.* Chicago: Nelson-Hall Company, 1974.

Cole, Stewart G. *The History of Fundamentalism.* Hamden, Conn.: Archon Books, 1963.

Dollar, George W. *A History of Fundamentalism in America.* Greenville, S. C.: Bob Jones University Press, 1973.

Hebert, Gabriel. *Fundamentalism and the Church.* Philadelphia: Westminster Press, 1957.

Jorstad, Erling. *The Politics of Doomsday: Fundamentalists of the Far Right.* Nashville: Abingdon Press, 1970.

Russell, Charles Allyn. *Voices of American Fundamentalism: Seven Biographical Studies.* Philadelphia: Westminster Press, 1976.

Sandeen, Ernest R. *The Origins of Fundamentalism: Toward a Historical Interpretation.* Philadelphia: Fortress Press, 1968.

———. *The Roots of Fundamentalism: British and American Millenarianism 1800–1930.* Chicago: University of Chicago Press, 1970.

Stevick, Daniel B. *Beyond Fundamentalism.* Richmond, Va.: John Knox Press, 1964.

## EVANGELICANISM

Barnhart, Joe E. *The Billy Graham Religion.* London: Mowbray, 1974.

Bloesch, Donald G. *The Evangelical Renaissance.* Grand Rapids, Mich.: W. B. Eerdmans Publishing Company, 1973.

Dayton, Donald W. *Discovering an Evangelical Heritage.* New York: Harper & Row, 1976.

Henry, Carl F. H. *Contemporary Evangelical Thought.* Great Neck, N.Y.: Channel Press, 1957.

———. *God, Revelation and Authority.* Waco, Texas: Word Books, 1976.

Jorstad, Erling. *That New-time Religion.* Minneapolis, Minn.: Augsburg Publishing House, 1972.

Lindsell, Harold. *The Battle for the Bible.* Grand Rapids, Mich.: Zondervan, 1976.

Padilla, C. René, ed. *The New Face of Evangelicalism: An International Symposium on the Lausanne Covenant.* Downers Grove, Ill.: Inter-Varsity Press, 1976.

Quebedeaux, Richard. *The Worldly Evangelicals.* New York: Harper & Row, 1978.

———. *The Young Evangelicals.* New York: Harper & Row, 1974.

Ramm, Bernard L. *The Evangelical Heritage.* Waco, Texas: Word Books, 1973.

Sernett, Milton C. *Black Religion and American Evangelicalism: White Protestants, Plantation Missions and the Flowering of Negro Christianity, 1787–1865.* Metuchen, N.J.: Scarecrow Press, 1975.

Shelley, Bruce L. *Evangelicalism in America.* Grand Rapids, Mich.: W. B. Eerdmans Publishing Company, 1967.

Sider, Ronald J., ed. *The Chicago Declaration.* Carol Stream, Ill.: Creation House, 1974.

Wells, David F. and Woodbridge, John D., eds. *The Evangelicals: What They Believe, Who They Are, Where They Are Changing.* Nashville: Abingdon Press, 1975.

Witte, Paul W. *On Common Ground: Protestant and Catholic Evangelicals.* Waco, Texas: Word Books, 1975.

# 2. Cooperative Agencies

## The American Council of Christian Churches

In 1941 Carl McIntire of the Bible Presbyterian Church and a number of other anti-Modernist churchmen called the American Council of Christian Churches into being in the conviction that the Federal Council of the Churches of Christ in America was a threat to Christianity, to freedom, to the capitalistic system, and to America. They announced the new council's purpose of becoming the voice of all anti-Modernist individuals and churches and of opposing the Federal Council at every point.[1]

In 1947 leaders of the American Council of Christian Churches professed deep concern about the Ecumenical movement as it was taking organizational shape in the World Council of Churches, and issued the call that led to the formation of the International Council of Christian Churches (in Amsterdam, in 1948), shortly before the first assembly of the World Council of Churches.

In the meeting held at Willow Grove, Pennsylvania, in 1968, the membership of the American Council voted McIntire down on all issues, including the selection of new officers. Thereby it eased McIntire out of its leadership, although he remained in firm control of the International Council of Christian Churches.

At its 1969 convention in Columbus, Ohio, the American Council expressed its forthright disapproval of McIntire's 1968 action in making International Christian Relief an arm of the International Council of Christian Churches without the consent of the American Council of Christian Churches. It warned that its continuing affiliation and support of the International Council of Christian Churches had thereby been placed in doubt.

At the 1970 meeting of the American Council of Christian Churches in Pasadena, California, McIntire, through a parliamentary maneuver that his critics described as "piracy of the worst order," had himself elected president in an unscheduled business meeting of the council. In the absence of most of the delegates to the assembly, the representatives from the International Council of Christian Churches, the Bible Presbyterian Church, the South Carolina Baptist Fellowship, and the United Christian Church (Brooklyn,

New York) voted McIntire in as president of the council. The other delegates, acting in a scheduled session, dropped from constituent membership the International Council of Churches and the church bodies whose delegates had backed McIntire. It also received the Westminster Biblical Fellowship, composed of former members of the Bible Presbyterian Church.

The American Council of Christian Churches states as its purpose "to raise a standard in behalf of Biblical Christianity and in opposition to religious liberalism." It stresses that it is "entirely separate from and opposed to the National Council of [the] Churches [of Christ in the United States of America]."[2] It sees its role as "that of a servant to the separated fundamental churches in America."[3]

The council's functional agencies include a radio and film commission, a commission on relief, and a commission on chaplaincy and related activities.

The American Council's Doctrinal Statement affirms the plenary divine inspiration of the Scriptures in their original languages and their consequent inerrancy and infallibility; the Trinity; Christ's deity, humanity, and virgin birth; his substitutionary, expiatory death; his resurrection and second coming; the total depravity of human beings; salvation as the effect of regeneration by the Spirit, not by works but by grace through faith; the everlasting bliss of the saved and the everlasting suffering of the lost; the spiritual unity in Christ of all whom his blood has redeemed; and the necessity of maintaining the purity of the church in doctrine and life.[4]

It requires general, local, and individual constituent members to signify their agreement with the entire Doctrinal Statement. The constitution stipulates that "no national church or associaion which is a member of the National Council of the Church of Christ in the U.S.A. is eligible for membership in this council so long as it retains connection with that body, nor shall local churches or individuals connected with national bodies holding membership in the said National Council be eligible for constituent membership."[5]

The general constituent members of the American Council at the present time are the Bible Protestant Church; the Congregational Methodist Church; the Evangelical Methodist Church of America; the Fundamental Methodist Church; the General Association of Regular Baptist Churches; Independent Bible Baptist Missions; Independent Churches, Affiliated; Independent Fundamental Bible Churches [Militant Fundamental Bible Churches, also known as Fundamental Evangelistic Association, Incorporated]; the Southern Methodist Church; the Tioga River Christian Conference; Ukrainian Baptist Churches [Ukrainian Evangelical Baptist Convention]; the Westminster Biblical Fellowship; the World Baptist Fellowship; individual congregations of the American Baptist Association; and many independent local congregations. The estimated total membership of the organized church bodies in the American Council (exclusive of local constituent members of the American Baptist Association) is about 300,000. Information on the number of local and individual constituent members is not available, but the American Council estimates that it represents "some 1,500,000 Christians throughout the United States."[6] The headquarters are at 15 Park Row, New York, New York 10038.

## National Association of Evangelicals

The National Association of Evangelicals, the major organizational embodiment of American Evangelicalism, looks back for its origin to April 7, 1942, when 150 delegates from some 40 denominations gathered in St. Louis for the National Conference for United Action among Evangelicals. They included leaders of smaller denominations that had never joined the Federal Council of Churches, as well as leaders from larger denominations that held membership in the Federal Council. For their own persons the participants felt that an unbridgeable theological and ideological chasm separated them from the Federal Council; at the same time they did not share either the ecclesiological views of the leaders of the American Council of Christian Churches or especially what they regarded as the latter body's exclusivist opposition to the Federal Council. By their subsequent association with the National Association of Evangelicals the participants in the St. Louis conference, whether they came from denominations that did or that did not belong to the Federal Council, turned their backs on the Federal Council (and on the later National Council of the Churches of Christ in the U.S.A.), and by devoting their energies to the National Association of Evangelicals they indicated their intention to oppose the liberal elements in the Federal Council denominations from without and from within.

The St. Louis conference drafted a tentative constitution and statement of faith. The constituting convention, held in Chicago in 1943, attracted a thousand conservative leaders from fifty denominations and scores of Christian organizations. The conference adopted without dissent a statement of faith[7] which members must sign when they join the National Association of Evangelicals and annually when they renew their membership.

The association provides opportunities through its office and commissions for cooperative effort in the areas of evangelism and the nurture of spiritual life, foreign missions, church extension and home missions, stewardship, united action in matters affecting religious liberty and its practice, social concern and welfare work, world relief, chaplaincies, education, publications, and radio-television. Among the organizations sponsored by or affiliated with the National Association of Evangelicals are Evangelical Churchmen Commission, the Women's Fellowship Commission, the National Sunday School Association, the National Association of Christian Schools, and the Religious Broadcasters. The association in turn is a member of the World Evangelical Fellowship, which it helped to found in 1951. The association has also played a role in the maturing theological development of the "New Evangelicalism" out of the Fundamentalism of the first quarter of the present century.

Sympathetic critics of the association see needs (1) for a solution to the nagging problem of finance and promotion; (2) for better communications between the association and the grass-roots level of church life; (3) for greater efficiency in operations through centralization and through making more explicit the ties that bind the affiliated organizations to the association; (4) for a positive program that will counteract the negative stance that marked the association in its early days and that will rally the support of evangelicals from various quarters; (5) for active recruitment of dynamic lay leadership; and (6) for an in-depth study of the doctrines of the church, the ministry, and the sacraments, that will produce unity in an area that in the past has divided Evangelicals and that will make it possible to exploit the possibilities of church federation.[8]

In addition to individuals, the National Association of Evangelicals has in its membership entire denominations,[9] conferences of churches within denominations that do not as such belong to the association,[10] individual churches in such denominations,[11] associations,[12] and organizations.[13] The National Association of Evangelicals represents an estimated 29,000 churches and 2.5 million Christians.

## National Fraternal Council of Churches

At the Rochester, New York, assembly of the Federal Council of the Churches of Christ in America in 1929 the late L. K. Williams, then president of the National Baptist Convention of America, Incorporated, suggested to the delegations of the black denominations attending the assembly the organization of a council that would bring them together for coordinated efforts to solve their common problems. The proposal caught on; a one-day meeting of denominational representatives at Howard University, Washington, D.C., drafted a plan of organization and selected Hampton Institute, Hampton, Virginia, as the site of the first plenary meeting. But the depression intervened, and the idea languished until 1933 when Bishop Reverdy C. Ransom of the African Methodist Episcopal Church sent out another call that led to the formal organization of the National Fraternal Council of Churches in the Mount Carmel Baptist Church, Washington, D.C., that same year.

The constitution of the council, which was incorporated in 1947, defines its purposes as (1) the development of cooperative relations among all the member denominations with a view to collective measures designed to bring about racial and economic justice, progressive measures of nonpartisan political legislation, and social reform; (2) creation of a center for coordinating the actions of the denominations in achieving common goals; and (3) cooperation with similar organizations in fostering the worldwide program of Christ. Although the council disavows partisan political activity, it is ready to endorse issues and legislation which it feels are in the best interest of the people as a whole.

The roster of denominations belonging to the council lists the African

Methodist Episcopal Church; the African Methodist Episcopal Zion Church; the African Orthodox Church; the Bible Way Churches of Our Lord Jesus Christ Worldwide, Incorporated; the Christian Methodist Episcopal Church; the Church of God in Christ; the Church of Our Lord Jesus Christ of the Apostolic Faith, Incorporated; the Holiness Church of God, Incorporated; and the National Baptist Convention of the United States of America, Incorporated. In addition individual churches and conferences of the International Convention of Christian Churches (Disciples of Christ), the United Methodist Church, and a number of Pentecostal denominations, as well as some black community churches, also belong to the council. Its headquarters are at 1225 N Street, Northwest, Washington, D.C. 20005.[14]

## The Canadian Council of Evangelical Protestant Churches

The Canadian Council of Evangelical Protestant Churches describes itself as "a loose federation of evangelical separatist groups," which came into being in 1953 "for Christian fellowship and mutual protest against the inroads of Modernism, Romanism, and other departures from the faith once for all delivered to the saints." It is committed to witness to the plenary inspiration, inerrancy, and infallibility of the Bible; the Trinity; Christ's deity and sinless humanity, virgin birth, substitutionary and expiatory death, resurrection, and second coming; "salvation, the effect of regeneration by the Spirit and the Word, not by works but by grace through faith"; the everlasting bliss of the saved and suffering of the lost; the "real spiritual unity in Christ" of all those whom His blood has redeemed; the necessity of purity of doctrine and life in the church; and the Apostles' Creed.[15]

Constituent membership is of three types: general constituent members (autonomous national churches or associations of Christians), local constituent members (local or regional congregations, churches, or association), and individual constituent members. Constituent members may not be affiliated directly or indirectly with the Canadian Council of Churches; auxiliary members connected with bodies affiliated with the Canadian Council of Churches must declare in writing to the Canadian Council of Churches and the affiliated member body that they should no longer regard themselves as representing the auxiliary member.

The Canadian Council of Evangelical Protestant Churches meets annually. An executive committee conducts the business of the congregation between the annual meetings. The organization functions through departments of evangelism, information and publication, home missions, foreign missions, Christian education, radio, and Sunday school materials, and through commissions on armed forces chaplains and the location of church property on government projects, and Men's and Women's Commissions. Its relief arm is International Christian Relief—Canada. The organization belongs to the International Council of Christian Churches; it regards the "compromise position" of the National Association of Evangelicals and the World Evangelical Fellowship as "Christ-dishonouring" and as "a position of expediency and disobedience to the Word of God," and it sees "the apostate cause" of the World Council of Churches as "one of unbelief."[16] No information is available about the size of the organization in terms of membership strength. The only autonomous church body association that holds general constituent membership in the council is the Association of Regular Baptist Churches of Canada; otherwise the constituent membership is composed wholly of local and individual members, chiefly Baptists.

The headquarters are at 130 Gerrard Street, East, Toronto, Ontario.

## National Black Evangelical Association

A group of black churchmen meeting in Los Angeles in April 1963 brought the National Black Evangelical Association into being "to promote and undergird a dynamic Christian witness among Afro-Americans living in the United States."[17] It sees itself as an association for fellowship, information, and service rather than as a denomination.

The National Black Evangelical Association believes that human beings are sinful and in need of salvation; that God provided a way of salvation through Christ; that to be redeemed human beings must exercise faith in Christ; and that redeemed human beings are expected to seek to enhance their relationship with Christ and to maintain a witness for the world around him.

Membership in the association is open both to individuals and to groups (local churches, denominations, evangelistic teams, missionary societies, and other organizations concerned for reaching American blacks with a Christian witness). The association operates through commissions on evangelism, missions, Christian education, youth, and social thought and action. A convention of the association meets annually. No information is available on the number of active individual members or on the number of active organizational memberships.[18] The address of the headquarters is Box 193, Pasadena, California 91102.

## Evangelical Fellowship of Canada

The Evangelical Fellowship of Canada was formed in 1964 as a cooperative agency for Canadian Evangelicals. Its membership is composed of denominations, other organizations, and individuals. Nine church bodies are members, and the Evangelical Fellowship claims to represent 300,000 members.

The organization assists its members in carrying out a threefold purpose, based on Philippians 1:5-12: (1) fellowship in the Gospel, (2) defense and confirmation of the Gospel, and (3) furtherance of the Gospel. Its platform of belief includes the infallibility of the Scriptures in their original form and salvation through Jesus Christ by faith apart from the works of the law.

The Evangelical Fellowship is subdivided into four provincial and regional associations in Alberta, British Columbia, Manitoba, and the Northwest Territories. Its headquarters are at 512 McNicoll Street, Willowdale, Ontario M2H 2E1 (P.O. Box 8800). Dr. Charles Seidenspinner is the current president. Repeated efforts to secure firsthand information from the organization were unsuccessful. The above information, based on material in the *Yearbook of American and Canadian Churches 1977*, was confirmed in a telephone conversation with Dr. Seidenspinner.

# NOTES

1. "Valiant for the Truth," *Accent: Newsletter of the American Council of Christian Churches* 1, no. 6 (September–October 1966): 1-5.
2. *Facts You Should Know about the American Council of Christian Churches* (undated 4-page pamphlet), p. 2.
3. *Accent! ! ! : Information Service,* 1, no. 1 (January 1970): 1.
4. Article II (Doctrinal Statement), *Constitution and Bylaws* (New York: American Council of Christian Churches, n.d.) (8-page pamphlet).
5. Section 4(a), Article III ("Membership"), ibid.
6. *Facts You Should know,* loc. cit.
7. See chapter 1, above.
8. Bruce L. Shelley, *Evangelicalism in America* (Grand Rapids, Mich.: W. B. Eerdmans Publishing Co., 1967), pp. 120-132.
9. Assemblies of God; Baptist General Conference; Brethren Church (Ashland, Ohio); Brethren in Christ; Christian Catholic Church (Evangelical Protestant); Christian Church of North America; Christian and Missionary Alliance; Christian Union; Church of God (Cleveland, Tennessee); Church of the United Brethren in Christ; Churches of Christ in Christian Union; Conservative Congregational Christian Conference; Elim Fellowship; Evangelical Church of North America; Evangelical Congregational Church; Evangelical Free Church of America; Evangelical Friends Alliance; Evangelical Mennonite Brethren Church; Evangelical Mennonite Church; Evangelical Methodist Church; Free Methodist Church; Full Gospel Pentecostal Association; International Church of the Foursquare Gospel; International Pentecostal Assemblies; Mennonite Brethren Church; Midwest Congregational Christian Fellowship; Missionary Church; Open Bible Standard Churches; Pentecostal Church of Christ; Pentecostal Church of God of America; Pentecostal Evangelical Church; Pentecostal Holiness Church; Primitive Methodist Church; Reformed Presbyterian Church of North America; Wesleyan Church.
10. For example, the Massachusetts, New Hampshire, and Northern California conferences of the Advent Christian Church.
11. Church bodies represented in the association by individual congregations include: American Baptist Convention; Berean Fundamental Church Council; Baptist Bible Fellowship; Church of the Brethren; Church of the Nazarene; Conservative Baptist Association; Disciples of Christ; Evangelical Covenant Church; General Association of General Baptists; General Conference Mennonite Church; National Fellowship of Brethren Churches; Kansas Yearly Meeting of Friends; North American Baptist Association; Presbyterian Church in the United States; Reformed Church in America; Southern Baptist Convention; United Baptists; United Methodist Church; United Presbyterian Church in the U.S.A.
12. Anchor Bay Evangelistic Association; Grace Gospel Evangelistic Association; National Holiness Association; Association of Fundamental Ministers and Churches; Full Gospel Church Association; New England Evangelical Baptist Fellowship.
13. American Association of Evangelical Students; Bethany Fellowship; Bible Meditation League; Gospel Association for the Blind; National Black Evangelical Association; Protestant Religious Education Services; The Railroad Evangelistic Association; The World Home Bible League.—Both

World Vision International and the World Evangelization Crusade, Fort Washington, Pennsylvania, have a doctrinal basis identical with statement of faith of the National Association of Evangelicals. Both are missionary service agencies, not denominations with churches in the United States and Canada.

14. Letter from Dr. Andrew Fowler, executive secretary, National Fraternal Council of Churches.

15. Preamble to the Constitution of the Canadian Council of Evangelical Protestant Churches, in *The Canadian Council of Evangelical Protestant Churches: Its Purpose and Constitution* (undated 6-page pamphlet), pp. 1-2. See also the editorial, "Why We Must Continue to Fight Modernism," *The Gospel Witness and Protestant Advocate* 32, no. 1 (April 23, 1953) (whole no. 1613): 1-2.

16. *To the Law and to the Testimony: A Comparative Study of the Church Councils and Associations* (4th ed.; Toronto: The Canadian Council of Evangelical Protestant Churches, n.d.), p. [5].

17. *The National Negro Evangelical Association* (undated 6-page folder), p. [2]; "Negro" was later changed to "Black."

18. Mr. James V. Geisendorfer, Minneapolis, Minnesota, kindly shared the information about the National Black Evangelical Association in his possession with the present writer. The latter's efforts to secure information directly from headquarters of the association were unsuccessful.

## BIBLIOGRAPHY

Gasper, Louis. *The Fundamentalist Movement*. The Hague: Mouton en Co., 1963. A survey of the renascence of conservative theological belief in the United States through the 1950s. The National Association of Evangelicals receives treatment particularly in chapter 2, "The Dual Alignment of Fundamentalism."

Murch, James DeForest. *Cooperation without Compromise: A History of the National Association of Evangelicals*. Grand Rapids, Mich.: W. B. Eerdmans Publishing Co., 1956. The standard historical record of the first fifteen years of the association's activity.

Nash, Ronald H. *The New Evangelicalism*. Grand Rapids, Mich.: Zondervan Publishing House, 1963. An effort to delineate the theological differences between the New Evangelicalism and "fundamentalism becoming intellectual."

Shelley, Bruce. *Evangelicalism in America*. Grand Rapids, Mich.: W. B. Eerdmans Publishing Co., 1967. This volume celebrates the 25th anniversary of the National Association of Evangelicals by providing a perceptive historical survey that clearly discloses the theological antecedents of contemporary Evangelicalism in the Reformed tradition and by offering a critically sympathetic evaluation of the National Association and its prospects.

# 3. The Christian and Missionary Alliance and the Missionary Church

## The Christian and Missionary Alliance

In 1881 a Canadian-born and -educated Presbyterian minister at Old Orchard, Maine, Albert Benjamin Simpson, felt that God was laying it upon his heart to plead for "a great missionary movement that would reach the neglected fields of the world."[1] The next year he established a Bible school at New York City (later moved to Nyack) for the training of young people as missionaries. In 1887 he founded two parallel societies. One was an inter-denominational spiritual fellowship that he called the Christian Alliance; the other was an international missionary society, the Evangelical Missionary Alliance. Ten years later the two were combined as the Christian and Missionary Alliance. Simpson attracted to his banner Henry Wilson, an Episcopalian; Kelso Carter, a Salvation Army officer; Albert Funk, a Mennonite; Stephen Merritt, a Methodist; and many others, notably from Baptist, Congregational, and Plymouth Brethren backgrounds.

In 1907 the impact of the Pentecostal movement, with its stress upon speaking in tongues as the evidence of the baptism of the Holy Spirit, began to make itself felt. Some members of the Christian and Missionary Alliance joined the Pentecostal movement; others remained within the alliance, which in that year on Simpson's urging adopted a policy of "seek not—forbid not." (The board of managers of the alliance reiterated this policy in 1963 as its answer to the revived tongues movement of the 1960s.[2])

In 1965 the General Council of the Christian and Missionary Alliance adopted a twelve-article statement of faith. It commits the alliance to the Trinity, Christ's deity and manhood, his substitutionary sacrifice on the cross, his resurrection, ascension, session, and return; the Holy Spirit; the Bible ("inerrant as originally given") as a complete revelation of God's will for the salvation of humankind; people's creation in God's image, their fall, and a destiny of everlasting joy and bliss in the case of the believers, and of eternal existence in conscious punishment in the case of the unbelieving;

20

God's provision of salvation for all people through Christ; God's will for the entire sanctification of believers, as both a crisis and a progressive experience that the Holy Spirit works after conversion;[3] provision in the atonement for healing of the body through prayer for the sick and anointing with oil; the church as the whole company of believers, who form Christ's body, with the local church a body of believers in Christ joined together for worship, edification, fellowship, proclamation of the Gospel, and observance of the ordinances of baptism and the Lord's Supper;[4] the bodily resurrection of the just and the unjust; and Christ's imminent personal and premillennial second coming[5] as the believer's blessed hope and an incentive to holy living and faithful service.[6]

Satisfactory evidence of regeneration and of belief in the Trinity, the verbal inspiration of the Bible as originally given, Christ's vicarious atonement, the eternal salvation of believers and the eternal punishment of those who reject Christ, and recognition of the truths of Christ as Savior, Sanctifier, Healer, and Coming King is an explicit condition of membership.[7]

The Christian and Missionary Alliance includes, in addition to its branch churches and foreign missions, individual Christians, groups of Christians of various Evangelical churches, undenominational churches, and city and highway missions. The General Council, the highest legislative body, meets annually. The headquarters are at 350 North Highland Avenue, Nyack, New York 10960. There are 21 districts in the United States and Canada, administering 1,179 churches and missions with a total membership of 145,833. The overseas constituency in the alliance's 24 foreign mission districts—in South America, Africa, the Middle East, India, Southeast Asia, Hong Kong, the Republic of China (Taiwan), Indonesia, the Philippines Republic, and Japan —is considerably larger than its North American membership.

## The Missionary Church

In 1954 a proposed union of the United Missionary Church with the Missionary Church Association went down to narrow defeat. Serious union discussions were renewed in December 1966. This time the union effort was successful and the two bodies united as the Missionary Church in March 1969.

The United Missionary Church was itself the result of a four-way union that took place over eight years in the last quarter of the nineteenth century. The Reformed Mennonites (Reforming Mennonite Society), founded in 1874 in Ontario by Solomon Eby and in Indiana by Daniel Brennemann, and the New Mennonites of Ontario joined in 1875 to create the United Mennonites. The Evangelical Mennonites, formally organized in 1858 after the congregations that were to comprise it had existed and worked separately for five years, joined the union to form the United Evangelical Mennonites in 1879. In 1860 the River Brethren (known as Brethren in Christ from 1863 on) in Ohio had divided into "Swankite" and "Wengerite" factions, primarily on the issue of baptism by single or triple immersion. In 1883 the Swankites and some of the Wengerites joined the United Evangelical Mennonites to form the Mennonite Brethren in Christ, a name which the merged body retained until 1947, when it took the United Missionary Church as its name.

Committed by its own history to revivals, protracted prayer and fellowship meetings, the use of the English language, and Sunday schools, the movement away from strict Mennonite traditions carried the United Missionary Church almost altogether out of the Mennonite orbit, as in the course of time it continued more and more to stress the new birth, entire sanctification as a second crisis experience after conversion, the Spirit-filled life, a premillennial view of the second coming of Christ, divine healing, evangelism, and missions.

In its rejection of unchristian practices the United Missionary Church was successful in keeping its members, as part of their separation from the world, from belonging to secret societies, frequenting dances and theaters, and using alcoholic beverages and tobacco. It was less successful in maintaining "a satisfactory standard" in proper dress and the wearing of jewelry. Simultaneously a limited trend toward participation in political matters manifested itself.

In spite of its history and official opposition to war and participation in it, by the time of World War II the failure of the ministers to stress the denominational doctrine had the result that in Canada half the eligible young men of the church entered the armed services and in the United States almost all of them did so. In 1955 the General Conference gave formal approval to noncombatant service.

The original prohibition of musical instruments and choirs, modified in 1916, was dropped in 1951, when the decision was left to each church. Official opposition to life insurance ended in 1928.[8]

In 1952 the Pennsylvania District Conference—the largest in the denomination—withdrew from the body for doctrinal and administrative reasons; initially it took the name of Mennonite Brethren in Christ Church of Pennsylvania, Incorporated, and later that of Bible Fellowship Church.

In spite of the loss of the Pennsylvania District, all but one of the statistical criteria had by 1957 compensated for the loss; the one exception was total church membership, which still lagged 3,000 behind the level of a decade previous.

The United Missionary Church had the very high ratio of one foreign missionary worker to every ninety-five North American members.

The Missionary Church Association came into being in August 1898 at Berne, Indiana. Its founders were clergymen of various denominational backgrounds, including Mennonites, German Baptists, Evangelicals, and members of the Christian and Missionary Alliance, whose association during the preceding decade had drawn them together into a binding fellowship and faith that emphasized the deeper Christian life.

One of the most influential among the founders of the association was a

General Conference Mennonite minister, A. E. Funk, who was a close associate of A. B. Simpson, founder of the Christian and Missionary Alliance.

Another was Joseph Eicher Ramseyer (1869–1944), originally a minister of the Defenseless Mennonite Church (now called the Evangelical Mennonite Church). A controversy about a number of issues had agitated his denomination for five years. In August 1896 he brought it to a crisis; he renounced his Mennonite baptism by pouring and received baptism by immersion at a Christian and Missionary Alliance conference in Cleveland. His church body expelled him four months later. Ramseyer became president of the Missionary Church Association in 1900 and continued in this office for forty-four years.

The constitution of the Missionary Church presents its Articles of Faith under six heads: (1) The Triune God; (2) the Bible ("the Bible, consisting of the sixty-six books of the Old and New Testaments, is the Word of God given by divine inspiration, inerrant in the original manuscript, and is the unchanging authority in matters of Christian faith and practice"); (3) man, his creation (as "a self-conscious personality capable of free and rational choice"), his fall, and his redemption ("God has provided redemption for all men through the mediatorial work of Christ"); (4) salvation, in terms of repentance, faith, justification and regeneration, sanctification and reception of the Holy Spirit ("while the divine work of making men holy begins in repentance and regeneration, yet through a subsequent crisis experience the believer is to die for self, to be purified in heart, and to be filled with the Holy Spirit"), resurrection and glorification; (5) the church; and (6) the last things, that is, Christ's descent into the clouds, the catching up of the waiting church, the tribulation judgments, the restoration of Israel, the return of the Christ and the church to the earth for the millennium, the great white throne judgment of the impenitent, and the consignment of the unrighteous and impenitent to hell and the everlasting bliss of the righteous in the new heaven and the new earth.

Eleven Articles of Practice affirm (1) the two ordinances of believer's baptism by immersion and the Lord's Supper, in which the emblems of bread and the fruit of the vine symbolize the death of Christ and which is open to all true believers of all denominations; (2) divine healing provided for Christ's redemptive work; (3) the obligation to honor the first day of the week as the Lord's day; (4) the obligation of Christian stewardship; (5) the propriety of formally dedicating little children in a public service of the church; (6) the sanctity of marriage and the home; (7) the wrongfulness of divorce; (8) the obligation devolving on each Christion to live in the recognition that he has become "the sole possession of Jesus Christ" ("he shall not marry an unbeliever, shall not hold membership in oath-bound secret societies, and shall not compromise Christian principles in partnerships; [nor shall he injure his] influence or body by the use of tobacco, intoxicating beverages, narcotics, and other harmful products"); (9) obedience toward civil government (except "where the demands of civil law would militate against the supreme law and will of God"); (10) the impropriety of a Christian promoting "strife between nations, classes, groups, or individuals" ("[but we] exercise tolerance and understanding and respect the individual conscience with regard to participation in war"); and the belief that the life of a Christian should exhibit such honesty and integrity "that his word can be fully trusted without the swearing of an oath either in personal or judicial situations."[9]

The General Conference of the Missionary Church meets every two years; district conferences meet annually.

The headquarters of the Missionary Church are at 3901 South Wayne Avenue, Fort Wayne, Indiana 46807. There are 273 churches in the United States with a total membership of 21,008, and 77 churches in Canada with a total membership of 4,887. The Missionary Church carries on foreign missions in Africa, India, South America, Japan, the Philippines Republic, the Middle East, the West Indies, and Bangladesh.[10]

## NOTES

1. J. H. Hunter, *Beside All Waters: The Story of Seventy-Five Years of Worldwide Ministry* [by] *the Christian and Missionary Alliance* (Harrisburg, Penn.: Christian Publications, 1964), p. 14.

2. *The Revived Tongues Movement* (New York: The Christian and Missionary Alliance, 1963) (8-page pamphlet reprinted from *The Alliance Witness* for May 1, 1963).

3. The Christian and Missionary Alliance does not believe in the "eradication" doctrine, nor does it see itself as rooted in the Wesleyan tradition.

4. Believer's baptism is administered by immersion "as a sign that our hearts have been washed from sin." The children of believing parents are dedicated to God, but this custom is not thought of as saving the children. In the Lord's Supper the bread and wine are "emblems of Christ's broken body and shed blood." (*Questions and Answers for Young Disciples* [Harrisburg, Penn.: Christian Publications, 1940] [40-page pamphlet], pp. 37-38.)

5. The idea of the "four-fold Gospel"— Christ our Savior, Christ our Sanctifier, Christ our Healer, Christ our coming Lord—originated with Simpson and is still the epitome of the message of the Christian and Missionary Alliance.

From the beginning the alliance has symbolized the four-fold Gospel with a cross, a laver ("the sanctifying grace of God, providing daily cleansing from the defilement of sin"), a pitcher of oil, and a crown.

6. *Statement of Faith Adopted by the Christian and Missionary Alliance General Council, Minneapolis—May 12-17, 1965* (2-page mimeographed document). From the standpoint of doctrine the Christian and Missionary Alliance regards the Missionary Church as closest to it.

7. Article III ("Membership") of the General Constitution in *Manual of the Christian and Missionary Alliance*, (rev. edn.; New York: Christian and Missionary Alliance, 1965), p. 6.

8. Everek R. Storms, *History of the United Missionary Church* (Elkhart, Ind.: Bethel Publishing Co., 1958), chap. 23, "Organizational and Doctrinal Developments."

9. *Constitution Proposed as Basis for Union of The Missionary Church Association and The United Missionary Church* (undated 34-page pamphlet), pp. 2-10.

10. Communication from church body headquarters.

# BIBLIOGRAPHY

Hunter, J. H. *Beside All Waters: The Story of Seventy-Five Years of World-wide Ministry [by] the Christian and Missionary Alliance.* Harrisburg, Penn.: Christian Publications, 1964.

# 4. The Plymouth Brethren Movement

## Plymouth Brethren (Christian Brethren)

"Plymouth Brethren" is the popular designation for a religious movement that originated in England and Ireland in the mid-1820s. The early adherents were unhappy about the baleful effects of the intimate connection that existed between the Established Church and the government, about what they considered unspiritual ecclesiasticism and dead formalism in worship, and about the denominationalism that divided Christians from one another. They took the self-designation "Brethren" directly from the Sacred Scriptures; other names by which they were known were Christians, Believers, and Saints. The name "Plymouth Brethren" derives from the fact that the largest and most important of the early congregations, or "assemblies," met in Plymouth, England. In the British Isles and Canada today many assemblies of "Open" Brethren (see below) call themselves Christian Brethren; in Canada they have registered themselves under this name with the Dominion government. The bulk of the Brethren in the United States call themselves "assemblies," and some use the designation "assemblies of Christians who meet in the name of the Lord Jesus alone," but there is a growing tendency to answer to the name "Plymouth Brethren." Nevertheless, the movement has never formally accepted any designation.

Early Brethren leaders included Anthony Norris Groves (1795–1853), an Exeter dentist who became the first of a long line of Brethren foreign missionaries; the German-born philanthropist-preacher George Müller (1805–1898) of Bristol orphanage fame; and, most prominently, John Nelson Darby (1800–1882). Darby, trained for the law and a graduate of Dublin's Trinity College at nineteen, was briefly a clergyman of the Anglican Church of Ireland. By 1828 he had associated himself with the Brethren. He spent the rest of his life preaching, writing prolifically, and traveling tirelessly in behalf of the Brethren movement.

Beginning in 1848 a series of "divergences" and secessions divided the movement. A split in the Plymouth Assembly led in 1848 to a fundamental division that persists to this day. It separated the "Open" Brethren from the "Exclusive" Brethren. In 1848 Open Brethren believed, as they generally do to this day, that they might receive to the Lord's table any believer who is personally sound in faith, even though the congregation or assembly from which he came might harbor questionable teaching. The Exclusive Brethren, under the informal leadership of Darby, regarded "separation from evil as God's principle of unity" and held that to receive to the Lord's table a brother from an assembly in which error is taught, even though he might personally reject it, disqualified the receiving assembly from participation in what often came to be called the "Circle of Fellowship." This circle is a joint body of mutually approved assemblies, with the decision of one binding on all; the influence of an individual leader in such a body is of course sometimes very great.

The only formal division among Open Brethren took place in 1889. Limited largely to the British Isles, it resulted in the organization of a relatively small number (fewer than 100) of "Needed Truth" assemblies, now called the Churches of God in the Fellowship of the Son of God, the Lord Jesus Christ. Otherwise all of the schisms, from 1881 on, have taken place among the Exclusive Brethren. These divisions reflect the seriousness with which the Exclusive Brethren take their role of representing visibly the purity of doctrine and life that the church is to have.

The divisions relate more to church discipline than to doctrine. Although they admit a degree of variety in teaching, the Brethren are still all in substantial doctrinal agreement.

While many assemblies and individuals have published statements of their beliefs, the Brethren regard and refuse creeds as unnecessary. They look on the Bible as verbally inspired and inerrant in the original writings, and they take it as their only authoritative guide. They are trinitarians. They stress both the deity and the complete humanity of Christ, as well as his virgin birth, resurrection, ascension, and intercession. They teach that God created the first human beings in his own image, but that as a result of sin all human beings have a sinful nature and are guilty, lost and without hope in themselves, and that they have incurred both physical death and the spiritual death of separation from God. In his amazing love God provided humankind with a Savior in the person of his Son. Few Brethren would affirm a predestination to reprobation; rather, they hold, God's will is for the salvation of all human beings, but he will not force anyone to receive this salvation. A right relationship with God comes alone through faith in Christ's all-sufficient sacrifice and shed blood, apart from works. Christ's own resurrection is proof that God accepted his atoning work. Those who receive Christ by faith are in that act born again and become children of God. Good works are the fruit of faith. True believers cannot be lost; they should be assured of their everlasting salvation, not on the basis of their feelings or their experience, but on the basis of God's Word. The believer's life should be one of devotion to Christ and of separation from all that is evil in the world.

The doctrine of the last things plays a prominent role in Brethren thinking. Christ, they hold, will come again to the earth's air to catch up ("rapture") all believers, living and dead. The Great Tribulation of Revelation 6-18 will follow, climaxed by Christ's return to establish his millennial reign. During the millennium the redeemed and reconstituted nation of Israel will play a special role among the peoples under the sovereignty of Christ and his raptured church. A short-lived rebellion will close the millennium, and the eternal age of the new heavens and the new earth will begin. The saved of all ages will enter eternal life and the unsaved will undergo eternal punishment and separation from God in hell.[1]

The Brethren's doctrine of the church reflects Darby's spiritualizing ecclesiology and the central dispensationalist distinction that he made between God's dealings with the church and with Israel. Unlike Israel, the true church does not include all that are born into it but only reborn believers. To maintain the relative purity of their assemblies Brethren require candidates for full fellowship to confess their faith in Christ as Lord and Savior and to give satisfactory evidence of the new birth. The Brethren receive them as members of Christ and do not think of them as having joined an ecclesiastical denomination. Brethren recognize that the overwhelming majority of those in the universal church are not Brethren.

Again unlike Israel, the church does not have a separate class of priests. This underlies the stress of the Brethren on the priesthood of all believers and their refusal to distinguish between the clergy and the laity. "Personal gift and spiritual power" from the Holy Spirit are proof of a call to ministry among the assemblies or on their behalf. Many Brethren preachers and teachers are not engaged in full-time ministries. Even those who do devote their full time to ministry are neither ordained, nor salaried, nor addressed by titles like "Reverend" or "Father." The means of support of these full-time workers are normally voluntary contributions from those co-religionists who care to "fellowship" with them, rather than stipulated remuneration. Unless they are engaged in missionary work at home or abroad, most full-time workers travel over a larger or smaller area. Brethren acknowledge and honor as elders and overseers (even though they may not always use the terms) the pious, gifted, and normally self-supporting individuals who provide for the assembly's spiritual needs. Brethren reject the idea of one person heading the congregation ("one-man ministry") as unbiblical and as inhibiting the exercise of the gifts that the Holy Spirit has imparted, but at the same time they do not practice an "any-man ministry." During the last generation a growing number of Open assemblies have invited full-time workers to associate themselves with a given assembly particularly, and these persons can become very much like conventional pastors. But even these men rarely do all the preaching or wholly give up itinerating, and they have no sacramental role.

The larger urban Open assemblies have often built attractive and functional "Bible Chapels." The smaller or rural Open assemblies and the Exclusive assemblies frequently call their meeting-places "Gospel Halls"; some meet in homes.

The Brethren observe two symbolical ordinances, baptism and the Lord's Supper. Open Brethren generally practice only believer's baptism by immersion. Exclusive Brethren allow and in some cases prefer infant baptism, also by immersion, of the children of parents in fellowship ("household baptism") on the analogy of Old Testament circumcision. Some Exclusive assemblies permit believer's baptism for those families who prefer it. In no case do Brethren think of baptism as conferring conversion. Brethren celebrate the Lord's Supper ("the breaking of bread") at a separate closed meeting—the only meeting at which Brethren take an offering—every Lord's day, usually in the morning. Any male who feels led to do so by the Holy Spirit may pray publicly, read and comment on a passage of the Bible, suggest a hymn to be sung, give thanks for the bread and wine, or pass the elements. Women may not speak in these meetings.

The Brethren aim at "apostolic simplicity" in their worship; there is no formal ritual or stated order of service. Brethren Sunday schools and preaching services resemble the parallel activities of nonliturgical denominations.

Open and Exclusive Brethren came separately to North America after the middle of the nineteenth century. Itinerant preachers from Scotland and Ireland planted most of the early Open assemblies. Darby himself visited the Exclusive assemblies several times. After his death the latter began to divide, sometimes because of issues on this continent, sometimes because of controversies in the British Isles. The United States Bureau of the Census used arbitrarily chosen roman numerals to differentiate them, and this mode of reference has persisted.

Brethren I ("Grant Brethren") were restricted to North America. They began in 1884, when about half of the Exclusives sided with Frederick W. Grant (1834–1901), whom the British assemblies had censured indirectly. From the 1920s on this group moved more and more toward an Open position. By the mid-1930s many of their urban assemblies had become Open; the remainder had formed Brethren VII and Brethren VIII. Their historic publishing house, Loizeaux Brothers, now of Neptune, New Jersey, the activities of which three generations of the same family have directed since 1876, became Open at this time.

Brethren II are the historically Open Brethren, with which many of the assemblies formerly a part of Brethren I have associated themselves. They generally welcome any born-again believers, regardless of denomination, to the Lord's table on the basis of a common *life* rather than a common *light*. They have no "Circles of Fellowship" and hold that discipline is a local matter for which each assembly is directly responsible to the ascended Lord of the Church. They generally practice believer's baptism, although some of the assemblies that were part of Brethren I still permit "household baptism."

Increasingly during the last generation a large percentage of these Brethren have had fellowship with individual Christians in the denominational church bodies and have participated in joint endeavors, such as Billy Graham Crusades, the Gideons, the Inter-Varsity Christian Fellowship, Christian Business Men's Committees, and other theologically conservative groups. Because they stress the independence of each local assembly there is considerable diversity in practice. A tenth or more of the assemblies in this group stress the "old paths" and view with concern the cited joint activities with other Christians, along with such activities and agencies as summer camps, a Bible school, and "expensive chapels." Although such assemblies appear in the same lists with the other Brethren II assemblies, they have preachers, conferences, and magazines that serve them alone.

Open Brethren have no central organization, but various service agencies have arisen on a regional or national basis in response to felt needs. *Letters of Interest*, a monthly periodical, reports on the activities of the assemblies of Open Brethren and of about 450 domestic full-time workers; its staff represents the Brethren with the national government concerned in such matters as the endorsement of military chaplains. The closely related Stewards Foundation in Chicago lends money for chapel construction or remodeling, issues bonds, and provides annuities for investors. It operates a few hospitals that are staffed as far as possible with Christian doctors and nurses and with one or more full-time chaplains, and it has become connected in an advisory way with a few Christian retirement homes. The Fields is another service organization; it publishes a magazine by that name that reports on the activities of over 1,200 Brethren foreign missionaries (some 400 of them commended by North American assemblies, the remainder by Brethren assemblies in other lands) in over 50 countries. In a purely advisory fashion, The Fields assists these missionaries in other ways as well, for instance by negotiating with foreign governments, receiving and transmitting funds, arranging for transportation, and aiding with furloughs. "Christian Missions in Many Lands" is a frequent designation for Open Brethren missionary activity. Literature Crusades is a newer, aggressive recruiter of young people for short-term missionary activity in various cities around the world. Many of those that it has recruited have subsequently become permanent missionaries. The triennial World Missions Congress that it sponsors attracts over 1,200 youthful participants.

In general, Open ministers are the only ones who go to graduate theological seminaries, usually conservative interdenominational schools like Trinity Seminary in Deerfield, Illinois; Dallas (Texas) Theological Seminary; and Fuller Theological Seminary. Proportionately the Open Brethren send out many more missionaries than Exclusive Brethren do and are more likely to have a higher percentage (sometimes a clear majority) of communicants from non-Brethren family backgrounds.

Brethren III, called the "Continental Brethren" because of the relative numerical strength of their European counterparts, came into being when the Brethren who had rejected Grant divided among themselves in 1890 over the ministry of a British leader, F. E. Raven (d. 1905). Brethren III rejected Raven. In 1926 they united with the so-called "Kelly Brethren," a group that had come out of a schism in 1881 and that was limited to England. In 1953 Brethren VII joined this worldwide circle.

Brethren IV, called the "Raven Brethren" because they supported Raven in the 1890 schism, were at least until recently the largest group of Exclusive Brethren worldwide, although not in North America. Raven had a mystical inclination and was not always precise in his doctrinal formulations. When he died, a New York businessman, James Taylor, Sr. (d. 1953), gradually assumed unofficial leadership among Raven's followers, but certain doctrinal novelties that he introduced accelerated the alienation of the Raven Brethren from other Exclusives. His son succeeded the elder Taylor as unofficial leader of this group. The junior Taylor's demands for increasingly rigorous separation from other Christians, for withdrawal from professional associations, for resigning offices in business corporations and for disposing of stock in them, and refusing to eat meals with anyone with whom the Brethren concerned were not in fellowship led to the schism that produced Brethren X. The leadership of the two Taylors had given Brethren IV the name "Taylor Brethren." In the United States the Taylor Brethren are strongest in New York, in the older industrial areas as far west as Detroit and Chicago, and on the West Coast. They are also well represented in Canada.[2]

Brethren V, served by Bible Truth Publishers, Oak Park, Illinois, is probably the largest Exclusive group in North America. They withdrew from Brethren III in 1909, when they sided with the Tunbridge Wells assembly in a jurisdictional dispute in England. Most of the English counterparts of this group entered the Kelly-Continental group in 1940, so that the "Tunbridge Wells Brethren" are now centered in North America and in certain foreign countries where they carry on missions. They hold that whole "Circles of Fellowship" may not properly reunite, but that the reconciliation must take place on an individual basis.

Brethren VI, the "Glanton Brethren," no longer exist in North America as a group. They withdrew from the Raven Brethren in 1908 in a dispute about centralizing tendencies within this group. Never a large circle, the North American assemblies immediately began to look for ties with the Grant Brethren; Brethren VIII absorbed them completely by the end of the 1930s.

Brethren VII withdrew from group I in 1928. The occasion for the schism was this group's rejection of the ministry of a visiting English Glanton Brethren preacher, James Boyd, and by its advocacy of the case of an aggrieved Philadelphia businessman, C. A. Mory. In 1953 Brethren VII united with Brethren III.

Brethren VIII, served by the Erie (Pennsylvania) Bible Truth Depot, began in the late 1920s as the Exclusive remnant of Brethren I, after the

Boyd and Mory controversies had caused many Grant Brethren assemblies to reexamine their principles and to become Open. At this time Brethren VIII linked up more closely with the Glanton Brethren in England. The most prominent preacher of the Brethren VIII circle was A. E. Booth (d. 1950). Brethren VIII and Brethren III are now carrying on conversations looking to the possible union of the two groups.

Brethren IX is a small circle that withdrew from Brethren VIII around 1949, supporting a preacher by the name of Ames in his distrust of the teaching and practice of the British Glanton Brethren.

Brethren X withdrew from the Taylor Brethren around 1960 because of their dissatisfaction with the pronouncements of the younger Taylor. They consist of a few assemblies who maintain ties with a number of overseas assemblies of former Taylor Brethren that have not found their way into other congregations.

There may perhaps be other very small groups in the United States and Canada that have withdrawn from one or the other of the circles listed.

There are over 700 Open assemblies in the United States and over 350 in Canada, with an estimated 70,000 communicants. Information about the Exclusive assemblies is harder to come by. A responsible estimate puts the total number of Exclusive assemblies in the United States and Canada at probably no more than 300 with a total of less than 10,000 communicants.[3]

### The Churches of God in the Fellowship of the Son of God, the Lord Jesus Christ (The Churches of God in the British Isles and Overseas)

The Churches of God in the British Isles and Overseas emerged out of the Open section of the Plymouth Brethren during the time-frame 1887–1893. The actual beginnings of the movement date back to the late 1870s, when some Open Brethren were disquieting many of their fellow Brethren by the ease with which they invoked the principle that "all believers are in the fellowship" to justify their association with other Christians. In 1876 *The Northern Witness*, a Plymouth Brethren magazine, began to raise questions in this area. A paper written in 1883 by Frederick A. Banks on "The Church and the Churches of God: A Suggestive Outline of Truth," proved to be particularly influential.[4] In 1888 a new journal, *Needed Truth*,[5] came into being; it began to sound the call for withdrawal in 1889. The bulk of the actual separations took place in 1892–1893. The fellowship began to expand into North America, Africa, Australia, New Zealand, and Asia early in the present century. About the same time a "deep division in the leadership of a Scottish church led to the breaking off" of a number of churches.[6]

Although from 1893 on "the Churches of God in united fellowship" often referred to themselves unofficially as "the Assemblies of God in the British Isles" and in the early 1900s began to use the designation "the Churches of God in the. British Isles and Overseas," the fellowship has never formally taken a name. When its congregations call themselves "Churches of God," they regard the appelation as a description rather than as a title. The Churches of God in the Fellowship of the Son of God, the Lord Jesus Christ, is the name under which the fellowship maintains its general purpose bank account.

The movement regards its historical origin less as a separation from the Plymouth Brethren than as the recovery of an essential part of the Christian faith and as a return to the perennially normative "blueprint laid down by our Lord and followed by his apostles" in establishing New Testament churches of God.[7]

Probably the most noteworthy feature about the teachings of the Churches of God in the Fellowship of the Son of God, the Lord Jesus Christ, consists in their definitions of the terms in which they frame their doctrine of the church. The inviolable "church which is [Christ's] body" is the church which Christ founded and of which human beings become members when they believe in him. The actual fellowship—specifically, the Churches of God in the Fellowship of the Son of God, the Lord Jesus Christ—comprises those who are together in obedience to the Lord after they have received the divine Word, have been baptized by other disciples, and have been "added" by the Lord. "Addition" is a distinct step beyond merely believing and relates to the association of baptized believers with Churches of God where the authority of Christ is expressed and maintained.[8] The Churches of God in the Fellowship of the Son of God, the Lord Jesus Christ, do not regard membership in their fellowship as a precondition or test of membership in the church which is Christ's body, but they believe that every believer, as a matter of obedience to God, ought to be in "the Fellowship" (understood as the total of their assemblies) and be governed by God's Word rather than by any humanly formulated rules or catechisms. "Church" in the narrow sense describes the believing and "added" Christians who form an assembly in one locality. A few assemblies may have more than one "meeting."

The Churches of God in the Fellowship of the Son of God, the Lord Jesus Christ, reject all nonbiblical names for officers in the church, all denominational designations, and all terms for individual members other than "saints," "brethren," "believers," and "disciples." True believers who are outside their assemblies are outside the "Churches of God," although not outside the "church that is Christ's body." Officially, the movement considers its meetings to be the only ones that have a legitimate title to call themselves "Churches of God."

Members may "embark on courtship" only with others who belong to the fellowship.[9] The fellowship holds that disciples should "marry only in the Lord" and any who marry persons outside the fellowship are "put away." Since 1947 membership in trade unions has been a matter of individual conscience. While the possession of radio sets is now widely tolerated, possession of television sets is still frowned on. "The Lord's disciple cannot . . . become a soldier of an earthly king or government to engage in war. . . . He may not serve in the . . . army, in any part thereof either combatant or non-combatant."[10] Members of the fellowship who join the armed forces are "placed under disability in the assembly," that is, they are debarred from leading the assembly in any spiritual exercise.

A local assembly generally aspires to have a hall ("meeting room") of its own in which to worship; the members of a small local assembly may meet for worship in private homes.

The Churches of God in the Fellowship of the Son of God, the Lord Jesus Christ, are committed to the inspiration of the Bible, the Trinity, the deity of Christ, the fall of man, and the atonement. They regard Christ's resurrection as lying at the basis of the Christian faith. They see baptism as a sign of willingness to follow Christ, a public confession of obedience to be administered in the presence of the church. Candidates must have reached an age of understanding, must be born again, and must show a disciple-spirit. A deacon or overseer totally immerses the candidate in the baptistry of the "meeting room," saying "I baptize you into the name of the Father and of the Son and of the Holy Spirit." Converts who have received believer's baptism in a Christian denomination are not baptized again.

The meeting for the "breaking of bread" in remembrance of Christ and in proclamation of his death is held every Sunday morning in every assembly. In addition each assembly normally has a "gospel meeting" aimed at the nonbeliever on Sunday evening. Larger assemblies may hold a prayer meeting during the week; the prayer meeting may be combined with a "ministry meeting" (Christian doctrine for believers). Worship is spontaneous. The main fellowship hymnbook is *Psalms, Hymns, and Spiritual Songs*; at the "gospel meetings" *Gospel Hymns of Grace and Glory* is likely to find use. The former is weighted toward traditional worship-type hymns, the latter toward nineteenth-century evangelistic hymns. Hymn singing in the church service is unaccompanied.[11]

The unity of the Churches of God is seen as based upon the unity of Christ's body and as consisting in a unity of the Spirit under the Lordship of Christ that finds expression in unity of doctrine and practice on the basis of the Word of God and in government by a united elderhood.[12] The fellowship opposes both congregational autonomy and federation; it holds that the Churches of God should be united in one partnership, after what it sees as the apostolic church's pattern. The local assemblies are the constituencies of overseers who function both at the local and at wider levels. The overseers, who are not thought of as being clergymen, form a self-perpetuating body, in which all overseers are nominally equal to one another, although older and more experienced men tend to enjoy greater regard. The overseers of the local assembly appoint the deacons; the ratio of elders and deacons to members varies from area to area. All overseers are also deacons; local overseers nominate candidates for elderhood to the district overseers and after interviewing them the district makes its decision. The Churches of God in the Fellowship of the Son of God, the Lord Jesus Christ, "put a premium on coordination of decision-making at a supra-assembly level."[13] A meeting of representative overseers takes place in Great Britain once a year; relatively few overseers from other countries are able to attend these conferences. Overseers meet at the district level at intervals of one, two, or three months. The fellowship has 106 churches worldwide, of which about one fifth are "overseas." The six churches in Canada (4 in Ontario, 2 in British Columbia) and the one church in the United States (at Trinidad, Colorado) have a total active membership that does not exceed 300. The Needed Truth Publishing Office is located at Assembly Hall, George Lane, Hayes, Bromley, Kent, England; its North American representative is Mr. J. Ramage, 44 Tweedsmuir Avenue, Dundas, Ontario, Canada.[14]

## NOTES

1. The doctrine of the last things here outlined is more or less common to Dispensationalists generally and is not the exclusive teaching of Brethren. While modern Dispensationalism traces its ancestry by way of the Scofield Reference Bible back to John Nelson Darby, there are today many more Dispensationalists in Baptist, Dunkard, Presbyterian, Pentecostal, and independent churches than there are in Brethren assemblies. In the Brethren community itself, there is not complete unanimity in this area. Most Open Brethren are Dispensationalists, but many in the younger generation seem to give it less than a central position in their thinking. In the Brethren assemblies of Great Britain there is a tradition going back to George Müller and others of his generation that does not accept Dispensationalism.

2. See Bryan R. Wilson, "The Exclusive Brethren: A Case Study in the Evolution of a Sectarian Ideology," in a volume that he edited, *Patterns of Sectarianism: Organisation and Ideology in Social and Religious Movements* (London: Heinemann Educational Books, 1967), chap. 9, pp. 287-342.

3. Students of comparative theology regularly lament the difficulty of obtaining authoritative information about the Brethren. This writer gratefully acknowledges the unofficial assistance so generously given by Mr. Paul F. Loizeaux, editor of *Help and Food*, Parkton, Maryland, and by Dr. Donald G. Tinder, assistant editor, *Christianity Today*, Washington, D.C.

4. This tract still possesses such historic importance for the ecclesiology of the Churches of God in the Fellowship of the Son of God, the Lord Jesus Christ, that the editors of *Needed Truth* reprinted it in full in vol. 74 (1967), pp. 181-188.

5. Hence the name "Needed Truth party," applied by outsiders to the group that became the Churches of God in the Fellowship of the Son of God, the Lord Jesus Christ.

6. See J. D. Terrell, "New Testament Churches of God: The Lessons of History," *Needed Truth* 74 (1967): 149-152; and T. M. Hyland, "New Testament Churches of God: The Position Today," ibid., pp. 165-169.

7. T. M. Hyland, "New Testament Churches of God: Introduction," ibid., p. 9. "Let them not trace their assembly origin to any phase of 'Plymouthism' or to any other 'ism'," Bank wrote in "The Church and the Churches of God: A Suggestive Outline of Truth," ibid., p. 188.

8. On these three stages see J. Drain, "New Testament Churches of God: Their Pattern," ibid., p. 39.

9. Particularly in a mobile social situation this endogamous pattern creates a web of kinship among the assemblies that undergirds conformity to the movement's norms.

10. "British Isles and Overseas Reports," *Summary of Minutes of the 1935 Conference of Representative Overseers of the Churches of God in the British Isles and Overseas*, pp. 22-23, quoted in Gordon Willis and Bryan R. Wilson,

"The Churches of God: Pattern and Practice," in Bryan R. Wilson, ed., *Patterns of Sectarianism: Organization and Ideology in Social and Religious Movements* (London: Heinemann's Educational Books, 1967), p. 281.
11. For a description of the worship of the fellowship, see ibid., pp. 285-286.
12. See A. F. Toms, "New Testament Churches of God: Their Unity," ibid., pp. 53-57, and R. T. H. Horne, "New Testament Churches of God: Their Government," *Needed Truth* 74 (1967): 68-70.
13. Willis and Wilson, p. 267.
14. Letters from Professor Byran R. Wilson, All Souls College, Oxford University, England; Mr. Gordon Willis, "High Croft," Highfield Road, Grange-over-Sands, Lancashire, England; and from an editor of *Needed Truth*, who desires that his name be withheld.

# BIBLIOGRAPHY

Bass, Clarence B. *Backgrounds to Dispensationalism: Its Historical Genesis and Ecclesiastical Implications.* Grand Rapids, Mich.: Wm. B. Eerdmans Publishing Co., 1960. An excellent narrative of the beginnings of the Brethren movement, with a careful critical evaluation of the theology of John Nelson Darby and a helpful bibliography.

Campbell, R. K. *The Church of the Living God: Comprehensive Meditations and Gleanings on Its Nature and Scriptural Order.* Wausau, Wis.: Scripture Truth Depot, 1950. The contents of the book appeared serially in *Grace and Truth* between 1943 and 1949. The author represents the Kelly-Continental tradition.

Coad, F. Roy. *A History of the Brethren Movement.* Exeter, England: Paternoster Press, 1968. The author is definitely pro-"Open" in outlook. The work concentrates on the first twenty-five years of the movement.

Darby, John Nelson. *The Collected Writings of John Nelson Darby.* Ed. William Kelly. 34 volumes, plus index volume. London: G. Morrish, 1867-1900[?].

———. *Letters of J.N.D.* 3 vols. Kingston-on-Thames: Stow Hill Bible and Tract Depot, n.d. A reissue of the edition published by G. Morrish, London, between 1886 and 1889.

Ehlert, Arnold D. "Plymouth Brethren Writers." In *Summary of Proceedings, Eleventh Annual Conference, American Theological Library Association . . . June 19-21, 1957* (Maywood, Ill.: American Theological Library Association, 1957), pp. 49-80. A very valuable bibliographic tool.

Grant, Frederick W. *A Divine Movement and Our Path with God Today.* New York: Loizeaux Brothers, 1895. Grant was an eminent Exclusive teacher.

Hoste, William. *Things Most Surely Believed among Us.* London: Pickering and Inglis, 1935 [?]. A 48-page pamphlet.

Ironside, Henry Allan. *A Historical Sketch of the Brethren Movement: An Account of Its Inception, Progress, Principles, and Failures, and Its Lessons for Present Day Believers.* Grand Rapids, Mich.: Zondervan Publishing House, 1942.

Neatby, William Blair. *A History of the Plymouth Brethren.* 2nd edn. London: Hodder and Stoughton, 1902.

Noël, Napoleon. *The History of the Brethren.* Ed. William F. Knapp. 2 vols. Denver: William F. Knapp, 1936. This history by a member of the Exclusive Continental Brethren must be used with caution. Its thorough documentation is valuable, but its account is partisan and tendentious.

Rendell, Kingsley, G., ed. [*Andrew*] *Miller's Church History, Extended to the Present Day.* London: Pickering and Inglis, 1967. Andrew Miller (1810–1883) represented the Exclusive tradition.

Ridout, Samuel. *The Church and Its Order according to Scripture.* New York: Loizeaux Brothers, n.d. Written before 1930 by a leading Exclusive teacher.

Rowdon, Harold H. *The Origins of the Brethren.* London: Pickering and Inglis, 1967. This work is based on the author's University of London doctor of philosophy dissertation. It is a fair and dispassionate presentation of information about the movement until 1850.

Tatford, Frederick A., ed. *The Faith: A Symposium.* London: Pickering and Inglis, 1952. A collection of essays on various commonplaces of systematic theology by prominent English Open Brethren.

Veitch, Thomas Stewart. *The Story of the Brethren Movement.* London: Pickering and Inglis, 1933.

Watson, J. B., ed. *The Church: A Symposium*. London: Pickering and Inglis, 1949. The authors of the individual essays are prominent British Open Brethren.

Willis, Gordon, and Bryan R. Wilson. "The Churches of God: Pattern and Practice." In: Bryan R. Wilson, ed., *Patterns of Sectarianism: Organization and Ideology in Social and Religious Movements* (London: Heinemann Educational Books, 1967), chap. 8, pp. 244-286.

Wilson, Bryan R. ed. *Patterns of Sectarianism: Organisation and Ideology in Social and Religious Movements*. London: Heinemann Educational Books, 1967. Of special relevance to the Plymouth Brethren are three chapters: (*a*) Peter L. Embley, "The Early Development of the Plymouth Brethren," chap. 7, pp. 213-243; (*b*) Gordon Willis and Bryan R. Wilson, "The Churches of God: Pattern and Practice," chap. 8, pp. 244-286; and (*c*) Bryan R. Wilson, "The Exclusive Brethren: A Case Study in the Evolution of a Sectarian Ideology," chap. 9, pp. 287-342. The approach of these chapters is primarily sociological, but they present important doctrinal and liturgical insights as well.

# 5. Dispensationalist Bodies

Taken in a general sense, Dispensationalism is the interpretation of history as a series of divine despensations. As the designation of a theological movement, the term derives from the translation of *oikonomia* ["management [of a household]") in I Corinthians 9:17; Ephesians 1:10; 3:2; and Colossians 1:25 (King James Version of the Bible).

While the idea of a series of divine dispensations has rabbinic and primitive Christian roots, modern Dispensationalism, as commonly understood, received a major impulse in the nineteenth century from John Nelson Darby, the early Plymouth Brethren leader. In twentieth-century North America the activity of Cyrus Ingerson Scofield (1843–1921), editor of the influential Scofield Reference Bible,[1] and of Lewis Sperry Chafer (1871–1952) popularized Dispensationalist patterns of "rightly dividing the word of truth," among conservative Evangelical Christians.

The Scofield Reference Bible defines a Dispensation as "a period of time during which man is tested in respect to his obedience to some specific revelation of the will of God."[2] The number of such dispensations varies from system to system; seven is popular. Other details also vary.

Dispensationalism has become a presupposition for many conservative Evangelical theologians in a wide spectrum of denominations that do not as denominations commit themselves to this pattern of biblical interpretation. Dispensationalism has likewise become an integral part of the official faith of a number of denominations that are not "Dispensationalist" in the sense that this pattern of interpretation seems to be their most characteristic feature. The movements described in this section are representative of those groups that have made the Dispensationalist principle determinative for their theology.

## Grace Gospel Fellowship

During the early 1930s J. C. O'Hair, the dispensationally oriented minister of the North Shore Church in Chicago, sponsored a series of Bible conferences in various midwestern cities. These laid special emphasis on what their sponsor regarded as the unique character of the revelation given to the apostle Paul concerning the church as the body of Christ. In 1939 some of the clergymen who had cooperated in these conferences met and formed a board to undertake the support of foreign missionaries. They called it Worldwide Grace Testimony; it is now called Grace Mission, Incorporated. In 1944 they formed the Grace Gospel Fellowship, a federation of individuals who shared a common view of Dispensationalism and most of whom were members of autonomous local congregations banded together on the same common basis. The next year the fellowship established the Milwaukee Bible Institute at Milwaukee, Wisconsin, to train evangelists, missionaries, pastors, and teachers "to rightly divide the Word of Truth in obedience to II Timothy 2:15."[3] In 1961 the school moved to Grand Rapids, Michigan, and took the name Grace Bible College. In addition to Grace Mission and Grace Bible College, the independent organizations recognized by and associated with the fellowship include the Things to Come Mission and Bethesda Missions.

The strongly (almost exclusively) Pauline doctrinal statement of the Grace Mission and of the Grace Gospel Fellowship affirms the verbal inspiration and plenary authority of the Bible, understood dispensationally; the Trinity; the total depravity of natural man; the unlimited provision but limited application of salvation; justification of sinners by grace on the ground of the blood of Christ, through the means of faith, apart from the individual's works and apart from sacraments; eternal security; regeneration, baptism, sealing, indwelling, enlightening and empowering of the saved by the personal Holy Spirit; one Bible church in the present dispensation, called the body of Christ and composed of all saved persons; the necessity of the gifts enumerated in Ephesians 4:7-16 (but of this passage only) for the ministry of the body of Christ; deliverance of believers from the power of sin, but without an eradication of the sinful nature of a human being during this life; the Lord's Supper as a commemoration (but not as "a means of grace whereby we receive the remission of sins") to be observed until Christ comes, with the bread and wine as symbols of Christ's body and blood; a divine baptism that identifies every member of the body of Christ with him in his death, burial, and resurrection, but that allows no place for water baptism in God's spiritual program for the body of Christ in this day of grace; the bodily resurrection of all human beings, the saved to eternal glory and the lost to everlasting condemnation in a state of conscious suffering;[4] Christ's personal and premillennial coming, first to receive the church to himself and then to receive the millennial Kingdom; and the mission and commission of the church to follow Paul (not the injunction of St. Matthew 28:18-20) and "to preach the Gospel in the regions beyond where Christ is not yet named."[5]

There are 43 churches throughout the United States and in Puerto Rico, with a total membership of about 3,200 within the fellowship. The strongest concentrations are in the Chicago-Grand Rapids area, southern California, and northern New Jersey. The fellowship conducts foreign missions in Africa, the Philippines Republic, the Netherlands, Bolivia, Curaçao, and Brazil. The fellowship does not regard itself as a denomination and neither the national Executive Council, which licenses and ordains the ministers of the fellowship, nor a national conference can bind a local church to any action. When a local church affiliates with the fellowship, each member of the congregation must do so for himself. The fellowship counts voting members only; some local churches admit women to voting membership, others do not. Although the fellowship has no formal headquarters, its activities center around the agencies in Grand Rapids, Michigan.[6]

## Gospel Tract Distributors

Around 1912 Danish-born Nels Thompson (d. 1935), who had come to the United States shortly before and was still in his early twenties, became a member of the Grant Brethren (Plymouth Brethren I) as a result of the preaching of Dr. Harry A. Ironside (1876–1951). Several years later Thompson began to devote his entire time to an evangelistic tent ministry up and down the Pacific Coast. In the early 1920s the Grant Brethren, then still strongly Exclusive, severed their connection with Thompson because of what they called his defiance of the group's regulations for its evangelists. Thompson thereupon continued his evangelistic work on his own. Meanwhile he came to the conviction that water baptism was a Jewish ordinance not intended for the present age. A fellowship of six assemblies of like-minded believers—the first of them in Oakland, California, in 1922—sprang up during his lifetime as a result of his work.

The beliefs and practices of the fellowship are similar to those of the Plymouth Brethren, particularly its meetings "to break bread" (the Lord's Supper) every Sunday and its rejection of "denominationalism," of a distinction between ordained clergymen and laypeople, of one-man ministries, and of titles like "Reverend." It affirms the verbal inspiration of the Bible; Christ's deity; the Trinity; the total depravity of human beings; the everlasting punishment of those who reject Christ; redemption by Christ's blood, not by works but by grace; everlasting life and the security of believers; the personality and punishment of Satan; the imminent resurrection of the believing dead and the rapture of the church at the end of the present age of grace (5th dispensation), followed by the seven years of the great tribulation (6th dispensation), Christ's visible return and millennial reign (7th dispensation), the great white throne judgment, and the expulsion of evil human beings from the earth.[7] It goes beyond the Plymouth Brethren in its Dispensationalism. The Gospels and a large part of Acts are still "on Israelitish ground." The revelation to Paul for the present dispensation was progressive, so that much of I Corinthians, for instance, is for the church in its infancy, while its grownup institutions are to be found in the prison epistles, especially Ephesians. Water baptism,[8] apostles, and prophets are no longer for this age, but evangelists, pastors, and teachers are.[9] Women may not preach in the meetings of the fellowship. Christmas, Easter, and other religious holidays are not to be celebrated. The local fellowships are called "assemblies" or "meetings"; the places of assembly are "meeting halls."

The publication center of the fellowship is at 8036 North Interstate Avenue (P.O. Box 17056), Portland, Oregon 97217. There are 15 assemblies and several small house-meeting groups in Arizona, the Pacific Coast states, and as far north as Rockglen, Saskatchewan. The total active membership is estimated at 600 families, or 1,800 persons.[10]

## "Prison Epistles" Dispensationalist Groups

Ethelbert W. Bullinger (1837–1913) was an ordained Anglican clergyman, an ardent Dispensationalist, the author of seventy-seven works, and for nineteen years the editor of a monthly, *Things to Come.* Of the seven or eight dispensations that his system originally envisioned, two fell between Pentecost and the end of the age of the church. The Gospels, all but a few verses of the Acts of the Apostles, and the General Epistles he placed under the law, and he saw the dispensation of the church beginning with the ministry of St. Paul after Acts 28:28, which he regarded the key verse for the right dispensational division. Thus he found the fullness of the revelation of the mystery of the present church age in the "prison letters": Ephesians, Philippians, Colossians, and Philemon. He denied that water baptism and the Lord's Supper are for this age.

During the last four years of his life Bullinger had as his associate Charles H. Welch (1880–1967), subsequently the principal of the Chapel of the Opened Book on Wilson Street, London, a prolific Dispensationalist author, and for over fifty years the editor of a monthly magazine of Bible exposition called *The Berean Expositor.* Like Bullinger, Welch saw Acts 28:23-31 as the "dispensational frontier,"[11] inaugurating the dispensation of the "church of the one body where Christ is recognized as Head." Stuart Allen succeeded Welch in London.

Broadly similar views have been affirmed in North America since World War I by a large number of persons, among them Robert A. Hadden, one of the founders of the Bible Institute of Los Angeles, and the contributors to the journal that he edited until his death in 1932, *The Christian Fundamental Magazine*; by Walter Bartz of Springfield, formerly of Bloomington, Illinois, and his circle; and by Harold P. Morgan of Riverton, New Jersey, editor of the magazine *Questions and Answers* from 1942 to his death in 1953.

Since the late 1940s Truth for Today, Incorporated, Route 2, Warsaw, Indiana, has provided materials to individuals and home study groups committed to this general type of Dispensationalism.[12] These home study groups, which reportedly exist in almost every state of the union and in a number of Canadian communities (such as Toronto, North Bay, and Victoria) have for the most part neither formal organization nor a stated membership.[13]

They hold that from Acts 28:28 to the Day of the Lord the Kingdom is held in abeyance. Jewish rituals and ordinances have been discontinued, repentance is not preached, worship is spiritual, and only faith is required. The truth of "the gospel of the dispensation of the mystery" is found neither in Moses and the prophets nor in the ministry of Christ and the Twelve; its biblical documents are the prison letters, the pastoral letters, and the letter to Philemon.[14] They likewise hold that God intended the Jewish Passover only for the circumcised. This implies that the church, with its heavenly calling, its seat with Christ at the right hand of God, and all its spiritual blessings in the heavenly places in Christ Jesus, can have no rituals with earthly elements. For that reason they do not baptize nor do they "observe the Lord's supper (Baal's supper) which came from the sun worship in Babylon."[15] The circulation of the monthly *Truth for Today*, which is supported by freewill offerings, is nearly 5,000.[16]

The Ewalt Memorial Bible School, P.O. Box 518, Atascadero, California, affirms and teaches a similar, although not identical, position. While Bullinger taught seven or eight dispensations and Welch saw as many as fifteen major movements in the Bible that he called dispensations, the Ewalt Memorial Bible School teaches only two vast dispensations. It likewise differentiates faith as receiving when it appropriates Christ's redemptive person and work, as obedient when it moves believers to walk in love, as motivating when it constrains believers to set their minds on things that are above, and as humble-minded when believers have among themselves the mind that was in Christ.[17]

The Northside Bible Church, Oklahoma City, Oklahoma, holds that the body of truth which Paul calls the mystery (Ephesians 3:3, 5, 9) is the revelation that Christ gave to Paul for the present dispensation and not any revelation that Christ gave Paul before the "prison letters" period. The church observes the Lord's Supper but does not practice water baptism. The congregations sponsor a bimonthly, *The Classics Expositor*, begun in December 1967 and published by the Classics Publishing Trust. It has an estimated circulation of 500. Associated with the Northside Bible Church are Calvary Tabernacle and Northminster Presbyterian Church in Oklahoma City and the Moore Bible Church in Moore, Oklahoma.[18]

## Concordant Publishing Concern

In 1907 Ethelbert W. Bullinger (1837–1913) published in *Things to Come* a series of articles on baptism by an American layman, Adolph Ernst Knoch (1874–1965), whom the Plymouth Brethren had expelled for having fellowship with other denominations.[19]

Knoch's work was chiefly literary. He translated the Concordant Version of the Scriptures. In this work, in the interest of consistency, he reproduced with a single English term a corresponding biblical vocable, and that vocable only. He likewise reproduced with an English "pattern" every occurrence of the same verb form in the original.[20] Knoch also produced *The Concordant Greek Text* as a companion to the *Concordant [Literal] New Testament*. With Vladimir Michael Gelesnoff (1877–1921) he published a bimonthly periodical, *Unsearchable Riches*, from 1909 on. After Gelesnoff's death, Knoch continued to publish the journal alone. His son, Ernst O. Knoch, who was co-editor from 1950 on, is continuing the periodical.

Knoch's system sees the history of the universe from various points of view in terms of five eons, five worlds, the three heavens and earths, two creations, twelve eras (*kairoi*), twelve administrations or economies, a week's work for the restoration of the present earth, four monarchies in regard to governing the earth's affairs, and the "unseen" (Sheol, Hades, and the final state).[21] Everything in the Old and New Testaments, Knoch held, has to do primarily with the Jews except the Pauline letters, which constitute a separate parenthesis for the present dispensation.[22] He "cuts the word of truth correctly" by differentiating the Kingdom from the present dispensation of grace. Knoch rejected the traditional doctrine of the Trinity. He saw Christ as a created being, although God's Son.[23] He taught that after the eonian times all created intelligences, including Satan and the demonic spirits, would be conciliated to God in the reconciliation of all things. He held that water baptism has no place in this dispensation, but observed the Lord's Supper at least once a month in the congregation in which he taught.

No formal organization has institutionalized Knoch's system. In addition to some groups in the Commonwealth and on the European continent, there are an estimated fifty groups in the United States and Canada that regularly turn to the Concordant Publishing Concern, 15570 West Knochaven Drive, Saugus, California 91350, for information and literature.[24]

### College Avenue Community Church
### (Fort Worth, Texas) and Associated Congregations

While attending Moody Bible Institute, Chicago, Ike T. Sidebottom served as associate pastor at the North Shore Church, under J. C. O'Hair. Upon his graduation from Moody Bible Institute in 1928 and his return to Fort Worth, Sidebottom began to teach a Bible class in a vacant store; the class grew into the College Avenue Community Church, with Sidebottom as its pastor. Upon his retirement in 1965 he was succeeded by Charles Wages. Over the years the church provided six other community churches in the area with pastors. Although there is no organization as such, these seven churches cooperate in sponsoring summer camps, midwinter conferences for students, and other programs.

Doctrinally conservative, the churches of the fellowship hold traditionally orthodox views on the Trinity, the verbal inspiration of the Bible, and Christ's deity and virgin birth. While rejecting the idea of a limited atonement, the churches of the fellowship stress salvation by grace and the eternal security of the believer. They see the church as the body of Christ, united in the Holy Spirit and composed of all true believers in Christ. While they attempt to maintain cordial relationships with other clergymen and churches of the local level, they deplore the ecumenism that seeks organic union, on the ground that, as they see it, this objective necessarily implies the compromise of basic convictions. They regard baptism and the Lord's Supper as being spiritual in the present dispensation and reject the ceremonies that use literal water or literal bread and wine; at the same time they do not make concurrence in this position a test of fellowship. In spite of the difference between this fellowship and the Grace Gospel Fellowship on the Lord's Supper, the churches of the former support missionaries of the Grace Gospel Fellowship and feel free to use Grace Gospel Fellowship personnel in their pulpits and camps. Most of the pastors in the fellowship support themselves as teachers, educational administrators, or business executives. The organ of the fellowship is *The Timely Messenger*, founded by Sidebottom in 1939 as a weekly, but now a monthly.

The total membership of the seven churches in the fellowship is estimated at 1,000.[25]

## Berean Mission, Incorporated

The Berean Mission, Incorporated, is an independent faith mission. The Denver (Colorado) Bible Institute organized the Berean Mission as its missionary arm in 1934. In 1937 the Berean Mission was incorporated as a separate organization. In 1943 it moved its headquarters to St. Louis. Since 1954 it has belonged to the Interdenominational Foreign Mission Association.

The doctrinal position of the Berean Mission, Incorporated, commits it to belief in the verbal inspiration and plenary authority of the Bible; the Trinity; the depravity and lost condition of all human beings; the personality of Satan; Christ's deity, virgin birth, blood atonement, resurrection, mediatorial intercession, imminent pretribulational and premillennial personal return, and millennial Kingdom; the justification of sinful human beings through faith in Christ alone; the personhood of the Holy Spirit and his work of convicting the world of sin and of regenerating and dwelling in those who believe in Christ; the eternal security of all believers in Christ; the spiritual gifts of God to all believers; the sufficiency of the gifts of evangelists, pastors, and teachers for the perfecting of the church today ("the apostolic age with signs, including tongues, ceased with the apostles . . . but God does hear and answer the prayer of faith, according to his own will for the sick and afflicted"); the church as those who are saved in the present dispensation; the establishment of local churches; the presence of two natures in those who are born again ("they may be victorious over the old through the power of the new, but . . . eradication of the old [nature] is unscriptural"); the call of all redeemed human beings to a life of separation from the world; the obligation of those who are saved to engage in missionary activity; the dispensational view of

Bible interpretation; eternal life for those who are saved and the conscious, eternal punishment of the wicked in hell; and believer's baptism by immersion and the Lord's Supper as the only ordinances for this age, but not as means of salvation.

The Berean Mission, Incorporated, rejects the "hyper-dispensationalism" that opposes the ordinances of the Lord's Supper and water baptism for this age; "traditional anti-Christian liberalism and modernism"; and the "more recent subtleties of pseudo-Christian thinking known as neoorthodoxy, neo-evangelicalism, and ecumenism," the last-named largely promulgated by the National Council of the Churches of Christ in the United States of America, the World Council of Churches, and the Roman Catholic hierarchy.[26]

The Berean Mission, Incorporated, draws its support chiefly from fundamental, Baptist, and independent Bible churches, and from individual members of these churches, as well as from other churches and individuals who share its doctrinal convictions.

Its headquarters are at 3536 Russell Boulevard, St. Louis, Missouri 63104. Its mission fields are primarily in Africa, the Republic of the Philippines, the West Indies, and South America, but it also operates missions in the United States among the Navajo Indians of New Mexico, the Spanish-speaking population of Las Vegas, New Mexico (formerly the Spanish American Bible Mission), and Cuban refugees in Miami, Florida. No estimate of the total active membership of these centers is available.[27]

## The True Light Church of Christ

In 1870 a Lake City (South Carolina) Methodist layman by the name of Cunningham Boyle (1831–1884) asserted that he had received a message from heaven declaring that the existing churches had deviated from Christ's teachings and were irretrievably lost. Accordingly he withdrew from the Methodist Church and began to preach with great zeal in the Lynchburg-Bishopville-Hartsville section of South Carolina the message that he had received. He won enough converts to establish the first congregation of the True Light Church of Christ, the High Hill Church near Lucknow, South Carolina. Two other congregations, the Rocky River Church and the Ebenezer Church, twelve miles north and south respectively of Monroe, North Carolina, also came into being in the 1870s. Members of the church body (locally known in the nineteenth century as Boyleites) recognize Boyle's claim to be the third in the series of angels forecast in Revelation 14[28] and hold that under him "the true light did shine back in its apostolic purity."

The teaching of the True Light Church of Christ is trinitarian. Its Articles of Faith affirm belief in one God, the creator, "a personal, spiritual being, occupying some part of glorified space," whose perfection consists in seven attributes (the "spirits" of Revelation 5:6)—mercy, justice, truth, omniscience, omnipotence, omnipresence, and immutability. They affirm the inspiration of the Bible.[29] They describe Christ as the only-begotten Son of God and Savior of the world, "capable of making all necessary arrangements for the salvation of the Adamic family."[30] Satan is a personal spiritual being who occupies "some part of space that God does not occupy. He is co-eternal with God, entirely unrighteous, possessing seven attributes essential to his nature—unmercifulness, injustice, untruthfulness, wisdom, power, omnipresence, and immutability. Each human being is composed of a body and a soul. Human souls exist in God from all eternity, "as the fruit exists in the tree," and are thus co-eternal with him; they were separated from God at creation to pass through probation, after which they will exist as separate spiritual beings for ever. When Adam voluntarily yielded to temptation he lost the Spirit of God and received the spirit of the devil instead. Christ overcame sin in the flesh, and through his suffering and death regained for human beings the Spirit of God, which enables them to overcome sin and keep the law of righteousness. To be saved, all Christians must belong to and be united in faith with the one true church of Christ; they become members of that church by voluntary repentance toward God and faith in Christ.[31] There are two ordinances: water baptism in the name of the Father, Son, and Holy Ghost: and the Lord's Supper. Sprinkling, pouring, and immersion are all valid modes of water baptism; water baptism is the privilege and duty of all who repent and become members of the church. Christian parents have the duty of having their children initiated into the church by water baptism and then to train them in the way they should go. The bread and wine of the Lord's Supper represent the body and blood of Christ; Christians have the right to observe the Lord's Supper as often as they see fit and to have it administered to those of their children "as are able to hear it."[32] The full time from creation to judgment is 7,000 years. The last generation began in 1870 and before it passes away the 6,000 years of probation will terminate with Christ's second advent to establish the millennial Kingdom, after the end of which the final judgment will take place. God, the devil, and souls of human beings were not created, and because they are spiritual beings they are immortal; time and space also were not created and are eternal and infinite.[33]

The church buildings of the group are functional. The worship is simple. Following the singing of hymns, a lay preacher designated by the elder (who has the oversight of doctrine in the congregation) proclaims the message that he believes that the Lord has given him for the occasion. An offering is taken only when there is a "need," such as a family in trouble or necessary repairs to the church building. The lay preachers and the congregational and denominational officers receive no pay.

The True Light Church of Christ forbids the use of tobacco and intoxicating beverages, but from the beginning its members have not regarded Sunday as possessing an intrinsic holiness. While they keep Sunday as a day of rest and worship, they observe every day alike ("Every day is the Lord's") and keep it holy to the Lord.[34]

The True Light Church of Christ regards war in any form as wrong.[35] Its members are conscientious objectors and are not permitted to serve in the armed forces.[36]

Beginning in December 1969, the True Light Church of Christ split over the choice of a successor for the then recently deceased head elder of the Shiloh Church (organized in 1907), near Mint Hill, North Carolina. Bishop Herman Flake Braswell (b. 1926) of Monroe claims to have been chosen head elder by the Conference Body, made up of elders, preachers, and deacons from all the congregations. In January 1970 Assistant Elder James Rommie Purser was elected elder by a majority of the members of the Shiloh Church.

Complicating the administrative issue was a doctrinal one. The entire True Light Church of Christ believes that the end of this age and the coming of the millennium will take place before the end of the century. The Braswell party believes that there are "thirty years of lost time back in the first century," resulting from the fact that "the early church probably recorded Christ's coming from the time he started his ministry." Consequently, without pinpointing the day or hour, this group believes that the world is "at the end of the probationary state of man, the 6,000 years that Adam's family had to work out their salvation."[37] The Purser group holds that the millennium is still up to thirty years away.

Although the Braswell group—which has begun to call itself the True Light Church of Christ of the Living God—insists that the True Church of Christ has never been "congregationally ruled," the judge in the first court test ruled that "the power of the churches of this denomination rests in the congregation" and confirmed Purser's eldership in the Shiloh Church,[38] in which he has 900 supporters. Bishop Braswell has the support of the High Hill, Ebenezer, and Rocky River congregations, and of a small group in the Shiloh Church;[39] they have a total membership of 300.

## Anonymous Assemblies

Maurice M. Johnson (b. 1893) began his career as a minister with ordination as a local preacher in the Methodist Episcopal Church, South, at Handley, Texas, in 1912. Except for a few months as assistant pastor of the North Shore Congregational Church, Chicago, in 1924, he continued in the service of the Methodist Church, chiefly in California, until 1925. In that year he withdrew because of his objections to the Methodist Church's Sunday school literature and its ministerial training course. With seventy-five followers he organized the Maranatha Tabernacle in Glendale, California. In 1927 he repudiated the latter organization, its membership, and his position as an employed and salaried pastor, and "began preaching only as a minister of Jesus Christ in the church which is Christ's body."[40]

Around 1930 Brother Johnson, as he now preferred to be called, began a local radio ministry. (The use of radio as a means of witness has become a characteristic feature of the anonymous assemblies here described.) In the years that followed Johnson traveled widely in the United States. Protégés of his whose call to be preachers he and the members of the assemblies recognized began to preach to congregations in California, Texas, Oklahoma, and Virginia.

The members of these anonymous assemblies see the Bible as their only charter, constitution, and by-laws. They regard any effort to supplement the Bible in these areas as impudent and crude. They refuse to carry "any denominational name" and hold that for them to incorporate "would be a denial of the very heart and essence of [their] most holy faith."[41] Accordingly the members of these assemblies own no property corporately, but only as individuals. They normally hold their meetings in private homes or in rented auditoriums. They describe themselves as "honest and sincere Christians who are associated together only because [they] are Christians."[42] At the same time they do not claim that they constitute the entire church which is Christ's body. They are "merely *some* members of the body of Christ who believe in the reality and practicality of that glorious church and have rejected all supplementary programs and human inventions"[43] to the best of their knowledge, intention, and desire.[44] Indeed, throughout the world, regardless of denomination, all people who have been personally convicted of their sins, who have been brought to personal faith in Christ, and who have then been added to his body of which he is the head are seen as fellow members of the church which is Christ's body. When two or more such believers gather for a Christian assembly in the Lord's name, there is a local manifestation of the church.

Their teaching about the Trinity and Christ's Incarnation is traditionally orthodox. The redemptive work of Christ is seen as finished and perfect. They hold that in the present dispensation, when there are no longer apostles and Christian prophets as there were at first, the divinely given officers of the church are evangelists,[45] pastors and teachers, elders, and deacons.[46] Ordination is not seen as the act of the ministry and/or of the assembly making an elder through the laying on of hands and prayer, but as the assembly's practical recognition that God has made the individual an elder.[47] The assemblies support their ministers, but do not pay them a fixed salary. The ministers perform marriage ceremonies, but water baptism and the observance of the Lord's Supper with material elements are not regarded as appropriate to the present dispensation. Members of the assemblies are aggressive in their evangelistic outreach. When an assembly has no minister regularly available, it may gather to sing and hear a tape-recorded sermon by one of the ministers, or a Bible study presented by a qualified person. They do not object to saluting the flag, nor do they endorse conscientious objection to military service.

Maurice M. Johnson receives mail at Box 74, Orangevale, California

95662; another mailing address is Box 42021, Los Angeles, California 90042. There are meetings in Los Angeles, San Diego, Riverside, San Luis Obispo, Sacramento, and elsewhere in California; Fort Worth, Texas; Tulsa, Oklahoma; and Charlottesville, Virginia. Ministers in these places frequently conduct meetings for other groups in communities at a distance. No membership records are kept, but an informed estimate places the number of people comprising the anonymous assemblies here described at between 1,000 and 1,100.

## NOTES

1. Begun in 1902 and published for the first time by the Oxford University Press in New York in 1909. The same publisher put out The New Scofield Reference Bible, revised by a nine-man editorial team headed by E. Schuyler English, in 1967.

2. In the comment on the heading the Scofield prefixed to Genesis 1:28 ("First Dispensation: Innocence [Gen. 1:28-3:6]").

3. J. C. O'Hair, "Foreword," in Charles F. Baker, Bible Truth: What We Believe and Why We Believe It (Milwaukee, Wis.: Milwaukee Bible College and others, 1956), pp. v-x; letter from the Reverend Charles F. Baker, president emeritus, Grace Bible College, 1011 Aldon Street, Southwest, Grand Rapids, Michigan.

4. The statement opposes Universalism, probation after death, annihilation of the unsaved dead, and the unconscious state of the dead as "thoroughly unscriptural and dangerous doctrines" (ibid., pp. 113-114).

5. For the complete text and an authoritative commentary that illuminates the dispensational nuances of the statement, see Baker, ibid., pp. 13-23. For a critique of this system from a more conventionally Dispensationalist view, see Charles Caldwell Ryrie, Dispensationalism Today (Chicago: Moody, Press, 1965), pp. 192-205.

6. This writer acknowledges gratefully the assistance of the Reverend Kenneth D. Mangelsdorf, pastor of Trinity Church, Edinburgh, Illinois, who established contact on this writer's behalf with the Reverend David Maysick, pastor of Grace Memorial Church (Grace Fellowship), Edinburgh, as well as of Pastor Maysick, who provided valuable information to this writer.

7. "We Believe In—", Last Day Messenger, vol. 6, no. 1 (January–February 1968), p. 2; Dee L. McCroskey, The Church: What and Where Is the True Church of the Bible? (Portland, Ore.: Gospel Tract Distributors, 1960) (35-page tract), pp. 18-19.

8. See Water and Spirit Baptisms: A Brief Outline of These Two Important Bible Baptisms (Portland, Ore.: Gospel Tract Distributors, n.d.) (4-page tract).

9. McCroskey, pp. 10-15.

10. Letter from Mr. Dee L. McCroskey, ed., Last Day Messenger.

11. Charles H. Welch, "The Dispensational Frontier: Acts 28:23-31," The Classics Expositor (Oklahoma City, Okla.), vol. 1, no. 2 (February–March 1968), pp. 4-22.

12. Another agency active in this field is the Philadelphia Bible Testimony, 1403 Alcott Street, Philadelphia, Pennsylvania, which takes a strong stand for the deity of Christ.

13. In 1955 Truth for Today co-sponsored a 10,000-mile speaking tour of the United States by Welch.

14. Oscar M. Baker, Dispensational Outline of the Books of the New Testament (Warsaw, Ind.: Truth for Today, n.d.) (4-page pamphlet), pp. [3]-[4].

15. Letters from Mr. Oscar M. Baker, Truth for Today, Incorporated, Route 2, Warsaw, Indiana.

16. Ibid.

17. Letter from the Reverend Russell H. Schaefer, director, Ewalt Memorial Bible School. The school's journal is Scripture Research.

18. Letter from the Reverend C. E. McLain, minister, Northside Bible Church, 100th Street at North McKinley, Oklahoma City, Oklahoma. On the board of the Classics Publishing Trust is Mr. Jack White, a Houston (Texas) businessman, who ministers to a con-

gregation in Pasadena, Texas, which rejects both water baptism and the Lord's Supper, along with tithing, as legalistic. He also provides a number of ministers with printed sermon outlines. (Letter from Mr. Jack White, 2400 West Loop, Houston, Texas).

19. Adolph Ernst Knoch, "A.E.K.'s Brethren Background as Told in His Own Words," *Unsearchable Riches,* vol. 56, no. 3 (May 1965), p. 36. The entire 48-page issue is a memorial to Knoch.

20. *The Story of the Concordant Version* (rev. edn.; Saugus, Calif.; Concordant Publishing Concern, 1967) (24-page pamphlet). Of the Old Testament only Genesis and Isaiah had been published by mid-1967; Daniel was soon to follow. As Knoch gives them, the divine names in the Old Testament are Al, Alue, and Alueim (for "God") and Ieue (for "Yahweh").

21. Adolph Ernst Knoch, *The Divine Calendar* (Saugus, Calif.: Concordant Publishing Concern, n.d.) (32-page pamphlet). The original edition came out in 1913.

22. Adolph Ernst Knoch, *The Sacred Scrolls of the Scriptures* (rev. edn.; Saugus, Calif.: Concordant Publishing Concern, 1955) (96-page brochure), pp. 94-96.

23. A[dolph] E[rnst] K[noch], "Christ Compared with Deity," *Unsearchable Riches,* vol. 22 [1931], pp. 200-214.

24. Letter from Ernst O. Knoch, executive editor, Concordant Publishing Concern. Among these congregations is Grace Fellowship, which conducts services in the Odd Fellows Hall in downtown Los Angeles and of which the Reverend Frank Neil Pohorlak and the Reverend Joseph E. Kirk are pastors.

25. Letters from the Reverend R. B. Shiflet, pastor, Eleventh Avenue Church, P. O. Box 473, Mineral Wells, Texas, and editor, *The Timely Messenger.* Beside the College Avenue Community Church, Fort Worth, and the Eleventh Avenue Church, Mineral Wells, the other five churches are the Liberty Heights Chapel, Lawton, Oklahoma; Peace Congregational Church, Indiahoma, Oklahoma; the Denton Bible Chapel, Denton, Texas; and the Johnson Station Church and the Arlington Community Church at Arlington, Texas.

26. *Berean Mission, Incorporated—Here We Stand* (8-page undated folder);

[*Questions*] *You Are Asking About Berean Mission, Incorporated* (8-page undated folder); *Our Doctrinal Platform* (4-page undated pamphlet).

27. Letters from the Reverend C. Reuben Lindquist, president, Berean Mission, Incorporated; *Berean Mission in Navajoland* (undated 8-page folder); *Navajoland, U.S.A.* (6-page undated folder).

28. Cunningham Boyle, *A Key to the Bible, or, the Book of Truth* (N.p.: N.p., n.d.), pp. 73-74. The first angel, says the True Light Church of Christ, was Martin Luther, but "not even Luther was made perfect, whom God had chosen to lead his people, for we find his wavering to the last, and partly acknowledging the Catholic church, which he could not have done had he possessed the full knowledge, for as a body they possess no part of the Christian church, but is the mother of all the corruption that now infects the earth" (ibid., pp. 67, 71-72). The second angel was Connecticut-born Theophilus Ransom Gates (1787–1846), a wandering lay preacher who went along the Middle Atlantic seaboard teaching that all these so-called churches were wrong, that they were but men-made systems, and were doomed to eternal destruction" (ibid., pp. 72-73). Roman Catholicism is the harlot of Revelation 17. It is also the dragon of Revelation 12; its seven heads are its seven sacraments (ibid., p. 66). It embraces traditionalism, mysticism, and natural rationalism (ibid., p. 62). The beast of Revelation 13 is the doctrine of natural rationalism; its ten horns are the movements established by natural reason through the Reformation—Episcopalianism, Presbyterianism, Baptism, Lutheranism, Unitarianism, Quakerism, Universalism, Spiritualism, Deism, and Arminianism (ibid., p. 68). The number of the beast—666—"is three sixes, which makes eighteen, equivalent to the number of letters it takes to spell 'Episcopal Methodist,' the name this beast or doctrine assumed" (ibid., p. 71).

29. In practice the True Light Church of Christ turns for its doctrine exclusively to the New Testament. The Old Testament in its view is good history, but since it has been fulfilled it does not require particular attention.

30. The True Light Church of Christ holds that the Son existed in the Father in

an embryonic state until the creation, when the Father separated the Son from himself; that he retained his perfect equality with God until his conception; that his judgment was then taken away until he was born and was not wholly restored until he passed through probation; and that he will retain it until the judgment (*Articles of Faith of the True Light Church of Christ* [Charlotte, N.C.: The True Light of Christ, 1965 (a reprint of the 1927 edition) (7-page pamphlet), p. (3)].

31. All human beings have inherited the sin of Adam and as a result do wrong naturally. Even the life of a believer is a constant struggle against the flesh. Salvation is limited to the "seed" that is saved from the fall of Babylon and from death and from the fires of hell; this "seed" the True Light Church of Christ sees limited to its own membership. Unbaptized infants, unconverted people past the age of infancy, and members of other denominations are doomed. The party in the True Light Church of Christ that follows Bishop Herman Flake Braswell states that it has "a knowledge . . . from God" that its six preachers are "the only six true preachers of the Gospel at the present time; all the rest are Anti-Christ or false teachers . . . making merchandise of the souls of men . . . teaching the doctrines of men or the devil, claiming it to be the doctrine of Jesus Christ for filthy lucre (money)" (letter of August 10, 1970).

32. Grape juice is used in place of fermented wine. Each communicant drinks from the same glass. The Lord's Supper is usually observed on Easter Sunday, but may be observed more often when circumstances warrant.

33. *Articles of Faith*, pp. 1-7. From A.D. 270 until 1870, when Boyle became the head bishop of the True Light Church of Christ, the visible body of Christ on earth remained destroyed, and the "spiritual church" was in a state of partial blindness, "worshiping the Lord in spirit and in truth, [but] not existing as an organized body" (open letter of the True Light Church of Christ, dated March 10, 1970 [3-page typescript]). During these 1,600 years only 144,000 were saved (ibid.; see Boyle, p. 71). On the 6,000-year

span, see Theophilus Ransom Gates, *Truth Advocated, or, the Apocalyptic Beast and Mystic Babylon,* in Gates, *The Trials, Experiences, Exercises of Mind, and First Travels of Theophilus R. Gates, Written by Himself* (Charlotte, N.C.: Washburn Printing Company, 1949), pp. 149-150.

34. See Boyle, pp. 89-90.

35. *Belief of the True Light Church of Christ Concerning War* (1 page undated broadside).

36. Letter from Bishop Herman Flake Braswell, Route 3, Monroe, North Carolina, dated June 20, 1970.

37. According to Dot Jackson, "They Expect the World to End This Year," *The Charlotte* [North Carolina] *Observer,* May 24, 1970, section B, pages 1-2, Braswell and many of his supporters had as of that date ceased to work for money anymore on the ground that the end of the world would come before December 31, 1970. In an undated letter to Purser and his supporters Braswell and his supporters stated: "We believe that the church of Christ was set back up in its apostolic purity in the year 1870 A.D. and will continue in that purity until our Lord makes his second advent in the end of this year, 1970 A.D." See also " 'True Light' Sect in Carolinas Bracing for End of the World," *New York Times,* December 20, 1970.

38. Order in the District Court Division of the General Court of Justice, State of North Carolina, County of Mecklenburg, 69-CVD-11258, Herman Flake Braswell and others *vs.* James Rommie Purser and others, February 20, 1970; Preliminary Restraining Order in the same court, 70-CVD-2332, James Rommie Purser and others *vs.* Herman Flake Braswell and others, March 13, 1970.

39. Two other societies, the Mossy Grove Church near Coward, South Carolina, and the Mount Hermon (or Samaria) Church near Leesville, South Carolina, lacking elders for a number of years, have merged with the High Hill Church.

40. Clarence L. Morey, complainant, *A Federal Court Acknowledges Christ's True Church in the District Court of the United States for the Southern District of California, Central Division* (Fort Worth, Texas: The Manney

Company, 1966), p. 56; Maurice M. Johnson, *Spiritual Separation versus Sensual* (1937) (undated [after 1963] 13-page pamphlet), pp. 1-5. The members of these anonymous assemblies reject any suggestion that Maurice M. Johnson is their founder, and profess to see his history as "totally irrelevant" (letter from Brother Jack W. Langford, 500 Norwood Drive, Hurst, Texas, minister of the anonymous assembly in Fort Worth, dated January 12, 1971). Another influential leader has been Brother Wilbur Johnson, Monterey Park, California, the son of Burnell Johnson and the grandson of Lyman H. Johnson. Lyman H. Johnson left the Presbyterian ministry shortly after the War between the States but continued to preach for about fifty years (Morey, p. 115). Burnell Johnson "supported his family by the building business, but he preached all his life" (ibid., p. 236). Toward the end of his life he and Maurice M. Johnson—who is not related to the other Johnsons here named—worked together (ibid., pp. 65-66). The anonymous assemblies here described distributed tracts written by Burnell and Lyman Johnson (ibid.).

41. Ibid., p. 132. See also Maurice M. Johnson, *The Body of Christ versus the Babylon of Christendom* (undated [after 1963] 9-page pamphlet). The present section was originally titled "The Church which is Christ's Body" on the basis of the "Findings of Fact, Conclusions of Law, and Judgment" of the Honorable Alfonso J. Zirpoli in 1962: "Plaintiffs are members of a church that has no distinctive identifying name, *other than the designation accepted by the members thereof as 'the church which is Christ's body'* "

(Morey, p. 331; emphasis added). The anonymous assemblies here described have distributed this volume widely to public libraries throughout the United States with no indication that the members of these assemblies disagreed with Judge Zirpoli's findings of fact. In the "Plaintiffs' Post Trial Brief of Law and Fact," Brother Dalford Todd, 1309 Main Street, Dallas, Texas, the attorney for the plaintiffs and himself a member of the Fort Worth assembly, repeatedly used the Latin *corpus Christi* ("Christ's body") (ibid., pp. 263-264, 269, 276). Brother Langford in the cited letter proposed that the present section be retitled "Some members of 'the church which is Christ's body' (Ephesians 1:22, 23) outside all man-made organizations.' "

42. Letter from Brother Todd, dated March 21, 1968.

43. Such as the "artificial Easter season," the use of "Reverend" as a form of address in the case of clergymen, and the distinction between "clergy" and "laity." See the 4-page tract, *Burning Hearts,* first preached as a radio sermon in 1941 by Maurice M. Johnson, and the 2-page undated tract by J[ames] D. C[ox], *Who Is "Reverend"?*

44. Letter from Brother Berl Chisum, Box 42021, Los Angeles, California. Brother Chisum is a "minister of Christ" recognized by the anonymous assemblies here described.

45. Johnson is so recognized (Morey, p. 116).

46. "Elder" and "Deacon" are not used as titles of address.

47. If an assembly calls or appoints a pastor or teacher of its choice, this is seen as frustrating the work of the men that Christ calls.

# BIBLIOGRAPHY

Bass, Clarence B. *Backgrounds to Dispensationalism: Its Historical Genesis and Ecclesiastical Implications.* Grand Rapids, Mich.: Wm. B. Eerdmans Publishing Company, 1960.

Boyle, Cunningham. *A Key to the Bible, or, the Book of Truth.* N.p.: N.p., n.d. This 91-page 1963 reprint notes that a copyright had been applied for, presumably by the author, but the title is not listed in the printed catalogue of the Library of Congress. The oldest edition the present writer has been able to trace was printed in 1932 by Knight Brothers, Sumter, South Carolina.

Cox, William E. *An Examination of Dispensationalism.* Philadelphia: Presbyterian and Reformed Publishing Company, 1963.

Ehlert, Arnold D. *A Bibliographic History of Dispensationalism.* Grand Rapids, Mich.: Baker Book House, 1965.

Gates, Theophilus Ransom. *The Trials, Experience, Exercises of Mind, and First Travels of Theophilus R. Gates, Written by Himself.* Charlotte, N.C.: Washburn Printing Company, 1949. This is an unaltered reissue of the second edition, printed for the author in 1818 by David Dickinson, Philadelphia. The 1949 reprint also contains Gates's *Truth Advocated, or, the Apocalyptic Beast and Mystic Babylon Clearly Delineated for the Serious Consideration of Christians Universally and Unbelievers of Every Description,* first published at Poughkeepsie, New York, by C. C. Adams in 1812, as printed by David Dickinson in Philadelphia in 1818, to which Gates appended *Observations on the Signs of the Times, or, Things as They Are Now in the World and as They Will Be Hereafter, Briefly Considered.* Also included are reissues of the second edition (1818) of Gates's *A Sincere Inquiry Concerning the Good, Acceptable, and Perfect Will of God, Addressed to All Such as Love the Lord Jesus Christ and Would Wish to Be Found of Him in Peace, Without Spot and Blameless* (1st edn., 1813); of the expanded second edition (1818) of his *Remarks on the Goodness and Severity of God*; of the expanded second edition (1818) of his *A View of the Last Dispensation of Light That Will Be in the World, Taking into Consideration Its Certainy, Its Effects upon Mankind, and the Time When the Light Will Be Dispensed* (1st edn., 1814); and of three of his shorter pamphlets.

Ryrie, Charles Caldwell. *Dispensationalism Today.* Chicago: Moody Press, 1965.

Scofield, Cyrus Ingerson. ed. *The New Scofield Reference Bible.* New edition by E. Schuyler English and others. New York: Oxford University Press, 1967.

# 6. Fundamental Churches

There are a number of church bodies in the United States and Canada that share as one of their most prominent features a conservative emphasis upon what came to be called "the fundamentals" during the first two decades of the twentieth century.

Some of them are associated with cooperative agencies like the National Association of Evangelicals and the American Council of Christian Churches. Others are strenuously independent.

### Bible Fellowship Church

In 1947 the Mennonite Brethren in Christ Church resolved to change its name to the United Missionary Church. But the Pennsylvania Conference, all the churches of which had grown out of the congregations which Elder William Gehman (1827–1918) began at Zionsville, Pennsylvania, in 1857,[1] elected to retain the old name. In 1952 the Pennsylvania Conference severed its connection with the United Missionary Church and in 1959, since it no longer held to Mennonite distinctives, took the name Bible Fellowship Church.

It combines a conservative Calvinism in theology with an emphasis on evangelism and missions. The twenty-seven Articles of Faith discuss the infallibility and divine inspiration of the Bible; the Trinity; the Father; the Son; the Holy Spirit; creation; Satan; man ("the guilt and consequence of Adam's sin are imputed to the whole human race so that all men are guilty, inherently corrupt, totally depraved, and subjects of the wrath of God"); sin ("the cause of the curse and defilement of the created universe"); free agency ("by the fall of Adam man forfeited his freedom of the will"); election ("those so chosen [God] redeemed by His Son and seals by His Spirit"); regeneration; sanctification ("a progressive work of the Holy Spirit"); perseverance of the saints ("they shall never totally or finally fall away"); the church ("all those redeemed by [Christ's] blood and born of His Spirit are members of [Christ's] body and are in mystical union and communion with Christ and fellow believers"); baptism by immersion of the believer ("it has no saving or cleansing power")[2] and the Lord's supper;[3] the Lord's day ("to be observed by all believers, voluntarily and in love, as a continuation of the sabbath principle. . . . Christians ought to engage only in duties of necessity and mercy"); divine healing ("healing whether by natural, medical or supernatural means must come from the omnipotent God"); civil government; resurrection; the second coming of Christ ("the resurrection of the righteous dead, the rapture of the saints, the salvation of Israel, the great tribulation, . . . the millennial reign, . . . the resurrection and judgment of the unrighteous"); the judgments; the millennium; and the eternal state.[4]

The annual conference transacts the business of the Bible Fellowship Church. The adjourned session of the annual conference elects a superintendent and the director of church extension. There are 45 churches in eastern Pennsylvania, New Jersey, and New York, with a total membership of 4,511. The Bible Fellowship Church carries on its foreign mission work through 16 conservative independent and interdenominational faith mission boards. About 50 adult members of the Bible Fellowship Church engage in foreign mission operations in Africa, India, Japan, Latin America, Thailand, New Guinea, Europe, and the French West Indies. The headquarters are at 2340 Union Street, Allentown, Pennsylvania 18104. Recent efforts to communicate with the church body have been unsuccessful.

## Social Brethren

The Social Brethren emerged as an organized movement in Saline County, Illinois, in 1867, in large part as a result of the War between the States. The founders, Frank Wright and Hiram T. Brannon among them, came from a variety of denominational backgrounds, chiefly Methodist and Presbyterian. They confessed that they "disagreed with their former brethren on certain points of Scriptures and rules of decorum,"[5] but a major concern was the bridging of the divisions in the American churches over the issue of slavery. The organizers of the Social Brethren regarded it as right and biblical to have fellowship with all churches that believed in the death, burial, and resurrection of Jesus Christ, regardless of their position on the slavery issue.

A ten-section Confession of Faith affirms the Trinity; the sufficiency of the canonical books of Holy Scripture as containing all things necessary to salvation; the agreement of the Old and New Testaments in offering everlasting life to humankind by the one mediator Jesus Christ; the visible church as a congregation of faithful men and women who have been changed from nature to grace and who have fully consecrated themselves to the service of God, among whom the pure word of God is preached and the sacraments duly administered; redemption, regeneration, sanctification, and salvation by the life, suffering, death, burial, resurrection, ascension and intercession of

Christ, but with the possibility of apostasy; the ordinances of Christ, that is, believer's baptism by sprinkling, pouring, or immersion and the Lord's Supper to be administered to all true believers; the rightfulness of giving suffrage and free speech to lay people and of receiving members into the church immediately in full connection; and the impropriety of political preaching or the proclamation of anything outside the Gospel.[6]

The Social Brethren have exhorters, licensed preachers, and ordained ministers. Each of three associations and the General Assembly meet annually. There are 34 churches in Illinois, Indiana, and Michigan with a total of 1,722 members. There are no central headquarters. The moderator resides at 54 Hudson Avenue, Pontiac, Michigan 48058.

## American Messianic Fellowship

William E. Blackstone founded the Chicago Hebrew Mission in 1887. In 1953 it took its present name. It is a faith mission designed to provide an interdenominational conservative and evangelical Christian testimony to Jews by means of visitation in Jewish neighborhoods, publications, radio, and evangelization and training institutes. Its headquarters are at 7448 North Damen Avenue, Chicago 60645. There are branches in Milwaukee, Minneapolis, Rock Island–Moline–Davenport, Miami, and Atlanta. Membership statistics are not available. It also operates a mission in Israel.

## The Christian Catholic Church

Edinburgh-born John Alexander Dowie (1847–1907) emigrated to Australia as a young man. He returned to his native Scotland for two years of preparatory study and in 1870 he entered the ministry of the Congregational Union in Australia. His criticism of the practice of pew rental and of the election of liquor manufacturers to positions of denominational leadership led to his withdrawal from the Congregational Church eight years later. During the independent ministry that followed he began to emphasize divine healing and established the International Divine Healing Association with headquarters in a tabernacle that he built in Melbourne. He came to the United States in 1888 and engaged in an itinerant ministry as a divine healer. The healing services that he conducted in his tabernacle near the 63d Street entrance to the World's Columbian Exposition at Chicago in 1893 attracted national attention.[7]

Dowie organized the Christian Catholic Church in Chicago in 1896 with 500 charter members, and in 1901—calling himself Elijah III and Elijah the Restorer—he founded the City of Zion half-way between Chicago and Milwaukee on the shores of Lake Michigan. Here he established a theocratic self-contained community with himself as "First Apostle"[8] and general overseer. Eloquent, colorful, and dynamic, he attacked unjust capitalists, greedy labor leaders, alcoholic beverages, tobacco, the medical profession, secret societies, the press, segregation and racial inequality, and the doctrine of eternal punishment, which he regarded as unworthy of a God of love. During his absences on a series of missionary tours in New York, London, and Mexico from 1903 to 1905 internal dissension racked the colony and led to Dowie's deposition. Under Wilbur Glenn Voliva (1870–1942), who succeeded Dowie in 1906, Michael Jonas Mintern, and Carl Q. Lee, the Christian Catholic Church established a strong foreign missionary program and underwent structural and doctrinal changes that have made it more completely "an evangelical Protestant fellowship."

Its affirmation of faith asserts that God created and sustains the world and that within the purpose of perfecting a universal fellowship of love God created human beings in His own image to live their lives in trust in God and in unselfish service to fellow human beings; that men have turned from God to "seek their own" and to succumb to pride, immorality, and injustice; that God has come to mankind in Christ, who identified himself with the need of human beings, died on the cross to save them from sin, rose in triumph, ascended to Lordship, and will come again to reveal openly the victory that he has won; that this good news impels people to respond in repentance and faith, by which they are born into a new relationship with God as members of his church and are constrained to loving service of their fellow human beings by the Holy Spirit that abides in them; that Christians are bound to the divinely inspired witness of prophet and apostle in the Bible, the norm of faith and life; that Christians proclaim the love of God not only through teaching and preaching but also through God's sacraments, the rite of triune immersion in the name of the Father, Son, and Holy Spirit and through the rite of the Lord's Supper; that in the observance of these ordinances the inward reality is more significant than the outward form; that God's healing grace provides infinite resources in Christ to restore broken minds and heal sick bodies; that Christians are bound to be interested in the advancement of human knowledge, the enrichment of human culture, and the achievement of justice and reconciliation under God in family life, social and economic relationships, national and international concerns, and in all affairs of men; that the church must take the Gospel everywhere; that the destiny of each person and the outcome of human history is in the hands of God the Judge and Redeemer; and that the expectation of Christians looks forward to Christ's coming, his Kingdom, and the life of eternal fellowship with God and his people.[9]

The basis of fellowship recognizes the infallible inspiration and sufficiency of the Bible as the rule of faith and practice; requires as conditions of church membership repentance for past sins and trust in Christ for salvation, the ability to make a good profession, and the possession of "the witness, in a measure, of the Holy Spirit"; and describes "all other questions of every kind" as matters of opinion that are not essential to church unity.[10]

The headquarters are on Dowie Memorial Drive, Zion, Illinois 60099. The convocation meets annually. The senior officer is the general overseer. There are six centers in Illinois, Indiana, and Arizona, with a total active membership of 2,000.[11] The church conducts foreign operations in Australia, Guyana, Jamaica, England, Jordan, India, the Philippines Republic, and South Africa.

### Christian Fellowship (People on "The Way," Disciples of Jesus, Friends, "Two-By-Twos")[12]

In 1886 Mr. John George Govan (1861–1927) of Edinburgh, Scotland, founded the Faith Mission for the evangelization of spiritually neglected rural and out-of-the way Scottish communities. The workers of the Faith Mission—known as "pilgrims"—went about in pairs, trusting in God for the supply of their needs. Initially the "pilgrims" were all male, but in 1885 the Faith Mission sent out the first pair of young women "pilgrims." In 1892 the Faith Mission extended its work to Ireland. William Irvine, a Scotsman, became a member of the Faith Mission in 1895. After a short period of service in Scotland, he went to work in Ireland. One of his most successful missions was at Nenagh, County Tipperary. Around 1897 he began to feel that the renunciation made by the Faith Mission "pilgrims" was not radical enough. He declared his independence of the Faith Mission and together with a nucleus of his converts he began to branch out on his own. In 1900 the Faith Mission publicly disavowed the independents and in the following year it announced the formal dropping of Irvine's name from the roster of its "pilgrims."[13]

About this time Edward Cooney gave up his secular work and associated himself with Irvine as a "tramp-preacher."[14] Cooney's strong personality and his flaming zeal soon won him a place of leadership in the movement, but differences between him and Irvine led to Cooney's early withdrawal.[15]

Missionaries of the new movement soon began to go into other English-speaking lands, including the United States (1903) and Canada (1904).[16] The first annual "conventions" (see below) in North America were held in 1906. In 1911/1912 two missionaries reportedly from America, Scots-born James Jardine and German-born Otto Schmid, established their first group in Germany at Lustnau-bei-Tübingen in Württemberg. Subsequently the movement has extended its outreach into other countries.

The fellowship regards as superfluous many features that other religious movements have found inescapable and even useful. It sees no need for an identifying name other than Christian, nor has it found legal incorporation necessary. Because the earliest Christians met in homes, it acquires no church property or real estate by purchase or in any other way. It issues no membership certificates or ministerial credentials. Most distinctive of all is its refusal to publish tracts, books of devotion, or other religious literature. It acknowledges the Bible (usually but not exclusively in the King James Version in English-speaking countries) as its only textbook, and the study and application of the Bible receives prominent emphasis in its program. To be effective, the movement holds, the communication of spiritual life must take place through the oral witness of person to person and cannot take place through printed matter or through mass-communications media like radio. It obtains its King James Version Bibles and its hymnals[17] from R. L. Allan and Son, Glasgow. It also rejects catechetical indoctrination and agencies of Christian education like the Sunday school, although it stresses Bible-centered home training, family life, and child discipline. It has shown considerable success in holding its young people.[18] In North America the fellowship is racially integrated.

The fellowship sedulously shuns publicity.[19] Members are generally reluctant to provide information about the fellowship that would come under the head of "communicating spiritual life" except to bona-fide seekers after association with the movement. The inquiries of others about the beliefs and the history of the fellowship are likely to be met with the reply, "You'll find it in the Bible."

In general, the theological views of the members of the fellowship conform broadly to most of the convictions and emphases of other unconfessional, evangelistic, biblically oriented, perfectionist movements that originated in the nineteenth century. An examination of the texts in *Hymns Old and New* confirms this impression.

Their views on the Trinity are those commonly held by conservative Christian groups. So are their positions on the deity and humanity of Christ and on the atonement through his death on the cross, published statements to the contrary notwithstanding.

Rebirth is seen as the indispensable condition of salvation. The new birth is the result of faith in the Word of God as proclaimed by a "servant" (short for "servant of God," the technical designation for a preacher in the fellowship). There is a strong stress both on God's grace and on holiness as the necessary and deliberate choice of Christ's followers.

In its teaching on the last things the movement is premillennial.

There is a strong in-group feeling in the fellowship and mutual aid, even to the point of sharing possessions in time of need, plays an important part. They profess no desire "to denounce and pull down others," but only "to uphold that which [they] believe in Christ." At the same time they relate the apostolic questions—"How are men to call upon him in whom they have not believed? And how are they to believe in him of whom they have never heard? And how are they to hear without a preacher? And how can men preach unless they be sent?"[20]—wholly to the activity of the preachers of their fellowship. Their teaching about the church tends to be exclusive and often they appear reluctant to concede that the Holy Spirit works through other Christian communities. At the same time, they declare that God is the judge of his people, not they. His Word, they hold, is both the basis of his judgment and the basis of their understanding of his will for their life here and now.

The fellowship rejects infant baptism and practices only believer's baptism by immersion in the name of the Father and of the Son and of the Holy Ghost. Converts who have been baptized in another Christian community are normally rebaptized.

The Lord's Supper ("breaking of bread") is observed every Sunday. Bread and unfermented wine in a common cup are used and only believers may take part. The service is understood as a memorial meal at which the communicants are to reflect on what Christ has done for them and what they owe him.

The individual's conscience determines for him if he may participate in war and military service. In practice most members of the fellowship accept noncombatant service.

As part of their rejection of "worldliness," the members of the fellowship wear no jewelry (except that a married person wears a wedding ring, as a witness to the sacredness of marriage). The women wear simple, modest dresses, use no makeup, and do not cut their hair. Possession of television sets is generally discountenanced.[21]

The movement commends the ideal of poverty on the basis of Luke 9:1-5; 10:1-9; and Matthew 10:5-42. While the ordinary members are free to pursue their respective secular callings, the preachers (who must have proved their ability to earn a living in an honorable occupation) are expected to devote their whole time and ability to the ministry, to take Christ's counsel of poverty literally, and to give up all their possessions and property.

From the beginning of the movement, the preachers—or "gospel workers"—have gone about in pairs,[22] two men or two women, persuaded that they are successors of the apostles and bearers of apostolic authority. They are normally unmarried and depend for their maintenance, housing, food, and other logistical support (including telephone and transportation) upon the members of the fellowship. The movement's stress on the command of Matthew 10:7, "As ye go, preach" (KJV), is the basis for "Go-Preachers" as an outsiders' designation for the movement's missionaries. In the rare cases where a minister subsequently marries, he normally renounces his ministry.

Their normal procedure in former years, still followed in rural areas, is for a pair of preachers to go into a community, enter the home of someone "worthy," and state that they have come to preach the Gospel the authentic "Jesus way." Public school buildings were at least at one time favored places for conducting meetings. In beginning work in a new urban area, a team of workers will enter a neighborhood and live among the residents for a few weeks while they conduct evangelistic meetings in a rented hall or vacant store until a nucleus of adherents has been won. Since the servants literally "live the life" that Christ commanded, going out two by two with nothing in their hands or pockets, their unqualified commitment tends to provide moral support for their authority.

The discipline within the fellowship appears to be very strict, and the servants enjoy great prestige and authority.

Communication within the fellowship is very good and makes extensive use of personal contacts and mail.

The membership is no longer as predominantly rural and small-town as it was originally or even as recently as a generation ago, and the fellowship is represented in all major cities.[23]

The preacher-missionaries are known as "brother-workers" and "sister-workers" as well as "servants of God." Newly appointed ministers are initially assigned to assist an experienced minister in evangelistic work and in ministering to assemblies of members. The supervision of a "field"—generally a state or province—is in the hands of an "overseer" ("senior servant" or "elder brother").

Each house-church is presided over by a "local elder" or "bishop." (The average membership of such a church is about twelve; some churches are smaller, and a few have as many as twenty or, occasionally even, more members.) Wherever possible, it is in the elder's home[24] that the members of the house-church meet on Sunday for the Lord's Supper ("breaking of bread"), exhortation, testimonies, and prayers. During the week they normally meet once or twice for Bible study and prayer. All members are expected to be present at these services, unless prevented by severe illness. Men and women alike may address the assembly on Bible passages of their own choice, and their understanding and interpretation of the passage is received respectfully. When servants conduct evangelistic meetings in a community, the members of all the house-churches of the area are expected to be present. These "gospel services" are usually held in a rented hall, a store, or a school building. One observer notes that, while the services appear bland, in his experience the congregations assemble with eager and quiet expectancy a full quarter of an hour before the scheduled time that the meeting is to begin.

The churches administered by a team of preachers form a "field." Members of a number of "fields" meet at an "annual Christian convention" or camp meeting. The usual site for such a convention—which lasts from three to four days—is a large farm, with tents pitched for the meeting, for meals, and for sleeping. This is the high point of the year's activities for the participants. Observers report that attendance at these conventions ranges from an estimated 500 to an estimated 2,000 and involves, in the words of a senior servant, "practically 100% of the members." At these conventions all matters pertaining to methods of work, doctrine, discipline of members, local elders, the ministry, and similar issues, are fully considered and settled. The "overseer" arranges definite fields of labor for all ministers within the area.

A state or province is the normal unit of supervision. There are house-churches of the fellowship in all fifty states and throughout Canada.[25] The number of conventions in a state or province varies with the number of members that the fellowship has. The "overseers" in North America, acting in fellowship with one another, exercise general supervision over the ministers and the membership on this continent. Since the fellowship keeps no membership records, the total number of active members is not determinable; conservative estimates place the movement's North American membership at between 15,000 and 30,000.[26]

### The Association of Evangelicals for Italian Mission
### (Continuing the Italian Baptist Association of America)

The Reverend Angelo di Domenica and five other pioneer Italian-American Baptist ministers organized the Italian Baptist Missionary Association at Mount Vernon, New York, in 1898.[27] It subsequently changed its name to the Italian Baptist Association of America. By the 1960s many of its ministers and many of its members were no longer of Italian descent and in May 1968 the organization changed its name to the Association of Evangelicals for Italian Mission. The change was to show that the association's doors were open to all evangelical Christians interested in the conversion of Italians, without distinction of denomination or national origin. In this way the association hoped to suggest that, although it had dropped Baptist from its name, it is "still Baptist, but . . . also Presbyterian and Methodist and Brethren and Pentecostal" and so on. "The tremendous power and influence of the Roman Catholic Church" is seen as one reason for an outreach particularly to Italians.[28]

In addition to its missionary efforts among Italians in North America and abroad, the association proposes "to be vigilant in the preservation of the great principle of separation of church and state and to make recommendations in those public questions relating to the welfare of our country and churches, especially those dealing with discrimination and religious freedom."[29]

The headquarters of the association are at 314 Richfield Road, Upper Darby, Pennsylvania 19082. No information is available about the number of churches that belong to the association, their denominational affiliation, or their total active membership.

### Hoomana Naauoa O Hawaii (The Enlightened Worship of Hawaii)

The Reverend J. H. Poliwailehua organized an independent church in Kohala, Hawaii, in 1853. Forty years later members of this congregation came to the island of Oahu and organized a church under the name of Hoomana Naauoa O Hawaii. Their pastor was the Reverend John Kekipi Maia. In 1897 they built a church at 910 Cooke Street, Honolulu. As the denomination expanded, the name of the Honolulu church attached itself to the whole church body. In addition to two churches in Honolulu, it has three branches on the island of Hawaii, one on Molokai, and one on Lanai. The total membership is estimated at 300. It has a tradition of strong family ties in its leadership; formerly Hawaiian was used exclusively at worship, but some English is now used in most services. Its beliefs and practices are basically those of a conservative Congregational church of the mid-nineteenth century.[30]

### Ka Makua Mau Loa (The Church of the Living God)

In 1896 Mrs. Rebekah Wise, née Nawaa, led a group of members of Hoomana Naauoa O Hawaii out of the church body and established an independent movement under the same name. In 1910 the parent body won a suit enjoining the rival group from using its name. Thereupon the latter took the name Ka Makua Mau Loa (The Church of the Living God). In the course of time it has spread to nine of the Hawaiian Islands.

Ka Makua Mau Loa accepts the teachings of the Old and New Testaments. Its faith is trinitarian and its beliefs stress healing, fasting, and the obligation of personal assistance to people who are in need of spiritual and material help. Its ministers serve without compensation. The Hawaiian language is to be used perpetually in its work.

The pastor of the mother church on Mokuea Street, Honolulu, is head of the entire body. There have been only three chief pastors since 1896: the Reverend John J. Mathews, whom the foundress nominated to rule in her place because she did not believe that a woman should be a minister and who served from 1896 to 1914; the Reverend John Wise, son of the foundress, from 1914 to 1932; and his daughter, the Reverend Ella Wise Harrison, since 1934. There are 10 churches with a total membership estimated at 3,480.[31] Ka Makua Mau Loa also maintains friendly contact with the independent Hawaiian congregation on Niihau which perpetuates the missionary efforts of Samuel Whitney.[32] The headquarters are at 1629 Bernice Street, Honolulu, Hawaii 96817.

### Ka Hale Hoano Hou O Ke Akua
### (The Hallowed House of God, the King of Kings and Lord of Lords)

Some of the members of Ka Makua Mau Loa on the island of Molokai withdrew in 1948 under the leadership of Lieutenant Commander W. H. Abbey and the Reverend Edward Ayau and established a new church, Ka Hale Hoano Hou O Ke Akua, in Kalihi Valley. It has since expanded to a total of six branches (the mother church at 45-252 Lilpuua Road, Honolulu; three on Molokai, where it is carrying on its most extensive work; one on Maui; and two on Hawaii). It describes itself as "Trinitarian independent

Protestant" and administers baptism in the name of the Father and Son and Holy Spirit. The Reverend Mr. Ayau is now the bishop of the church body. The total active membership is estimated at less than 500. Services are normally conducted in Hawaiian.[33]

## Associated Gospel Churches of Canada

In the course of the Fundamentalist-Modernist controversy of the early decades of the twentieth century, many individuals and in some cases whole congregations withdrew from their denominational affiliations and organized as independent churches: As these churches were becoming increasingly— even though slowly—aware of one another's existence, four congregations in Ontario, under the leadership of Dr. P. W. Philpott of Hamilton and Mr. H. E. Irwin, a Toronto lawyer, banded together in 1922, under a charter that Dr. Philpott had secured some years before, as the Christian Workers' Church of Canada. To avoid confusion with other religious groups with similar names, the growing church body took the name Associated Gospel Churches of Canada in 1925.[34]

Theologically, the Associated Gospel Churches of Canada are funda-mental, premillennial, and dispensational. The Articles of Faith and Doctrine —which each minister and congregation must reaffirm annually—commit the denomination to the divine authority and plenary inspiration of the whole canonical Scriptures; the Trinity; the fall of man; the total depravity of human beings; the necessity of regeneration by the Holy Spirit before a person can enter the Kingdom of God; Christ's substitutionary atonement; salvation by grace through faith; the assurance of the present salvation and eternal safety of all those who are actually born again; Christ's deity and virgin birth; the unity of the true church in the mystical body of Christ; the personality and deity of the Holy Spirit and his continuing present mission to the church; a distinction between the indwelling of the Spirit in all be-lievers and being filled with the Spirit, which is the believer's privilege and duty; sanctification as perfected by the one offering of Christ's blood and progressive through the constant washing of water by the Word, by Christ's blood, and by the Spirit's presence and power; Christ's premillennial return; his own resurrection, the resurrection of the believers at his return, and the resurrection of the unbelievers at the end of the millennium; the eternal blessedness of the saved and eternal punishment of the lost; the personality of Satan; Christ's death for sin but not for the effects of sin, so that divine healing is not in the atonement as salvation and the forgiveness of sins are in the atonement; believer's baptism by immersion; and the Lord's Supper as a memorial of Christ's death. A service of public dedication of infants is available to Christian parents.[35]

The supreme governing body of the Associated Gospel Churches of Canada is the Conference, which normally meets once a year. Between sessions an Executive Council transacts the denomination's business. The individual congregations are autonomous.

The headquarters are at 280 Plains Road West, Burlington, Ontario L7T 1G4. There are 105 churches in 7 provinces from coast to coast. The total inclusive membership is 12,500. Missionaries ordained by the Associated Gospel Churches of Canada work in Africa, India, Indonesia, the Philippines Republic, Latin America, the West Indies, and Europe. The denomination itself carries on no foreign missions, but the member congregations are free to formulate their own missionary programs and to support evangelical missions, faith missions, and individual missionaries as each church may choose.

### United Christian Church, Incorporated
### (The United Christian Church of America)

The oldest congregation of record in what has become the United Christian Church was incorporated in Baltimore, Maryland, in 1893. By 1925 the church body that grew out of this congregation had expanded into Pennsylvania and New York. It was incorporated under its present name in 1938 and, after an era of expansion during the World War II years, the General Conference adopted new Articles of Association in 1945. It belongs to the American Council of Christian Churches.

The United Christian Church's "statement of fundamental scriptural truth" affirms the church body's belief in the verbal inspiration of the Bible; the Trinity; the deity of Christ and of the Holy Spirit; the total depravity of all human beings; the atonement by Christ's blood; the salvation of sinners by grace through faith; the resurrection of the body; everlasting life for believers; the endless punishment of the lost; the reality and personality of Satan; and Christ's premillennial coming. The church body's "elaborated statement of fundamental truth" develops the articles on the inspiration of the Bible; the one true God; the fall and redemption of human beings; the salvation of human beings; believer's baptism;[36] the Lord's Supper as a memorial feast; and the church as Christ's body, of which each Spirit-born believer is an integral part. The official English translation of the Bible for local churches is the King James Version.[37]

The polity of the United Christian Church is episcopal. The ministry consists of the bishop (who holds office for life), elders, deacons, and licentiates. The Conference, of which only the ministers are members, meets annually. Local churches may call their own pastors, provided that the candidates are in good standing in the Conference of the United Christian Church, and transact all other business pertaining to their existence as local units, but the Conference has the right to approve or disapprove matters pertaining to conduct and doctrine. The work of the United Christian Church is carried on through free-will offerings; local churches may not raise funds by means of fairs, festivals, suppers, concerts, and other "mercenary and questionable means."[38]

The headquarters of the United Christian Church, Incorporated, are at 117 Rose Lane, New Hyde Park, New York 11040. No information is available on the number of churches or the active membership.[39]

## Fundamental Evangelistic Association, Incorporated

Marion H. Reynolds, Sr., organized the Fundamental Evangelistic Association, Incorporated in 1927. It shares the fifteen-article Statement of Doctrine of Grace Fundamental Church, 205 North Union Avenue, Los Angles.[40] This affirms the verbal inspiration of the Scriptures, Christ's deity and virgin birth, the indwelling of the Holy Spirit in all regenerated people, the church as the sum of "all those who in the present dispensation truly believe and accept Jesus Christ as Lord and Savior," the Trinity, the Holy Spirit as "the infallible Interpreter of the infallible Scriptures," Christ's substitutionary atonement and resurrection, justification "on the single ground of faith in the shed blood" of Christ, the eternal security of all believers, Christ's kingship and his premillennial and imminent return, separation from the world, evangelism, the personality of Satan, the universality of sin, heaven and hell as places, and the need for maintaining good works.[41] The association operates a Bible school, Fundamental Bible Institute, for the training of pastors, missionaries, and Christian workers. It strongly opposes the National Council of the Churches of Christ in the U.S.A. and the World Council of Churches and is a member of the American Council of Christian Churches[42] and the International Council of Christian Churches.

The association claims that over fifty independent Fundamental churches have been organized under its leadership.[43] No information is available about the number of churches (other than Grace Church) currently connected with the association or the size of the association's membership.[44] The association's Fundamental World Wide Mission raises and transmits funds for missionary work.

## Independent Fundamental Churches of America

In the late 1920s the American Conference of Undenominational Churches came into being in the Middle West. Early in 1930 several independent "fundamental" leaders joined the organization. In June of that year it held its convention at the Cicero Bible Church, adopted a new constitution and doctrinal statement, elected a new panel of officers, and took the name Independent Fundamental Churches of America. Under the slogan "independent but not isolated," it affirms its stand "for the full authority of the Bible, purity of doctrine, Biblical separation both ecclesiastically and individually, and the freedom under God of the local church and of the individual minister."[45]

The organization declares that knowledge, belief, and acceptance of the sixteen articles in its doctrinal statement are "essential to sound faith and fruitful practice, and therefore requisite for Christian fellowship in the I.F.C.A." These sixteen articles cover the Bible ("the verbally inspired Word of God, the final authority for faith and life, inerrant in the original writings, infallible, and God-breathed"); the Trinity; Christ's deity, virgin birth, "representative, vicarious, substitutionary sacrifice," resurrection, ascension, and exaltation; the person and work of the Holy Spirit; the total depravity of human beings; salvation ("the gift of God brought to man by grace and received by personal faith in the Lord Jesus Christ"); the eternal security and assurance of believers; the two natures of the believer; separation from all religious apostasy, and all worldly and sinful pleasures, practices and associations; missions; the ministry and spiritual gifts ("speaking in tongues and the working of sign miracles gradually ceased as the New Testament Scriptures were completed and their authority became established"); the church ("the body and the espoused bride of Christ is a spiritual organism made up of all born-again persons of this present age"); Dispensationalism ("we believe in the dispensational view of Bible interpretation but reject the extreme teaching known as 'hyperdispensationalism' . . . which opposes either the Lord's table or water baptism as a scriptural means of testimony for the church in this age"); the personality of Satan; the "personal, imminent, pretribulation and premillennial coming" of Christ; and the eternal state.[46]

The Independent Fundamental Churches of America see as their distinctive emphases a regenerated church membership, open Communion, the support of the local church by the free-will offering of saved persons, and the spiritual unity of all believers.[47] The fellowship warns insistently against Roman Catholicism, the organized ecumenical movement, "the prevailing dangers of neo-orthodoxy, the dangerous compromises of the 'New Evangelicalism,' and the deceptive allurements of uniting believers and unbelievers in spiritual efforts."[48]

Organizations and individual ministers and full-time Christian workers must have "separated from all denominational affiliation" before becoming eligible for membership in the organization. Local congregations own their own property, but are "urged to refrain" from calling as pastors or leaders one who is not or will not within a reasonable time become a member of the organization. A thirteen-member Executive Committee transacts the business and conducts the work of the organization between the annual conventions.

The headquarters are at 1860 Mannheim Road, Westchester, Illinois 60153. The fellowship has 614 churches with 87,582 members in the United States.

## Association of Fundamental Ministers and Churches, Incorporated

In 1931 at Kansas City, Missouri, the Reverend Fred Bruffett, his wife, Hallie, the Reverend Paul Bennett, the Reverend George Tasker, and six others organized the Association of Fundamental Ministers and Churches, Incorporated, "for the purpose of preaching and teaching the Gospel of Jesus Christ as set forth in the Old and New Testament Scriptures and [to] promote Christian fellowship and unity in the church."[49] Bruffett, Bennett, and Tasker had all been associated with the Church of God (Anderson, Indiana), to whose fellowship Tasker later returned.

The association defines five fundamentals for which it stands: the Trinity; the divine inspiration of the Bible and its entire sufficiency as the sole creed of the church; "the body of Christ, with Christ as the Head, including in it all Christians, organized into local autonomous churches, administered to by evangelists, pastors, elders, teachers, and deacons, under the supervision of the Holy Spirit"; the new birth as the basis of fellowship and unity; definite experimental knowledge of salvation through Christ's blood; the practice of Christian forbearance in other matters and liberty in all questions of conscience.[50] At least some ministers in the association stress divine healing as included in the atonement and available to individuals through the prayer of faith.[51]

The association meets annually. Four elected officers manage its business affairs. The headquarters are at 8605 East 55th Street, Kansas City, Missouri 64129. The Association directory lists twenty-five state (regional) conventions from coast to coast, with foreign mission stations in Guatemala and Hong Kong.[52] No membership statistics are available; reportedly about 1,200 Christian workers of both sexes belong to the association. In spite of the corporate name, according to the constitution the membership consists only of ordained and unordained ministers and Gospel workers, not of churches. Beyond refusing to issue credentials where this action seems indicated, the association exercises no control over its member workers, the churches to which they minister, its home missionaries, or its foreign missionaries.[53]

## Slavic Gospel Association, Incorporated

In 1920 Peter Deyneka, who had come to the United States from Russia in 1914, was converted in the Moody Church at Chicago, Illinois. After completing Bible school in 1925, he undertook a number of missionary journeys to Byelorussia and to other countries with Russian refugee and immigrant populations.

In 1934 he helped found the Russian Gospel Association. In 1945 it took the present name. In 1952 it absorbed the remnants of the World Christian Fundamentals Association, organized after 1919 and presided over until 1930 by William Bell Riley (1861–1947).

Its unalterable doctrinal statement affirms belief in the verbal inspiration of the original biblical writings; the Trinity; Christ's true deity and humanity; the sinful nature of all human beings, with spiritual death as its consequence; Christ's death as a representative and substitutionary sacrifice; justification on the ground of Christ's blood; Christ's resurrection, ascension, and heavenly life as the high priest and advocate of believers; his imminent, personal, and premillennial return; the rebirth through the Holy Spirit of all who receive Christ by faith; the bodily resurrection of all human beings, the everlasting blessedness of the saved, and the everlasting, conscious punishment of the lost; and the evangelistic duty of Christians.[54]

The international headquarters of the association are at 2434 North Kedzie Boulevard, Chicago, Illinois 60639. The address of the Canadian office is Box 2, Station K, Toronto, Ontario M4P 2G1. In addition to its work in 20 countries of Europe, Latin America, Asia, and Australia, it has 32 churches and missions including 6 in Alaska, 4 in Canada, 10 in Europe, and 12 in South America. The total active membership of these churches and missions is estimated at 3,500, chiefly persons of Russian, Byelorussian, Ukrainian, and Polish extraction, but including Slavic people of all nationalities.[55]

## Berean Fundamental Church Council, Incorporated

The Reverend Ivan E. Olsen completed his studies in the Denver Bible Institute in 1936 and organized an independent congregation in North Platte, Nebraska, that same year. He soon began Bible classes in neighboring communities and they became nuclei for new congregations. In 1947 these congregations formed the Berean Fundamental Church Council, Incorporated.

As a fundamental church the fellowship sees itself committed to "the inerrancy of the Bible not only in faith and morals, but also in reference to such matters as creation, the virgin birth, the literal bodily resurrection, the reality of heaven and hell, and so on." It also sees its position as distinguished both from modernism and from "the extremes of fanaticism."[56] Its objectives are evangelism and instructing its converts in Christian living.

It regards the fact that the fellowship is not aligned with one of the historic denominations as an advantage, in that it is free to secure leaders, teachers, and pastors without denominational restrictions and to support interdenominational missionary societies such as the China Inland, Sudan Interior, Team, and Africa Inland missions. Similarly, it feels no urgency to establish its own educational institutions or publish its own literature; instead, it avails itself of existing fundamental schools and Christian literature agencies. It disavows any connection with the National Council of the Churches of Christ in the United States of America. Its ministers and churches are free, if they wish to do so, to affiliate with organizations like the National Association of Evangelicals and the American Council of Christian Churches.

The headquarters are at North Platte, Nebraska 69101. A delegate assembly meets twice a year, an executive committee monthly. There are

40 churches in Nebraska, Kansas, Colorado, Wyoming, South Dakota, and California, with a total membership of 2,000.

## Central Alaskan Missions, Incorporated

In 1936 Vincent J. Joy (1914–1966), of Methodist background, founded and incorporated Central Alaskan Missions as an independent "faith" mission without denominational affiliation. He began a program of village missions in the Copper Valley of south-central Alaska the following year. Various supporting activities were added subsequently—an itinerant plane ministry that gradually gave way to ground transportation as the road network of the area improved, a medical program that climaxed in the erection of a hospital in 1956, a radio station, and the Alaska Bible College for the training of indigenous Christian leadership.[57]

The doctrinal statement of the Central Alaskan Missions includes belief in the Trinity; Christ's deity, incarnation, vicarious and substitutionary death, resurrection, ascension, and imminent personal and premillennial return; the Holy Spirit and his work; the verbal inspiration of the Bible ("inerrant in the original writings"); the universal sinfulness and guilt of human beings; salvation solely by grace through faith in Christ's blood sacrifice, death, and resurrection; the eternal security and everlasting blessedness of the saved; the personality of Satan; the bodily resurrection of the saved to eternal life and of the lost to everlasting punishment; the Lord's Supper; and the church as exclusively the company of those who have been redeemed, regenerated, and sealed by the Holy Spirit; the church's missionary obligation; and the requirement that members of the church live lives separated from everything that might dishonor God, discredit his cause, or weaken their testimony.[58]

Central Alaskan Missions practice believer's baptism by immersion "in the name of the Father and of the Son and of the Holy Ghost." Baptism is encouraged but not required for membership. Children are dedicated, not baptized.[59]

The headquarters of Central Alaskan Missions are at Glennallen, Alaska 99588. There are congregations and missions in nine communities. The membership fluctuates with population movements.[60]

## United Fundamentalist Church, Incorporated

Leroy M. Kopp founded the United Fundamentalist Church at Los Angeles in 1939 for the purpose of licensing and ordaining ministers and missionaries to preach the whole Bible to the whole world with a minimum of organizational restrictions.

The United Fundamentalist Church subscribes to the doctrinal statement of the National Association of Evangelicals, of which it is a member. Membership in a local church of the organization is open to any person who has genuinely repented, who has been born of the Spirit of God, and who knows that he is saved. Members are encouraged to seek sanctification and the baptism of the Holy Spirit at its altars and to exercise any of the spiritual gifts that they may have received. The United Fundamentalist church holds that the blood which Christ shed for believers obtains redemption for sinners who will accept this payment. It sees the divine healing of the sick as either the response of God to the prayer of faith or as a sign confirming his written or proclaimed word. While the United Fundamentalist Church believes that the Bible explains itself if every passage bearing on a given subject is examined, it provides in its constitution for a Doctrinal Council—consisting of the general officers, territorial supervisors, and state and district superintendents—which meets at the call of the president to endeavor to determine the true meaning of a Bible passage when marked confusion arises in the church over the interpretation of any portion of the Bible.

The present president, E. Paul Kopp, succeeded his father in 1964.

An estimated 250 licensed and ordained pastors, evangelists, and missionaries belong to the United Fundamentalist Church. No information about the number of churches and missions or about the total membership is available. The headquarters of the United Fundamentalist Church receive mail at Box 28, Los Angeles, California 90053. The church sponsors Zion Christian Mission in Jerusalem.[61]

## Associated Gospel Churches

Sixteen Methodist Protestant pastors and congregations that preferred not to become a part of the Methodist Church organized the Associated Gospel Churches in 1939.[62] Its letterhead describes it as "an independent fellowship of fundamental autonomous churches" and as "a service agency for chaplains, missionaries, pastors, churches, Christian schools, etc." The masthead of its journal, the *A.G.C. Reporter*, carries the statement: "Not affiliated with any Council of Churches in any manner."

The fellowship affirms the absolute sovereignty and independence of the local church. It describes itself as "baptistic in polity and belief" and as standing "for complete separation from all apostasy and compromise."[63]

Its Basis of Fellowship specifically asserts belief in the Trinity; Christ's deity and virgin birth; the personality of the Holy Spirit; the supernatural and verbal inspiration of the Bible; Christ's substitutionary blood atonement; the necessity of the new birth; the maintenance of good works; Christ's literal, bodily, imminent, and premillennial return; the resurrection of the saved and the lost; the reality and personality of Satan; the endless punishment of unbelievers and the endless blessedness of true believers; the Lord's Supper and baptism by immersion as the Christian ordinances; and the dire need of cleansing and revival in Fundamentalism.[64]

The headquarters are at 1919 Beech Street, Wilkinsburg, Pennsylvania 15221. The Associated Gospel Churches reports "about 25,000 in its entire fellowship."[65]

The Commission on Chaplains of the Associated Gospel Churches represents, in addition to its own constituency and various independent local congregations, the American Baptist Association, the Anglican Orthodox Church, the Baptist Bible Fellowship, the Brethren in Christ Fellowship, Christian Crusade, and the Southwide Baptist Fellowship, as well as various theological seminaries.[66] In 1967 the Associated Gospel Churches sponsored the organization of the American Association of Christian Schools of Higher Learning as "a fundamental accrediting agency that would also stand for separation."[67] Associated Gospel Missions, the missionary arm of the fellowship, sponsors foreign operations in South Africa, Nigeria, the Philippines Republic, Sri Lanka, Spain, and Italy.[68]

## National Association of Kingdom Evangelicals (NAKE)

In the 1930s C. O. Stadsklev, a minister in the Christian and Missionary Alliance, withdrew from that organization because of its opposition to his emphatically expressed conviction that the divine message is not chiefly for the individual but for the nation. Stadsklev proceeded to organize and incorporate the Gospel Temple in Minneapolis as the forum for his message. He took to the radio throughout the country, and in community after community local evangelists found themselves in substantial agreement with Stadsklev's message. The situation seemed to demand an organization of these likeminded religious leaders, and Stadsklev ultimately organized the National Association of Kingdom Evangelicals. The credo which ministerial members of the association affirm is printed on the second page of Stadsklev's monthly journal, *Truth and Liberty Magazine*. It asserts that the Bible is the Word of God; that Jesus the Christ was God in human form; the new birth and the blood atonement; that the Anglo-Saxons are Israel and that the national laws of the Bible must become the law of the land; the ministry of the Holy Spirit to the believer's spirit, mind, and body; and Christ's return and literal reign here on earth.[69]

The association holds that the Anglo-Saxon, Celtic, Nordic, and racially allied peoples are the Israel of biblical prophecy. It also sees some truth in the British-Israel theory. At the same time, it regards this theory as usually propounded with some reserve because of the movement's conviction that the United States in particular is the national fulfillment and eschatological embodiment of the promised Zion, and that God has been preparing the United States for its mission ever since the first Anglo-Saxon colonists established permanent settlements in North America in the seventeenth century. The association also believes that the Union of Soviet Socialist Republics, as the standard-bearer of world Communism, will attack the United States with an air armada, but that God will tear this force into bits.[70]

The association opposes the "Babylonian money system" that underlies our present economy in favor of a method that issues money interest-free and debt-free at its source and that will back the national currency not with gold but with the nation's faith, credit, and productivity.[71]

The doctrine of the Trinity is generally held by the ministers belonging to the association, but it is not insisted upon. The usual formula of baptism, administered only to believers by immersion, includes the words "in the name of the Father and of the Son and of the Holy Ghost." The movement makes no stipulations regarding its adherents' participation in military service.

Although itself basically conservative, the movement faults Fundamentalists for failing to preach the "national message" of the Bible, for refusing to admit that in this generation God has an earthly servant race through whom he works and blesses other races, for their "unscriptural concept" that hell involves torment for from 90 to 95 percent of the human race and for their antagonism to "Paul's doctrine of the reconciliation of all things."[72]

The Gospel Temple, now located at 16205 Highway 7 in suburban Minnetonka, is the headquarters of the association and the site of its Annual Conference. The association reportedly links seven autonomous churches in various parts of the United States. No information is available on their total active membership. In addition there are many small study groups, some family-sized, others larger, which play the tapes of the services in the Gospel Temple as the core of their own worship.[73]

## American Mission for Opening Closed Churches, Incorporated

In 1940 the Reverend Lyle C. Anderson (b. 1903) left his settled pastorate in the Ridge Road Union Church near Lewiston, New York, and with his wife, Ruth, undertook a new task, that of reopening churches that had been closed. Their success with four churches in the Adirondacks north of Amsterdam, New York, led to the organization of the American Mission for Closed Churches as an independent faith mission at Niagara Falls, New York, in 1943.

After the mission determines that a closed church has a potential future, it secures the property by gift, agreement, purchase, or in some other acceptable way; provides the field with a missionary; helps him establish a comprehensive program of witness and service; and assists him in recruiting a congregation. When the congregation has become self-governinge and self-supporting, the mission turns the property over to the church and relinquishes control. Thereupon the missionary normally moves on to another field. The congregation itself is free to decide if it will remain independent or affiliate with some denomination.

During the first quarter of a century of its existence the mission restored fifty-five churches to vitality, chiefly in New York and New England, but in some cases as far south as Maryland and as far west as Illinois and Wisconsin. About three fifths of these are now undenominational and independent community churches; about one third are Baptist, the remainder Christian and Methodist. The mission continues ready to supply counsel and help to the congregations it has established as they need and request it. The deed contains a reversion clause specifying that if the church should again close its doors the property will revert to the mission.

The missionaries whom the mission employs in reestablishing these churches are not required to sever their connection with their own denominations when they affiliate with the mission, but they are expected to conform to the doctrinal stand, the policies, and the established procedures of the mission.

The mission also stands ready to open new churches, particularly in suburban areas where planning for churches has been inadequate.

The statement of doctrine of the American Mission for Opening Closed Churches commits it to belief in the divine inspiration of the Bible; the Trinity; Christ's deity and supernatural birth; the sinfulness of human beings and their need of a savior; Christ's atoning work, bodily resurrection, ascension, and premillennial and personal return; the bodily resurrection of the just and unjust; and the eternal blessedness of the saved and the eternal punishment of the lost.[74] Its missionaries normally practice believer's baptism by immersion.

The address of the headquarters of the American Mission for Opening Closed Churches, Incorporated, is Box 130, Olcott, New York 14126. The number of congregations under the supervision of the mission varies from year to year.[75]

## American Evangelical Christian Churches

G. W. Hyatt founded the American Evangelical Christian Churches in Chicago in 1944 as an association both of ministers and of local congregations "dedicated to the spread of the Gospel in home and foreign lands." Local congregations usually call themselves Evangelical Christian Churches; in some cases they call themselves community churches and identify their affiliation by adding the initials A.E.C.C. in parentheses.

Fervently evangelical, the denomination affirms seven cardinal points of doctrine: (1) the Bible as the written Word of God; (2) Christ's virgin birth; (3) his deity; (4) salvation through the atonement; (5) the guidance of the individual Christian's life through prayer; (6) the return of the Savior; and (7) the establishment of the Kingdom of God on earth.[76] Its theology tries to bridge the chasm between Reformed orthodoxy of the Synod of Dort type and Arminian teaching.

The leaders of the denomination hold an annual conference at Pala Mar, the American Evangelical Christian Churches' training center in Pineland, Florida, at which they plan the national program. Local congregations are autonomous, but their association with the denomination obligates them to cooperate with the national headquarters.

The denomination has 303 ministers and 22 exhorters on its list and claims about 250 local congregations with an estimated total membership of 34,500. Its headquarters are at Pineland, Florida 33945. A branch of the American Evangelical Christian Churches operates in Great Britain as the Ministry of Evangelism.[77]

### Fellowship of Independent Evangelical Churches

The Independent Fundamental Ministers Meeting came into being in 1949 largely through the efforts of Dr. L. Poindexter McClenny (b. 1907), then a clergyman in Charlotte, North Carolina, and more recently pastor of the Wheaton College Church at Wheaton, Illinois, and of Dr. Robert C. McQuilkin (1886–1952), a Presbyterian minister and the president of Columbia (South Carolina) Bible College. In 1951 the membership of the meeting incorporated itself in South Carolina as the Fellowship of Independent Evangelical Churches, with headquarters in Spartanburg. The corporate purpose was defined as "the forming of a religious organization of Bible-believing churches," ministers, evangelists, missionaries, Christian workers, and officers of local churches, "with authority to ordain men into the Christian ministry."[78]

The fellowship's doctrinal statement affirms the verbal inspiration and inerrancy of the Scriptures; the Trinity; Christ's deity, virgin birth, substitutionary atonement on the cross, literal and bodily resurrection, intercession, and personal return; the work of the Holy Spirit; the corruption of all human beings in body, mind, and spirit; salvation by grace through personal faith in Christ as Savior and Lord; rebirth by the Holy Spirit; the eternal preservation of those who are truly saved; the invisible church as the body and bride of Christ, of which all who are born again are members; the visible church as those who associate themselves for worship, edification, spiritual growth, and service; baptism and the Lord's Supper as enduring ordinances; angels as creatures of God; Satan as a personal being who led a host of angels in rebellion and as the "god of this age"; Christ's premillennial return, his messianic Kingdom, and the bodily resurrection of the just to eternal glory and of the unjust to everlasting conscious punishment in hell.

The fellowship asserts the total independence of member churches; declares its willingness to enter into Christian fellowship with members of any church body or denomination whose creed and practice holds fast to the historic Christian faith and which subordinates its authority to that of the Word of God; calls for separation from the world; and regards the marriage of Christians with unbelievers as prohibited by the Bible.[79]

The secretary of the Fellowship of Independent Evangelical Churches resides at 2311 Anderson Street, Bristol, Tennesssee 37620. There are 55 active ministerial members and 10 member churches in the fellowship. The active membership of the latter is estimated at 2,800. The active membership of the churches that do not belong to the fellowship but whose pastors do is estimated at 3,000.[80]

### Evangelical Ministers and Churches International, Incorporated

In 1950 a number of clergymen joined to form the Evangelical Ministers and Churches International, to be a fellowship of ordained ministers, Gospel workers, and churches. Incorporation took place in 1956. The organization has legal authority to ordain Christian workers to the work of the Gospel ministry, to issue credentials to ordained ministers empowering them to perform all the duties commonly connected with the office of the ministry, to establish educational institutions, and to organize and establish churches and missions.

The association's doctrinal platform affirms the inspiration of the Bible; its infallibility as a rule for faith and life; the Trinity; the teachings of the Bible about creation, the fall of man, the sinful state of human beings by nature, the miracles of both Testaments, and Christ's deity, virgin birth, life, death, burial, resurrection, and imminent return; salvation by grace through faith and through the blood of Christ shed on the cross; and the necessity of a strong and consistent Christian testimony by believers, of a life "unspotted from the world," and of active work for the salvation of souls and the edification of Christ's body.[81]

The fellowship owns and operates Colorado Bible College and Seminary, Manitou Springs, Colorado, a "home study" (that is, correspondence) theological college founded in 1927 as Pikes Peak Bible Seminary by C. J. Burton. Prior to adopting its present name, the institution was known as Burton College and Seminary.

Currently the fellowship numbers an estimated 150 clergymen in the United States. Some of these are pastors of "fundamental" Baptist, Presbyterian, Methodist, and other congregations not directly affiliated with the fellowship. There are about 100 congregations in the United States, with an estimated total membership of 15,000 that hold church or group membership in the association. A number of churches in South Korea also belong to the fellowship.[82] The headquarters are at 105 West Madison Street, Chicago, Illinois 60602. The association meets annually; the international Executive Board transacts the business of the association between the annual sessions.

### Independent Churches Affiliated

Independent Churches Affiliated came into being in 1953. The organization is a general constituent member of the American Council of Christian Churches.

It depends for its literature requirements on the American Council of Christian Churches, the General Association of Regular Baptist Churches, and other church bodies that stand in the "true fundamental" tradition, and share the council's doctrinal position.

No information is available about the number of churches in the association or about the inclusive membership.[83] There are no central headquarters.

### The Church of the New Testament

In 1954 Bill Jones, a black ex-gambler,[84] Roland Allen, and Mary Fasley founded the Church of the New Testament in Austin, Texas, as an independent organization. They did this, they said, in order not to be bound by human and sectarian traditions that depart from the Word of God and in order to be free to preach God's Word without compromise.

The Church of the New Testament teaches that the Bible is God the Creator's inspired and unchangeable Word; that Christ is God's only begotten Son and the Savior of the world, whose blood was shed for the forgiveness of sins; that salvation is not of works, but by God's grace through faith; that Christ's Gospel is the power of God to every one who believes it; that every sinner who comes to Christ for salvation must repent and believe the Gospel; that Christ was God incarnate, virgin-born, crucified, buried, and resurrected; that heaven is a place for born-again believers to live in forever and hell a place of eternal punishment for all who do not believe Christ's Gospel; that human beings are fallen creatures who must be born again; and that God is redeeming his people out of every nation by the proclamation of Christ's Gospel. The Church of the New Testament administers believer's baptism by immersion in the name of the Father and of the Son and of the Holy Ghost; serves the Lord's Supper; and practices foot washing. It prefers the King James Version to other translations of the Bible into English. Its ministry includes visiting and praying with the sick, prison evangelism, the publication of Gospel tracts, witnessing in homes, radio broadcasting, and holding street-corner meetings.

The headquarters of the Church of the New Testament are at 1602 Harvey Street, Austin, Texas 78702. The total nominal membership of the Church of the New Testament is about 200.[85]

### Missionary and Soul Winning Fellowship (Christians in Action)

The Missionary and Soul Winning Fellowship, established in 1957 by the Reverend Lee Shelley, a minister of the Christian and Missionary Alliance, is a nondenominational international and interracial agency that carries on a missionary ministry chiefly in eighteen countries outside the United States. In the interest of its program it operates a vocational training school with a six-week "soul-winning" institute for basic training in personal evangelism and a nine-month missionary training program.

The seven-point Statement of Faith of the fellowship is a paraphrase of the Statement of Faith of the National Association of Evangelicals. It commits the missionaries of the fellowship to belief in the Bible as the only infallible Word of God; the Trinity; Christ's deity, virgin birth, sinless life, miracles, atonement, resurrection, and second coming; the necessity of the transformation of sinful human beings by the Holy Spirit; the power to lead a godly life and to witness to others as a consequence of the indwelling of the Holy Spirit; the resurrection of Christians to eternal life and of the lost to perdition; and the spiritual unity of all believers in Christ.[86]

The headquarters of the Missionary and Soul Winning Fellowship are at 350 East Market Street, North Long Beach, California 90805. Its centers in the United States are limited to the activities of the headquarters chapel, a mission to Jews in Los Angeles, and a mission among the Apache Indians in Arizona. No estimate of the total active membership of these agencies is available. The fellowship also sponsors four centers on Okinawa.[87]

## This Testimony

This Testimony is the result of the unplanned confluence in North America of several streams of conviction. These streams have widely diverse geographical origins in the twentieth century, but they have this in common that while they stand outside the denominational main current of historic Christianity they believe firmly that the church is God's primary concern in this dispensation. Two names bulk particularly large, Watchman Nee and T. Austin-Sparks.

In 1920 Chinese university student Nee To-sheng became a Christian during the visit of a native evangelist to Nee's birthplace, Fuchow. In the course of the next eighteen years Nee developed out of his study of the Bible a faith that he communicated to his converts and disciples and that combined the traditional theology of the nineteenth-century missionary revival with a radically undenominational doctrine of the church. The Christian name Watchman that he took reflects his understanding of his own apostolic mission. Under his leadership and that of his followers a reported 636 local assemblies committed to his views, with a total membership estimated at 118,000, ultimately came into being in the Orient prior to the communist takeover of mainland China.

In 1949, when the Nationalist government of China transferred its capital to Taiwan, Nee followed. After his return to the mainland, the communists arrested him in 1952 on the charges of "counterrevolutionary activities and multiple adultery" and sentenced him to fifteen years in prison in Shanghai. When his sentence expired in April 1967, his captors refused to release him.[88]

In the 1940s and 1950s Nee became increasingly well known in English-speaking religious circles through transcriptions of his addresses in tracts and magazine articles. In 1957 his reputation was greatly enhanced by the publication in Bombay of *The Normal Christian Life,* an outline of his theology (on the basis of Romans 1–8) that his followers drew from addresses which he had delivered during and shortly after a visit of his to Europe in 1938/1939. This work was followed by an English version of a slender ecclesiological study, *The Normal Christian Church Life.* Other works of his available in English include *The Spiritual Man,* a three-volume series, as well as *The Glorious Church, Love Not the world,* and *The Release of the Spirit.*

Nee's Bible-oriented theology largely assumes the inherited teaching of the historic church about the Trinity and the person of Christ without extensively articulating it. In the description of Christ's work, it differentiates the blood of Christ from his cross. By his death as the substitute for human beings, Christ obtained for them forgiveness, justification, and reconciliation. Christ's blood deals with sins and guilt; Christ's cross deals with sin, flesh, and the natural man; Christ's life is made available to dwell in, recreate, and empower believers; the working of death in the natural man makes the indwelling life progressively manifest.[89]

Nee's theology understands baptism as believer's baptism by immersion, although he does not make the mode a condition of fellowship. The baptism of the Holy Spirit is an identifiable gift in addition to rebirth, but need not be accompanied by "Pentecostal" phenomena. Nee's eschatology is premillennial.

Nee lays great stress on the universal church as the body of Christ, of which individual Christians are the members. The purpose of the proclamation of the Gospel he sees as the creation of local churches—meetings for the "breaking of bread" or the Lord's Supper. He holds that the only basis for dividing the universal church into churches is the "God-ordained method of division on the basis of locality," with a "locality" understood as a city or as a comparable administrative unit in a metropolis or in the country.

Spiritual leadership, the human instruments that God uses in the salvation of believers, denominationalism and sectarianism, doctrinal, racial, or national differences, and social distinctions are not justifiable bases of division. As examples of nondivisive doctrinal issues Nee lists differences in eschatology, differences in the mode of baptism, vegetarianism, and sabbatarianism.

Each church is independent of the others before God and is responsible to him alone. The elders are to be chosen from the membership of the local church, are not to devote themselves exclusively to spiritual work, and are not to be transferred to another church. Nee holds that his followers must remain nonsectarian but that they cannot make this a condition of fellowship. If they proclaim the gospel in a locality where there is no local church as Nee understands the term, the converts to Christianity that come to faith are to initiate one. If a denominational church already exists in the unit-locality, the converts are to establish a local nonsectarian church. The members of this local church are to engage in fellowship with other Christians as far as this is possible, but such a local nonsectarian church is not to cooperate with a denominational church.

Two of Nee's intimate co-workers, Stephen Kaung and Witness Lee, brought Nee's message to North America personally. Kaung came to this continent in 1954 and ultimately settled in New York. Lee came over in 1960 and made Los Angeles the base of his operations. Much of Lee's work has been done among Chinese students on West Coast campuses and among their compatriots in the nonacademic community.[90]

Another Asian Christian who has played a significant role in the This Testimony movement in North America is Bakht Singh (b. 1904), leader of some two hundred indigenous groups in his native India. He toured almost thirty North American cities in the early 1960s and is represented in the English literature of the movement by translations of a number of tracts.

In the early 1920s, about the time that Watchman Nee was establishing his first indigenous churches in Fuchow, the Reverend T. Austin-Sparks, a Baptist clergyman in London, found himself compelled to find larger premises for a ministry that was overreaching denominational boundaries. He found the buildings that he needed at 13 Honour Oak Road, Forest Hill, London. Here he established the Honour Oak Christian Fellowship Centre. With the move to the new site of his labors, his personal connection with the Baptist denomination lapsed. He continued to head the center for the next four decades.[91]

Through his ministry at the center, through the conferences that he was invited to conduct, through the journal that, in his words, "spontaneously came into being" in 1922, *A Witness and a Testimony*, and through his many books and tracts, Austin-Sparks exerted a considerable influence in the English-speaking world.[92]

The impact of Austin-Sparks's ministry increased markedly in North America from the 1930s on and reached a climax in the 1960s.[93]

The local groups that have come into being in the United States and Canada as the unintended result of his ministry have no affiliation with the Honour Oak Christian Fellowship Centre in London, and Austin-Sparks disclaims any responsibility for them. They see what they call denomination-alism as a menace to spiritual growth and fullness, and a hindrance to the full purpose of God. At the same time, they refuse to proselytize on the ground that everything spiritual must proceed from the Holy Spirit and dare not be of human arrangement. Committed to "the principle of the organic," that is, growth from the indwelling Christ, they appoint no officers, official bodies, committees, or organizers. They have no spokesmen and sense no need of a state of doctrinal principles and practice. The single human authority that they respect is the spiritual authority that God's anointing upon a person manifests.

They administer believer's baptism by immersion as a testimony of union with Christ in death and resurrection. They see the "Lord's table" as a testimony to Christ's death for them, their death in him, and the oneness of all believers in and with him as one loaf. They hold that in the Christ who is present with his worshiping people the fullness of the Trinity is embodied and the redeemed sinners that constitute his body are made complete.

Since This Testimony lacks a central organization, statistics about the groups adhering to This Testimony are necessarily only approximations. Estimates on the number of functioning local assemblies in the United States and Canada range from 75 to 100. Estimates of the total number of persons actively participating in these assemblies range from 5,000 to 7,000.[94]

### The Church of All Christian Faiths

In February 1964 the Reverend Charles S. Poling, D.D. (b. 1892), pastor of the First Presbyterian Church, Phoenix, Arizona, withdrew from the United Presbyterian Church in the United States of America in protest against what he called "the N[ational] C[ouncil of the] C[hurches of Christ in the United States of America] takeover of the United Presbyterian Church" and the latter's capture by the "ultra-liberals."[95] In April of the same year he and a number of like-minded individuals who had withdrawn from their respective churches in protest against the "new social gospel" and what they described as "the general apostasy" of their former denominations organized the Church of All Christian Faiths as a free church, "not affiliated with any other denomination whatsoever."

Membership in the church requires acceptance of the Bible as inspired by God and as the only infallible rule of faith, obedience, and life, and of the Church of All Christian Faiths revision of the Apostles' Creed. This revision substitutes "the grave" for the traditional "hell" and "Christian" for the traditional "Catholic." The articles of faith acknowledge the help that the Church of All Christian Faiths has received from its study of the statements of faith of the National Association of Congregational Churches (Continuing Congregational Church) as well as of other denominations. The Articles of Faith further commit the Church of All Christian Faiths to the congregational form of church government; assert that God alone is the Lord of conscience; describe the Holy Spirit speaking in the Scriptures as the supreme judge that is to determine all controversies of religion; affirm the authority of the Bible; declare that all human beings properly using the ordinary means can attain to a sufficient understanding of those things which they must know, believe, and observe for salvation; propose to emphasize the essentials of Christianity and to leave freedom for diversity of interpretation concerning details; recognize baptism and the Lord's Supper as sacraments instituted by Christ, with the mode of baptism left to the individual conscience; and incorporate the 1629 one-sentence covenant of the Salem (Massachusetts) Congregationalist Church, the Congregationalist Statement of Faith adopted at Kansas City in 1913, and the Church of All Christian Faiths version of the Apostles' Creed.[96]

The headquarters of the Church of All Christian Faiths are at 4222 East

Lincoln Drive, Paradise Valley, a suburb of Phoenix, Arizona 85253. The Paradise Valley congregation has about 500 members; a second congregation in Topeka, Kansas, has about 300 members, and a third, in Douglas, Arizona, has about 150 members.[97]

## Independent Fundamental Bible Churches

At the convention of the American Council of Christian Churches in Mobile, Alabama, in 1965, a group of pastors and laymen affiliated with independent churches organized the Independent Fundamental Bible Churches. They designed the new organization to be a fellowship that would offer a unified stand and witness for the cause of Christ through the spread of the Gospel of God's grace and against ecumenism (as represented by the National Council of the Churches of Christ in the United States of America), modernism, liberalism, Communism, and immorality. Leaders in the movement were the Reverend W. C. Standridge, pastor of the Interstate Baptist Church of Memphis, and Dr. Harland O'Dell, pastor of the Canton (Ohio) Gospel Center, and Dr. Marion H. Reynolds, Jr., associate pastor of Grace Fundamental Church, Los Angeles. The American Council of Christian Churches received the new organization as a constituent member body in 1967.

The doctrinal statement of the Independent Fundamental Bible Churches affirms belief in the absolute sovereignty and independence of the local church, and commits the membership "without reservation to all of the doctrines of the historic Christian faith." These include the verbal inspiration, inerrancy, and infallibility of the Bible as originally written; the Trinity; the deity and humanity of Christ, his virgin birth, substitutionary death, blood atonement and bodily resurrection, and his literal, personal, bodily and premillennial return; the deity and personality of the Holy Spirit; the total depravity of human beings; salvation by grace through faith in Christ's finished work on the cross; the eternal security of all truly born-again persons; good works in response to the divine will; the eternal blessedness of the saved and the everlasting conscious suffering of the lost; the unity of all whom Christ has redeemed; the reality and personality of Satan; the need for maintaining the church's purity of doctrine and life; the church as the body and bride of Christ; the establishment and continuance of local churches as a teaching of the New Testament; believer's baptism by immersion and the Lord's Supper as the two ordinances given to the church; separation from all apostasy and scripturally forbidden alliances; and civil government as a divine ordinance.[98]

The office of the secretary of the Independent Fundamental Bible Churches is at 2400 Cleveland Avenue, Northwest, Canton, Ohio 44709. There are 11 churches in the fellowship with an estimated membership of 1,700.[99]

# NOTES

1. Bright N. and Thelma N. Heist, *Centennial Anniversary, Bible Fellowship Church, formerly Mennonite Brethren in Christ Church, Zionsville, Pennsylvania, 1859–1959* (Zionsville, Penn.: Bible Fellowship Church, 1959).

2. The Bible Fellowship Church heartily encourages its "people to dedicate their children to the Lord by prayer and laying on of hands of the Elders" (N. H. Wolf, ed., *Proceedings, Eighty-Third Annual Conference of the Bible Fellowship Church, 1966* [N.p.: N.p., 1966], p. J.

3. The bread and wine are described as "emblems" ("Local Church Order," p. 6, in *Faith and Order of the Bible Fellowship Church* [N.p.: N.p., 1961]) (33-page pamphlet).

4. "The Articles of Faith," pp. 1-13, ibid.

5. *Discipline of the Social Brethren Church, Revised and Approved by the General Assembly, March 3, 1949* (N.p.: Social Brethren Church, 1950), p. 3.

6. Ibid., pp. 4-7.

7. Because of Dowie's stress on divine healing, Pentecostalist historians regard him as one of the precursors of the Pentecostal movement. Some of the early leaders of the latter movement, among them John G. Lake, Daniel C. O. Opperman, and William J. Mitchell, had been supporters of Dowie.

8. The office of apostle was abolished in the late 1930s.

9. "Christian Catholic Church: Affirmation of Faith," *Leaves of Healing,* vol. 102 (1966), p. 63. The Constitution of 1966 makes this affirmation of faith "with deep respect for the Apostles' Creed, the writings of the church Fathers, the work of the early church Councils, the evangelical insights of the Reformers, and all reverent Christian scholarship" (ibid., p. 51). The strong interest in millennial teaching that formerly characterized the Christian Catholic Church has diminished in recent years. The observance of the Mosaic eating codes, including abstention from pork, is understood not as a religious require-

ment, but as part of the movement's health regimen.

10. Ibid.

11. General Overseer Carl Q. Lee states in a letter that the nominal membership is probably three times as great.

12. The bulk of the information in this section derives from reports of a number of observers across the continent whose integrity the present writer has no reason to doubt, from a letter by a senior servant of the fellowship, and from a personal interview with two state overseers. (The observers are not themselves members of the fellowship, but their attitudes toward it range from neutral to highly appreciative.) The designation "The Way" (or "the Jesus Way") reflects New Testament usage (Acts 9:2; 18:25; 19:23; 22:4; 24:14, 22). Members of the fellowship frequently refer to one another as "friends." They themselves hold that they stand in a succession of communities that goes back to apostolic times and that they are merely perpetuating an unbroken tradition almost 2,000 years old.

13. Irvine's family name is sometimes given incorrectly as Erwin. The information about the Faith Mission and Irvine's early connection with it has kindly been provided in a letter to the present writer by Mr. John G. Eberstein, 5 Corstorphine House Avenue, Edinburgh, Scotland, a member of the Faith Mission since 1922, its president for some twenty years, and the editor of its magazine for more than three decades. See also his article, "Faith Mission," in Burton L. Goddard, ed., *The Encyclopedia of Modern Christian Missions: The Agencies* (Camden, N.J.: Thomas Nelson and Sons, 1967), no. 523, p. 279. On Govan see Isobel Rosie Govan, *Spirit of Revival: Biography of J. G. Govan, Founder of the Faith Mission* (London: The Faith Mission and Marshall, Morgan, and Scott, 1938).

14. From him comes the much resented name "Cooneyites" that nonmembers have often derisively applied to members of the fellowship. "Tramp-preacher" appears to have been Cooney's own designation for himself;

the term has long been used by outsiders for the missionaries of the movement.

15. According to one unverifiable report, Cooney came to the United States, settled in the West, and began a rival movement. The cited letter from Mr. Eberstein states that Cooney died in Ireland in the mid-1960s.

16. One of the first to emigrate to North America was Irvine Weir. The identity of this first name with the family name of the organizer of the movement has misled some into referring to the organizer by the conflate name William Weir Irvine. Other early missionaries to North America were George Walker; James Nicol, and Walter Jardine; William and John Hendy; George and Ella Johnson, one of the fairly few married couples in the leadership of the movement; Samuel Charlton; Anna Groves; and May Underwood (d. 1968). The fellowship's growth in Alberta is more or less typical of its spread in western Canada. It came to the province between 1910 and 1914, grew slowly at first, expanded rapidly during the depression, and by the mid-1940s had between 1,200 and 1,800 members in the province, with three summer camps (William Edward Mann, *Sect, Cult, and Church in Alberta* [Toronto, Ontario: University of Toronto Press, 1955], pp. 23, 30, 45, 56, 70, 108-110, 116). David Christie (d. 1969) and his wife, Emily, née Wilson, came to Hawaii in December 1923 and began working on the island of Oahu the next month. Attending ministers (elders) conduct services in homes on all four of the main islands. Although membership rosters are not maintained, the number of active believers is estimated at between 150 and 200, according to a local leader of the movement who prefers to remain unnamed. John F. Mulholland, *Hawaii's Religions* (Rutland, Vt.: Charles E. Tuttle Company, 1970), p. 205, calls the fellowship "a church without a name."

17. *Hymns Old and New*, their current hymnal in English-speaking communities, makes extensive use of Gospel songs and choruses, although it contains a moderate number of classics out of the British tradition of hymnody. About one tenth of the 335 hymns in *Hymns Old and New* are listed in the indices of the revised edition of John Julian, ed., *A Dictionary of Hymnology* (London: John Murray, 1915). On the other hand, only 3 of the 118 hymns in the relatively sophisticated and deliberately ecumenical selection in Luther Noss, ed., *Christian Hymns* (Cleveland, Ohio: World Publishing Company, 1963), are in *Hymns Old and New*—"Abide with Me," "Jesus, Thou Joy of Loving Hearts," and "O God of Bethel." There is one explicitly trinitarian doxology, stanza 4 of no. 239, "Cease Not to Praise God for All He Has Done," by "C.H.L." Reportedly this hymn is in frequent use in the services of the fellowship. Of the texts in *Hymns Old and New* many are by adherents of the movement. Eighty-nine bear the names or initials of the authors. Most of the authors have contributed only one text identified with their name, but S. Jones is represented by twenty-two, Fanny Crosby and Frances Havergal have six apiece, Horatio Bonar has five, Isaac Watts three, and Ada R. Haberson, Gerhard Tersteegen, N. Norton, and A. A. Pollard two each. The German version of the hymnal, *Alte und neue geistliche Lieder,* has 195 hymns in alphabetical sequence, without tunes or indications of authorship. The hymns stress renunciation of the world, the bliss of the hereafter, and personal religion generally.

18. The permanence of the local fellowships varies. In one case that the present writer was able to check personally, the Reverend Theodore Dautenhahn, later of St. Louis, but in 1938 pastor of Trinity Church, Stewardson, Illinois, reported that at that time the movement had made a considerable number of converts in and around Brownstown and Neoga, Illinois. His successor in the pastorate of the Stewardson parish in 1967, the Reverend George C. Williams, reported to the present writer that he had not been able to find any trace of the movement in the area. (It is possible that the churches in question had moved to nearby communities upon the death or removal of the bishops.) On the other hand, the present writer knows of two "sister-workers," one at work in Denmark, the other in the United States, who were born

into families on "The Way." The fellowship in Trenton, New Jersey, has been in existence at least since 1948. One of the churches in Appleton, Wisconsin, goes back to the period of World War I. Of the three conventions in Wisconsin the one at Marion has been meeting at the same place for over fifty years, the one in Menominee at the same place for over thirty years.

19. The literature on the fellowship is very scanty and does not differentiate between the original movement and the "Cooneyite" schism. One of the longest discussions known to this writer is an article by W. M. R[ule], "The Cooneyites or Go-Preachers: A Warning," *Our Hope*, vol. 30 (1923/1924), pp. 426-436. It has been reprinted under the same title as a 16-page pamphlet (New York: Loizeaux Brothers, n.d.). Rule also published a very similar 24-page pamphlet, *The Cooneyites or "Go-Preachers" and Their Doctrines* (5th edn.; London: Central Bible Truth Depot, n.d.). This pamphlet appears in an abridged form with editorial annotations under the same title as a chapter in William C. Ervine, ed., *Heresies Exposed: A Brief Critical Examination in the Light of the Holy Scriptures of Some of the Prevailing Heresies and False Teachings of Today* (4th edn., 33rd printing; Neptune, N.J.: Loizeaux Brothers, 1964), pp. 73-78. Rule's strongly polemical evaluation, written from a conservative Dispensationalist viewpoint, charges the adherents of the fellowship with teaching that "the Lord Jesus Christ had sinful flesh in him that needed to be overcome"; that they have "no room for the precious atoning blood of Christ as the ground of salvation"; and that they ignore "the sovereign work of the Holy Spirit in the souls of men" (*The Cooneyites or "Go-Preachers" and Their Doctrines*, pp. 18-20). Adherents of the movement reject these charges as unwarranted misrepresentations. Other discussions of the fellowship include an anonymous and undated 12-page tract, *A Cunning Cult* (Coffeyville, Kan.: Gospel Tract Mission, n.d. [after 1951]); William E. Paul, *The "Two by Twos": Who Are They? What Do They Believe?* (North Platte, Neb.: News and Truths, 1968) (18-page tract); a 55-line article, "Die Jünger Jesu," in Kurt Hutten, ed., *Seher—Grübler—Enthusiasten: Sekten und religiöse Sondergemeinschaften der Gegenwart* (6th edn.; Stuttgart: Quell-Verlag der Evangelischen Gesellschaft, 1960), pp. 441-442; a 41-line article, "Disciples of Jesus," at no. 0871 in Johannes Gründler, *Lexikon der christlichen Kirchen und Sekten* (Vienna, Austria: Herder, 1961), vol. 1, pp. 411-412; a 15-line item, "Cooneyites," in J. Oswald Sanders and J. Stafford Wright, *Some Modern Religions* (2nd edn.; London: Tyndale Press, 1956), p. 60, almost identical with the 15-line summary under the same heading in J. Oswald Sanders, *Cults and Isms* (rev. edn.; Grand Rapids, Mich.: Zondervan Publishing House, 1962), p. 166; an 11-line paragraph in Elmer T. Clark, *The Small Sects in America* (rev. edn.; Nashville: Abingdon-Cokesbury Press, 1949), p. 184; and a 9-line article by Theodore G. Tappert, "Cooneyites," in Lefferts A. Loetscher, ed., *Twentieth Century Encyclopedia of Religious Knowledge* (Grand Rapids, Mich.: Baker Book House, 1955), vol. 1, p. 298.

20. Romans 10:14-15.

21. One of the local nicknames by which the movement has sometimes been known is "Black Stockings" or "Black Sox."

22. Hence the name "Two by Twos" for the movement.

23. In late 1967 a district fellowship that covered the not too densely populated Snohomish County in the state of Washington reportedly had 14 house-churches; King County, of which Seattle is a part, was said to have at least 50 house-churches. Denver, Colorado, reportedly has about 24 house-churches, Greater Los Angeles 37, New Orleans only one (but several in upstate Louisiana). The 1966–1967 roster of "servants" for Wisconsin lists 12 teams (24 servants) in that state. The 1968–1969 roster of servants for New York, New Jersey, and New England list 18 teams (36 members). The 1967 roster of conventions lists three each in Wisconsin and North Dakota, and two each in Minnesota and South Dakota.

24. On the basis of these meetings, the members of the fellowship sometimes refer to it as "the Church in the House." The term "cell" to describe house-churches is explicitly repudiated.

25. Within the space of a few months in 1967–1968 the present writer received reports of missionaries of the movement currently at work in every region of the continental United States, as well as in British Columbia, Alaska, the West Indies, and the Republic of China (Taiwan), and behind the Iron Curtain in Europe. Since then he has received reports of active elements of the movement in Scandinavia, Africa, and South America.

26. The present writer has not succeeded in determining if the rival movement reportedly begun by Cooney has survived. Leaders of the fellowship profess to have no knowledge of its existence.

27. Angelo di Domenica, *Protestant Witness of a New American: Mission of a Lifetime* (Chicago: The Judson Press, 1956), p. 38.

28. Robert Santilli, "What's in a Name?" *The New Aurora,* vol. 67, no. 2 (October 1968), p. 3. *The New Aurora* is the association's monthly organ.

29. "Constitutions of the Association of Evangelicals for Italian Mission Continuing the Italian Baptist Association of America," *The New Aurora,* vol. 67, no. 5 (January 1969), p. 11.

30. John Field Mulholland, *Hawaii's Religions* (Rutland, Vt.: Charles E. Tuttle Company, 1970), pp. 222-223. The present writer gratefully acknowledges the assistance of the Reverend Mr. Mulholland, who visited the Cooke Street Church on this writer's behalf and secured the information here provided.

31. Letter of the Reverend Ella Wise Harrison, pastor, Ka Makua Mau Loa.

32. John Field Mulholland, *Religion in Hawaii* (Honolulu, Hawaii: The Kamehameha Schools, 1961), p. 32.

33. John Field Mulholland, *Hawaii's Religions* (Rutland, Vt.: Charles E. Tuttle Company, 1970); pp. 223-224; letter from the Reverend Mr. Mulholland; telephone conversation with the Reverend Robert A Farley, assistant pastor of the mother church.

34. *What Is the A.G.C.?*" (Hamilton, Ontario: Associated Gospel Churches of Canada, 1965) (8-page pamphlet), p. 3. A letter from Miss D. Schultz, secretary to the president, Briercrest Bible Institute, Caronport, Saskatchewan, indicates that the Association of Gospel Churches referred to in William

Edward Mann, *Sect, Cult, and Church in Alberta* (Toronto, Ontario: University of Toronto Press, 1955), pp. 89 and 106, ought to have been referred to as the Associated Gospel Churches of Canada.

35. "Articles of Faith and Doctrine," in *Constitution of the Associated Gospel Churches* (rev. edn.; Hamilton, Ontario: Associated Gospel Churches of Canada, 1963) (50-page pamphlet), pp. 3-10, as amended in *Associated Gospel Churches Yearbook 1968* (Hamilton, Ontario: Associated Gospel Churches of Canada, 1968), p. 34. The constitution permits member congregations of the Associated Gospel Churches to admit to fellowship believers who have not been immersed. It also directs the regular observance of the Lord's Supper, preferably on the first Lord's day of the month, under the presidency of the pastor or any duly authorized person.

36. The section on baptism in the Articles of Faith specifies neither the mode (beyond stating that it "should be observed as commanded in the scriptures") nor the formula (*The History, Doctrine and By-Laws of the United Christian Church, Inc., Adopted at Annual Conference, May 11, 1963* [Brooklyn, N. Y.: United Christian Church, 1963] [16-page pamphlet], p. 7).

37. Ibid., pp. 5-7.

38. Ibid., pp. 7-14.

39. Ralph Lord Roy, *Apostles of Discord: A Study of Organized Bigotry and Disruption on the Fringes of Protestantism* (Boston: Beacon Press, 1953), p. 397, credits the United Christian Church of America with "a few legitimate churches" and quotes Bishop Elliott as estimating the total active membership of the denomination at that time as "several thousand."—The present writer gratefully acknowledges the assistance of the Reverend Carl J. Kruger, then pastor of Trinity Church, New Hyde Park, New York, who kindly established contact on this writer's behalf with the Reverend Herbert J. Elliott, Th.D., D.D., presiding bishop, United Christian Church, Incorporated.

40. The Reverend Marion H. Reynolds, Sr., president of the Fundamental Evangelistic Association, Incorporated, is the pastor of Grace Fundamental

Church; the Reverend Marion H. Reynolds, Jr., superintendent of the association, is associate pastor of the church.

41. *Statement of Doctrine, Grace Fundamental Church* (undated pamphlet).

42. The 1966 roster of member denominations of the American Council of Christian Churches listed the Fundamental Evangelistic Association under the name of Militant Fundamental Bible Churches. A 1960 survey listed the Militant Fundamental Bible Churches as having 1,268 members (*Christianity Today*, vol. 9, no. 9 [January 29, 1965], p. 11 [431]). In 1966 Dr. Marion H. Reynolds, Jr., became president of the American Council of Christian Churches.

43. Communication from the Reverend Marion H. Reynolds, Sr. The present writer acknowledges gratefully the assistance of the Reverend Barry Stephenson Hughey, Caracas, Venezuela, then seminarian-assistant at the Church of the Good Shepherd, Ingleside, California, who interviewed Dr. Reynolds, Sr., on this writer's behalf.

44. Grace Fundamental Church, but not the Fundamental Evangelistic Association, Incorporated, has become a member of the Independent Fundamental Bible Churches, of which Dr. Marion H. Reynolds, Jr., is president.

45. J. Ellwood Evans, "Here Is the I.F.C.A.," in *1965 National I.F.C.A. Sunday* (Chicago: Independent Fundamental Churches of America, 1965) (2-page tract), p. 2.

46. Article IV ("Faith and Doctrine"), *Constitution of the Independent Fundamental Churches of America, Incorporated* (Chicago: Independent Fundamental Churches of America, 1964) (12-page pamphlet), pp. 3-5. Benjamin R. De Jong, Harold Pothover, and Laurel W. Hanely, *This We Believe* (Chicago: Independent Fundamental Churches of America, n.d.) (83-page brochure, plus 12-page appendix), in a commentary on this statement. The appendix discusses the ordinances of believer's baptism by immersion in the name of the Father and of the Son and of the Holy Spirit as the outward symbol of the baptism of the Holy Spirit, and the Lord's Supper as a "sacred, symbolic and scriptural means" of remembering Christ's death for our sins.

47. *What Is an Independent Fundamental Church?* (Chicago: Independent Fundamental Churches of America, n.d.) (8-page tract), pp. 6-7.

48. *What Is the I.F.C.A.?* (Chicago: The Independent Fundamental Churches of America, 1966) (6-page tract), p. 5. Among its better-known member churches are the Church of the Open Door, 5455 York Road, Philadelphia, Pennsylvania, founded in 1936 by the Reverend Merril T. MacPherson, D.D., after he had left the Presbyterian Church in the U.S.A. (see his *Why I Left the Presbyterian Church U.S.A.* [Philadelphia: The Church of the Open Door, 1945] [23-page pamphlet]) and the Conversion Center, Incorporated, Havertown, Pennsylvania, a "mission specializing in winning Roman Catholics to Jesus Christ" (*Program, 37th National Convention IFCA* [Chicago: Independent Fundamental Churches of America, 1966], p. [15]).

49. Article 4, "Constitution and Articles of Agreement of the Association of Fundamental Ministers and Churches, Incorporated," in Fred Bruffett, *Christian Evangelism—Christian Unity—A Triumphant Church* (Kansas City. Mo.: Association of Fundamental Ministers and Churches, 1957) (63-page brochure), p. 3.

50. Article 8, ibid., pp. 4-5. Pp. 6-63 of the cited brochure contain sermons by the author which explicate in various ways the implications of these fundamental doctrines.

51. Ibid., pp. 28-38.

52. *Fundamental News,* January–February 1967, p. 2.

53. The present writer gratefully acknowledges the assistance of the Reverend Joel F. Ingebritson, Wabag, New Guinea, then séminarian-assistant at Calvary Church, Kansas City, who interviewed the Reverend Fred Bruffett, D.D., editor of *Fundamental News* and former chairman of the Association of Fundamental Ministers and Churches, Incorporated, on this writer's behalf.

54. *Constitution and Principles and Practices of the Slavic Gospel Association, Incorporated* (rev. edn.; Chicago: Slavic Gospel Association, 1967) (29-page pamphlet), pp. 7-9.

55. Communication from the Reverend Andrew Semenchuk, assistant director,

Slavic Gospel Association, Incorporated.

56. Carl M. Goltz, *Let's Get Acquainted* (North Platte, Neb.: Berean Fundamental Church, n.d.) (6-page tract), p. 1.

57. "In Memoriam Rev. Vincent J. Joy 1914–1966," *Alaskan Nuggets,* special edition, Winter 1966–1967.

58. *Central Alaskan Missions, Incorporated* (6-page undated folder), p. [6].

59. Letter from Miss Faye E. Crandall, publicity chairman, Central Alaskan Missions, Incorporated, Glennallen, Alaska.

60. *World Christian Handbook 1968,* p. 112, estimated the membership at 350.

61. Letter from the Reverend E. Paul Kopp, president, United Fundamentalist Church, Incorporated, 3236 Larga, Los Angeles, California. This writer gratefully acknowledges the efforts put forth on his behalf by Mr. Jerry Raedeke, then seminarian-assistant at the First Lutheran Church, Van Nuys, California, to obtain information about the United Fundamentalist Church.

62. Communication from the Reverend W. O. Higgett Garman, Th.M., D.D., president, Associated Gospel Churches. Ralph Lord Roy, *Apostles of Discord: A Study of Organized Bigotry and Disruption on the Fringes of Protestantism* (Boston: Beacon Press, 1953), p. 394, states that the Associated Gospel Churches began when about twenty-five congregations broke with the Methodist Protestant Church in 1939 to form the American Bible Fellowship Association. Dr. Garman reports in the *A.G.C. Reporter* for September 1967, p. 1: "When we affiliated with the AGC, we had been led to believe that it was made up of 30 churches. We later discovered to our great chagrin that there were perhaps only 3 which were active." Since then, he states, the picture has been "gloriously changed." The "service agency" aspect of the association is receiving increasing emphasis.

63. "Basis of Fellowship," *Where Does Your Church Stand?* (Pittsburgh, Penn.: Associated Gospel Churches, n.d.) (4-page pamphlet), p. [2].

64. Ibid.

65. Communication from Dr. Garman.

66. *A.G.C. Reporter,* September 1967, p. 1. The Gospel Fellowship Association,

listed as one of the agencies which the Commission on Chaplains of the Associated Gospel Churches represents, is related to Bob Jones University, Greenville, South Carolina, and is an association of individuals, not of congregations (letter from Dr. Gilbert Stenholm, director of ministerial training and extension, Bob Jones University).

67. *A.G.C. Reporter,* September 1967, p. 1.

68. Ibid., p. 2.

69. See, for instance, *Truth and Liberty Magazine,* September 1968, p. 2. On some of Stadsklev's past activities, see Ralph Lord Roy, *Apostles of Discord: A Study of Organized Bigotry and Disruption on the Fringes of Protestantism* (Boston: Beacon Press, 1953), pp. 112-113.

70. C. O. Stadsklev, *The United States Is Zion of Bible Prophecy* (Hopkins, Minn.: Gospel Temple, 1955) (91-page brochure); Stadsklev, *Our Christian Beginnings* (Hopkins, Minn.: Gospel Temple, n.d.) (35-page tract); Stadsklev, *America in the Kingdom Parables* (Hopkins, Minn.: Gospel Temple, 1959) (91-page brochure); Stadsklev, *From Abram through Armageddon and A Defence of Armageddon by F. E. Pitts, 1857* (Hopkins, Minn.: Gospel Temple, 1960); C. O. Stadsklev, *United States in Bible Prophecy and Will Russia Attack America?* (Hopkins, Minn.: Gospel Temple, n.d.) (47-page brochure).

71. C. O. Stadsklev, *The Inevitable Collapse of Our Debt Money System* (Hopkins, Minn.: Gospel Temple, 1957) (56-page brochure); Stadsklev, *New Money for the New Age* (Hopkins, Minn.: Gospel Temple, n.d.) (76-page brochure).

72. C. O. Stadsklev, *Errors of Fundamentalism* (Hopkins, Minn.: Gospel Temple, n.d.) (34-page tract).

73. The repeated efforts of the present writer to secure information about the National Association of Kingdom Evangelicals (NAKE) directly from the Reverend Mr. Stadsklev by mail were unsuccessful.

74. *Once an Active, Thriving Church . . .* (Olcott, N.Y.: American Mission for Opening Closed Churches, 1966) (8-page pamphlet), p. 7.

75. Letter from the Reverend Lyle C. Anderson, general director, American

Mission for Opening Closed Churches, Incorporated.

76. *1967 Directory of the American Evangelical Christian Churches* (Chicago: American Evangelical Christian Churches, 1966), pp. 6, 20.

77. Ibid., pp. 9-18; letter of Dr. G. W. Hyatt, moderator, American Evangelical Christian Churches.

78. Certificate of Incorporation, State of South Carolina, for the Fellowship of Independent Evangelical Churches (Spartanburg, South Carolina), dated February 5, 1951.

79. Articles III-V, *Constitution of the Fellowship of Independent Evangelical Churches,* 1968 edition (11-page mimeographed document).

80. Letter from the Reverend Howard Boyll, secretary, Fellowship of Independent Evangelical Churches.

81. Section I, Bylaws, *Constitution and By-Laws of Evangelical Ministers and Churches International [E.M.C.I.]* (rev. edn.; Chicago: Evangelical Ministers and Churches International, 1965) (10-page pamphlet), p. 5.

82 Letters from the Reverend Jacob W. Stauffer, D.D., Litt.D., president, Evangelical Ministers and Churches International, Incorporated.

83. Letter from the Reverend Paul M. Cell, D.D., pastor emeritus of the First Baptist Church of Willowick, 224 East 315th Street, Willowick, Ohio; telephone conversation with the Reverend Ralph I. Yarnell, D.D., 327 Seventh Street, Marietta, Ohio. In 1960 a survey by *Christianity Today* listed the membership of Independent Churches Affiliated at 14,100 (*Christianity Today*, vol. 9, no. 9 [January 29, 1965], p. 11 [431]).

84. Bill Jones, *A Gambler's Testimony* (Austin, Texas: The Church of the New Testament, n.d.) (4-page tract).

85. Letter from Brother Bill Jones, pastor, Church of the New Testament, Austin, Texas.

86. "Statement of Faith," *Christians in Action* (Long Beach, Calif.: Missionary and Soul Winning Fellowship, n.d.) (20-page brochure), p. 7.

87. Letter from Miss Lyn Klippenstein, secretary, Missionary and Soul Winning Fellowship, Box 7271, Long Beach, California.

88. See George N. Patterson, *Christianity in Communist China* (Waco, Texas: Word Books, 1969), pp. 72-73, 143.

89. Watchman Nee, *The Normal Christian Life* (3rd edn., 3rd printing; Fort Washington, Penn.: Christian Literature Crusade, 1967).

90. Lee is editor of a quarterly magazine, *The Stream,* published at Box 18782, Los Angeles. This writer's repeated efforts to obtain information about his work directly from him were unsuccessful. Although Nee and Austin-Sparks have known one another since the 1930s and although Austin-Sparks has twice visited Taiwan at Lee's invitation and lectured at his conferences and Lee in turn has ministered at the Honour Oak Christian Fellowship Centre in London, there is no official or organized connection between the work of Austin-Sparks and that of Nee and Lee.

91. The center is described by Austin-Sparks as "simply a meeting-place for Christian fellowship, and not the center of a community." In the early 1950s a woman minister of the Reformed Church in Holland who claimed to have studied at the center circulated a long report among evangelical leaders in which she asserted the existence at the center of a secret fellowship of "Sons of God" under Austin-Sparks's direction. This secret fellowship allegedly had as its purpose the penetration of the denominational church bodies and missionary societies with a view to spreading the deeper revelation that the House of God at Honour Oak possesses. The center officials immediately repudiated the charges and branded the report a complete fabrication. Nevertheless, the Dutch minister's allegations were revived a dozen years later in an expanded form by Andrew Stenhouse in an article, "A Sinister Movement," in a British journal. The Plymouth Brethren publication *Letters of Interest* for September 1966, pp. 12-13, republished it under the title, "Destruction by Infiltration." The British journal in question invited Austin-Sparks to submit answers to eleven questions that the Stenhouse article raised. Austin-Sparks explicitly denied the existence of an Honour Oak Fellowship in the sense in which the Stenhouse article had used the term, rejected the views and teachings that the Stenhouse article had ascribed to the center, and declared that "for some years" he had not had personal

responsibility for the work at Honour Oak. *Letters of Interest* for November 1966, pp. 22-23, carried the entire statement under the title, "T. Austin-Sparks Rebuts Andrew Stenhouse Article."

92. Among the independent congregations in North America that have had informal links with the ministry of Austin-Sparks and the Honour Oak Christian Fellowship Centre is Westmoreland Chapel (Ambassadors for Christ, Incorporated), 1505 South Westmoreland Avenue, Los Angeles, originally founded in 1942 by former members of the Church of the Open Door, Los Angeles, led by Dr. James Graham after he had resigned from the Presbyterian ministry over the issue of divorce and remarriage. Austin-Sparks took part in the conferences there for a number of years and in 1957 Mr. C. J. B. Harrison (d. 1967), an elder of the Honour Oak Fellowship, came to Los Angeles to help the Westmoreland Chapel reestablish itself. The congregation gathers in the conviction that Christ is the head of the church and a living person who leads his people through the Holy Spirit, that all preaching should be derived from the Bible, and that creeds and doctrinal emphases separate God's people into sects. It holds a strict view on divorce and remarriage. It practices baptism by immersion and observes the Lord's table every week as a rule, although neither practice is a basis of fellowship. (Letters from Mr. Russell D. Blomberg, treasurer, Ambassadors for Christ, Incorporated, 1505 South Westmoreland Avenue, Los Angeles, California.)

93. Since 1966 the Atlantic States Christian Convocation, held annually at Camp Wabanna, Mayo, Maryland, has brought together in a joint ministry representatives of This Testimony like Austin-Sparks, Stephen Kaung, and DeVern Fromke of Indianapolis.

94. Much of the information contained in this section has been taken from letters received in September 1968 from a proponent of This Testimony who has been intimately associated with it for over three decades. Of the voluntary and unsolicited contributions acknowledged in *A Witness and a Testimony* during 1966 and 1967, 31.2 percent of the total sum came from the United States of America and 1.7 percent from Canada. Except for one gift of $600 from the Atlantic States Christian Convocation, the remittances from the United States came from 161 post offices in thirty states and averaged slightly over $9.00 each. The only communities that appear five times or more were the Twin Cities (13), Birmingham, Alabama (12), the New York metropolitan area (5), and St. Petersburg, Florida (5).

95. Charles S. Poling, *"Choose Ye This Day"* (Phoenix, Ariz.: Church of All Christian Faiths, n.d.) (11-page pamphlet), pp. 3, 11.

96. *The Denomination of the Church of All Christian Faiths: A Free Church—Constitution (Articles of Incorporation), By-laws, Articles of Faith* (rev. edn.; Phoenix, Ariz.: Church of All Christian Faiths, 1967) (28-page pamphlet), pp. 14, 23-26.

97. Letters from Mrs. L. W. Staley, office secretary, Church of All Christian Faiths, Phoenix, Arizona.

98. Article V ("Doctrinal Statement"), *Constitution and Doctrinal Statement of the Independent Fundamental Bible Churches* (Los Angeles, Calif.: Independent Fundamental Bible Churches, n.d.) (4-page leaflet), pp. [1]-[2].

99. Letter from the Reverend Kenneth L. Barth, secretary, Independent Fundamental Bible Churches.

# PART II

## OTHER CHURCHES IN THE CHRISTIAN TRADITION

# 7. Friends

## Friends in America

Charles Fox (1624–1691), the offspring of a devout Puritan household in England, gained religious peace in 1646 through the conviction that God gives to each person a gift of divine Inner Light. For Fox the Divine Light meant that revelation was no longer limited to the Scriptures. He spoke out against outward ceremony, paid ministry, establishment of religion, taking oaths, and waging war. With his followers, he had to endure severe persecution for his beliefs. Fox's movement was organized as the Religious Society of Friends, and its followers were labeled Quakers.

Mary Fisher and Ann Austin were the first Friends to come to America, arriving in Boston in 1656, but they were quickly expelled. Quakers continued to come to New England and, after enduring persecution which for some led to execution, they were tolerated after 1675. Rhode Island and the middle colonies provided a refuge for Quaker missionaries. The first Yearly Meeting was held in Newport, Rhode Island, in 1661. Following a visit of George Fox to the colonies in 1672–1673, the Quaker movement spread through New Jersey.

William Penn, a convert to the Quaker movement in 1667, visited the colonies and from the Duke of York received a large grant of land in America which he named after his father. He successfully appealed for colonists in a holy experiment which called for freedom of religion, and settlers came to Pennsylvania from Great Britain and Germany in considerable numbers.

The Religious Society of Friends became a leading denomination during the colonial period of American history. Through their separatism they were not affected substantially by the Great Awakening of the eighteenth century. The Friends divided over the issue of preparation for the military action of the Revolutionary War. Growing opposition to slavery among the Friends, especially on the part of John Woolman (1720–1772) and Anthony Benezet (1713–1784), helped eliminate slavery from the middle and northern colonies.

The evangelicalism which issued from the Second Awakening in the nineteenth century had consequences for the Friends. Many Friends found the evangelical impulse congenial. In England Joseph John Gurney (1788–1847) had an "evangelical" influence on the Quakers. Elias Hicks (1748–1830) of Long Island, New York, opposed the evangelical influence as inconsistent with the Quaker emphasis on the Inner Light. In 1827 the Philadelphia Yearly Meeting divided into Orthodox and Hicksite camps. Toward the mid-nineteenth century the Quakers of the Philadelphia meeting and elsewhere divided between those who followed Gurney and those who were loyal to John Wilbur (1774–1856), a moderate Quaker who opposed the Gurneyites.

In the latter part of the nineteenth century the Quaker Yearly Meetings participated in a series of advisory General Conferences. Out of these a Five Years Meeting developed as a consultative body for many Friends. New organizations developed among those who found the Five Years Meeting too liberal and that meeting was reorganized as the Friends United Meeting. The influence of the Evangelical movement among the Friends expressed itself organizationally in the formation of the Evangelical Friends Alliance in 1965.

## General Conference of the Religious Society of Friends

The General Conference of the Religious Society of Friends is the oldest (by two years) and second largest of the four major Friends groupings in the United States. Although it was formally organized in 1900, its antecedents go back at least to 1868 when members of the "Hicksite" Yearly Meetings called into being the First-day School General Conference for the promotion of Quaker Sunday schools. Another predecessor organization was the Friends Union for Philanthropic Labor, created in 1881; it perpetuated the concern for peace and social reform of the Friends who had been active in the Underground Railroad a generation earlier. A third forerunner was the Friends Religious Conference, organized in 1893, in part as a result of Friends' contact with the World's Congress of Religions at Chicago that year. A fourth precursor was the Friends Education Conference, established in 1894 to bring together every two years those members of the "Hicksite" Yearly Meetings who had a special concern for the denomination's schools and colleges. These four conferences and the seven yearly meetings that supported them reorganized as the Friends General Conference in 1900.

Although the General Conference has no creed to which its members must subscribe, and although cooperation with the other major groupings of Friends has mitigated some of the sharply chiseled features, along with the misunderstandings and hostilities, of the nineteenth and early twentieth centuries, the "Hicksite" liberal tradition is still apparent. It finds expression in three emphases.

The first is on the centrality for Friends of the authority of the Inner

Light or the Christ Within. Linked with this are a cluster of other convictions, that God has written his law on every human heart, that salvation is the continuing process of spiritual renewal, and that the individual human spirit is the primary unit of spiritual value. This constellation made it possible for "Hicksite" Friends to affirm their allegiance to Christ while rejecting the necessity of traditional orthodoxy's christological definitions.

A second emphasis is on waiting for divine guidance as the central feature of worship.

A third emphasis is on the positive desirability of a variety of approaches within the local fellowship, within the yearly meeting and the denomination, and within the Christian community as such.

While the General Conference has never had a place in its program for foreign missions, its Committee for the Advancement of Friends Principles (now simply the Advancement Committee) has been a kind of surrogate. It has been active in recent years in the production of literature designed to interest potential members in the society, in providing channels of publicity at local and higher levels, and in caring for the spiritual needs of some 7,000 nonresident members of its yearly meetings. The Committee on Christian Unity concerns itself with the ecumenical relations of the General Conference. The religious education, religious life, school and college education, and peace and social order committees provide channels for the expression of the continuing historic concern of the yearly meetings in these areas.

There are four yearly meetings in the United States with membership exclusively in the General Conference—Philadelphia (with well over half of the total membership of the conference), Illinois, Indiana, and South Central. The Green Pastures Quarterly Meeting of the otherwise unaffiliated Lake Erie Yearly Meeting also belongs to the conference. The New England, New York, Baltimore, and Southeastern Yearly Meetings belong to both the General Conference and the United Meeting. These meetings have a total of 233 local meetings in the United States, with an inclusive membership of 26,184. The Canadian Yearly Meeting also belongs to both the General Confrence and the United Meeting.[1] The headquarters of the General Conference of the Religious Society of Friends are at 1520-B Race Street, Philadelphia, Pennsylvania 19102.

## Philadelphia Yearly Meeting of the Religious Society of Friends

The Philadelphia Yearly Meeting of the Religious Society of Friends, the largest yearly meeting of Friends in North America, is the continuation into the present of the Friends General Meeting that met for the first time at Burlington, New Jersey, in 1681 and that four years later took the name "The General Yearly Meeting for Friends of Pennsylvania, East and West Jersey and of the Adjacent Provinces." A major schism took place in 1827. Two thirds of the membership, followers of Elias Hicks, formed the Race

Street Meeting; the "Orthodox" third formed the Arch Street Meeting. In 1933 both bodies made changes in their respective disciplines to provide for the establishment of United Monthly Meetings. In 1945 they arranged for the establishment of the Philadelphia General Meeting of the Religious Society of Friends. The reunion of the two meetings was completed in 1955. The Philadelphia Yearly Meeting belongs to the Friends General Conference.

Its *Discipline* disavows a formal creed. "Each person must humbly and prayerfully seek individual guidance and follow his understanding of God's leading. He will be helped by studying the developing interpretation of God in the Bible and especially by pondering the deep obligations imposed upon us by the teachings and sacrificial death of Jesus. With all those who sincerely try to follow Him in spirit and truth, Friends find themselves in unity."[2] The Light Within—given to all people everywhere since the beginning of the human race but not to be identified with the human conscience—is "a spiritual power known to [Friends] by its working in their lives and exemplified in the life of Jesus. For all it has been a fertile seed waiting to be quickened." Each human being is "in a large measure the arbiter of his own destiny, having the power of choice. Salvation, in the Quaker sense, comes through this power given to man to make right choices under the guidance of the Light."[3]

The Bible bears witness to the faith "that there is in every man a spark of the divine, and that through its Light man can have the experience of God speaking to his condition." The Old Testament is "the foundation of the great Judeo-Christian religious heritage by which devout worshipers cooperate in upholding righteousness." The New Testament climaxes "a progressive revelation of God's nature and His will, culminating in the revelation of Himself in the life and teachings of Jesus Christ." In the impact of His life on His contemporaries, "one finds the beginning of the Christian Church." As the Spirit produced the Scriptures, "they are fully understood and accepted only through the same Spirit," so that the discovery of the meaning of the Bible and the application of its teachings to life calls for "spiritual insight as well as modern scholarship."[4]

As Friends are less reliant than many groups on the written word of Scripture, creed, or ritual, so they are less affected by conflicts between science and religion. As long as religion finds its basis in experience and "a language exists for communicating religious insights with reasonable precision," there is no opposition between religion and scientific laws considered as the simplest correlations of data, correlations that at the same time are productive of further discoveries. In the process of biological evolution, the coming of man has made possible the rapid transformation of communities through planning and education. For harmonious life in communities, "the Old Testament describes the development of a high system of ethics" that became more complex as it confronted new situations. Jesus pointed out the impossibility of living up to the limitless demands of an ethical life solely by one's own efforts. He demonstrated the possibility of a higher level, on which the human being is freed from the distorted perspective where he looks at everything from himself as a center. Then a new creative power—the Holy Spirit, the Light of Christ, the Inward Light, the Spirit of God—sets human beings free from worry and fear and transforms them "into sensitive, strong personalities, centers of radiating love, illuminating and confirming others."[5]

The Philadelphia Yearly Meeting has neither a trained ministry nor an outward observance of the sacraments of the Lord's Supper and of water baptism. It opposes gambling, presses the cause of total abstinence, and counsels "its members to refuse to bear arms or to accept membership in military forces."[6] Its 17,000 members carry on an outreach in Japan through the Japan Committee and among North American Indians; provide very substantial support for the American Friends Service Committee; maintain many Quaker schools and colleges; and have a strong concern for peace, for right race relations, for social order, and for the religious education and spiritual life of their membership.[7] It reports its statistics through the General Conference of the Religious Society of Friends. The headquarters of the Philadelphia Yearly Meeting are at 1515 Cherry Street, Philadelphia, Pennsylvania 19102.

## The Religious Society of Friends (Conservative)

The three mainly rural Conservative yearly meetings of the Religious Society of Friends—Iowa, North Carolina, and Ohio (Barnesville)—are, together with a few independent meetings, the modern heirs of the Wilburite tradition among Orthodox Friends. They constitute about one fiftieth of the American Quaker community. The name "Conservative" does not describe necessarily either their theology or their social and political attitudes. It merely indicates that like their spiritual forebears of the mid-nineteenth century they continue to be concerned about the preservation of what they see as the essential Friends convictions and practices, especially belief in the Inner Light.

At the beginning of the present century the Conservatives had been extensively disowned by and isolated from the rest of the Religious Society of Friends. As defenders of a beleaguered subculture they were long engaged in a losing struggle. They suffered serious losses both in the number of yearly meetings, in inclusive membership, and in the number of their schools. The changing economy and the changing environment made it difficult to retain many cherished customs for which they once stood—the plain clothing, the plain language, the division of the meetinghouse into men's side and women's side, the ban on music in the home, and the strict discipline which, for instance, disowned the Friend who "married out."

Since World War II the decline seems to have been arrested and Conservative Friends are returning more and more to the mainstream of Quaker life. They have joined other Friends in the agencies that support conscientious objectors and the pacifist ideal, although they have not abandoned their insistence that pacifism must basically be the outcome of a total transformation of the whole person by the power of the Inner Light. There are additional measures of their newfound cooperation with other Friends. The Conservative Yearly Meetings have resumed correspondence with all other yearly meetings. They have been giving increasing all-around support to more and more national and international agencies of the Friends. Since 1945 two Conservative yearly meetings—New England and Canada—have merged with other yearly meetings in their respective territory. Interest in cooperation and intervisitation with neighboring Friends has increased in each of the three Conservative yearly meetings; in some cases this has led to dual membership. Young people are receiving new attention and regard, and interest in Friends schools at both the elementary and secondary level has revived. Two of the yearly meetings have reorganized and rewritten their disciplines in modern language and with regard to contemporary psychological insights. Theological differences are wide, but "the average conservative does tend to agree on the importance and necessity of Divine Guidance, and on the need for depth—regardless of the words used—in worship."[8]

The three Conservative meetings have a total of 26 local meetings with 1,840 members. Each meeting has its own clerk; there are no general headquarters.

### Friends United Meeting

By the late 1880s difficulties of communication, accommodation in varying degrees to prevailing patterns in American Christianity of the nineteenth century, and growing divergence in practice among Friends of the "Orthodox" tradition combined to create a situation that seemed to require a new definition of purpose and practice by which the Friends in North America could guide themselves. For that reason a conference of representatives of all North American yearly meetings in official correspondence with the "mother" London Yearly Meeting was convened at Richmond, Indiana, in 1887. The immediate outcome was an awakened desire for closer cooperation. The conference found a sense of unity in a statement of belief known as the Richmond Declaration of Faith.[9]

Another outcome was a delayed one. After two more meetings at five-year intervals, the Five Years Meeting of Friends in America came into being formally in 1902, uniting twelve yearly meetings that had adopted the uniform discipline: New England, New York, Baltimore, Canada, Wilmington (Ohio), Indiana, Western (in Indiana), Iowa, Kansas, California, Oregon, and North Carolina. In the course of time the Kansas and Oregon yearly meetings withdrew because of theological differences. A new yearly meeting was organized in Nebraska in 1908. As a result of overseas mission work a number of yearly meetings and smaller associations of Friends in foreign countries joined the Five Years Meeting. From 1960 on, the representatives of the yearly meetings assembled at three-year rather than five-year intervals; as a result the organization adopted the name of Friends United Meeting in 1965. Today it includes a little more than half the Friends in the world.

The Friends United Meeting has no binding creed, but it has a number of "common testimonies." Its members believe that through his Spirit God can reveal his will through anyone and use any worshiper as his minister in any meeting for worship. About one fifth of the meetings (local congregations) follow the tradition of unprogrammed worship and wait together in silence for God to inspire some worshipers to speak, pray, or sing. The remaining meetings avail themselves of pastors who are able to provide inspired preaching, skilled teaching, pastoral care, and the kind of leadership that develops the latent gifts of the other members of the meeting in a pattern of shared leadership.

The Friends United Meeting holds that its members can know communion with Christ and the baptism of his Spirit without the use of symbolic ceremonies and the material means historically associated with these sacraments. All members have equal responsibilities in the search for guidance in the divine ordering of the meeting's business affairs. They believe in the sacredness of personality as a gift of the Creator, and in varying degrees they support the historic Friends testimonies for peace (and its corollary not to kill another human being), good race relations, and concern for the less privileged. They hold that life is to be lived in a sense of stewardship; thus they practice integrity in business affairs, speak the truth without oaths, and discourage the use of narcotics, alcoholic beverages, and tobacco. They believe that the Spirit of God stands ready not only to usher human beings into everlasting life but also to guide them in their day-by-day living. They emphasize the redeeming grace of God through Christ; affirm the inspiration of the Bible; and base their statements of faith on the life and teachings of Christ and their own experiences of God. Their missionary concern embraces both the spiritual welfare of others and the achievement of justice and harmony in the community.

The Friends United Meeting functions through seven boards for Christian social concerns, missions, publications, evangelism and church extension, Christian education, stewardship and finance, and vocation and ministry. Between the triennial meetings, an Executive Council meets semiannually to conduct the United Meeting's interim business. The Friends United Meeting is active in ecumenical affairs and is a member of the National Council of the Churches of Christ in the United States of America.

The headquarters are at 101 Quaker Hill Drive, Richmond, Indiana 47374. There are 519 local meetings in the United States with an inclusive membership of 66,680. The Canadian Yearly Meeting of the Religious Society of Friends belongs to both the Friends United Meeting and the Friends General Conference. Overseas meetings are located in Kenya, Jamaica, Cuba, Mexico, and Jordan.

## The Canadian Yearly Meeting of the Religious Society of Friends

A considerable number of Friends, who refused to fight either on the side of the United Colonies or on the side of the British crown in the Revolutionary War, accompanied the Loyalist refugees to Canada. Around the end of the eighteenth century they founded the first Friends meetings in what was to become the Dominion of Canada—in Nova Scotia, in Upper Canada near the east end of Lake Ontario, and in the Niagara peninsula.[10] The Canada Yearly Meeting was established in 1867. It maintains ties with Quakers in the United States by holding membership in both the Friends United Meeting and the Friends General Conference. At the same time it retains a link with Friends in the British Isles by using as its own the London Yearly Meeting's anthology-type manual, *Christian Faith and Practice in the Experience of the Society of Friends*. In the classic Friends tradition, the cited manual stresses that "the Society of Friends is tolerant of varied judgments amongst its members. It does not expect acceptance of a precise definition of its faith. It does not adopt an order of service for its public worship. It leaves its members wide freedom in working out the application of its testimonies."[11] An important arm of the meeting is the Canadian Friends Service Committee, through which the meeting implements its social concerns. There are 28 local meetings in 8 provinces; the total membership is 1,066.

## Evangelical Friends Alliance

In 1965 four regional groupings of Friends joined together to form the Evangelical Friends Alliance.

One participating group was the Kansas Yearly Meeting of Friends, which two decades earlier had played a prominent role in the organization of the Association of Evangelical Friends. Organized in 1872, the Kansas Yearly Meeting of Friends grew out of the great westward migrations of the late nineteenth century. In 1902 it was one of the eleven meetings that united to form the Five Years Meeting of Friends, now the Friends United Meeting. A great rural meeting that has given many leaders to the Friends movement and is strongly conservative, the Kansas Yearly Meeting withdrew from the Five Years Meeting in 1937 out of concern for the inroads that secularism, humanism, and a preoccupation with "works of mercy" at the expense of a spiritual interest appeared to be making in the larger confederation. In the same year the Kansas Yearly Meeting established its own mission in Burundi. Its present headquarters are at 2018 Maple Street, Wichita, Kansas 67213.

Another group which helped to form the Evangelical Friends Alliance in 1965 was the Northwest Yearly Meeting. It was formed in 1893 (as the

Oregon Yearly Meeting) by the Iowa Yearly Meeting to provide for the spiritual needs of the Friends who had migrated into Washington, Oregon, and Idaho, chiefly from Iowa and Kansas. The antecedents of the Northwest Yearly Meeting inclined it toward theological conservatism, and in 1926 it withdrew from the Five Years Meeting. The withdrawal was a protest against what the Oregon Yearly Meeting regarded as tendencies to depreciate the inspiration and the place of the Scriptures, to minimize the Friends teaching on holiness, to adulterate the Gospel, and to call the verities of the Christian faith into question. The mailing address of its headquarters is Box 190, Newberg, Oregon 97132.

A third group which helped form the Evangelical Friends Alliance was the Rocky Mountain Yearly Meeting of Friends, established in 1957 out of the constituency of the Nebraska Yearly Meeting. Concern over theological liberalism was a primary issue in the formation of the Rocky Mountain Yearly Meeting; most of the members were opposed to membership in the National Council of the Churches of Christ in the United States of America on the part of the Five Years Meeting of Friends (since 1965 the Friends United Meeting). The Rocky Mountain Yearly Meeting is a member of the National Holiness Association and of the National Association of Evangelicals, whose theological platform it endorses. It has 25 local meetings with a total of about 1,500 members and carries on a mission among the Navajos of Arizona. Its headquarters are at 2460 Orchard, Grand Junction, Colorado 81501.

The fourth group which helped form the Evangelical Friends Alliance was the Evangelical Friends Church—Eastern Region. Established in 1813 as the Ohio Yearly Meeting by Friends who had moved into the Ohio Territory in large numbers, the organization suffered two severe schisms during its first century—the Hicksite split and the Wilbur–Gurney separation. The Evangelical movement penetrated deeply into the Ohio Yearly Meeting, especially in the latter half of the nineteenth century. The extreme quietism and emphasis on the doctrine of the Inner Light of the past gave way to Bible reading and Bible study, the singing of Gospel songs with organ accompaniment, revival meetings, the pastoral system, and—in some cases— the observance of the outward ordinances of baptism and the Lord's Supper. In 1886 the Ohio Yearly Meeting ruled that nonobservance of these outward ordinances would no longer be a test of membership.[12] In addition the Holiness tenet of sanctification as a second work of grace and the teaching of the premillennial return of Christ also began to appear. A new theological vocabulary came into use, which attempted to clothe the essentials of early Friends teaching in new terminology.

In 1902 the Ohio Yearly Meeting did not join the ten other meetings that formed the Five Years Meeting. Given the meeting's evangelical stance, it was only natural that the Association of Evangelical Friends would attract many members of the Ohio Yearly Meeting. In 1971 the organization took its present name.

There are fifteen doctrinal articles in the *Discipline* of the Evangelical Friends Church—Eastern Region. They affirm the Trinity, redemption through the blood of the virgin-born Son of God, Jesus Christ, his deity and his manhood, the satisfactory nature of his propitiation and atonement for the sins of the whole world, the personality of the Holy Spirit, the inspiration and divine authority of the Holy Scriptures, the existence of Satan, and man's loss of the image of God through the fall. God imputes sin to human beings only when they transgress the divine law after having received sufficient capacity to understand it. Infants are heirs of grace. With Fox, Barclay, and Gurney the Evangelical Friends Church—Eastern Region asserts that "Our Lord Jesus Christ bestows a measure of the enlightening influence of the Holy Spirit on all," but it rejects the teaching that there is the "gift of a portion of the Holy Spirit in the soul of every man." Repentance and confession of sins is a prerequisite of justification, which is by faith in the merits of Christ's atonement for our sins of omission and commission and which includes regeneration, adoption, and initial sanctification. In entire sanctification Christians receive the baptism with the Holy Ghost and fire. The *discipline* further affirms the resurrection of the dead, Christ's judgment of the living and the dead on the great day of judgment, deep humiliation and subjection of soul before God as the essential qualification of worship, individual liberty of conscience in the observance or nonobservance of the external ordinances of baptism and the supper of the Lord, the duty of prayer and praise, the divine origin of the gifts of the Gospel ministry, and Christ's premillennial return for the rapture of his bride prior to his coming reign.[13]

The Evangelical Friends Church—Eastern Region maintains the traditional Friends position against war and upholds conscientious objection to military service. It prohibits oaths, endorses the keeping of Sunday as the New Testament Sabbath, forbids divorce (except in cases of adultery), opposes the use of alcoholic beverages and tobacco, commends simplicity of dress, observes that while God has not declared his purpose to heal all the sick he often does heal in response to believing prayer, and earnestly entreats its members to avoid harmful practices such as speaking in tongues.[14]

Through a series of historical developments over its more than 150 years of existence, the Evangelical Friends Church—Eastern Region includes monthly (local) meetings not only in Ohio, but also in Michigan, Iowa, Pennsylvania, Virginia, North Carolina, Rhode Island, Florida, and Ontario. It recently moved its headquarters to Canton, Ohio 44709. There are 88 churches with an inclusive membership of nearly 9,000. It carries on foreign missions in India, Nepal, the Republic of China (Taiwan), and (in cooperation with the Evangelical Friends Alliance) in Mexico.[15]

The Evangelical Friends Alliance emerged out of movements among Friends which included an Evangelical revival and a reappropriation of the Evangelical nature of the views of seventeenth-century Friends. Those associated with the Evangelical Friends Alliance are conservative and Evangelical in theology and utilize pastors locally. Their Sunday morning worship, while providing for a period of open worship, includes a sermon by the pastor in addition to Scripture reading and singing.

Among the Yearly Meetings of the Evangelical Friends Alliance are 254 churches with an inclusive membership of 27,206. At present the Evangelical Friends Alliance is seeking to serve its constituent groups as a common agency for mission through a proposed Evangelical Friends Mission.

### Pacific Yearly Meeting of the Religious Society of Friends

The oldest monthly (local) meeting of the Pacific Yearly Meeting was founded in 1881. Fifty years later, at the initiative of the Friends leaders, Howard and Anna Brinton, the Pacific Coast Association of Friends was formed. After years of discussion, the Pacific Yearly Meeting was established in 1947 within the Pacific Coast Association and met concurrently with it until the latter organization was "laid down" in 1958.

While the meeting has no formal set of words in which it fixes its faith, its *Discipline* affirms the great value that the members of the Pacific Yearly Meeting put on the record of God's dealing with people in the Scriptures and the need of interpreting them "in the Spirit which inspired them and which continues to reveal Truth to men." It stresses the experience of the divine Life at the heart of the universe that Friends call "the Light within" and that enlightens every person. The life of Jesus on earth revealed this Light, and when Friends live and walk in it they feel that they answer to this same Light of God in other persons. The *Discipline* sees a creative tension between the particular and universal character of the Friends interpretation of Christianity, between its Christ-centered and its God-centered orientation, and between its mystical and its practical demands.[16] In receiving an applicant for membership, the Visiting Committee concerns itself about what the applicant's experience has revealed to him so far concerning God, the Inward Light, Jesus, the question of evil, the place of the Bible, and immortality.[17]

Worship in the Pacific Yearly Meeting is an unprogrammed and silent waiting on the Lord. The worshipers come together in silence for about an hour; a spoken message that one or the other participant is moved to give occasionally breaks the silence. The meeting has no ordained clergy.

There are 37 monthly (local) meetings on the West Coast of the United States and in Hawaii, with an inclusive membership of 1,600. There are also local meetings in Canada and Mexico. It is the largest unaffiliated Friends Yearly Meeting in North America. Its journal, *Friends Bulletin*, is published from 2635 Emerald Street, Eugene, Oregon 97403.[18]

### Central Yearly Meeting of Friends

By 1924 a considerable number of Evangelical Friends in Hamilton County, Indiana, asked their monthly meetings to transfer them to the Ohio

Yearly Meeting because they felt they could no longer in good conscience continue in connection with the Five Years Meeting, which they had come to regard as an unorthodox body. Most of the applicants had their requests refused. As a consequence several groups of individuals withdrew between 1924 and 1926 from their respective monthly meetings and set up monthly and quarterly meetings of their own. The organization of the Central Yearly Meeting of Friends in the latter year climaxed this development.[19]

In its Statement of Belief, the Central Yearly Meeting accepts the Bible as its rule of faith and conduct. It affirms belief in the inspiration of the Bible "both as to words and matter"; in the Trinity; in the Father ("the Son and the Holy Ghost, though of equal essence, are subordinate in office [to the Father]"); in the Son and in his person, work and bodily premillennial return; and in the Holy Ghost. It teaches the reality of Satan; the creation and fall of man ("in consequence of his disobedience and fall, sin and death were entailed upon all men; but we believe infants do not have sin imputed to them until they have a consciousness that they are sinners in God's sight . . . because the atonement covers that for which they are not personally responsible"); the redemption of man ("only by and through the vicarious sacrifice of Jesus Christ on the cross"); regeneration; sanctification ("the second definite work of grace . . . for all who have been born again"); and the resurrection of both the just and the unjust.[20]

It calls for Bible schools on the First-day before meetings for worship; approves a regular and salaried ministry of pastors and evangelists; recommends tithing; holds that Christians are not bound to submit to any outward ordinances or practice any form or ceremony that serves only as the outward symbol of an inward work (such as baptism and Communion);[21] and describes the first day of the week as the Christian Sabbath.[22] It honors "that type of courage which refuses all military service for conscience' sake and patiently endures the penalty inflicted"; counsels against participation in partisan politics or running for office; admonishes its members to avail themselves of the legal privilege of affirming rather than swearing; urges those who intend to marry to submit the matter to the monthly meeting; disowns persons who seek divorce except on well-proved biblical grounds; discountenances the wearing of jewelry and conformity to the vain and changeable fashions of the world in dress; and recommends that members neither own nor voluntarily watch television.[23]

The Central Yearly Meeting stresses that it is not associated or connected with the American Friends Service Committee, the Friends World Committee, the Friends Coordinating Committee, the World Council of Churches, or the National Council of the Churches of Christ in the United States of America.[24]

There are 12 local meetings with a total membership of 492.[25] The Newby Book Room, Route 1, Box 296, Noblesville, Indiana 46060, serves in lieu of a headquarters. The meeting maintains a foreign mission in Bolivia.

## Unaffiliated Meetings of Religious Society of Friends

In addition to the Pacific Yearly Meeting and the Central Yearly Meeting already described, there are other yearly meetings of Friends which are not formally associated with larger organizations. Among these are the Southern Appalachian Yearly Meeting with headquarters at 301 Hayes Street, Crossville, Tennessee 38555; the Alaska Yearly Meeting at Box 268, Kotzebue, Alaska 99752; the Missouri Valley Conference Yearly Meeting at 1123 South Topeka, Wichita, Kansas 67211; and the Intermountain Yearly Meeting at 4 Arco, Northwest, Albuquerque, New Mexico 87120. The number of unaffiliated yearly meetings is estimated to be near 90 with an inclusive membership of about 6,000.

## The Wider Quaker Fellowship

The Wider Quaker Fellowship came into being in 1936, in response to a proposal of the Quaker mystic and historian Rufus Matthew Jones (1863–1948). Sponsored by the American Section and Fellowship Council of the Friends World Committee, it is intended to be a means of enabling non-Quakers to associate themselves in spiritual fellowship with the Religious Society of Friends without becoming members of it and to maintain another religious affiliation while doing so.

The reasons why individuals have joined this "existent fellowship of friendly expectant sympathizers"—which Jones called "a kind of Franciscan Third Order"—vary from member to member. Some have become "friends of the Friends" to have the spiritual foundations of their peace testimony fortified. Others have done so to record their approval of the way in which Friends express their religious faith in programs of social action. The mystical approach to God of the Religious Society of Friends has attracted still others. No religious test is imposed as a condition of membership.

Members of the fellowship make voluntary contributions to meet the costs that the fellowship incurs in keeping in touch with its constituents. Where several members of the fellowship live in the same community they are encouraged to meet for worship or study both to strengthen one another and to reach out to sympathetic friends and neighbors. Here and there a local or regional Friends meeting establishes contact with members of the fellowship. Members of the fellowship in a given area are invited to attend the bimonthly meeting of the American Section of the Friends World Committee when it meets in their vicinity, but relatively few accept the invitations.

About 2,900 mailings[26] (many of them to husbands and wives) go out three times a year to members in the United States, just under 60 to Canada, just over 1,000 to members in fifty-five foreign countries. The number of Friends who belong to the fellowship slightly exceeds 100; many of these are members because they are unable to attend a Friends meeting near their respective places of residence. Only a small number of non-Quaker members of the fellowship ever become Friends; when this happens, the individual in question may either resign or remain a member, as he prefers.[27] The headquarters of the Wider Quaker Fellowship is at 152a North Fifteenth Street, Philadelphia, Pennsylvania 19102.

## NOTES

1. See Lawrence McK. Miller, "Friends General Conference," in Edwin B. Bronner, ed., *American Quakers Today* (Philadelphia, Penn.: American Section and Fellowship Council, Friends World Committee, 1966), pp. 43-57, and William Hubben, *Who Are the Friends? Their Principles and Organization* (Philadelphia, Penn.: Friends General Conference, 1965) (20-page pamphlet).

2. "Quaker Faith," in *Faith and Practice of the Philadelphia Yearly Meeting of the Religious Society of Friends: A Book of Christian Discipline* (rev. edn.; Philadelphia, Penn.: Philadelphia Yearly Meeting of the Religious Society of Friends, 1965), p. 9.

3. Ibid., p. 10.

4. Ibid., pp. 12-13.

5. Ibid., pp. 14-15.

6. "Practice and Procedure," ibid., p. 41.

7. Letter from Mr. Edwin B. Bronner, curator, the Quaker Collection, Haverford College, Haverford, Pennsylvania.

8. William P. Taber, Jr., "Conservative Friends," in Edwin B. Bronner, ed., *American Quakers Today* (Philadelphia, Penn.: Friends World Committee, American Section and Fellowship Council, 1966), p. 83. This writer acknowledges his indebtedness to the entire cited essay. The author, a "released Friend," that is, one who is financially released so that he can follow his religious concerns, is the first salaried leader that the Ohio Yearly Meeting, Conservative, has ever had. See also *The Book of Discipline of Ohio Yearly Meeting of the Religious Society of Friends* (rev. edn.; Barnesville, Ohio: Ohio Yearly Meeting of the Religious Society of Friends, 1963) (51-page brochure); *Friends' Book of Discipline* (rev. edn.; Woodland, N.C.: North Carolina Yearly Meeting of the Religious Society of Friends [Conservative], 1967).

9. For the text of the Richmond Declaration of Faith of 1887, see *Faith and Practice: Unofficial Statements and the Official Provisions for Organization and Procedures of the Friends United Meeting* (Richmond, Ind.: Friends Book and Supply House, 1966), pp. 128-150. This statement is not used as much now as it was a few decades ago, but there seems to be no current attempt under way to prepare and issue a new statement to replace the Richmond Declaration (letter from Mr. David O. Stanfield, secretary, Board for Stewardship and Finance, Friends United Meeting).

10. Arthur Garratt Dorland, *The Quakers in Canada* (Toronto, Ontario: Canadian Friends Service Committee, n.d.) 8-page pamphlet), p. 3.

11. *Christian Faith and Practice in the Experience of the Society of Friends* (3rd edn.; London: London Yearly Meeting of the Religious Society of Friends, 1963), p. [3] of the "Introduction."

12. Elton Trueblood, *The People Called Quakers* (New York: Harper & Row, 1966), p. 145, observes: "In [the Ohio Yearly Meeting] freedom has reached the ultimate limit, in that the Discipline permits the physical celebration of the Lord's Supper on occasion, if the local congregation desires this experience. In short, they have gone the whole way in that they have both "freedom from' and 'freedom to.' Though Ohio Friends have sometimes been criticized for this departure from former Quaker practice, the criticism is clearly not justified. The whole idea is that of freedom from *any* ceremonial requirements, after which other freedoms are possible."

13. "Doctrine," in *Book of Discipline of Ohio Yearly Meeting of the Friends Church* (rev. edn.; Damascus, Ohio: Ohio Yearly Meeting of the Friends

Church, 1961), pp. 5-12.
14. "Testimonies," ibid., pp. 12-20; *Friends' Way* (Damascus, Ohio: Ohio Yearly Meeting of the Friends Church, 1961), pp. 19-28.
15. Communication from Galen Weingart, presiding clerk, 2130 31st Street Northwest, Canton, Ohio 44709.
16. *Discipline of Pacific Yearly Meeting of the Religious Society of Friends: A Quaker Guide to Christian Faith and Practice* (Fremont, Calif.: Pacific Yearly Meeting [Wanda Underhill], 1965) (pamphlet), p. 9.
17. Ibid., p. 43.
18. Letters from Virginia B. Harris, 1739 Delaware Street, Berkeley, California.
19. "History of the Friends," in *Declaration of Faith and Discipline for Central Yearly Meeting of Friends* (3rd edn.; n.p.: n.p., 1960) (74-page brochure), pp. 5-9.
20. "Statement of Belief," ibid., pp. 10-13. See also J. Edwin Newby, *Teachings of Evangelical Friends as Gleaned from George Fox's Journal and Friends Disciplines* (N.p.: n.p., 1952) (24-page pamphlet, containing the messages given at the Central Yearly Meeting of 1952).
21. *Some Distinctive Views of Friends, Prepared by a Committee of Central Yearly Meeting of Friends* (2nd printing; N.p.: n.p., 1957) (32-page pamphlet), pp. 13-31, argues that neither Christ nor the apostles commanded compulsory water baptism and that Christ did not institute the "Lord's supper."
22. "Worship," ibid., pp. 14-19.
23. "General Subjects," ibid., pp. 50-57.
24. *Minutes of Central Yearly Meeting of the Friends Church, 1966*, p. 37.
25. Ibid., annexed statistical report.
26. A typical year of mailings (March, July, and November 1968) brought members three newsletters from the office staff; an 8-page leaflet from the Kvakera Esperantista Societo (Quaker Esperanto Society), an 8-page leaflet describing new programs of the Friends World Committee, *Friends Around the World*; a reprint of an article by John Keats from *The New York Times Magazine* for March 24, 1968, "There is Something Called Quaker Power"; copies of two issues of the Wells News Service semimonthly newsletter, *Between the Lines* (published in protest against the "narrow provincialism and . . . traditional prejudices" of American news coverage and the "political fanaticism and military extremism" that it sees threatening "sound democratic practice and a rational defense system"); and three newly published Pendle Hill pamphlets.
27. Letter from Yolanda G. Stevens, the Wider Quaker Fellowship; *Wider Quaker Fellowship: Purpose—Membership —Program* (Philadelphia, Penn.: Wider Quaker Fellowship, 1968) (6-page folder), which contains significant portions of the letter of invitation that Jones sent in 1936 to "those who would like closer fellowship with Friends"; Margaret E. Jones "The Wider Quaker Fellowship," *Friends World News*, no. 86 (Winter 1968), pp. 282-283; Emma Cadbury, *The Wider Quaker Fellowship: Its History and Purpose* (Philadelphia, Penn.: Wider Quaker Fellowship, 1964) (8-page tract by the chairman of the fellowship from 1943 to 1963); Mary Hoxie Jones, *Rufus M. Jones and the Wider Quaker Fellowship* (Philadelphia, Penn.: Wider Quaker Fellowship, n.d.) (12-page tract by Jones's daughter reprinted from *The American Friend* for July 31, 1952).

# BIBLIOGRAPHY

*Book of Discipline of Ohio Yearly Meeting of the Friends Church.* Revised edition. Damascus, Ohio: Ohio Yearly Meeting of the Friends Church, 1961.

Bronner, Edwin B., ed. *American Quakers Today.* Philadelphia, Penn.: American Section and Fellowship Council, Friends World Committee, 1966.

*Christian Faith and Practice in the Experience of the Society of Friends.* Third edition. London: London Yearly Meeting of the Religious Society of Friends, 1963.

*Constitution and Discipline of Oregon Yearly Meeting of Friends.* Newberg, Oregon: Barclay Press, 1958. See especially chapter 2, "Fundamental Truths."

Doherty, Robert W. *The Hicksite Separation: A Sociological Analysis of Religious Schism in Early Nineteenth Century*

*America.* New Brunswick, N.J.: Rutgers University Press, 1967.

Dorland, Arthur Garratt. *The Quakers in Canada.* Toronto, Ontario: Ryerson Press, 1968. This definitive work is the second edition of *A History of the Society of Friends (Quakers) in Canada* (Toronto, Ontario: The Macmillan Company, 1927).

Escolme, Edward, and others. *Handbook for Friends.* Revised edition by Walter R. Williams. Damascus, Ohio: Ohio Yearly Meeting of the Friends Church, 1963.

*Faith and Practice of the Philadelphia Yearly Meeting of the Religious Society of Friends: A Book of Christian Discipline.* Revised edition, fourth printing. Philadelphia, Penn.: Philadelphia Yearly Meeting of the Religious Society of Friends, 1965. This volume has separate parts on faith and thought (pp. 1-42); practice and procedure (pp. 45-102); and the Quaker witness to the faith (pp. 105-250), an anthology.

*Faith and Practice: Unofficial Statement and Official Provisions for Organization and Procedures of the Friends United Meeting.* Richmond, Ind.: Friend Book and Supply House, 1966.

Forbush, Bliss. *Elias Hicks, Quaker Liberal.* New York: Columbia University Press, 1956.

*Friends' Way.* Damascus, Ohio: Ohio Yearly Meeting of the Friends Church, 1961. A catechism for children describing the history and organization of the Friends Church, the Bible and its teachings, general views and points of emphasis of Friends, and the enterprises and institutions of the Ohio Yearly Meeting.

Hubbin, William. *Who Are the Friends? Their Principles and Organization.* Philadelphia, Penn.: Friends General Conference, 1965.

Trueblood, D. Elton. *The People Called Quakers.* New York: Harper & Row, 1966.

Willcuts, Jack L. *A Family of Friends: Friends Church Membership Course.* Newberg, Ore.: Barclay Press, 1960. The author created this training course, a pamphlet of 89 pages, in response to a recommendation of the Oregon Yearly Meeting's Ministry and Oversight "that a brief training course in Friends doctrine and procedures be presented to all new members."

# 8. Churches of the Living God

## Church of the Living God (Motto: C.W.F.F.)

Chief William Christian (d. 1928), organized the church body now known as the Church of the Living God (Motto: C[hristian] W[orkers] f[or] F[ellowship]) at Wrightsville, Arkansas, in 1889. In the course of time the movement sustained a number of divisions and secessions. Two of these breakaway groups later returned: the Church of the Living God (Apostolic Faith), later called the Church of the Living God, General Assembly; and the Church of Christ in God. In 1925 a number of seceding groups consolidated under the leadership of the Reverend E. J. Cain as the House of God, Which Is the Church of the Living God, the Pillar and Ground of the Truth, Incorporated.

The Articles of Faith of the Church of the Living God assert belief in the Trinity; the fatherhood of God and the brotherhood, native freedom, and equality of all human beings; Christ as the redeemer of mankind and the only door to eternal life; his death, burial, resurrection, and ascension; salvation through living by every word pertaining to salvation that proceeds from God's mouth; the unity in Christ of all those who do his will; the Bible as the book which points the way to eternal life through obedience; the Golden Rule; and in three ordinances ordained by Christ in the new covenant, believer's baptism by immersion, the Lord's Supper in unleavened bread and water, and the washing of feet.[1]

It regards the Scriptures as profitable for teaching, for reproof, for correction, and for training in righteousness; holds that the Old Testament is "a Jewish guide to bring many souls to Christ"; describes the four Gospels as the ritual through which "the church should receive its government and instructions of the doctrine as can be found in the various epistles of the apostles," while the Acts are the bylaws and the history of the apostolic work; and holds that God gave the Revelation to John for the correction of Christ's disciples. The organization forbids the use of wine or strong drink in any form.[2]

The organization has borne a strong fraternalistic imprint from the beginning. The founder held that Freemasonry was the true expression of religion and regarded the movement that he established as a kind of "operative Masonry," with baptism, the holy Supper, and foot washing "the first three corporal degrees."

Local centers are called temples rather than churches. Members are expected to tithe their incomes for the support of the organization.

There are twelve bishops, headed by a chief and a vice-chief. The other ranks of the ministry are overseer, evangelist, pastor, missionary, and local preacher. The General Assembly meets every four years. The National Assembly meets annually. The Executive Board oversees the operation of the entire organization.

The chief bishop resides at 801 Northeast 17th Street, Oklahoma City, Oklahoma 73105. There are nearly 300 temples, with an overall membership of about 50,000. Recent efforts to contact the church body have not been successful.

### The House of God, Which Is the Church of the Living God, the Pillar and Ground of the Truth Without Controversy, Incorporated

"Mother" M. L. Ester Tate (1870–1930)—or Saint Mary Magdalena Tate, as she is known in the organization—was a Black Pentecostal evangelist. She began the House of God, Which Is the Church of the Living God, the Pillar and Ground of the Truth Without Controversy, Incorporated, around 1907. Co-founders were her two sons, W. C. Lewis and F. C. Lewis, both of whom became bishops in the church in 1914. By 1908 several local churches had begun in the Deep South, and the first General Assembly met at Greenville, Alabama, in 1908 and elected Mother Tate as the first overseer. After a number of secessions and the death of Mother Tate, the church was reorganized into three semiautonomous dominions in 1931, with a chief overseer over each of the dominions.

The church body is trinitarian and stresses the necessity of its biblical name, which it derives from I Timothy 3:15–16; conversion, sanctification, and baptism with the Holy Spirit as distinct works of grace; water baptism by immersion in the name of the Father and of the Son and of the Holy Ghost; prayer and fasting. It recognizes women as Gospel workers and emphasizes obedience to central authority.

The three dominions hold their annual conference in May, June, and July respectively. The three dominions comprise an estimated 500 churches in 40 states with an estimated 20,000 members. The church conducts foreign operations in Jamaica, Nassau, and Spain. The headquarters are at Nashville, Tennessee.

### The House of God, Which Is the Church of the Living God, the Pillar and Ground of the Truth, Incorporated (Philadelphia, Pennsylvania)

The House of God, Whis Is the Church of the Living God, the Pillar and Ground of the Truth, Incorporated, withdrew from the similarly named Black Pentecostal church body which has its headquarters in Nashville, Tennessee, and organized as a separate fellowship in 1919. Like the parent body, it emphasizes conversion, sanctification, and baptism with the Holy Spirit as distinct works of grace, water baptism by immersion, prayer, and fasting. Its basis of union is an expanded adaptation of the Nicene-Constantinopolitan Creed. Its form of government is episcopal. The General Assembly of the church body meets annually. Its monthly journal, *The Spirit of Truth Magazine*, is published from 3943 Fairmont Avenue, Philadelphia, Pennsylvania 19104. It reports 103 churches with an estimated total of 25,860 members.[3]

### The (Original) Church of the Living God, Pillar and Ground of Truth

Frank S. Cherry, who died in 1965, asserted that many years ago, when he was in a distant foreign country, God appointed him as prophet in a vision, led him back to his native United States, and directed him to establish the (Original) Church of the Living God, Pillar and Ground of Truth, at 2132 Nicholas Street, Philadelphia, Pennsylvania. The foundation of the church is "the Ten Commandments and Jesus Christ and his Twelve Apostles, which taught the people the commandments as did Moses in the Wilderness."[4] The (Original) Church of the Living God demands the abolition of the terms "Negroes" and "colored people" and holds that the "black peoples in America" are the original Ethiopian Hebrews, "the descendants of Abraham, Isaac, and Jacob, the first Jew," all of whom were black, and the land of Canaan is their home.[5] White Jews are regarded as interlopers and frauds.

The ideology of the (Original) Church of the Living God is in the vehemently antiwhite tradition of the late nineteenth-century emergence of black self-consciousness. Theologically, the (Original) Church of the Living God reveals a strong Holiness movement influence, especially on its moral standards, coupled with a strong rejection of competing Christian denominations, especially of the Pentecostal type. Jesus, who came not to abrogate the Old Testament but to fulfill it, was himself black.[6] In 2000 he will return to usher in the millennium.

The (Original) Church of the Living God has taken over many Old Testament and Jewish features.[7] It extends the prohibition of making "graven images" to include allowing one's photograph to be taken[8] and having pictures on the walls of one's home. It keeps the Sabbath from sundown Friday to sundown Saturday, and begins the year with the Passover month of April. While it observes baptism, it does not celebrate either Christmas or Easter; for the Holy Communion it substitutes the Passover. It forbids its members to eat pork. Male members of the church wear skull-caps of the Jewish type. But on the basis of Revelation 3:9 it rejects the designation "synagogue" for its center.

The (Original) Church of the Living God forbids marriage of its members outside its circle (unless the outsider agrees to join the church), divorce (even for infidelity, unless the offended spouse surprises the marriage partner in the adulterous act), secular dancing, and drunkenness, but it encourages moderate use of alcoholic intoxicants. It derives its support from tithes, voluntary offerings, and special fees for participation in certain services such as the Passover meal.

The Philadelphia center is the only one. Its membership is estimated at about 400 persons.[9] The founder has been succeeded by his son, Benjamin Cherry.[10]

# NOTES

1. The washing of the saints' feet is required only once, when a new member unites with the church.
2. Communication from the Reverend F. C. Scott, chief bishop, Church of the Living God (Motto: C.W.F.F.).
3. Communications from Bishop A. H. White, 6107 Cobbs Creek Parkway, Philadelphia, Pennsylvania. Subordinate jurisdictions, incorporated under a variety of names, include: The House of God, Which Is the Church of the Living God, the Pillar and Ground of the Truth Without Controversy in New Jersey, Incorporated; the Elect Church of the Living God in New York; and The House of God Which Is the Church of the Living God, the Pillar and Ground of the Truth and Without Controversy (1923).
4. Letter of Elder Daniel Lewis, pastor, and Elder Rothalz Mason, assistant pastor, to the Adjutant General, United States Army.
5. During the lifetime of Founder Cherry, the letterhead of the Original Church of the Living God featured the six-pointed star of David, with Ṣiyyon (Zion) written in square Hebrew characters inside it. Both the church's letterhead and the cards advertising its services carried phrases from Genesis 28: 16-17 in Hebrew (with the Masoretic pointings), while the advertising cards also carried the invitation in Yiddish: "Notice! All nations can come to hear the black Hebrew prophet."
6. Since most pictures of Christ show him as a white person, Prophet Cherry offered $10,000 for an authentic "picture of Jesus Christ or any other prophet."
7. Although the members of the (Original) Church of the Living God are sometimes called "Black Jews," they should be carefully distinguished from the black Jewish synagogues which practice a consistent and exclusive Judaism.
8. The biblical basis given is Numbers 33:52; Deuteronomy 4:15-18; Isaiah 2:16. This prohibition has caused difficulty for members of the church who enter the armed services, which require photographs for identification-card purposes.
9. This writer gratefully acknowledges the helpfulness of the Reverend Gary Schubert, then pastor of Nazareth Church, Philadelphia, in his efforts to secure information about the Original Church of the Living God.
10. Letter from Mr. Edward Blackshear, the Church of the Living God, Pillar and Ground of the Truth, Philadelphia.

# 9. Independent Nondenominational Churches and Associations

There is no feasible way of discovering how many independent non-denominational churches there are in the United States and Canada. Those described in this chapter[1] are representative of the variety of such churches. Also described are three associations by which some churches of this kind maintain contact with each other and coordinate some of their efforts without jeopardizing the independence that they prize so highly.

## The Church of the Open Door

The Church of the Open Door, 550 South Hope Street, Los Angeles, was organized in 1915 by eighty-six charter members. Although it has no organizational link with the Bible Institute of Los Angeles, the two institutions have consistently cooperated for nearly half a century. The doctrinal position of the Church of the Open Door, described as "very similar to that stated in the Westminster Catechism," is evangelical and premillennial. The church has no formal connection with any national or international ecclesiastical organization. Its membership of 4,000 supports 27 missionaries in the United States and 87 foreign missionaries.[2]

## Erieside Church on the Boulevard

The ministry of Herbert MacKenzie (1868?–1945) at the now defunct Gospel Church, Cleveland, Ohio, extended from 1908 to 1943. In 1924 he founded the Erieside Gospel Church in Willowick, Ohio, an eastern suburb of Cleveland, as an independent congregation. In 1935 he organized another congregation at 221 East 320th Street and called it the Erieside Church on the Boulevard.

Its theology is Bible-oriented, evangelical, Calvinistic, and premillennial. It practices believer's baptism by immersion and open Communion.

The church is located at 221 East 320th Street, Willowick, Ohio 44094. The congregation has a membership of 300.[3]

### Berachah Church (Houston, Texas)

Charles Y. Colgan, a graduate of the Philadelphia School of the Bible, began a Bible class in his home in Houston, Texas, in the 1930s. In April 1934 he organized it as an independent church in downtown Houston and called it Berachah Church.[4] In 1959 it moved to its present location at 2815 Sage Road in the southwestern part of the city. Its constitution commits it "to stand unequivocably [unequivocally] for the fundamentals of the faith as contained in the Holy Scriptures." Its statement of doctrine affirms the Bible as the "authoritative, inerrant, God-breathed" Word of God; the Trinity; the total depravity of man; Christ's deity, incarnation, substitutionary sacrifice, resurrection, and exaltation; the personality of the Holy Spirit and the duty of every believer to be filled with the Holy Spirit; salvation as God's gift by grace received by personal faith in Christ; the eternal security of believers; the church as "a spiritual organism made up of all born-again persons of this age irrespective of their affiliation with Christian organizations"; the personality of Satan; the rapture and the translation of the church; the tribulation; Christ's premillennial return; the eternal state of believers and unbelievers determined at death; the responsibilities of believers; and the ordinances of baptism by immersion and the Lord's Supper. The congregation's constitution prohibits it from becoming a member of, sanctioning, or supporting "the National Council of [the] Churches of Christ in [the United States of] America, the World Council of Churches, or any such organization."[5] The stress of the congregation's program is on the systematic teaching of the Bible and on a worldwide ministry through recorded tapes and printed publications. It supports home missionaries in nine states and foreign missionaries in Africa, Latin America, the Philippines Republic, Thailand, and Belgium. Information about the size of the congregation is not available.

### Billy Sunday Memorial Tabernacle (Sioux City, Iowa)

The late Harry Clark (1889–1957), for eight years song leader for the evangelist Billy Sunday, founded the Billy Sunday Memorial Tabernacle now located at 6100 Morningside Avenue, Sioux City, Iowa, as an independent church in 1938. Doctrinally it takes a Baptist position. It has about 700 members, supports 35 missionaries, many of them members of the congregation, in foreign countries, and conducts a retirement home and a private elementary school. Its weekly journal, *The Sawdust Trail*, has a national circulation of 3,000.[6]

### Chinese Christian Church of New England

The Chinese Christian Church of New England was incorporated in 1946 as an independent, undenominational, interracial, and bilingual congregation. Its basis of membership is acceptance of Jesus as Lord and Savior. Its motto is that of the Church of Christ in China: "We agree to differ, but resolve to love and unite to serve." Since 1947 its pastor has been Dr. Peter Y. F. Shih, for six years instructor at the Nanking Theological Seminary and for six more years dean of the West China Union Theological Seminary in Chengtu; in 1969 his son, the Reverend David Peter Shih, ordained in the United Presbyterian Church in the United States of America, became his associate.

The church is supported by American Baptist, Protestant Episcopal, United Church of Christ, United Methodist Church, and United Presbyterian Church giving. In addition to worship services it conducts a day-care center and language classes; provides social services for the aged, for refugees, and for foreign students from Southeast Asia; carries on an intensive intercultural program; and is projecting a ten-story Chinese-American Christian Life Center to house its activities. Since 1947 it has trained and sent out 11 missionaries to Hong Kong, the Republic of China (Taiwan), and Java. Its headquarters are at 62 Tyler Street, Boston, Massachusetts 02111. It has about 100 active members.[7]

### The Church of the Saviour, Washington, D.C.

While serving in Europe as a Baptist Army chaplain in World War II, the Reverend Gordon Cosby conceived the idea of a committed community of Christians with a distinctive ecumenical spirit and approach. It would endeavor to enter into full fellowship with all Christian groups and denominations, and would seek close relationship and, if possible, affiliation with all organizations and movements representing united or cooperating Christian churches. It would allow freedom of worship, practice, and belief among its constituents, while remaining true to the basic values in the stream of historic evangelical Christianity. It would attempt to bear a unique witness of spiritual power, while recognizing the validity, integrity, and rights of self-determination of all Christian groups and denominations. These ideas were written into the constitution of the Church of the Savior that he and a handful of associates organized in the Washington, D.C., area in October 1946.[8]

The commitment of membership is the profession of faith of the Church of the Saviour. Adopted in 1947 on the occasion of the first service in the church's first permanent building, it affirms that the church is "the body of those on whom the call of God rests to witness to the grace and truth of God"; that its function "is to glorify God in adoration and sacrificial service, and to be God's missionary to the world, bearing witness to God's redeeming grace in Jesus Christ"; and that "Jesus is the Christ, the Son of the Living God." In making the commitment, members promise that they will "unreservedly and with abandon commit" their lives and destiny to Christ, "promising to give him a practical priority in all the affairs of life"; to become informed and mature Christians "regardless of the expenditures of time, energy, and money" involved; to "be lavish and cheerful" in their regular gifts because God is the total owner of their lives and a lavish giver; to "seek to be Christian in all relations" with their fellow beings of all nations, groups, classes, and races; to bring every phase of life under Christ's Lordship; and when moving elsewhere to "join some other expression of the Christian church."[9]

Members covenant "with Christ and with one another" as a minimum discipline to engage in a set time of prayer daily, to let God confront them through the Scriptures, to grow in love for the brotherhood and all people, to worship weekly, to be vital contributing members to one of the groups, to give proportionately beginning at a tithe, and to confess and ask the help of the fellowship if they fail in these expressions of devotion.[10]

Children are baptized or dedicated according to the wishes of the parents. The Holy Communion is administered once a month in a larger congregation, whenever there is a members' meeting, and at other less formal occasions.

The headquarters of the Church of the Saviour are at 2025 Massachusetts Avenue, Northwest, Washington, D.C. 20036. Services are held regularly both at the headquarters and at the Potter's House, 1658 Columbia Road, Northwest (20009), the coffee shop and art center of the church. Twelve "mission groups" of from two to twenty persons each function in metropolitan Washington in a variety of activities all of which are designed both "to serve the world redemptively by bringing to it in action the saving word of the Gospel" and "to nurture the spiritual growth of its members." The Church of the Saviour distinguishes "totally committed" members from "associate members," chiefly those who are "moving forward toward full belonging," but have not yet said, "We belong to Christ and we belong to you in Christ." No information is available on the number of members of either type.

### Christian Crusade

Christian Crusade is headed by the Reverend Billy James Hargis (b. 1925), of Tulsa, Oklahoma. He was ordained to the ministry in 1943 by the Rosehill Christian Church, Texarkana, Texas, an independent congregation that cooperated with a loose fellowship of independent Christian churches and Churches of Christ. In 1947, while he was pastor of the First Christian Church in Sapulpa, Oklahoma, he organized the Christian Crusade to fight "Communism and its allies." Some of the clergymen that he has ordained since then have affiliated with independent Christian churches, while others are affiliated with the Church of the Christian Crusade in Tulsa, which Hargis founded and of which he is pastor.

The Christian Crusade espouses a militant Bible-centered conservatism of the "fundamental" type. With this theological orientation it combines the conviction that the United States of America has always been a Christian country, and that it is God's chosen nation in our time. It inculcates a profound reverence for the Constitution as the Founding Fathers formulated it, and energetically opposes atheism, political and religious liberalism, all forms of what Hargis calls "socialism," Communism, the United Nations in its present form, pacifism, proponents of one-world government, and the National Council of the Churches of Christ in the United States of America.

The Christian Crusade makes extensive use of radio and television, carries on an energetic program of magazine, pamphlet, and book publication, sponsors a continuing series of anticommunist rallies throughout the United States, produces phonograph records and tapes, and has organized an "anti-Communist youth university" at Manitou Springs, Colorado, where two-week summer courses train young people of high school and college age to organize youth groups that promote the crusade in their home communities. In 1967 it discontinued its local chapters. The contributors to the Christian Crusade make up a loose fellowship of conservatives throughout the United States; some conduct local study groups, but most of them do not.

A "Cathedral of the Christian Crusade" has been built in Tulsa to house the Church of the Christian Crusade. Staffed by clergymen with various denominational backgrounds, the Tulsa congregation itself has no denominational affiliation. In its worship and its practice of serving the Lord's Supper every Sunday it follows the Disciples-Christian tradition.

The Tulsa congregation counts about 300 resident and nonresident members in its fellowship.[11]

### Blessed Martin Spiritual Church

In 1942 the Reverend R. Viola Bankston, now Mrs. R. Viola Melville, granddaughter of a Methodist local preacher, founded the Blessed Martin Spiritual Church in her kitchen in Atlanta with three members. She incorporated it in 1948. She named the denominationally unaffiliated congregation after St. Martin de Porres (1579–1639) of Peru, a Dominican lay-brother and the natural son of a Spanish knight by a Panamanian black freedwoman, and envisioned it as ministering to the needs of the poor and underprivileged. It observes the ordinances of baptism by immersion in the name of the Father and of the Son and of the Holy Ghost, and the Lord's Supper, and practices divine healing and prophecy. Admission to membership is by baptism or Christian experience. The church is located at 694 Pryor Street, Southwest, Atlanta, Georgia 30315. It has 250 members.[12]

### Bethany Bible Church and Other Independent Bible Churches of the Phoenix (Arizona) Area

In the mid 1950s Dr. John L. Mitchell, a graduate of Dallas (Texas) Theological Seminary, came to the Bethany Bible Church in Phoenix, Arizona, then newly founded for people who had left the Presbyterian, Baptist, and other denominations because they felt that these denominations had deviated from the theological stand that they had once occupied. Since then four other graduates of the same seminary have organized independent "Bible churches" in the Phoenix area. While there is no organic connection among them or between any of them and the Bethany Bible Church, they all hold a substantially identical doctrinal position.

The statement of faith of the Bethany Bible Church affirms belief in the verbal inspiration and complete inerrancy of the Bible; the Trinity; Christ's virgin birth, deity, and manhood; the sinful nature of human beings from birth; Christ's representative and substitutionary sacrifice and the justification of those who believe in him on the ground of his shed blood; Christ's resurrection, ascension, and intercession; his premillennial and imminent return; the eternal security of those who receive him by faith and are born of the Spirit; the bodily resurrection of all human beings; the everlasting blessedness of the saved; and the everlasting conscious punishment of the lost.[13] Its mild dispensationalism is nurtured on an eclectic use of the Scofield Reference Bible.

The Bethany Bible Church practices believer's baptism by immersion, but it does not insist on the mode of baptism and it is not concerned about the question of rebaptism. It serves the Lord's Supper monthly and sees it as an act of remembrance; reception of the elements is open to all believers. The church is governed by a self-perpetuating board. It carries on its foreign missionary activity, for which it raises about $80,000 annually, through various "faith" mission boards. Individual and corporate Bible study is a major stress of the church.

The Bethany Bible Church is located at 6060 North Seventh Avenue, Phoenix 85013. It has an adult membership of about 1,100. The other four Bible churches in the Phoenix area have from 100 to 400 members each.[14]

### The Free Church of Berkeley (South Campus Community Ministry)

The Free Church of Berkeley (California) came into being in 1967 as the South Campus Community Ministry under the direction of the Reverend Richard York (b. 1940), who later became pastor of the center, and the Reverend Anthony Nugent (b. 1940), who later became the administrator. (The Reverend John Pairman Brown, Th.D. [b. 1923] joined them in 1968 as "theologian-in-residence.") The Free Church derives the bulk of its financial support from the Board of National Missions of the United Presbyterian Church in the United States of America and from the Protestant Episcopal Diocese of California. Although originally designed as "an ecumenical youth church with one foot in and one foot out of the church establishment," the Free Church, in the words of the Reverend Mr. York, began "to open up the Bible on its own, to start celebrating the Freedom

Meal on its own, [and] to pass its members through the waters of baptism." In the Bible it found for itself "a manifesto for human liberation, a radical Jesus, [and] a Good News for its own problems." It makes its appeal to "alienated runaways, drug users, and street people." Persuaded that it is too late to build bridges between the "Establishment" and alienated youth, its staff proposes to offer an "alternative life style" while addressing itself to what it sees as the causes of youthful alienation, defined as "war, the draft, racism, police oppression, injustice and corruption in high office, exploitation, and [the] manipulation of personal freedom."[15]

The Free Church has devised its own liturgical forms—frequently changed—for services, baptisms, weddings, and the "freedom meal," the Free Church's form of the Lord's Supper (held every Friday evening). Its general philosophy "calls for an end to war, the end of racism, and helping one's fellow man." The only rules are no drugs and no violence on the premises of the "liberated zone."

The statement of doctrine of the Free Church reads: "God is not dead. God is bread. The bread is rising. Bread means revolution. God means revolution. Murder is no revolution. Revolution is love. Win with love. The radical Jesus is winning. The world is coming to a beginning. The whole world is watching. Organize for a new world. Wash off your brother's blood. Burn out the mark of the Beast. Join the freedom meal. Plant the peace garden. The asphalt church is marching. The guerrilla church is recruiting. The people's church is striking. The submarine church is surfacing. The war is over. The liberated zone is at hand."[16]

The Free Church of Berkeley is located at 2200 Parker Street. It recognizes informal (but not structural) links between itself and the Action Training Coalition, the Switchboards[17] and Switchboard-like projects throughout the country, and about 60 churches, communities, and centers in 28 states and the District of Columbia with aims that the Free Church of Berkeley sees as broadly parallel to its own concerns for peace and liberation. Some of these churches, communities, and centers are independent; others are explicitly ecumenical and interdenominational; and still others have Eastern Orthodox, Roman Catholic, Lutheran, Protestant Episcopal, Presbyterian, Methodist, United Church of Christ, and Friends affiliations.

## International Ministerial Federation, Incorporated (Fresno, California)

William E. Opie, pastor of Bethel Independent Full Gospel Temple, Fresno, California, organized the International Ministerial Federation in 1930. In March 1939 he and two other ministers incorporated the association as the International Ministerial Federation of California.[18] The amended Articles of Incorporation list as some of the purposes of the corporation "to maintain a religious denomination for the purpose of teaching the precepts of the Christian religion at home and abroad; to further the spirit of fellowship among the ministers of the gospel and to enlarge and open the field of evangelism to evangelists; to ordain and to issue certificates of ordination to, and to license, any person who shall in the opinion of the credential committee of this corporation, be qualified to conduct services consistent with the principles, creed, precepts, practices, and discipline of the Christian religion as described by this denomination."[19]

Membership is restricted to ministers; congregations are not eligible for membership. The only creedal requirement that applicants must meet is an affirmative answer to the question if they believe in the commonly accepted evangelical doctrine embraced by every orthodox Christian church. In general, applicants must be ordained prior to becoming members of the federation, but the federation will in exceptional cases authorize the ordination of an unordained person by a congregation that may want to support the individual in question for a special missionary work.

Membership in the federation is not exclusive, and Baptists, Methodists, Presbyterians, Pentecostals, as well as members of other denominations, are among the 400 ministers in the United States and Canada who belong to the federation.

The headquarters are at 724 Clark Street, Fresno, California 93701. The federation does not hold conventions of its own and exercises no discipline over its member ministers.[20]

## American Ministerial Association, Incorporated

A small group of unaffiliated ministers organized the American Conference of Undenominational Ministers in 1929 for mutual fellowship and consultation in professional matters. In the course of a reorganization in 1944 it became the American Ministerial Association. It disavows trying to assume the functions of the church and proposes to offer a vehicle through which its minister-members can become articulate in matters of common interest and concern, to foster brotherhood among them, to provide recognition and protection to them, and to supply a means of cooperation without coercion or compromise.

It describes its doctrinal position as mediating. It embraces "the customary Christian positions," but allows its members to live their religious lives unrestricted by tradition, unhampered by creedal obligations, and untrammeled by sectarian barriers. It holds to the autonomy of the local church and its independence from all ecclesiastical control. It professes to be Bible-based and its members recognize no other written creed or confessions of faith.

It provides qualified applicants, according to their circumstances and without regard to sex, with recognition of previous ordination, with ordination, or with a ministerial licence. Although primarily a ministerial fellowship, it offers churches, missions, and other agencies institutional membership;

the association desires that such institutional members cooperate with one another but does not try to compel them to do so. To heighten the spirit of cooperation it maintains boards of national and international missions, a council on schools and colleges, a commission on ministerial training, and evangelistic and benevolent councils. It sponsors the Order of St. Luke the Physician of America as its healing arm. The association reports a membership of over 500 ministers and 300 churches and missions. Information on the total membership of these churches is not available.[21]

## The Council of Community Churches

The Council of Community Churches came into being in 1946 at the initiative of a number of independent local congregations seeking a racially integrated fellowship free from what the council calls the organizational shackles of ecclesiasticism. It stresses that it is a council of churches, not a church or a denomination. In the continuing and challenging "tension between loneliness and fellowship" it finds freedom for the creativity of the Gospel to manifest itself in the local congregation.

Theologically it describes itself as "Christian-oriented." It imposes no interpretation of the Christian faith on its member congregations. "Final authority in faith and order," it holds, "resides in persons as they relate to each other in the local congregation." It affirms the possibility of "unity in diversity and disagreement without division." It believes that "ecumenicity in the spirit of Jesus is the community of God's people where they are, and exists as a spirit irrespective of merging denominations and organizational unity."[22] One leader of the movement has summed up the intention of the council in the motto: "We agree to differ, resolve to love, unite to serve."[23] A local congregation becomes a member of the council "by declaring itself in sympathy with the principles set forth in the constitution" and by paying the annual membership fee. The council recognizes the ordination of both male and female clergy by recognized denominations as well as "by the local church in accordance with the time honored congregational tradition widely practiced by free churches." It affirms its intention to maintain relations with "all ecumenical movements," specifically the National Council of the Churches of Christ in the United States of America and the World Council of Churches, and encourages its member churches to cooperate with local, state, national, and international councils of churches. To execute its policies the Annual Conference elects a National Board of Trustees; between meetings of the trustees the Executive Committee of the board has power to act on the board's behalf.[24]

The headquarters of the council are at the Chittenden Hotel, 18 West Spring Street, Columbus, Ohio 43215. Its membership comprises 173 churches in 26 states from coast to coast and in the District of Columbia, and one community church in Mexico.[25] The congregations reportedly range in size from 25 to 6,800; but no information is available on the total membership. The council conducts no foreign missionary activities of its own, but it provides member congregations with "an annotated list of possibilities" that gives the names, addresses, and brief descriptions of the work of 29 foreign and worldwide agencies as well as of 15 agencies and institutions in the United States.[26]

# NOTES

1. Most of them are churches about which the present writer received requests for information while this volume was in preparation.
2. Letter of the Reverend Elliott R. Cole, D.D., associate pastor; *Church of the Open Door: Golden Anniversary 1915–1965* (Los Angeles: Church of the Open Door, 1965).
3. Letters from the Reverend Milton Cox Sealey, pastor, Erieside Church on the Boulevard, Willowick, Ohio.
4. "Berachah" is explained as the Hebrew word for "blessing."
5. *Berachah Church: Constitution* (rev. edn.; Houston, Texas: Berachah Church, 1964) (28-page pamphlet), pp. 1-5.
6. Letters from the Reverend Martin Mosier, pastor, Billy Sunday Memorial Tabernacle, Sioux City, Iowa.
7. Letter from the Reverend David Peter Shih, B.D., associate pastor, Chinese Christian Church of New England.
8. Elizabeth O'Connor, *Call to Commitment: The Story of the Church of the Saviour, Washington, D.C.* (New York: Harper & Row, 1963), p. 19.
9. Ibid., pp. 20-21.
10. Ibid., p. 34.
11. Letters from the Reverend Billy James Hargis, D.D., LL.D., 2808 South Sheridan, Tulsa, Oklahoma 74129.
12. Letters from the Reverend Frederick W. Melville, pastor, Blessed Martin Spiritual Church. The designation "Spiritual" in the church's name refers not to spiritualism but to the "spiritual" nature of its teachings.
13. *Faith and Life: Bethany Bible Church* (4-page undated leaflet), p. [2].
14. The present writer gratefully acknowledges the assistance of the Reverend Eugene A. Beyer, pastor of Mount Calvary Church, Phoenix, Arizona, who interviewed the Reverend Lewis C. Lawton, Jr., Th.M., director of Christian Education, Bethany Bible

Church, on this writer's behalf.
15. Trudy Rubin, "Berkeley Free Church: For 'an Alternative Life Style,' " *The Christian Science Monitor,* July 19, 1969; Lawrence E. Davies, "Berkeley Hears Far-Out Liturgy," *The New York Times,* June 15, 1969; 2-page typewritten transcript of an "Address by the Rev. Richard L. York, Berkeley Free Church, at a City-Wide Meeting," May 25, 1969.
16. *Win with Love: A Directory of the Liberated Church in America,* no. 1 (July 1969), inside front cover.
17. "Switchboards" are telephones manned at least afternoons and evenings, and sometimes twenty-four hours a day, to provide help to runaways and prisoners and information on local peace activities.
18. "Articles of Incorporation of International Ministerial Federation of California," filed in the office of the Secretary of State of the State of California March 3, 1939, p. 1.
19. "Certificate of Amendment of Articles of Incorporation of International Ministerial Federation of California," filed in the office of the Secretary of State of the State of California November 4, 1946, p. 1. The membership at the time was 207 (ibid., p. 4).
20. Letters from Dr. William E. Opie, executive secretary, International Ministerial Federation, Incorporated. The present writer gratefully acknowledges the helpfulness of the Reverend Martin Schabacker, Jr., pastor, Peace Church, Fresno, California, and of Miss Virginia Johansen, secretary to the Reverend Egon W. Gebauer, M.A., pastor, Emmanuel Church, Fresno, in connection with this writer's efforts to secure information about the International Ministerial Federation.
21. Letters from the Reverend Grant Timothy Billett, Ph.D., D.D., president of the American Ministerial Associa-

tion; *American Ministerial Association (Incorporated): International—Independent—Interdenominational* (undated pamphlet). Dr. Billett is also primate of the Old Catholic Church in North America. The vice-president of the American Ministerial Association is Archbishop Hermann Adrian Spruit, primate of the Church of Antioch, Malabar Rite.

22. "The Council of Community Churches: Its Nature and Its Purpose," approved by the Board of Trustees of the Council of Community Churches and reproduced from *The Christian Community* for July 1962.

23. Marvin Neff, "What Is a Community Church?" reprinted from the same issue of *The Christian Community*.

24. Articles VI-VIII, XI-XII, *Constitution* and *By-Laws of the Council of Community Churches* (Columbus, Ohio: The Council of Community Churches, 1964) (4-page pamphlet).

25. 1967–1968 Yearbook Issue, *The Christian Community*, pp. 3-5. The largest number of member-congregations belonging to the council is reported to have been 250.

26. *Your Community Church Shares in World Mission* (Columbus, Ohio: The Council of Community Churches, 1966) (2-page broadside). The present writer gratefully acknowledges the assistance of the Reverend Philip Schroeder, S.T.M., then pastor, University Lutheran Chapel, Columbus, Ohio, who personally interviewed the secretary of the Council of Community Churches on this writer's behalf.

## BIBLIOGRAPHY

Brown, John Pairman. *The Liberated Zone*. Richmond, Va.: John Knox Press, 1969.

Hargis, Billy James. *Communism, the Total Lie!* Tulsa, Okla.: The Christian Crusade, 1963.

———. *The Far Left*. Tulsa, Okla.: Christian Crusade, 1964.

O'Connor, Elizabeth. *Call to Commitment: The Story of the Church of the Saviour, Washington, D.C.* New York: Harper & Row, 1963. The author is a member of the staff of the Church of the Saviour.

———. *Journey Inward, Journey Outward*. New York: Harper & Row, 1968. The author continues in this volume the account that she began in *Call to Commitment*.

Penabaz, Fernando. *"Crusading Preacher from the West": The Story of Billy James Hargis*. Tulsa, Okla.: Christian Crusade, 1965.

Pope, Gerald S., ed. *Christian Crusade*. A monthly magazine published by Hargis since 1949.

Redekop, John M. *The American Far Right: A Case Study of Billy James Hargis and Christian Crusade*. Grand Rapids, Mich.: Wm. B. Eerdmans Publishing Company, 1968. A strongly critical evaluation by a political scientist on the faculty of Pacific College, Fresno, California.

# 10. Christadelphians and Related Movements

## Christadelphians

John Thomas (1805–1871) studied medicine in London and emigrated to North America in 1832. In Brooklyn, New York, he joined the Disciples of Christ, but when his studies in the Bible led him to deny many of their tenets, they cut him off from their fellowship. He gathered a number of persons who shared his convictions and formed them into an ecclesia, or assembly of believers. From about 1844 on ecclesias began to be formed in many parts of North America as well as in Great Britain. In order to secure deferment from military duties during the War between the States, the movement had to take a name and chose "Christadelphians," explained as meaning "brothers in Christ."

Christadelphians see much modern theological teaching as a mixture of pagan speculation with the original Christian doctrine that false teachers have corrupted; they regard themselves as the restoration of primitive Christianity.

Christadelphians list twenty-seven tenets as "divine requirements for salvation." On the basis of these, Christadelphians hold that the Bible is the inspired Word of God (their motto is "The Bible True"); that the only God is not a Trinity but a simple unity; that Jesus Christ is the son of God, not God the Son, and by nature a mortal man like us; that his death was an offering for the sin of the world, but not a means of appeasing the anger of an offended God; that God raised him from the dead and thereby exalted him to immortality; that he is now a priestly mediator between the Father and those who come to him; that salvation can be obtained only through Jesus Christ; and that the Holy Spirit is not a person but the power that proceeds from God, the medium and influence by which God penetrates all space and executes his will. They teach that the kingdom of Israel was in the Old Covenant the Kingdom of God on earth; that God himself overturned this Kingdom; that the Jews have been restored to their own land of Israel in fulfillment of prophecy; and that this will be the future Kingdom of God. God, Christadelphians say, made covenants concerning this King-

124

dom with Abraham, Isaac, and Jacob; Jesus Christ was the confirmation of these promises; and both Jews and Gentiles are concerned in them. God also made a covenant of promise with David, Christadelphians affirm, and Christ is the realization of this covenant also.

Christadelphians believe that Christ will soon make a second visible appearance on earth, to be followed by the resurrection of the "responsible" classes of humanity, that is, those who heard the Gospel, defined as the things concerning the Kingdom of God and the name of Jesus Christ, and who responded with either acceptance or rejection; the "irresponsible" classes, who never heard the Gospel, will pass away in death and never be resurrected.[1]

For a thousand years, Christadelphians say, Jesus will reign from Jerusalem over the whole earth in a political kingdom that will be built on the ruins of all existing governments, and the righteous, that is, those who have believed the Gospel and served God faithfully during this life of probation, will reign with him. At the judgment the faithful will receive everlasting life and the unfaithful will suffer the promised second death. Human beings are naturally mortal, Christadelphians teach, and immortality or everlasting life is the reward only of the righteous. Hell, say the Christadelphians, is the grave, not a place of punishment, and the devil is sin in the flesh personified, and not a supernatural being. Christadelphians hold that baptism by immersion in water is an act of obedience that God requires of all who believe the Gospel and hope for salvation.[2]

Christadelphians keep the first day of the week and on it they observe the "breaking of bread" together. They hold strict views on marriage, divorce, and temperance, and forbid their members to participate in war in any form, whether as combatants or noncombatants, although in most ecclesias members may serve as conscientious objectors in hospitals at their option.

Admission to an ecclesia requires a satisfactory confession of faith in Christadelphian principles, followed by baptism by immersion. Each ecclesia is autonomous and elects its own "serving brothers," who serve without compensation. There is no general organization and no dependable information is available either on the number of ecclesias or on the total number of Christadelphians. Informed estimates of the number of ecclesias in the United States and Canada range from 850 to 2,000, and the number of members from 12,000 to 15,800.[3]

## Megiddo Mission Church

During the War between the States Indiana-born L. T. Nichols[4] (1844–1912) was drafted into the Union Army. A Christadelphian in faith (although probably not by formal membership), he secured by means of an appeal to President Lincoln an assignment to a Madison (Wisconsin) base hospital to escape having to take human life in battle. After the war he remained in Wisconsin, where his preaching attracted a group of loyal followers, whom he and his wife led to Oregon in 1874. He maintained himself by farming and by manufacturing his inventions, and spent his leisure in religious work. In 1880 Nichols saw in his newfound insight "that no man could be saved apart from knowing and keeping every commandment of God," the True Reformation.[5] He moved the base of his ecclesia's operations to Ellington, Minnesota, three years later; here he continued to enlist converts to his views from as far away as Ohio and to form them into congregations. In 1901 about thirty families who had sold their farms to follow him built a 205-foot river steamboat with their own hands and launched it at Lyons, Iowa, under the name *Megiddo*. For two years it provided a home for the ninety members of the group as they plied the Mississippi, Ohio, and Cumberland rivers and held meetings in each major city. In late 1903, when persistent low water made navigation on the Ohio River hazardous, the community, reduced to seventy-two members, sold the steamboat and settled in Rochester, New York. Here in 1904 they established their present headquarters at 481 Thurston Road. From Rochester the power cruisers *Megiddo I* and *Megiddo II* successively spread the Megiddo Mission's message over the waterways of New York State between 1915 and 1924. With the advent of the automobile the Megiddo Mission Gospel Car replaced the motor cruisers from 1924 to 1931. Since then the mission has depended chiefly on its monthly magazine, *Megiddo Message* (begun in 1914 as *The Megiddo News*), for its evangelistic outreach.[6]

The Megiddo Mission Church regards the Bible as fully and completely the sacred Word of God. It believes in a single all-powerful Creator and Ruler. The account of creation in Genesis 1-3 is not to be taken literally, because then it would be absurd, unreasonable, and unscientific. It is a spiritual allegory or forecast of God's entire plan for people's salvation and the building of his Kingdom.[7]

The Megiddo Mission Church holds that the doctrine of the Trinity is of pagan origin and defies both reason and mathematics.[8] Christ is not God and had no existence before his human birth of the virgin Mary.[9] He was not sinless; his life was perfect in that he never transgressed the law of God after he knew it. Since he was mortal, he died in the crucifixion, but was raised from the dead, ascended into heaven, was glorified, and will return to begin his kingly reign.[10] The Holy Spirit is not a person, but the Power of God. It was withdrawn in the year 70 and since then human beings can work no miracles (including miracles of healing) by divine power.[11]

The soul of man is mortal and corruptible; death is a sleep.[12] After death there is neither a purgatory nor the hell of traditional theology. Christ bestows immortality conditionally. By nature human beings are strangers and aliens, not God's children; they become children of God by learning of his plan of salvation and agreeing to keep his commandments.[13]

The day of salvation is 6,000 years long. Christ's return—which will be preceded by the advent of Elijah the prophet and the "latter rain" or renewal of the Holy Spirit—will precipitate the Battle of Armageddon and inaugurate the millennium. Then Christ will begin his reign (which will continue on earth forever), ruling jointly with the 144,000 faithful who in their lifetime acquired the knowledge of God and of his plan of salvation, agreed to serve him, and kept his law involate.[14]

The innumerable multitude of subjects of the Kingdom will be developed during the millennium. After the second resurrection and final judgment, the faithful will be made immortal and the earth will become a finished handiwork of God. Those who never knew the true God or never covenanted to serve him will remain in the grave and be as if they had not been.[15] The devil is not a supernatural or immortal being, but only sin as an abstraction and all sinners.[16] The doctrine of original sin is unjust and unbiblical; the divine principle from the beginning is individual responsbility. Similarly the doctrine of the vicarious atonement is an impossible, unjust, and pagan theory; Christ's role in the salvation of human beings was to leave them a perfect example to follow. By dying to sin as Christ died, an at-one-ment with the moral character of Christ takes place.[17]

Water baptism is a symbolic rite that ceased with the apostles. God's present commission requires a spiritual washing in the water of life, the word of truth. The Lord's Supper is to be observed annually on the evening of Abib 13; the elements used are symbolic emblems of the Word of God and of obedience to it. Eternal life is a future attainment, a reward that human beings can secure only by perfect obedience to the law of God as revealed in his Word, and by becoming mentally, morally, and (at Christ's return) physically like God.

In the area of ethics the Megiddo Mission Church prescribes strict honesty, exemplary family life, and separation from the world in politics,[18] religion,[19] and social life. The Golden Rule must govern all aspects of life. Divorce is forbidden, except in cases of marital unfaithfulness. Modesty in dress,[20] good stewardship of material possessions, unity and harmony among the members of the community, total abstinence from alcohol and tobacco, ungrudging hospitality, conscientious objection to military service,[21] and missionary activity are energetically inculcated.[22]

No members of the communty receive salaries for their contributions to the religious work of the church. Women hold parity with men in the leadership of the group.

Members residing in the Rochester area number about one hundred. "Members by correspondence" live in many parts of the United States and Canada, as well as in the British Isles, Australia, Poland, and Liberia. The church has active distributors of literature in India, some parts of Africa, and the Philippines.[23]

**Church of God General Conference**
**(Church of God of the Abrahamic Faith)**

In the middle of the nineteenth century Joseph Marsh of Rochester, New York, Benjamin Wilson (1817–1900)[24] of Geneva, Illinois, and other Bible students in Texas, Minnesota, Iowa, and Pennsylvania began to publish journals which gained moderately wide circulation. These publications provided a means for individuals to discover the existence of others of a like mind. Circuit preachers circulated back and forth among these different local groups, and new churches grew up in other communities. At a later date state conferences came into being and, in 1888, a general conference emerged that had a brief life of only five years. A permanent general conference came into being in 1921.

The Church of God claims no single founder and regards no other church body as its ancestor. It sees itself as Fundamentalist in its acceptance of the Bible as the only inspired Word of God and as the church's sole authority for faith and doctrine. It sees itself as unitarian (and hence contratrinitarian) in that it believes that God is one, the Father and Creator who is above all, and that his Son Jesus Christ came into existence through God's power by birth out of the Virgin Mary. It sees itself as baptist in that it believes in the immersion of adult believers for the remission of sins. It is premillennial in that it believes that Christ's imminent return will take place before the millennium but that the Kingdom of God will not be established on earth before then. It is conditionalist in that it believes that a human being will inherit immortality only on the condition that the person accepts Christ as Savior and is found in Christ at the latter's second coming and that the wicked will be destroyed. It describes itself as being "of the Abrahamic faith" (on the basis of Galatians 3:29) because it believes that the promises of God to Abraham will find fulfillment in the church and in the faithful of Israel through Christ.[25]

It regards its "Simple Statement of Faith" not as a creed, but as a summary of the doctrines believed and taught within it. It affirms that God is a literal, corporeal being; that Christ did not personally preexist; that the Holy Spirit is not a person but is God's divine power and influence manifest in God's work and in his people's lives; that the Bible is God's Word; that the death resulting from human fall into sin is "the cessation of all life and consciousness" and that all human beings are both sinful and mortal and thus in need of salvation; that salvation by God's grace through Christ's atoning blood consists of God's forgiveness of sin, the imparting of his Spirit, and the gift of immortality at the resurrection when Christ returns; that this salvation has four steps: (*a*) belief in the Gospel of the Kingdom and the things concerning Jesus Christ, (*b*) sincere repentance, evidenced if necessary by confession and restitution, (*c*) immersion in the name of Jesus for the remission of sons,[26] and (d) growth in grace and in the knowledge of Christ; that the church is the body of people called out from among all nations through obedience to the Gospel plan of salvation; that the Christian life of consecrated discipleship will be characterized by prayerful dependence on God, study of his word, and faithful stewardship ("with tithing as a practical expression"); that Israel will be restored to Palestine as the head over the Gentile nations in the Kingdom of God; that during the millennium Christ and the church will reign visibly in Jerusalem over the whole earth; and that after the final judgment and destruction of the wicked the restitution of all things will take place and God will establish new heavens and a new earth in which there will be no death and God will be all in all.[27]

The Church of God undertakes to "recognize those members who, because of their religious convictions, claim exemption from military service."[28]

The address of the headquarters of the Church of God General Conference is Box 231, Oregon, Illinois 61061. There are 134 churches in the United States and Canada, with a total membership of 7,485. The Church of God General Conference carries on foreign missions in Mexico, India, Nigeria, Lebanon, and the Philippines Republic.

The individual churches are autonomous, and the degree of cooperation with the general conferences varies from full to more or less marginal. A number of independent churches that are not in fellowship with the Church of God General Conference but that have identical or all but identical beliefs go by the name Church of God of the Faith of Abraham. They are located near Hartford City, Indiana; and in El Paso, Texas.

### The Church of the Blessed Hope

Under the guidance of Mark Allen of Woburn, Massachusetts, a visiting missionary of the Church of God movement that the Wilson family had initiated at Geneva, Illinois, in the 1840s,[29] "fourteen obedient ones" met in Cleveland, Ohio, on Sunday evening, October 4, 1863, and organized a local Church of God. In 1865 the congregation affirmed the principle of noncombatancy in wartime. In 1888 the group, which had established associated congregations in Salem and Unionville, Ohio, incorporated itself as the Church of the Blessed Hope. As late as 1908 it secured a pastor from the Church of God of Oregon, Illinois. When he resigned in 1922, the Cleveland group obtained a Christadelphian leader for five years.[30]

In its beliefs the Church of the Blessed Hope is close to the Christadelphians, whose literature and hymnals it uses. It also admits Christadelphians to its Communion services, although the Christadelphians do not reciprocate.

The Church of the Blessed Hope accepts the Bible as God's only written revelation, as a unique and exclusive authority, and as the criterion of God's blessings upon obedience and his curses on disobedience. It holds the "gospel of the kingdom" to be the only true Gospel, which sinners must hear, believe, confess, and obey to be saved. It defines the Kingdom of God as "a divine political dominion established upon the earth" by Christ in person at the close of the times of the Gentiles. God's judgment upon the nations for their unbelief will be severe. Only a remnant will survive. The subjects of his Kingdom will consist almost entirely of infants and children, plus a residue of meek, willing, and well-disposed people who are alive at the time of the Kingdom's establishment. The Kingdom's rulers will be Christ and his associated saints, the resurrected righteous believers who have died and the righteous believers who are still living; collectively they form the seed of Abraham. During his millennial reign Christ will destroy all human governments and all religions except his own; other phenomena will include the end of war and of premature death and a sevenfold increase of solar and lunar light. At the end of the millennium the righteous will be approved and immortalized, the wicked consigned to shame and the second death, death itself destroyed, and God's supremacy will supersede that of Christ.

The Church of the Blessed Hope rejects the doctrine of the Trinity as polytheistic, and affirms that only the Father is God. Christ is God's virgin-born Son, and the divinely appointed mediator and advocate. The Church of the Blessed Hope also rejects purgatory and all form of posthumous probation. It affirms that the sacrifice of Christ has destroyed the devil, that is, sin. The Spirit of God is the Father's radiant power and energy in diffusion and official manifestation; the gifts of the Holy Spirit were only temporary and are not extant today. There is no intrinsically immortal principle in human beings and they are mortal because of sin. Those who are ignorant of the Gospel are irresponsible and are not raised from the dead; only those who have known the Gospel and have either accepted it (the righteous) or rejected it (the unjust) will be raised. Only the immersion of believers is a valid baptism. Among Christ's commandments that believers must keep is the weekly observance of the breaking of bread and drinking of the cup as a memorial of his death. Another commandment of Christ is the prohibition of participation in war as combatants.[31]

The Church of the Blessed Hope in Cleveland Heights is in complete fellowship with congregations at Unionville and Salem, Ohio; Miami, Florida; Perryville, Kentucky; Roll, Indiana; and El Paso, Texas; and with several Christadelphian groups. The total membership of the 7 churches is about 430. The Church of the Blessed Hope is located at Fairmount Boulevard and Taylor Road, Cleveland Heights, Ohio 44118. A new location is being constructed at 7450 Wilson Mills Road, Chesterland, Ohio 44026.[32]

## NOTES

1. Some Christadelphians think that only those that have been baptized into Christ after coming to faith and confessing their sins will have their names written in the books that will be opened at the judgment after Christ's return, while others believe that those who have the requisite knowledge, whether baptized or not, will be resurrected and brought to judgment

(letter from Mr. Edwin A. Zilmer, Waterloo [Iowa] Christadelphian Ecclesia, 2126 West Ninth Street, Waterloo, Iowa).

2. *Divine Requirements for Salvation* (Washington, D.C.: The Washington Christadelphian Ecclesia, n.d.) (4-page pamphlet), pp. 2-3. See also John Thomas, *A Synopsis of the One Faith Taught by the Apostles* (Washington, D.C.: The Northwest Christadelphian Ecclesia, 1932) (4-page pamphlet), pp. 2-3, drafted by him in 1867 and later referred to by him as "the definer's creed."

3. Cited letter of Mr. Zilmer. Although it describes British Christadelphians rather than those in North America, part three, "The Christadelphians," of Bryan R. Wilson, *Sects and Society: A Sociological Study of Three Religious Groups in Britian* (London: William Heinemann, 1961), pp. 219-314, is instructive.

4. "L.T." were his father's initials.

5. See *The Great Apostasy (or Departure from True Religion)* (Rochester, N.Y.: The Megiddo Mission Church, 1958). The Megiddo Mission Church holds that by the seventh century error had swallowed up Christian truth. The Megiddo Mission rejects Roman Catholicism; Martin Luther's "Pseudo-Reformation"; the Protestant denominations (Rome's "harlot daughters"); the work of John Calvin, John Knox, John Wesley, George Whitefield, Dwight L. Moody, Charles Taze Russell, William Miller, Mary Baker Eddy, and Billy Graham; and Spiritualism.

6. *History of the Megiddo Mission* (Rochester, N.Y.: The Megiddo Mission Church, 1965), pp. 1-57; Arch Merrill, "From River Boat to Rochester," *The Democrat and Chronicle Sunday Magazine* (Rochester, N.Y.), April 4, 1943, pp. 4-5.

7. See Percy J. Thatcher, ed., *God's Spiritual Creation: A Treatise on the First Three Chapters of Genesis* (Rochester, N.Y.: The Megiddo Mission Church, 1956). This 79-page brochure summarizes forty-eight lectures of the Reverend L. T. Nichols on the subject.

8. See L. T. Nichols, *The Trinity; Sacrifice, Death and Blood of Christ; His Sonship* (Rochester, N.Y.: The Megiddo Mission Church, 1966), pp. 1-12. This brochure was first published in 1909.

9. Ibid., pp. 8-29. The Megiddo Mission Church annually celebrates the birth of Christ on Abib 1 (the first new moon after the vernal equinox), the "True Christmas and New Year's Day." The other "special occasions" of the community are Independence Day, the anniversary of Captain Nichols's birth on October 1, and Thanksgiving Day. The weekly holy day is Sunday, but only because members of the Megiddo Mission Church "live where Sunday is the order of the 'laws that be' "; see L. T. Nichols, *The Sabbath* (Rochester, N.Y.: The Megiddo Mission Church, n.d.), especially p. 35.

10. Although a 1904 newspaper report quotes Nichols as declaring that "Christ is coming back in 1941 as sure as you and I are here now" (Merrill, p. 4, quoting the Rochester (N.Y.) *Democrat and Chronicle* for January 28, 1904), the actual position of the Megiddo Mission Church then as now has consistently been to refuse to set a date for Christ's return and the events that will attend it ("A Summary of the Principal Beliefs of the Megiddo Mission," question 20, in *History of the Megiddo Mission,* pp. 69-70).

11. See *A Treatise on the Holy Spirit* (Rochester, N.Y.: The Megiddo Mission Church, 1954).

12. See L. T. Nichols, *Man—What Is He? A Material or Immaterial Being,* and Maud Hembree, *After Death: What?* (Rochester, N.Y.: Megiddo Mission, 1921).

13. See L. T. Nichols, *What Must We Do to be Saved?* (Rochester, N.Y.: Megiddo Mission, 1905).

14. See *The Coming of Jesus and Elijah and the Great Battle of Armageddon* (Rochester: Megiddo Mission, n.d.).

15. See *The Kingdom of God* (Rochester, N.Y.: The Megiddo Mission Church, 1963).

16. See L. T. Nichols, *The Devil and Hell of the Bible* (Rochester, N.Y.: The Megiddo Mission Church, n.d.).

17. See Nichols, *What Must We Do to Be Saved?* and *The Trinity,* pp. 48-76.

18. Normally members of the colony do not vote in elections, except where their program is at stake, as in the case of educational issues.

19. Separation in religion includes renunciation of paganized holidays, such as

the celebration of Christmas on December 25.

20. The dress of the women of the community continues to be that of the late nineteenth century.

21. In lieu of military service in the armed forces, members of the Megiddo Mission Church stand ready to serve under civilian direction in work of national importance, such as industry, forestry, and hospitals.

22. *Synopsis of the Principal Beliefs of the Megiddo Mission Church* (Rochester, N.Y.: The Megiddo Mission Church, 1958); "A Summary of the Principal Beliefs of the Megiddo Mission," in *History of the Megiddo Mission,* pp. 64-71.

23. Letters of the Reverend Kenneth E. Flowerday, pastor and president of the Megiddo Mission.

24. Wilson was the author of *The Emphatic Diaglott,* a Greek-English New Testament first published at New York in 1864. He and his family had emigrated from England.

25. Harold J. Doan, "An Introduction to the Church of God," *The Restitution Herald,* vol. 51, no. 3 (special get-acquainted issue, 1960), pp. 4-5.

26. The Church of God holds that Communion is an ordinance which pictures the continuation of the redemptive relationship of which baptism pictures the establishment. In the Communion "the bread respresents the body of Christ; the fruit of the vine in the cup represents the blood of Christ" (Alva G. Huffer, *Systematic Theology* [3rd printing; Oregon, Ill.: The Restitution Herald, 1965], pp. 456-457).

27. "Statement of Faith," quoted from the constitution and by-laws of the Church of God General Conference in *The Restitution Herald,* ibid., p. 5.

28. Section H, "Statement of Faith," ibid.

29. Later this movement took institutional form as the Church of God of the Abrahamic Faith (Church of God General Conference), with headquarters at Oregon, Illinois. The Church of the Blessed Hope severed its connection with this body around 1909/1910.

30. B. H. Lang and others, *History of the Church of the Blessed Hope 1863–1963* (Cleveland Heights, Ohio: The Church of the Blessed Hope, 1963) (11-page brochure).

31. *Our Confession of Faith* (Cleveland, Ohio: The Church of God, n.d.) (30-page pamphlet). The Cleveland Heights and Unionville congregations differ from the others in that the former permit their members to accept noncombatant service in the armed forces, while the other churches require their members to accept alternative civilian service. For the text of the position of the Roll congregation on this issue, see *Statements of Religious Bodies on the Conscientious Objector,* 6th edition edited by P. Wayne Wisler and J. Harold Sherk (Washington, D.C.: National Service Board for Religious Objectors, 1968), pp. 23-24. Some of the congregations call themselves Church of God of the Faith of Abraham (Roll) or Church of God of the Abrahamic Faith (Miami, El Paso). (Letters from Mr. Vaughn Long, Perryville, Kentucky; from Elder Ernest R. Drabenstott, Huntington, Indiana, leader of the Roll congregation; and from Mr. Carol E. Jaggars, 3917 North Piedras Street, El Paso, Texas.

32. Letters from Mr. Lawrence E. Gibbs and the Reverend Allan Greif, Church of the Blessed Hope, Cleveland Heights, Ohio.

# 11. Sabbatarians

## The Bible Sabbath Association

After the exchange of many letters among Sabbath-keepers of various beliefs and affiliations over a two-year period, the Bible Sabbath Association was organized in 1945 for Sabbath promotion and defense.

Its platform calls for worldwide restoration of the seventh-day Sabbath; for imparting to everyone "an appreciation of the permanency of the universal scriptural decalog"; the restoration to honor and respect of the Ten Commandments as a whole, with special emphasis on the commandment "Remember the Sabbath day to keep it holy"; study of the Old and New Testaments and the inclusion in all editions of the New Testament "of a full and accurate presentation of the entire Ten Commandments"; repeal of all Sunday legislation; opposition to any civil calendar that destroys the continuity of the seven-day week; restoration of the designation "Sabbath" for "Saturday"; and building "the true Scriptural Sabbath into the conscience of mankind."

Membership is composed of individuals. The association meets every two years. Its executive agency is the twelve-member Board of Directors, on which the Seventh Day Baptist General Conference, the Seventh-day Adventist General Conference, the Church of God (Seventh Day) (Denver, Colorado), and the General Council of the Churches of God (Seventh Day) are represented. The publications program includes issuance of *The Sabbath Sentinel*, a monthly periodical, Sabbath-keepers' annual calendars, localized sunset tables, tracts, and leaflets.

The headquarters are located at Fairview, Oklahoma 73737. The association has about 500 active members.

## Seventh Day Baptist General Conference

The Seventh Day Baptist General Conference perpetuates a Sabbath practice that can be traced back almost three centuries in the history of Baptists in America and fifty years beyond that in England. The first Seventh-

133

Day Baptist church in this country was organized under English influence at Newport, Rhode Island, in 1672. Around 1700 some six Seventh Day Baptist churches came into being in the Philadelphia area and the biblical research of a member of the Baptist church at Piscataway, New Jersey, led to the establishment of a Seventh Day Baptist church there in 1705. The movement grew by emigration from these centers.[1] The Seventh Day Baptist General Conference was organized in 1802 and incorporated in 1927. Currently 62 churches—chiefly in Rhode Island, New Jersey, New York, West Virginia, California, and Wisconsin—claim 5,177 communicants. Linked to the American body are churches in England, Holland, Germany, Poland, the Republic of China, Burma, Mexico, Brazil, Guyana, Jamaica, New Zealand, Nigeria, and South Africa. In 1966 eleven national groups joined in forming the Seventh Day Baptist World Federation. The conference carries on an energetic tract ministry.

Theologically, the Seventh Day Baptists stand in the historic Baptist tradition. They have no binding creed to which members must subscribe. There have been both Calvinists and Arminians, Fundamentalists and Modernists in their ministry, and there are now conservatives and liberals among their laity, but the dominant stress is on an intermediate position. Their polity is congregational, their worship nonliturgical. The inconvenience and persecution that were the lot of their membership when Sunday laws were more rigidly enforced have made them even more sensitive than other Baptists to problems arising out of a mixing of state and church. In the early days of the movement, until the seventeenth-century "Exclusive Acts" made it impossible in England for them to do so, and again from early in the present century, Seventh-Day Baptists have taken an ecumenical stance. In connection with this they have consistently urged the freedom of the individual conscience and have discouraged the proliferation of administrative agencies in ecumenical organizations. They believe in God as creator; in Jesus Christ as the Son of God and Son of Man who revealed God in a clearer light and whose life, death, and resurrection carried God's plan for the salvation of humanity to its culmination; and in the Holy Spirit as the indwelling Comforter who makes actual the salvation that Christ made accessible by his finished atoning work on the cross. They see the human personality as coming from the God who created the human being capable of love and faith and obedience. The Bible, the only authoritative source of their faith, is a record written by inspired men to show forth God's dealings with people and to reveal His will for them. They believe in individual interpretation of the Scriptures under the guidance of the Holy Spirit. The universal church, the whole company of redeemed people gathered in one body with Christ as head, takes local form in the autonomous individual church. Burial by immersion in the baptismal waters is the initial overt act of the Christian believer in personal consecration of his life to God and a witness to others of that dedication. The Lord's Supper offers Christians the opportunity to partake of the emblems of the body of Jesus. The seventh-day Sabbath antedates Moses and has the sanction of Jesus; it is a symbol of God's presence in time and a pledge of eternal Sabbath rest, made sacred by divine appointment. Seventh Day Baptists stress that they keep Saturday as a day of worship and rest not because of slavish fear or to earn salvation, but out of winning and loving obedience to the law of God, which in their view nowhere sanctions a change in the day which God commanded people to keep. Evangelism—the preaching of the Gospel which holds the only hope for mankind—and religious education as a part of evangelism are an obligation on both the universal and the local church.[2]

The headquarters are at 510 Watchung Avenue, Plainfield, New Jersey 07061. The conference carries on foreign missions in Guyana, Jamaica, and Malawi.

### The General Conference of German Seventh-Day Baptists

The members of the General Conference of German Seventh-Day Baptists are not, strictly speaking, Baptists at all, but Dunkards or Brethren. Their founder, Johann Conrad Beissel (1690–1768), a Pietist from the Palatine, emigrated to America in 1720 "to devote the residue of his days to a hermit's life."[3] He turned first to John Kelpius's colony of Rosicrucians on the Wissahickon, known as "The Woman in the Wilderness (*Das Weib in der Wüste*)," only to find it in a state of near-dissolution following its leader's death. After a brief stay in Germantown, where he was apprenticed to the minister of the German Dunkard congregation, Peter Becker, he retired to Conestoga as a hermit and baptized himself. In 1723 he received baptism at Becker's hands at Conestoga and took the name Friedsam Gottrecht. Beissel thereupon founded a congregation of his own in the Conestoga and Pequa valleys. It split in 1728 over the keeping of Saturday as the Sabbath, as Beissel had come to insist Christians must do. Beissel renounced his Dunkard baptism, baptized one of his followers, and was rebaptized by him.

In 1732 Beissel moved on to a new hermitage at Ephrata, near Lancaster, Pennsylvania. Here he attracted a number of capable followers, among them the German Reformed minister, Peter Miller, who later handled the European foreign-language diplomatic correspondence for the Continental Congress, and, for a time, Conrad Weiser. In 1733 Beissel began the erection of the buildings of the Brotherhood of Zion at Ephrata, a rigorously disciplined, quasimonastic, perfectionist community, around which a secular congregation of Saturday-observing Dunkards gathered. Until around 1786 ownership of private property was forbidden to the members of the Brotherhood. Voluntary celibacy was the rule; married men and women who entered the community were required to live apart with the other members of their sex in separate houses. The requirements of community of property and of celibacy were not imposed on the secular congregation, which incorporated as the German Seventh-Day Baptists in 1814. The Ephrata community enjoyed considerable success, but in the late nineteenth century it began to dwindle rapidly and in 1905 it became extinct, although some of the buildings still stand.[4]

After the Revolutionary War the movement expanded into western Pennsylvania. Snow Hill (Schneeberg), near Waynesboro, Franklin County, became the chief center of the faith with the establishment of a congregation in 1829. Here a second monastic settlement, "The Nunnery," which still stands, was erected. During World War I the General Conference dropped "German" from its name and pronounced unqualifiedly against all war in order to secure conscientious-objector status for its members. "German" was restored to the group's name after World War I to differentiate it from other Saturday-observing bodies in the region.

The theological position of the German Seventh-Day Baptists is typically Dunkard: no creed but the Scriptures; the inspiration and inerrancy of the Bible; the Trinity; the Saviorhood and Mediatorship of Christ; believer's baptism in running water by threefold forward immersion; foot washing as the prelude to the Lord's Supper; anointing of the sick; refusal to bear arms and take oaths; separation from the world; abolition of the ceremonial law in the era of grace but the persistence of the Decalogue as the only rule of righteousness for all men. Since baptism is a symbol of the believer's repentance and infants have no sins to confess, infant baptism is not practiced. Instead, infants are blessed in a special ceremony in the course of their first year; baptism upon personal confession takes place at about age twelve. The Lord's Supper, formerly observed quarterly, is now an annual observance. The most noteworthy difference between the German Seventh-Day Baptists and others of the Dunkard tradition is the former's strict observance of the Sabbath from sundown on Friday to sundown on Saturday.

The number of members has declined to 82 in two churches. The General Conference met as such for the last time in 1962.[5]

## Church of God (Seventh Day) (Denver, Colorado)

The organization of the Seventh Day Baptist General Conference in 1802 united most of the Gentile keepers of the Saturday Sabbath, in North America, but here and there some independent congregations of Sabbath-keepers managed to maintain themselves. The witness of Seventh-Day Baptists won over to Sabbath-keeping some of the leaders of the movement that ultimately developed into the Seventh-day Adventists—William Miller, Elder Joseph Bates, and Elder and Mrs. James White. An article in Miller's journal *The Midnight Cry* in 1843 persuaded Elder Gilbert Cranmer (1814–1904) of Michigan to become a Sabbath-keeper. For a while he associated himself with the Seventh-day Adventists, but because he found himself unable to endorse some of Mrs. White's teachings, he severed his connection with them. He continued to preach and recruited a considerable following, including a number of clergymen. In 1860 he organized the Church of God in Michigan and became its first president. In 1863 the new church body began to publish *The Hope of Israel* (now *The Bible Advocate*); this journal played a vital role in the expansion of the Church of God (Seventh Day) eastward into Pennsylvania, New York, and New England, northward into Canada, southward into Ohio, Indiana, and Illinois, and westward into Iowa. In 1866 the headquarters of the church were moved to Marion, Iowa. In 1887 they were moved again, this time to Stanberry, Missouri, where the Church of God (Seventh Day) was incorporated in 1899.

A schism divided the church in 1933; one group continued to look to the headquarters at Stanberry, the other established headquarters at Salem, West Virginia. An effort at healing the breach in 1949 enjoyed some success, and new headquarters were established at Denver, Colorado. Some of the members of the West Virginia group successfully challenged the validity of the merger through legal action and continued the Salem headquarters.

The Church of God (Seventh Day) does not regard its thirty-seven-article statement of doctrinal beliefs as a closed creed, but as a summary of the cardinal teachings "determined and accepted by the ministerial council of the church." The individual articles treat the Bible ("infallible in its teaching"); God the Creator; Jesus the Son of God; the Holy Spirit;[6] Satan; the fall of man; the plan of salvation ("The Father accepted His Son's death as payment of the death penalty, thus making possible a pardon for sin and eternal life for all who will accept this plan of salvation"); the blood of Christ; accepting Christ ("an individual must believe on the Lord Jesus Christ and accept Him as his personal Saviour, obey the terms of the gospel, and pattern his life after the example set by Christ"); the terms of the Gospel ("faith in God and in His Son Jesus Christ, confession of and repentance for sin, restitution [where possible] for wrongs committed, and baptism[7] by immersion"); the Ten Commandments ("they are still to be observed in their entirety"); the Sabbath ("it is to be observed as sacred and holy from sunset Friday until sunset Saturday"); the Lord's Supper ("to be observed annually on the beginning of the day corresponding to the fourteenth day of the Hebrew month Nisan [or Abib]; unleavened bread and the 'fruit of the vine' [unfermented grape juice] should be used in this service as emblems of the broken body and shed blood of Christ"); foot washing ("to be practiced in connection with the observance of the Lord's supper"); church organization; church name ("the Bible name for the church is: Church of God"); church financing ("to pay tithes[8] and give offerings"); law of clean and unclean ("God's people are to use for food only those animals, birds, and fishes which were given by Him for that purpose, as distinguished from those designated as unclean for human use [pork, for example]"); unclean and defiling habits ("[including] smoking, chewing, and snuffing tobacco, the drinking of intoxicating liquors, and . . . using narcotic drugs unless prescribed by a licensed physician"); carnal warfare ("the Church of God stands opposed to carnal warfare");[9] prayer; prayer for the sick; Christ's preexistence ("[Christ] was in the plan of salvation before the foundation of the world"); Christ's crucifixion ("[on] Wednesday") and resurrection ("just before sundown the following weekly Sabbath"); the kingdom ("three phases: [1] the spiritual kingdom of grace, [2] the millennial reign of Christ, and [3] the eternal kingdom of God"); Christ's millennial reign; the new earth ("[the] renovated earth will become the eternal home of the redeemed"); the regathering of a portion of literal Israel to the land of Palestine; Christ's second coming; prophecy and signs of its fulfillment; state of the dead ("there is no consciousness in death"); punishment of the wicked ("they will be completely destroyed"); worldliness ("Christians should not patronize . . . movie theaters, pool halls, taverns, and night clubs; they should not take part in any form of social or ballet dancing; they should avoid the excessive use of jewelry"); pagan days ("Christmas, Lent, Easter, Good Friday, and Sunday are of pagan origin and . . . should not be observed"); the seven last plagues of Revelation 16 ("events in the world which cause great trouble and distress"); the third angel's message ("being preached by the Church of God as a warning against ['the beast']"); and marriage and divorce.[10]

The headquarters are at 330 West 152nd Avenue (Box 2370), Denver, Colorado 80201. The General Conference, composed of all the members of the church worldwide, meets every two years; consciously following a biblical pattern, the conference elects a twelve-man Executive Board to act for the conference between sessions. The board elects a chairman who is also chairman of the General Conference. The seventy-member ministerial council is the final authority in establishing and clarifying church doctrine.[11] There are 104 churches and missions in the United States and Canada, with a total membership of 8,000. Foreign operations are carried on in Latin America, the West Indies, the Philippines Republic, Nigeria, India, England, and Germany.

### The Church of God (Seventh Day) (Salem, West Virginia)

Efforts in 1949 to end the sixteen-year-long schism in the Church of God (Seventh Day) proved unsuccessful when members of the group with headquarters in Salem, West Virginia, successfully challenged by legal action the merger which others of the group tried to effect with the faction with headquarters in Stanberry, Missouri. As a result of the litigation the right of the West Virginia group to the property and publishing house in Salem was affirmed, and the Salem group continued its independent existence.

The constitution of the Salem Church of God (Seventh Day) includes a forty-point position on doctrine which was increased to fifty statements by action of the church body's Apostolic Council in 1951. Listed in the doctrinal position as "essentials of our faith" are the affirmations that "the Bible . . . is inspired as no other writing is, and is complete, infallible, and expresses God's complete will to man," that Jesus, the virgin born Son of God, Savior, and Redeemer "proved His Messiahship by remaining in the tomb exactly three days and three nights, rising in the end of the Sabbath," that "the inspired Bible name for God's called out assembly is the 'Church of God,'" that "the Lord's Supper is to be observed annually, on the beginning of the Passover, the 14th of Nisan, and after the example of Jesus," that "we ought to wash one another's feet," that "we should observe the seventh day of the week from even to even, as the Sabbath of the Lord," that "the return of Jesus will be literal, visible, personal and is imminent," and that "the throne of David will be established at Jerusalem in the person of Jesus Christ."[12]

Organizationally the Apostolic Council conducts the church's affairs, meeting on the first Sundays in January and July annually. From among the church body's elders twelve are chosen by lot to be apostles, seventy to be prophets. Seven of the church's members are chosen to be financial stewards. *The Advocate of Truth*, published semimonthly, is the church body's periodical. Headquarters are at Salem, West Virginia 26426. The church body appeals to II Samuel 24 for its decision not to make "a practice of taking a census."[13] Mission work is carried on in India, the Philippines Republic, the West Indies, Mexico, and Central America.

## The Worldwide Church of God

The true church of God has four basic characteristics, according to the Worldwide Church of God: (1) The Bible is the Maker's instruction book for mankind, the source of the only true religion, and the foundation of all knowledge, and man must live by its every word. (2) The name of the church is The Church of God. (3) Sin is the transgression of the spiritual law, summarized by the Ten Commandments, and repentance of sin and faith in Jesus Christ as personal Savior are the required conditions of receiving the Holy Spirit and becoming a child of God. (4) The church is to proclaim the Gospel of the Kingdom of God, understood as the divine government that will be set up on earth at Christ's return.

On the basis of these four characteristics the Worldwide Church of God traces the succession of true believers from apostolic times by way of the groups that the world knew as the Quartodecimanians, the Paulicians, the Bogomils, the Waldenses, the Lollards (who received the truth from "a German Waldensian preacher, Walter Lollard"), the Sabbatarian Baptists of England and America, the Church of God Brethren among the followers of William Miller, and the Church of God (Seventh Day). In 1931 Herbert W. Armstrong, a businessman, received ordination as "a minister of Jesus

Christ" in the last-named church body, but in 1933 it, like its predecessors, succumbed in Armstrong's view to spiritual death. The leadership attempted to put the local congregations under human government, in the form of a financial board of seven members, while at the same time "certain" leading ministers demanded that no more *new* truth be preached to the brethren. Armstrong withdrew from the Church of God (Seventh Day) and began broadcasting on his own in 1934.[14]

The Worldwide Church of God describes the doctrine of the Trinity as pagan.[15] Its "Fundamentals of Belief" affirm belief in one God; in Jesus of Nazareth as "the Christ, the divine Son of the living God, begotten of the Holy Spirit, born in the human flesh of the virgin Mary, and that He is true God and true man"; in the Holy Spirit "as the Spirit of God and of Christ Jesus, the power of God with which all things were created and made; that through the Holy Spirit God is everywhere present; that the Holy Spirit is divine "Love, Faith, Understanding, Power, Joy, and all the attributes of God"; in the inspiration of the Scriptures ("infallible in the original writings"); in the fact of the personality of Satan, who now has dominion over the world for six thousand-year days for "his labor of deception"; in man as created in God's image, formed of flesh, "which is wholly mortal, subject to corruption and decay, without possibility of eternal life inherent in himself," and in Adam's sin, by which he incurred "the death penalty without having received eternal life"; in sin as the transgression of the Law; in the Law, "which reveals to us the only right and true way to life—the only possible way of happiness, peace, and joy"; in the representative and substitutionary sacrifice of the sinless Son of God as "making it legally possible for man's sins to be forgiven and for God to release him from their penalty"; in Christ's resurrection as "making immortality possible for mortal man" and in his ascension and intercession; in the justification of repentant believers who accept "Jesus Christ as personal Saviour in faith"; in water baptism by immersion into Jesus Christ "for the remission of sins, following genuine repentance"; in what is commonly called the Lord's Supper "as continuation of the Passover, observed at night on the anniversary of the death of our Saviour, the 14th of Abib"; in the Sabbath "from Friday sunset to Saturday sunset"; in the observance by the true church today, as the "spiritual Israel," of the seven annual holy days "given to ancient Israel by God through Moses"; and in the necessity of avoiding "certain foods called 'unclean.' "

It is a fundamental doctrine that Christ and God's commandments forbid Christians "in any manner directly or indirectly to take human life by whatsoever means" and members of the Worldwide Church of God "conscientiously refuse to bear arms or to come under the military authority." There is a strong Dispensationalist strain in the theology of the Worldwide Church of God. The covenants, including the New Covenant, and the promises pertain only to Israel. As the descendants of Ephraim and Manasseh, or more generally of the "ten lost tribes of Israel," the white English-speaking peoples enjoy the national phases of the promises, the material blessings or "birthright." The spiritual phase of the promises, including Christ and salvation through him, is freely open to Gentiles who through Christ became Abraham's children. The object of redemption is to rescue mankind from the practice and penalty of transgressing the fundamental spiritual law, and "the object of the present dispensation is to fit those whom God now calls, with their consent, through a life of trial and test and overcoming sin . . . to possess the Kingdom"; Christians must therefore live clean, pure, holy lives by faith according to the Bible standard. "The church is merely that body of believers who have and are led by the Holy Spirit"; its inspired name is "The Church of God." Each local assembly is "The Church of God" and collectively they are "the Churches of God." The church's mission in this time is to preach the Gospel of the coming Kingdom of God to all nations, "with special stress on the warning to America and Britain of the prophecies pertaining to them." The only hope of eternal life for mortal men "lies in the resurrection through the indwelling (now) of the Holy Spirit." There will be a bodily resurrection of the just to eternal life as spirit beings on earth and of the unjust to the second and final death in Gehenna, "in which they shall perish in eternal punishment." Christ will return personally, visibly, premillienially, and imminently "to rule the nations of earth as King of Kings, and to continue his priestly office as Lord of Lords"; during the millennium he will restore all things and "establish the Kingdom of God upon earth forever."[16]

Herbert W. Armstrong is pastor general; his son, Garner Ted Armstrong, is executive vice-president. There are over 525 local churches worldwide with regional offices serving Canada, British Isles, Australia, South Africa, New Zealand, Switzerland, Netherlands, Philippines, Scandinavia, Central–South America, West Germany, and the West Indies. Worldwide membership is estimated at 67,000. (These figures represent baptized *adults*. Average church attendance worldwide is estimated at 94,000.)[17] The Worldwide Church of God is headquartered in Pasadena, California 91123, at the campus of Ambassador College.[18] The Feast of Tabernacles is observed annually at over seventy sites worldwide, in thirty-eight countries. The Worldwide Church of God sponsors a radio and television program entitled, Garner Ted Armstrong Presents, a monthly magazine, *Plain Truth*, and mails out over 28 million pieces of literature annually.[19]

## General Council of the Churches of God (Seventh-Day)

The Church of God (Seventh Day) that emerged as an organized body in Michigan in the 1860s was congregational in its polity. After the schism of 1933 the Salem (West Virginia) group adopted a so-called "biblical" or "apostolic" type of church government, in which the twelve apostles had twentieth-century counterparts who presided over the spiritual affairs of the church, with a council of seventy and a board of seven business stewards. Part of the cost of the reunion of the two factions in 1949 was an accommodation of the polity of the reunited church in the direction of the Salem pattern as well as compromises in doctrine in areas where differences had arisen in the half a generation of separation. A major issue was the conviction of some of the members of the Salem group that the Old Testament prohibition of "unclean meats" antedated the revelation of the Decalogue on Sinai and therefore bound New Testament Christians. Some of the members of the Stanberry group felt that the concessions made to Salem positions constituted a forsaking of the ancient landmarks. Accordingly they called a meeting in the summer of 1950 at Meridian, Idaho, at which they organized the General Council of the Churches of God (Seventh Day).

Although it has no binding creed to which members must subscribe, the General Council has a Statement of Faith that reads: "We believe the Bible to be the inspired word of God. We believe that God the Father is the supreme Deity, Jesus Christ the only begotten son of God, and the Holy Spirit the promised Comforter.[20] We believe in the deity of our Lord Jesus Christ, in his virgin birth, in his sinless life, in his miracles, in his vicarious and atoning death, in his bodily resurrection late on the Sabbath day,[21] in his ascension to the right hand of God in heaven, and His personal return to earth to establish his kingdom and rule this earth in great power and glory.[22] We believe the only means of being cleansed from sin[23] is through repentance and faith in the precious blood of Jesus and obedience to our Lord's command to be baptized (immersed) in the name of Christ for the remission of sins. We believe that by faith we may receive healing for our bodies.[24] We believe the scriptures enjoin the observance of the seventh day Sabbath (commonly called Saturday) to be observed from sunset on Friday until sunset on Saturday.[25] We believe the Lord's supper and foot washing should be observed once a year at the appointed time (14th of Nisan). We believe in the resurrection of the dead, both the just and the unjust, the just to eternal life and the unjust to eternal death. We believe the dead are in a state of unconsciousness.[26] We believe the true church organization taught in the Bible is local autonomy[27] and that the Bible name of the church is 'The Church of God.' [We believe] that the test of Christian fellowship is the commands of God and the faith of Jesus."[28]

The standing resolutions of the General Council endorse tithing and giving freewill offerings, oppose worldliness, discountenance all fleshly lusts (including tobacco, narcotic drugs, and intoxicating liquors), and condemn divorce "except for the Bible reason." The General Council opposes "carnal warfare," but since there is a difference of opinion on a Christian's duty with reference to military service, with some opposing any participation in war, and with "others believing that they can conscientiously serve the cause of righteousness through such participation," the General Council recognizes the need of maintaining fellowship in spite of these differences of opinion and pledges "moral support and protection to those who follow the voice of conscience."[29]

The doctrine of a definite experience with God or the "new birth," accompanied by strong, but quiet and undemonstrative, manifestations of the Holy Spirit, especially at camp meetings and revivals, is gaining general acceptance.[30]

The General Council meets annually. Between sessions a seven-member board administers policies of the General Council. The headquarters are at 302 East Gruber Street, Meridian, Idaho 85642. There are 41 churches from coast to coast (including 2 in British Columbia), with an estimated total membership of 2,000. The major concentrations are on the West Coast, in Missouri, and in Oklahoma. About 12 other congregations maintain associations ranging from independent to very close.[31]

The General Council supports missionaries in Jamaica and in St. Vincent, West Indies.

### The Seventh Day Church of God

In 1953 Elder A. N. Olson, secretary-treasurer of the Church of God (Seventh Day) (Salem, West Virginia), and Elder Joe Ling, chairman of the twelve apostles, separated from the parent body. Together with Elder Paul Groshans and Elder Martin Ogren they formed a fellowship which they called the Seventh Day Church of God and which established its headquarters in Caldwell, Idaho, in 1954. All the founders except Elder Ogren subsequently withdrew.

The fellowship holds the "Forty Doctrinal Points of Faith" adopted by the Salem, West Virginia, fellowship in 1933, revised and expanded to forty-one at Richland, Washington, in 1965. These teach the unique inspiration of the Bible; the sole Godhead of Jehovah; Jesus of Nazareth as the only begotten Son of God and our Lord, Savior, and Redeemer; his crucifixion on Wednesday and his resurrection on the Sabbath; the Holy Spirit as the Comforter who manifests himself by the power and fruits of the Spirit; the personality of Satan; the fall of man through disobedience; Christ as the pattern of the Christian's life; the Church of God as an inspired Bible name; the apostolic organization and government of God's Kingdom; pure religion personally experienced by those whom its power has regenerated; the necessity of preaching repentance; the essentiality of conversion; the sanctification of holy living as God's command for his people; baptism by immersion as typical of Christ's burial and resurrection; the efficacy of prayer; salvation of the sick through prayer and anointing; the laying on of hands; celebration of the Lord's Supper on the 14th of Abib; foot washing; observance of the seventh day from sunset to sunset as the Sabbath; observance of the seven annual holy days of the Old Covenant calendar; tithing of all increase; condemnation of all carnal warfare and of participation therein; observance of the law of the clean and unclean; condemnation of "the use of intoxicatinng liquors, alcoholic stimulants, narcotics, tobacco, and any habit-forming drugs"; observance of the law of God as the law of life in Christ; sin as the transgression of the law; justification through Christ alone; the literal, visible, personal, and imminent return of Christ; his establishment of the throne of David at Jerusalem; "the institution of the millennial reign of the kingdom of heaven" at Christ's return; judgment on the house of God during the Gospel age; the resurrection and reward of the righteous at the coming of Jesus; the inheritance of the earth by the meek; a final regathering of the dispersed nation of Israel; the resurrection of the wicked dead to final judgment and destruction and not to probation; the contemporary applicability of the message of the third angel of Revelation 14:9; the seven plagues of Revelation 14:9-10 as literal events at the end of the Gospel age; and the practice of fellowship in the brotherhood of Christ.[32]

The Seventh Day Church of God does "not keep strict membership records."[33] The membership of the Caldwell congregation is very small; whether there are other organized congregations in the United States and Canada that wholly share its position and are in full fellowship with it cannot be determined.

### United Seventh Day Brethren

In 1947 two small independent churches, both of them premillennial and committed to the observance of the seventh day of the week as "the sabbath of the Lord thy God," joined to form the General Association of United Seventh Day Brethren. Subsequently the organization suffered both gains and losses. The four churches in the association (located in Missouri, Oklahoma, Iowa, and Nebraska), with an overall membership of less than 100, retain their local independence. The position of the United Seventh Day Brethren varies from the positions of the Seventh-day Adventists, the Church of God (Seventh Day), and the Seventh Day Baptists. At the same time they do not consider themselves a denomination, and there are considerable differences of viewpoint within the association.[34] There are no general headquarters; the president receives mail at Box 225, Enid, Oklahoma 73701.

### NOTES

1. The assertion that William Miller, the spiritual ancestor of the Seventh-day Adventists, was originally a Seventh Day Baptist, seems to be unfounded. There is at least no record that he ever belonged to a Seventh Day Baptist church. But there is some evidence that Ellen Gould White, one of the most influential early leaders of the Seventh-day Adventists, received her instruction on the significance of the Saturday Sabbath from Seventh Day Baptist friends.

2. Without official ties to, but in fellowship with, the Seventh Day Baptist General Conference is the Pine Street

Gospel Chapel, 219 Pine Street, Middletown, Connecticut. The basic tenets of its faith include belief in the Trinity; the inspiration of the Bible; the duty of repentance and faith in Christ as the only hope of salvation; believer's baptism by immersion; the binding force of the Decalogue—including the commandment to observe the Sabbath —on all redeemed believers in Christ as the will of God for their present lives on earth; foot washing; the Lord's Supper; tithing; Christ's visible return to establish his Kingdom on earth; the resurrection of the just and the unjust; and the obligation of believers to treat their bodies with the greatest care and therefore to refrain from the use of alcohol and tobacco. The church, which has forty-one adult members, began as a Seventh-day Adventist church in 1905, but broke with that denomination over matters of doctrine and became independent in 1915. It supports the foreign missions of the Seventh Day Baptist General Conference. (Letter from the Reverend William J. Kimshel, Haddam Quarter Road, Durham, Connecticut, pastor, Pine Street Gospel Chapel, Middletown.)

3. Walter Conrad Klein, *Johann Conrad Beissel, Mystic and Martinet, 1690–1768* (Philadelphia: University of Pennsylvania Press, 1942), p. 34.

4. For a comprehensive listing of literature through the early 1940s, see Eugene E. Doll and Anneliese M. Funke, compilers, *The Ephrata Cloisters: An Annotated Bibliography* (Philadelphia: Carl Schurz Memorial Foundation, 1944).

5. Letter of the Reverend Walter H. Koenig, pastor of St. Matthew's Church, Pittsburgh, reporting on an interview which he had with Mr. Crist M. King, president of the General Conference of Seventh-Day Baptists, Pittsburgh, at this writer's request.

6. The Church of God (Seventh Day) (Denver, Colorado) does not hold the dogma of the Trinity as the historic traditions conventionally receive it. It considers that Jesus is the Son of God —not the person, God, manifest in the flesh. It believes that Jesus is God in his essential nature, as opposed to being human, and that he existed before his birth to the Virgin Mary. It holds that there are two distinct persons in the Godhead, Jesus being the only begotten Son of God. It does not regard the Holy Spirit as one of the hypostases of the Godhead, but as the manifestation of God the Father and of Jesus, his Son. God and Jesus have influence on human lives and this holy influence is the Holy Spirit.

7. The Church of God (Seventh Day) (Denver, Colorado) does not prescribe a formula for baptism. This one is widely used: "Upon confession of your faith, by authority of God the Father and under the direction of the Holy Spirit, I baptize you in the name of the Lord Jesus Christ for the remission of sins."

8. Tithing is, however, not a test of fellowship in the Church of God (Seventh Day).

9. The Church of God (Seventh Day) (Denver, Colorado) is opposed to participation in carnal warfare as a member of the armed forces. As a pacifist church body it advises its young men to accept neither combatant nor noncombatant status in any branch of the armed services.

10. *Doctrinal Beliefs of the Church of God (Seventh Day) with Supporting Scriptures* (Stanberry, Mo.: The Bible Advocate Press, n.d.) (31-page pamphlet).

11. On the organization of the church body, see *Church Manual of Organization and Procedure for Use in the Church of God (7th Day)* (rev. edn.; Stanberry, Mo.: Church of God Publishing House, 1962) (62-page booklet).

12. The Constitution of the Church of God, printed pamphlet, pp. 6-8.

13. Letter from Chris W. Royer, Church of God Publishing House.

14. Herman L. Hoeh, *A True History of the True Church* (Pasadena, Calif.: Ambassador College, 1959) (31-page brochure), pp. 14-27.—Herbert W. Armstrong and Garner Ted Armstrong, *The Wonderful World Tomorrow: What It Will Be Like* (Pasadena, Calif.: Ambassador College Press, 1966), p. 3, sees the millennium as having begun "in just ten or fifteen short years." On p. 35 the authors state: "This NEW World Tomorrow appears to be not *too* much farther off than 1977—or even 1987—it's coming IN OUR TIME!"

15. Hoeh, p. 23.
16. *Fundamentals of Belief* (Pasadena, Calif.: Radio Church of God, n.d.) (5-page typescript).
17. The literature on the Worldwide Church of God from sources outside itself is fairly limited. Walter R. Martin, *The Kingdom of the Cults: An Analysis of the Major Cult System in the Present Christian Era* (rev. edn.; Grand Rapids, Mich.: Zondervan Publishing House, 1968), furnishes a critique of the Worldwide Church of God from a conservative Baptist point of view in chapter 15, "Anglo-Israelism—Herbert W. Armstrong and the Radio Church of God"; this chapter has been separately reprinted as *Herbert W. Armstrong and the Radio Church of God in the Light of the Bible* (3rd rev. printing; Minneapolis, Minn.: Bethany Fellowship, 1968) (32-page pamphlet). Other tract-length discussions include George Darby, *The Delusions of Herbert W. Armstrong* (Minneapolis, Minn.: Religion Analysis Service, n.d.) (16-page tract); Robert L. Sumner, *Herbert W. Armstrong: A False Prophet* (Murfreesboro, Tenn.: Sword of the Lord Foundation, 1961) (24-page tract); and Paul Wilson, *The Armstrong Heresy: A Brief Examination* (Denver, Colo.: Wilson Foundation, n.d. [1960 or later]) (23-page tract).
18. In November 1977 six former students of Ambassador College published a 92-page magazine alleging that the college, the church, and its leaders misused funds and violated the civil rights of its members. One of the magazine articles was a five-page interview with Bobby Fischer, the chess expert who defeated the Russian champion Boris Spassky for the world title in 1972. In the article Fisher alleges that his gifts to the Worldwide Church of God led to his impoverishment and warns against the church's domination of its members' lives. Officials of the church body rejected the charge as "untrue, scurrilous, and exaggerated." Cf. *The New York Times,* November 6, 1977, p. 27.
19. Statistical information provided by Randal G. Dick, personal aide to Garner Ted Armstrong.
20. The General Council of the Churches of God (Seventh Day) regards the traditional doctrine of the Trinity as "a Catholic innovation" and holds that the Holy Spirit is a presence and not a person in the sense that the Father and the Son are persons. In the past its pastors have commonly baptized "in the name of the Father and of the Son and of the Holy Ghost," but in recent years other formulas have reportedly come into use, such as "in the name of Jesus" and "in the name of the Father and of the Son and of the Holy Ghost into Jesus Christ."
21. "Jesus was crucified . . . on the day we call Wednesday, and he was in the tomb three days and three nights. He arose toward the end of the Sabbath day (Saturday)" (*A Declaration of Those Things Most Commonly Believed among Us* [10-page pamphlet], Article 3). *A Declaration of Those Things Most Commonly Believed among Us* was formally adopted by the General Council in 1963 (ibid., p. [10]).
22. The signs of the times, "such as the regathering of Israel," are seen as indicating that Christ's return is "even at the doors" (ibid., Article 13).
23. "Sanctification is effected instantaneously, at the time of conversion, and continuously, each day, as the believer walks with God" (ibid., article 7).
24. "We believe in the 'laying on of hands' of the elders and the prayer of faith for divine healing" (ibid., Article 11).
25. The sabbath law is thought of as not being a part of "the handwriting of ordinances that was against us [and that] was blotted out and taken out of the way by Christ nailing it to his cross" (ibid., Article 10).
26. "Death is a condition of unconsciousness (sleep) to all persons, both the just and the unjust, a condition which shall remain unchanged until the great resurrection at Christ's second advent, at which time the righteous will receive eternal life, while at their appointed time the wicked will be 'punished with everlasting destruction,' suffering the complete extinction of being; this is the second death" (ibid., Article 5).
27. The General Council of the Churches of God sees itself as exemplifying the Bible pattern "in both local autonomy and general cooperation" (see Frank Walker, *"Workers Together with Him":*

*Local Autonomy* [9-page undated pamphlet]).
28. *General Council of the Churches of God* (Seventh Day) (Meridian, Idaho: Church of God Publishing House, n.d.) (9-page pamphlet), p. 9.
29. *A Declaration,* pp. [8]-[10].
30. Letter from Elder F. Mark Burnham, General Council of the Churches of God (Seventh Day), Meridian, Idaho.

31. Letter from Carl Palmer, president.
32. *Doctrinal Points of the Faith of the Church of God* (rev. edn.; N.p.: The Church of God, 1966) (7-page pamphlet).
33. Communication from Elder Martin Ogren, the Seventh Day Church of God.
34. Communication from Myrtle J. Ortig of the Enid Assembly.

## BIBLIOGRAPHY

Burdick, William L. and Corliss Fitz Randolph. *A Manual of Seventh Day Baptist Procedure.* Rev. edn.; Plainfield, N.J.: American Sabbath Tract Society, 1926.

Ernst, Jameo Emanuel. *Ephrata: A History.* Ed. John Joseph Stoudt. Harrisburg: Pennsylvania Historical and Museum Commission, 1963.

Holloway, Mark. *Heavens on Earth: Utopian Communities in America 1680–1880.* 2nd edn. New York: Dover Publications, 1966. Pp. 38-52.

Klein, Walter Conrad. *Johann Conrad Beissel, Mystic and Martinet, 1690–1768.* Philadelphia: University of Pennsylvania Press. 1942.

Randolph, Corliss Fitz. *The Sabbath and Seventh Day Baptists.* 4th edition. Plainfield, N.J.: American Sabbath Tract Society, 1936.

*Sabbath Handbook and Directory of Sabbath-Observing Organizations.* 2nd edn. Fairview, Okla..: The Bible Sabbath Association, 1961. A 43-page brochure. Since publication of the first edition a number of the organizations listed in the "Directory" have disbanded.

Sachse, Julius Friedrich. *The German Sectarians of Provincial Pennsylvania, 1708–1800: A Critical and Legendary History of the Ephrata Cloister and the Dunkers.* 2 vols. Philadelphia: Privately printed, 1899–1900.

# 12. Sabbatarians: "Sacred Names" Movement

## The "Sacred Names" Movement

The "Sacred Names" movement reflects the conviction of its proponents that the Father must be referred to by the Sacred Name of Yahweh and Jesus Christ by the name of Yahshua (or Yahvahshua) the Messiah.[1] The origins of the movement are somewhat obscure. In a sense it represents a delayed revival of the interest in the original form of the divine names generated by the book *Yahveh Christ, or The Memorial Name*, which Alexander MacWhorter of Yale University published in 1857,[2] and renewed by the lectures on "Names of the Deity" delivered around the turn of the century by Frederick Leonard Chapell of the A. J. Gordon Missionary Training College in Boston.[3] A parallel movement that began in England before World War I had some effect in North America. The insistence of Jehovah's Witnesses on the name Jehovah also played a role.

The focus of the revived interest during the early 1930s was the Church of God (Seventh-Day) (Salem, West Virginia). With the exception of Elder Angelo Benedetto Traina, now of Buena, New Jersey, all of the major leaders in the early phases of the movement in North America were ministers or members of this denomination. In 1934 Elder Squire LaRue Cessna, head of the Assembly of Jehovah in Detroit, renamed his congregation the Assembly of Yahvah. The use of Yahshua in public prayer has been traced back as far as 1936. The "Kadesh [*sic*] Name Society" in Detroit was in existence in 1936; it may have been organized earlier. In 1939 the Assembly of YHVH was chartered in Michigan as a general organization.[4]

One of the leaders in the organization of the Church of God (Seventh Day) (Salem, West Virginia) was Elder Clarence O. Dodd (1899–1955) of Salem, an initial member of the Seven and secretary-treasurer of the denomination until 1936. In that year he was asked to resign because of a difference of opinion between him and the other leaders of the church body about the feasts that were to be kept. Dodd withdrew and in 1937 he began to publish a monthly journal *The Faith*, primarily to promote his position on the feasts issue. Soon afterward he became interested in the Sacred Names question. By

October 1938 he had committed *The Faith* to the Sacred Names movement and had organized the Faith Bible and Tract Society.[5]

Upon Dodd's death the leadership of the movement devolved on Elder Beecher C. Wright, who continued to publish *The Faith* from the Kansas City, Missouri, headquarters of his Faith Scriptural Truths, Incorporated. Among the leading proponents of the movement during this period were Wright's editorial associate, W. L. Bodine of Van Buren, Arkansas,[6] and Elder Haig M. Mardirossian of Providence, Rhode Island, author of a formidable volume, *The Forgotten Faith of the True Worshippers*,[7] and head of a group which called itself the Assemblies of Yahweh and of Messiah. For this group Mardisossian devised *The Rules of Faith Laid Down by the Word of Yahweh*.[8] Illness has forced him to retire from active promotion of the movement in recent years.[9]

After Wright's withdrawal from the editorship of *The Faith* in 1961 because of his disagreement with the message promoted in the magazine, Dr. D. G. Werner, Post Office Box 261, Washington, D.C., edited the monthly until 1966.[10] After he resigned this position the editing and publication of the magazine became the full responsibility of an editorial committee of leaders of the Assembly of Yahweh of Morton, Pennsylvania; in 1969 the Assembly of Yahweh at Holt, Michigan, took over the editorial task. An average of 2,500 copies is published each month. The magazine serves as a link among independent local assemblies of somewhat divergent beliefs in 14 states and 6 Canadian provinces, as well as in the Philippines Republic, Jamaica, Africa, and India.[11]

### Kingdom Truth Assembly (Irvington, New Jersey) and Associated Assemblies of Yahweh

Elder Angelo Benedetto Traina was one of the speakers at the camp meeting at Warrior, Alabama, in 1938 that gave the North American "Sacred Names" movement much of its early impetus. In 1950 he published the *Sacred Name New Testament*, and in 1963 the Scripture Research Association of Irvington, New Jersey, which he heads, brought out his version of both the Old and the New Testaments, *The Holy Name Bible*. The Kingdom Truth Assembly at 1125 Stuyvesant Avenue, Irvington, which Traina organized in 1925, is in fellowship with other assemblies in Brandywine, Maryland, and in Miami and Cassia, Florida, each of which calls itself the Assembly of Yahweh. The estimated total membership of all four assemblies is 200.

The rules of faith that constitute the doctrinal beliefs of these assemblies include the insipiration of the Bible in its original form; acceptance of Yahweh as the only name of the Creator, and rejection of trinitarianism as a false doctrine derived from pagan sources; redemption through Yahshua, the virgin-born son of Yahweh; salvation through the atonement for sin that

Yahshua made through his blood; water baptism of believers through immersion; the permanent validity of the Decalogue given at Sinai as the standard of righteousness for believers in Yahweh; the obligation to abstain from food defined as unclean in Leviticus 11 and Deuteronomy 14, as well as from alcoholic beverages, tobacco, and narcotic drugs; the annual observance of Passover, Pentecost, and Tabernacles; Yahshua's memorial supper kept annually with unleavened bread and fermented wine on the day corresponding to the 15th of Abib; foot washing before the Communion, since the believers of the New Covenant are a royal priesthood; tithes and free-will offerings as the means of supporting the assembly and carrying forth the good news; prohibition of divorce and subsequent remarriage (except for fornication); the mortality of the soul and the unconscious state of the dead; the punishment of the wicked in the lake of fire, from which there is no resurrection; the restoration of Judah and Israel before the end of this age and the emergence of the Antimessiah as their head; and the return of Yahshua to set up a millennial kingdom during which he will rule over the nations with a rod of iron; the destruction of those who do not stand with him at the end of the millennium; and the eternal home of the saved on earth under Yahweh as all in all.[12]

The journal of the Kingdom Truth Assembly is called *The Way*.

### The Assembly of Yahvah

In 1945 Elder and Mrs. Loranze Dow Snow began to publish *The Yahwist Field Reporter*[13] at Fort Smith, Arkansas. In 1949 Elder Snow organized the Assembly of Yahvah at Emory, Texas, and became its overseer. In 1956 it was incorporated in Texas and began "to teach the restoration of the apostolic organization of the Assembly of Yahvah as it existed in the wilderness, in the days of Moses, and under the Messiah."[14] A revised constitution was adopted at Bristow, Oklahoma, in 1964. It calls for an apostolic organization with the Twelve (who constitute the Assembly Council), the Seven, the Elders, and the Seventy, all chosen by lot, and for an overseer and assistant overseer appointed by the Assembly Council. All members of the organization, whatever their capacity, are required to obey those over them.

The section on doctrine affirms the inspiration of the Bible; the necessity of using Yahvah, Yahshua, and Assembly of Yahvah as divinely revealed names; the Messiah's resurrection late on the Sabbath after remaining in the tomb exactly three days and three nights; the availability of the baptism and nine gifts of the Holy Spirit to Yahvah's followers today; the fall of Adam as bringing death and Yahvah's wrath on all human beings; experimental salvation, repentance, conversion, water baptism by immersion in the name of Yahvah-shua the Messiah (as meeting the requirements of Matthew 28:19), and healing of the sick through prayer and anointing; the annual observance of the Passover in unleavened bread and grape juice on the dark part of the 14th of Abib; the Saturday sabbath; tithing; condemnation of "all carnal warfare," of intoxicants, alcoholic stimulants, narcotics, tobacco, and habit-forming drugs; the law of the clean and unclean; the perfection and continuity of the Ten Commandments; the impending literal, visible, and personal return of Yahshua and the resurrection and reward of the righteous, to be followed by his millennial reign with his saints on the throne of David in Jerusalem;[15] the unconscious state of the dead; the resurrection of the wicked to final judgment and eternal destruction, not to a second chance; and the literal character of the seven last plagues at the end of this age. The Assembly of Yahvah holds that the 144,000 were the first to hear the Kingdom message and that no contemporary movement can be the 144,000; and that Yahvah-shua made the New Testament with the twelve tribes of Israel and Judah "when he was there the first time." Women can fulfill any obligation that the Spirit places on them, but they cannot be evangelists, apostles, bishops, pastors, or overseers. The Assembly of Yahvah does not object to, but refuses to advocate, the keeping of Pentecost and the Feast of Tabernacles.[16] There are four organized assemblies in North America: the headquarters assembly at 6th and Elm Streets, Junction City, Oregon 97448; one in Moline, Illinois; and two in Alabama. The total active membership is estimated at 100. The assembly carries on foreign missions in India, the Philippines Republic, Africa, and Jamaica. Its monthly journal, *The Eliyah Messenger and Field Reporter*, goes out to 1,500 domestic and foreign recipients.[17]

## NOTES

1. Other forms used by various individuals at different times have included IHVH, JHVH, JHWH, YHVH, YHWH, Jehovah, Jahovah, Jahaveh, Jahvah, Yahveh, Yahvah, Yahovah, and Yahwe, and Jahoshuah for Jesus. The pronunciation has also varied. The principle has been extended to other names, for example, Eliyahu for Elijah and Miriam for Mary.

2. Alexander MacWhorter, *Yahveh Christ, or The Memorial Name* (Boston, Mass.: Gould and Lincoln, 1857).

3. Published by John J. Scruby in *The Standard Bearer* (Dayton, Ohio), nos. 150-152 (January–March 1911).

4. It took the name the Assembly of Yahweh in 1945. Detroit's Yahver Beth Israel, now located at 5629 Dudley, Dearborn Heights, Michigan, reportedly antedated the Assembly of YHVH.

5. Its present address is 61 Oak Street, Salem, West Virginia. Dodd's views on the Sacred Names are summarized in *The Name of the Father and of the Son* (Salem, West Va.: Faith Bible and Tract Society, n.d. [1948 or later]) (22-page pamphlet).

6. From 1961 on Bodine was associated with Norman Warner in the direction of the Assembly of Yahvah with headquarters in Lebanon, Oregon. Both of them have withdrawn from the organization.

7. Haig M. Mardirossian, *The Forgotten Faith of the True Worshippers* (New York: Vantage Press, 1958). After his name Mardirossian used the initials V. Y. M., which he explained as the abbreviation of "Verba [*sic*] Yahweh Minister."

8. Haig M. Mardirossian, *The Rules of Faith Laid Down by the Word of Yahweh* (Kansas City, Mo.: Faith Scriptural Truths, n.d.) (26-page tract).

9. For the early history of the Sacred Names movement, the present writer has drawn extensively on Loranze Dow Snow, "A Brief History of the Movement in America," *The Elijah Messenger and Field Reporter*, vol. 20, no. 11 (May 1966), pp. 1, 4, 7, 12, and no. 12 (June 1966), pp. 5-6.

10. *The Faith*, vol. 29, no. 2 (February 1966), p. 13. Werner, reared in the Evangelical Church in his native Germany, was a Seventh-day Adventist minister in Europe and North America from 1907 to 1947, when he joined the Church of God (Seventh Day) (Salem, West Virginia). He severed his connections with the latter body and joined the Yahweh movement in 1952. (*The Faith*, vol. 24, no. 7/8 [July–August 1961], p. 17.)

11. Communications from Elder Alfred J. Francis, Assembly of Yahweh, and from Brother Richard H. Francis, treasurer, Assembly of Yahweh.

12. "The Rules of Faith Constituting the Doctrinal Beliefs of the Assembly of Yahweh" (4-page typewritten document, accompanying a letter of Elder Angelo B. Traina, Box 142, Buena, New Jersey).

13. Later the *Kingdom Messenger and Field Reporter*, now *The Eliyah Messenger and Field Reporter*.

14. Loranze Dow Snow, "A Brief History of the Name Movement in America," *The Eliyah Messenger and Field Reporter*, vol. 20, no. 11 (May 1966), p. 12.

15. The Mosaic or sacrificial system will not be reinstated in the millennium.

16. *The Constitution of the Assembly of Yahvah as Revised June 1964, Bristow, Oklahoma* (Junction City, Ore.: Assembly of Yahvah, 1965) (4-page document).

17. Letter from Elder Loranze Dow Snow, former bishop-overseer, Assembly of Yahvah, 1632 North Evanston Place, Tulsa, Oklahoma.

# 13. Seventh-day Adventists and Related Bodies

## Adventism

Adventism[1] centers in the belief that there are two advents of Christ (both visible and personal), that the second coming of Christ is imminent, and that the central feature of this event is the establishment of his millennial reign. While Adventism has existed throughout the history of the church, especially in times of stress, the most significant Adventism movement of modern times originated with William Miller (1782–1849).

A former army officer, a farmer, a licensed Baptist preacher, and an ardent student of the "chronological portions" of the prophetic writings of the Bible, Miller believed that the dates for all important events in sacred history have been fixed in prophecy. Since the exact dates of the Flood, the sojourn of Israel in Egypt, the destruction of the Canaanites, the duration of the Exile had been foretold, the exact date of Christ's second coming must also have been prophesied. Miller believed that he found the date of Christ's second coming in Daniel 8:13,14, which speaks of 2,300 days until the cleansing of the sanctuary. He fixed the date of the beginning of this period in 457 B.C., the year in which the command to rebuild Jerusalem was given, Daniel 9:25, and following the practice of most time setters that according to Numbers 14:34 a day in prophecy denotes a year, he proclaimed that the cleansing of the sanctuary would occur within a year after March 21, 1843. The 70 weeks of Daniel 9:24, totaling 490 years and ending A.D. 33, would constitute the first part of the 2,300 "days," and the 1,335 days of Daniel 12:12 would constitute the second part of this period and end in 1843. Miller held that the cleansing of the sanctuary was figurative language denoting the personal return of Christ to cleanse the world of all its pride and power, pomp and vanity and to establish the peaceful Kingdom of the Messiah in place of the kingdoms of this world.

In 1831 Miller opened a vigorous campaign to gain adherents for his views, and by 1843 his followers numbered 50,000. When March 21, 1844, passed without the Lord's visible return, there was keen disappointment, and

153

Miller admitted his mistake. However, several prominent leaders believed that the coming of the Lord was to occur on the Festival of the Atonement, October 22, 1844, and not on the Jewish New Year, as Miller had predicted. This encouraged the Adventists, and they made extensive preparations for the Lord's glorious appearance, only to be bitterly disappointed again.

The belief that Christ would appear at an early date to establish his millennial reign persisted, and in 1845 a group of Adventists met at Albany, New York, to define their position and to adopt principles embodying the views of Miller concerning the character of Christ's second advent, the resurrection, and renewal of the earth. The salient points agreed on at Albany are: (a) The present world is to be destroyed by fire, and a new earth is to be created for the believers. (b) There are only two advents of Christ, both visible and personal. (c) The second advent is imminent. (d) The condition of sharing in the millennial reign of Christ is repentance and faith, a godly and watchful life. (e) There are two resurrections, that of the believers at Christ's second coming and that of the unbelievers after the millennium. (f) The departed saints do not enter Paradise in soul and spirit until the final blessedness of the everlasting Kingdom shall be revealed at Christ's second coming. However, differences arose within the group concerning the nature of Christ's coming, the immortality of the soul, the condition of the dead in the intermediate state, and the observance of the Sabbath. Controversies on these points led to the organization of various groups of Adventist bodies, the largest being the Seventh-day Adventist denomination.

## General Conference of Seventh-Day Adventists

Doctrinally the Seventh-day Adventists are heirs of the nineteenth-century Adventist movement and of the specific teaching of William Miller.[2] Though they agreed with Miller that 1844 was the date of the cleansing of the sanctuary, they differed with him on how to interpret the event. They held that the cleansing of the sanctuary did not refer to the rejuvenating of the world, as Miller taught, but to an "investigative judgment" by Christ in the sanctuary of heaven. According to this view Christ began in 1844 to judge his people according to the standard of the Decalogue.

The groups of people who were to organize as Seventh-day Adventists were influenced also by the teachings of Seventh Day Baptists that the keeping of the Old Testament Sabbath was an unalterable and everlasting command of God. An increasing number of Adventists held that Christ was cleansing the sanctuary according to "the fourth principle of the Decalogue," that is judging people as to their attitude over against the commandment to observe the Sabbath according to the Mosaic law.

In 1847 a leader of the group, Ellen G. White (1827–1915), reported visions in support of the interrelation between Adventist and Sabbatarian views. In one vision she saw two angels standing by the heavenly Ark of the Covenant in the sanctuary of heaven and Jesus raising the cover of the ark containing the Ten Commandments, the fourth surrounded by a halo. In another vision she was informed that the message of the third angel in Revelation 14:9-12 referred to the papacy and that according to Daniel 7:25 the great antichristian sin is the changing of the Old Testament Sabbath into Sunday.[3]

With Ellen G. White providing the inspiration and her husband, James, the leadership and organization, the Seventh-day Adventists drew together in conference in the 1850s. Several publications were launched, including the still influential *Review and Herald* in 1850, and a publishing house was established in Rochester, New York, and then moved in 1855 to Battle Creek, Michigan, which soon became the headquarters for the emerging denomination. In a general meeting at Battle Creek in 1860 the denominational name was adopted. The Seventh-day Adventist Publishing Association was incorporated in 1861. In 1863 a General Conference was held and a constitution for the organization was drafted.

The Seventh-day Adventists were soon engaged in a vigorous missionary endeavor. In 1868 evangelists went west and launched work on the Pacific Coast. In 1874 the General Conference sent John Nevins Andrews (1829–1883) to Europe and began a worldwide expansion. By the 1880s Seventh-day Adventists could be found from the British Isles to Russia and from Scandinavia to Italy with Switzerland as the center for missionary operations. Further outreach brought the movement to Central and South America, to Australia and New Zealand, and to India and Japan. Today the worldwide membership is more than 2,500,000.[4]

Placing major emphasis on the second Advent of Christ and on the observance of the seventh day as the Sabbath, the Seventh-day Adventist denomination is "a conservative Christian body, . . . evangelical in doctrine, and professing no creed but the Bible."[5] Though Seventh-day Adventists have insisted that "the Bible and the Bible only" should be the Christian's creed, they have over the years issued various statements of belief which resulted ultimately in the publication of twenty-two "Fundamental Beliefs" in the denominational *Yearbook* since 1931. Not considered a creed, the document professes only to embody "the principal features" of belief as they "may be summarized."[6]

Most helpful for understanding Seventh-day Adventist teaching is the publication, *Seventh-day Adventists Answer Questions on Doctrine: An Explanation of Certain Major Aspects of Seventh-day Adventist Belief*. It was prepared by a representative group of Seventh-day Adventist leaders, Bible teachers, and editors and published in 1957 in response to questions about the relation between Seventh-day Adventist teaching and orthodox Christian beliefs. The publication distinguishes three categories of teaching: (1) nineteen basic truths which Seventh-day Adventists share with evangelical Protestant Christians, (2) twelve doctrines held by Seventh-day Adventists on which Protestant denominations are divided, and (3) five distinctive doctrines held only by Seventh-day Adventists.[7]

Among the teachings which Seventh-day Adventists assert they hold in common with evangelical Protestants are the beliefs in God as Triune, the creator and ruler of the universe; in the Scriptures as "the inspired revelation of God" and the "sole rule of faith and practice"; in Jesus as "very God," who "became incarnate through the miraculous conception and the virgin birth," whose "vicarious, atoning death . . . is all-sufficient for the redemption of a lost race," who "arose literally and bodily from the grave" and "ascended literally and bodily into heaven," and who will return "in a pre-millennial, personal, imminent second advent"; in the Holy Spirit as "a personal being" who shares "the attributes of deity"; in "salvation through Christ . . . by grace alone, through faith in His blood"; in "the new life in Christ . . . by regeneration"; and in "the resurrection or translation of the saints" and "a judgment of all men."[8]

Among the teachings which Seventh-day Adventists claim they hold on which evangelical Protestants disagree are the beliefs that people are "free to choose or reject the offer of salvation through Christ"; that the moral law of the Ten Commandments is binding on all people of all ages; that baptism is by single immersion; that the human being has "conditional immortality," not an immortal soul; that the wicked are completely destroyed and do not suffer torment in an eternal hell; that the seventh day of the week is the Sabbath, which must be observed as such by people of all times; that tithing is God's plan not only for the Jews but for the church; that church and state "operate in entirely separate fields"; that foot washing at the time of the Lord's Supper is an "ordinance instituted by Christ"; that there should be abstinence from the use of alcohol and tobacco.[9]

The five doctrines listed as distinctively Seventh-day Adventist are the following:

1. That there is a sanctuary in heaven where Christ, our High Priest, ministers in two distinct phases of His mediatorial work.

2. That there is to be an investigative judgment in which the destinies of all men are decided before Christ comes in the clouds of glory.

3. That the Spirit of prophecy, or the prophetic gift, is one of the gifts of the Spirit promised to the church in the last days, and that that gift was manifested to the Seventh-day Adventist Church in the work and writings of Ellen G. White.

4. That the seal of God and the mark of the beast, mentioned in Revelation, are the symbols of the opposing forces of good and evil in the last great conflict before Christ comes the second time.

5. That the three angels of Revelation 14 represent the proclamation of God's last message to the world in preparation for the coming of our Lord.[10]

Seventh-day Adventists are noted for their use of the mass media of communications. They sponsor regular programs over approximately 1,000 radio and more than 150 television stations. They operate 50 publishing houses, printing in over 200 languages and issuing 400 magazines. Seventh-day Adventists are noted also for their stress on education. They sponsor approximately 5,000 elementary and 300 secondary schools. In medicine and health they operate over 100 hospitals and sanitoria.

Seventh-day Adventists have 3,386 congregations with a total membership of 495,699. Their headquarters are at 6840 Eastern Avenue, Northwest, Washington, D.C. 20012.

## The Advent Christian General Conference of America

When Christ did not return visibly to earth in 1844, as William Miller and his followers expected, consternation and confusion developed in the "Adventist" ranks. With a view to restoring their shattered conference, a "Mutual Conference of Adventists" assembled in Albany, New York, in April 1845, reached a consensus on the central teachings of Adventism, and organized the loosely knit American Millennial Association (later the Evangelical Association of Adventists).

In 1852 two leaders of this group, Jonathan Cummings and F. H. Berrick, concluded that Miller had made an error of ten years in his calculations and that Christ would appear visibly in 1854. In January of that year they began to publish *The World's Crisis* and succeeded in persuading a very small percentage ("perhaps one in fifty") of Adventists. This date failed, too, but the journal continued publication as an advocate of "conditional immortality." Under the new editorial leadership of Horace L. Hastings and Miles Grant, it recruited additional supporters for this teaching. In July 1860 its proponents organized a "Christian Association" in order to spread the two tenets of Christ's imminent return and conditional immortality more effectively, particularly through the publication of literature. At the new organization's first annual meeting later in the same year, they took the name "The Advent Christian Association" and set up their publication activities as a separate venture. Officers in the new body included Hastings, Daniel T. Taylor, Charles F. Hudson, and George F. Adams. Advent Christians regard 1860 as the beginning of their existence as an organized denomination. In 1865 the American Advent Mission Society began work among the liberated slaves of the American South and in 1891 it began its foreign missionary outreach in the conviction that the evangelization of the nations must precede Christ's return. In 1964 the three surviving congregations of the Life and Advent Union, a denomination organized in 1863, united with the Advent Christian General Conference.

Although the Advent Christian Church has an eleven-article statement of doctrinal principles, adopted in 1900, it regards itself as a noncreedal church. Its geographical dispersion, its decentralized control, and its dependence upon a largely untrained ministry have brought about considerable theological diversity. This has led to some tensions in the denomination in the area of revelation and inspiration between those who hold a fundamentalistic position and those who espouse a mediating, although still conservative view.

The two eschatological tenets of the imminent nonmillennial return of Christ and conditional immortality—conceived of in biblical terms rather than in terms of a Platonic immortality of the soul—remain prominent features of Advent Christian teaching. The latter article tends to color almost every other doctrine. In its simplest terms, this teaching affirms that God, who alone possesses immortality, created man with the potential either of obeying God or of rebelling against him. Had men lived in obedience they would never have died. The rebellion of our first parents made them and all their posterity mortal. At death all men enter a state of unconsciousness that continues until the resurrection when Christ returns. The Christian Gospel offers men the hope of participating in God's immortality through faith in Jesus Christ. If they accept God's gracious saving acts—Christ's atoning sacrifice, death, resurrection, and ascension—in faith, they have a hope that finds partial fulfillment in this life that will find its consummation in the eschatological and eternal kingdom that God will establish upon earth. If persons remain finally incorrigible and impenitent, they are lost and—as Advent Christians understand Matthew 10:28 and Mark 9:43-49—God will destroy them, along with the devil and his minions, in Gehenna's fire after the last judgment. The result of their destruction by burning will be eternal, but not the process itself.

Advent Christians are conventional trinitarians, but their doctrine of God reflects the doctrine of conditional immortality in that they see the eternal punishment of sinners in the fires of Gehenna as contradicting the image of a loving God revealed in and through Christ. They also see the doctrine of conditional immortality as demanding that human beings be free moral agents, who can choose to respond to the divine love revealed in Christ or to rebel against God and as a consequence to be utterly destroyed.

Advent Christians have not fully articulated a doctrine of the church. They keep Sunday as the weekly day of worship and regard believer's baptism by immersion and the Lord's Supper as ordinances that Christ instituted. By his burial in the baptismal waters the believer gives a symbolic witness to his belief in Christ's atoning death, burial, and resurrection and to his own death to sin in repentence and his own regeneration by which the Holy Spirit empowers him to walk in newness of life. In the Lord's Supper the elements are the emblems of Christ's death, which the communicants confess with joy in the awareness of his spiritual presence in the midst of his people as they participate in this memorial meal.

Advent Christian polity is basically congregational. The democratically structured local church is the final authority in most aspects of church life, although Advent Christians see the ordination of ministers as requiring a broader sanction. For that reason local conferences—of which there are thirty-three in the United States, divided into five regions—administer ordination. The General Conference, which meets every two years, is over the regions. The authority of these various levels of supervision and administration is moral rather than legislative.

Advent Christians treat the ethical norms of Sacred Scripture very seriously but try to avoid legalism. They seek for purity of life while striving faithfully to be ready for Christ's return. Tithing is a biblical and therefore desirable practice, but not a requirement. Historically they have opposed the use of alcoholic beverages, and they have discountenanced the use of tobacco. Until recently they have urged their people to avoid social dancing, card-playing, and attendance at motion pictures, although now they find it increasingly difficult to implement these standards.

Since the beginning of the century, Advent Christians have made the achievement of higher educational standards for their ministry a primary emphasis, along with a closer coordination of denominational efforts. The ecumenical stance of the denomination as a whole is one of interest without strong commitment; some local churches and denominational agencies have related themselves to the National Council of the Churches of Christ in the U.S.A. and some to the National Association of Evangelicals.

Membership in the twentieth century has tended to remain on a plateau. Currently about 400 churches have an inclusive membership of about 31,000 persons. Denominational headquarters' address is Box 23152, Charlotte, North Carolina 28212. The existing foreign missions of the denomination are in India, Japan, the Philippines Republic, Malaysia, and Mexico.[11]

### The Primitive Advent Christian Church of West Virginia

Before the turn of the century the Reverend Silas P. Whitney (1835–1912) of Sand Hills, New York, an Advent Christian disciple of William Miller, came to the Poca River area of West Virginia. He identified himself with the people of the region and in spite of opposition by the organized churches—mostly Baptists and Methodists—he attracted a considerable following in Roane, Jackson, Clay, Kanawha, and surrounding counties.[12] In the late 1920s the preaching of the Reverend Freemont Whitman, pastor of the First Advent Christian Church in Charleston, West Virginia, against rebaptizing backsliders and foot washing precipitated a schism. The proponents of both practices organized the Primitive Advent Christian Church (or Conference) of West Virginia in 1931. Since 1950 the economic decline of part of the region due to the reduction in timber, natural gas, and oil operations has resulted in a decline in the number of churches.[13]

A twelve-section Declaration of Faith affirms belief in the Trinity; the inspiration, authority, and truthfulness of the historic statements of the Bible; the sufficiency of the teachings of Christ and his apostles about the church's duties and faith ("and we reject all modern visions and revelations, so-called"); conditional immortality; Christ's death for our sins, resurrection to immortality, session and intercession, and imminent personal return; death as a condition of unconsciousness for all, changing at the coming of Christ to everlasting life for the righteous and to everlasting destructions through "extinction of being" for the wicked; salvation as free to all who in this life meet the conditions God imposes, repentance toward him and faith in Jesus Christ with a life of consecration to God's service ("thus excluding all hope of a universal salvation or future probation"); the establishment of an eternal home for the redeemed on the new earth; the final judgment of all according to their works on the day of Christ's return; baptism by immersion, the Lord's Supper in unleavened bread and wine, and the saints' washing of one another's feet as biblical ordinances; baptism of penitent backsliders; and a renunciation of opposition to other denominations.[14] The church makes Christian character the only test of fellowship and Communion and opposes "taking up arms against our fellow man in case of war."[15]

Elkview, West Virginia 25071, is a major center of the denomination, which has 10 churches, all in West Virginia, with an inclusive membership of 350.

## People's Christian Church

Rejecting as false the claims of Mrs. Ellen Gould White to be a prophetess, Elmer E. Franke (d. 1946) left the Seventh-day Adventists in 1916 and founded the People's Christian Church in New York City. Seven years later a second congregation was established in Schenectady, New York. A third congregation was founded the following year in New Bedford, Massachusetts.

The articles of Belief of the People's Christian Church affirm the movement's faith in God the Creator; Jesus Christ, "one in nature with the Father"; the Holy Spirit, "one with the Father and the Son"; the divine inspiration and sufficiency of the Bible; believer's baptism by immersion into the name of the Father and of the Son and of the Holy Spirit; the Lord's Supper, in which the unleavened bread symbolizes Christ's body and the wine his blood, celebrated usually on the first Sabbath of the month with no one excluded from participation in it; the release of the Gospel church from observing the Mosaic ceremonial law, with its shadows and symbols that ceased when Christ was nailed to the cross; the Ten Commandments, including the seventh-day Sabbath, as the eternal moral law of God; a new birth as necessarily entailed by conversion; the autonomy of the local church, whose officers are the ordained minister, the ordained elder, and the ordained deacon; tithes and free-will offerings as the biblical way of supporting the Lord's work; and Christ's imminent, personal, and visible second coming, at which those who have died in Christ shall arise first and the living Christians will be translated.[16]

There are no central headquarters. The New York mother-church is located at 165 West 105th Street 10025. There are two churches each in New York and Massachusetts, and scattered members throughout the country. The total active membership is estimated at 1,000.[17]

## Seventh-day Adventist Reform Movement

At the beginning of World War I in Europe in 1914, the Seventh-day Adventists in sixteen countries on that continent agreed to bear arms and to do so even on the Sabbath. The small percentage of members that insisted on what they regarded as their movement's original teaching on nonparticipation in military service and on Sabbath-keeping were put out of their churches. Even when peace was restored, they found that they could not be reunited with the majority without giving up their views. Accordingly, they organized in 1925 as the Seventh-day Adventist Reform Movement. They teach respect for and loyalty to the civil authorities at all levels, but they decline all participation in military service, although they are willing to perform under civil direction prescribed alternative service that is not inconsistent with what they regard as the divine requirements. In the conviction that a healthy body is conducive to spiritual development and increases the individual's capacity for service, they are vegetarians and strict abstainers from alcoholic beverages, tobacco, tea, coffee, and all foods that they deem unhealthful. The movement describes itself as "founded upon the Advent message of 1844," and takes the doctrinal positions held generally by Seventh-day Adventists in 1914.[18]

The headquarters of the movement are at 3031 Franklin Boulevard, Sacramento, California 95817. There are 10 congregations and missions in the United States and Canada, with an estimated total active membership of more than 200. The major part of the movement's worldwide strength of about 10,000 is in South America, Western Europe, the Balkan countries, the Union of Soviet Socialist Republics, and Australia. The chief mission fields of the movement are in Africa, the Philippines Republic, the Iberian peninsula, and Central America.[19]

## Seventh-day Christian Conference

In 1934 Victory Tabernacle, New York, dropped its Seventh-day Adventist affiliation and became the headquarters church of the Seventh-day Christian Conference.

The conference differs doctrinally from Seventh-day Adventism at a number of points, chiefly in accepting as its rule of faith and practice only such teachings and prophetic utterances as it finds in the Old and New Testaments.

The New York church is located at 252 West 138th Street (10030). There are churches in Cambridge, Massachusetts; Montclair, New Jersey;

and St. Louis, Missouri; and a mission in the Gordon Heights district of New York. The total active membership is estimated at 450. In addition there are four congregations in Jamaica and one in the Republic of Panama.[20]

## Unification Association of Christian Sabbath Keepers, Incorporated

Between 1942 and 1956 a series of unsuccessful efforts were made to unite the independent black Sabbath-keeping conferences and churches in the metropolitan New York area. The leader in these efforts was Elder (now Bishop) Thomas I. C. Hughes of the Advent Sabbath Church (founded in 1941) in Manhattan. The missionary outreach of his church into Antigua in 1951, into Jamaica and the United States Virgin Islands in 1952, and into Nigeria and New Zealand in 1956, provided in the last-named year the basis for establishing a joint missionary effort with the New York United Sabbath Day Advent Church and the formation of the Unification Association of Christian Association of Christian Sabbath Keepers (incorporated in 1957).[21]

The association rejects elaborate statements of faith on the ground that they erect walls of partition between believers. It stresses the relationship with Christ's person and love for him as the basis of fellowship. "Our statement of faith is the entire Bible, its teachings our doctrines, its Lord our Savior."[22] In addition to stressing observance of the seventh-day Sabbath, it teaches believer's baptism by immersion. It practices the dedication of children in place of infant baptism. It believes that the conscience of a Christian will forbid "his serving in the direct, first-hand business of blood shedding," but that he can and should assist his government when it fights "on the side of righteous principle," including noncombatant service in the armed forces.[23]

The headquarters are at 145 Central Park North, New York, New York 10026. The churches in the continental United States meet for fellowship annually. The international General Conference, which meets every four years, is the final authority. A General Board of Evangelism meets monthly between sessions of the quadrennial conference. The office of bishop, created in 1964, implies no authority over the member congregations. There are four churches in New York and New Jersey, and two Sabbath schools in the United States Virgin Islands. The total membership of these churches is estimated at 400. In addition, the church has affiliates in the Caribbean, England, Germany, Australasia, India, South America, and Africa. The bulk of the association's membership is in India and Africa.

## The Remnant Church

In the early 1950s Texas-born Mrs. Tracy B. Bizich, née Stevens, of Sewickley, Pennsylvania, had many dreams, visions, and ecstatic trancelike experiences in which, as she believed, God spoke to her as he had spoken to his servants in the past. In 1951 the late Mrs. Ellen G. White reportedly appeared to her. In this vision Mrs. Bizich heard the Seventh-day Adventist prophetess tell her that the Seventh-day Adventists had backslidden irretrievably. She also heard Mrs. White tell her that the spiritual name of Mrs. Bizich was "the Bee" and that she would be joined by a man whose spiritual name was "the Fly."[24] Their common mission would be to begin to gather the 144,000 chosen and sealed saints of God referred to in Revelation 14:1, 3 who were to be the only ones to enter the new earth after the imminent destruction of the present world.

In 1957 Mrs. Bizich came into contact with Elsworth Thomas Kaiser (b. 1902) of Rochester, New York, a native of Jersey Shore, Pennsylvania, a railroad worker, and a former marine. A former Seventh-day Adventist, he belonged at the time to a Seventh-day Adventist offshoot, the Shepherd's Rod, defunct since 1959. Kaiser too had had many visions, dreams, and trance-experiences that he identified as coming from the angels. She recognized him as "the Fly," interpreted his dreams and visions for him, and designated him an elder and the first minister of the Remnant Church that he was to organize under her spiritual direction. Elder Kaiser founded a church of the new movement in Rochester that same year.[25]

The Remnant Church sees 1957 as marking the beginning of the end of the world. Its "Doctrines, Rules, and Bylaws" prescribe obedience to superiors; observance of the Sabbath; community of goods; the Lord's Supper only once a year; and full baptism, both of water and of the Holy Spirit, administered in a public stream to candidates that have reached the age of understanding (normally fourteen years). They forbid recourse to physicians; suits at law in human courts; distinctions based on race or color; the use of tobacco, alcohol, and drugs; taking money collections on the Sabbath; attendance at commercial motion pictures; and infant baptism.[26] Some of the 144,000 have already risen from their graves, according to the Remnant Church, and have preached in the spirit to friends and relatives.

The headquarters of the Remnant Church are at 56 Manhattan Street, Rochester, New York. The single center has a membership of five.[27]

## NOTES

1. The material in this section is based on a description written by Arthur Carl Piepkorn and previously published as part of the item "Adventist Bodies" in *Lutheran Cyclopedia*, Erwin L. Lueker, ed. (St. Louis: Concordia Publishing House, 1975), pp. 6-7.
2. See the previous section on Adventism.
3. The preceding description is based on ibid., p. 7.
4. The historical material in the two preceding paragraphs is based on

*Seventh-day Adventist Encyclopedia,* rev. edn., Don F. Neufeld, ed. (Washington, D.C.: Review and Herald Publishing Association, 1976), pp. 1326–1328.
5. Ibid., p. 1325.
6. The "Fundamental Beliefs," reprinted regularly in the denomination's *Yearbook* and *Church Manual*, are presented in ibid., pp. 396-398.
7. *Seventh-day Adventists Answers Questions on Doctrine: An Explanation of*

*Certain Major Aspects of Seventh-day Adventist Belief* (Washington, D.C.: Review and Herald Publishing Association, 1957), pp. 21-25.

8. Ibid., pp. 21-23.

9. Ibid., pp. 23-24.

10. Ibid., pp. 24-25.

11. The present writer acknowledges his indebtedness to an unpublished paper by Moses C. Crouse, Ph.D., Aurora College, Aurora, Illinois, for many of the insights of this presentation. The Orrin Roe Jenks Collection of Adventual materials in the Charles B. Phillips Library of Aurora College contains one of the completest files of early Millerite and Adventist periodicals and papers in existence.

12. He took a wife from the Poca River area. He is buried at Walton, West Virginia.

13. Letters of Mr. Hugh W. Good, Primitive Advent Christian Church, Elkview, West Virginia.

14. "Declaration of Faith," *Constitution of the P[rimitive] A[dvent] Church [of West Virginia]* (Charleston, West Va.: Jones Printing Co., n.d.), pp. 3-6.

15. "Church Covenant," ibid., p. 1.

16. "Articles of Belief" (Schenectady, N.Y.: Schenectady People's Christian Church, n.d.) (2-page mimeographed document).

17. Letters from the Reverend A. Warren Burns, minister, People's Christian Chapel, 401 Melrose Street, Schenectady, New York, and from Mrs. Helen G. Loede, clerk, People's Christian Church, New York. The churches sponsor a four-station radio program, "A Faith That Lives."

18. See *Principles of Faith and Church Order of the Seventh Day Adventist Reform Movement* (Sacramento, Calif.: Reformation Herald Publishing Association, 1957) (40-page brochure). These principles were first issued by the General Conference of the Seventh-day Adventist Reform Movement at its session in Gotha, Germany, in 1925. When the American Union of the Seventh-day Adventist Reform Movement reorganized itself in 1949, it adopted these principles to govern its activities (ibid., p. 2).

19. Letter from Mr. Alex N. Macdonald, secretary Seventh-day Adventist Reform Movement General Conference, Sacramento, California.

20. Letter from Mr. Hubert A. Gauntlett, secretary-treasurer, Seventh-day Christian Conference. The present writer acknowledges gratefully the assistance of the Reverend Clemonce Sabourin, LL.D., former pastor, Mount Zion Church, New York, who interviewed Elder Henry Alexander Grant, minister, Victory Tabernacle, and vice-president, Seventh-day Christian Conference, on behalf of this writer.

21. See the history of the movement, "The Story of Unification," published serially in the movement's monthly, *Unification Leader*, vol. 10, no. 2 (February 1966), through vol. 11, no. 6 (June 1966). The New York United Sabbath Day Adventist Church was organized in 1910 as a Seventh-day Adventist congregation. It withdrew from that denomination in 1930 and became the headquarters church of the United Sabbath Day Adventist Conference. It withdrew from the latter conference in 1954 over the congregation's right to use its tithes and offerings for the construction of a proposed building.

22. Thomas I. C. Hughes, "It's Already Written," ibid., vol. 11, no. 2 (February 1967), p. 2. In a letter to this writer Bishop Hughes states: "Most of the churches in the Unification Association are trinitarian, believe in the deity of our Lord and Savior Jesus Christ, and use the triune formula of Matt. 28:19 at baptism."

23. George R. Farrow, *The Christian and War* (Elizabeth, N.J.: Mount Zion Sanctuary Publishing Society, n.d. [around 1945]) (8-page leaflet), pp. 6-7. In the cited letter Bishop Hughes says of this leaflet, which he provided for the present writer's information, that the Unification Association fully endorses the leaflet as the association's "stand on war and service in the military."

24. See Isaiah 7:18.

25. Letter from Elder Elsworth Thomas Kaiser, minister, the Remnant Church.

26. "Doctrines, By-Laws, [and] Rules of the Remnant Church (Revelation 14)" (3-page typescript document).

27. Letter from Elder Kaiser.

# BIBLIOGRAPHY

Gedney, Edwin K. *A Primer of Prophecy*. Concord, N.H.: Advent Christian Publications, 1964. An introduction to the teachings of the Advent Christian General Conference of America.

Hoekema, Anthony A. *The Four Major Cults*. Grand Rapids, Mich.: W. B. Eerdmans Publishing Co., 1963. Seventh-day Adventism is described as a cult, pp. 89-169.

Johnson, Albert C. *Advent Christian History*. Mendota, Ill.: The Western Advent Christian Publication Society, 1918. Background for the history of the Advent Christian General Conference of America.

Lewis, Gordon R. *Confronting the Cults*. Philadelphia: Presbyterian and Reformed Publishing Company, 1966. Part V, pp. 101-130, assesses Seventh-day Adventist beliefs from an Evangelical perspective.

Martin, Walter R. *The Kingdom of the Cults*. Grand Rapids, Mich.: Zondervan Publishing House, 1965. Seventh-day Adventism is dealt with in an appendix, pp. 359-422, where the author distinguishes the church body in its present form from its cult-like past.

————. *The Truth about Seventh-day Adventism*. Grand Rapids, Mich.: Zondervan Publishing House, 1960. A case made for Seventh-day Adventism as a Christian denomination.

Mitchell, David. *Seventh-Day Adventists: Faith in Action*. New York: Vantage Press, 1958. A description of the growth and influence of Seventh-day Adventists around the world.

*Seventh-Day Adventist Encyclopedia*. Rev. edn. Dan F. Neufeld, ed. Washington, D.C.: Review and Herald Publishing Association, 1976.

*Seventh-day Adventists Answer Questions on Doctrine: An Explanation of Certain Major Aspects of Seventh-day Adventist Belief*. Washington, D.C.: Review and Herald Publishing Association, 1957. Prepared by a representative group of Seventh-day Adventist leaders, Bible teachers, and editors.

Wellcome, Isaac C. *History of the Second Advent Message and Mission, Doctrine and People*. Boston: Advent Christian Publication Society, 1874.

# 14. The Catholic Apostolic Movement

## Catholic Apostolic Church

About the beginning of the second quarter of the nineteenth century, an Anglican clergyman, J. Haldane Stewart, wrote a tract on the prophecy of Joel, "I will pour out my spirit on all flesh." In it he urged the necessity of prayer for the outpouring of the Holy Spirit upon the contemporary church. The burden of this tract was of a piece with the preaching of Edward Irving (1792–1834), the Scottish minister of the Presbyterian church in Regent Square, London, and a member of an eschatologically oriented group that had gathered around Henry Drummond (1786–1860). Drummond was a wealthy former businessman and political figure, who later became an apostle, prophet, and evangelist, as well as the "angel for Scotland," in the Catholic Apostolic Church.

Stewart's tract had a wide circulation both in Great Britain and on the European continent. Among the persons into whose hands it fell, the first to begin to speak in tongues and to prophesy was a Scottish Presbyterian woman, Mary Campbell. During the next two years many others had the same experience, including members of Irving's congregation. (As a result the adherents of the movement came to be known then and later as "Irvingites.") A recurring feature of the early prophecies was the reference to a "body," which was taken to imply the creation of a community in which all the ministries of the primitive church would be revived. This community began to take shape between 1832, when Drummond as prophet formally "called" the first apostle, John Bate Cardale (1802–1877), and 1835, when the "college of apostles" had become complete and the first congregation was formally organized. In the latter year the church held its first council in London. In January 1836 it sent a "testimony" to the episcopate and clergy of the Church of England, and in 1838 a more elaborate document (The Great or Catholic Testimony) to the political and spiritual leaders throughout Europe. In these documents they undertook to trace the evils of society back to their spiritual source in the departure of the churches from God; they held up the promise of Christ's coming as the only promise of deliverance; and they declared that the original structure and endowments of the primitive church had begun to be recovered in preparation for the coming reign of Christ. In a series of missionary journeys to the European continent and to North America, the apostles spread their message and organized their converts into congregations.

Although the movement refused to take a distinctive name, it became generally known as the Catholic Apostolic Church. Its ministry was fourfold— apostles, prophets, evangelists, and pastors. The apostles were thought of as directly chosen by God; God chose the others through the apostolic authority. (From the 1860s on there were also apostles' coadjutors.) The chief pastor of a local church bore the title "angel." The local churches had each a body of priest-elders, as well as deacons, deaconesses, and underdeacons.

The church committed itself to the Apostles', Nicene, and Athanasian creeds, while its theology stressed the person and work of the incarnate Word of God, the activity of the Holy Spirit, God's "election according to grace," and a premillennial eschatology.

The service book of 1842 combined Anglican, Roman Catholic, and Eastern Orthodox elements. The clergy wore vestments; the sacramentals included incense and holy water. The two Dominical sacraments are the Eucharist and baptism. The Eucharist was celebrated every Lord's day and was reserved in a tabernacle with a sanctuary lamp burning before it; but the Catholic Apostolic Church denied both that the eucharistic element ceased to be bread and that the eucharistic sacrifice is a repetition of the death of Christ. Infant baptism was retained. In addition to rites for ordination and for marriage, there were rites for private confession and absolution and for the anointing of the sick. There was also a rite of "sealing" based on Revelation 7:3–8 and administered by the apostles only to candidates who were at least twenty years old. (Ordinations and sealings ceased in 1901.) In addition to the hours of prayer, nonliturgical services provided opportunities for the exercise of the gifts of the Spirit, such as speaking in tongues and prophecy.

A schism began to develop in the German branch (established in 1842) in the late 1850s after the death of half of the original apostles. Some of the German leaders demanded the replacement of the deceased apostles; the English leadership refused. The result was the withdrawal of most of the German churches in 1862 and the organization of the New Apostolic Church.

By 1879 only one of the original apostles was left; his death in 1901 was a severe blow to the remaining members of the church, who had hoped that the Parousia would take place before the last apostle died. The year 1901 marks the beginning of the "period of silence." With the death of more and more of the clergy, the services of the Catholic Apostolic Church had to be abbreviated and simplified. Finally, they have had to be discontinued in most places. The youngest priests would now be in their late eighties.

The Catholic Apostolic Church ceased its evangelistic outreach long ago. Its relatively few surviving members still hold fast to the hope of the Lord's imminent appearing for which he restored the apostolate to the church in the nineteenth century, even though they are compelled to attend the services of other denominations and received the sacraments in these churches (usually Protestant Episcopal churches) as far as this is canonically possible. By 1936 the number of Catholic Apostolic congregations in the United States had declined to 7, with 2,577 reported members. Since then no statistical information has been published. Two churches reportedly still exist. Assuming a normal sex ratio, a normal pattern of fertility and mortality, a normal age structure as of 1936 (with a median weighted toward over 45), normal additions to the group through natural increase, and a relatively stable aging of the group, a reasonable estimate of the size of the group as of 1970 would indicate a membership of between 120 and 180. The office of the custodian of records of the Catholic Apostolic Church is at 417 West 57th Street, New York, New York 10019.

## The New Apostolic Church of North America

Six of the apostles whom John Cardale (1802–1877) had ordained in 1835 had already died and the date of Christ's second coming had been postponed five times (1835, 1838, 1842, 1845, 1855) by 1860. In that year, while attending a meeting of the Apostolic Council of the Catholic Apostolic Church in Albury, England, Heinrich Geyer of Berlin, a prophet in the church (that is, a member of what was then the second order of the Catholic Apostolic ministry) designated two evangelists (that is, members of what then was the third order of the Catholic Apostolic ministry) as apostles. The surviving apostles refused to recognize these new appointees as fellow apostles but accepted them merely as apostle-coadjutors, whose duty it was to assist the authentic apostles in their task. This compromise satisfied Geyer for the moment, but while he was on a trip to Königsberg (Kaliningrad) in the company of Apostle Francis V. Woodhouse the next year, Geyer, acting without his companion's knowledge or consent, appointed the Königsberg presbyter Rosochatsky as apostle. (Rosochatsky repented and recanted shortly afterward.) The assistant bishop-angel of Hamburg, F. W. Schwartz (d. 1895), endorsed Geyer's action. When what Geyer had done became generally known, the Catholic Apostolic Church excommunicated both Geyer and Schwartz in 1862. They proceeded to form the General Christian Apostolic Mission in 1865, with Schwartz, appointed an apostle by Geyer, at its head. In 1908 it took the name of New Apostolic Community. Geyer's withdrawal was the first of some ten schisms—which in turn have often subdivided. Nevertheless, the New Apostolic Church is the largest free church in Germany. Outside Europe—including North America—it has made its greatest progress among people of German background. Between 1884 and 1938 the New Apostolic Church made a number of unproductive overtures to the Catholic Apostolic Church looking toward reunion. Fritz Krebs (d. 1905), Schwartz's successor, developed the doctrine of the Chief Apostle (*Stammapostel*), a title which he took for himself. Walter Schmidt of Dortmund succeeded to the position in 1960, as the follower of Johann G. Bischoff (1871–1960), who in 1951 declared that Christ would return in his lifetime.

The New Apostolic Church regards itself as the perfecting of the redemptive activity that Christ and his apostles began. It is the primitive church restored as the church of the last times. The apostles are God's messengers, with unique authority. As Christ's vicegerents the apostles administer Christ's heritage and provide the sole channel through which God imparts his Holy Spirit.

The apostles, of whom there are now nearly fifty, with the chief apostle at their head, are organs of divine revelation. Their words supplement the Bible, God's revelation for a time that is now past. When the New Apostolic Church has achieved the necessary degree of perfection, the rapture of the New Apostolic Church will inaugurate the Parousia.

The creed of the New Apostolic Church has ten articles. The first three reproduce the Apostles' Creed, with some variations, the most important of which is the affirmation in Article 3: "I believe in a holy apostolic church." Article 4 affirms that Christ rules his church through living apostles until his own return, and that he has sent and continues to send these apostles with the commission to teach, to forgive sins in his name, and to baptize with water and the Holy Spirit. Article 5 makes the apostles responsible for choosing and instituting the incumbents of all ministerial offices in the church—bishops, district elders, evangelists, pastors, priests, deacons, subdeacons, and so on. (The office of prophet was abrogated in the 1940s). Article 6 declares that water baptism—which the New Apostolic Church administers to infants with the conventional trinitarian formula—is a part of rebirth and that the person baptized thereby obtains the right to receive the Holy Spirit. This takes place when an apostle seals him. Sealing is the third sacrament, the essential part of rebirth, the baptism with the Spirit and with fire, the most exalted sacramental impartation of grace that a human being can receive. (The New Apostolic Church has rites for the vicarious baptizing and sealing of the departed.) Article 7 describes the Lord's Supper as the remembrance of the sacrificial death of Christ and the assurance of a common life with him. The New Apostolic Church administers the Lord's Supper in the form of unleavened hosts upon which drops of wine have been placed in the process of preparation. Infants, children, and adults all receive the sacrament. Article 9 affirms Christ's return to transform the first-fruits who hope in his coming. Article 10, formulated in the language of Romans 13, affirms that the government is the servant of God.

The Dutch Reformed tradition made a great impact on the New Apostolic Church under the leadership of Schwartz. One result was the early abolition of many of the liturgical features (including the traditional vestments) that had characterized the worship of the Christian Apostolic Church and a radical simplification of New Apostolic worship.

The international headquarters are at Frankfurt-am-Main, West Germany.

The United States headquarters are at 3753 North Troy Street, Chicago, Illinois 60618. Two districts—with 314 churches and an inclusive membership of 23,267—are administered by the president of the Canadian district, who has oversight over churches and missions in seven other countries as well.

## BIBLIOGRAPHY

Andrews, William Watson [1810–1897]. *The History and Claims of the Body of Christians Known as the "Catholic Apostolic Church."* 7th edn. Wembley, Middlesex: H. B. Copinger, 1950. This 48-page brochure by one of the leaders and chief exponents of the movement in the United States was originally published as an article in *Bibliotheca Sacra* for January and April 1866.

Shaw, P. E. *The Catholic Apostolic Church, Sometimes Called Irvingite: A Historical Study.* New York: King's Crown Press, 1946. The definitive study by an outsider.

# 15. Unitarians and Universalists

The American Unitarian Association and the Universalist Church of America agreed to unite in 1958. Both bodies confirmed the agreement in 1959 and ratified it in simultaneous but separate meetings in 1960. In May 1961 the Unitarian Universalist Association formally came into being.

An understanding of this relatively new body requires a knowledge of the background of the two uniting denominations.

### Unitarianism

Historically the term "Unitarian" describes a person who does not believe in the Trinity as the creeds of the church—notably the so-called Athanasian Creed—define this dogma and who asserts that God exists in only one hypostasis or "person." In this sense the term does not adequately describe modern Unitarianism. American Unitarians accepted the name only under protest. They view their position as less a denial of the Trinity than as an attempt to practice religion on the highest ethical plane untrammeled by creed or dogma.

The historic roots of Unitarianism go back at least to the Renaissance and the radical Antitrinitarians of the sixteenth century. Among the latter were Martin Borrhaus (Cellarius) (1499–1564), Louis Hetzer (beheaded in 1529 at Zurich), the Dutch mystic John Campanus (1500–1575), the Italian free thinkers George Biandrata (1515–1588), Matthew Gribaldi (d. 1564), and Valentine Gentile (1520?–1566), and particularly the Spaniard Michael Servetus (1511?–1553).

The movement took firmest root in Transylvania, then nominally a part of Hungary, and in Poland.

In Transylvania—where King John II Sigismund (Zápolya) himself inclined to Unitarianism—his court preacher, Francis Dávid (1510–1579), established a Unitarian movement that has survived down to the present, with some 170 churches in modern Romania and Hungary. Dávid's adherents became known as "Nonadorantists," because they allegedly denied the propriety of giving adoration to Christ. In Poland the Antitrinitarians in the Reformed community came to be known as the Minor Reformed Church. Upon arriving in Poland from Transylvania in 1579, Faustus Socinus (1539–1604), whom many regard as "the architect of modern Unitarianism" on the European continent, became the accepted leader of the Minor Reformed Church, although it is not certain that he was ever admitted to its membership or to participation in its observance of the Lord's Supper. Socinianism survived in Poland until 1658, when the Jesuits secured passage of a decree in the Diet requiring "Arians" to leave the country within three years (subsequently reduced to two) or suffer capital punishment. Therewith organized Socinianism in Poland came to an end.

According to the Racovian Catechism of 1605—so-called from the Community that the Polish Antitrinitarians founded at Raków in 1569—the essence of Christianity consists in fulfilling God's will as the Bible reveals it and as reason approves it. This "systematic statement of Socinian doctrine for propaganda purposes" retains a considerable quantity of Calvinian thinking, including the doctrines of election and of Christ's threefold office. It views man as fully capable of working out his spiritual destiny. It describes the dogma of the Trinity as irrational. It sees Christ as more than a mere man, but denies that he has a divine nature. Because of the innocency of Christ's life, God endowed him with divine powers and after his resurrection exalted him to serve as eternal Priest, Prophet, and King over his church. The Racovian Catechism describes Christ's work primarily as revealing God's commandments and promises, and makes faith in the Lord Jesus Christ and obedience to his commandments the two requisites of eternal life.

After the expulsion of the Socinians from Poland, their doctrine was tolerated on the continent of Europe only in Holland.[1] Traces of Unitarianism appear in England in the sixteenth and early seventeenth centuries, but the real father of English Unitarianism was John Biddle (1615–1662). In England too the proponents of Unitarianism met with persecution, and the Act of Toleration of 1689 excluded Antitrinitarians from its provisions. But in the late seventeenth and eighteenth centuries, increasing numbers of Anglican and Nonconformist clergymen began to hold Socinian views, along with nontheologians like Isaac Newton and John Locke.

Among the leaders in the Unitarian movement in England were Theophilus Lindsey (1723–1808), who organized the first Unitarian congregation in England, and Joseph Priestley (1733–1804), who emigrated in 1794 and established at Northumberland, Pennsylvania, the first congregation in North America to call itself Unitarian. James Martineau (1805–1885), successively a Presbyterian and a Unitarian preacher, became the recognized leader in England after the formal organization of the British and Foreign Unitarian Association in 1825.

American Unitarianism developed primarily within New England Congregationalism. Here theological liberalism and a concern for morals in preference to doctrine were nothing new, while more and more preachers were stressing the role of reason in religion, casting doubt on the dogma of the Trinity and on the doctrine of the total depravity of human beings, and affirming the basic goodness of the individual and the freedom of the human will. The Halfway Covenant of 1662 had admitted the children of baptized, although noncommunicant, parents to baptism, on the condition that the parents subscribed to the main tenets of the Gospel "by intellectual belief" and promised "to walk under the discipline of the church." Solomon Stoddard (1643–1729) advocated admitting to full membership in the church persons who led blameless lives even though they were unconverted. The Great Awakening (1735–1745) under Jonathan Edwards, Stoddard's grandson, led to the abrogation of the Halfway Covenant, but in the reaction against the excesses that marked the revival, Unitarian or Arian ministers like Ebenezer Gay (1696–1787), Lemuel Briant (d. 1754), Charles Chauncy (1705–1787), Jonathan Mayhew (1720–1766), and William Bentley (1759–1819) —to name only a few—became ministers of many Congregational churches without evoking perceptible commotion among their parishioners. Indeed, in Boston twelve of the city's fourteen Congregationalist churches reportedly had "Arian" preachers at the end of the eighteenth century.[2]

In 1805 the liberal Henry Ware, Jr., became Hollis Professor of Divinity at Harvard College. Alarmed, the conservative Congregationalist ministers dissolved their fellowship with the liberal group. The liberals gradually took on a distinctly denominational form and in 1825 they organized the American Unitarian Association.

Internal strife soon weakened the new denomination. Three schools of thought emerged, each with its leader. William Ellery Channing (1780–1842), whose epochal "Baltimore sermon" of 1819 on "Unitarian Christianity" gave American Unitarianism a platform, was an Arian. Ralph Waldo Emerson (1803–1882) was a pantheist and a philosophical idealist who represented the extreme left wing of early nineteenth-century Unitarianism. Theodore Parker (1810–1860) was a radical theologian in the spirit of the nascent German type of liberalism to which the executive committee of the American Unitarian Association in 1853 opposed its "creed" affirming "the divine origin, the divine authority, the divine sanctions of the religion of Jesus Christ." The organization of the National Convention (later Conference) of Unitarian Churches in 1865 at New York under the conservative leadership of Henry W. Bellows assuaged some of the strife and contributed to the development of a denominational consciousness, although it also led to the withdrawal of some of the more liberal leaders, who founded the Free Religious Association. After a decline in the early 1900s, the Unitarian Association undertook in the mid-twentieth century to capitalize on the post-World War II interest in religion and to propagate its teachings more energetically.

Over the years the Unitarian Association's influence has been proportionately much greater than its membership would indicate. Its uncreedal personal commitment to high ethical ideals has attracted many statesmen and educators. Its liberal approach to religion has found many allies in other denominations. In one sense there have generally been more Unitarians outside the American Unitarian Association than inside it.

Unitarians have no formal creed, but they do have certain basic beliefs.

1. Individual freedom in the area of religious conviction is fundamental. The range of Unitarian theological views brackets every variety of belief from atheism, agnosticism, and humanism to the relative orthodoxy of the minority "who consider themselves Catholic Christians . . . and who do not have the slightest desire to separate from the mainstream of Christianity."[3] While from the early sixteenth into the eighteenth centuries only the followers of Francis Dávid among the forerunners of modern Unitarianism refused to affirm the Apostles Creed, modern Unitarians generally deny that Jesus was anything more than a great moral and spiritual teacher, and reject His virgin birth, resurrection, and second coming.

2. Unitarians usually formulate their second basic assumption as "the Fatherhood of God," intending to symbolize thereby what Charles Eliot has called "the best human combination of justice, tenderness, and infinite sympathy."

3. The third basic assumption of Unitarian theology is the perfectibility of human beings. Unitarians concede the existence of evil in the world and acknowledge the responsibility of human beings for it. Human beings, Unitarians hold, are imperfect but not fundamentally sinful. Every individual has within him "a spark of the divine" that gives him limitless power and endless possibilities. The primary responsibility for human progress lies with human beings themselves. They can create the environment and impart the education that will enable mankind to realize more and more fully its ideals and aspiration.

4. Unitarians regard the brotherhood of man as a tenet that all religions hold.

5. The final assumption is "salvation by character." Unitarians see the traditional teaching of the historic churches about salvation by grace for Christ's sake as incredible and incompatible both with the character of God and with the dignity of human beings. Enlightened religion can inspire human beings to do what needs to be done in our time in order to create a world of peace, justice, and brotherhood that is built on moral values and spiritual insight and that makes possible the sharing of the benefits of increasing scientific knowledge with all people.

Unitarian practice on baptism and Communion has varied. Although Unitarians do not regard baptism as essential, many Unitarian ministers baptize infants as a symbolic act of naming and dedication; the baptism of adults is less usual. Communion, when observed, is a memorial ceremony designed to recall a great spiritual religious teacher who dedicated his life to the achievement of peace and good will on earth.

Particularly in recent years Unitarians have demonstrated a desire to enrich their services of corporate worship by utilizing the common heritage of religious literature, music, and art.

### Universalists

In the language of theology "universalism" is the doctrine that God will ultimately save all people. Proponents of this doctrine have arisen from time to time throughout the history of the church.

Universalism as a modern denomination traces its origins to the middle of the eighteenth century, when here and there in Europe and America preachers began to affirm publicly that it was unthinkable that a loving heavenly Father could doom any of his children to everlasting punishment. Some historians have called George de Benneville (1703–1793) the "father of American Universalism." Frequently imprisoned in Europe for expounding heretical views, he came to Pennsylvania in 1741. Here he absorbed the universalism of some of the German mystics who had settled in that colony, and in association with the Universalist-minded Quaker printer Christopher Sower (Sauer) (1693–1758) de Benneville disseminated his views widely through the printed page. John Murray (1741–1815), expelled from British Methodism for heresy, came to New Jersey in 1770. He traveled extensively, capitalizing on a growing discontent with the traditional Reformed theology current in New England. A group of sixty-one members of the Gloucester (Massachusetts) Parish, moved both by their own studies of Universalist writings and by Murray's sermons, in 1779 withdrew from the church, signed Articles of Association, and established The Independent Church of Christ—the first formally organized Universalist congregation in North America—with Murray as its minister.

The year before Caleb Rich had organized the first "General Society" of Universalists in New England. In 1785 the General Society met in Oxford, Massachusetts, with representatives from congregations in Massachusetts and Rhode Island, and decided to meet annually and to adopt a charter. It grew and after a number of changes in name it became in 1866 the Universalist General Convention and subsequently the Universalist Church of America. The Universal Baptist Church, formed at Philadelphia in 1786, became the mother-church of the Philadelphia Universalist Convention. In 1790 this body, with Murray representing the New England Universalists, adopted the Philadelphia Declaration of Faith. The declaration acknowledged the Scriptures as containing "a revelation of the perfection and will of God and the rule of faith and practice" (Section 1). It affirmed the unique Mediatorship of Christ "in whom dwelleth all the fullness of the Godhead bodily, who by giving himself a ransom for all, hath redeemed them to God by his blood, and who, by the merit of his death and the efficacy of his Spirit, will finally restore the whole human race to happiness" (Section 3). It accepted "the obligation of the moral law as a rule of life" and held "that the love of God manifest to man in a Redeemer is the best means of producing obedience to that law and promoting a holy, active, and useful life" (Section 5).

The Universalists are a distinctly American denomination and their membership is confined almost wholly to North America.[4] The one factor that united the early Universalists was their common opposition to the doctrine of eternal punishment. On other points of theology the divergence was wide. Murray's view was "an improved Calvinism." He based his universalism on the view that God's grace made Christ the actual Head of the human race, who expiated the sins of all people. He accepted the classic Reformed position that God decreed the salvation only of the elect, but saw all people as elected.

Elhanan Winchester (d. 1797), a Baptist converted to Universalism by reading a German Universalist work that Christopher Sower had printed in an English version, was an Arminian. He saw the final conflagration as purifying the unbelievers and rebels so that at last all men and angels will enjoy eternal bliss.

In 1803 the New England Universalists adopted the Winchester (New Hampshire) Confession of Faith in the Scriptures "as a revelation of the character of God and of the duty, interest and final destination of mankind," in "one God, whose nature is love, revealed in one Lord Jesus Christ, by one Holy Spirit of Grace, who will finally restore the whole family of mankind to holiness and happiness," and in the inseparable connection of holiness and true happiness. To keep this from becoming a creed binding on a society or individual, the framers added the "Liberty Clause," leaving it to the several churches, societies, or smaller associations "to continue or adopt within themselves such more articles of faith" as their circumstances might seem to require.

The real architect of Universalist theology of the early nineteenth century and the individual who did most to lead the Universalists into Unitarian patterns of theological thinking was Hosea Ballou (1771–1852). His Treatise on Atonement (1805) rejected as unbiblical and irrational the doctrines of the Trinity, the fall, the depravity of the human race, salvation by faith alone, and everlasting punishment. It affirmed the rationality of the Christian religion, the unchanging love of God as the supreme divine trait, God's everlasting Fatherhood, the divine sonship of human beings, the mission of Jesus as the reconciler of humankind with God, the certainty of punishment for sin, and the final salvation of all souls. Christ's atonement, Ballou taught, was a moral, not a legal work. In his death, Christ only demonstrated God's loving concern for the moral cure of the human soul. God cannot punish arbitrarily; the wages of sin cannot be an aimless torment and a wicked vengeance, but all punishment of sin must be corrective.

In 1831 the radical views of Ballou led to the withdrawal of a group that formed the Massachusetts Association of Universal Restorationists, which survived only until 1841.

The original basic Universalist tenet, the restoration of all things, received less and less emphasis as the denomination became more and more Unitarian. An effort in 1870 to halt the influence of German rationalism on some of the younger ministers by incorporating the Winchester Profession of Faith—without the "Liberty Clause"—into the convention's constitution proved futile. In 1899 the General Convention adopted five "Essential Principles of the Universalist Church": (1) the universal fatherhood of God; (2) the spiritual authority and leadership of his Son, Jesus Christ; (3) the trustworthiness of the Bible as containing a revelation from God; (4) the certainty of just retribution for sin; (5) the final harmony of all souls with God. The same convention reinstated the "Liberty Clause."

In the mid-1930s the Universalist Church of America in convention adopted as its last statement of essential beliefs the "Washington Avowal of Faith." This document defines the bond of fellowship in the denomination as "a common purpose to do the will of God as Jesus revealed it and to cooperate in establishing the kingdom for which he lived and died." It affirms the church's faith in "God as eternal and all-conquering love, the spiritual leadership of Jesus, the supreme worth of every human personality, the authority of truth known or to be known, and in the power of men of good will and sacrificial spirit to overcome all evil and progressively to establish the kingdom of God." The majority of delegates accepted this statement not as dogma, but as the foundation for a theological structure. But some of them felt that to be truly Universalist, the church should have formally acknowledged the contributions of other world religions. Most Universalists regarded baptism and the Holy Communion as "sacred symbols."

## Unitarian Universalist Association

The convergence of Universalists and Unitarians into a single denomination had already gone on for a century when in 1953 both groups appointed a joint Commission to Study Federal Union. The same year saw the Liberal Religious Youth supersede the two denominational youth organizations. In 1954 came the formation of the Council of Liberal Churches (Universalist-Unitarian), disbanded when the two churches opted for organic union. In 1961 the union took place. A small group of Universalist societies organized the Committee for Continuing Universalist Churches in April of that year; in 1964 the Committee became the Christian Universalist Church of America.

In the united body, each church is free to retain its original name. The constitution guarantees the independence and autonomy of local congregations. Local churches call and ordain their ministers, but the association grants fellowship. The annual General Assembly is the overall policy-setting and directing body. The constitution requires no minister, church, or member to subscribe to any particular interpretation of religion or to any particular religious belief or creed. In formulating the statement of purposes and objectives of the new organization, the drafters of the statement, after debate, determined to omit the name of Jesus from the statement.[5] The six listed purposes are:

1. To strengthen one another in a free and disciplined search for truth as the foundation of our religious fellowship;

2. To cherish and spread the universal truths taught by the great prophets and teachers of humanity in every age and tradition, immemorially summarized in the Judeo-Christian heritage as love to God and love to man;

3. To affirm, defend, and promote the supreme worth of every human personality, the dignity of man, and the use of the democratic method in human relationships;

4. To implement our vision of one world by striving for a world community founded on ideals of brotherhood and peace;

5. To serve the needs of member churches and fellowships and to extend and strengthen liberal religion;

6. To encourage cooperation with men of good will in every land.

The association reports 942 churches with an inclusive membership of 142,501. Headquarters are at 25 Beacon Street, Boston, Massachusetts 02108.

## The Christian Universalist Church of America
### (The Committee for Continuing Christian Universalist Churches)

Shortly before the union of the Universalist Church of America with the American Unitarian Association took place, some of the more conservative Universalist societies, concerned about "retaining Christian philosophy" and a liberal orientation, formed the Committee for Continuing Universalist Churches in April 1961 under the leadership of the Reverend John M. Schofield. It subsequently added "Christian" to its name and in 1964 it was incorporated in South Carolina as The Christian Universalist Church of America.

*A Universalist Catechism*, published with the committee's imprint, describes as the essential principles of the Universalist Church "the universal fatherhood of God; the spiritual authority and leadership of His Son Jesus Christ; the trustworthiness of the Bible as containing a revelation from God; the certainty of just retribution for sin; [and] the final harmony of all souls with God." In contrast to the principal emphasis of Universalism in the eighteenth century on "the truth that all men will be saved," its chief emphasis today is on "the universal fatherhood of God, implying universal brotherhood among men, and upon the certainty of retribution for sin." This shift in stress has taken place, the catechism asserts, "because men have come to see the importance of applying faith to life." Christ saves from sin "by revealing God and His love; by teaching the evil of sin and the suffering that follows it; [and] by showing the kind of life men may and ought to live."[6]

The address of the headquarters is P.O. Box 323, Deerfield Beach, Florida 33441. Statistical information is difficult to obtain. The organization of the body is informal. Membership in the Christian Universalist Church of America is not exclusive, and a congregation that is sympathetic to the aims of the Christian Universalist Church of America may hold membership both in the Unitarian Universalist Association and in the Christian Universalist Church of America.[7]

## NOTES

1. In a letter to the present writer, Dr. George Hunston Williams, Hollis Professor of Divinity in the Divinity School of Harvard University, observes that although Socinus refused to submit to rebaptism, the group for which he was spokesman practiced believer's baptism by immersion and that "the practice of immersion by English Baptists is probably a consequence of the Socinian influence on English Baptist refugees among the Collegiants in Holland."

2. Unitarianism invaded other communions as well. Thus King's Chapel, Boston's first Anglican house of worship (1686), also, under James Freeman, became the city's first church to turn Unitarian (1785). It still functions under its original covenant and charter.

3. See Ronald M. Mazur, "Unitarians and the Dialogue," *The Christian Century,* vol. 78 (1961), pp. 205-208.

4. In 1890, after twenty-four years of discussion and planning, the Universalist

Church opened a mission in Japan. In 1954 the Universalist Church of Japan joined the Japan Free Religion Association.

5. Because of its theological position the Unitarian Universalist Association is excluded from membership in the National Council of the Churches of Christ in the U.S.A. and the World Council of Churches.

6. *A Universalist Catechism* (Hopkinsville, Ky.: The First Universalist Church, 1963) (8-page tract), pp. 4, 6, 7.

7. The present writer gratefully acknowledges the assistance of the Right Reverend H. Kenneth Means, Deerfield Beach, Florida, one of the founders of the Christian Universalist Church of America, and of the Reverend Eugene O. Krug, pastor of St. Paul's Church, Boca Raton, Florida, in connection with this writer's efforts to secure information about the Christian Universalist Church of America.

## BIBLIOGRAPHY

Bainton, Roland H. *Hunted Heretic: The Life and Death of Michael Servetus, 1511–1553.* Boston: Beacon Press, 1960.

Bartlett, Laile E. *Bright Galaxy: Ten Years of Unitarian Fellowships.* Boston: Beacon Press, 1960.

Brown, Arthur W. *Always Young for Liberty: A Biography of William Ellery Channing.* Syracuse, N.Y.: Syracuse University Press, 1956.

Buehrer, Edwin T. "Unitarianism," in Vergilius Ferm, ed., *The American Church of the Protestant Heritage.* New York: Philosophical Library, 1953. Pp. 149-163.

Cassara, Ernest. *Hosea Ballou.* Boston: Beacon Press, 1961.

Channing, William Ellery. *Unitarian Christianity and Other Essays,* ed. Irving H. Bartlett. New York: The Liberal Arts Press, 1957.

Channing, William T., Ralph Waldo Emerson, and Theodore Parker. *Three Prophets of Religious Liberalism: Channing, Emerson, Parker.* Boston: Beacon Press, 1961.

Cheetham, Henry H. *Unitarianism and Universalism: An Illustrated History.* Boston: Beacon Press, 1962.

Commager, Henry Steele. *Theodore Parker: Yankee Crusader*. Boston: Beacon Press, 1960.

Crompton, Arnold. *Unitarianism on the Pacific Coast: The First Sixty Years*. Boston: Beacon Press, 1957.

Cummins, Robert. "The Universalist Church of America," in Vergilius Ferm, ed., *The American Church of the Protestant Heritage*. New York: Philosophical Library, 1953. Pp. 333-349.

Geffen, Elizabeth M. *Philadelphia Unitarianism 1796–1861*. Philadelphia: University of Pennsylvania Press, 1961.

Kot, Stanislas. *Socinianism in Poland: The Social and Political Ideas of the Polish Antitrinitarians in the Sixteenth and Seventeenth Centuries*, trans. from Polish by Earl Morse Wilbur. Boston: Starr King Press, 1957.

Mendelsohn, Jack. *Why I Am a Unitarian-Universalist*. New York: Thomas Nelson and Sons, 1966.

Parke, David B., ed. *The Epic of Unitarianism: Original Writings from the History of Liberal Religion*. Boston: Starr King Press, 1957.

Persons, Stow. *Free Religion: An American Faith*. Boston: Beacon Press, 1963.

Scott, Clinton Lee. *The Universalist Church of America: A Short History*. Boston: Universalist Historical Society, 1957.

Wilbur, Earl Morse. *A History of Unitarianism*. Vol. I: *Socinianism and Its Antecedents*; 1945. Vol. II: *In Transylvania, England, and America*; 1952. Boston: Beacon Press.

Wintersteen, Prescott Browning. *Christology in American Unitarianism*. Boston: The Unitarian Universalist Christian Fellowship, 1977.

Wright, Conrad. *The Beginnings of Unitarianism in America*. Boston: Beacon Press, 1966.

———. *The Liberal Christians: Essays on American Unitarian History*. Boston: Beacon Press, 1970. A description of the impact of "rational religion" on eighteenth-century America by an eminent Unitarian scholar.

# Index